French for Reading

French
for
Reading

Karl C. Sandberg
UNIVERSITY OF ARIZONA

Eddison C. Tatham
PRESCOTT COLLEGE

PRENTICE-HALL, INC., *Englewood Cliffs, New Jersey*

PRENTICE-HALL INTERNATIONAL, INC., *London*
PRENTICE-HALL OF AUSTRALIA, PTY. LTD., *Sydney*
PRENTICE-HALL OF CANADA, LTD., *Toronto*
PRENTICE-HALL OF INDIA PRIVATE LIMITED, *New Delhi*
PRENTICE-HALL OF JAPAN, INC., *Tokyo*

To the Student

Purpose

A few years ago in one of the major universities in the United States a graduate student of botany was preparing to defend his doctoral dissertation. He had "passed" his French reading knowledge examination, but he was not sure of the meaning of a certain article in French in the general area of his dissertation. When he had someone from the French Department translate it for him, he found that all of his research had been only the duplication of experiments performed by a French botanist two years before.

His experience and that of a multitude of other scholars demonstrates that the ability to read a foreign language with accuracy and at least moderate ease is always a valuable research tool and indeed is sometimes indispensable to the serious researcher.

This text will not teach you to speak or write French, but it will prepare you, in a relatively short time, to read readily and accurately in your major field. If you follow the instructions given, after having finished the course you will be able to recognize the meanings of all of the grammar forms in *Le Français fondamental* (the French government list prepared for overseas French schools). You will have a recognition vocabulary of about 1,500 basic French words, plus several thousand cognates, and will have developed a number of techniques of reading in a foreign language. With some additional outside reading in the professional literature of your field, to acquaint you with its particular vocabulary, you should be able to demonstrate the proficiency in reading French which most graduate schools require, and should be able to use French practically in research.

Format

Each lesson is built around a general reading passage or passages drawn from the journals or texts of the various disciplines. In order to prepare you to read the passages, the lessons include: (1) explanations of grammar points, (2) self-correcting exercises which test recognition of the grammar, introduce new vocabulary, and review grammar and vocabulary introduced in previous lessons, (3) a vocabulary development section which shows you how to proliferate your recognition skills, and (4) a testing exercise which permits you to verify your mastery of the material introduced in the chapter. The time necessary to complete the entire course has varied from 70 to 120 hours of actual study time.

Procedure

Because a graduate student's time is usually at a premium, this text has been designed to enable you to work at your own speed. To use it with maximum effectiveness, you should proceed in the following way:

1. Read the grammar explanation and study each of the examples several times to fix the point in your mind. If you have forgotten grammatical terminology, consult the Glossary of Grammatical Terms in the Appendix.

2. Proceed to the exercises which follow the grammar section. On the right side of the page you will find a reading column in French and on the left side a verification column in English. *Cover the English with a card or a slip of paper.* As you read through the exercises, respond to the questions which are asked about the sentences, or else simply determine the meaning of the sentences. Occasionally, you will have alternatives presented to you for your choice (e.g. **Que**=*what/who*). Choose the one which expresses the meaning in the context of the sentence given.

When you have determined upon a meaning, move your card down and verify your attempt. *Do not look at the English until you have genuinely tried to read the French, and do not write any English in the French column.* The speed and permanency with which you learn French will depend to a great extent on how closely you follow this instruction.

3. Circle the words in each exercise which you do not immediately recognize. When you finish the exercise reread the circled words or phrases until they are perfectly familiar to you.

This kind of review is indispensable to the most effective use of this text. In order for you to advance as rapidly as possible toward the goal of reading authentic, unedited French, this text has been programmed in fairly large steps. Tests have shown that steps of this size can be accommodated by most graduate students. In order to avoid being inundated in the later chapters, however, you must master the material presented in each lesson as you go along. You should therefore develop the habit of making a periodic review of the difficult items which you will have circled the first time through.

4. When you finish the exercises of a given chapter, do the grammar testing exercise. It will tell you if more review is in order before continuing.

5. Read the passages at the end of the chapter, and answer the questions on them. Develop the habit of looking for the meaning of whole phrases, sentences, and paragraphs rather than of individual words. Again, circle new or unrecognized words for future review.

6. Set aside a regular time each day for French. Reading is a skill which must be built. It is not a body of information which can be "crammed." Intensive but sporadic concentration on a foreign language is less effective than a smaller amount of time spent at regular intervals. If you have six hours a week to devote to French, for example, you would do better to divide them into twelve periods of one half hour each than into two periods of three hours each. Moreover, since most of the sections in this text can usually be completed in fifteen to thirty minutes, they lend themselves to

being sandwiched into short periods of time which might otherwise be lost.

7. Keep in mind that there is seldom any linguistic success without motivation. Get acquainted, therefore, with the French journals and literature in your field. They will make the learning of French more meaningful and practical for you.

The role of translation

Translation from French to English has been de-emphasized in this course in favor of comprehension. Translation is time-consuming and laborious, and from a technical or literary point of view it is probably the most demanding of linguistic tasks. It involves the full and complete expression in one language of thoughts already expressed in another and can adequately be undertaken only by someone possessing an expert stylistic command of both languages. The ability to understand French, moreover, does not depend necessarily on the ability to make a polished translation.

But if we think of translation as the use of the native language to establish and verify the meaning contained in phrases of a foreign language, translation has a legitimate role in the teaching of reading. Some of the exercises in this text will therefore test your comprehension of the French sentences by asking you to express their meanings in English. When you make your translation, you may find that your version differs from the one in the verification column. If the meaning you express is substantially the same, it does not matter (for these purposes) if your wording differs from that given by the text. There are usually several adequate translations for the same phrase. Furthermore, in order to clarify the meaning of the French structure, the translations in the verification column sometimes follow the French more closely than would be desirable from a strictly literary point of view. Do not hesitate, therefore, to use any translation which expresses the meaning of the sentence.

To the Teacher

This text presents the basic elements of French syntax, grammar, and vocabulary in a programmed format: material is introduced in regular steps, it is reviewed often, and the accuracy of the student's response is verified immediately. The use of programming does not replace the teacher in the classroom, but on the contrary, permits him to speed up and reinforce the learning process and, consequently, to use the classroom time more effectively.

With some approaches, the student usually writes out a translation of a passage or an exercise outside of class and spends most of the class time *verifying* his comprehension and *correcting* his mistakes. Moreover, having no immediate confirmation or correction of his attempts, the student must wait until the next class meeting to have his errors pointed out to him. If new vocabulary is presented in the reading or exercises, as much as one-third to two-thirds of the student's study time is spent in the mechanical process of thumbing through the vocabulary section or through the dictionary.

The use of a programmed approach, however, eliminates or greatly diminishes these obstacles. New vocabulary is explained as it is encountered and is usually reviewed several times in succeeding exercises. The vocabulary encountered in the reading passages at the end of each chapter has therefore been presented and drilled in the Reading Preparation exercises or has been made known by marginal notes. Moreover, since the student is asked to circle, review, and learn new or unfamiliar vocabulary items before going to the reading passage, he will more likely recognize the words of the passage immediately or else will be able to deduce their meaning from the context.

At the end of the reading passage is a set of questions with an answer key provided. The student can independently verify the degree of his comprehension.

Since most of the fundamental work of presentation, verification, and correction can be handled by the student on his own, the teacher is able to devote the class time to more productive activities. Probably some time still will have to be spent on verification of meaning, but much more may be spent on active *practice* and *reinforcement*, without which the student cannot realistically hope for much fluency or permanent gain.

The following procedure has worked well in the classroom:

1. Assuming that the exercises, grammar, testing, and reading have previously been assigned for outside preparation, the teacher first discusses the student's answers to the testing questions and examines the student to find out how he arrived at the answer: "How do you know that this verb is in

the present tense and not in the imperfect?"; "What tells you that the subject is plural and not singular?"; "What tells you that *le* in this sentence means *the* and not *him?*" With the multiple choice questions, the teacher could ask: "Why can't the answer be # 3 instead of # 4?" The same procedure can be used on parts of the text not covered by the written questions. With such questions the student is able to reinforce his previously acquired knowledge by repeating it, and to enlarge his understanding of the grammar signals by the careful textual analysis which this questioning entails.

2. Depending on the degree of student preparation, the teacher may then use any combination of the following techniques:

(a) *A review of exercises in text.* The students cover the English with their cards, and the teacher indicates various exercises and calls on students in irregular order. If the student hesitates the first time, the teacher calls on him a second and third time for the same sentence at an interval of two or three questions. Variations of the text exercises also can be used here by putting key words on the blackboard. If the student shows a lack of preparation on any given grammar point, the teacher assigns a section for review.

(b) *A recognition drill.* The teacher puts a pattern sentence on the board with a number of possible substitute items in the manner of an oral substitution drill. If the subject is the interrogative adverbs and pronouns, the following pattern might be used:

Quand est-il parti? Pourquoi? Comment? Avec qui?

The teacher then points variously to the alternatives and calls on students in rapid succession and in irregular order to supply the meaning. The students in response give the meaning in a complete sentence.

(c) *A deduction of the meaning of words from context.* In the reading passage of Ch. XVI, for example, one finds *"Le jeune garçon reçut ainsi sa première formation* **au sein de** *la communauté juive."* Assuming that the student does not readily understand the phrase *au sein de,* the teacher might ask such questions as the following: "What information does the context give you?"; "Does association of this phrase with a community probably indicate a location or a time?"; "Do the previous sentences probably mean a location within or without?" This type of exercise is very helpful in connection with the textual analysis that is described in (1).

(d) *A review of grammar and vocabulary.* The Reading Passages offer many opportunities to review and illustrate grammatical points which have already been covered or which are being studied at the time. In addition, these passages pave the way for the gradual introduction of new points that will be studied in detail in subsequent chapters. This preliminary introduction often greatly facilitates subsequent understanding.

It goes without saying that one of the primary functions of the instructor is to satisfy the questions the students ask. To accomplish this, it has been found effective to elicit questions that will enable the student, as much as possible, to answer his own question. The student might ask, for example, "What does the sentence mean?" The teacher would then answer, "What does *que* do in this sentence? Does it ask a question or does it join two clauses?" He would pursue this line of questioning until the student could see the answer for himself. The great diversity of subject matter presented in this text makes this Socratic method especially applicable. Furthermore, this approach will enable the slower student to understand both the answer and other pertinent questions that he may not have thought of or may have been reluctant to ask.

The reading and testing passages, both in the first part of the text and in the last section (devoted solely to reading), are especially valuable to the student in that they permit him, practically from the beginning, to realize that he is already able to understand material in a variety of fields. This achievement tends to give him a feeling of confidence that the teacher should attempt to develop by urging him to do additional outside reading in the field of his interest.

In the reading tests sometimes there will be two choices which seem possible. One, however, will be more correct in the context indicated. It would be well to point out to the students that this is the type of question which they might expect to find on a reading proficiency test such as the Educational Testing Service examination (the Princeton Exam).

If this text is used in a two-semester course, the class usually comes to the Reading Passages, at the end of the book, about mid-way through the second semester. These passages lend themselves to all the drills and activities described above. Students who are still unfamiliar with the basic grammar structures should be assigned review drills in the appropriate chapters.

Contents

Chapter Seven

Chapter Eight

Chapter Nine

Chapter Ten

Chapter Eleven

Chapter Twelve

Chapter Thirteen

Chapter One

1. *Cognates—Definition*

1. The task of learning French vocabulary is both simplified and hindered for the American student by a large number of **cognate** words (words with similar spellings) which exist in the two languages.

2. It is simplified by **true cognates,** that is, words which look alike and which have similar or nearly similar meanings (e.g., **géologie** and *geology*; **décembre** and *December*). These cognates give you an immediate working vocabulary of many hundreds of words and account for thirty to fifty per cent of the words occurring on an average page of French scientific prose.

3. The task is hindered by **partial cognates** (words which look alike but which have some similar and some divergent meanings) and **false cognates,** that is, words with similar spellings but no related meanings. (See sections 8 and 9.)

4. As a first step in learning to read French, you should learn how to take advantage of true cognates and to be alert to the presence of partial and false cognates.

2. *Nouns—Gender and Cognate Patterns*

1. French nouns have been arbitrarily designated as either masculine or feminine. They are almost always preceded by **le, la, les, l'** (*the*) or **un, une**

1

(*a*). **Le** and **un** precede singular masculine nouns, and **la** and **une** precede singular feminine nouns. **Les** precedes plural nouns of both genders, and **l'** precedes singular nouns of both genders which begin with a vowel sound.

2. A number of French and English nouns ending in **–ion, –itude** and **–age** have identical or nearly identical spellings and meanings: **nation, altitude, passage.** Other groups of words have characteristic patterns which make them easily identifiable:

FRENCH		ENGLISH
Final **–ie**	usually corresponds to	*–y*
l'anthologie (f.)		*the anthology*
une théorie		*a theory*
Final **–é**	usually corresponds to	*–y*
la légalité		*the legality*
la gaieté		*the gaiety*
Final **–eur**	usually corresponds to	*–or*
le directeur		*the director*
un pasteur		*a pastor*
Final **–iste**	usually corresponds to	*–ist*
un artiste		*an artist*
un radiologiste		*a radiologist*
Final **–ment**	usually corresponds to	*–ment*
les gouvernements		*the governments*
l'accomplissement (m.)		*the accomplishment*
Final **–re**	sometimes corresponds to	*–er*
une lettre		*a letter*
l'offre (f.)		*the offer*

READING PREPARATION

INSTRUCTIONS: *Cover the left–hand column (the verification column) with a card or a sheet of paper. Examine the words in the right–hand column and give their meanings. Move your card down as you read if you feel you need to verify your answer.*

	1. l'anthologie
1. the anthology	**2.** l'angularité

2.	the angularity	3.	la légalité
3.	the legality	4.	un gladiateur
4.	a gladiator	5.	un moniteur
5.	a monitor	6.	un dentiste
6.	a dentist	7.	le métallurgiste
7.	the metallurgist	8.	le centre
8.	the center	9.	un mètre
9.	a meter	10.	la densité
10.	the density	11.	la nativité
11.	the nativity	12.	le conducteur
12.	the conductor	13.	les législateurs
13.	the legislators	14.	un fataliste
14.	a fatalist	15.	l'oculiste
15.	the oculist	16.	un monstre
16.	a monster	17.	le théâtre
17.	the theater	18.	la festivité
18.	the festivity	19.	la maturité
19.	the maturity	20.	une odeur
20.	an odor	21.	l'intérieur
21.	the interior	22.	le juriste
22.	the jurist	23.	un baptiste
23.	a Baptist	24.	décembre
24.	December	25.	les offres
25.	the offers	26.	les gouvernements
26.	the governments	27.	les accomplissements
27.	the accomplishments	28.	les monuments

28. the monuments	29. les jugements
29. the judgments	Could you recognize all of the above? Oui?
Magnifique! Go on to the next section.	

3. *Adjectives—Agreement and Cognate Patterns*

1. French adjectives take the gender and number of the noun which they describe. The most common means of agreement is by adding **—e** for the feminine singular, **—s** for the masculine plural, and **—es** for the feminine plural.

2. The following adjective endings often suggest reliable cognates in English:

Final **—en** (m.) **—euse** (f.)	usually correspond to	*—ous*
anxieux **généreux**		*anxious* *generous*
Final **—ique** (m. and f.)	usually corresponds to	*—ic* or *—ical*
cosmique **mécanique**		*cosmic* *mechanical*
Final **—able** (m. and f.)	usually corresponds to	*—able*
agréable **gouvernable**		*agreeable* *governable*
Final **—eux** (m.) **—elle** (f.)	usually correspond to	*—al*
annuel, annuelle **réel, réelle**		*annual* *real*
Final **—el** (m) **—ive** (f.)	usually correspond to	*—ive*
abusif, abusive **subjectif, subjective**		*abusive* *subjective*
Final **—if** (m.) **—enne** (f.)	usually correspond to	*—an*

indien, indienne		*Indian*
épicurien, épicurienne		*Epicurian*
Final **–ant** (m.)	usually correspond to	*–ing*
–ante (f.)		
charmant, charmante		*charming*

READING PREPARATION

INSTRUCTIONS: *Cover the left-hand column (the verification column) with your card. Examine the words in the right-hand column and give their meanings. Move your card down as you read if you feel you need to verify your answer.*

	1. anxieux	
1. anxious	**2.** lumineux	
2. luminous	**3.** atlantique	
3. Atlantic	**4.** électrique	
4. electric, electrical	**5.** déclinable	
5. declinable	**6.** formidable	
6. formidable	**7.** intellectuel	
7. intellectual	**8.** sensuel	
8. sensual	**9.** décisif	
9. decisive	**10.** subjonctif	
10. subjunctive	**11.** formel	
11. formal	**12.** paternel, paternelle	
12. paternal	**13.** irritable	
13. irritable	**14.** affable	
14. affable	**15.** physique	
15. physical	**16.** identique	
16. identical	**17.** curieux	
17. curious	**18.** dynamique	

18.	dynamic	19.	miraculeux
19.	miraculous	20.	instinctif
20.	instinctive	21.	maternel, maternelle
21.	maternal	22.	naturel
22.	natural	23.	coercitif
23.	coercive	24.	manuel
24.	manual	25.	hérétique
25.	heretical	26.	hideux
26.	hideous	27.	subjectif
27.	subjective	28.	coupable
28.	culpable	29.	fantastique
29.	fantastic	30.	charmant
30.	charming	31.	indien
31.	Indian	32.	épicurienne
32.	Epicurian	33.	américain
33.	American		

4. *Adjective Word Order*

1. In English the adjective occasionally follows but usually precedes the noun which it modifies. In French the adjective may precede the noun, but it usually follows it. In translating a noun-adjective combination, you would, of course, use the English word order:

le résultat identique   *the identical result*
une abondante bibliographie   *an abundant bibliography*

READING PREPARATION

INSTRUCTIONS: *Read the following cognate phrases and express their meaning in English. Keep the English verification column covered until you have made a real attempt to read the French. Circle the phrases which you find difficult.*

	1. un volume important
1. an important volume	2. les volumes importants
2. the important volumes	3. une méthode technique
3. a technical method	4. les méthodes techniques
4. the technical methods	5. une technique méthodique
5. a methodical technique	6. une analyse thermique
6. a thermic analysis	7. une analyse thermique différentielle
7. a differential thermic analysis	8. une abondante bibliographie
8. an abundant bibliography	9. les méthodes modernes
9. the modern methods	10. une détermination structurale
10. a structural determination	11. un spécialiste capable
11. a capable specialist	12. un jugement important
12. an important judgment	13. un phénomène curieux
13. a curious phenomenon	14. une tendance instinctive
14. an instinctive tendency	15. une déclaration formelle
15. a formal declaration	16. les sciences physiques
16. the physical sciences	17. les jugements subjectifs
17. the subjective judgments	18. une lettre instructive
18. an instructive letter	19. les lettres instructives
19. the instructive letters	20. une lettre charmante
20. a charming letter	21. un sujet charmant
21. a charming subject	22. une tendance épicurienne
22. an Epicurian tendency	23. le gouvernement indien
23. the Indian government	When you can recognize the phrases which you circled, go on to the next section.

5. *Cognate Adverbs*

1. The ending **–ment,** attached to an adjective, tells you that the word is an adverb and is usually translated by an English word ending in *–ly:*

rapidement	*rapidly*
anxieusement	*anxiously*
intellectuellement	*intellectually*

2. Remember, however, that some nouns also have an **–ment** ending:

un accomplissement	*an accomplishment*
un jugement	*a judgment*

READING PREPARATION

INSTRUCTIONS: *Read the following French phrases. What ideas do they express? Cover the verification column on the left with your card and consult it only when necessary. Circle the phrases which give you difficulty.*

	1. une réponse catégoriquement négative
1. a categorically negative answer (response)	2. un volume particulièrement important
2. a particularly important volume	3. une phrase curieusement formulée
3. a curiously formulated phrase	4. une idée logiquement impossible
4. a logically impossible idea	5. un effort absolument admirable
5. an absolutely admirable effort	6. une méthode essentiellement moderne
6. an essentially modern method	7. une bibliographie essentiellement complète
7. an essentially complete bibliography	8. une bibliographie complètement essentielle
8. a completely essential bibliography	9. une décision substantiellement correcte
9. a substantially correct decision	10. un jugement essentiellement erroné
10. an essentially erroneous judgment	Review the phrases which you circled before you go on to the next section.

6.   *Cognate Verbs*

1.   French verbs in their infinitive form end in **–er, –ir,** or **–re.** These endings correspond to the English word *to* as the sign of the infinitive: **continuer**=*to continue.* Certain classes of French verbs likewise suggest possible equivalents in English:

FRENCH		ENGLISH
Final **–er**	sometimes indicates	*–e* or is dropped entirely
admirer		*to admire*
continuer		*to continue*
accepter		*to accept*
présenter		*to present*
Final **–er**	sometimes indicates	*–ate*
germiner		*to germinate*
amputer		*to amputate*
Final **–yser** or **–iser**	usually indicate	*–yze* or *–ize*
analyser		*to analyze*
moraliser		*to moralize*
Final **–ier**	often indicates	*–y*
crier		*to cry out*
purifier		*to purify*
Final **–ir**	often indicates	*–ish*
démolir		*to demolish*
nourrir		*to nourish*
Final **–rir**	sometimes indicates	*–er*
offrir		*to offer*
couvrir		*to cover*
Final **–quer**	usually indicates	*–cate*
abdiquer		*to abdicate*
indiquer		*to indicate*

READING PREPARATION

INSTRUCTIONS: *Remember to use your card to cover the English word until you have made an effort to express the meaning of the French. Continue to circle difficult words.*

	1. admirer
1. to admire	**2.** examiner
2. to examine	**3.** accepter
3. to accept	**4.** présenter
4. to present	**5.** analyser
5. to analyze	**6.** terroriser
6. to terrorize	**7.** électrifier
7. to electrify	**8.** raréfier
8. to rarify	**9.** indiquer
9. to indicate	**10.** célébrer
10. to celebrate	**11.** émaner
11. to emanate	**12.** accomplir
12. to accomplish	**13.** languir
13. to languish	**14.** suffoquer
14. to suffocate	**15.** équivoquer
15. to equivocate	**16.** lamenter
16. to lament	**17.** charmer
17. to charm	**18.** condamner
18. to condemn	**19.** civiliser
19. to civilize	**20.** diversifier
20. to diversify	**21.** démolir
21. to demolish	**22.** chérir
22. to cherish	**23.** finir
23. to finish	**24.** humilier
24. to humiliate	**25.** méditer
25. to meditate	**26.** fabriquer

26. to fabricate	**27.** périr
27. to perish	**28.** stupéfier
28. to stupefy	**29.** punir
29. to punish	**30.** immortaliser
30. to immortalize	**31.** familiariser
31. to familiarize	**32.** exister
32. to exist	**33.** communiquer
33. to communicate	**34.** abdiquer
34. to abdicate	**35.** nourrir
35. to nourish	**36.** identifier
36. to identify	**37.** agiter
37. to agitate	Review the words which you circled above until you can recognize them easily.

7. *Assorted Cognates*

1. Prefixes, initial letters, and accents may likewise suggest cognates:

FRENCH		ENGLISH
Initial **es–** or **é–**	often becomes	*s–*
espace		*space*
étudier		*to study*
une étude		*a study*
Initial **dé–** or **dés**	often becomes	*dis–*
déshonorer		*to dishonor*
dédaigner		*to disdain*

A circumflex accent (ˆ) often suggests an **s** which has dropped out:

une forêt	*a forest*
un mât	*a mast*
coûter	*to cost*
rôtir	*to roast*

READING PREPARATION

INSTRUCTIONS: *Give the English word which the French cognate suggests. Remember to use your card.*

	1. un espace
1. a space	**2.** un estomac
2. a stomach	**3.** étrange
3. strange	**4.** un esturgeon
4. a sturgeon	**5.** une forêt
5. a forest	**6.** une île
6. an isle	**7.** désengager
7. to disengage	**8.** déguiser
8. to disguise	**9.** une étude
9. a study	**10.** déplacer
10. to displace	**11.** étrangler
11. to strangle	**12.** un mât
12. a mast	**13.** désorganiser
13. to disorganize	**14.** désassembler
14. to disassemble	**15.** une éponge
15. a sponge	**16.** une étable
16. a stable	**17.** rôtir
17. to roast	**18.** un hôpital
18. a hospital	**19.** un rôti de porc
19. a pork roast	**20.** coûter
20. to cost	

INSTRUCTIONS: *The following cognates have developed slightly differently in French than in English, but their meaning can be deduced with a little intelligent guessing.*

	1. un ancêtre
1. an ancestor	2. une espèce
2. a species	3. nombreux
3. numerous	4. vulgaire
4. vulgar, common	5. un kangourou
5. a kangaroo	6. un wagon–restaurant (*part of a train*)
6. a dining car	7. zigzaguer
7. to zigzag	8. un chapitre
8. a chapter	9. un géant
9. a giant	10. un drame
10. a drama	11. un hôtel
11. a hotel	12. pittoresque
12. picturesque	13. irrégulier
13. irregular	14. linéaire
14. linear	

8. *Cognates—Partially Similar Meanings*

1. If the meanings of all French words could be deduced by similarities which they bear to English, the learning of vocabulary would be very easy. But language is not so simple. Some cognates have meanings which are related but not equivalent. A French word may have some but not all of the meanings of an English cognate:

marcher	= *to march*	but also	*to walk* or *to function*
saluer	= *to salute*		*to greet, to acclaim*
saisir	= *to seize*		*to understand*
défendre	= *to defend*		*to prohibit*
comprendre	= *to understand*		*to include*

2. The meanings of partial cognates must be derived from the context or from a dictionary.

READING PREPARATION

INSTRUCTIONS: *Using your card, work through the following discussion.*

	1. **L'arbitre a disqualifié l'équipe de baseball =** The _____ disqualified the baseball team. The French **arbitre** suggests the English *arbitrator* or *arbiter*, but in this sentence either word would be awkward and imprecise. In English the man who "arbitrates" between baseball teams is the _____.
1. umpire	2. You would know that you should use the word *umpire* instead of *arbiter* because of the context specified by the word _____.
2. baseball	3. **L'arbitre a arrêté le match de boxe =** The _____ stopped the boxing match. The context specified by the reference to boxing tells you that **arbitre** here would not be translated by *umpire*, but by _____.
3. referee	4. The word *referee* is suggested by the _____.
4. context	5. **Les expériences effectuées par le professeur Duchesne donnent des résultats inattendus =** The _____ performed by Professor Duchesne give unexpected results. Here the context suggests that **expériences** would be translated by _____.
5. experiments	6. **Les expériences de la vie sont parfois désagréables =** The _____ of life are sometimes unpleasant. Here the context suggests that **expériences** would be translated by _____.

6. experiences

9. *False Cognates*

1. Some words in French look like English words, but they have completely different meanings which may not always be apparent from the context of the sentence. Examples are:

FRENCH	ENGLISH
actuel, actuelle	*current, present*
actuellement	*currently, presently*
la lecture	*the reading*
la conférence	*the lecture*
le bout	*the extremity, end*
la chair	*the flesh*
attirer	*to attract*
rester	*to remain*
avertir	*to warn*

In the appendices there is a table of many common false cognates of which you should be aware.

TESTING EXERCISE

INSTRUCTIONS: *The following testing exercise will permit you to verify your mastery of the French-English cognates. Write the English in the space provided. The answers are at the end of the chapter. If you miss the answer, go back to the section indicated at the right of the blank space and review the point. If you get them all right, go to the reading passage*

1. beauté _____ (2)
2. continuer _____ (6)
3. mécanique _____ (3)
4. abusif _____ (3)
5. démolir _____ (6)
6. une forêt _____ (7)
7. une étable _____ (7)
8. déplacer _____ (7)
9. actuellement _____ (9)
10. particulièrement _____ (5)
11. une bibliographie complètement
    essentielle _____ (4 and 5)

READING PASSAGE

INSTRUCTIONS: *The following book review consists of extracts from the* Bulletin de la Société chimique de France.[1] *Only three words have been changed from the original. Write out a translation of it in clear, natural English, using the English supplied as cues.*

Cet ouvrage présente une série d'études sur des * méthodes récentes de caractérisation
This work _____ __ ___ *of* ___ *on* _____ _____ *of* _____

et de détermination structurale des composés macromoléculaires. Il est l'oeuvre collective
and of _____ _____ *of* _____ _____. *It is the* _____ *work*

de plusieurs spécialistes et constitue un volume particulièrement important. . . .
of several _____ *and* _____ __ _____ _____ _____

L'auteur commence par une étude sur la microactivité et sur les méthodes de détermination
_____ _____ *by a* ___ *on* _____ *and on the* _____ __ _____

de la stéréorégularité à l'état solide et en solution . . . Deux importants chapitres traitent
of _____ *in* ___ ___ *and in* _____. *Two* _____ _____ *treat*

de la diffusion des rayons X aux petits angles et de la diffraction des électrons. La résonance
the _____ *of* _____ *at short* _____ *and the* _____ *of* _____. _____

magnétique nucléaire fait l'objet d'un chapitre, avec son emploi pour la détermination
_____ _____ *is the* ___ *of one* _____, *with its utilization for the* _____

de la configuration et de la structure des chaînes macromoléculaires. L'analyse thermique
of the _____ *and of the* _____ *of* _____ _____. _____ _____

différentielle . . . est ensuite largement développée . . . Une abondante bibliographie
_____ *is then* _____ *at length. An* _____ _____

complète chaque chapitre. Une table des matières termine l'ouvrage, qui sera certainement
_____ *each* _____. *A* ___ __ *contents* _____ *the work, which will* _____

accueilli avec beaucoup de faveur.
be received with much _____.

---

[1] From a review by G. Champetier of *New Methods of Polymer Characterization* in *Bulletin de la Société chimique de France* (septembre, 1965), p. 2666.
* *Do not translate.*

ANSWERS TO THE TESTING EXERCISE, PAGE 15:

1 beauty	5 to demolish	9 currently
2 to continue	6 a forest	10 particularly
3 mechanical	7 a stable	11 a completely essential
4 abusive	8 to displace	bibliography

Chapter Two

10. *Subject Pronouns and Present Tense of* −er *Verbs*

1. The subject pronouns and the present tense of **−er** verbs are as follows:

trouver	*to find*
je trouve	*I find, am finding, do find*
tu trouves	*you find, are finding, do find*
il (m.), **elle** (f.) **trouve**	*he, she, it finds, is finding, does find*
on trouve	*one finds, is finding, does find*
nous trouvons	*we find, are finding, do find*
vous trouvez	*you find, are finding, do find*
ils (m.), **elles** (f.) **trouvent**	*they find, are finding, do find*

2. **Tu** and **vous** are both translated as *you.* **Tu** is always a singular form and indicates that the speaker is addressing someone with whom he is on close personal terms or to whom he feels superior. **Vous** is either singular or plural and is used in speaking to strangers, superiors, or acquaintances. Notice also that **il, elle, ils,** and **elles** may refer either to persons or things.

3. While there is only one form of the present in French, there are three in

17

English. In translating the present tense into English, choose the form of the English present indicated by the context. (Sometimes two or all three will be possible.)

Parfois la connaissance de la fonction résulte de l'expérimentation directe.	*Sometimes the knowledge of the function results from direct experimentation.*
A la Jamaïque, l'université joue actuellement un rôle primordial dans le développement de la nouvelle nation.	*In Jamaica the University is presently playing a primordial role in the development of the new nation.*
Malgré les suppositions contraires l'université joue un rôle important.	*In spite of contrary suppositions the University does play an important role* (or *is playing*, or *plays*).

READING PREPARATION

INSTRUCTIONS: *Match the verb ending with the appropriate pronoun. Continue to circle difficult words for future review.*

	1. _____ trouv**ez** (1) vous (2) nous (3) ils
1. (1) **vous** trouv**ez**	**2.** _____ trouv**ons** (1) vous (2) nous (3) ils
2. (2) **nous** trouv**ons**	**3.** _____ trouv**ent** (1) il (2) tu (3) ils
3. (3) **ils** trouv**ent**	**4.** _____ trouv**es** (1) je (2) tu (3) vous
4. (2) **tu** trouv**es**	**5.** _____ trouv**e** (1) je (2) vous (3) elles
5. (1) **je** trouv**e**	**6.** Vous étudiez actuellement le français. (The presence of **actuellement** indicates that **étudiez** will be best translated as—*are studying/study*.)
6. *are studying* You are presently studying French.	**7.** **toujours**=*always* Nous étudions toujours le français. (**Toujours** suggests that **étudions** will best be translated by—*are studying/study*.)

7. *study* We always study French.	**8.** **sembler**=*to seem* La lecture semble facile.
8. Reading seems easy. (Remember that **la lecture** is a false cognate.)	**9.** Elle semble toujours facile. (To which word of #8 does **elle** refer?)
9. **la lecture** It always seems easy.	**10.** Marie trouve la lecture facile.
10. Mary finds the reading easy.	**11.** Elle trouve la lecture facile. (To which word of #10 does **elle** refer?)
11. **Marie** She finds the reading easy.	**12.** Je trouve l'article intéressant.
12. I find the article interesting.	**13.** **ce, cet, cette**=*this* Je trouve ce sujet intéressant.
13. I find this subject interesting.	**14.** Ce sujet semble toujours intéressant.
14. . This subject always seems interesting.	**15.** Vous trouvez cette lecture facile.
15. You find this reading easy.	**16.** Au contraire, nous trouvons cette lecture difficile. (Being contrasted with **facile, difficile** must mean _____ _____.)
16. *difficult* To the contrary, we find this reading difficult.	**17.** **le pays**=*the country* L'auteur présente une étude concernant le pays de la Jamaïque.
17. The author presents a study concerning the country of Jamaica.	**18.** **parler de**=*to speak of* Il parle de l'effort pour moderniser le pays. (With reference to #17, does **il** refer to **l'auteur** or **une étude**?)
18. **l'auteur—il,** being masculine, cannot refer to **une étude,** which is feminine. He speaks of the effort to modernize the country.	**19.** Cet effort semble particulièrement énergique à la Jamaïque. (Since the sentence speaks of a location, **à** here probably means—*in/to.*)
19. *in* This effort seems particularly energetic in Jamaica.	**20.** L'auteur parle longuement de l'éducation à la Jamaïque.
20. The author speaks at length of education in Jamaica.	**21.** L'auteur trouve cet effort admirable.

21. The author finds this effort admirable.	**22.** **avec**=*with* Il parle de cet effort avec admiration.
22. He speaks of this effort with admiration.	**23.** Les observateurs objectifs parlent de cette étude avec dédain.
23. The objective observers speak of this work with disdain.	**24.** Ils parlent de cet article avec enthousiasme.
24. They speak of this article with enthusiasm.	**25.** **chaque**=*each* L'auteur parle de chaque aspect de l'éducation à la Jamaïque.
25. The author speaks of each aspect of education in Jamaica.	**26.** Il traite chaque aspect de ce sujet. (Your previous encounters with **de** suggest that here it would be translated as—*at/of*.)
26. *of* He treats each aspect of this subject.	**27.** Une abondante bibliographie complète chaque chapitre.
27. An abundant bibliography completes each chapter.	Before going on to the next section, be sure that you are perfectly familiar with the words you circled above.

11. Le, la, les, l' *as Definite Articles*

1. Le, la, les, l' serve two grammatical functions in French: as pronouns and as definite articles.

2. When they are used as definite articles, they precede a noun, and their meaning is sometimes expressed by *the*:

l'université (f.) **nationale**	*the national university*
l'esprit (m.) **de collaboration**	*the spirit of collaboration*
la religion anglicane	*the Anglican religion*
le développement de la nouvelle nation	*the development of the new nation*
les ressources (f.) **principales de l'île**	*the principal resources of the island*

les services (m.) **gouvernementaux du pays**	*the governmental services of the country*
l'histoire (f.) **de France**	*the history of France*

3. On the other hand, they may signal a meaning which in English is expressed simply by a general noun or a plural:

La France est en Europe.	*France is in Europe.*
Le fer est dur.	*Iron is hard.*
Les hommes sont mortels.	*Men are mortal.*
La science et la technique posent un grand nombre de problèmes.	*Science and Technology pose a great number of problems.*

When *the* sounds awkward as a translation (e.g. "The France is in Europe") omit *the*. Let your ear be your guide.

READING PREPARATION

INSTRUCTIONS: *Cover the English with your card. Then try to work out the meaning of the French. Move your card down only to verify or correct your answer.*

	1. sont=*are* Les ressources principales de l'île sont:
1. The principal resources of the island are:	**2.** la bauxite
2. bauxite	**3.** la canne à sucre
3. sugar cane	**4.** le tourisme
4. tourism (or the tourist industry)	**5.** les bananes
5. bananas	**6.** le rhum
6. rum	**7.** le café
7. coffee	**8. est**=*is* Le fer est un métal commun.
8. Iron is a common metal.	**9.** La France est en Europe.

9. France is in Europe.	**10.** **par** = *by* Cette étude traite des problèmes posés par la science.
10. This study treats the problems posed by science.	**11.** Le sujet de l'article en question est la Jamaïque.
11. The subject of the article in question is Jamaica.	**12.** Les problèmes posés par la technologie sont toujours difficiles.
12. The problems posed by technology are always difficult.	**13.** **diriger** = *to guide, to lead* Le président dirige la nation.
13. The president leads (guides) the nation.	

12. Le, la, les, l' *as Pronouns*

1.   As a pronoun **le** is translated by *him* or *it*, **la** by *her* or *it*, and **les** by *them*, depending on the antecedent. When they precede verbs, they are pronouns and not articles:

(l'article) **Je le trouve intéressant.**	*I find it interesting.*
(l'auteur) **Je le trouve capable.**	*I find him capable.*
(Marie) **Je la trouve belle.**	*I find her beautiful.*
(la lecture) **Je la trouve intéressante.**	*I find it interesting.*
(les problèmes) **Je les trouve difficiles.**	*I find them difficult.*

2.   **L'** is the elision of either **le** or **la** with a word beginning with a vowel sound.

READING PREPARATION

INSTRUCTIONS: *Cover the English with your card. Then try to work out the meaning of the French. Move your card down only to verify or correct your answers.*

	1. L'étude est solide. Ils la trouvent solide.

1. The study is sound (solid). They find it sound.	**2.** **bon**=*good, correct* La réponse est bonne. Je la trouve bonne.
2. The answer is correct. I find it correct. (You have probably guessed that **bonne** is the feminine form of **bon**.)	**3.** **très**=*very* Mme Curie est très célèbre. On la trouve très célèbre. (What cognate does **célèbre** suggest in English?)
3. *celebrated*, or *famous* Mme Curie is very famous. One finds her very famous.	**4.** Les spécialistes sont nécessaires. On les trouve nécessaires.
4. Specialists are necessary. One finds them necessary.	**5.** Les réponses sont bonnes. Nous les trouvons bonnes.
5. The answers are correct. We find them correct.	**6.** L'auteur semble très capable. Nous le trouvons très capable.
6. The author seems very capable. We find him very capable.	**7.** Les auteurs modernes semblent réalistes. Nous les trouvons réalistes.
7. Modern authors seem realistic. We find them realistic.	Are you continuing to circle and review the words which you find difficult?

13. *Preposition*—de (du, des)

1. The most common meanings of the preposition **de** are expressed in English by *of* and *from*:

les ressources *de* l'île   *the resources **of** the island*

Il arrive *de* France.   *He is arriving **from** France.*

2. Many French verbs and nouns are followed by **de**+an infinitive. Since the correspondence of meaning between French and English prepositions is sometimes slight, translate the expression as a whole, choosing the preposition which English usage requires. Often there will be no "one–for–one" translation of **de** or other prepositions.

Les dirigeants essaient de moderniser le pays.   *The leaders are trying to modernize the country.*

la volonté de contribuer à la grandeur d'un pays . . .   *the will to contribute to the greatness of a country . . .*

> **Les dirigeants cherchent le moyen de moderniser le pays.**
>
> *The leaders are looking for the means of modernizing the country.*

3. Du is the contraction of **de + le. Des** is the contraction of **de + les.** They are translated as *of the* or *of, from the* or *from,* depending on the context:

> **la maturité des dirigeants**
>
> *the maturity of the leaders*

> **la grandeur du pays**
>
> *the greatness of the country*

> **la détermination structurale des composés macromoléculaires**
>
> *the structural determination of macro-molecular compounds*

READING PREPARATION

INSTRUCTIONS: *Give the meanings of the following phrases.*

1. les impressions du visiteur

1. the impressions of the visitor

2. **la volonté** = *the will*
la volonté des dirigeants

2. the will of the leaders

3. **vif** = *quick, active, keen*
la volonté des forces vives (f. pl.) de la nation

3. the will of the active forces of the nation

4. la maturité des dirigeants

4. the maturity of the leaders

5. **jouer** = *to play*
La volonté des dirigeants joue un rôle important dans le gouvernement.

5. The will of the leaders plays an important role in the government.

6. Le souvenir de l'esclavage reste vif. (The context suggests that **souvenir** here means—*souvenir/memory.*)

6. *memory*
The memory of slavery remains keenly alive.
(Remember that **rester** is a false cognate.)

7. **grand** = *great, large*
Le souvenir de l'esclavage joue un grand rôle dans la formation d'un esprit nationaliste.

7. The memory of slavery plays a large role in the formation of a nationalist spirit.

8. Le souvenir de la grandeur du pays reste vif.

8. The memory of the greatness of the country remains keenly alive. (Notice that it is sometimes possible, or preferable, to use a paraphrase instead of a word-for-word translation.)	**9.** L'intention de l'auteur reste obscure.
9. The intention of the author remains obscure.	**10.** La majorité des problèmes scientifiques restent difficiles.
10. The majority of scientific problems remain difficult.	**11.** La majorité des problèmes scientifiques concernent la structure d'une fonction.
11. The majority of scientific problems concern the structure of a function (math.).	

14. *Preposition*—à (au, aux)

1. The most common meanings of **à** are expressed in English by *at, to,* or *in.*

2. Many French verbs are followed by **à** + the infinitive. There are a good number of nouns which are followed by **à** in special constructions. In these phrases **à** does not have a "one–for–one" equivalent. Read the phrase as a whole and not as a series of unrelated words.

Des spécialistes anglo-saxons aident à industrialiser le pays.	*Anglo-Saxon specialists are helping to industrialize the country.*
la canne à sucre	*sugar cane*
un thermomètre à mercure	*a mercury thermometer*

3. **Au** is the contraction of **à** + **le.** **Aux** is the contraction of **à** + **les.** They are usually translated as *to the, at the,* or *in the,* depending on the context.

La ville est au centre de l'île.	*The city is in the center of the island.*
une référence à l'effort pour moderniser le pays . . .	*a reference to the effort to modernize the country . . .*

READING PREPARATION

INSTRUCTIONS: *Give the meanings of the following phrases and sentences. Cover the English with your card until you have attempted to read the French.*

	·1. une contribution à la grandeur d'un pays
1. a contribution to the greatness of a country	**2.** une lettre adressée au président
2. a letter addressed to the president	**3.** une référence à l'effort d'industrialisation
3. a reference to the effort of industrialization	**4.** **ville** = *city* L'université est au centre de la ville.
4. The university is at (in) the center of the city.	**5.** La ville est au centre de l'île.
5. The city is at (in) the center of the island.	**6.** Ils contribuent au développement du pays.
6. They contribute to the development of the country.	**7.** **nouveau** (m.) = *new* **nouvelle** (f) = *new* Je parle aux dirigeants de la nouvelle nation.
7. I am speaking to the leaders of the new nation.	**8.** Nous parlons des dirigeants du nouveau pays.
8. We are speaking of the leaders of the new country.	**9.** Nous parlons à l'auteur d'une étude importante.
9. We are speaking to the author of an important study.	**10.** **diriger** = *to lead* **un dirigeant** = *a leader* **étudier** = *to study* **un étudiant** = _____
10. *a student*	**11.** Cette étude contient une description de l'éducation à la Jamaïque. (Which cognate verb does *contient* suggest?)
11. *contains* This study contains a description of education in Jamaica.	**12.** Il parle aux étudiants de l'université nationale à Paris.

12. He is speaking to the students of the national university at Paris.	**13.** Les étudiants de l'université nationale jouent un rôle important dans le développement du système d'éducation à la Jamaïque.
13. The students of the national university are playing an important role in the development of the system of education in Jamaica. (Remember that English usage omits the article with countries.)	If you circled any of the above phrases, make sure that you know them before continuing.

15. *Prepositions*—dans, sur, par, parmi, entre, pendant, avec

1. The meanings of these prepositions are usually indicated as follows:

dans	*in, into*
sur	*on*
par	*by, through*
parmi	*among*
entre	*between*
pendant	*during, for*
avec	*with*

2. When you are translating, remember that relatively few words in any one language have exact "equivalents" in another language, that is, words which have all the meanings and only the meanings of the words in the first language. This is especially true of prepositions. Be guided by the normal English usage. In translating the phrase "une étude sur la révolution," a possible rendering might be, "a study on the revolution." It would be a better translation, however, to say "a study about the revolution." But "un chapitre sur la découverte de l'or" could very well be translated as "a chapter on the discovery of gold."

READING PREPARATION

INSTRUCTIONS: *Give the meanings of the following phrases and sentences. Cover the English with your card until you have made a genuine effort to read the French.*

		1.	dans le domaine de l'éducation
1.	in the field of education	**2.**	les ressources principales sont, dans l'ordre . . .
2.	the principal resources are, in order . . .	**3.**	dans un ouvrage médiocre
3.	in a mediocre work	**4.**	dans un chapitre brillant sur des découvertes récentes
4.	in a brilliant chapter on recent discoveries	**5.**	L'auteur présente une étude sur l'implantation d'entreprises industrielles nouvelles.
5.	The author presents a study of the implantation of new industrial enterprises.	**6.**	**deux**=*two* Parmi les impressions du visiteur anglo-saxon, deux dominent.
6.	Among the impressions of the Anglo-Saxon visitor, two predominate.	**7.**	Parmi les accomplissements du nouveau pays, deux sont exceptionnels.
7.	Among the accomplishments of the new country, two are exceptional.	**8.**	Le chapitre commence par une étude sur la découverte de l'or.
8.	The chapter begins by (with) a study of the discovery of gold.	**9.**	**un an**=*one year* pendant un an pendant deux ans
9.	during (for) one year during (for) two years	**10.**	**les savants**=*the scholars* Nous citons la collaboration entre les savants européens et américains.
10.	We cite (make special mention of) the collaboration between European and American scholars.	**11.**	**sain**=*wholesome, healthy* On admire l'esprit de saine collaboration entre les universités du pays.
11.	One admires the spirit of wholesome collaboration among the universities of the country.	**12.**	Parmi les études sur ce sujet, deux dominent.
12.	Among the studies of (on) this subject, two predominate.	**13.**	On parle toujours favorablement du nouvel ouvrage.

13. One always speaks of the new work with favor.
(**Nouvel** masculine singular is the form of **nouveau** which is used before a vowel sound.)

14. **travailler**=*to work*
Les spécialistes anglo–saxons travaillent avec les dirigeants de la nouvelle nation.

14. The Anglo-Saxon specialists work with the leaders of the new nation.

15. **où**= *where*
La Jamaïque est un pays où le souvenir de l'esclavage reste toujours vif.

15. Jamaica is a country where the memory of slavery still remains keenly alive.

16. **un endroit**=*a place*
L'université est un endroit où on étudie.

16. The university is a place where one studies.

17. Le laboratoire est un endroit où on travaille.

17. The laboratory is a place where one works.

18. L'auteur admire l'esprit de saine collaboration entre les diverses institutions du nouveau pays.

18. The author admires the spirit of wholesome collaboration between the diverse institutions of the new country.

19. Les dirigeants travaillent à la modernisation du pays.

19. The leaders are working to modernize the country.

20. Un candidat au doctorat travaille toujours à une thèse.

20. A doctoral candidate is always working on a thesis.

21. **un livre**=*a book*
On trouve un grand nombre de livres à la bibliothèque. La bibliothèque est un endroit où on étudie.
(The association of place, books, and study indicates that the **bibliothèque** is the _____.)

21. library
One finds a great number of books at the library. The library is a place where one studies.

22. Notamment, le nouveau département de pédagogie de l'université continue à travailler avec les institutions gouvernementales.
(English usage suggests that **pédagogie** should be translated as— *education/pedagogy*.)

22. *education*
Notably, the new department of education of the university continues to work with the governmental institutions.

23. **régner**=*to reign*
Notamment, un esprit de saine collaboration règne entre les services gouvernementaux.

23. Notably, a spirit of healthy collaboration reigns between the governmental services.	24. Un désir de contribuer à la grandeur du pays règne à l'université.
24. A desire to contribute to the greatness of the country reigns at the university.	

TESTING EXERCISE

INSTRUCTIONS: *Circle the word which makes the sentence grammatically correct or gives the best translation into English. If you miss any of them, go back and review the appropriate section. The number in parentheses indicates the section that treats the material. If all your answers are correct, go on to the reading passage. Do the entire test before checking your answers.*

   1. **Le** travail commence bien.
      A. the   B. it   c. they   D. them

1. A
(11)
   2. Je **le** trouve incapable.
      A. him   B. the   c. her   D. them

2. A
(12)
   3. Nous _____ l'esprit de progrès qui domine dans la nouvelle nation.
      A. admirez   B. admirons   c. admirer   D. admirent

3. B
(10)
   4. La majorité des problèmes posés par **la science** restent sans réponse.
      A. the science   B. science   c. some science   D. the sciences

4. B
(11)
   5. Je parle _____ futurs professeurs.
      A. au   B. à les   c. à le   D. aux

5. D
(14)
   6. On parle du nouvel ouvrage _____ beaucoup d'enthousiasme.
      A. pendant   B. avec   c. parmi   D. sur

6. B
(15)
   7. Ce livre est **l'oeuvre collective** de plusieurs spécialistes.
      A. the works   B. the collective work   c. collective work   D. a collective work

7. B
(11)
   8. **La canne à sucre** est un des produits du Cuba.
      A. the sugar cane   B. the cane of sugar   c. the can of sugar   D. sugar cane

8. D
(14)
   9. Vous travaillez probablement **dans** un laboratoire de physique.
      A. in   B. among   c. during   D. on

9. A
(15)
   10. Elle _____ l'Europe tous les étés.
      A. visiter   B. visitons   c. visitez   D. visite

10. D
(10)
   Score _____

READING PASSAGE

INSTRUCTIONS: *Read the following paragraphs. The words that are in darker print and have footnotes following them are translated at the bottom of the page. Circle the words which you do not immediately recognize but do not look them up right away. Read for the overall content. When you have finished reading, verify your comprehension by answering the questions at the end. If two alternatives seem plausible, choose the one which more nearly expresses the meaning stated in the text. Then come back to the circled words and work out their meaning more precisely, if necessary.*

Description de l'île de la Jamaïque

From Gilbert L. de Landsheere, "Education et la formation du personnel enseignant dans un pays en plein développement," *International Review of Education*, VIII (1962), 42–43.

Les ressources principales de l'île **sont**,[1] dans l'ordre: la bauxite, la canne à sucre, le tourisme, les bananes, le rhum, et le café. Le pays **fait un gros** [2] effort d'industrialisation; l'implantation d'entreprises industrielles nouvelles et la construction d'hôtels sont **encouragées** [3] par une exemption de **tous les**
5 **impôts** [4] pendant sept [7] ans . . .

Parmi les impressions qui **assaillent** [5] le visiteur, deux dominent: la volonté des forces vives de la nation de contribuer à la grandeur d'un pays où le souvenir de l'esclavage reste vif, et la compétence et la maturité des dirigeants—**qui** [6] continuent **d'ailleurs de s'entourer** [7] de spécialistes
10 anglo-saxons partout où **ils en sentent le besoin. . . .**[8]

La religion anglicane est **la plus répandue:** [9] on trouve ensuite **des** [10] baptistes, des méthodistes, des presbytériens, des catholiques romains et des juifs. . . .

L'Université joue un rôle primordial dans le développement de la nouvelle
15 nation. Dans le domaine de l'éducation, notamment, **on ne peut qu'**[11]admirer l'esprit de saine collaboration **qui** [12] règne entre les services gouvernementaux, les **anciennes** [13] institutions d'enseignement et le nouveau département de pédagogie de l'Université.

1. The main idea of the first paragraph is that
   A. many tourists visit the island, making tourism the principal industry
   B. the island is doing much to develop its economy
   C. hotels pay a heavy tax
   D. the resources of the island remain unexploited

---

1. B

2. The main idea of the second paragraph is that
   A. the development of the island is progressing slowly

1 *are*	6 *who*	10 Here **des** simply indicates
2 *is making a great*	7 *moreover to surround*	plurality.
3 *encouraged*	*themselves with*	11 *one cannot but*
4 *all taxes*	8 *they feel the need of it*	12 *which*
5 *which beset*	9 *the most widespread*	13 *former*

B. slavery is still found in some parts of the island but is disappearing

C. some leaders are mature but the country is still dominated by Anglo-Saxon specialists

D. there is a powerful spirit of nationalism at work in the country

2. D   **3.** The fourth paragraph states that

A. the various governmental and university agencies work harmoniously with each other

B. the university is relatively unimportant

C. education on a large scale is still not a reality

D. there is a healthy competition between governmental agencies.

3. A

Chapter Three

16. Etre (*to be*) *and Impersonal Pronouns*

1. The verb **être** does not follow the regular pattern of conjugation. Its present tense forms, with three new impersonal pronouns, are as follows:

je suis	*I am*
tu es	*you are* (sing.)
il est	*he is, it is*
elle est	*she is, it is*
on est	*one is, people are, they are*
ceci, cela est	*this, that is*
c'est	*it is, she is, he is*
nous sommes	*we are*
vous êtes	*you are*
ils sont	*they are* (m.)
elles sont	*they are* (f.)
ce sont	*they are*

2. Notice that **il, elle,** and **ce** may refer either to persons or things. In order to be sure of the correct translation, you must read the word in its entire context:

On rejette communément la théorie de Picard—elle est intenable.

People commonly reject the theory of Picard—it is untenable.

Sa conférence traite de Mme Curie —elle est très célèbre.	*His lecture deals with Mme Curie— she is very famous.*
Le travail joue un grand rôle dans cette théorie—il explique la nature de la valeur.	*Work plays a large role in this theory— it explains the nature of value.*
Il est professeur de chimie.	*He is a professor of chemistry.*
Il est dix (10) heures.	*It is ten o'clock.*
C'est facile.	*It is easy.*
Le professeur Picard donne une conférence ce soir. C'est un savant distingué.	*Professor Picard is giving a lecture tonight. He is a distinguished scholar.*

3. Many idioms are constructed with **être.** Some common ones are:

être en train de	*to be in the process of*
être au courant de	*to be aware of, or conversant with*
être d'accord avec	*to be in agreement with*

4. Il and **on** have other uses and meanings, which are explained in Chapter VI.

READING PREPARATION

INSTRUCTIONS: *Express the meaning of the following phrases. Cover the English verification with your card until you have worked out the entire meaning. Circle the words you do not immediately recognize.*

1. un fait = *a fact*
Je suis sûr des faits.
(Since **sûr** has an accent, it is not the preposition **sur,** *on.* Look for a cognate.)

1. I am sure of the facts.		**2.** Je suis au courant de ce fait.	
2. I am aware of this fact.		**3.** Je suis naturellement d'accord avec ce fait.	
3. I am naturally in agreement with this fact.		**4.** Nous hésitons à accepter cette théorie.	
4. We hesitate to accept this theory.		**5.** Nous sommes en train d'étudier cette théorie.	

5. We are in the process of studying this theory. (Notice that English usage requires *studying* and not *to study* in this case.)

6. **ces** = *these*
Nous sommes naturellement d'accord avec ces théories.

6. We are naturally in agreement with these theories.

7. Elle est sûre de la réponse.

7. She is sure of the answer.

8. **aussi** = *also*
L'étude est aussi riche en faits historiques.

8. The study is also rich in historical facts.

9. **la vérité** = *the truth*
Nous sommes aussi incertains de la vérité de cette théorie.

9. We are also uncertain of the truth of this theory.

10. Vous semblez incertain de la vérité de ces faits.

10. You seem uncertain of the truth of these facts.

11. Ils semblent trouver ces théories incertaines.

11. They seem to find these theories uncertain.

12. Ils les trouvent incertaines.

12. They find them uncertain.

13. **vrai** = *true*
Cela est vrai—elles sont difficiles à établir.

13. That is true—they are difficult to establish.

14. Ceci est certain—la vraie raison reste obscure.

14. This is certain—the true reason remains obscure.

15. **mais** = *but*
Cette théorie est intéressante, mais elle est aussi fausse.
(faux × vrai)

15. This theory is interesting, but it is also false.
(fausse = feminine form)

16. **d'ailleurs** = *moreover*
Marie est belle. D'ailleurs elle est intelligente.

16. Marie is beautiful. Moreover, she is intelligent.

17. Nous sommes ambitieux, mais nous sommes aussi fatigués.

17. We are ambitious, but we are also tired.

18. **néanmoins** = *nonetheless*
Vous êtes beau, mais vous êtes néanmoins intelligent.

18. You are handsome, but you are nonetheless intelligent.

19. La leçon est facile, mais elle est néanmoins importante.

19. The lesson is easy, but it is nonetheless important.

20. La leçon est très intéressante. Elle est d'ailleurs d'une grande importance.

20. The lesson is very interesting. It is moreover of great importance.

21. **si**=*if*
Si les observations de Walras sont simples, elles sont néanmoins importantes.

21. If the observations of Walras are simple, they are nonetheless important.

22. Si les faits historiques sont difficiles à établir, ils sont néanmoins nécessaires.

22. If historical facts are difficult to establish, they are nonetheless necessary.

23. **peut-être**=*perhaps*
découvrir=*to discover*
une découverte=*a* _____
Vous êtes peut-être au courant des découvertes de Cook.

23. **discovery**
You are perhaps aware of the discoveries of Cook.

24. Vous êtes peut-être d'accord avec l'hypothèse de Cook sur l'origine des comètes.

24. You are perhaps in agreement with the hypothesis of Cook concerning the origin of comets.

25. Vous êtes peut-être en train de l'étudier.
(To which word in #24 does l' refer?)

25. **l'hypothèse**
You are perhaps in the process of studying it.

26. Je suis au courant des progrès en météorologie.

26. I am aware of the progress in meteorology.

27. Il est d'accord avec l'hypothèse de Norgren.

27. He agrees with Norgren's hypothesis.

28. C'est très facile.

28. It is very easy.

29. C'est difficile.

29. It is difficult.

30. Le professeur Raton est en train de formuler une belle théorie économique.

30. Professor Raton is in the process of formulating a splendid economic theory.

31. C'est un professeur célèbre.

31. He is a famous professor.

32. C'est une théorie très ingénieuse.

32. It is a very ingenious theory.

33. **un appareil**=*an apparatus*
L'appareil de Véfour enregistre les phénomènes atmosphériques.
(Does the combination of *apparatus*

	and *atmospheric phenomena* suggest a cognate for **enregistre?**)
34. *registers, records* The apparatus of Véfour records atmospheric phenomena.	**35.** C'est un appareil très ingénieux.
35. It is a very ingenious apparatus.	**36.** Le professeur Véfour est l'inventeur de cet appareil—c'est un véritable génie.
36. Professor Véfour is the inventor of this apparatus—he is a veritable (true) genius.	Now reread the sentences of this section which you marked on your way through the first time. When you can recognize all of the phrases, go on to the next section.

17. Avoir (*to have*)

1. The verb **avoir** is also irregular in its conjugation pattern. Its present tense forms are as follows:

j'ai	*I have*
tu as	*you have* (sing.)
il a	*he has*
elle a	*she has*
on a	*one has, they have, people have*
nous avons	*we have*
vous avez	*you have*
ils ont	*they have* (m.)
elles ont	*they have* (f.)

Do not mistake **à** (prep.) for **a** (verb).
Do not mistake **ils ont** (*they have*) for **ils sont** (*they are*).

2. **Il y a** is an **avoir** idiom indicating existence and is translated by *there is . . .* or *there are . . .*

Il y a des choses qui ont une valeur naturelle.	*There are things which have a natural value.*
Il y a une valeur naturelle dans le sol cultivable.	*There is a natural value in cultivable soil.*

READING PREPARATION

INSTRUCTIONS: *Cover the English verification with your card. Verify your answer only after a genuine attempt to express the meaning of the French. Continue to circle unrecognized words.*

	1. Le sujet de cette discussion est l'origine de la valeur.
1. The subject of this discussion is the origin of value.	**2.** **selon**=*according to* Selon certains économistes, le travail est l'origine de la valeur.
2. According to certain economists, labor (work) is the origin of value.	**3.** **un arbre**=*a tree* Mais selon Walras, les arbres, par exemple, ont une valeur naturelle. (**Par exemple**=*for* _____)
3. *example* But according to Walras, trees, for example, have a natural value.	**4.** Les animaux sauvages, par exemple, ont une valeur naturelle. (**Les animaux sauvages** must be— *domesticated/wild*.)
4. *wild* Wild animals, for example, have a natural value.	**5.** Les plantes, par exemple, ont une valeur naturelle.
5. Plants, for example, have a natural value.	**6.** **la terre**=*the earth* Selon cette théorie, la terre et le sol cultivable ont une valeur naturelle. (Because of its association with **cultivable, sol** probably means _____.)
6. *soil* According to this theory, the earth and the cultivable soil have a natural value.	**7.** **une chose**=*a thing* La terre et le sol cultivable sont des choses, mais elles ont néanmoins une valeur naturelle.
7. The earth and the cultivable soil are things, but they nonetheless have a natural value. (Notice that here **des** simply indicates plurality.)	**8.** **qui**=*which* Selon Walras, il y a des choses qui ont une valeur naturelle.
8. According to Walras, there are things which have a natural value.	**9.** Il a une hypothèse intéressante sur l'origine de la valeur.
9. He has an interesting hypothesis about the origin of value.	**10.** Il y a une théorie amusante sur l'origine de la valeur.

10.	There is an amusing theory of the origin of value.	**11.**	Vous avez probablement des doutes sur la vérité de cette hypothèse. (The sentence means that you probably—*do/do not* accept the hypothesis.)
11.	*do not* You probably have some doubts about the truth of this hypothesis.	**12.**	Il a un appareil qui enregistre les phénomènes de l'atmosphère.
12.	He has an apparatus which records the phenomena of the atmosphere.	**13.**	Il y a un appareil qui enregistre automatiquement les phénomènes atmosphériques.
13.	There is an apparatus which automatically records atmospheric phenomena.	**14.**	Nous avons des doutes sur la valeur de cet appareil.
14.	We have doubts about the value of this apparatus.		Review the circled words before going on to the next section.

18. Avoir *idioms*

1. A number of very common **avoir** idioms are expressed in English by *to be* and not by *to have*.

avoir faim	*to be hungry*
avoir soif	*to be thirsty*
avoir chaud	*to be warm*
avoir froid	*to be cold*
avoir sommeil	*to be sleepy*
avoir peur de	*to be afraid of*
avoir besoin de	*to be in need of*, or *to need*
avoir raison	*to be right*
avoir tort	*to be wrong*

READING PREPARATION

INSTRUCTIONS: *The following exercise gives you practice in recognizing verb forms and in using the context to establish meaning. When there are blanks, match the correct pronouns with the verb. Cover the left hand column and consult it only for verification.*

1. **l'après-midi**=*the afternoon*
Ordinairement, à cinq (5) heures de l'après-midi, nous avons faim.

1. Ordinarily at five o'clock in the afternoon, we are hungry.

2. Il est cinq heures de l'après-midi. _____ avez peut-être faim.
(1) Ils   (2) Nous   (3) Vous

2. (3) **Vous**
It is 5:00 P.M. You are perhaps hungry.

3. **le soir**=_the evening_
Ordinairement, à onze (11) heures du soir, on a sommeil.

3. Ordinarily at eleven o'clock at night, one is sleepy.

4. Il est onze heures du soir. _____ ont peut-être sommeil.
(1) Il   (2) Ils   (3) Nous

4. (2) **Ils**
It is 11:00 P.M. They are perhaps sleepy.

5. A cinq heures du matin, j'ai toujours sommeil.
(If **matin** is not _the afternoon_ or _the night_, it must be the _____.)

5. _morning_
At five o'clock in the morning, I am always sleepy.

6. **manger**=_to eat_
Si on a faim, on a besoin de manger.

6. If one is hungry, one needs to eat.

7. **Quand**=_when_
Quand on a besoin de manger, on a faim.

7. When one needs to eat, one is hungry.

8. **parfois**=_sometimes_
Quand on a faim, on a parfois soif aussi.

8. When one is hungry, one is sometimes thirsty also.

9. Quand vous avez soif, vous avez besoin de boire.
(What meaning does the context suggest for **boire**?)

9. _to drink_
When you are thirsty, you need to drink.

10. **le soleil**=_the sun_
Ordinairement quand le soleil brille, nous avons chaud.
(**Briller** is obviously something the sun does. It must mean _____.)

10. _to shine_
Ordinarily, when the sun shines, we are warm.

11. Quand la température est −20° nous avons toujours froid.

11. When the temperature is −20°, we are always cold.

12. D'habitude (ordinairement) quand nous avons chaud, _____ avons soif aussi.
(1) Vous   (2) Elle   (3) Nous

12. (3) **Nous**
Usually, when we are warm, we are also thirsty.

13. Quand vous travaillez longtemps, vous avez d'habitude chaud et soif.

13. When you work for a long time, you are usually warm and thirsty.

14. A onze heures du soir, le soleil ne brille pas.
(**Ne brille pas** must mean _____
_____.)

14. *does not shine*
At 11:00 P.M., the sun does not shine.

15. Parfois, quand le soleil ne brille pas, _____ avez froid.
(1) je   (2) tu   (3) vous

15. (3) **vous**
Sometimes, when the sun does not shine, you are cold.

16. A minuit, on a parfois sommeil.
(Being associated with **sommeil**, **minuit** must mean—*noon/midnight*.)

16. *midnight*
At midnight, one is sometimes sleepy.

17. Quand on a sommeil, on a besoin de dormir.
(**Dormir** probably means _____
_____.)

17. *to sleep*
When one is sleepy, one needs to sleep.

18. Les enfants ont toujours peur des dragons et des monstres.

18. Children are always afraid of dragons and monsters.

19. Les étudiants ont parfois peur des examens.

19. Students are sometimes afraid of examinations.

20. **Sans doute**=*no doubt* (*without doubt*)
La température est 95°. Vous avez chaud, sans doute.

20. The temperature is 95°. You are warm, no doubt.

21. Oui, vous avez raison. J'ai chaud.

21. Yes, you are right. I am warm.

22. La température est −20°. Ils ont froid, sans doute.

22. The temperature is −20°. They are no doubt cold.

23. Oui, vous avez raison. Ils ont très froid.

23. Yes, you are right. They are very cold.

24. Il est minuit. Elle a sommeil, sans doute.

24. It is midnight. She is no doubt sleepy.

25. Si vous avez chaud, vous avez sans doute soif aussi.

25. If you are warm, you are no doubt thirsty also.

26. S'il a faim, il a peut–être soif aussi.

26. If he is hungry, he is perhaps thirsty also.	27. S'ils sont très fatigués, ils ont peut-être sommeil aussi.
27. If they are very tired, they are perhaps sleepy also.	28. Si vous avez besoin d'étudier, vous avez aussi besoin de sommeil.
28. If you need to study, you are also in need of sleep.	29. Selon certains économistes, Walras a raison.
29. According to some economists, Walras is right.	30. **d'autres**=*others* Selon d'autres, il a tort.
30. According to others, he is wrong.	31. Il a peut-être tort d'insister sur cette hypothèse.
31. He is perhaps wrong in insisting on this hypothesis.	32. Il a peut-être raison de l'affirmer. (To which word in the preceding sentence does **l'** refer?)
32. **cette hypothèse** He is perhaps right in affirming it.	33. Il y a peut-être d'autres raisons de l'affirmer.
33. There are perhaps other reasons for saying so (affirming it).	How many did you miss? Review the checked phrases until you recognize the meaning of all of them. Then go on to the next section.

19. *Negation*—ne . . . pas

1. Ne preceding the verb and **pas** following it indicates *negation*. This form may be translated variously according to English usage:

Ces observations ne sont pas pertinentes.	*These observations are not pertinent.*
On ne trouve pas la cause de la valeur dans le travail.	*One does not find the cause of value in labor.*
Les frais de production n'expliquent pas la valeur.	*The costs of production do not explain value.*
Cette explication n'a pas de valeur.	*This explanation has no value* (or *doesn't have any value*).

READING PREPARATION

INSTRUCTIONS: *Are you covering the verification column with your card? Remember to derive the meaning as much as possible from the French context. Continue to circle unfamiliar words.*

	1. **un produit**=*a product* La terre et le sol cultivable ne sont pas les produits du travail.
1. The earth and the cultivable soil are not the products of labor.	2. Les fruits spontanés de la terre ne coûtent pas de travail. (The circumflex accent in **coûtent** suggests what cognate?)
2. *cost*—the (ˆ) often marks an **s** which has dropped out. The spontaneous fruits of the earth do not cost (require) any labor.	3. Ces choses ont néanmoins une valeur naturelle.
3. These things have nonetheless a natural value.	4. **seulement**=*only, solely* Il n'est pas possible d'attribuer la valeur seulement au travail.
4. It is not possible to attribute value solely to labor.	5. **donc**=*therefore* Il n'est donc pas possible de trouver l'origine de la valeur seulement dans le travail.
5. It is therefore not possible to find the origin of value solely in labor.	6. **fonder**=*to create, to found* Donc le travail ne fonde pas la valeur.
6. Therefore, labor does not create value. (Value is not founded upon labor.)	7. Cette réponse n'explique toujours pas l'origine de la valeur.
7. This answer still doesn't explain the origin of value.	8. Cette idée n'est pas très compliquée.
8. This idea is not very complicated.	9. Elle n'est pas très difficile à saisir. (**Saisir** would best be expressed by—*to seize/to understand.*)
9. *to understand* It is not very difficult to understand.	10. Cela n'est pas très difficile.
10. That is not very difficult.	11. Néanmoins, nous ne sommes pas d'accord avec cette hypothèse.
11. Nonetheless, we are not in agreement with this hypothesis.	12. Néanmoins, je ne suis pas très au courant des développements récents dans ce domaine.
12. Nonetheless, I am not very aware of (or up to date with) the recent developments in this area.	13. Quand on n'a pas sommeil, on n'a pas besoin de dormir.
13. When one is not sleepy, one does not need to sleep.	14. Quand il n'y a pas de soleil, on a froid.

14. When there is no sun, one is cold.	**15.** Quand on n'a pas faim, on n'a pas besoin de manger.
15. When one is not hungry, one does not need to eat.	**16.** Les découvertes de Pasteur ne sont pas très récentes.
16. Pasteur's discoveries are not very recent.	**17.** Si une théorie n'est pas vraie, elle est fausse.
17. If a theory is not true, it is false.	

20.   *Expressions of Quantity*

1.   The following words indicate quantity or degree:

(1)	**tant de livres**	*so many books*
	tant de temps	*so much time*
(2)	**assez de clarté**	*enough (or quite a bit of) clarity*
	une idée assez claire	*a quite (rather) clear idea*
(3)	**trop de difficultés**	*too many difficulties*
	trop d'espace	*too much space*
	un livre trop difficile	*too difficult a book*
(4)	**moins de théories**	*fewer theories*
	moins d'eau	*less water*
	une étude moins théorique	*a less theoretical study*
(5)	**beaucoup d'astronomes**	*many astronomers*
	beaucoup d'énergie	*much energy*
	un livre beaucoup trop difficile	*much too difficult a book*
(6)	**bien des hommes intelligents**	*many intelligent men*
	un homme bien intelligent	*a very intelligent man*
(7)	**plusieurs savants**	*several scientists (scholars)*
(8)	**quelques ingénieurs**	*some (a few) engineers*
(9)	**la plupart du temps**	*most of the time*
	la plupart des hommes	*most of the men, most men*

2.   You have learned that **de** sometimes expresses the meanings of *of* or *from*, but before deciding upon its meaning, you should look at its context and the kind of phrase it is used with. When it is used with the above expressions of quantity, it is not translated at all. When **des, du,** or **de la**

are used with expressions of quantity (except **bien des**) they are usually translated as *of the:*

Beaucoup de théories sont intenables.	*Many theories are untenable.*
Beaucoup des théories de Pelletier sont intenables.	*Many of the theories of Pelletier are untenable.*

READING PREPARATION

INSTRUCTIONS: *See how many of the following phrases you can read without consulting the left-hand column. Continue to circle the unfamiliar words.*

	1. **les frais** (m.) =*the costs* la plupart des frais de production
1. most of the costs of production	2. la plupart des produits du travail
2. most of the fruits of labor (work)	3. Plusieurs produits du travail contribuent à fonder la valeur.
3. Several products of labor contribute to the establishing of value.	4. Quelques frais de production ne sont pas nécessaires.
4. A few (some) costs of production are not necessary.	5. **comporter**=*to entail, to involve, to include* Bien des théories comportent assez de variantes.
5. Many theories entail quite a few variants.	6. Bien des services productifs sont bien nécessaires.
6. Many productive services are very necessary.	7. Plusieurs de ces théories comportent quelques difficultés énormes.
7. Several of these theories entail some enormous difficulties.	8. Beaucoup de théories sont assez intenables.
8. Many theories are quite untenable.	9. Tant de théories sont fausses.
9. So many theories are false.	10. Moins de théories sont vraies.
10. Fewer theories are true.	11. La théorie de Pelletier comporte trop de difficultés.
11. Pelletier's theory entails too many difficulties.	12. Trop de théories comportent des difficultés.

12. Too many theories entail difficulties.	**13.** Plusieurs observations de Walras sont assez pertinentes.
13. Several observations of Walras are quite pertinent.	**14.** connu=*known* Les expériences de Pelletier ne sont assez connues.
14. The experiments of Pelletier are not known well enough.	**15.** Moins des théories de Pelletier sont très connues.
15. Fewer of the theories of Pelletier are well known.	**16.** Assez des variantes sont connues.
16. Enough (or quite a few) of the variants are known.	**17.** Assez de difficultés persistent.
17. Quite a few difficulties remain (persist).	**18.** Trop de théories restent obscures.
18. Too many theories remain obscure.	**19.** Les variantes de l'hypothèse de Hoeft sont assez importantes.
19. The variants of Hoeft's hypothesis are quite important.	Review the words you have circled before going on.

21. *Meanings of* peu

1. Un peu (de) has the meaning of *a little:*

un homme un peu naïf	*a slightly naive man*
un peu de pain	*a little bread*
un peu de volonté	*a little will power*

2. Peu de (without **un**) means *little* or *few:*

peu de théoriciens	*few theoreticians*
peu d'hommes	*few men*
peu de volonté	*little will power*

3. When **peu** is used alone before an adjective, the adjective can often be translated by its opposite:

un mécanisme compliqué	*a complicated mechanism*
un mécanisme peu compliqué	*a simple mechanism,* or *uncomplicated mechanism*
un appareil efficace	*an effective apparatus*
un appareil peu efficace	*an ineffective apparatus*

READING PREPARATION

INSTRUCTIONS: *Give the meaning of the following sentences. Do not uncover the English until you have made a real attempt to understand the French.*

	1. Un peu du sol de cette région est assez cultivable.
1. A little of the soil of this region is quite cultivable.	**2.** Peu de ce sol est très cultivable.
2. Not very much of this soil is very cultivable.	**3.** Le sol de cette région est peu cultivable.
3. The soil of this region is not very cultivable.	**4.** La théorie de Walras est peu connue.
4. The theory of Walras is little known.	**5.** Elle est un peu difficile à établir.
5. It is a little difficult to establish.	**6.** Elle est peu difficile à établir.
6. It is not very difficult to establish.	**7.** Elle comporte quelques difficultés.
7. It entails a few difficulties.	**8.** Elle comporte peu de difficultés.
8. It involves few difficulties.	**9.** Plusieurs frais de production sont peu nécessaires.
9. Several costs of production are little needed (or are unnecessary).	**10.** Peu des théories de Walras sont bien connues.
10. Few of the theories of Walras are well known.	**11.** Ces théories restent un peu obscures.
11. These theories remain a little bit obscure.	

22. Du, de la, des *as Expressions of Quantity*

1. Du, de la, de l', or **des,** in addition to meaning *of the* or *from the,* may also indicate an unspecified quantity. This meaning is expressed in English by *some, any* or simply the plural, depending on the context.

une étude sur des méthodes récentes	*a study of recent methods,* or *a study of some recent methods*
J'ai du pain.	*I have some bread.*
Avez-vous du vin?	*Do you have any (some) wine?*

| **2.** Notice that **des** is the plural form of **un, une.**

READING PREPARATION

INSTRUCTIONS: *Give the meaning of the following phrases. Do not uncover the English until you have made a real attempt to understand the French.*

---

1. **souvent** = *often*
Au restaurant nous commandons souvent du vin.

---

1. At the restaurant we often order wine.

2. Nous mangeons rarement du porc.

---

2. We rarely eat pork.

3. Nous commandons souvent de la bière.

---

3. We often order beer.

4. Je mange souvent de la soupe.

---

4. I often eat soup.

5. **une loi** = *a law*
Les corps célestes obéissent à des lois naturelles.
(The association with **lois** suggests that **obéissent** probably means _____.)

---

5. *obey*
Heavenly bodies obey natural laws.

6. Les comètes décrivent des orbites très elliptiques.
(*A comet d_____cribes an orbit.*)

---

6. *describes*
Comets describe very elliptical orbits.

7. La valeur du travail est imputable à des conditions naturelles.

---

7. The value of labor is attributable to natural conditions.

8. **permettre** = *to permit*
Des méthodes récentes permettent la formation de théories moins obscures.

---

8. Recent methods permit the formation of less obscure theories.
(Are you circling unrecognized words?)

9. Les fruits spontanés de la terre ont souvent de la valeur.

---

9. The spontaneous fruits of the earth often have (some) value.

10. La théorie de Moore comporte des difficultés énormes.

---

10. The theory of Moore entails (some) enormous difficulties.

11. Ordinairement, les produits du travail ont de la valeur.

---

11. Ordinarily, the products of work have (some) value.

12. Bien des économistes diffèrent sur la cause de la valeur.

---

12. Many economists differ on the cause (source) of value.

13. Les fruits spontanés de la terre sont des choses qui ont une valeur naturelle.

13. The spontaneous fruits of the earth are things which have a natural value.	**14.** Des appareils modernes permettent souvent des études avancées sur les comètes.
14. Modern apparatus (instruments) often permit (make possible) advanced studies of comets.	

23. *Possessive Adjectives*

1. You will note that the form of possessive adjectives, like all adjectives in French, differs according to the gender and number with the noun they modify. They can therefore have three forms, masculine singular, feminine singular, and masculine and feminine plural. The possessive adjectives in French always precede the noun:

MASCULINE SINGULAR	FEMININE SINGULAR		MASCULINE AND FEMININE PLURAL	
mon	**ma**	*my*	**mes**	*my*
ton	**ta**	*your* (sing.)	**tes**	*your* (sing.)
son	**sa**	*his, her, its*	**ses**	*his, her, its*
notre	**notre**	*our*	**nos**	*our*
votre	**votre**	*your*	**vos**	*your*
leur	**leur**	*their*	**leurs**	*their*

2. Note that **son, sa, ses** can mean *his, her,* or *its,* because the adjective takes the gender of the thing possessed and not the possessor:

    sa mère   can mean, *his, her* or *its mother*
    son père   can mean *his, her* or *its father*

3. Before feminine nouns beginning with a vowel or a mute *h,* the masculine form of the possessive adjective is used.

    une histoire, son histoire   *a story, his story*
    une auto, mon auto   *a car, my car*

READING PREPARATION

INSTRUCTIONS: *In the following exercises, pay special attention to the various meanings of* **son** *and* **sa.**

	1.	**un père**=*a father* Une lettre arrive de mon père.
1. A letter is arriving from my father.	**2.**	Un chèque arrive de ton père.
2. A check is arriving from your father.	**3.**	**un ami**=*a friend* Il y a une lettre de ton amie. (Is the friend a man or a woman?)
3. A woman. The final **e** indicates the gender. There is a letter from your girl friend.	**4.**	Il y a une lettre de tes amis.
4. There is a letter from your friends.	**5.**	Marie est contente—un chèque arrive de **son** père.
5. Mary is happy—a check is arriving from *her* father.	**6.**	**une mère**=*a mother* Il y a une lettre de **sa** mère.
6. There is a letter from *her* mother.	**7.**	Pierre est content—un chèque arrive de **son** père.
7. Pierre is happy—a check is arriving from *his* father.	**8.**	Il y a aussi une lettre de **sa** mère.
8. There is also a letter from *his* mother.	**9.**	L'oeuvre de Mme Curie est très célèbre. **Son** oeuvre est très célèbre.
9. The work of Mme Curie is very famous. *Her* work is very famous.	**10.**	L'oeuvre de Pierre Curie est bien connue. **Son** oeuvre est bien connue.
10. The work of Pierre Curie is well known. *His* work is well known.	**11.**	On ne trouve pas l'origine de la valeur dans le travail. On ne trouve pas **son** origine dans le travail.
11. One does not find the origin of value in work. One does not find *its* origin in work.	**12.**	Elle n'a pas **sa** cause dans le travail.
12. It does not have *its* cause in work.	**13.**	Mme Curie est célèbre dans l'histoire de France—**ses** contributions à la science moderne sont énormes.
13. Mme Curie is famous in French history—*her* contributions to modern science are enormous.	**14.**	**donner**=*to give* Quelques économistes essaient de donner des explications de la valeur, mais leurs explications restent parfois obscures.

14. A few economists try to give explanations of value but their explanations sometimes remain obscure.	**15.** L'ouvrage de Cook sur ce point est bien intéressant, mais son étude ne donne pas d'explication de ce fait.
15. The work of Cook on this point is very interesting, but his study gives no explanation of this fact.	**16.** Ses observations ne semblent pas convaincantes.
16. His observations do not seem convincing.	**17.** L'oeuvre de Pierre et Marie Curie est d'une grande importance dans le développement d'une théorie atomique.
17. The work of Pierre and Marie Curie is of a great importance in the development of an atomic theory.	**18.** Leur oeuvre est d'une grande importance.
18. Their work is of great importance.	**19.** Son importance est grande.
19. Its importance is great.	**20.** Leurs travaux en commun donnent la première description adéquate du radium.
20. Their work (efforts) in common gives the first adequate description of radium.	**21.** Ma théorie personelle est essentiellement différente.
21. My personal theory is essentially different.	**22.** Nos conclusions sur ce point sont essentiellement vraies.
22. Our conclusions on this point are essentially true.	**23.** L'oeuvre de Cook est vraiment essentielle.
23. Cook's work is truly essential.	**24.** Vos conclusions sont nécessairement vraies.
24. Your conclusions are necessarily true.	**25.** Votre collaboration est vraiment nécessaire.
25. Your collaboration is truly necessary.	Master the new vocabulary in this section before continuing.

24.   *Irregular Plurals for Nouns and Adjectives*

   1.   Most French nouns form the plural by adding an *s:*

le service, les services	*the services*
l'accomplissement, les accomplissements	*the accomplishments*

2. Nouns ending in −s, −x, or −z in the singular have the same form for the plural. In this case, you must consult the accompanying article to determine the number:

le pays (*the country*)	les pays (*the countries*)
le choix (*the choice*)	les choix (*the choices*)
le gaz (*the gas*)	les gaz (*the gases*)

3. Some nouns have irregular plural endings. The ending **−aux** indicates the plural of nouns ending in **−au** and **−al**:

le niveau (*the level*)	les niveaux (*the levels*)
l'animal (*the animal*)	les animaux (*the animals*)
le journal (*the newspaper*)	les journaux (*the newspapers*)

4. **−aux** is also the masculine plural ending for adjectives ending in **−au** and **−al**:

le nouveau pays	*the new country*
les nouveaux pays	*the new countries*
l'élément principal	*the principal element*
les éléments principaux	*the principal elements*

READING PREPARATION

INSTRUCTIONS: *As you read through these phrases, notice the cognate pattern between English and French. Continue to mark the words which you do not immediately recognize.*

	1. (un) égal = (*an*) *equal* Dans une démocratie les hommes sont considérés comme égaux.
1. In a democracy, men are considered as equals.	**2.** Les deux théories (f) sont d'une importance égale.
2. The two theories are of equal importance.	**3.** Beaucoup de nos intérêts nationaux sont commerciaux.
3. Many of our national interests are commercial.	**4.** un rapport = *a relation* Les rapports généraux entre les deux pays sont amicaux. (Are the countries friends or enemies?)
4. friends The general relations between the two countries are amicable.	**5.** Les rapports généraux entre les deux nations restent normaux.

5. The general relations between the two nations remain normal.	**6.** **un bureau**=*an office* Les fonctionnaires travaillent dans les bureaux gouvernementaux. (What is one called who works in a governmental office?)
6. a civil servant (or bureaucrat) Civil servants work in the governmental offices.	**7.** Dans les cas spéciaux, nous avons besoin de solutions spéciales.
7. In special cases we need special solutions.	**8.** **le mal**=*evil, misfortune* La faim et la pauvreté sont parmi les grands maux de la société.
8. Hunger and poverty are among the great evils of society.	**9.** Ces maux semblent exister dans toutes les sociétés.
9. These evils seem to exist in all societies	**10.** Ces maux influent souvent sur les rapports internationaux. (noun=l'influence; verb=influer sur)
10. These evils often influence (or have an influence upon) international relations.	

TESTING EXERCISE

INSTRUCTIONS: *Are you ready to go on? Do the following testing exercise, choosing the answer which makes the sentence grommatically correct or which best expresses the meaning of the underlined word. Circle any that you miss and review the indicated sections before continuing.*

     1. Beaucoup de théories _____ intenables.
       A. ont   B. est   C. sont   D. êtes

1. C **2.** In French "his mother" would be expressed as _____.
(16)   A. son mère   B. sa mère   C. ma mère   D. ton mère

2. B **3.** Les comètes sont très intéressantes—**leurs** orbites semblent capricieuses.
(23)   A. its   B. their   C. your   D. his

3. B **4.** _____ suis reconnaissant de vos efforts.
(23)   A. Je   B. Il   C. Ils   D. Vous

4. A **5.** Il est totalement impossible de construire le barrage. Le projet comporte
(16)   _____ difficultés.
     A. trop de   B. peu de   C. moins de   D. très

5. A **6.** On abandonne sa théorie— elle est _____ solide.
(20)   A. bien   B. peu   C. tant   D. plusieurs

6. B   **7.** On accepte généralement la théorie de Moore sur les frais de production—
(21)   il présente _____ évidence.
            A. un peu d'   B. assez d'   C. moins d'   D. peu d'

7. B   **8.** Les corps célestes obéissent à **des** lois naturelles.
(20)   A. of the   B. to the   C. at some   D. omitted in translation

8. D   **9.** Ils parlent souvent de **leur** voyage en Espagne.
(22)   A. our   B. your   C. his   D. their

9. D   **10.** Le professeur Charat confirme les résultats de **nos** expériences.
(23)   A. our   B. your   C. their   D. my

10. A   **11.** On **n'accepte pas** la théorie ptolémaïque—sa base est peu solide.
(23)   A. seldom accepts   B. accepts   C. does not accept   D. advocates

11. C
(19)

READING PASSAGE

INSTRUCTIONS: *Read through the following discussion of an economic theory of value. Then answer the questions at the end. Do the same for the subsequent passage also.*

Sur l'origine de la valeur

Résumé d'un sujet traité par Gaétan Pirou, *Les Théories de l'équilibre économique; L. Walras et V. Pareto.* Paris, 1938. (F. Loviton & Cie)

Selon des théoriciens anglais, la valeur a sa cause dans la production. Cette théorie de la valeur comporte deux variantes: (1) le travail fonde la valeur; (2) **l'ensemble** [1] des frais de production, l'ensemble des services productifs fondent la valeur.

5 Deux observations d'Auguste Walras sur la variante "travail" sont assez pertinentes. **En premier lieu,** [2] il note qu'il y a des choses qui ont une valeur et qui ne coûtent pas de travail.

Par exemple, les fruits spontanés de la terre, **tels que** [3] les arbres, les plantes, les animaux sauvages, la terre ou le sol cultivable sont des choses qui
10 ont certainement une valeur. Néanmoins, elles ne sont pas les produits du travail. Il est donc impossible de trouver l'origine de la valeur seulement dans le travail ou dans les frais de production.

Le travail n'est donc pas la source **ni** [4] la cause de la valeur, **puisqu'** [5] il y a des choses qui ont une valeur et qui ne nécessitent pas de travail.
15 En deuxième lieu, **si on dit que** [6] la valeur a sa cause dans le travail, on

1 *the entirety*   3 *such as*   5 *since*
2 *in the first place* 4 *nor*   6 *if one says that*

n'explique toujours pas **pourquoi** [7] le travail a une valeur. **Quelle** [8] est la cause de la valeur du travail? Sur ce point, néanmoins, l'argumentation d'Auguste Walras semble avoir un peu moins de force.

1. What are the two variants of the theory in question (paragraph #1)?
2. What is the first observation made by Auguste Walras (paragraph #2)?
3. What examples does he give (paragraph #3)?
4. What is the second observation he makes (paragraph #5)?
5. What reservation does the author have concerning the reasoning of Walras?

Les Comètes

Compte rendu d'un sujet traité par Rudaux et Vaucouleurs, *Astronomie: Les Astres, l'Univers*, Paris, 1948. (Larousse, Editeur)

Les comètes offrent un spectacle singulier et étrange, mais leur origine et leur nature restent peu connues. Ces corps **obéissent** [1] néanmoins à des lois naturelles. **En vertu de** [2] ces lois, les comètes décrivent des orbites très elliptiques. Si leurs courses semblent capricieuses, c'est seulement en
5   conséquence d'orientations diverses et très changeantes **par rapport à nous.** [3]

L'action du soleil modifie notablement l'aspect des comètes **au** [4] cours de leur **déplacement.** [5] Leur **changement** [6] d'aspect est aussi imputable à des effets de perspective variable.

1. How much is known about the origin and nature of comets?
2. What governs their movements?
3. Do their courses seem erratic or stable? Why?
4. What two factors influence the appearance of comets?

Le Météorographe

d'après Le Grand Dictionnaire Universel P. Larousse

Un météorographe est un appareil qui enregistre automatiquement les phénomènes appréciables de l'atmosphère, et qui sont l'objet de la météorologie. Les principaux appareils de **ce genre** [1] sont **celui** [2] de M. Salleron et celui du Père Secchi, directeur de l'observatoire du Collège
5   romain, à Rome. Le météorographe de M. Salleron, à l'Ecole d'agriculture de Grignon, diffère de l'appareil du Père Secchi par le mécanisme et par l'absence de toute indication relative à la température.

7 *why*	8 *what*	
1 *obey*	3 *in relation to us*	5 *movement*
2 *by virtue of*	4 *in the*	6 *change*
1 *this kind*	2 *the one*	

1. What is a **météorographe**?
2. Should **romain** be translated as *Catholic* or *Roman*?
   What part of the context gives you the answer?
3. What is the difference between the two instruments mentioned?

Chapter Four

REVIEW: Immediate recognition of new vocabulary comes only after numerous encounters. Go back over the circled words in Chapters Two and Three before going on to the material in Chapter Four.

25. *Present Tense of* –ir *Verbs*

1. The following endings are those of the present tense of regular **–ir** verbs: **–is, –is, –it, –issons, –issez, –issent.**

finir	*to finish*
je fin*is*	*I finish, am finishing, do finish*
tu fin*is*	*you finish, are finishing, do finish*
il fin*it*	*he finishes, is finishing, does finish*
nous fin*issons*	*we finish, are finishing, do finish*
vous fin*issez*	*you finish, are finishing, do finish*
ils fin*issent*	*they finish, are finishing, do finish*

2. Remember that the present tense in French has three possible meanings which are expressed in English by three different forms, as above.

READING PREPARATION

INSTRUCTIONS: *Many of the following phrases are drawn from previous reading passages and from the reading passage at the end of this chapter. Read the French and try to express its meaning. Refer to the English only to verify your first attempt.*

	1. _____ établissez (1) nous (2) ils (3) vous
1. (3) **vous** établ**issez**	2. _____ obé**issent** (1) je (2) tu (3) vous (4) elles
2. (4) **elles** obé**issent**	3. _____ obé**is** (1) j' (2) il (3) ils
3. (1) **j'**obé**is**	4. Les comètes obéissent à des lois naturelles.
4. Comets obey natural laws. (Are your circling unfamiliar words?)	5. Le soleil obéit à des lois naturelles.
5. The sun obeys natural laws.	6. Nous obéissons toujours aux lois de notre pays.
6. We always obey the laws of our country.	7. Les expériences de Bruno établissent la solidité de sa théorie.
7. The experiments of Bruno establish the soundness of his theory.	8. **la lumière**=*light* La lumière joue parfois un assez grand rôle dans les transformations chimiques.
8. Light sometimes plays quite a large role in chemical transformations.	9. **agir**=*to act* Elle agit parfois comme agent chimique.
9. It sometimes acts as a chemical agent.	10. **la puissance**=*power* La lumière agit comme puissance chimique.
10. Light acts as a chemical power.	11. La lumière agit parfois comme un puissant agent chimique. (**Puissant** is an *adjective* or a *noun?*)
11. *adjective* Light sometimes acts as a powerful chemical agent.	12. Elle fournit de l'énergie aux transformations chimiques.
12. It (light) furnishes energy for chemical changes.	13. **l'eau** (f.)=*water* La lumière et l'eau agissent comme puissances chimiques.
13. Light and water act as chemical powers (agents).	14. Elles fournissent des éléments nécessaires à la plante.
14. They furnish elements necessary to the plant.	15. **réussir à**=*to succeed in* Personnellement, je ne réussis pas à

	définir le rôle de la lumière et de l'eau dans cette transformation.
15. Personally, I do not succeed in defining the role of light and water in this transformation. (If you said, "I am not successful," your translation is still correct.)	**16.** Le professeur Mesnard réussit brillamment à définir le rôle de la lumière. (Is the result of his efforts doubtful or certain?)
16. certain Professor Mesnard succeeds brilliantly in defining the role of light.	**17.** Il l'établit brillamment. (To which word in #16 does l' refer?)
17. le rôle He establishes it brilliantly.	**18.** Vous ne réussissez pas à établir solidement vos conclusions.
18. You do not succeed in establishing your conclusions solidly.	**19.** Par la solidité de vos expériences, vous établissez fermement vos conclusions. (Are the conclusions doubtful or certain?)
19. certain By the soundness of your experiments, you firmly establish your conclusions.	Reread the phrases which you circled. When you can recognize the meaning of each of them, go on to the next section.

26. *Present Tense of* –re *Verbs*

1. The present tense of most **–re** verbs is indicated by the following endings: **–s, –s, –, –ons, –ez, –ent.**

permettre	*to permit*
je permets	*I permit, am permitting, do permit*
tu permets	*you permit*, etc.
il permet	*he permits*, etc.
nous permettons	*we permit*, etc.
vous permettez	*you permit*, etc.
ils permettent	*they permit*, etc.

2. A number of **–ir** verbs also take this ending:

partir	*to leave*
je pars	*I leave, am leaving, do leave*
tu pars	*you leave*, etc.

il **part**	*he leaves,* etc.
nous partons	*we leave,* etc.
vous partez	*you leave,* etc.
ils partent	*they leave,* etc.

Notice that the stem for the singular forms is irregular.

READING PREPARATION

INSTRUCTIONS: *Read the following phrases based upon the reading passage and express their meanings. After you have finished the exercise, reread the ones you have circled until you can recognize their meanings without looking at the English.*

	1. Je pars dans quelques moments.
1. I am leaving in a few moments.	**2.** Vous partez sans doute dans quelques heures.
2. You are no doubt leaving in a few hours.	**3.** Tu pars sans doute dans quelques heures. (Is this sentence translated in the same way as the preceding one?)
3. Yes—**tu** and **vous** are both translated as *you*.	**4.** **une fleur**=*a flower* Dans son étude l'auteur parle de la transformation des substances odorantes des fleurs.
4. In his study the author speaks of the transformation of the scents (odoriferous substances) of flowers.	**5.** La transformation et la destruction des substances odorantes des fleurs dépendent de l'action de la lumière et de l'eau.
5. The transformation and destruction of the scents of the flowers depend on the action of light and water.	**6.** L'auteur tend à attribuer à la lumière et non pas à l'oxygène le rôle principal dans cette transformation.
6. The author tends to attribute the principal role in this transformation to light and not to oxygen.	**7.** **prétendre**=*to maintain, to claim* D'autres botanistes prétendent le contraire.
7. Other botanists maintain the contrary.	**8.** **la pression**=*pressure* Ce dégagement est imputable à la pression de l'eau.
8. This emission is attributable to the pressure of water.	**9.** L'auteur prétend prouver l'influence de la lumière sur la pression de l'eau.

9. The author claims to prove the influence of light on the water pressure.	10. **le parfum**=*the scent* **dégager**=*to give off, to emit* La plupart des fleurs tendent à dégager leurs parfums.
10. Most flowers tend to give off (emit) their scents.	11. L'intensité du parfum des fleurs dépend toujours de l'action de la lumière et de l'eau.
11. The intensity of the scents of flowers always depends on the action of light and water.	12. **au dehors**=*to the outside, outward* La pression de l'eau tend à refouler au dehors les parfums de la plante. (**Refouler** must mean _____)
12. *expulse, push toward,* or equivalent The pressure of the water tends to cause the emission of the scents of the plant.	13. L'action de la lumière combat cette tendance.
13. The action of light opposes this tendency.	14. **cependant**=*however* Cependant, la vérité de cette théorie dépend de la solidité de nos expériences.
14. However, the truth of this theory depends on the soundness of our experiments.	15. Cependant, les résultats de mes expériences tendent à établir la vérité de cette hypothèse. (Who performed the experiments?)
15. I did (*mes*) However, the results of my experiments tend to establish the truth of this hypothesis.	16. Les expériences de M. Mesnard tendent, cependant, à contredire les conclusions de ses prédécesseurs. (Does he oppose or agree with his predecessors?)
16. He opposes their conclusions. The experiments of M. Mesnard tend to contradict the conclusions of his predecessors.	17. Bien des savants prétendent le contraire.
17. Many scientists claim (maintain) the contrary.	18. **connaître**=*to know* Peu de botanistes connaissent cette théorie.
18. Few botanists know of this theory.	19. Nous ne connaissons toujours pas cette théorie.
19. We still don't know this theory.	20. Quelques botanistes combattent cette théorie.

20. A few botanists oppose this theory.	**21.** **reconnaître**=*to realize, to recognize* Plusieurs des confrères de M. Mesnard reconnaissent la vérité de son hypothèse.
21. Several of the colleagues of Mr. Mesnard recognize the truth of his hypothesis.	**22.** Je connais cette théorie en général, mais elle reste obscure dans les détails.
22. I know this theory in general, but it remains obscure in the details.	**23.** Je ne la connais pas dans les détails.
23. I do not know it in detail.	**24.** Si vous ne reconnaissez pas les verbes, vous ne les connaissez pas.
24. If you do not recognize the verbs, you do not know them.	

27. *Past Participles—Formation*

1. The past participles of regular verbs are identified by the following endings attached to the stem:

INFINITIVE		PAST PARTICIPLE	
—er verbs		**–é**	
donner	*to give*	**donné**	*given*
trouver	*to find*	**trouvé**	*found*
montrer	*to show*	**montré**	*shown*
exposer	*to disclose*	**exposé**	*disclosed*
–ir verbs		**–i**	
finir	*to finish*	**fini**	*finished*
agir	*to act*	**agi**	*acted*
accomplir	*to accomplish*	**accompli**	*accomplished*
réussir	*to succeed.*	**réussi**	*succeeded*
–re verbs		**–u**	
descendre	*to descend*	**descendu**	*descended*
dépendre	*to depend*	**dépendu**	*depended*
vendre	*to sell*	**vendu**	*sold*

2. In addition, there are many verbs whose past participles do not follow this pattern. Examples are:

INFINITIVE		PAST PARTICIPLE	
être	*to be*	**été**	*been*
avoir	*to have*	**eu**	*had*
découvrir	*to discover*	**découvert**	*discovered*
connaître	*to know*	**connu**	*known*
produire	*to produce*	**produit**	*produced*
écrire	*to write*	**écrit**	*written*

Past participles will be given with each new irregular verb or set of verbs. It is very important to memorize them, because they frequently occur as adjectives, nouns and indicators of time.

28.   *Past Indefinite Tense*—avoir *Verbs*

1.   The combination of the helping verbs **avoir** or **être** with the past participle indicates past time.

2.   This tense has two different meanings in French: (1) action which took place at a past moment which is neither specified nor implied—e.g., "I have finished my work," or (2) action which took place at a specified or implied moment—e.g., "I finished my work (last night)." The meaning of this tense is therefore expressed in English by either of the above forms, according to the context:

ils ont été	*they were, they have been*
elles ont eu	*they had, they have had*
j'ai donné	*I gave, I have given*
elle a fini	*she finished, she has finished*
nous avons agi	*we acted, we have acted*
vous avez trouvé	*you found, you have found*

READING PREPARATION

INSTRUCTIONS: *Cover the English with your card and give the possible renderings of the following phrases. Whenever you meet an unfamiliar word, put a circle around it.*

	1. Ils ont été . . .
1. They were, they have been . . .	**2.** Ils ont eu . . .
2. They had, they have had . . .	**3.** Il a été . . .

3. He was, he has been . . .

4. There were (was), there have (has) been . . .

5. I knew, I have known . . .

6. I recognized, I have recognized . . .

7. One found, one has found . . .

8. She recognized, she has recognized . . .

9. I succeeded, I have succeeded . . .

10. He (it) seemed, has seemed . . .

11. We obeyed, have obeyed . . .

12. She (it) seemed, has seemed . . .

4. Il y a eu . . .

5. J'ai connu . . .

6. J'ai reconnu . . .

7. On a trouvé . . .

8. Elle a reconnu . . .

9. J'ai réussi . . .

10. Il a semblé . . .

11. Nous avons obéi . . .

12. Elle a semblé . . .

Now read the following sentences for meaning in the context.

13. **ci-dessus**=*above*
Nous avons parlé ci-dessus de quelques phénomènes botaniques.

13. We have spoken above of a few botanical phenomena.

14. Nous n'avons pas fini de parler de ce sujet.

14. We have not finished speaking of this subject.
(Notice that here the infinitive—**parler**—is translated by an English present participle.)

15. Dans les expériences ci-dessus la lumière a agi comme puissance chimique.

15. In the above experiments light acted as a chemical agent.

16. **montrer**=*to show*
Par cette série d'expériences l'auteur a montré l'influence de la lumière sur le dégagement des parfums.

16. By this series of experiments the author has shown the influence of light on the discharge of fragrances.

17. **éclairer**=*to enlighten, to cast light*
Il a bien réussi à éclairer la question.

17. He (has) succeeded very well in casting light on the question.

18. Cependant, il n'y a pas eu beaucoup d'exemples de ce phénomène.

18. However, there have not been many examples of this phenomenon.
(Notice that **il y a eu** is the past indefinite of **il y a.**)

19. Ce fait n'a pas toujours été connu.

19. This fact has not always been known.

20. Cependant, je n'ai pas été toujours au courant des développements dans ce domaine.

20. However, I have not always been up to date with the developments in this field.

21. Vous n'avez pas toujours été d'accord avec cette hypothèse, peut-être.

21. You have not always been in agreement with this hypothesis, perhaps.

22. Ses raisons ont été bien convaincantes.

22. His reasons were very convincing.

23. Il a donné des raisons peu convaincantes.

23. He gave some unconvincing reasons.

24. On n'a pas toujours reconnu la vérité de la théorie.

24. One has not always recognized the truth of the theory.

25. **exposer**=*to exhibit, to set forth*
Le 20 septembre, M. Dupont a exposé ses découvertes à l'Académie.

25. On September 20, Mr. Dupont exhibited his discoveries to the Academy.

26. Il a bien traité son sujet.

26. He treated his subject well.

27. **expliquer**=*to explain*
Il a très bien expliqué son point de vue.

27. He explained his point of view very well.

28. Il a exposé son point de vue.

28. He set forth his point of view.

29. **dernier**=*last*
Pendant sa dernière expédition, il a trouvé une lampe préhistorique dans une grotte.

29. During his last expedition he found a prehistoric lamp in a cave (grotto).

30. Il a découvert cette grotte pendant sa dernière expédition.

30. He discovered this cave during his last expedition.

31. Il a découvert plusieurs objets préhistoriques.

31. He discovered several prehistoric objects.

32. **laisser**=*to leave*
La combustion d'une matière d'origine animal a laissé quelques traces dans cette lampe.

32. The combustion of a material of animal origin (has) left a few traces in this lamp.

33. **gras**=*fat, fatty*
On a sans doute utilisé une substance grasse dans la lampe.

33. They no doubt utilized a fatty substance in the lamp.

34. **pour**=*for, in order to*
Ils ont peut-être utilisé cette lampe pour éclairer la grotte.

34. They perhaps utilized this lamp to light the cave.

35. **noir**=*black*
La combustion a laissé une substance noire dans la lampe.

35. The combustion (has) left a black substance in the lamp.

36. J'ai reconnu la composition de cette matière noire par une analyse chimique.

36. I recognized the composition of this black material by (means of) a chemical analysis.

37. Il a montré des objets préhistoriques.

37. He showed some prehistoric objects.

38. Il les a montrés.

38. He showed them.

39. **un confrère**=*a colleague*
Il a eu l'audace de contredire ses confrères.

39. He had the audacity to contradict his colleagues.

40. Il a eu l'audace de les contredire.

40. He had the audacity to contradict them.

41. **accueillir**=*to receive*
Ils ont accueilli son exposé avec peu d'enthousiasme.

41. They received his talk (account) with little enthusiasm.

29. *Past Participles Used as Adjectives*

1. Past participles supply many of the adjective forms in French. In such cases they agree in gender and number with the noun they are modifying by adding an **—e** for the feminine singular, **—s** for the masculine plural, and **—es** for the feminine plural:

Il a parlé de quelques phénomènes isolés.
He spoke of a few isolated phenomena.

Il a utilisé une substance enrichie.
He used an enriched substance.

Ce sont des idées (f.) developpées par ses prédécesseurs.
They are ideas developed by his predecessors.

2. When the past participle is part of an elliptical expression, it appears after the verb in English:

C'est une expérience perfectionnée par le professeur Charrat.	*It is an experiment (which has been) perfected by Professor Charrat.*
C'est un gaz isolé par Pradel.	*It is a gas (which has been) isolated by Pradel.*

READING PREPARATION

INSTRUCTIONS: *In the following phrases and sentences, past participles are used as adjectives. Cover the left hand column with your card and give the meanings of the phrases.*

1. Il a utilisé une méthode récente developpée par le professeur Bouvier.

1. He (has) used a recent method developed by Professor Bouvier.

2. **décrire**=*to describe*
   Il a décrit des expériences perfectionnées par M. Ribaudet.

2. He described some experiments perfected by Mr. Ribaudet.
   (Notice that the past participle of **décrire** does not end in **–u** but in **–it.**)

3. C'est une leçon compliquée par l'abondance des matières.

3. It is a lesson complicated by the abundance of the material.

4. **écrire**=*to write*
   Il a écrit un ouvrage accueilli avec beaucoup de faveur.

4. He wrote (has written) a work received with much favor.

5. Il a décrit des entreprises industrielles encouragées par une exemption d'impôts.

5. He (has) described industrial enterprises encouraged by an exemption from taxes.

6. Il écrit sur la plupart des problèmes posés par la science.

6. He writes about (on) the majority of the problems posed by science.

7. Il a montré une lampe préhistorique trouvée dans la grotte de La Mouthe.

7. He showed (has shown) a prehistoric lamp found in the cave of La Mouthe.

8. Il a décrit une matière noire constituée par une substance charbonneuse.

8. He (has) described a black material made up of a carbonaceous substance.

9. Il a montré des matières laissées par la combustion.

9. He showed (has shown) some substances left by combustion.

10. Il a décrit une matière grasse utilisée pour éclairer la grotte.

10. He (has) described a fatty substance utilized to light the cave.

11. Il a analysé les résidus laissés par la combustion.

11. He (has) analyzed the residues left by combustion.	**12.** Il a écrit un exposé sur une lampe préhistorique découverte dans la grotte.
12. He wrote (has written) an account of a prehistoric lamp discovered in the cave.	**13.** Son ouvrage traite de l'action combinée de la lumière et de l'eau.
13. His work treats the combined action of light and water.	**14.** Il écrit actuellement sur l'action mécanique exercée par la lumière. (**Actuellement** tells you that **écrit** is to be translated as—*writes/is writing.*)
14. He *is* presently *writing* on the mechanical action exerted by light.	**15.** **une cellule**=*a cell* Les cellules contiennent de l'eau.
15. The cells contain water.	**16.** Il parle de l'eau contenue dans les cellules.
16. He speaks of the water contained in the cells.	**17.** Il a décrit les parfums contenus dans l'épiderme de la plante.
17. He (has) described the scents contained in the epidermus of the plant.	**18.** La pression de l'eau dans les cellules tend à refouler au dehors les parfums contenus dans l'épiderme de la plante.
18. The pressure of water in the cells tends to cause the emission of the odors contained in the epidermis of the plant.	**19.** Le dégagement du parfum des plantes dépend de l'action combinée de la lumière et de l'eau.
19. The release of odors from plants depends upon the combined action of light and water.	When you can read all of the above phrases readily, go on to the next section.

30. *Past Participles in Dependent Statements*

1. Past participles are often used to introduce dependent statements. In this case, you must look to the following clause to find the subject:

Trouvée dans une grotte, la lampe offre un grand intérêt historique.	*Having been found in a cave, the lamp offers a great historical interest.*
Ecrit par un auteur célèbre, le livre est bien connu.	*Having been written by a famous author, the book is well known.*

2. Notice in the above examples that the French past participle may be translated by the English past participle, or by *having been + past participle*, as the situation requires.

READING PREPARATION

INSTRUCTIONS: *Read the French and try to express its meaning. Refer to the English only to verify your first attempt.*

1. Trouvée dans une grotte, la lampe révèle beaucoup sur la vie préhistorique.

1. Having been found in a cave, the lamp reveals much about prehistoric life.

2. Trouvés dans une grotte, ces objets sont révélateurs de la vie préhistorique.

2. Having been found in a cave, these objects are revealing of prehistoric life.

3. Montrée aux membres de l'Académie, elle a été l'objet d'une grande curiosité.

3. Having been shown to the members of the Academy, it has been the object of a great curiosity.

4. Laissées par la combustion, ces matières noires révèlent distinctement leur origine.

4. Left by combustion, these black materials distinctly reveal their origin.

5. Reconnue pour authentique, la lampe est d'une grande valeur historique.

5. Recognized as authentic, the lamp is of great historical value.

6. Utilisée pour l'éclairage de la grotte, la lampe est recouverte d'une matière noire.
(Which makes more sense in the context?—*covered with/recovered with*)

6. Having been used for the lighting of the cave, the lamp is *covered with* a black substance.

7. Perfectionnée par le professeur Bouvier, cette méthode est très utile.
(**utiliser** = *to utilize, to use*)
(**utile** = _____)

7. Having been perfected by Professor Bouvier, this method is very *useful*.

8. Ecrit par un savant célèbre, le livre est très utile.

8. Having been written by a famous scholar, the book is very useful.

9. Ecrit par un auteur savant, le livre est bien utile.
(Here **savant** is an adjective describing **auteur**. Savant must mean _____.)

9. *scholarly*, or *learned*
Having been written by a learned author, the book is very useful.

After you have mastered the material above, go on to the next section.

VOCABULARY DEVELOPMENT

INSTRUCTIONS: *Since many past participles may be used as nouns, you may increase your vocabulary rapidly by learning to recognize them as such. Give the meaning of the following past participles.*

1. **donner**=*to give*
Les données du problème sont claires.

1. *the givens* (or *data*)

2. **durer**=*to last*
D'habitude, **la durée** de la séance n'est pas longue.

2. *the duration*

3. **entrer**=*to enter*
On a applaudi **l'entrée** du président.

3. *the entry*

4. **voir**=*to see*
Cette **vue** sur l'océan est impressionnante.

4. *view*

5. **résumer**=*to summarize*
Le résumé de son discours a été très intéressant.

5. *the summary*

6. **produire**=*to produce*
Les arbres ne sont pas des **produits** du travail.

6. *products*

7. **contenir**=*to contain*
Le livre est beau, mais son **contenu** est médiocre.

7. *contents*

8. **fumer**=*to smoke*
La fumée a couvert la ville.

8. *the smoke*

TESTING EXERCISES

INSTRUCTIONS: *Cover the left-hand column with your card, and in the right-hand column mark the answer which makes the sentence grammatically correct or which makes the best*

sense in the context. Then verify your answers by consulting the left-hand side of the page.
If you miss any questions, review the section indicated before going on to the reading.

1. _____ agissent comme puissances chimiques.
    A. J'   B. Nous   C. Vous   D. Elles

---

1. D
(25)

2. La pression de l'eau _____ à dégager le parfum des plantes.
    A. tend   B. trouve   C. connais   D. vend

---

2. A
(26)

3. M. Ricanier a _____ ses découvertes devant l'Académie.
    A. exposer   B. expose   C. exposé   D. exposez

---

3. C
(27)

4. J'ai enfin _____ à trouver la réponse.
    A. réussissais   B. réussi   C. réussir   D. réussis

---

4. B
(27, 28)

5. Il a _____ l'audace de contredire son professeur.
    A. été   B. eu   C. accueilli   D. fini

---

5. B
(27, 28)

6. C'est une thèse _____ par nos prédécesseurs.
    A. développer   B. développeur   C. développant   D. développée

---

6. D
(29)

7. Par une analyse chimique, on a mesuré le _____ physique de la
    lampe.
    A. contient   B. contenu   C. contenant   D. contenir

---

7. B
(Vocabu-
lary De-
velopment
Section)

8. **Cependant,** il n'a pas établi la valeur de ses expériences.
    A. Moreover   B. Therefore   C. However   D. Also

---

8. C
General
vocabu-
lary

9. The past participle of **dépendre** is _____.
    A. dépendi   B. dépendu   C. dépendé   D. dépend

---

9. B
(26)

10. The past participle of **écrire** is _____.
    A. écrit   B. écru   C. écrié   D. écri

---

10. A
(26)

READING PASSAGES

INSTRUCTIONS: *The following passages are representative of the type of French found in
learned journals. Read the following passages and write out the answers to the questions.
Circle any unfamiliar words for future review.*

Une lampe préhistorique

Résumé d'une note intitulée "Sur une lampe préhistorique, trouvée dans la grotte de La Mouthe" dans *Comptes rendus de l'Académie des Sciences*, vol. 133, page 666.

Dans la séance du 20 septembre, M. Rivière a exposé à l'Académie quelques découvertes **faites** [1] dans la grotte de La Mouthe. Entre autres objets il a montré une lampe préhistorique **creusée dans un galet de grès rouge.**[2] La face interne est recouverte d'une matière noire. M. Berthelot, chimiste bien connu, a fait une analyse chimique de cette matière. Laissée par la combustion, elle est constituée par une substance charbonneuse, et elle contient des composés fixes. Ces résidus charbonneux ressemblent aux matières laissées par la combustion d'une matière grasse d'origine animale. C'est probablement une matière de **ce genre** [3] qui a été utilisée pour l'éclairage de la grotte.

1. What did Mr. Rivière show to the Academy other than the lamp?
2. What did the lamp look like?
3. What kind of material coated it?
4. Where did this material come from?
5. What was it used for?

Influence de la lumière et de l'eau

Note de M. Eugène Mesnard, "Sur l'action combinée de la lumière et de l'eau dans le dégagement du parfum des plantes", dans *Comptes rendus de l'Académie des Sciences*, tome 122, p. 493.

En résumé, c'est la lumière et non pas l'oxygène, **comme on l'a prétendu,**[1] qui est la principale cause de transformation et de destruction des substances odorantes; mais ces deux agents semblent, dans beaucoup de circonstances, combiner leurs efforts.

L'action de la lumière **se fait sentir de** [2] deux manières différentes: **d'une part,**[3] elle agit comme puissance chimique capable de fournir de l'énergie à **toutes** [4] les transformations des produits odorants: **d'autre part,**[5] elle exerce une action mécanique qui joue un rôle important dans la biologie générale des plantes, et cette propriété explique, **en somme,**[6] le mode de dégagement périodique des parfums des fleurs. L'intensité du parfum d'une fleur dépend, **en effet,**[7] de l'équilibre qui **s'établit,**[8] à toute heure de la journée, entre la pression de l'eau dans les cellules, qui tend à refouler au dehors les parfums contenus dans l'épiderme, et l'action de la lumière qui

---

1 *made*   2 *hollowed out in a piece of*   3 *this kind*
                              red sandstone

---

1 *as has been claimed*   4 *all*   7 *in fact*
2 *makes itself felt in*   5 *on the other hand*   8 *is established*
3 *on the one hand*   6 *in short*

¹⁵ combat cette turgescence. Toute la physiologie des plantes à parfums découle de cette simple notion.

On s'explique **ainsi pourquoi,**[9] dans les contrées de l'Orient, les fleurs sont moins odoriférantes **que** [10] dans nos contrées . . . on s'explique aussi pourquoi la végétation générale dans l'Orient est épineuse et squelettique: il y a, dans ces contrées, trop de lumière et **pas** [11] assez d'eau.

1. What is the chief agent in the transformation of fragrances in flowers?
2. What is the effect of light on a plant?
3. What is the effect of the water in the cells?
4. How do the flowers in European countries differ from those in Oriental countries?
5. What is the cause of these differences?

---

9 *thus, why*   **10** *than*   **11** *not*

Chapter Five

REVIEW: Language learning is a cumulative process. Be sure that you have mastered previous sentence forms and vocabulary before going on to new material. Review the items you circled in Chapters Three and Four before going on to Chapter Five.

31. *Past Indefinite of* être *Verbs*

1. The following verbs form the past indefinite tense with **être** instead of **avoir.** Their meanings are expressed in English by *have* (*has*) +past participle or by the English simple past (but see **naître,** below) :

arriver	je suis arrivé	*I arrived, I have arrived*
partir	tu es parti	*you left, have left*
aller	il est allé	*he went, has gone*
venir	je suis venu	*I came, I have come*
entrer	elle est entrée	*she came in, has come in*
sortir	elles sont sorties	*they* (f.) *went out, have gone out*
monter	nous sommes montés	*we* (m. pl.) *went up, have gone up*
descendre	nous sommes descendues	*we* (f. pl.) *came down, have come down*
tomber	vous êtes tombées	*you* (f. pl.) *fell, have fallen*
mourir	ils sont morts	*they died, they have died*
rester	elles sont restées	*they* (f. pl.) *remained, have remained*

| retourner | je suis retourné | *I went back, have gone back* |
| naître | vous êtes nés | *you* (m. pl.) *were born* |

2. When these verbs are conjugated with **être,** you will notice that the ending of the past participle always changes to agree in gender and number with the subject. This ending helps you to identify the subject but it makes no difference to the meaning.

3. Compounds of the above verbs are also conjugated with **être:**

rentrer	*to re-enter, to go back, to return home*
revenir	*to come back*
devenir	*to become*

4. **Apparaître** (*to appear*) and **disparaître** (*to disappear*) are conjugated with **être** or **avoir,** according to whether one is emphasizing the state or the action.

READING PREPARATION

INSTRUCTIONS: *Practice recall of the meanings of these intransitive verbs. Look at the English only to verify your surmises. Give both possible meanings.*

	1. Je suis arrivé.
1. I arrived (have arrived).	**2.** Elle est entrée.
2. She came in (has come in).	**3.** Elle est sortie.
3. She went out (has gone out).	**4.** Ils sont entrés.
4. They came in (have come in).	**5.** Vous êtes venu.
5. You came (have come).	**6.** Je suis sorti.
6. I went out (have gone out).	**7.** Elles sont venues.
7. They came (have come).	**8.** **aller en ville**=*to go to town.* Je suis allé en ville.
8. I went (have gone) to town.	**9.** Ils sont allés en ville.
9. They went (have gone) to town.	**10.** Ils sont sans doute partis.
10. They no doubt left (have left).	**11.** Elles sont donc restées.
11. They therefore remained (have remained).	**12.** Cependant, nous sommes partis.

12. However, we left (have left).	**13.** Il est néanmoins parti.
13. He nonetheless left (has left).	**14.** Elle est donc venue.
14. She therefore came (has come).	**15.** D'ailleurs, elle est restée.
15. Moreover, she remained (has remained).	**16.** Nous sommes tombés.
16. We fell (have fallen).	**17.** **Heureusement**=*fortunately* Heureusement, il n'est pas tombé.
17. Fortunately, he did not fall.	**18.** Je suis rentré pendant l'après-midi.
18. I came back during the afternoon.	**19.** Heureusement, je ne suis pas rentré le matin.
19. Fortunately, I did not come back in the morning.	**20.** Il est retourné pendant la nuit.
20. He went back (has gone back) during the night.	**21.** **vers**=*toward* Vers la fin, son exposé est devenu obscur. (**fin** × **commencement**)
21. Toward the end his talk became obscure.	**22.** **malheureusement** × **heureusement** Malheureusement, il n'est pas retourné.
22. Unfortunately, he did not go back (hasn't gone back).	**23.** Malheureusement, il a essayé de diriger ses remarques vers la politique.
23. Unfortunately, he tried to steer his remarks toward politics. (Notice that an English plural is needed to translate a French singular.)	**24.** Il est arrivé difficilement à la matière centrale de son exposé.
24. He arrived with difficulty at the main subject of his talk.	**25.** Il a essayé d'arriver à la matière centrale de son exposé.
25. He tried to arrive at the main subject of his talk.	**26.** Malheureusement, ses auditeurs sont restés sceptiques.
26. Unfortunately, his listeners remained skeptical.	**27.** Ses auditeurs sont partis vers la fin de son exposé.
27. His listeners left toward the end of his talk.	**28.** Il a tant parlé que ses auditeurs sont partis vers la fin de son discours.

28. He talked so much that his listeners left toward the end of his speech.

29. She was born rich.

30. She died poor.

31. Mr. Berthelot descended into the cave of La Mouthe in order to look for prehistoric objects.

32. He became famous by (because of) his research.

33. Many scientists (scholars) have gone into the oriental lands (countries) to study the general vegetation of those regions.

34. When the rocket re–entered the atmosphere, some alterations appeared in its trajectory.

35. The only alterations appeared at the time of the re–entry into the atmosphere.

36. The rocket disappeared at the time of its entry into space.

37. Modern chemistry was born of atomic physics.
(Are you circling unrecognized words?)

38. *to give birth to*
Atomic physics gave (has given) birth to a considerable number of technical applications.

39. The discoveries in the area of atomic physics gave (have given) birth to several military applications.

29. Elle est née riche.

30. Elle est morte pauvre.

31. M. Berthelot est descendu dans la grotte de La Mouthe pour chercher des objets préhistoriques.

32. Il est devenu célèbre par ses recherches.

33. Bien des savants sont allés dans les contrées orientales pour étudier la végétation générale de ces régions.

34. **la fusée**=*the rocket*
Quand la fusée est rentrée dans l'atmosphère, des altérations sont apparues dans sa trajectoire.

35. **lors de**=*at the time of, during*
Les seules altérations sont apparues lors de la rentrée dans l'atmosphère.

36. La fusée a disparu lors de son entrée dans l'espace.

37. La chimie moderne est née de la physique atomique.

38. La physique atomique a donné naissance à un nombre considérable d'applications techniques.
(**naître** = *verb*, **naissance** = *noun*
donner naissance à=_____)

39. Les découvertes dans le domaine de la physique atomique ont donné naissance à plusieurs applications militaires.

40. **à partir de**=*starting with, from the time of*
Les découvertes effectuées à partir de 1930 ont donné naissance à un grand nombre de technologies.

40. The discoveries made starting in 1930 (or from 1930 on) have given birth to a great number of technologies.

41. A partir de 1930, les applications de la physique atomique sont devenues extrêmement nombreuses.

41. Starting in 1930, the applications of atomic physics became extremely numerous.

Review! Reread the circled words until you know them readily.

32. *Irregular Verbs* pouvoir (*to be able*) *and* vouloir (*to want, to desire*)

1. Present tense:

POUVOIR		VOULOIR	
je peux (puis)	*I can (am able to)*	je veux	*I want*
tu peux	*you can*	tu veux	*you want*
il peut	*he can*	il veut	*he wants*
nous pouvons	*we can*	nous voulons	*we want*
vous pouvez	*you can*	vous voulez	*you want*
ils peuvent	*they can*	ils veulent	*they want*

2. The past participles are **pu** and **voulu**:

il a pu   *he was able to (could)*
il a voulu   *he wanted*

3. You will often find **pouvoir** and **vouloir** followed by an infinitive:

Nous pouvons partir à six heures.   *We can leave at six o'clock.*
Nous voulons arriver à six heures.   *We want to arrive at six o'clock.*

READING PREPARATION

INSTRUCTIONS: *Express the meanings of the following phrases, paying special attention to the distinction of tenses.*

1. **dire**=*to say*
On peut dire . . .

1. One can say . . .

2. On a pu dire . . .

2. One was able to (could) say . . .

3. We can ascertain several historical errors in the official documents.

4. You can establish at least the possibility of this theory.

5. They can give at least two explanations of this phenomenon.

6. I can recognize at least the possibility of this phenomenon.

7. The project can succeed if you have enough money.

8. We can be right, but it is not probable.

9. You can produce good results if you have enough time.

10. You can no doubt give an explanation of your absence.

11. We were not able to leave on time.

12. Doubts can arise (be born) concerning the possibility of this project.

13. She was at least able to come, but she was not able to stay.

14. We can leave at eight o'clock if you want to.

15. We want to leave at eight o'clock.

16. He will not (does not want to) recognize the value of your work.

17. I do not want to stay too long—I want to leave at eight o'clock.

3. Nous pouvons constater quelques erreurs historiques dans les documents officiels.

4. **au moins**=*at least*
    Vous pouvez établir au moins la possibilité de cette théorie.

5. Ils peuvent donner au moins deux explications de ce phénomène.

6. Je peux reconnaître au moins la possibilité de ce phénomène.

7. Le projet peut réussir si vous avez assez d'argent.

8. Nous pouvons avoir raison, mais ce n'est pas probable.

9. Vous pouvez produire de bons résultats si vous avez assez de temps.

10. Tu peux sans doute donner une explication de ton absence.

11. Nous n'avons pas pu partir à temps.

12. Des doutes peuvent naître de la possibilité de ce projet.

13. Elle a au moins pu venir, mais elle n'a pas pu rester.

14. Nous pouvons partir à huit heures si vous voulez.

15. Nous voulons partir à huit heures.

16. Il ne veut pas reconnaître la valeur de votre ouvrage.

17. Je ne veux pas rester trop longtemps— je veux partir à huit heures.

18. **un chat**=*a cat*
     grâce à=*thanks to, because of*
     Grâce à ce vol de fusée, on a pu constater les altérations dans la respiration du chat.

18. Thanks to this rocket flight, they were able to notice (ascertain) the alterations in the cat's respiration.	**19.** Grâce aux besoins militaires, l'industrie nucléaire a pu connaître un développement rapide.
19. Thanks to military needs the nuclear industry was able to experience (know) a rapid development.	**20.** Grâce aux découvertes effectuées à partir de 1930, nous avons pu réaliser des progrès considérables.
20. Thanks to the discoveries made in 1930 and after, we were (have been) able to realize considerable progress. (Notice that **progrès** which is plural in French is translated by the singular in English.)	

33. Que *as a Conjunction*

1. One of the uses of **que** is to join two independent clauses. As such it is translated as *that.*

On dit que l'expérience n'a pas réussi.	*They say that the experiment did not succeed.*
Je proteste que cela n'est pas vrai.	*I protest that that is not true.*

READING PREPARATION

INSTRUCTIONS: *Continue to circle unfamiliar words and phrases as you read these exercises.*

	1. On dit qu'un laboratoire français a effectué une expérience intéressante en 1963.
1. They say that a French laboratory performed an interesting experiment in 1963.	**2.** **le comportement**=*the behavior* On a voulu mesurer le comportement de quelque animal dans l'espace.
2. They wanted to measure the behavior of some animal in space.	**3.** On a voulu mesurer le comportement d'un chat dans l'espace.
3. They wanted to measure the behavior of a cat in space.	**4.** Le laboratoire a rapporté que cette expérience a parfaitement réussi. (**rapporté** in this context=*brought back/reported*)

4. *reported*
The laboratory reported that this experiment succeeded perfectly.

5. Le laboratoire rapporte qu'on a placé un chat sur une fusée.
(Was the cat in the rocket or on the rocket?)

---

5. Probably in the rocket, even though **sur** is usually translated *on*.
The laboratory reports that they placed a cat in a rocket.

6. On dit que la fusée a rapporté le chat.
(**rapporté** in this context=*reported/ brought back*)

---

6. *brought back*
They say that the rocket brought back the cat.

7. **supporter**=*to endure, to bear, to tolerate*
On a observé que le chat a bien supporté les effets de son voyage dans l'espace.

---

7. They observed that the cat tolerated the effects of its trip in space well.

8. **voler**=*to fly*
un vol=_____

---

8. *a flight*

9. On a constaté que le chat a bien supporté son vol en fusée.

---

9. They ascertained that the cat endured (tolerated) its rocket flight well.

10. **au cours de**=*in the course of*
Au cours de ce vol, on a pu étudier le comportement de l'animal.

---

10. In the course of this flight, they were able to study the behavior of the animal.

11. **peser**=*to weigh*
la pesanteur=_____

---

11. *weight*

12. On a constaté que le chat a pu supporter les périodes de non–pesanteur.

---

12. They ascertained that the cat was able to tolerate the periods of weightlessness.

13. **voir**=*to see*
On voit que le chat a assez bien supporté les périodes de non–pesanteur.

---

13. We see (one sees) that the cat tolerated the periods of weightlessness quite well.
(Remember that *on* may be translated by *any of the persons.*)

14. Nous voyons par cette expérience, effectuée par des savants français, que les périodes de non–pesanteur ne présentent pas de grandes difficultés pour le voyageur dans l'espace.

---

14. We see by this experiment, performed by French scientists, that periods of weightlessness do not present great difficulties to the traveler in space.

Review the above circled items until they are thoroughly familiar to you. Then go on to the next section.

34.   Que *as a Relative Pronoun*

1.   Que may also join two statements as a relative pronoun. In this case, it becomes the direct object of one of the statements and may be translated as *which* or *whom* (or *that*), according to whether it refers to a person or a thing.

Les savants sont partis. Nous connaissons ces savants.=**Les savants que nous connaissons sont partis.**	*The scholars whom (that) we know have left.*
Il a exposé ces objets. Il a découvert ces objets.=**Il a exposé les objets qu'il a découverts.**	*He displayed the objects which (that) he discovered.*

2.   Notice in the above examples that the past participles agree in gender and number with the preceding direct object. The agreement helps you to identify the preceding direct object, but it does not change the meaning.

READING PREPARATION

INSTRUCTIONS: *Continue to read, mark, and review.*

	1. L'expérience qu'on a réalisée a donné des résultats très utiles.
1. The experiment which they performed gave some very useful results.	**2. un singe**=*a monkey* Les savants que nous avons consultés veulent étudier le comportement d'un singe au cours d'un vol en fusée.
2. The scientists whom we have consulted want to study the behavior of a monkey in the course of a rocket flight.	**3. semblable**=*similar* Les savants que nous avons mentionnés projettent d'autres vols semblables.
3. The scientists whom we have mentioned are projecting (planning) other similar flights.	**4.** Les périodes de non-pesanteur, que le chat a d'ailleurs assez bien supportées, n'ont pas posé de grandes difficultés.
4. The periods of weightlessness, which moreover the cat tolerated rather well, did not pose any great difficulties.	**5. sans**=*without* Le chat qu'on a placé sur la fusée est revenu sans difficulté.
5. The cat which they placed in the	**6.** La lampe et d'autres objets semblables,

rocket came back without difficulty.

que nous avons trouvés dans la grotte, datent des temps préhistoriques.

6. The lamp and other similar objects, which we found in the cave, date from prehistoric times.

7. Nos confrères, que nous avons consultés pour dater ces objets, ont été très aimables.
(*they helped us/they did not help us*)

7. *they helped us*—the related cognate **aimable** suggests it.
Our colleagues, whom we consulted in order to date these objects, were very helpful.

8. Les découvertes qu'on a pu effectuer à partir de 1930 ont contribué énormément au développement d'une technologie moderne.

8. The discoveries which they were able to make starting in 1930 have contributed enormously to the development of a modern technology.

9. **maintenant** = *now*
L'évidence que nous voyons maintenant suggère une autre interprétation.

9. The evidence which we see now suggests another interpretation.

10. Les faits que nous voyons maintenant imposent une autre interprétation.
(Is another interpretation *necessary* or *merely possible?*)

10. *necessary*
The facts which we now see impose another interpretation.

11. Maintenant que je connais ses écrits, ses idées deviennent claires.
(**ses écrits** = *his sayings/his writings*)

11. *his writings*
Now that I know his writings, his ideas are becoming clear.

12. Les spécialistes que nous connaissons maintenant contredisent complètement leurs confrères.

12. The specialists whom we now know contradict their colleagues completely.

13. Maintenant que nous connaissons leurs écrits, nous voyons qu'ils contredisent complètement leurs confrères.

13. Now that we know their writings, we see that they contradict their colleagues completely.

14. **jusqu'à** = *until, as far as, up to the time of*
L'évidence que nous avons vue jusqu'à maintenant suggère une interprétation contraire.
(**vu**—p.p. of **voir**)

14. The evidence which we have seen up to now suggests an opposite interpretation.

15. Les économistes que nous avons consultés jusqu'à maintenant avancent une théorie semblable.

15. The economists whom we have consulted up to now advance a similar theory.

16. Vous pouvez comparer ces notions populaires avec les faits établis dans les documents officiels.

16. You may (can) compare these popular ideas with the facts established in the official documents.	**17.** L'industrie nucléaire a pu connaître un développement rapide.
17. The nuclear industry was able to make (know) a rapid development.	**18.** A partir de 1930 ils ont pu effectuer bien des découvertes nucléaires.
18. Starting in 1930 they were able to make many nuclear discoveries.	**19. presque**=*almost* Ces progrès suggèrent un avenir presque sans limites.
19. This progress suggests an almost limitless future.	

35. Qui *as a Relative Pronoun*

1. Qui joins two statements but becomes the subject of one of them. **Qui** may also refer either to persons or things and is translated *that, which,* or *who,* depending on the context.

Il y a des choses qui ont une valeur naturelle.
There are things which (that) have a natural value.

C'est M. Walras qui a formulé cette théorie.
It is Mr. Walras who formulated this theory.

2. Que contracts with a following vowel and becomes **qu'**. **Qui** never contracts. Therefore, **qu'** is always **que** and never **qui.**

READING PREPARATION

INSTRUCTIONS: *As you read the following sentences, notice that* **qui** *may refer either to persons or to things. Circle the phrases which you cannot read without hesitation.*

	1. Les savants qui ont réalisé cette expérience ont placé un chat sur une ´fusée.
1. The scientists who performed this experiment placed a cat in a rocket.	**2.** Cette expérience, qui a d'ailleurs bien réussi, a donné des résultats extrêmement utiles.
2. This experiment, which moreover succeeded very well, gave some extremely useful results.	**3. fort**=**très** Les savants qui ont placé le chat sur la fusée ont trouvé cette expérience fort instructive.

3. The scientists who placed the cat in the rocket found this experiment very instructive.

4. Les résultats de cette expérience, qui sont fort utiles, permettent au laboratoire de projeter une autre expérience semblable.

4. The results of this experiment, which are very useful, permit the laboratory to project another similar experiment.

5. **entraîner**=*to entail*
La rentrée dans l'atmosphère, qui a néanmoins entraîné quelques difficultés, n'a pas posé de problème vraiment grave.
(**l'entrée**=*the entry, the entrance*
la rentrée=_____)

5. *the re–entry, or re–entrance*
The re–entry into the atmosphere, which nonetheless entailed a few difficulties, did not pose any truly serious problem.

6. L'expérience qu'ils ont effectuée a bien réussi.
(**Qu'** is the contraction of—**que/qui**.)

6. **Que—qui** is never contracted.
The experiment which they performed succeeded very well.

7. Les résultats indiquent que le chat, qui a fort bien supporté les périodes de non–pesanteur, a mal supporté la décélération et la rentrée dans l'atmosphère.

7. The results indicate that the cat, which tolerated the periods of weightlessness very well, tolerated poorly the deceleration and the re–entry into the atmosphere.

8. Les savants qui effectuent cette série d'expériences veulent étudier le comportement d'un singe ou d'un autre animal semblable au cours d'un vol en fusée.

8. The scientists who are performing this series of experiments want to study the behavior of a monkey or another similar animal in the course of a rocket flight.

9. M. Pradel, qui a découvert cette lampe, l'a montrée à ses confrères.
(**l'** refers to which preceding word?)

9. **lampe**
M. Pradel, who discovered this lamp, showed it to his colleagues.

10. M. Pradel a montré cette lampe qui date des temps préhistoriques.

10. M. Pradel showed this lamp, which dates from prehistoric times.

Go on to the next section only after you are familiar with all the material above.

36. *Inversion of Subject and Verb Following* que

1. Very often in clauses following **que,** the subject and the verb are inverted. Do not mistake **que** for **qui.** (This mistake is one of the most frequent made

by American students in reading French.) **Que** as a relative pronoun is always an object and is followed by a subject and verb. **Qui** is itself the subject of the verb which follows it.

La quantité de tanin que contient ce liquide est constante.	*The quantity of tanin which this liquid contains is constant* (not *"which contains this liquid"*).
La tendance que combat l'action de la lumière est fort évidente.	*The tendency which the action of light opposes is very evident* (not *"which opposes the action of light"*).
La tendance *qui combat* l'action de la lumière est fort évidente.	*The tendency **which opposes** the action of light is very evident.*
Ce sont les objets qu'a trouvés M. Rivière.	*These are the objects which Mr. Rivière found* (not *"which found Mr. Rivière"*).

READING PREPARATION

INSTRUCTIONS: *Express the meaning of the following phrases and sentences. Verify your rendering only after you have made a genuine attempt to read the French.*

1. La quantité de tanin que contient ce liquide n'est pas constante.

1. The quantity of tanin which this liquid contains is not constant.

2. La plante qui contient ce liquide est fort rare.

2. The plant which contains this liquid is very rare.

3. Le livre qu'explique notre théorie est bien connu.

3. The book which our theory explains is well known.

4. Le livre qui explique notre théorie est bien connu.

4. The book which explains our theory is well known.

5. Il a exposé les objets préhistoriques qu'ont trouvés ses confrères.

5. He displayed the prehistoric objects which his colleagues found.

6. Il a parlé de ses confrères qui ont trouvé ces objets préhistoriques.

6. He spoke of his colleagues who found these prehistoric objects.

7. Nous citons le rôle primordial que joue l'université dans le développement du nouveau pays.

7. We cite the primordial role which the university is playing in the development of the new nation.

8. Un esprit de collaboration règne parmi les dirigeants qui jouent un rôle primordial dans l'université.

8. A spirit of collaboration reigns among the leaders who play a primordial role in the university.	**9.** La lampe est recouverte des résidus que laisse la combustion d'une matière grasse d'origine animale.
9. The lamp is covered with residues which the combustion of a fatty, animal material leaves.	**10.** On a sans doute utilisé une matière qui laisse des résidus charbonneux.
10. They no doubt used a material which leaves carbonaceous residues.	**11.** C'est de cette manière que sont produits des résidus charbonneux.
11. It is in this way (manner) that carbonaceous residues are formed.	**12.** Les expériences qu'ont effectuées ces savants n'ont pas fort bien réussi.
12. The experiments which these scientists performed did not succeed very well.	Review the circled items, and then continue.

37. *Verbs Followed by* avoir (être) + *Past Participle or by an Infinitive*

1. When certain verbs such as **prétendre, croire, affirmer** are followed by **avoir (être)** + the past participle or by the infinitive, they are usually translated by two clauses in English:

Il prétend avoir établi solidement ses conclusions.	*He claims he has established his conclusions solidly.*
Je crois être arrivé à la fin de mes difficultés.	*I believe I have arrived at the end of my difficulties.*
Je crois pouvoir établir solidement cette théorie.	*I believe I can establish this theory solidly.*

READING PREPARATION

INSTRUCTIONS: *Express the meaning of the following phrases in English. Be sure to keep the left hand column covered with your card.*

	1. **croire** = *to believe* Nous croyons pouvoir établir la solidité de nos conclusions.
1. We believe we are able to establish the soundness of our conclusions.	**2.** Je crois avoir établi que ma théorie n'est pas fausse.

2. I believe I have established that my theory is not false.	**3.** Il prétend avoir prouvé la solidité de ses conclusions.
3. He claims to have proved the soundness of his conclusions. (Are you circling unfamiliar items?)	**4.** Ils croient pouvoir dater avec précision ces objets qu'ils ont trouvés.
4. They believe they can date precisely these objects which they have found.	**5.** Il prétend avoir démontré la vérité de son hypothèse.
5. He claims he has demonstrated (or to have demonstrated) the truth of his hypothesis.	**6.** Vous croyez sans doute pouvoir fonder votre hypothèse sur des faits sûrs.
6. You no doubt believe you are able to found (base) your hypothesis on sure facts. (Notice the difference between the adjective **sûr** and the preposition **sur.**)	**7.** Vous croyez peut–être avoir fondé votre hypothèse sur des faits sûrs.
7. You perhaps believe you have founded your hypothesis on sure facts.	**8.** Il croit d'ailleurs avoir fondé ses théories sur des faits établis empiriquement.
8. He moreover believes he has founded his theories on facts established empirically.	**9.** Il prétend pouvoir dégager des parfums des fleurs seulement par l'action de la lumière.
9. He claims he is able to release fragrances from flowers by nothing more than the action of light.	**10.** Il prétend avoir dégagé des parfums des fleurs seulement par l'action de la lumière.
10. He claims he has released perfumes from flowers by nothing more than the action of light.	Review and then continue.

VOCABULARY DEVELOPMENT

INSTRUCTIONS: *Try to arrive at the meaning of the new words from the meaning of the root word.*

	1. des principes fondamentaux= *fundamental principles* Vous êtes **fondamentalement** en erreur.
1. You are fundamentally in error.	**2.** On dit que le **fondement** de la valeur est le travail.

2. They say that the *basis* (*foundation*) of value is labor.	**3.** **une fleur**=*a flower* En mai les arbres **fleurissent.**
3. In May the trees *blossom*.	**4.** Dans une société civilisée les arts **fleurissent.**
4. In a civilized society the arts *flourish*.	**5.** Les découvertes effectuées à partir de 1930 ont donné naissance à une **floraison** d'applications pratiques.
5. The discoveries made starting in 1930 gave birth to an *efflorescence* (*a flourishing*) of practical applications.	**6.** **investir**=*to invest* Grâce aux **investissements** militaires, les technologies ont fleuri.
6. Thanks to the military *investments*, the technologies have flourished.	

TESTING EXERCISES

INSTRUCTIONS: *Circle the answer which makes the sentence grammatically correct or which best expresses the meaning of the italicized word. Check your answers below. If you miss any, review the indicated section before going on to the reading.*

1. L'industrie nucléaire **a pu** connaître un développement rapide.
    A. may   B. might   C. is able to   D. was able to

---

1. D
(32)

2. _____ peuvent donner naissance à des conséquences fâcheuses.
    A. On   B. Nous   C. Ils   D. Il

---

2. C
(32)

3. Le conférencier a parlé des découvertes **qu'**il a faites.
    A. who   B. whom   C. which   D. what

---

3. C
(34)

4. Il y a des choses **qui** ont une valeur naturelle.
    A. who   B. what   C. whom   D. which

---

4. D
(35)

5. C'est M. Pollard **qui** a formulé cette théorie.
    A. who   B. whom   C. which   D. what

---

5. A
(35)

6. C'est M. Pollard **que** nous avons entendu.
    A. who   B. whom   C. which   D. what

---

6. B
(34)

7. On a montré l'objet **qu'a trouvé M. Rivière.**
    A. which M. Rivière found   c. who found M. Rivière
    B. which found M. Rivière   D. whom M. Rivière found

---

7. A
(36)

8. Il **est tombé** sur la glace.
    A. falls   B. is falling   c. fell   D. does fall

8. C (31)	9.	Elle **est née** riche.
		A. was born B. was found C. died D. lived

9. A (31)	10.	Nous **sommes venus** à dix heures.
		A. left B. came C. went out D. went up

10. B (31)	11.	On dit **que** l'expérience a réussi.
		A. that B. whom C. which D. who

11. A
(33)

READING PASSAGE

INSTRUCTIONS: *Read the following passages and write out the answers to the questions. Circle any unfamiliar words for future review.*

Un vol en fusée

Résumé d'une note dans *La Recherche spatiale* (août–septembre, 1965), pp. 44–45.

En octobre 1963 le CERMA (Centre d'Enseignement et de Recherches de Médecine Aéronautique) a effectué des expériences pour mesurer le comportement d'un chat sur une fusée VERONIQUE et a mesuré au cours du vol un certain nombre d'effets physiologiques et neurophysiologiques spontanés ou
5   évoqués.

Cette expérience, qui a parfaitement réussi, a donné des résultats intéressants. Le chat qu'on a placé sur la fusée a bien supporté les périodes de propulsion et de non–pesanteur. En effet, les seules altérations qu'on a observées sont apparues lors de la rentrée dans l'atmosphère, quand la
10 décélération a entraîné des **troubles** [1] marqués dans la sphère végétative.

Enfin, le CERMA prépare, pour le début de 1966, une expérience **destinée** [2] à étudier le comportement d'un singe lors d'un vol en fusée.

1. What was the purpose of the experiment?
2. Did the cat have any difficulty during the flight?
3. What plans does CERMA have for the future?

Les étapes de la physique atomique

Compte rendu des remarques de M. Louis Leprince-Ringuet dans "A la découverte de l'infiniment petit," *Revue des applications de l'électricité*, No. 209 (1965), p. 17.

L'auteur trace le développement de la physique de la structure atomique. Connue dans ses principes fondamentaux **dès avant** [1] la première **guerre**,[2]

---

1 *disturbances*   2 *intended*

1 *from before*   2 *war*

elle a donné naissance à une floraison considérable d'applications dans **tous** [3] les domaines de la technique avancée. En effet, nous pouvons dire que c'est
5 grâce aux notions de base sur la constitution des atomes que la connaissance des cristaux, la chimie moderne, et l'électronique ont connu un si grand développement. Ensuite il parle de **l'étape suivante** [4] dans la connaissance fondamentale, **celle** [5] de la physique nucléaire entre les deux guerres et un peu après la dernière guerre. Les découvertes de laboratoires effectuées
10 essentiellement à partir de 1930 ont permis aux diverses technologies de se développer, et grâce aux immenses investissements effectués aux Etats–Unis pendant la deuxième guerre, l'industrie nucléaire **a pris un départ** [6] exceptionnellement rapide. **Dès** [7] la fin de la guerre on **disposait de** [8] réacteurs atomiques de puissances considérables et aussi des premiers explosifs
15 nucléaires. En effet, ces progrès suggèrent un avenir presque sans limite.

1. Lines 2–4 state that
   A. the principles of atomic physics were used militarily in World War I, though in a rudimentary state
   B. the application of atomic principles has been quite limited up to now
   C. much technology owes its development to the knowledge of atomic physics
   D. we are really still in the incipient stages of atomic progress.

1. C   **2.**   Lines 5–7 state that progress in electronics is due to
   A. concurrent progress in modern chemistry
   B. developments in the knowledge of crystals
   C. fundamental concepts of atomic structure
   D. all of the above.

2. C   **3.** Lines 8–15 state that
   A. the war hindered the development of a civilian nuclear industry.
   B. the basic atomic notions were not highly developed before 1930
   C. nuclear explosives put an end to World War II
   D. the reactors of World War II were of small capacity compared to the ones now available.

3. B

3 *all*   **5** *that*   **7** *since*
4 *the following stage*   **6** *made a start*   **8** *had at one's disposal*

Chapter Six

REVIEW: Before going on to Chapter Six, be sure that you can recognize all of the new vocabulary and constructions introduced in Chapters Four and Five.

38. *Irregular verb* faire (*to do, to make*)

1. This is a very common and consequently a very important verb. You must be able to recognize it immediately in any of its forms.

PRESENT TENSE

je fais	*I do, am doing, do do*
tu fais	*you do*
il fait	*he does*
nous faisons	*we do*
vous faites	*you do*
ils font	*they do*

Past participle–**fait** (*done, made*)

Past indefinite–**j'ai fait**   *I have done (made), did, made*

2. Faire has many meanings, but the most basic ones are expressed in English by *to do* or *to make:*

Je fais mes devoirs.	*I am doing my homework.*

On fait des montres exquises en Suisse	*They make exquisite watches in Switzerland.*

3. Many expressions using **faire** must be translated as a whole and not as individual words. Some common **faire** idioms are:

faire attention à	*to pay attention to*
faire de son mieux ⎱	
faire son possible ⎰	*to do one's best*
faire peur à	*to frighten*
faire plaisir à	*to please, to give pleasure to*

READING PREPARATION

INSTRUCTIONS: *Respond to the following exercises.*

	1. Which pronouns go with the following verb forms? _____ **faites** (1) **je** (2) **tu** (3) **vous**
1. (3) **vous**	**2.** _____ **font** (1) **il** (2) **ils** (3) **nous**
2. (2) **ils**	**3.** _____ **faisons** (1) **vous** (2) **elles** (3) **nous**
3. (3) **nous**	**4.** _____ **fais** (1) **je** (2) **il** (3) **vous**
4. (1) **je**	**5.** What are the infinitive forms of the following verbs? **Ils sont** (1) **être** (2) **avoir** (3) **faire**
5. (1) **être**	**6.** **Ils ont** (1) **être** (2) **faire** (3) **avoir**
6. (3) **avoir**	**7.** **Ils font** (1) **être** (2) **faire** (3) **avoir**
7. (2) **faire**	**8.** On dit que vous faites des progrès considérables en français. (**faites**=*are doing/are making*)
8. *are making* They say that you are making considerable progress in French.	**9.** On dit que vous faites beaucoup de travail ces jours–ci. (**faites**=*are doing/are making*)

9. *are doing*
They say that you are doing a lot of work these days.

10. Je crois que vous faites une étude très profonde des verbes français.
(**faites**=*are doing/are making*)

10. *either one*
I believe that you are doing (or making) a very extensive (deep) study of French verbs.

11. Je vois que vous faites très peu d'erreurs.
(**faites**=*do/make*)

11. I see that you *make* very few errors.

12. On dit que vous faites une étude en français.
(**faites**=*are doing/are making*)

12. *either one*
They say that you are doing (or making) a study in French.

13. Vous voyez qu'il n'a pas réussi, mais il a fait de son mieux.
(Do you have to consult the verification column to be sure of the meaning?)

13. If so, circle the phrase you were not sure of.
You see that he did not succeed but he did his best.

14. Je crois qu'il ne parle pas très bien le français, mais il fait de son mieux.

14. I believe that he does not speak French very well, but he does his best.

15. Si vous ne faites pas attention aux verbes, vous ne faites certainement pas de progrès.

15. If you are not paying (or don't pay) attention to the verbs, you are certainly not making any progress.

16. Si tu ne fais pas attention aux verbes, tu ne fais certainement pas de progrès.

16. Same as #15—usually the familiar **tu** form and the **vous** form are both translated the same way in English.

17. Je crois qu'il essaie de faire attention à son professeur.

17. I believe that he tries to pay attention to his professor.
(Did you remember the meaning of **essayer**? If not, circle the word.)

18. **chanter**=*to sing*
Nous ne chantons pas bien, mais nous faisons de notre mieux.

18. We do not sing well, but we do our best.

19. Quand elle ne fait pas attention à la musique, elle ne chante pas bien.

19. When she does not pay attention to the music, she does not sing well.

20. Ils ont peur des enfants.
(**enfants**=*children/infants*)

20. *children*
They are afraid of children.

21. Ils sont peureux comme des enfants.

21. They are timid like children.

22. Quand ils chantent, ils font peur aux enfants.

22.	When they sing, they frighten the children. (Notice the **ils** form of the three preceding verbs.)	**23.**	Néanmoins, ils font de leur mieux.
23.	Nonetheless, they are doing their best.	**24.**	Ils font leur possible pour faire plaisir à leurs auditeurs.
24.	They are doing their best to please their listeners.	**25.**	Quand ils chantent, nous faisons notre possible pour être polis.
25.	When they sing, we do our best to be polite.	**26.**	Quand il parle, je fais mon possible pour faire attention.
26.	When he speaks, I do my best to pay attention.	**27.**	Quand ses discours ne sont pas trop longs, ils font presque toujours plaisir à ses auditeurs.
27.	When his speeches are not too long, they almost always please his listeners.	**28.**	Les discours qu'ils font ne font pas plaisir.
28.	The speeches they give do not please.		Review the words you have circled, and then go on to the next section.

39. *Impersonal Expression* il fait

1. **Il fait** + adjective or phrase is a common way to describe the weather:

Il fait beau (mauvais) temps.   *It is good (bad) weather.*

Il fait chaud (froid).   *It is hot (cold).*

Notice that **il** is used impersonally (it does not refer to any person or thing).

READING PREPARATION

INSTRUCTIONS: *The ability to read French requires more than the memorization of vocabulary. See how many of the following new words you can read without looking at the English to establish the meaning.*

1. Les noms des saisons sont le printemps, l'été, l'automne, et l'hiver.
En hiver il fait froid, d'habitude.
(**l'hiver** = _____)

1. *winter* In winter it is usually cold.	**2.** En hiver, le sol est souvent couvert de neige. (**neige,** covering the ground, must be _____)
2. *snow*	**3.** Quand il y a de la neige, la terre est blanche. (**blanche**=_____)
3. *white*	**4.** Quand il y a de la neige, il fait froid.
4. When there is snow, it is cold.	**5.** Au printemps, les arbres fleurissent. Il fait beau temps. (**le printemps**=_____)
5. *spring* The weather is good.	**6.** Au printemps, les feuilles reviennent sur les arbres. (**feuilles**=_____. What comes back on the trees in the spring?)
6. *leaves*	**7.** La neige est blanche. Les feuilles des arbres sont vertes. (**vertes**=_____)
7. *green*	**8.** Au printemps, les oiseaux chantent dans les arbres. (**les oiseaux**=_____)
8. *the birds* In the spring the birds sing in the trees.	**9.** Il fait un temps splendide.
9. The weather is splendid.	**10.** En été, il fait chaud. (**en été**=_____)
10. *in the summer* In the summer, it is hot. (Do not confuse **l'été**–summer–with **été**–p.p. of **être**.)	**11.** L'été dernier a été très long.
11. Last summer was very long.	**12.** **parce que**=*because* En été, les plantes poussent parce qu'il fait chaud. (**pousser**=_____. What do plants do in summer?)
12. *grow* In summer the plants grow because it is warm.	**13.** Il a travaillé six ans à son étude très poussée. (**l'étude est**=*profonde/peu profonde.*)

13. **profonde**=*deep*, or *exhaustive*	**14.** En été, la plupart des plantes sont vertes.
14. In summer most of the plants are green.	**15.** En automne, les feuilles tombent des arbres. (If you do not remember **tomber,** the context of leaves and autumn should tell you that it means _____.)
15. *to fall* In autumn the leaves fall from the trees.	**16.** Il ne fait pas souvent beau temps.
16. The weather is not often good.	**17.** En automne, les feuilles sont souvent rouges, oranges ou jaunes. (If **jaune** describes autumn leaves and is not *red* or *orange*, it must be _____.)
17. *yellow* In autumn, the leaves are often red, orange or yellow.	**18.** **ou . . . ou**=*either . . . or* En automne, la plupart des feuilles sont ou rouges ou jaunes.
18. In autumn most of the leaves are either red or yellow.	**19.** Il fait souvent mauvais temps.
19. The weather is often bad.	**20.** En automne, le ciel n'est pas souvent bleu. Il est gris la plupart du temps. (**ciel**=_____ **gris**=_____)
20. *sky* *gray* In autumn the sky is not often blue. It is gray most of the time.	**21.** La plupart du temps, il fait mauvais temps.
21. Most of the time, the weather is bad.	**22.** Le ciel est souvent ou bleu ou gris.
22. The sky is often either blue or gray.	

40. *Numbers (Cardinal and Ordinal)*

1. The cardinal numbers in French are as follows:

0	**zéro**	3	**trois**	6	**six**
1	**un, une**	4	**quatre**	7	**sept**
2	**deux**	5	**cinq**	8	**huit**

9	neuf	34	trente–quatre	88	quatre–vingt–huit
10	dix	40	quarante	90	quatre–vingt–dix
11	onze	41	quarante et un	91	quatre–vingt–onze
12	douze	47	quarante–sept	99	quatre–vingt–dix–neuf
13	treize	50	cinquante	100	cent
14	quatorze	51	cinquante et un	101	cent un
15	quinze	52	cinquante–deux	200	deux cents
16	seize	60	soixante	316	trois cent seize
17	dix–sept	61	soixante et un	500	cinq cents
18	dix–huit	70	soixante–dix	580	cinq cent quatre–vingts
19	dix–neuf	71	soixante et onze	1.000	mille
20	vingt	75	soixante–quinze	1.001	mille un
21	vingt et un	77	soixante–dix–sept	3.000	trois mille
23	vingt–trois	80	quatre–vingts	100.000	cent mille
30	trente	81	quatre–vingt–un		
31	trente et un				

2. Notice that in French numerals, periods are used where English uses commas: 4.000 (Fr.)–4,000 (Eng.)

3. The ending **–ième** indicates an ordinal number:

1st	premier, première		11th	onzième
2nd	{ deuxième		16th	seizième
	{ second, seconde		17th	dix–septième
3rd	troisième		20th	vingtième
4th	quatrième		21st	vingt et unième
5th	cinquième		34th	trente–quatrième
6th	sixième		100th	centième
7th	septième			
8th	huitième			
9th	neuvième			
10th	dixième			

READING PREPARATION

INSTRUCTIONS: *Pouvez-vous faire de l'arithmétique en français?*

	1. Deux et deux font quatre. $2+2=4$
1. Two and two make four.	**2.** Deux fois trois font six. $2\times3=6$
2. Two times three make six.	**3.** Deux fois quatre font—**huit/neuf.**
3. **huit** (8)	**4.** Quatre et cinq font—**huit/neuf.**

4. **neuf** (9) (Are you circling unfamiliar items?)	5. Quatre fois cinq font—**dix/vingt**.
5. **vingt** (20)	6. Cinq et cinq font—**vingt–cinq/dix**.
6. **dix** (10)	7. Cinq fois cinq font—**vingt–cinq/dix**.
7. **vingt–cinq** (25)	8. Cinq fois dix font—**cinquante/quinze**.
8. **cinquante** (50)	9. Cinq et dix font—**cinquante/quinze**.
9. **quinze** (15)	10. Quatre et dix font—**quatorze/quarante**.
10. **quatorze** (14)	11. Dix et six font—**seize/soixante**.
11. **seize** (16)	12. Quatre fois dix font—**quatorze/quarante**.
12. **quarante** (40)	13. Six fois dix font—**seize/soixante**.
13. **soixante** (60)	14. Trois fois dix font—**treize/trente**.
14. **trente** (30)	15. Trois et dix font—**treize/trente**.
15. **treize** (13)	16. Trois et trois font—**neuf/six**.
16. **six** (6)	17. Trois et quatre font—**douze/sept**.
17. **sept** (7)	18. Quatre fois trois font—**douze/sept**.
18. **douze** (12)	19. Quatre et quatre font—**huit/seize**
19. **huit** (8)	20. Sept et huit font—**quinze/dix–sept**.
20. **quinze** (15)	21. Neuf et huit font—**dix–neuf/dix-sept**.
21. **dix–sept** (17)	22. Huit fois huit font—**seize/soixante-quatre**.
22. **soixante–quatre** (64)	23. Sept fois neuf font—**seize/soixante-trois**.
23. **soixante–trois** (63)	24. Sept fois dix font—**dix–sept/soixante–dix**.
24. **soixante–dix** (70)	25. Huit fois neuf font—**soixante-douze/dix–sept**.

25. soixante–douze (72)

26. Quatre fois vingt font—**vingt–quatre/quatre–vingts.**

26. quatre–vingts (80)

27. Quatre et vingt font—**vingt–quatre/quatre–vingts.**

27. vingt–quatre (24)

28. Quatre–vingt–huit moins quatre font—**quatre–vingt–quatorze / quatre–vingt–quatre.**

28. quatre–vingt–quatre (84)

29. Quatre–vingt–huit et six font—**quatre–vingt–seize/quatre–vingt–quatorze.**

29. quatre–vingt–quatorze (94)

30. Quatre–vingt–deux et douze font—**quatre–vingt–quatre/quatre–vingt–quatorze.**

30. quatre–vingt–quatorze (94)

31. Quatre–vingts moins quatre font **soixante–seize/soixante–six.**

31. Soixante–seize (76)

32. Soixante–seize moins huit font soixante–huit.

32. Seventy–six minus eight makes sixty–eight.

33. Vingt–quatre moins huit font seize.

33. Twenty–four minus eight make sixteen.

34. La première guerre mondiale a commencé en dix–neuf cent quatorze. (What is the date given?)

34. 1914

35. What must **guerre mondiale** mean?

35. *world war*

36. La deuxième guerre mondiale a commencé en dix–neuf cent trente–neuf. (What is the date given?)

36. 1939

37. **s'élever à**=*to rise, to amount to* Nos impôts s'élèvent à un vingtième de notre revenu, parfois à un dixième.

37. Our taxes amount to 1/20 of our income, sometimes to 1/10.

38. Je répète cette histoire pour la centième fois.

38. I repeat this story for the hundredth time.

41. *Determiners*—ce, cette, cet, ces

1. You have already encountered these words in your readings. They serve to point out or specify. They are translated by *this* or *that, these* or *those,* according to the context:

ce livre	(masculine singular noun)	*this, (that) book*
cette méthode	(feminine singular noun)	*this, (that) method*
cet hôtel	(masculine singular noun beginning	*this, (that) hotel*
cet arbre	with vowel or mute h)	*this, (that) tree*
ces livres	(plural of either masculine or	*these, (those) books*
ces méthodes	feminine nouns)	*these, (those) methods*
ces hôtels		*these, (those) hotels*
ces arbres		*these, (those) trees*

2. **–ci** and **–là** affixed to nouns designated by **ce, cet, cette, ces** intensify the specificity and indicate proximity, spatially or figuratively, in relation to the speaker. They are translated by *this* or *that, these* or *those,* respectively.

ce livre–ci	*this book*
ce livre–là	*that book*
cet arbre–ci	*this tree*
cet arbre–là	*that tree*
cette structure–ci	*this structure*
cette structure–là	*that structure*
ces méthodes–ci	*these methods*
ces théories–là	*those theories*

READING PREPARATION

INSTRUCTIONS: *Give the meaning of the following phrases in English. Work with your card, as usual.*

	1. cet ouvrage
1. this (that) work	**2.** cette théorie
2. this (that) theory	**3.** ces arbres
3. these (those) trees	**4.** ces lois
4. these (those) laws	**5.** ce pays

5. this (that) country	6. cet esprit de collaboration
6. this (that) spirit of collaboration	7. cette matière–là
7. that material	8. cette matière–ci
8. this material	9. ces matières–là
9. those materials	10. ces matières–ci
10. these materials	11. ce résidu–là
11. that residue	12. ces résidus–ci
12. these residues	13. cet agent–ci
13. this agent	14. ces deux agents–là
14. those two agents	

42. *Demonstrative Pronouns*—celui, celle, ceux, celles

1. Celui, celle, ceux, celles refer to previously mentioned persons or things, and their meanings are expressed in English as follows, according to context:

celui (m. sing.)	*that, the one*
celle (f. sing.)	*that, the one*
ceux (m. pl.)	*those, the ones*
celles (f. pl.)	*those, the ones*
Les principaux textes de ce genre sont celui de M. Salleron et celui du Père Secchi.	*The main texts of this kind are the one of Mr. Salleron and the one of Father Secchi.*
L'expérience de M. Robineau diffère de celle de M. Moulin.	*The experiment of Mr. Robineau differs from that of Mr. Moulin.*
les textes de M. Salleron et ceux du Père Secchi	*the texts of Mr. Salleron and those of Father Secchi*
les expériences de M. Robineau et celles de M. Moulin	*the experiments of Mr. Robineau and those of Mr. Moulin*

READING PREPARATION

INSTRUCTIONS: *Give the meanings of the following phrases. Work with your card, as usual.*

1. Le chemin de fer de St. Etienne et celui de Lyon datent des années 1820. (**chemin**=*road*, **fer**=*iron*, **le chemin de fer**=_____)

1. *the railroad*
The railroad of St. Etienne and the one of Lyons date from the 1820's.

2. L'histoire de France et celle des Etats–Unis diffèrent substantiellement.

2. The history of France and that of the United States differ substantially.

3. Le système lymphatique du chat diffère de celui des humains.

3. The lymph system of the cat differs from that of humans.

4. Les principes de la physique atomique et ceux de la chimie ont fait une contribution énorme à la technologie moderne.

4. The principles of atomic physics and those of chemistry have made a great contribution to modern technology.

5. **influer sur**=*to influence*
Les découvertes effectuées pendant la première guerre et celles effectuées pendant la deuxième guerre ont beaucoup influé sur l'industrie nucléaire.

5. The discoveries made during the first war and those made during the second have greatly influenced the nuclear industry.

6. L'atmosphère de la terre diffère de composition de celle de Vénus.

6. The atmosphere of the earth differs in composition from that of Venus.

7. Le gouvernement a accordé la concession du chemin de fer de St. Etienne en 1826 et celle du chemin de fer de Roanne en 1828.

7. The government granted the concession for the St. Etienne railroad in 1826 and that of the Roanne railroad in 1828.

43. *Comparatives*

1. The following patterns indicate degrees of comparison.

(A) **aussi . . . que**   *as . . . as*

Vénus est presque aussi grande que la terre.   *Venus is almost as large as the earth.*

La deuxième expérience a réussi aussi parfaitement que la première.	The second experiment succeeded as perfectly as the first one.
(B) plus . . . que	more (–er) . . . than
La terre est légèrement plus grande que Vénus.	The earth is slightly larger than Venus.
La deuxième expérience a réussi plus parfaitement que la première.	The second experiment succeeded more perfectly than the first.
(C) (le, la, les) plus . . .	the most (–est) . . .
Jupiter est la plus grande planète du système solaire.	Jupiter is the largest planet in the solar system.
Homère et Virgile sont les plus grands auteurs de l'antiquité.	Homer and Virgil are the greatest authors of antiquity.

READING PREPARATION

INSTRUCTIONS: *Give the meanings of the following sentences.*

	1. La terre est plus grande que Vénus.
1. The earth is larger than Venus.	**2.** Vénus est presque aussi grande que la terre.
2. Venus is almost as large as the earth.	**3. près de ✕ distant de** Mercure est la planète la plus près du soleil.
3. Mercury is the planet nearest to the sun.	**4.** Vénus est la planète la plus près de la terre.
4. Venus is the planet nearest to the earth.	**5.** La lune est un satellite de la terre. (**la lune** = _____)
5. *the moon* The moon is a satellite of the earth.	**6.** La lune est plus près de la terre que Vénus.
6. The moon is nearer to the earth than Venus (is).	**7.** La lune est plus près de la terre que de Vénus.
7. The moon is nearer to the earth than to Venus. (Notice the difference of meaning indicated by the preposition **de**.)	**8. la plus éloignée = la plus distante** Pluton est la planète la plus éloignée du soleil.

8. Pluto is the most distant planet from the sun.

9. Venus, which is the planet most comparable to the earth, revolves (turns) less rapidly than the latter.

10. Jupiter and Saturn are the largest of the planets.

11. Saturn, which is a smaller planet than Jupiter, is more distant from the sun than is the latter.

12. Mercury revolves more rapidly around the sun than the earth does.

13. Pluto revolves much less quickly around the sun than does Mercury.

14. Certain astronomers believe that the earth revolves as fast as does Venus.

15. The moon revolves around the earth.

16. According to some astronomers, Venus appears to rotate much less quickly than the earth.

17. The twelve moons of Jupiter appear to revolve more quickly than the one of our planet.

18. The earth appears to have fewer satellites than Jupiter does.

19. The atmosphere of the earth appears less dense than that of Venus.

20. The importance of the sun is great, and that of the moon is less (er).

9. **moins . . . que**=*less . . . than*
Vénus, qui est la planète la plus comparable à la terre, tourne moins rapidement que celle–ci.

10. Jupiter et Saturne sont les plus grandes des planètes.

11. Saturne, qui est une planète moins grande que Jupiter, est plus éloignée du soleil que celle–ci.

12. **autour de**=*around*
Mercure tourne plus rapidement autour du soleil que la terre.

13. **vite**=**rapidement**
Pluton tourne beaucoup moins vite autour du soleil que Mercure.

14. Certains astronomes croient que la terre tourne aussi vite que Vénus.

15. La lune tourne autour de la terre.

16. **paraître**=*to appear, to seem*
Selon quelques astronomes, Vénus paraît tourner beaucoup moins vite que la terre.

17. Les douze lunes de Jupiter paraissent tourner plus vite que celle de notre planète.

18. La terre paraît avoir moins de satellites que Jupiter.

19. L'atmosphère de la terre paraît moins dense que celle de Vénus.

20. L'importance du soleil est grande, et celle de la lune est moindre.

21. Les orbites des comètes sont plus elliptiques que celles des planètes.

21. The orbits of comets are more elliptical than those of the planets.

22. efficace = *efficient*
Il a réalisé un appareil plus efficace que celui de M. Heiseman.

22. He has constructed a more efficient apparatus than that of Mr. Heiseman.

23. L'atmosphère est souvent plus froide que la terre.

23. The atmosphere is often colder than the earth.

24. L'atmosphère de Vénus est au moins aussi chaude que celle de la terre.

24. The atmosphere of Venus is at least as warm as that of the earth.

25. une couche = *a layer*
Les couches d'air inférieures sont moins froides que les couches supérieures.

25. The lower layers of air are less cold than the upper layers.

26. La moyenne de cinq et trois est quatre.
(la moyenne = _____)

26. *the average*
The average of five and three is four.

27. La densité moyenne du globe vénusien est un peu plus faible que celle du globe terrestre.

27. The average density of the Venutian globe is a little less than that of the earth.

28. tandis que = *while, whereas*
Notre globe a 12.756 kilomètres de diamètre tandis que celui de Vénus est estimé à 12.333 kilomètres.

28. Our globe has a diameter of 12,756 kilometers while that of Venus is estimated at 12,333 kilometers.

29. Notre globe a plus de douze mille sept cent kilomètres de diamètre tandis que c'est à 12.333 qu'est estimé celui de Vénus.
(Qu' is the contraction of–qui/que.)

29. que–qui is never contracted
Our globe has a diameter of more than 12,700 kilometers whereas that of Venus is estimated at 12,333.

30. La température moyenne de cette région est soixante–six degrés.

30. The average temperature of this region is 66 degrees.

31. Il fait plus froid en hiver qu'au printemps.

31. It is colder in the winter than in the spring.

32. Il fait moins chaud en automne qu'en été.

32. It is cooler (less warm) in autumn than in the summer.

33. On voit moins d'oiseaux en hiver qu'en été.

33. One sees fewer birds in winter than in summer.

34. Ce printemps dernier a été moins long que l'été.

34. This last spring was shorter than the summer.	**35.** **L'amour—propre** = *self—love, conceit* L'amour—propre est le plus grand de tous les flatteurs. La Rochefoucauld.
35. Conceit is the greatest of all flatterers.	**36.** **habile** = *clever* L'amour—propre est plus habile que le plus habile homme du monde. La Rochefoucauld
36. Self—love is cleverer than the cleverest man in the world.	**37.** **fin** = **habile** On peut être plus fin qu'un autre, mais non pas plus fin que tous les autres. La Rochefoucauld
37. One can be cleverer than another person, but not cleverer than all others.	Review and then continue.

44. Celui—ci, celui—là

1. Do not confuse **celui—ci** or **celui—là** with **celui. —ci** and **—là**, when added to the demonstrative pronouns express the meanings of *"the latter"* and *"the former."*

celui—ci
celle—ci
ceux—ci   *the latter*
celles—ci

celui—là
celle—là
ceux—là   *the former*
celles—là

READING PREPARATION

INSTRUCTIONS: *In the following exercises, notice the difference of meaning between* **celui** *and* **celui—là,** *etc. Keep the left hand column covered with your card.*

1. **conclure** = *to conclude*
Nous avons conclu, d'après les obser- vations de M. Crookes et celles de M. Ravier que le sel d'uranium devient notablement moins actif dans une solu-

tion de baryum à l'état sulfaté.
Celles–là sont les plus convaincantes.
(**Celles–là** refers to **les observations de Crookes/les observations
de Ravier/une solution.**)

---

1. **Les observations de Crookes**—it
cannot refer to **solution,** which is singular.
We (have) concluded, from the observations of Mr. Crookes and those of
Mr. Ravier that the salts of uranium
become notably less active in a solution
of barium in the sulfatic state. The
former are the most convincing.

2. Les premiers chemins de fer français
sont celui de Saint–Etienne à Andrezieux et celui de Saint–Etienne à Lyon.
Celui–ci date de dix–huit cent vingt-
six et celui–là de dix–huit cent vingt-
trois.

---

2. The first French railroads are the one
from Saint–Etienne to Andrezieux and
the one from Saint–Etienne to Lyons.
The latter dates from 1826 and the
former from 1823.

3. **pourtant**=*however*
Pour établir ce fait on a consulté des
documents officiels et des ouvrages
historiques. Ceux–là semblent pourtant plus authentiques que ceux–ci.

---

3. In order to establish this fact, they
consulted official documents and historical works. The former seem, however, more authentic than the latter.

4. La première guerre mondiale a commencé en dix–neuf cent quatorze et la
deuxième en dix–neuf cent trente-
neuf. Celle–là a fini en dix–neuf cent
dix–huit et celle–ci en dix–neuf cent
quarante–cinq.

---

4. The first World War started in 1914
and the second in 1939. The former
ended in 1918 and the latter in 1945.

5. Grâce aux recherches de M. Porte et
à celles de M. Sévenne, on a pu établir
les faits historiques. Celles–ci semblent plus convaincantes que celles–là.

---

5. Thanks to the research of Mr. Porte
and that of Mr. Sévenne, one has been
able to establish the historical facts.
The latter (research) seems more convincing than the former.
(Here is another example of a French
plural being translated by an English
singular.)

6. **avant**=*before*
Les Anglais et les Espagnols sont
venus dans le Nouveau Monde. Ceux-
ci sont arrivés avant ceux–là.
(**une guerre mondiale**=*a world
war*
le Nouveau Monde=_____)

---

6. *the New World*
Both the English and the Spanish
came to the New World. The latter
arrived before the former.

Review the circled items before going
on.

VOCABULARY DEVELOPMENT

INSTRUCTIONS: *Try to enlarge your vocabulary by using the root word to discover the meanings of the other words.*

	1. faible=*feeble, weak* Selon Machiavelli le prince intelligent essaie toujours d'**affaiblir** son ennemi.
1. *to weaken*	**2.** Il paraît **affaibli** parce qu'il a été très malade.
2. *weak, weakened*	**3.** On a observé au cours de l'expérience **un affaiblissement notable** de la radioactivité du sel d'uranium.
3. *a noticeable weakening*	**4. conduire**=*to lead, to conduct, to guide* Les recherches les plus récentes **conduisent à considérer** la question comme peu importante.
4. *lead (one) to consider*	**5.** Il n'a pas travaillé, il a trop mangé, il a bu trop de vin. **Sa conduite** dans cette circonstance est fort blâmable.
5. *his conduct*	**6.** Il a démoli son auto parce qu'il est **incapable de la conduire.**
6. *incapable of driving it*	**7.** J'ai enfin obtenu mon **permis de conduire.**
7. *driver's license*	**8.** Leonard Bernstein est **un conducteur bien connu.**
8. *a well–known conductor*	

TESTING EXERCISE

INSTRUCTIONS: *Are you ready to go on? Answer the following questions by circling the answer which best completes the sentence or which expresses the most accurate translation of the underlined phrase. If you miss any, review the section indicated.*

1. Jean est **aussi grand que** Charles.
    A. smaller than   B. larger than   C. as large as

1. C (43)	2. **Il fait mauvais temps.**

2. Il fait mauvais temps.
A. He is late.   c. The weather is not good.
B. It is about time.   D. The weather is splendid.

2. C
(39)

3. Quatre–vingts moins quatre font
A. seize   B. soixante–dix   c. quatre–vingt–quatorze   D. soixante–seize

3. D
(40)

4. On dit qu'elle **chante** assez bien.
A. sings   B. acts   c. speaks   D. works

4. A
(Make General Vocabulary Review)

5. C'est un professeur qui **fait peur à ses étudiants.**
A. pleases his students   c. makes his students pay attention
B. frightens his students   D. makes his students do their best

5. B
(40)

6. Quarante et trente–quatre font
A. cinquante–quatre   c. soixante–quatre
B. soixante–quatorze   D. quatre–vingt–quatre

6. B
(40)

7. J'ai **fait** une grosse erreur.
A. did   B. made   c. repeated   D. feared

7. B
(41)

8. Ces méthodes–là sont peu efficaces.
A. these   B. those   c. this   D. that

8. B
(42)

9. Cette expérience de Robineau diffère de _____ de M. Moulin.
A. ceux   B. celui   c. celle   D. cette

9. C
(42)

10. Les expériences du Père Louvain et du professeur Barnard suggèrent une interprétation nouvelle. Cependant, celui–ci est le plus convaincant. **Celui–ci** *refers to*
A. les expériences   c. le professeur Barnard
B. le Père Louvain   D. une interprétation

10. C
(44)

READING PASSAGE

INSTRUCTIONS: *As you read the following passage, circle for future review the words and phrases which you do not immediately recognize. Do not look them up the first time through, but instead read for the overall meaning of the passage. Verify your understanding by means of the reading test and then work out the meanings of the circled items. In answering the questions, choose the alternative that is most nearly correct.*

Vénus

Renseignements extraits de *L'Astronomie* par Rudaux et de Vaucouleurs (Larousse, Editeur)

Parmi les principales planètes, Vénus est la plus comparable à la terre. Celle–ci est cependant légèrement plus grande que celle–là. Notre globe a 12.756 kilomètres de diamètre, tandis que c'est à 12.333 qu'est estimé celui de Vénus. La densité moyenne des matériaux qui constituent le globe
5   vénusien est égale à 5 (eau=1), c'est–à–dire, un peu plus faible que celle du globe terrestre (5,52). Cette donnée signifie qu'à la surface de ce monde–là l'intensité de la pesanteur est un peu moindre qu'ici–bas. Notre poids **y serait abaissé** [1] aux 88 centièmes de sa valeur habituelle.

Mais quand nous voulons établir d'autres rapprochements fondés sur
10   les connaissances les plus récentes, nous rencontrons une diversité peu con- ciliable dans les résultats fournis par l'observation. Certains savants ont attribué à Vénus une rotation moins rapide que celle de la terre. Selon d'autres, la rotation de Vénus s'élève à soixante–huit heures (McEwen), à vingt–quatre jours, huit heures (Bianchini), ou à deux cent vingt–cinq jours
15   (Schiaparelli). Selon ce dernier, la durée de la rotation est égale à celle de la révolution. Si cette hypothèse est bien fondée, un même côté du globe est toujours tourné vers le soleil, et l'autre toujours plongé dans la nuit. Cette opinion semble trouver aujourd'hui une acceptance de plus en plus générale.

On peut distinguer directement l'enveloppe gazeuse de la planète, et parce
20   que l'atmosphère de Vénus paraît très chargée de troubles, il est difficile d'apercevoir les détails du sol. **Les meilleures** [2] recherches modernes con- duisent, cependant, à considérer l'atmosphère de Vénus comme assez peu importante, et surtout très différente de composition de celle de la terre.

1. The first paragraph states that
    A. Venus is slightly larger than the earth
    B. the earth is slightly larger than Venus
    C. for a long time most people thought them to be almost exactly the same size

1. B   **2.** The first paragraph states that if a given object were weighed on the earth and on Venus
    A. it would be heavier on the earth
    B. it would be lighter on the earth
    C. it would weigh the same in both places

2. A   **3.** The second paragraph states that
    A. the earth turns more rapidly than Venus
    B. Venus turns more rapidly than the earth
    C. the opinion of astronomers is not completely unanimous on the subject

---

1 *would there be lowered*   **2** *best*

3. C   **4.** The third paragraph states that
    A. Venus and Earth are thought to have basically the same kind of atmosphere
    B. the nature of the soil on Venus can be deduced by the nature of its atmosphere
    C. the atmosphere of Venus seems to be unstable and in great commotion.

4. C

Chapter Seven

REVIEW: The degree of vocabulary retention depends in part on the number of times you encounter a word. Review the phrases you circled in Chapters Five and Six before you continue with Chapter Seven.

45. *Passive Constructions—Present Tense*

1. Some of the most common constructions in scientific French are passive. In an active construction the receiver of the action is the object. In a passive construction the receiver of the action is the subject. Compare the following sentences:

ACTIVE

Subject	*Verb*	*Object*
L'auteur	**développe**	**sa thèse.**
The author	*develops*	*his thesis.*
Le gouvernement	**encourage**	**le tourisme.**
The government	*encourages*	*tourism.*

113

PASSIVE

Subject	Verb	Agent
La thèse	**est développée**	**par l'auteur.**
The thesis	is developed	by the author.
Le tourisme	**est encouragé**	**par le gouvernement.**
Tourism	is encouraged	by the government.

2. As you see above, the passive is formed by the combination of **être** with the past participle.

3. You will remember that there is a small group of verbs which form the active Past Indefinite with **être** (**aller, venir,** etc.—see sec. 31). You should memorize these verbs in order to avoid confusing them with the Present Passive. Compare the examples below.

Le problème est devenu difficile.	*The problem became difficult.*
La solution du problème est obtenue par le calcul d'équations.	*The solution of the problem is obtained by the calculation of equations.*

READING PREPARATION

INSTRUCTIONS: *Cover the English with your card and express the meaning of the following phrases. Look at the English only to verify your answer.*

	1. **ce genre**=*this kind* Les mineurs utilisent une lampe de ce genre pour l'éclairage des mines de charbon. (What kinds of mines contain carbonaceous material?)
1. Miners utilize a lamp of this kind for lighting *coal* mines.	**2.** Une lampe de ce genre est utilisée pour l'éclairage des mines de charbon.
2. A lamp of this kind is utilized for lighting coal mines.	**3.** Une lampe de ce genre est utilisée par les mineurs. (Note the difference between **par** and **pour** above.)
3. A lamp of this kind is utilized by the miners.	**4.** Le gouvernement encourage la construction de nouveaux hôtels.
4. The government encourages the construction of new hotels.	**5.** La construction de nouveaux hôtels est encouragée par le gouvernement.

5. The construction of new hotels is encouraged by the government.	6. Un thermomètre est employé pour mesurer la température.
6. A thermometer is employed to measure the temperature. (**Pour** here has the meaning of *in order to*.)	7. La température est mesurée par un thermomètre.
7. The temperature is measured by a thermometer.	8. Les phénomènes de l'atmosphère sont étudiés par un météorologiste.
8. The phenomena of the atmosphere are studied by a meteorologist.	9. Un météorologiste étudie les phénomènes de l'atmosphère.
9. A meteorologist studies the phenomena of the atmosphere.	10. La nature de la valeur est expliquée par plusieurs facteurs.
10. The nature of value is explained by several factors.	11. Plusieurs facteurs peuvent expliquer la nature de la valeur.
11. Several factors can explain the nature of value.	12. **sous**=*under* L'étudiant introduit ce liquide sous pression dans des sacs lymphatiques.
12. The student introduces this liquid into lymphatic sacs under pressure.	13. Un liquide est introduit dans ces sacs sous pression.
13. A liquid is introduced into these sacs under pressure.	14. Le liquide est ensuite projeté dans le système artériel.
14. The liquid is then projected into the arterial system.	15. Vous pouvez déterminer par cette expérience les effets de l'intoxication.
15. You can determine the effects of intoxication (poisoning) by this experiment.	16. Les effets de l'intoxication sont déterminés par cette expérience.
16. The effects of intoxication are determined by this experiment.	17. Les effets de l'intoxication peuvent être déterminés par cette expérience.
17. The effects of intoxication can be determined by this experiment.	18. Les problèmes posés par la science sont restés difficiles. (**Rester** is an **être** verb.)
18. The problems posed by science (have) remained difficult.	19. Les problèmes posés par la science sont étudiés constamment.
19. The problems posed by science are constantly studied.	20. Les données de la physique nucléaire sont devenues nombreuses.

20.	The data of nuclear physics have become numerous.	**21.**	De nombreux physiciens nucléaires ont contribué au développement de la physique nucléaire. (**Physiciens**=*physicists/physicians*)
21.	**physicists** Numerous nuclear physicists have contributed to the development of nuclear physics.	**22.**	De nombreux physiciens nucléaires ont vérifié les théories de la physique nucléaire.
22.	Numerous nuclear physicists have verified the theories of nuclear physics.	**23.**	Les théories des physiciens nucléaires sont vérifiées par des expériences.
23.	The theories of nuclear physicists are verified by experiments.	**24.**	**loin**=*far* Quelques physiciens sont allés trop loin dans leurs spéculations.
24.	A few physicists have gone (went) too far in their speculations.		

46.   *Passive Constructions—Past Indefinite Tense*

1.   The past Passive in French is formed by the Present of **avoir**+**été**+ the past participle of the main verb:

L'ouvrage a été accueilli favorablement.	*The work was received, or has been received, favorably.*
Ces découvertes ont été effectuées à partir de 1930.	*These discoveries were made after 1930, or have been made starting in 1930.*

2.   With the verb **pouvoir,** the Passive is formed by **être**+the past participle:

Ces couches peuvent être produites indépendamment l'une de l'autre.	*These layers can be produced independently of one another.*

INSTRUCTIONS: *Notice the contrast between the Active and the Passive as you read through the following phrases. Look at the English only to verify your answer.*

		1.	L'auteur a largement développé cette thèse.
1.	The author (has) developed this thesis at length.	**2.**	Cette thèse a été largement développée.

2.	This thesis has been (was) developed at length.	**3.**	Nous avons vérifié les conditions de l'expérience.
3.	We (have) verified the conditions of the experiment.	**4.**	Les conditions de l'expérience ont été vérifiées.
4.	The conditions of the experiment were (have been) verified.	**5.**	Pendant l'expérience, le liquide a été injecté dans le système artériel.
5.	During the experiment, the liquid was injected into the arterial system.	**6.**	Ses confrères ont fait plusieurs découvertes importantes dans cette grotte–là.
6.	His colleagues (have) made several important discoveries in that cave.	**7.**	Plusieurs découvertes importantes ont été faites dans la grotte de La Mouthe.
7.	Several important discoveries have been made in the cave of La Mouthe.	**8.**	Le conférencier a facilement obtenu la solution du problème.
8.	The lecturer easily obtained the solution to the problem.	**9.**	La solution du problème a été obtenue par des calculs ingénieux.
9.	The solution to the problem was obtained by some ingenious calculations.	**10.**	La solution du problème peut être obtenue par la plupart des étudiants.
10.	The solution of the problem can be obtained by most of the students.	**11.**	Ces couches de nuages peuvent être produites indépendamment les unes des autres.
11.	These layers of clouds can be produced independently of one another.	**12.**	La nature de la valeur a été expliquée par plusieurs facteurs.
12.	The nature of value was (has been) explained by several factors.	**13.**	La nature de la valeur peut être expliquée par plusieurs facteurs.
13.	The nature of value can be explained by several factors.	**14.**	La nature de la valeur est peut–être expliquée par ces facteurs–ci. (**peut–être**=*can be/perhaps*)
14.	*perhaps*—the hyphen tells you that it is not the verb phrase. The nature of value is perhaps explained by these factors.	**15.**	Le public a favorablement accueilli cet ouvrage.
15.	The public has received this work favorably.	**16.**	L'ouvrage a été favorablement accueilli par le public.
16.	The work has been (was) received with favor by the public.	**17.**	L'accueil par le public a été généralement favorable.

17. The reception by the public has been (was) generally favorable.	**18.** Plusieurs astronomes ont établi la densité moyenne de l'atmosphère vénusienne.
18. Several astronomers (have) established the average density of the atmosphere of Venus.	**19.** La densité moyenne de l'atmosphère de Vénus a été établie par plusieurs astronomes.
19. The average density of the atmosphere of Venus has been (was) established by several astronomers.	**20.** Cependant, il n'y a pas beaucoup d'astronomes qui ont été d'accord sur cette question.
20. However, there are not many astronomers who have been in agreement on this question.	

47. *Translation of* on, l'on

1. You have encountered **on** in contexts where it means **one** or **they**. Actually, being an indefinite pronoun, it can refer to any of the persons and can be translated as *I, you, we they, he, she, one, people,* or *someone,* depending on the context:

Qu'est–ce qu'on a fait hier soir? (**Vous et Marie**)	*What did you do last night?*
On est allé au cinéma.	*We went to the movie.*
On parle anglais en Angleterre.	*One speaks English in England. People speak English in England. They speak English in England.*
On est sorti.	*I, you, he, she, we, they, someone went out* (depending on *who* went out.)

2. Very often a smoother translation may be obtained with **on** constructions by placing the verb in the Passive voice: e.g. *English is spoken in England.*

3. Note that even though **on** is often plural in meaning (*they, people in general*), the verb is always in the third person singular.

4. An **l'** is often placed before **on** for the sake of euphony. Pay no attention to this **l'** in translating. It has no grammatical function or meaning. Compare the examples below.

Les plans que l'on prépare . . .	*The plans that one prepares* . . .
Les plans qu'on prépare . . .	*The plans that one prepares* . . .

READING PREPARATION

INSTRUCTIONS: *Translate the following phrases in two ways whenever possible; use an active construction for one and a passive for the other when you can.*

	1. On reconnaît à l'heure actuelle que . . .
1. One recognizes at the present time, *or* it is recognized at the present time that . . .	2. Grâce à cette expérience, on a reconnu l'influence de la lumière.
2. Thanks to this experiment, one (has) recognized the influence of light, *or* the influence of light was (has been) recognized.	3. On a effectué en France des expériences semblables.
3. One (has) performed similar experiments in France, *or* similar experiments have been (were) performed in France.	4. Grâce à la compétence du personnel du laboratoire, plusieurs expériences semblables ont été effectuées.
4. Thanks to the competence of the laboratory personnel, several similar experiments have been (were) performed.	5. On observe plusieurs couches de nuages.
5. Several layers of clouds are observed.	6. En France on parle français.
6. In France, French is spoken (one speaks French, they speak French).	7. **tout(e)** = *all, any* Hier soir, je suis allé au cinéma avec Marie. On a parlé français toute la soirée.
7. Last night (yesterday evening) 1 went to the movies with Mary. *We* spoke French all evening (or *Mary*, or *I*).	8. On parle allemand en Allemagne. (Berlin est en Allemagne)
8. German is spoken in Germany (*or* one speaks, *or* they speak, etc).	9. Plusieurs Allemands ont posé des questions au professeur. On a répondu en allemand.
9. Several Germans asked the professor some questions. He answered in German.	10. On constate que . . .
10. One ascertains that . . . *or* It is ascertained that . . .	11. On peut constater que . . .

11. One may ascertain that . . . *or* It may be ascertained that . . .	**12.** Le plaisir de l'amour est d'aimer, et l'on est plus heureux par la passion que l'on a que par celle que l'on donne. La Rochefoucauld
12. The pleasure of love is in loving, and one is happier in the love that one feels than in the one that one causes.	

48. *Impersonal Expressions* (il s'agit de, *etc.*)

1. When a verb is used impersonally, the subject pronoun **il** does not refer to a previously mentioned person or thing. In the following phrases **il** is translated by *it*:

il s'agit de ⎫ **il est question de** ⎭	*it is a question of,* *it concerns*
il importe que(de)	*it is important that (to)*
il paraît que ⎫ **il semble que** ⎭	*it seems that, it appears that*
il arrive que(de)	*it happens that (to)*
il suffit que(de)	*it is sufficient that (to)*

2. **Paraître, sembler, arriver** and **suffire** can also be used personally. You must examine all of the context to determine whether **il** is to be translated as *he* or *it:*

Pierre n'a pas d'argent.	*Peter has no money.*
Il semble préoccupé.	*He seems worried.*
Il semble qu'il est préoccupé.	*It seems that he is worried.*

READING PREPARATION

INSTRUCTIONS: *Express the meaning of the following sentences. Continue to circle the phrases you do not immediately recognize.*

1. Il s'agit de deux éléments différents.

1. It concerns two different elements.	**2.** Il s'agit de ne pas confondre les deux éléments.
2. It is a question of not confusing the two elements.	**3.** Il s'agit d'une expérience simple.
3. It is a question of (concerns) a simple experiment.	**4.** Il importe d'examiner les résultats.
4. It is important to examine the results.	**5.** **un procédé**=*a procedure* Il importe de bien décrire les procédés utilisés.
5. It is important to describe well the procedures utilized.	**6.** Il s'agit dans ce chapitre de décrire un simple procédé chimique.
6. In this chapter it is a question of describing a simple chemical procedure.	**7.** **empêcher**=*to prevent, to hinder* Il est question d'un procédé destiné à empêcher le noircissement du cidre.
7. It concerns a procedure intended to prevent the darkening of cider.	**8.** Il s'agit d'une expérience destinée à empêcher le noircissement du cidre.
8. It concerns an experiment intended to prevent the darkening of cider.	**9.** Il paraît que l'auteur veut partir des faits connus. (**partir**=*to leave/to start from*)
9. *start from* It appears that the author wants to start from (take as the point of departure) known facts.	**10.** L'auteur note qu'il arrive souvent que le cidre noircit à l'air. (**à l'air**=*to the air/in the open air.* Don't look at the verification until you re–examine the context.)
10. *in the open air* The author notes that it often happens that cider turns dark in the open air.	**11.** Il arrive à la conclusion que le liquide noircit à l'air. (Is **il arrive** used *personally* or *impersonally?*)
11. *personally*–**il** refers to **auteur** He arrives at the conclusion that the liquid darkens in the open air.	**12.** Le liquide ne reste pas inaltéré; au contraire, il paraît noircir. (Does **il** refer to a *previously mentioned object,* or is it used *impersonally?*)
12. It refers to **le liquide.** The liquid does not remain unchanged; to the contrary, it appears to darken.	**13.** Il ne paraît pas que le liquide reste inaltéré.

13. It does not appear that the liquid remains unchanged.

14. prendre = *to take*
Il paraît que la solution prend une teinte brune.

14. It appears that the solution takes on a brown tint.

15. alors = *then*
Il est alors arrivé au liquide de prendre une teinte brune.

15. It then happened that the liquid took on a brown tint.

16. Il arrive alors que la solution ne reste pas inaltérée.

16. It then happens that the solution does not remain unchanged.

17. verser = *to pour*
Il paraît que le liquide, versé dans un vase ouvert, ne reste pas inaltéré.
(Which is the most probable meaning of vase ouvert = *open vase/open receptacle?*)

17. *open receptacle*
It appears that the liquid, (when) poured into an open receptacle does not remain unaltered.

18. ajouter = *to add*
Il est arrivé que l'auteur a ajouté une petite quantité d'acide citrique au cidre.

18. It happened that the author added a small quantity of citric acid to the cider.

19. Il suffit d'ajouter une petite quantité d'acide citrique au cidre.

19. It is sufficient to add a small quantity of citric acid to the cider.

20. Il importe d'ajouter au cidre l'acide nécessaire.

20. It is important to add to the cider the necessary acid.

21. Il importe de ne pas ajouter trop d'acide au cidre.

21. It is important not to add too much acid to the cider.

22. Versé dans le cidre, l'acide citrique empêche le cidre de noircir à l'air.

22. (Having been) poured into the cider, the citric acid keeps the cider from turning black (darkening) in the open air.

23. Il suffit de verser un peu d'acide citrique dans le cidre pour empêcher le noircissement de celui-ci.

23. It is sufficient to pour a little citric acid in the cider in order to prevent the darkening of the latter.

24. Il semble qu'on a trouvé le secret d'empêcher aussi le noircissement des vins.

24. It seems that they have found the secret to prevent the darkening of wines also.

25. d'autant moins = *all the less, proportionately less*
Il semble que le cidre est d'autant moins altéré que la solution ajoutée contient plus d'acide.

25.	It seems that the cider is proportionately less changed as the added solution contains more acid.	26.	Il paraît que les cidres noircissent d'autant plus qu'ils sont riches en tanin.
26.	It appears that ciders discolor (darken) all the more as they are rich in tanin.	27.	Le cidre prend une teinte d'autant plus brune qu'il est exposé à l'air.
27.	Cider takes on a browner color in proportion to its exposure to the air.		

49. *Impersonal Expressions Indicating Existence*

1. The following impersonal expressions indicate existence and may be translated by singular or plural forms, depending on the context:

Il est un procédé pour déterminer la densité de l'atmosphère.	*There is a procedure to determine the density of the atmosphere.*
Il est des procédés pour la déterminer.	*There are procedures for determining it.*
Il y a un soleil.	*There is a sun.*
Il y a plusieurs soleils.	*There are several suns.*
Il reste une partie.	*There remains one part,* or *one part remains.*
Il reste dix–huit francs.	*There remain eighteen francs,* or *eighteen francs remain.*
Il existe un procédé . . .	*There exists a procedure,* or *a procedure exists.*
Il existe dans le cidre des sels de fer.	*There exist ferric salts in cider,* or *ferrous salts exist in cider.*

READING PREPARATION

INSTRUCTIONS: *Determine whether the following impersonal verbs should be translated by the singular or the plural.*

	1. Il y a une certaine obscurité dans son explication. (**Il y a** = *There is/There are*)
1. *There is* a certain obscurity in his explanation.	2. Il y a pourtant des obscurités dans cette explication. (**Il y a** = *There is/There are*)

2. *There are,* however, some obscurities in this explanation.	**3.** Il y a une valeur naturelle dans les forêts.
3. There is a natural value in the forests.	**4.** Il y a des choses qui ont une valeur naturelle.
4. There are things which have a natural value.	**5.** Il reste des obscurités dans son explication.
5. Some obscurities remain in his explanation.	**6.** Il existe des cidres qui ne noircissent pas à l'air.
6. There are some ciders which do not darken in the open air.	**7.** Il existe toujours dans le cidre des sels de fer.
7. There are always some ferrous salts in cider.	**8.** **foncé**=*dark* Il reste une coloration beaucoup plus foncée.
8. A much darker coloration remains.	**9.** Il reste toujours des doutes dans l'esprit du lecteur. (**l'esprit**=*the spirit/the mind*)
9. *the mind* Doubts still remain in the mind of the reader.	**10.** Il existe un procédé pour prévenir le noircissement du cidre.
10. There exists a procedure to prevent the darkening of cider.	**11.** Il est pourtant des procédés très peu efficaces.
11. There are, however, some very ineffective procedures.	

50. *Irregular Verb* savoir (*to know*)

1.   Present

je sais	*I know*
tu sais	*you know*
il, elle, on sait	*he, she, one knows*
nous savons	*we know*
vous savez	*you know*
ils, elles savent	*they know*

Past Participle: **su** (*known*)

2.   In addition to its basic meaning of *to know*, **savoir** can also mean *to learn* or, when followed by an infinitive, *to know how to*, or *to be able to*.

Nous ne savons pas l'heure de votre arrivée.	*We do not know the time of your arrival.*
Nous avons su par cette expérience que . . .	*We have learned by this experiment that . . .*
Nous ne savons pas écrire le français.	*We do not know how to write French (we are not able to).*

READING PREPARATION

INSTRUCTIONS: *Pay special attention to the uses of* **savoir** *in the following phrases.*

		1.	On sait que le cidre noircit à l'air.
1.	It is known that cider darkens in the open air.	**2.**	Nous savons qu'il existe des sels de fer dans le cidre.
2.	We know that ferrous salts exist in cider.	**3.**	**se trouvent**=*are found* On sait que d'autres substances se trouvent dans le cidre.
3.	It is known that other substances are found in cider.	**4.**	**Pourquoi**=*why* On sait pourquoi d'autres substances se trouvent dans le cidre.
4.	We know (or equivalent) why other substances are found in cider.	**5.**	Nous avons su par cette expérience que . . .
5.	We learned by this experiment that . . .	**6.**	Nous avons su empêcher le noircissement du cidre.
6.	We were able to prevent the darkening of the cider.	**7.**	Je ne sais pas exactement pourquoi il veut empêcher le noircissement du cidre.
7.	I do not know exactly why he wants to prevent the darkening of the cider.	**8.**	Il a su obtenir le même résultat que ses confrères.
8.	He was able to obtain the same result as his colleagues.	**9.**	Vous ne savez pas s'il a su obtenir les mêmes résultats que ses confrères.
9.	You do not know if (whether) he was able to obtain the same results as his colleagues.	**10.**	Il sait parler français.
10.	He knows how to speak French.	**11.**	Il a su trouver la cause du noircissement des vins.
11.	He was able to find the cause of the darkening of wines.		

51. *Uses of* aussi

1.   Aussi has three main meanings, depending on its use and position in the sentence: (1) used with **que** it indicates comparison; (2) at the beginning of the sentence, followed by an inversion of the subject and verb, it indicates consequence and is translated as *therefore;* and (3) its most common meaning is *also.*

Un résultat aussi étonnant que celui de notre première expérience . . .	*A result as astonishing as that of our first experiment . . .*
Aussi existe–t–il des cidres qui ne noircissent pas à l'air.	*Therefore there are some ciders which do not turn black in the open air.*
Il existe aussi des cidres qui se conservent facilement.	*There are some ciders which are easily preserved.*

READING PREPARATION

INSTRUCTIONS: *Point out the difference of meaning between the following phrases.*

		1.	Ils le savent aussi.
1.	They know it, also.	**2.**	Ils le savent aussi bien que nous.
2.	They know it as well as we do.	**3.**	Aussi savent–ils . . .
3.	Therefore they know . . .	**4.**	On peut constater aussi . . .
4.	One can also ascertain (or determine) . . .	**5.**	Aussi peut–on constater . . .
5.	Therefore one may ascertain (or determine) . . .	**6.**	Il y a aussi . . .
6.	There is (are) also . . .	**7.**	Aussi y a–t–il . . .
7.	Therefore there is (are) . . .	**8.**	Il y a eu aussi . . .
8.	There was (were) also (*or* there have also been) . . .	**9.**	Aussi y a–t–il eu . . .
9.	Therefore there was (were) (*or* have been) . . .	**10.**	Nous avons pu constater aussi que . . .
10.	We were also able (*or* have been able) to ascertain . . .	**11.**	Aussi avons–nous pu constater que . . .

11. Therefore we were able (or have been able) to ascertain that . . .	**12.** Nous pouvons rester aussi longtemps que nous voulons.
12. We can remain as long as we want.	**13.** Aussi pouvons–nous rester.
13. Therefore we can remain.	

52. *Uses of* même

1.   Même also changes meanings according to its position in the sentence. Preceding a noun, it has the meaning of *the same* or *a like:*

ces mêmes solutions	*these same solutions*
la même quantité	*the same quantity*
un même volume	*a like volume*

In this case it is often used as a term of comparison:

Ils ont obtenu le même résultat que leurs prédécesseurs.	*They obtained the same result as their predecessors.*

2.   Immediately following a noun it emphasizes or particularizes:

ces solutions mêmes	*these very solutions*
ce volume même	*this very volume* (*or amount*)
les plantes mêmes	*the plants themselves*
l'empéreur lui-même	*the emperor himself*

3.   Elsewhere in the sentence it has the meaning of concession and is translated by *even:*

. . . des cidres, qui même riches en tanin . . .	*. . . ciders, which even rich in tannin . . .*
Même si l'opinion est combattue . . .	*Even if the opinion is opposed . . .*
. . . des nuages qui même marchent dans des directions opposées . . .	*. . . clouds which even move in opposite directions . . .*

INSTRUCTIONS: *As you read the following phrases, look for the differences of meaning indicated by the position of* **même.** *Continue to circle the phrases you do not recognize automatically.*

	1. **obtenir**=*to obtain* Nous avons obtenu le même résultat que nos confrères.
1. We obtained the same result as our colleagues.	2. Nous avons même obtenu le résultat que . . .
2. We even obtained the result that . . .	3. J'ai ajouté la même quantité d'acide citrique au cidre.
3. I added the same amount of citric acid to the cider.	4. J'ai ajouté une même quantité . . .
4. I added a like quantity . . .	5. J'ai même ajouté une quantité d'acide citrique au cidre.
5. I even added an amount of citric acid to the cider.	6. J'ai ajouté au cidre une quantité de cet acide même.
6. I added to the cider an amount of this very acid.	7. **se trouve**=*is found* Cette même substance se trouve dans l'épiderme des plantes.
7. This same substance is found in the epidermis of the plants.	8. Cette substance se trouve même dans l'épiderme des plantes.
8. This substance is found even in the epidermis of the plants.	9. Cette substance se trouve dans l'épiderme des plantes mêmes.
9. This substance is found in the epidermis of the plants themselves.	10. J'ai même constaté le fait que . . .
10. I even ascertained the fact that . . .	11. J'ai pu constater le même fait que M. Roberteau.
11. I was able to determine the same fact as Mr. Roberteau.	Review!! Reread the items circled above before going on.

VOCABULARY DEVELOPMENT

INSTRUCTIONS: *Try to give the meaning of the following words by analogy with the key word.*

	1. **noircir**=*to turn black* **brunir**=
1. *to turn brown*	2. **blanchir**=
2. *to turn white*	3. **jaunir**=

3. *to turn yellow*	4. **rougir**=
4. *to turn red*	5. Je rougis de mes stupidités.
5. I blush because of my stupidities	6. **une teinte foncée**=*a dark color* (*hue*) une teinte plus foncée=
6. a darker color	7. une teinte de plus en plus foncée=
7. a darker and darker color	8. une teinte de moins en moins foncée=
8. a lighter and lighter color (less and less dark)	

TESTING EXERCISE

INSTRUCTIONS: *Circle the answer which makes the sentence grammatically correct or which best expresses the meaning of the indicated word or phrase. If you miss any, review the indicated section before continuing.*

1. La solution du problème **est obtenue** par des calculs ingénieux.
   A. was obtained   B. is obtained   C. has been obtained

---

1. B   2. Les données de la physique nucléaire **sont devenues** nombreuses.
   A. are becoming   B. are become   C. have become

---

2. C   3. Ces couches de nuages **peuvent être produites** indépendamment les unes des autres.
   A. are to be produced
   B. can be produced
   C. were able to be produced
   D. are produced

---

3. B   4. **Il s'agit de** deux expériences différentes.
   A. He is performing two different experiments.
   B. He is reacting to two different experiences.
   C. He performed two different experiments.
   D. It concerns two different experiments.

---

4. D   5. **Il existe un procédé** pour prévenir le noircissement du cidre.
   A. A procedure exists.
   B. It exists in a procedure.
   C. One proceeds through existing methods.

---

5. A   6. **On** reconnaît facilement les dangers de son procédé.
   A. I   B. You   C. We   D. One
   E. any of the above, depending on context.

6. E   7. D'autres causes peuvent **aussi** donner naissance aux nuages.
               A. also   B. therefore   C. as

7. A   8. On observe ce phénomène **aussi** souvent sur les montagnes **que** sur les lieux humides.
               A. also   B. therefore   C. as . . . as

8. C   9. **Aussi** observe–t–on ce phénomène souvent sur les lieux humides.
               A. also   B. therefore   C. as

9. B   10. Cette **même** substance se trouve dans l'épiderme des plantes.
               A. same   B. even   C. itself

10. A   11. La nature de la valeur est expliquée _____ plusieurs facteurs.
               A. par   B. pour   C. entre   D. dans

11. A   12. Nous **savons** parler français.
               A. know   B. know how   C. are learning

12. B

READING PASSAGE

INSTRUCTIONS: *As you read the following passage, circle the words which you do not immediately recognize, but do not look them up the first time through. When you finish reading the passage, verify your comprehension by taking the test at the end. Then go back over the passage and work out the meaning of the circled words more carefully. If you make notes, make them in the margin and not between the lines.*

Procédé pour prévenir le noircissement du cidre

Note de MM. Léon DUFOUR et Lucien DANIEL dans *Comptes rendus de l'Académie des Sciences*, Tome 122, p. 494.

On sait que le cidre présente parfois la propriété **de se colorer** [1] à l'air, en brun d'abord, puis en noir: on dit alors vulgairement que le cidre se tue. Nous avons **remarqué** [2] que le noircissement du cidre est en relation avec la quantité de tanin que contient ce liquide. Il suffit de noter,
5 **avant** [3] l'analyse, si le cidre, versé dans un vase ouvert, reste inaltéré, ou s'il se tue légèrement, ou beaucoup: **en comparant** [4] ces indications avec le contenu en tanin on arrive à cette conclusion que les cidres se tuent d'autant plus qu'ils sont plus riches en tanin.

Nous allons voir toutefois [5] que d'autres substances, qui se trouvent
10 dans le cidre, combattent l'effet du tanin: aussi existe–t–il des cidres qui, même riches en tanin, ne noircissent pas à l'air.

---

1 *to change color*   3 *before*   5 *we will see, however*
2 *noticed*   4 *by comparing*

Les solutions de tanin s'oxydent à l'air **en prenant** [6] une teinte brune de plus en plus foncée. **D'autre part, toute** [7] cause qui augment l'altération des solutions de tanin, augmente aussi le noircissement du cidre. On sait, par
^15 exemple, que les solutions alcalines produisent une coloration brune et immédiate des solutions de tanin; ces mêmes solutions alcalines accentuent beaucoup le noircissement du cidre.

Une autre cause accentue le noircissement pour certains cidres: il existe toujours dans le cidre des sels de fer qui, comme on le sait, précipitent le
^20 tanin en noir; il en résulte une coloration beaucoup plus foncée **que** [8] celle qui **serait** [9] produite par la simple oxydation du tanin.

Pour combattre le noircissement du cidre, nous **partons** [10] de ce fait connu, que la présence d'acides empêche les solutions de tanin de brunir à l'air.
^25 Si dans une série de tubes à essais, **contenant** [11] la même quantité de cidre, on ajoute un même volume de solutions acides diversement concentrées, on constate, au bout d'un certain temps, que le cidre est d'autant moins altéré que la solution ajoutée contient plus d'acide. Parmi les divers acides (malique, citrique, tartique, etc.) **dont** [12] nous avons étudié l'action, c'est
^30 l'acide citrique qui nous a fourni les **meilleurs** [13] résultats. La dose à employer dépend du contenu en tanin et de la proportion d'acides libres **existant** [14] naturellement dans le cidre. **En ajoutant** [15] 10 g. à 15 g. d'acide citrique par hectolitre, on obtient un effet suffisant avec un cidre qui ne s'altère pas très rapidement.

1. In the first paragraph we can infer that
   A. some ciders tend to turn brown and others to turn black.
   B. cider always becomes discolored in the open air.
   C. **se tuer** is a common expression indicating the discoloration of cider.
   D. cider is often the object of vulgar remarks.

2. The first paragraph states that
   A. the more tannin there is in the cider, the more the cider discolors.
   B. the less tannin the cider has the more easily it discolors.
   C. there is little relation between tannin and the discoloration of cider.

3. The second paragraph states that
   A. because of other circumstances some ciders do not discolor in the open air.
   B. tannin is the only darkening agent usually found in cider.
   C. actually the richest ciders do not discolor in the open air.

4. Paragraph three states that
   A. alkaline solutions combat the process of discoloration.

6 while taking on	**9** would be	**13** best
7 furthermore, any	**10** start with	**14** existing
8 than	**11** containing	**15** by adding
	12 of which	

B. solutions of tannin turn a light brown when they oxidize.

C. the more alkaline solutions the tannin contains, the darker the cider becomes.

5. The basic ingredients used in preventing discoloration are
    A. ferrous salts
    B. oxidized tannin
    C. alkaline solutions
    D. acids

Answers: 1–C;   2–A;   3–A;   4–C;   5–D

FOR CLASS DISCUSSION:

1. Underline all of the past participles and be able to tell whether they are used as nouns, as adjectives, or as part of the past indefinite tense of the verb.

2. Describe the experiment suggested by the author in the last paragraph.

Chapter Eight

REVIEW: Before going on to Chapter Eight, verify your retention of the new vocabulary and structures of Chapters Six and Seven.

53. *Reflexive Verbs—Present Tense*

1. Reflexive verbs often indicate an action which the subject does to itself (they "reflect" the action back upon the doer). **S'habiller** (to dress oneself), **se laver** (to wash oneself) are both reflexive verbs. They are identified by the presence of the following object pronouns which precede the verb:

je *me* **lave**	*I wash (myself)*
tu *te* **laves**	*you wash (yourself)*
il *se* **lave**	*he washes (himself)*
elle *se* **lave**	*she washes (herself)*
on *se* **lave**	*one washes (oneself)*
nous *nous* **lavons**	*we wash (ourselves)*
vous *vous* **lavez**	*you wash (yourself, yourselves)*
ils *se* **lavent**	*they (m.) wash (themselves)*
elles *se* **lavent**	*they (f.) wash (themselves)*

2. Reflexive verbs can also indicate reciprocal actions:

Nous nous parlons.	*We speak to each other.*
Ils se connaissent.	*They know each other.*

133

3. They are also used in a more general, impersonal way which is translated into English by the passive:

Il s'oppose à cette action.   *He is opposed to this action.*

Cette loi se déduit des données.   *This law is deduced from the data.*

Sometimes a simple present verb in the active voice, or *to become*, is sufficient to express the meaning:

Si un vent s'élève . . .   *If a wind comes up* . . .

Les nuages se déplacent rapidement.   *The clouds move rapidly.*

L'atmosphère se refroidit.   *The atmosphere becomes cool.*

4. Notice that the reflexive pronoun **se** can suggest *himself, herself, itself, oneself, themselves*, according to the subject pronoun.

5. A definite article used with a reflexive verb is usually translated by the possessive adjective:

Je me lave *les* mains.   *I wash my hands.*

READING PREPARATION

INSTRUCTIONS: *Express the meanings of the following sentences. Cover the English with your card until you have worked out a meaning which you want to verify.*

	1. L'eau se compose d'oxygène et d'hydrogène.
1. Water is composed of oxygen and hydrogen.	**2.** L'eau est composée d'oxygène et d'hydrogène.
2. Same as above.	**3.** Les nuages se produisent de différentes manières.
3. Clouds are produced in different ways.	**4.** Les nuages sont produits de différentes manières.
4. Same as above.	**5.** Les nuages peuvent se produire de différentes façons.
5. Clouds can be produced in different ways.	**6.** Les nuages peuvent être produits de différentes façons.

6. Same as above.	**7.** **une prairie**=*a meadow* Les nuages se forment sur les prairies.
7. Clouds are formed over the meadows.	**8.** Les nuages peuvent se former sur les prairies.
8. Clouds can form (be formed) over the meadows.	**9.** Lorsqu'on se trouve isolé sur une montagne . . .
9. When one finds oneself alone on a mountain . . .	**10.** On voit les nuages se former dans les lieux humides.
10. One sees the clouds forming (being formed) in humid places.	**11.** **ensuite**=*next, then* Ensuite les nuages se déplacent.
11. Then the clouds move.	**12.** Ensuite, on voit les nuages se déplacer.
12. Next, one sees the clouds move.	**13.** Les nuages peuvent se former très vite.
13. Clouds can be formed very quickly.	**14.** Les nuages peuvent se déplacer très vite.
14. Clouds can move very quickly.	**15.** Lorsque le soleil commence à réchauffer l'atmosphère, les nuages se dissolvent. (Does **réchauffer** mean *to warm again* or *to cool?*)
15. When the sun begins to warm the atmosphere again, the clouds dissolve (*or* are dissolved). *to warm again*	**16.** Lorsqu'un vent s'élève, les nuages se déplacent.
16. When a wind arises, the clouds move.	**17.** Le soleil se lève le matin. (**se lever**=_____)
17. The sun comes up in the morning. *to come up*	**18.** Lorsque le soleil se lève, il fait jour.
18. When the sun comes up, it gets light.	**19.** Lorsqu'on voit le soleil se lever, on se lève. (**on se lève**=_____)
19. When one sees the sun coming up, one gets up. *one gets up*	**20.** Quand le soleil se couche, il fait noir. (**se coucher**=_____)
20. When the sun goes down, it gets dark. *to go down*	**21.** Quand on voit le soleil se coucher, le ciel est parfois rouge.

21. When one sees the sun going down, the sky is sometimes red.	**22.** A dix heures du soir, je me couche. (**se coucher**=_____)
22. At 10:00 P.M. I go to bed. *to go to bed*	**23.** Il y a d'autres substances qui se trouvent dans le cidre.
23. There are other substances which are found in cider.	**24.** Un cidre riche en tanin s'altère très rapidement.
24. A cider rich in tannin changes (*or* is changed) very rapidly.	**25.** Quand je suis fatigué, je me couche.
25. When I am tired, I go to bed.	**26.** Quand il est dix heures, nous nous couchons.
26. When it is ten o'clock, we go to bed.	**27.** Vous ne vous levez pas avant six heures du matin, probablement.
27. You do not get up before 6:00 A.M., probably.	**28.** Je me lave les mains. (**les mains**=*the hands/my hands*)
28. I wash *my hands*	**29.** Nous nous lavons les mains. (**les**=*the/our*)
29. We wash *our* hands.	**30.** On se lave la figure. (**la figure**=*the face/one's face*)
30. *one's face*	**31.** Je me brosse les dents. (**les dents**=*the teeth/my teeth*)
31. I brush *my teeth.*	**32.** Ils se brossent les dents. (**les dents**=*the teeth/their teeth*)
32. They brush *their teeth.*	**33.** **tromper**=*to deceive* Le vrai moyen d'être trompé, c'est de se croire plus fin que les autres. La Rochefoucauld
33. The true way of being deceived is to believe oneself more clever than the others.	**34.** **perdre**=*to lose* Les vertus se perdent dans l'intérêt, commes les fleuves se perdent dans la mer. La Rochefoucauld
34. Virtues become lost in self-interest as rivers become lost in the sea.	

54. *Reflexive Verbs—Past Indefinite*

1. The Past Indefinite tense of reflexive verbs is recognized by the combination of the reflexive pronoun, the Present tense of **être** (not **avoir**) and the past participle as follows:

PRESENT	PAST
je me couche	**Je me suis couché(e)** *I went (have gone) to bed*
tu te couches	**tu t'es couché(e)**
il, elle, on se couche	**il, elle, on s'est couché(e)**
nous nous couchons	**nous nous sommes couché(e)s**
vous vous couchez	**vous vous êtes couché(e)s**
ils, elles se couchent	**ils, elles se sont couché(e)s**

2. The presence of the reflexive pronoun signals the difference between the Present Passive and the Past Indefinite. The times indicated by the Past Indefinite of reflexive verbs are the same as for the regular patterns of the Past Indefinite: *I went to bed* or *I have gone to bed.*

READING PREPARATION

INSTRUCTIONS: *Give the meanings of these sentences.*

	1. Les nuages se sont produits de différentes manières.
1. The clouds were formed in different ways.	**2.** Les nuages ont été produits de différentes manières.
2. Same as above.	**3.** Ils se sont formés sur les prairies.
3. They were formed over the meadows.	**4.** Ils ont été formés sur les prairies.
4. Same as above.	**5.** Ensuite, les nuages se sont déplacés.
5. Next, the clouds moved.	**6.** Un vent s'est élevé.
6. A wind came up.	**7.** Le soleil s'est levé.
7. The sun came up.	**8.** Je me suis levé.
8. I got up.	**9.** Je me suis lavé.
9. I washed up.	**10.** Le soleil s'est couché à six heures.

10.	The sun went down at six o'clock.	**11.**	Nous nous sommes couchés à dix heures.
11.	We went to bed at ten o'clock.	**12.**	Beaucoup de tanin s'est trouvé dans le cidre.
12.	Much tannin was found in the cider.	**13.**	Le cidre s'est altéré rapidement.
13.	The cider changed rapidly.	**14.**	Une coloration très foncée s'est produite.
14.	A very dark discoloration was produced.	**15.**	Elle s'est produite bien vite.
15.	It was produced very rapidly.	**16.**	**s'habiller**=to get dressed Vous vous êtes habillé bien vite ce matin.
16.	You dressed very quickly this morning.	**17.**	Elle est habillée en bleu aujourd'hui.
17.	She is dressed in blue today.	**18.**	Vous êtes fatigué.
18.	You are tired.	**19.**	Vous vous êtes fatigué.
19.	You tired yourself out (you got tired).	**20.**	Je me suis brossé les dents.
20.	I brushed my teeth.	**21.**	Il s'est lavé la figure.
21.	He washed his face.	**22.**	Nous nous sommes vus.
22.	We saw each other.	**23.**	Nous nous sommes parlé.
23.	We spoke to each other.	**24.**	**quitter**=to leave Nous nous sommes quittés.
24.	We left (took leave of) each other.	**25.**	Je me suis vite habillé.
25.	I got dressed quickly.	**26.**	Elle est habillée en noir.
26.	She is dressed in black.		

55. *Impersonal Expression*—falloir (*to be necessary*)

1.   Falloir is used only impersonally and only in the third person singular. The present is **il faut.**

2.   Followed by an infinitive **il faut** can be translated by *it is necessary* or *one (we, you, etc.) must +infinitive.*

Pour prévenir le noircissement du cidre il faut employer de l'acide citrique.	*In order to prevent the darkening of cider it is necessary to (one must) use citric acid.*

3. Followed by a noun, it may be translated by *one needs* or *is needed:*

Pour assurer le succès de l'expérience il faut une bonne méthode.	*In order to assure the success of the experiment, a good (correct) method is needed (or "one needs a good method").*

4. The meaning of **il ne faut pas** is *one must not* (not *it is not necessary to).* necessary to).

Il ne faut pas oublier que les langues artificielles n'ont pas souvent réussi.	*One must not forget that artificial languages have not often succeeded.*

READING PREPARATION

INSTRUCTIONS: *Continue to circle new or unfamiliar words as you read.*

	1. Pour maintenir la qualité du cidre, il faut empêcher le cidre de noircir.
1. In order to maintain the quality of the cider, it is necessary to (one must) prevent it from turning black.	**2.** Il faut l'empêcher de noircir. (With reference to #1, **l'** refers to = **la qualité/le cidre**)
2. *le cidre* It is necessary to (one must) keep it from turning black.	**3.** Pour constater l'effet du tanin, il faut laisser un peu de cidre dans un vase ouvert.
3. In order to ascertain the effect of the tannin, it is necessary to leave a little cider in an open receptacle.	**4.** Pour empêcher le noircissement du cidre il ne faut pas l'exposer à l'air.
4. In order to prevent the darkening of cider, it must not be exposed to the open air.	**5.** **se rencontrer** = *to meet, to encounter* Quand deux vents inégalement chauds se rencontrent, il se forme souvent des nuages. (Is **il se forme** used *personally* or *impersonally?*)
5. When two winds of unequal warmth meet, clouds are often formed. *impersonally*	**6.** Il faut expliquer que les nuages peuvent se former par la rencontre de deux vents inégalement chauds.

(Is **rencontre** used as a noun or as a verb?)

6. *as a noun*
It must be explained that clouds may be formed by the encounter of two winds of unequal warmth.

7. Pour observer la formation des nuages, il faut se placer sur une montagne d'où on peut voir des lieux humides. (Does **d'où** mean *where* or *from where?*)

7. *from where*
In order to observe the formation of clouds, one must place oneself on a mountain, from where one can see some humid places.

8. De là on peut voir la rencontre des couches d'air plus froides et de la vapeur qui s'élève du sol.

8. From there one can see the encounter of colder layers of air and the vapor which arises from the ground.

9. **se noircir**=*to become black, to turn black*
se refroidir=_____

9. *to become cold, or to cool off*

10. **oublier**=*to forget*
Il ne faut pas oublier que le soir l'atmosphère se refroidit.

10. It must not be forgotten that in the evening the atmosphere cools off.

11. Il faut ajouter que le matin, après que le soleil se lève, l'atmosphère se réchauffe.

11. One must add that in the morning after the sun comes up, the atmosphere becomes warm (warms up) again.

12. **se souvenir**=*to remember*
Il faut se souvenir que la formation des nuages est due à la présence de la vapeur d'eau dans l'air.

12. It must be remembered that the formation of clouds is due to the presence of water vapor in the air.

13. Il faut ajouter qu'il faut aussi un air plus froid que le sol.

13. It must be added (one must add) that an air colder than the ground is also needed.

14. Il faut également des lieux humides.

14. Humid places are also needed.

15. Pour mesurer la température, il faut un thermomètre.

15. To measure the temperature, one needs a thermometer.

16. Il faut se souvenir que la formation des nuages est due à la présence de la vapeur d'eau dans un air saturé d'humidité et plus froid que le sol.

16. One (we) must remember that the formation of clouds is due to the presence of water vapor in air saturated

17. Il ne faut pas dire toutefois que tous les nuages se forment de cette même manière.

with humidity and which is colder than the ground.	
17. One must not say, however, that all clouds are formed in this same way.	**18.** **mettre**=*to put* Il y a beaucoup de choses qu'il faut laisser dans la vie et qu'il ne faut pas mettre dans un livre. <div align="right">Joubert</div>
18. There are many things which must be left in life and which must not be put in a book.	Review the words you have circled. When you can recognize them all immediately, go on to the next section.

56. *Prepositions of Place*

1. The following high frequency prepositions may indicate location or place:

devant	*before, in front of*
derrière	*behind, in back of*
en arrière de	*behind, backward*
à droite de	*to the right of*
à gauche de	*to the left of*
au milieu de	*in the middle of*
au—dessus de	*above*
au—dessous de	*beneath*
en face de	*opposite, facing*
à côté de	*beside*
au fond de	*at the bottom of*
au bout de	*at the end of*

2. They may also be used figuratively as well as literally:

L'auto est stationnée devant la maison.	*The car is parked in front of the house.*
Devant un si grand besoin, nos efforts sont inutiles.	*Before such a great need, our efforts are useless.*
L'église est juste à gauche de l'hôtel.	*The church is just to the left of the hotel.*
Le Parti communiste est à gauche du centre.	*The Communist Party is to the left of center.*

READING PREPARATION

INSTRUCTIONS: *Express the meanings of the following sentences. Cover the English with your card until you have worked out a meaning which you want to verify.*

1. **tout à fait**=*completely*
En face de l'évidence qu'il présente, il ne faut pas rejeter sa théorie tout à fait.

1. In face of the evidence which he presents, one must not entirely reject his theory.

2. **s'incliner**=*to bow, to yield*
Quand on est tout à fait raisonnable, on s'incline devant l'évidence.

2. When one is completely reasonable one bows before (yields to) the evidence.

3. Pasteur ne s'est pas incliné devant les traditions de son temps.

3. Pasteur did not yield to the traditions of his time.

4. **cacher**=*to hide*
Quand il pleut, les montagnes se cachent derrière les nuages.

4. When it rains, the mountains are hidden behind the clouds.

5. Les montagnes se cachent alors à l'observateur.
(Does **à** here mean *to* or *from?*)

5. *From*—it is the English verb which determines the preposition to be used in the translation.
The mountains are then hidden from the observer.

6. Les nuages se forment près des lieux humides.

6. Clouds form near humid places.

7. **bas**=*low*
Quand un vent s'élève, les nuages bas sont emportés vers les montagnes.

7. When a wind comes up, the low clouds are carried away toward the mountains.

8. Les lacs se trouvent le plus souvent près des forêts.

8. Lakes are most often found near forests.

9. Les nuages se forment loin des lieux humides.

9. Clouds form far from humid places.

10. Loin de la forêt et des montagnes se trouve un petit lac isolé.

10. Far from the forest and the mountains is found a small isolated lake.

11. **les airs** (pl.) =*the atmosphere*
Il faut ajouter que les nuages peuvent aussi se former directement au milieu des airs.

11. It must be added that clouds can also be formed directly in the middle of the atmosphere.

12. **tout à coup**=*suddenly*
Quelquefois les nuages apparaissent tout à coup au milieu d'un ciel pur.

12. Sometimes clouds appear suddenly in the middle of a clear sky.

13. **ainsi**=*thus*
Il faut ajouter que les nuages se

forment souvent ainsi au–dessus des forêts.

---

13. It must be added that clouds are often formed this way above forests.

14. Il ne faut pas oublier que les nuages se forment quelquefois ainsi au–dessus des lieux humides.

---

14. We must not forget (it must not be forgotten) that clouds sometimes are formed in this way above humid places.

15. La vapeur d'eau qui s'élève au–dessus de l'eau bouillante est comme celle qui s'élève au–dessus du sol.
(La température de l'eau bouillante est à 212° F.)

---

15. The water vapor which arises above boiling water is like that which arises from the ground.

16. **pour ainsi dire**=*so to speak*
Au–dessous de la couche supérieure se trouve une autre couche qui constitue, pour ainsi dire, un nouveau sol.

---

16. Beneath the upper layer is found another layer which constitutes, so to speak, a new ground.

17. **la mer**=*the sea, the ocean*
La couche d'au–dessous devient, pour ainsi dire, un nouveau sol ou une nouvelle mer qui intercepte les rayons solaires.

---

17. The lower layer becomes, so to speak, a new ground or a new sea which intercepts the solar rays.

18. Au bout de quelques heures, quand l'atmosphère se refroidit, on peut voir des nuages translucides se former au–dessus des prairies.

---

18. At the end of a few hours, when the atmosphere cools off, one can see translucent clouds being formed above the meadows.

19. **haut x bas**
Au bout de quelques temps, il arrive que ces nuages sont emportés dans les hautes régions de l'atmosphère.
(Is **il** used *personally* or *impersonally?*)

---

19. *Impersonally*
After a little while it happens that these clouds are carried away into the upper (high) regions of the atmosphere.

20. Loin des lieux humides, on voit peu de nuages.

---

20. Far from moist places, few clouds are seen.

21. Au–dessous de ces nuages se trouve une couche moins blanche.

---

21. Beneath these clouds is found a darker layer (which is less white).

22. **partout**=*everywhere*
Vers midi, on peut voir des nuages partout.

22.	Toward noon, one can see clouds everywhere.	**23.**	**les yeux**=*eyes* (sing. **un oeil**) Il est parfois possible de voir se former des nuages devant ses yeux.
23.	It is sometimes possible to see clouds form before one's eyes.	**24.**	Il y a partout des sources de vapeur d'eau.
24.	There are sources of water vapor everywhere.	**25.**	Les forêts se trouvent souvent à côté des lacs.
25.	Forests are often found beside lakes.	**26.**	On trouve quelquefois des chemins de fer à côté des routes.
26.	Sometimes one finds railroads beside the highways.	**27.**	**la gare**=*the railroad station* L'église est en face de la gare.
27.	The church is opposite the station.	**28.**	L'église est près de la gare.
28.	The church is near the station.	**29.**	L'église est loin de la gare.
29.	The church is far from the station.	**30.**	L'église est à côté de la gare.
30.	The church is beside (next to) the station.	**31.**	Le Parti socialiste est à la gauche du centre.
31.	The Socialist Party is to the left of center.	**32.**	Le Parti communiste est tout à fait à gauche.
32.	The Communist Party is completely to the left.	**33.**	Les conservateurs sont à la droite du centre.
33.	The conservatives are to the right of center.	**34.**	Pour trouver l'église il faut prendre à gauche.
34.	To find the church you must take a left.		

57.   *Disjunctive pronouns*

1. The disjunctive pronouns are so-called because they are separated from the verb. For emphasis the adjective **même** is often affixed to the pronoun. They most often refer to persons but **lui, elle, eux, elles** may also refer to things:

moi	*I, me*	**moi–même**	*myself*
toi	*you*	**toi–même**	*yourself*
lui	*he, it, him,*	**lui–même**	*himself, itself*

elle	she, it her	elle–même	herself, itself
soi	himself, oneself	soi–même	himself, itself, oneself
nous	we, us	nous–mêmes	ourselves
vous	you	vous–mêmes	yourselves
eux	they, them	eux–mêmes	themselves
elles	they, them	elles–mêmes	themselves

2. The disjunctive pronouns are used

(a) in comparisons:

Jean est plus grand que moi.   *John is bigger than I.*

(b) after prepositions:

Il va venir avec moi.   *He will come with me.*

(c) in answers of one word:

Qui est là? Moi.   *Who's there? I am.*

(d) after the expressions **c'est** or **ce sont**:

C'est lui. Ce sont eux.   *It is he. It is they.*

(e) for emphasis:

**Lui, il est prêt, mais elle est   *He is ready, but she is late as usual.*
en retard comme toujours.**

Je les ai vus, lui et elle.   *I saw them, him and her.*

3.   The pronouns **soi** and **soi–même** have both the same meaning in English *oneself, itself, himself,* and *herself.*

Chacun pour soi.   *Each one for himself.*
**Quand on pense constamment à   *When one constantly thinks of oneself,*
soi–même, on est égoïste.**   *one is an egoist.*
Cela va de soi.   *That is obvious.*

READING PREPARATION

INSTRUCTIONS: *Give the meanings of the following sentences. Continue to make a check by the ones which contain new or unrecognized vocabulary. Review the checked sentences after you finish the exercise and again in a day or two.*

1. **la voix**=*the voice*
    Françoise a une belle voix.

1.	Françoise has a beautiful voice.	**2.**	**meilleur** (adj.) = *better* Elle a une meilleure voix que son frère.
2.	She has a better voice than her brother.	**3.**	Elle a une meilleure voix que lui.
3.	She has a better voice than he has.	**4.**	**mieux** (adv.) = *better* Elle chante mieux que lui.
4.	She sings better than he does.	**5.**	Il chante pis qu'elle. (**Pis,** being contrasted with *better,* must mean _____)
5.	He sings *worse* than she does. *worse*	**6.**	**les affaires** = *business* Les affaires vont de mieux en mieux.
6.	Business is going better and better.	**7.**	**mal x bien** Les affaires vont de mal en pis.
7.	Business is going from bad to worse.	**8.**	Les affaires vont pis cette année que l'année dernière.
8.	Business is worse this year than last year.	**9.**	**pire x meilleur** La situation est pire cette année que l'année dernière.
9.	The situation is worse this year than last year.	**10.**	En tout cas, elle n'est pas meilleure que l'année dernière.
10.	In any case, it is not better than last year.	**11.**	Vous le savez mieux que nous.
11.	You know it better than we do.	**12.**	Vous le savez mieux qu'eux.
12.	You know it better than they do.	**13.**	Vous le savez, mais ils ne le savent pas, eux.
13.	You know it, but they don't.	**14.**	Tu l'as dis toi–même.
14.	You said it yourself.	**15.**	Je sais fort bien que vous vous trompez. Vous le savez vous–même.
15.	I know very well that you are mistaken. You know it yourself.	**16.**	**car** = *for* Il sait que c'est un bon livre, car il l'a écrit lui–même.
16.	He knows that it is a good book, for he wrote it himself.	**17.**	Elle l'a dit elle–même.
17.	She said it herself.	**18.**	Elles l'ont dit elles–mêmes.

18. They said it themselves.

19. Il ne faut pas penser tout le temps à soi.

---

19. One must not think of oneself all the time.

20. **aimer**=*to love, to like*
On n'aime pas se comparer à quelqu'un de plus intelligent que soi.

---

20. One does not like to be compared to someone more intelligent than oneself.

21. Une bonne mère aime ses enfants.
(**aime**=*loves/likes*)

---

21. A good mother loves her children.

22. Une mère dévouée n'aime pas quitter ses enfants.
(**n'aime pas**=*does not like/does not love*)

---

22. A devoted mother *does not like* to leave her children.

23. Un philanthrope aime faire du bien à ses frères.

---

23. A philanthropist likes to do good to his brothers.

24. Un avare n'aime pas donner son argent.
(**un avare**=_____)

---

24. *A miser* does not like to give away his money.
a miser

25. Un avare aime l'argent.
(**aime**=*likes/loves*)

---

25. A miser *loves* money.

26. Selon lui, tous les hommes sont frères.

---

26. According to him, all men are brothers.

27. Nous les avons vus, lui et elle.

---

27. We saw them, him and her.

28. **une faute**=*a fault*
Les jeunes gens souffrent moins de leurs fautes à eux que de la prudence des vieillards.
Vauvenargue

---

28. Young people suffer less from their own faults than from the prudence of old people.

29. **maudire**=*to curse.*
S'il est quelqu'un tourmenté par la maudite ambition de mettre toujours tout un livre dans une page, toute une page dans une phrase, et cette phrase dans un mot, c'est moi.
Joubert
(Is **S'il est** used *personally* or *impersonally?*)

---

29. *Impersonally*
If there is someone tormented by the

30. L'amour–propre est l'amour de soi— même, et de toutes choses pour soi—

cursed ambition of always putting a whole book in one page, a whole page in one phrase, and that phrase in one word, it is myself.

il rend les hommes idolâtres d'eux–mêmes.

30. L'amour–propre is the love of oneself and of everything for oneself—it makes men idolatrous of themselves.

31. On ne peut se consoler d'être trompé par ses ennemis, et l'on est souvent satisfait de l'être par soi–même.
La Rochefoucauld
(**l'être** refers to the previously stated idea of _____.)

31. *being deceived*
One cannot be consoled at being deceived by one's enemies, and one is often satisfied to be deceived by oneself.

58. *Irregular Verb*—venir

1. The Present tense of **venir** and its compounds is recognized by the following conjugation:

je viens	*I come, am coming*
tu viens	*you come, are coming*
il, elle, on vient	*he, she, one comes, is coming*
nous venons	*we come, are coming*
vous venez	*you come, are coming*
ils, elles viennent	*they come, are coming*

2. Other **–ir** verbs which are conjugated the same way are:

contenir	*to contain*
obtenir	*to obtain*
retenir	*to retain*
tenir	*to hold*
convenir	*to agree, to be appropriate*
prévenir	*to forestall, to warn, to prevent*
revenir	*to come back* (conjugated with **être**)
parvenir	*to reach, to succeed* (conjugated with **être**)
devenir	*to become* (conjugated with **être**)
provenir	*to come from, to originate from* (conjugated with **être**)

3. The past participle of this group of verbs ends in –**u**:

INFINITIVE	PAST PARTICIPLE
tenir	*tenu*
contenir	*contenu*
venir	*venu*
devenir	*devenu*
etc.	

---

1. plutôt que = *rather than*
Il s'agit d'un genre de lecture qui convient aux spécialistes plutôt qu'au public.

1. It concerns a kind of reading which is appropriate for specialists rather than for the public.

2. Je conviens que vous avez raison.

2. I agree that you are right.

3. Le noircissement du cidre provient plutôt du tanin que de l'acide.

3. The darkening of the cider comes rather from the tannin than from the acid.

4. C'est un sujet qui a perdu plutôt que retenu son intérêt.

4. The subject has lost rather than retained its interest.

5. Après une assez longue digression, le conférencier est revenu à son sujet.

5. After a rather long digression the lecturer came back to his subject.

6. L'obscurité de son exposé est provenu de ces longues digressions.

6. The obscurity of his talk came from those long digressions.

7. Il est parvenu cependant à convaincre ses auditeurs.

7. He succeeded, however, in convincing his listeners.

8. La lettre n'est pas parvenue à son destinataire.

8. The letter did not reach its addressee.

9. Il faut ajouter que l'expérience n'a pas obtenu les résultats voulus.

9. It must be added that the experiment did not obtain the desired results.

10. Le problème devient d'autant moins difficile que les données sont connues.

10. The problem becomes all the less difficult as the data are known.

11. Le cidre contient une quantité de tanin.

11. Cider contains a quantity of tannin.

12. Il convient aux savants de travailler soigneusement.

12. It befits (is appropriate for) scholars to work carefully.

13. They have found a procedure to prevent the darkening of beers.

14. Mr. Dupont warned the Academy of the difficulties of this undertaking.

15. There are two kinds of heat rays—those which come from the sun and those which come from the earth.

13. On a trouvé un procédé pour prévenir le noircissement des bières.

14. M. Dupont a prévenu l'Académie des difficultés de cette entreprise.

15. Il y a deux sortes de rayons caloriques—ceux qui viennent du soleil et ceux qui viennent de la terre.

VOCABULARY DEVELOPMENT

INSTRUCTIONS: *Use the root meaning and the context to determine the meaning of the indicated phrases.*

1. **haut**=*high*
   Puisque plusieurs personnes s'intéressent à la lettre, il faut la lire **à haute voix**.

1. *aloud*

2. Les nuages se forment parfois à une grande **hauteur**.

2. *height*

3. Il a offensé beaucoup de ses auditeurs, parce qu'il a parlé avec **trop de hauteur**.

3. *too haughtily*, or *equivalent*

4. Il ne faut pas être découragé—il y a toujours **des hauts et des bas** dans la vie.

4. You must not be discouraged—there are always *ups and downs* in life.

5. On ne vous entend pas—il faut parler **plus haut**.

5. *louder.*

6. **brouiller**=*to mix together, to confuse, to blur*
   Il a tant parlé que mes pensées sont complètement **brouillées**.

6. He spoke so much that my thoughts are completely *confused.*

7. A Londres il y a quelquefois des **brouillards** très épais.

7. In London there are sometimes very thick *fogs.*

8. **des œufs**=*eggs*
   Pour le petit déjeuner (*breakfast*) on aime les **œufs brouillés**.

8. *scrambled eggs*	**9.** Les nuages se forment le plus souvent des **brouillards.**
9. Clouds are most often formed from *fog.*	**10.** Le conférencier connaît si mal son sujet qu'il va certainement **s'embrouiller.**
10. The lecturer knows his subject so poorly that he is certainly going to become *confused* (muddled, tangled, up, or *equivalent*).	**11.** Il se trouve souvent dans des situations difficiles, mais il parvient toujours à se **débrouiller.**
11. He often finds himself in difficult situations, but he always manages *to get out of them* (extricate himself, disentangle himself, or *equivalent*).	

TESTING EXERCISE

INSTRUCTIONS: *Circle the letter which gives the best translation of the indicated phrases.*

1. Ils s'entendent bien.
 A. They hear well.   C. They understand each other well.
 B. They heard each other well.   D. They intend well.

1. B **2.** Elle s'est lavée.
(53)   A. She got up.   C. She washed.
        B. She is washing.   D. She raised her hands.

2. C **3.** Elle s'est lavé les mains.
(54)   A. She is washing her hands.   C. She washed her hands.
        B. She is raising her hands.   D. She raised her hands.

3. C **4.** Les nuages **se sont vite déplacés.**
(54)   A. are moving rapidly   C. were moving rapidly
        B. moved rapidly   D. are moved rapidly

4. B **5.** **Lorsqu'on se dépêche** on se trompe souvent.
(54)   A. When one hurries   C. When one is depleted
        B. When one goes fishing   D. When one deprecates

5. A **6.** Il ne faut pas le laisser se refroidir.
(53)   A. It must be allowed not to cool.   C. It need not be allowed to cool.
        B. It must not be allowed to cool.   D. It is not necessary to allow it to refrigerate.

6. B **7.** Il n'avait rien **devant lui.**
(55)   A. to the side of him   C. behind him
        B. in front of him   D. to the right of him

7. B   **8.** La maison **elle-même** était neuve.
(56)   A. herself   B. itself   C. even   D. the same

8. B   **9.** Je les ai trouvés, **lui** et sa soeur.
(57)   A. herself   B. him   C. to her   D. her

9. B   **10.** Plus on étudie, plus **on devient sage.**
(57)   A. divines wisdom   C. loses wisdom
               B. becomes wise   D. seeks wisdom

10. B   **11.** **On parvient à** se faire comprendre.
(58)   A. One prevents   C. One comes by
               B. One comes from   D. One succeeds in

11. D.
(58)

READING PASSAGE

Les nuages

Pierre Larousse, *Grand Dictionnaire universel*,
p. 1146.

La formation des nuages est due à la présence de la vapeur d'eau dans un
air saturé d'humidité et plus froid que le sol, où cette vapeur devient visible,
exactement comme celle qui s'élève au–dessus de l'eau bouillante. Les nuages
peuvent se produire de différentes manières. "Lorsque, pendant **une soirée**
5   **d'été,**[1] on se trouve isolé sur une montagne, dit Lecoq, on voit bientôt, **à
mesure que** [2] l'atmosphère se refroidit, des nuages translucides se former
sur les prairies et dans tous les lieux humides; peu à peu, ils augmentent de
densité et cachent la terre aux yeux de l'observateur. Si alors un vent s'élève,
il arrive que ces nuages bas sont emportés dans les hautes régions de
10   l'atmosphère. Souvent ils se forment de cette manière au–dessus des forêts,
sur les plateaux élevés, sur la **cime** [3] des pics isolés, et ils se déplacent ensuite
pour flotter dans l'air. Ces nuages sont le résultat du refroidissement de l'air;
ils augmentent, en général, pendant la nuit, au point même de recouvrir le ciel,
et le matin, quand le soleil commence à réchauffer l'atmosphère, ils se
15   dissolvent . . .
"D'autres causes peuvent aussi donner naissance aux nuages. Ils peuvent
se former directement au milieu des airs par la condensation des vapeurs qui
s'élèvent à une grande hauteur dans des couches d'air plus froides ou par la
rencontre de deux vents humides inégalement chauds. C'est presque toujours

---

1 *a summer evening*   **3** *top*
2 *as (to the degree that)*

20 de cette manière que se produisent les nuages qui apparaissent **tout à coup** [4] au milieu d'un ciel pur.

"On observe encore fréquemment plusieurs couches de nuages superposées et qui même **marchent** [5] quelquefois (parfois) dans des directions opposées. En général, ces couches sont d'autant plus élevées qu'elles sont plus blanches.
25 Elles peuvent être produites indépendamment l'une de l'autre; mais fort souvent, c'est la couche inférieure qui donne naissance à la supérieure. La couche inférieure constitue alors, pour ainsi dire, un nouveau sol ou une nouvelle mer qui intercepte les rayons caloriques, ceux qui viennent du soleil et ceux qui viennent de la terre. L'évaporation y [6] acquiert une nouvelle
30 activité et produit, à une certaine hauteur, une seconde couche de nuages qui peut elle–même en produire une troisième et **ainsi de suite**". [7] En somme, les nuages se forment le plus souvent des brouillards.

1. Lines 1—15 state that
  A. clouds are formed when the atmosphere is dry
  B. clouds are formed in the evening when the atmosphere becomes warmer
  C. clouds are generally more prevalent in the mountains in the evening because of the cooling of the atmosphere
  D. when the sun begins to warm the atmosphere they become more dense.

2. Lines 22–24 state that
  A. clouds can also form when two equally warm winds come together
  B. the position of the sun often explains the sudden appearance of clouds in a clear sky
  C. successive layers of clouds always move in the same direction
  D. in general, the higher the cloud layers are, the whiter they appear.

3. Lines 25–32 state that
  A. often a low cloud layer causes the formation of the one above it
  B. evaporation of the humidity precipitates in the form of rain
  C. clouds are rarely formed from fog
  D. fog is not usually found over the ocean.

Answers:
    1–C   2–D   3–A

4 *suddenly*   **6** *there*   **7** *and so forth*
5 *move*

Chapter Nine

REVIEW: The vocabulary and grammar structures introduced in earlier lessons serve as a foundation for future progress. Review the items encircled in Chapters Seven and Eight before going on to Chapter Nine.

59. *Negation*—ne . . . pas, point, jamais, guère, plus

1. You have learned that **ne** in front of the verb and **pas** after it indicate negation:

La science n'avance pas.   *Science is not advancing.*

Do not confuse the negation **ne . . . pas** with the noun **un pas** (*a step*):

La science avance pas à pas.   *Science is advancing step by step.*

2. Other expressions of negation, following the pattern of **ne . . . pas** are:

ne (verb) **guère**	*hardly, scarcely*
ne (verb) **jamais**	*never*
ne (verb) **point**	*not at all*
ne (verb) **plus**	*no more, no longer*
Il n'est guère possible de calculer la pression.	*It is hardly possible to calculate the pressure.*

Les langues artificielles n'ont jamais réussi.	Artificial languages have never succeeded.
Le français n'est plus difficile.	French is no longer difficult.
Le français n'est point difficile.	French is not at all difficult.

3. When an infinitive is negated, the two elements of the negation are generally written together and placed before the infinitive:

| Etre ou ne pas être . . . | To be or not to be . . . |
| Ne jamais s'amuser c'est ne pas vivre. | Never to enjoy oneself is not to live. |

READING PREPARATION

INSTRUCTIONS: *In the first frame can you distinguish between the meanings indicated by the negative expressions?*

	1. Nous ne parlons plus des sujets météorologiques—nous parlons d'un nouveau sujet, celui des langues artificielles.
1. We are no longer speaking of meteorological subjects—we are speaking of a new subject, that of artificial languages.	2. La facilité d'acquisition des langues naturelles n'a jamais été suffisante.
2. Natural languages have never been easy enough to acquire. (The facility (ease) of acquisition of natural languages has never been sufficient.)	3. Les savants n'emploient plus le latin comme langue universelle.
3. Scholars no longer use Latin as an international language.	4. On n'a pas assez insisté devant l'Académie sur le besoin de communication entre les savants des divers pays.
4. One has not insisted enough before the Academy on the need for communication between the scholars of the various countries.	5. On n'a jamais insisté sur cette question devant l'Académie.
5. One has never insisted on this question before the Academy.	6. Devant un si grand besoin, les langues naturelles ne paraissent plus suffisantes.
6. Before such a great need, natural languages no longer seem sufficient.	7. **diminuer × augmenter** Cependant, le besoin de quelque idiome universel n'a jamais diminué.

7. However, the need of an international language has never diminished.

8. Ce besoin d'une langue universelle n'a guère diminué.

---

8. This need of an international language has scarcely diminished.

9. **compter**=*to count, to include*
Les érudits ne comptent pas moins de cent cinquante langues internationales que l'on a au moins projetées.

---

9. Scholars (the learned) count not less than 150 international languages which have at least been projected.

10. Le latin ne répond plus aux besoins du monde savant.

---

10. Latin no longer answers the needs of the scholarly world.

11. Le Volapük, proposé en 1879, n'a point répondu aux espérances des premiers jours.
(**espérer**=*to hope*
les espérances=_____)

---

11. *the hopes*
The Volapuk language, proposed in 1879, has not fulfilled (answered) the hopes of the first days (its beginnings).

12. On ne compte plus sur le latin pour répondre à nos besoins actuels.

---

12. We no longer count on Latin to answer our present needs.

13. Il ne faut plus compter sur le latin comme langue internationale.

---

13. We must no longer count on Latin as an international language.

14. Les adhérents du Volapük sont peu nombreux, mais ils ne se sont point découragés.

---

14. The adherents of Volapuk are few in number, but they have not become at all discouraged.

15. Mais ils n'ont guère connu un succès brillant.

---

15. But they have scarcely had (known) a brilliant success.

16. **donc**=*therefore*
Donc, ils n'ont plus leur enthousiasme premier.

---

16. Therefore, they no longer have their original enthusiasm.

17. Les savants qui ne parlent pas une même langue nationale ont besoin d'un idiome artificiel.

---

17. The scholars who do not speak the same national language need an artificial language.

18. Les linguistes n'ont jamais pu créer une langue assez facile pour les savants de diverses nationalités.

---

18. Linguists have never been able to create a language easy enough for scholars of diverse nationalities.

19. Donc, les efforts des linguistes n'ont guère répondu à ce besoin impérieux.
(Is the need *urgent* or *moderate?*)

19. *urgent*
Therefore, the efforts of the linguists have scarcely answered this imperative need.
(Notice that the French verb **répondre** is followed by a preposition whereas the English verb is not.)

20. Le Volapük ne compte plus les nombreux adeptes (adhérents) des premiers jours.

20. Volapuk no longer has (counts) the numerous adherents it had in the beginning.

21. L'Espéranto ne présente point les mêmes difficultés que le Volapük.

21. Esperanto does not present at all the same difficulties as Volapuk.

22. La facilité d'acquisition de celui–ci n'est guère suffisante.

22. The ease of acquisition of the latter is hardly sufficient.

23. **apprendre** = *to learn*
On apprend plus facilement celui–là que celui–ci.

23. The former is more easily learned than the latter.

24. La grammaire du Volapük n'a jamais été expliquée assez clairement.

24. The grammar of Volapuk has never been explained clearly enough.

25. La grammaire de l'Espéranto, au contraire, n'est point compliquée.

25. The grammar of Esperanto, on the other hand, is not at all complicated.

26. Ses adeptes ne sont pas peu nombreux.

26. Its adherents are not few in number.

27. Il ne compte pas moins de 40.000 adeptes.

27. It counts no fewer than 40,000 adherents.

28. On apprend plus facilement les langues artificielles que les langues naturelles.
(Is **plus** here used as *a negation* or as *a term of comparison?*)

28. *A term of comparison.* There is no **ne** in the phrase.
One learns artificial languages more easily than natural languages.

29. Il faut plus de temps pour apprendre celles–ci que celles–là.

29. More time is needed to learn the latter than the former.
(If you could not read the phrase readily, circle it.)

30. On n'apprend jamais une langue étrangère sans difficulté.
(**étrangère** = *foreign/strange*)

30. *foreign* One never learns a foreign language without difficulty.	**31.** La plupart des étrangers qui viennent aux Etats–Unis ont besoin d'apprendre une nouvelle langue. (**étrangers**—*foreigners/strangers*)
31. *foreigners* Most of the foreigners who come to the United States need to learn a new language.	**32.** Etre ou ne pas être, c'est là la question. Shakespeare.
32. Oui, votre réponse est correcte.	**33.** Travailler ou ne pas travailler—c'est là une autre question.
33. To work or not to work—that is another question.	**34.** Il s'agit de ne pas confondre les deux problèmes. (**confondre**—*to confound/confuse*)
34. *to confuse* It is a question of not confusing the two problems.	**35.** Il faut essayer de ne pas confondre les deux cas.
35. One must try not to confuse the two cases.	**36.** Si vous reconnaissez les formules de négation, vous avez fait un grand pas en avant.
36. If you recognize the structures of negation, you have taken a great step forward.	**37.** Même si vous ne faites pas de rapides progrès, vous avancez du moins pas à pas.
37. Even if you do not make rapid progress, you are at least advancing step by step (steadily).	Review the phrases you have circled and then go on.

60. *Negation*—rien, personne, aucun, nul, ni . . . ni

1. Other words which indicate negation are:

ne (verb) **rien**	*nothing*
ne (verb) **personne**	*nobody, no one*
ne (verb) **aucun** (m.), **aucune** (f.)	*no, not any*
ne (verb) **nul** (m.), **nulle** (f.)	*no, not any*

2. These expressions may precede the verb, in which case they become the subject of the sentence, or they may follow the verb:

Je n'ai rien trouvé.	*I found nothing.*
Rien n'est arrivé.	*Nothing happened.*

Je n'ai vu personne.	*I saw no one.*
Personne n'est venu.	*No one came.*
Elle n'a nul intérêt aux langues.	*She has no interest in languages.*
Nul n'est prophète dans son pays.	*No man is a prophet in his own country.*
Aucune des expériences n'a réussi.	*Not one (none) of the experiments succeeded.*

3. The meaning of **ne . . . ni . . . ni** is expressed in English by *neither . . . nor:*

Je n'ai ni talent ni argent.	*I have neither talent nor money.*
Ni l'Espéranto ni le Volapük n'a réussi comme langue internationale.	*Neither Esperanto nor Volapuk has succeeded as an international language.*

4. **Aucun** and **nul** also have adverb forms: **aucunement** and **nullement.**

Elle ne s'intéresse nullement aux langues.	*She is not at all interested in languages.*
Tel n'est aucunement le cas de l'Esperanto.	*Such is not at all the case with Esperanto.*

5. Often you will find no second element of negation after the verbs **pouvoir** (*to be able*), **savoir** (*to know*), **cesser** (*to cease*), **oser** (*to dare*):

On n'a pu réussir à créer une langue internationale.	*They have not been able to succeed in creating an international language.*

INSTRUCTIONS: *What do the following sentences mean? Distinguish carefully between the meanings of the various expressions of negation.*

1. Until the present moment no international language has been perfected.

2. Until the present moment, no artificial language has succeeded.

3. Until now, no one has created a truly universal language.

1. Jusqu'à présent, on n'a perfectionné aucune langue universelle.

2. Jusqu'au moment actuel, aucune langue artificielle n'a réussi.

3. Jusqu'à maintenant, personne n'a créé une langue vraiment universelle.

4. **rendre** = *to render, make, cause*
La diversité des langues nationales rend difficile la communication entre les savants de nationalités différentes.

4. The diversity of national languages makes it difficult for scholars of different nationalities to communicate with each other.

5. Rien n'a répondu au besoin que la diversité des langues naturelles rend si pressant.

5. Nothing has answered the need which the diversity of natural languages renders so pressing.

6. Jusqu'à ce jour, personne n'a rien fait pour répondre à ce besoin.

6. Until now, no one has done anything to answer this need.

7. **Servir de**=*to be used as, to serve as* Aucune langue naturelle ne peut servir d'interprète entre tous ceux qui ne parlent pas une même langue nationale.

7. No natural language can serve as a medium of communication (an interpreter) between all those who do not speak the same national language.

8. Jusqu'à maintenant, personne n'a répondu aux besoins des savants de diverses nationalités.

8. Until now no one has answered the needs of the scholars of diverse nationalities.

9. Aucune des langues artificielles n'a donné satisfaction.

9. None of the artificial languages has given satisfaction.

10. Rien n'a répondu à ce besoin.

10. Nothing has answered this need.

11. Le Volapük n'a donné nulle satisfaction.

11. Volapuk has given no satisfaction.

12. **l'élève**=**l'étudiant** Ni l'élève ni le professeur ne l'ont trouvé assez efficace.

12. Neither the student nor the teacher has found it sufficiently effective.

13. Cette langue–là n'a répondu aux espérances ni des élèves ni des professeurs.

13. That language has not fulfilled the hopes either of the students or of the teachers.

14. **résoudre**=*to resolve, solve* Les efforts de nos prédécesseurs n'ont nullement résolu le problème.

14. The efforts of our predecessors have not at all solved the problem.

15. Les efforts qu'on a faits jusqu'à maintenant n'ont nullement répondu à nos besoins.

15. The efforts which have been made up to this time have not at all answered our needs.

16. **contre**=*against* Presque personne n'a été contre les langues artificielles, mais celles–ci n'ont jamais réussi.

16. Almost no one has been against artificial languages, but they (the latter) have never succeeded.

17. **un défaut**=*a defect*
Le Volapük a contre lui des défauts que l'Espéranto n'a pas.

17. Volapuk has defects against it that Esperanto does not have.

18. Parce que cette langue–là est fort compliquée, presque personne ne peut l'apprendre.

18. Because that language is very complicated, almost no one can learn it.

19. Il ne faut pas oublier que l'Espéranto n'a pas contre lui les défauts du Volapük.

19. It must not be forgotten that Esperanto does not have against it the defects of Volapuk.

20. La langue n'est point compliquée, mais je n'ai pu l'apprendre.

20. The language is not at all complicated, but I was not able to learn it.

21. Nous ne pouvons parler à ceux de nationalités différentes.

21. We cannot speak to those of different nationalities.

22. **lire**=*to read*
Je peux lire plusieurs langues, mais je ne peux les parler.

22. I can read several languages, but I can not speak them.

61. Ne . . . que

1. **Que,** used with a negative construction, expresses an exception to the general statement of negation. It is often translated by *only, nothing but,* or *nothing except:*

La lumière ne joue qu'un rôle secondaire.

Light plays only a secondary role.

Son œuvre n'a qu'un intérêt historique.

His work has nothing but an historical interest (nothing except).

2. The exception applies to the phrase which **que** immediately precedes:

On n'a projeté des langues artificielles que pendant le cours des deux derniers siècles.

They have projected artificial languages only during the course of the last two centuries.

On n'a que projeté des langues artificielles pendant le cours des deux derniers siècles.

They have only projected artificial languages during the course of the last two centuries.

3. Ne faire que+*infinitive* expresses the meaning of *to do nothing else but; all one does is . . .*

On n'a fait que projeter des langues artificielles.	*They did nothing else but project artificial languages.*
On se fatigue quand on ne fait qu'étudier.	*One gets tired when one does nothing but study.*

INSTRUCTIONS: *Distinguish carefully between the negations and **ne . . . que** patterns.*

	1. Une langue artificielle n'est utile qu'à ceux qui ne parlent pas une même langue nationale.
1. An artificial language is useful only to those who do not speak the same national language.	2. On dit que l'Espéranto ne peut servir d'interprète qu'aux spécialistes linguistiques.
2. It is said that Esperanto can serve as a means of communication only between linguistic specialists.	3. Les érudits ne comptent pas moins de cent cinquante langues universelles.
3. Scholars count not less than 150 international languages.	4. Les érudits ne comptent que cent cinquante langues universelles.
4. Scholars count only 150 international languages.	5. Je ne parle pas de l'influence de la lumière.
5. I am not talking about the influence of light.	6. Je ne parle que de l'influence de la lumière.
6. I am speaking only of the influence of light.	7. L'Espéranto n'a été proposé qu'en dix-huit cent quatre–vingt–sept.
7. Esperanto was proposed only in (was not proposed until) 1887.	8. Les variations de température n'exercent qu'une influence secondaire sur les plantes.
8. The variations of temperature exert only a secondary influence on the plants.	9. Les variations de température n'exercent une influence directe que sur les plantes.
9. The variations of temperature exert a direct influence only upon the plants.	10. Nous n'avons étudié que l'histoire de France l'année dernière.
10. We studied nothing but (or only) the history of France last year.	11. Nous n'avons étudié l'histoire de France que l'année dernière.

11. We studied the history of France only last year.	**12.** Le Volapük n'a trouvé des adeptes qu'en Hongrie.
12. Volapuk found adherents only in Hungary.	**13.** Les adeptes du Volapük ne sont nombreux qu'en Hongrie.
13. The followers of Volapuk are numerous only in Hungary.	**14.** Le célèbre écrivain russe Tolstoï n'a eu besoin que de deux heures pour apprendre l'Espéranto. (**écrire**=*to write* **un écrivain**=_____)
14. *a writer* The famous Russian writer Tolstoy needed only two hours in order to learn Esperanto.	**15.** Un élève vraiment diligent ne fait que travailler.
15. A truly diligent student does nothing but study.	**16.** **dernièrement**=**récemment** J'ai remarqué que dernièrement vous ne faites que travailler.
16. I have noticed that lately (recently) you do nothing but work.	**17.** Il n'a pas travaillé dernièrement—il ne fait que parler.
17. Lately, he hasn't been working—all he does is talk.	Review the phrases you just circled until you know them well.

62. Ne . . . que *with Other Negative Constructions*

1. The meanings of other negative constructions with **ne . . . que** are as follows:

ne . . . plus que	*no longer (anything, anybody) except*
La lumière ne joue plus qu'un rôle secondaire.	*Light no longer plays any but a secondary role.*
ne . . . jamais que	*never (anything, anybody) except*
La lumière ne joue jamais qu'un rôle secondaire.	*Light never plays any but a secondary role.*
ne . . . rien que	*nothing but, nothing except*
Il n'y a rien que la lumière qui joue un rôle important.	*There is nothing but light which plays an important role.*
ne . . . guère que	*scarcely (anything, anybody), except*

La lumière ne joue guère qu'un rôle secondaire.   *Light plays scarcely more than a secondary role.*

2. Remember that a 'translation' is only an expression of meaning from one language to another and may therefore take several forms. Any translation is adequate if it expresses the meaning and is not awkward.

INSTRUCTIONS: *Can you distinguish the meanings of the different negations? Circle the ones which give you trouble.*

		1.	Je ne parle plus de l'action de la lumière.
1.	I am no longer speaking of the action of light.	2.	Je ne parle plus que de l'action de la lumière.
2.	I am no longer speaking of anything but the action of light.	3.	Les variations de température ne jouent qu'un rôle secondaire.
3.	The variations in temperature play only a secondary role.	4.	Les variations de température ne jouent plus un rôle secondaire.
4.	The variations in temperature no longer play a secondary role.	5.	J'ai montré que les variations de température ne jouent plus qu'un rôle secondaire.
5.	I have shown that the variations in temperature no longer play anything but a secondary role, *or* . . . no longer play more than a secondary role . . .	6.	Ces expériences n'ont plus d'intérêt historique.
6.	These experiments no longer have any historical interest.	7.	Leurs expériences n'ont plus qu'un intérêt historique.
7.	Their experiments no longer have anything but an historical interest.	8.	Leurs expériences n'ont qu'un intérêt historique.
8.	Their experiments have only historical interest.	9.	Il ne reste plus que la lumière comme agent possible.
9.	Only light remains as a possible agent.	10.	Il n'y a plus que les savants qui s'intéressent à l'Espéranto.
10.	No one is interested in Esperanto anymore except scholars.	11.	On n'a jamais constaté que des variations fort limitées.
11.	They have never ascertained anything except very limited variations.	12.	Le Volapük n'a jamais connu qu'un succès assez restreint. (Was the success *limited* or *widespread?*)

12.	*limited* Volapuk has never had any but a rather limited success.	**13.**	Il n'y a jamais eu que des érudits parmi ses adeptes.
13.	There has never been anyone except the learned among its adherents.	**14.**	L'Espéranto n'a guère été utile que pour les érudits.
14.	Esperanto has scarcely been useful except for the learned.	**15.**	Vous n'avez rien prouvé.
15.	You have proved nothing.	**16.**	Vous n'avez jamais rien prouvé.
16.	You have never proved anything.	**17.**	Vous n'avez rien prouvé que la présence de l'eau.
17.	You have not proved anything except the presence of water.	**18.**	**un échantillon**=*a sample* Ces observations ne sont fondées que sur un examen peu exact de 300 échantillons.
18.	These observations are based only upon an inexact examination of 300 samples.	**19.**	Ces observations ne se fondent sur un examen que de 300 échantillons.
19.	These observations are based upon an examination of only 300 samples.	**20.**	**un rapport**=*a relationship* On ne peut établir par cette expérience qu'un rapport indirect entre ces deux éléments.
20.	One can establish by this experiment only an indirect relation between these two elements.	**21.**	On ne peut établir un rapport direct qu'entre ces deux éléments.
21.	One can establish a direct relationship only between these two elements.	**22.**	Les variations de la température n'exercent qu'une influence secondaire.
22.	The variations in temperature exert only a secondary influence.	**23.**	Les variations de la température n'exercent plus qu'une influence secondaire.
23.	The variations in temperature no longer exert any but a secondary influence.	**24.**	Il n'y a eu que de bons échantillons dans la collection de M. Lambert.
24.	There were only good samples (specimens) in Mr. Lambert's collection.	**25.**	Il n'y a eu de bons échantillons que dans la collection de M. Lambert.
25.	There weren't any good specimens except in Mr. Lambert's collection.	**26.**	Il n'a montré que des échantillons incomplets.

26. He showed only some incomplete samples.

27. **déjà**=*already*
Vous n'avez rien prouvé que des faits déjà connus.

27. You have proved nothing but facts already known.

28. Vous n'avez guère réussi à prouver l'influence de la lumière.

28. You have hardly succeeded in proving the influence of light.

29. Vous n'avez guère réussi à prouver que l'influence de la lumière.

29. You have hardly proved anything except the influence of light.

30. **nettement**=*clearly, distinctly*
L'influence des événements historiques sur les idées politiques s'est affirmée très nettement au XVIIème siècle.
(Was the influence *strong* or *weak?*)

30. *strong*
The influence of historical events on political ideas asserted itself very clearly in the 17th century.

31. L'influence des événements historiques ne s'est affirmée très nettement qu'au XVIIème siècle.

31. The influence of historical events did not assert itself very clearly except in the 17th century.

32. Jamais l'influence des événements historiques ne s'est affirmée plus nettement qu'au XVIIème siècle.
(Does **qu'** here signal an *exception* or a *comparison?*)

32. *a comparison*
Never did the influence of historical events assert itself more clearly than in the 17th century.

33. **incommode**=*inconvenient*
l'incommodité=_____

33. *the inconvenience*

34. On n'a pas assez insisté sur l'incommodité de la diversité des langues naturelles.

34. We have not insisted enough on the inconvenience of the diversity of natural languages.

35. **infliger**=*to inflict*
On n'a insisté que sur l'incommodité infligée aux savants par la diversité des langues naturelles.

35. We have insisted only on the inconvenience inflicted on scholars by the diversity of natural languages.

36. On n'a insisté que sur la grave incommodité que les langues naturelles infligent à tous les hommes civilisés.

36. We have insisted only on the serious inconvenience which the natural languages inflict on all civilized men.

37. On n'insiste plus sur l'incommodité qu'inflige la diversité des langues naturelles à tous les savants.

37. We no longer insist on (emphasize) the inconvenience which the diversity

of natural languages inflicts upon all
scholars.

63. *Irregular Verb* suivre (*to follow*)

1. Suivre is conjugated as follows:

Je suis	*I follow, am following, do follow*
Tu suis	*You follow*, etc.
Il, elle, on suit	*He, she, one, it follows*, etc.
Nous suivons	*We follow*, etc.
Vous suivez	*You follow*, etc.
Ils, elles suivent	*They follow*, etc.

2. Do not mistake the first person singular of **suivre** for the first person singular of **être**:

Je suis étudiant de chimie.	*I am a chemistry student.*
Je suis un cours de chimie.	*I am taking (following) a chemistry course.*

3. The past participle of **suivre** is **suivi** (*followed*). The present participle of **suivre** is **suivant** (*following*).

4. An impersonal compound of **suivre** is **s'ensuivre** (*to follow from*):

Il s'ensuit que . . .	*It follows that . . .*

INSTRUCTIONS: *What do the following phrases mean?*

	1. Les observations qui suivent . . .
1. The observations which follow . . .	**2.** L'observation qui suit . . .
2. The observation which follows . . .	**3.** La note suivante . . .
3. The following note . . .	**4.** Le cas qui va suivre . . .
4. The case which follows (is going to follow) . . .	**5.** Les données suivantes . . .
5. The following data . . .	**6.** Dans cette expérience nous avons suivi le procédé de Cook.

6. In this experiment we followed Cook's procedure.	**7.** Les résultats suivants . . .
7. The following results . . .	**8.** souvent
8. often	**9.** suivant
9. following	**10.** Je suis étudiant de chimie.
10. I am a student of chemistry.	**11.** Je suis un cours de chimie.
11. I am taking a chemistry course.	**12.** Il s'ensuit que . . .
12. It follows that . . .	**13.** Nous ne suivons que les méthodes établies.
13. We only follow established methods.	**14.** Vous n'avez suivi qu'un cours élémentaire.
14. You took only an elementary course.	**15.** Il s'ensuit que . . .
15. It follows that . . .	

VOCABULARY DEVELOPMENT

INSTRUCTIONS: *Use the root word to arrive at the meaning of the related words.*

	1. écrire=*to write* Tolstoï est un des plus grands **écrivains** russes.
1. *writers*	**2.** Parmi ses **écrits** est le grand roman *La guerre et la paix.*
2. *writings*	**3.** Il n'a pas appris à écrire cette langue, mais il a du moins appris à la lire. (He did not learn to write it but he learned to _____.)
3. *read it*	**4.** On peut lire ses lettres très facilement—il a une belle **écriture.**
4. He writes a very good hand, or he has beautiful *handwriting.*	**5.** Les écrits de St. Paul se trouvent dans **les Ecritures saintes.**
5. *The Holy Scriptures*	

TESTING EXERCISE

INSTRUCTIONS: *Circle the letter which best completes the sentence grammatically or which indicates the best translation of the italicized words and phrases.*

1. *Vous n'avez jamais prouvé que la lumière est de première importance.*
   A. You have scarcely proved the primary importance of light.
   B. You have never proved anything except the primary importance of light.
   C. You have never proved that light is of primary importance.
   D. You have proved only the primary importance of light.

1. C
(59)

2. *Vous n'avez jamais prouvé que l'importance de la lumière.*
   A. You have never proved the importance of light.
   B. You have never proved anything about the importance of light.
   C. You have scarcely proved the importance of light.
   D. You have never proved anything except the importance of light.

2. D
(62)

3. *Il ne s'agit point* de cette expérience.
   A. It no longer concerns . . .   C. It never concerns . . .
   B. It does not at all concern . . .   D. It concerns nothing . . .

3. B
(59)

4. Les langues artificielles *n'ont guère connu* un succès brillant.
   A. have never known   C. have scarcely known
   B. no longer knew   D. have not known

4. C
(59)

5. _____ des appareils réalisés jusqu'ici n'a donné satisfaction.
   A. personne   B. aucun   C. aucunement   D. rien

5. B
(60)

6. *On n'a établi qu'un rapport indirect entre les blés divers.*
   A. One has established that there is an indirect relation between the various wheats.
   B. One has established only an indirect relation between the various wheats.
   C. One has never established any but an indirect relation between the various wheats.
   D. One has not established that even an indirect relation enters into the question of the various wheats.

6. B
(61)

7. *Je suis* un cours de géologie.
   A. I am   B. I am taking   C. I know

7. B
(63)

8. *Je suis* étudiant de géologie.
   A. I am   B. I follow   C. I know

8. A
(63)

9. *On n'a rien constaté que des variations limitées.*
   A. One has ascertained that the variations are limited.
   B. One has ascertained only that the variations are limited.
   C. One has ascertained nothing except limited variations.
   D. One has ascertained that the variations are really nothing.

9. C   **10.** *Je ne fais qu'étudier le français.*
(62)   A. I do not study French.   C. I say that I study French.
                B. I study only French.   D. I do nothing except study French.

10. D
(61)

READING PASSAGE

INSTRUCTIONS: *Read the following passage through, circling but not looking up any of the unfamiliar words. Take the test at the end to verify your comprehension and then come back to the difficult phrases and work out their meaning.*

Une langue internationale

"Sur les services que peut rendre aux Sciences la langue auxiliaire internationale de M. le Dr Zamenhof, connue sous le nom d'Espéranto". Note de M. C. Méray, dans *Comptes rendus de l'Académie des Sciences*, v. 128, pp. 874–75.

Il **serait** [1] puéril d'insister **devant** [2] l'Académie sur la très grave incommodité qu'infligent à tous les hommes civilisés, aux savants en particulier, la diversité des langues naturelles et la difficulté de leur acquisition pour les étrangers. Cette situation trop connue a **fait naître,** [3] elle rend de plus en plus
5   pressant le besoin de quelque idiome artificiel facile qui **pût** [4] immédiatement servir d'interprète entre tous ceux qui ne parlent pas une même langue nationale; et ce besoin est **si** ancien, **si** [5] impérieux qu'à cette heure les érudits ne comptent pas moins de 150 langues internationales **ayant** [6] été au moins projetées pendant le cours des deux derniers siècles. Un instant il a
10   **paru** [7] trouver satisfaction dans le Volapük, proposé en 1879 par M. l'abbé Schleyer, très savant linguiste allemand, puis essayé presque **partout** [8] avec un **entrain** [9] extraordinaire. Mais l'événement n'a pas répondu aux efforts, aux espérances des premiers jours: le Volapük **avait** [10] contre lui de graves défauts dans sa construction, une facilité d'acquisition beaucoup trop
15   insuffisante, et partout aussi, il a été successivement abandonné, **quoiqu'en** [11] Autriche–Hongrie, pays particulièrement tourmenté par la confusion des langues, une **poignée** d'adeptes, dit-on, **lui resterait encore fidèle.** [12]
         Tel [13] n'est aucunement le cas de l'Espéranto, langue auxiliaire entièrement différente, due à un médecin russe, M. le Dr Zamenhof, de Varsovie,
20   qui **en** [14] a publié les principes en 1887 sous le pseudonyme "doktoro

---

1 *would be*
2 *before*
3 *given rise to*
4 *might* (imp. subj. of **pouvoir**)
5 *so*

6 *having*
7 **paru**—p.p. of **paraître**
8 *everywhere*
9 *enthusiasm*
10 *had*
11 *although in*

12 *handful . . . still remains faithful to it*
13 *such*
14 *of it*

Espéranto", **d'où** [15] le nom resté à son oeuvre. La valeur linguistique intrinsèque de l'Espéranto a été sanctionnée par les suffrages d'hommes comme M. Max Muller, Associé étranger de l'Académie des Inscriptions et Belles–Lettres; comme M. Ernest Naville, Associé étranger de l'Académie

25 des Sciences morales et politiques; comme le célèbre écrivain russe I. Tolstoï qui a écrit **à son propos:**[16] ". . . Il est si facile à apprendre qu'**ayant reçu,**[17] **il y a six ans,**[18] une grammaire, un dictionnaire et des articles sur cet idiome, j'ai pu arriver, **au bout de** [19] deux petites heures, sinon à écrire, du moins à lire **couramment** [20] la langue". Sa valeur pratique **lui a déjà**

30 **attiré environ** [21] 40.000 adeptes disséminés sur tous les points du globe, principalement en Russie, en Suède et dans les pays de langue française.

1. The first sentence states that
A. all civilized people should be familiar with other languages.
B. one cannot really be termed a scholar without knowing more than one language.
c. that foreigners have difficulty in learning natural languages.

1. C　**2.** Lines 4–9 state that
A. at least 150 different languages have been planned for the next two years
B. the need for an international language, though old, is still urgent
c. the need is really not generally realized.

2. B　**3.** Volapuk did not succeed because (lines 9–17)
A. it was too hard to learn
B. of European prejudice against the Hungarians
c. the Volapukians were too nationalistic.

3. A　**4.** Esperanto was invented by a
A. Hungarian professor　　c. a Polish diplomat
B. a French scientist　　　D. a Russian doctor.

4. D　**5.** Tolstoy wrote concerning Esperanto that (lines 26–29)
A. he could speak it but not write it
B. he could read it but not write it
c. he easily learned to speak, read, and write it
D. he got tired of it after two hours

5. B　**6.** When the article was written the popularity of Esperanto was
A. growing　　　　c. remaining constant
B. decreasing　　　D. confined to the European countries.

6. A

15 *whence*　　　　18 *six years ago*　　　21 *has already drawn to it*
16 *concerning it*　　19 *at the end of*　　　　*about*
17 *having received*　20 *fluently*

Chapter Ten

REVIEW: A foreign language becomes valuable to you only when you recognize its grammar signals and vocabulary without hesitation. Before going on to Chapter Ten, review the items you circled in Chapters Eight and Nine.

64. Tout

1. Tout as an adjective agrees with the noun that it modifies and when followed by **le, la** or **les** means *all* or *every:*

tout le matin (m. sing.)	*all* (*the*) *morning*
toute l'année (f. sing.)	*all* (*the*) *year*
tous les matins (m. pl.)	*all* (*the*) *mornings,* or *every morning*
toutes les années (f. pl.)	*all* (*the*) *years,* or *every year*

When followed by a noun without the definite article, **tout** carries the meaning of *any* or *each:*

tout homme	*any* (*each*) *man*
toute plante	*any* (*each*) *plant*

2. As indefinite pronouns, **tout** means *everything* and **tous** and **toutes** mean *all* or *everyone:*

172

Tous sont venus.	*All came.*
Tout a réussi.	*Everything succeeded.*

3. As adverbs **tout, toute, toutes** may be translated by *completely, very,* or *quite:*

Les fleurs sont toutes fraîches.	*The flowers are quite fresh.*
A cette nouvelle, il est devenu tout pâle.	*At this news, he became quite pale.*

4. Some common idioms with **tout** are:

tout le monde	*everyone, everybody*
tout de suite	*immediately*
tout à fait	*entirely, quite*

INSTRUCTIONS: *Distinguish between the different meanings of* **tout** *in the following sentences. Continue to circle the phrases which you do not immediately recognize.*

1. Exposé à l'air, tout cidre tend à noircir.

1. When exposed to air, any cider tends to go dark.

2. Le liquide devient tout noir.

2. The liquid becomes completely black.

3. **puis**=*then*
   Versé dans un vase ouvert, le liquide brunit d'abord, puis noircit tout à fait.

3. (When) poured in an open receptacle, the liquid first turns brown, then turns entirely black.

4. Ajouté au cidre, l'acide citrique agit tout de suite comme agent chimique.

4. Added to cider, citric acid acts immediately as a chemical agent.

5. Il s'agit d'un procédé tout nouveau.

5. It concerns a completely new process.

6. Quelques linguistes ont fait tout leur possible pour créer une langue internationale.

6. A few linguists have done all they could to create an international language.

7. On peut constater tout de suite que c'est en effet un effort tout à fait inutile.

7. One can ascertain immediately that it is in fact a completely useless effort.

8. Néanmoins, toute langue est plus ou moins utile.

8.	Nevertheless, any language is more or less useful.	**9.**	Toute langue artificielle offre un intérêt linguistique.
9.	Any artificial language offers a linguistic interest.	**10.**	Les langues artificielles ne sont pas toutes d'utilité égale.
10.	Artificial languages are not all of equal usefulness.	**11.**	Tous les savants ne parlent pas la même langue nationale.
11.	All scholars do not speak the same national language.	**12.**	Chimistes, botanistes, ingénieurs—tous ont besoin de communiquer les uns avec les autres.
12.	Chemists, botanists, engineers—all need to communicate with one another.	**13.**	Tout savant qui étudie l'histoire de Rome est obligé de savoir lire le latin.
13.	Any scholar who studies the history of Rome is obliged to know how to read Latin.	**14.**	Pour bien apprendre à lire, il faut lire tous les jours.
14.	In order to learn how to read well, one must read every day.	**15.**	Après avoir étudié plusieurs langues on sait que toutes sont difficiles.
15.	After having studied several languages, one knows that all are difficult.	**16.**	Il n'est pas possible de tout savoir.
16.	It is impossible to know everything.	**17.**	Tous ces points de vue sont possibles.
17.	All these points of view are possible.	**18.**	Il y a plusieurs points de vue, et tous sont possibles.
18.	There are several points of view, and all are possible.	**19.**	Tout le monde est d'accord sur ce point.
19.	Everyone agrees on this point.	**20.**	Tout le monde n'est pas au courant de tous ces développements.
20.	Everyone is not acquainted with (up to date with) all of these developments.	**21.**	Tout est bien qui finit bien.
21.	All is well that ends well.		Review the phrases you circled and then continue.

65. *Past Definite Tense* (passé simple)—*Regular Conjugations*

   1. The following endings attached to the stem of the verb tell you that the verb is in the Past Definite tense:

—er		*—ir*	
je trouvai	(*I found*)	**je finis**	(*I finished*)
tu trouvas	(*you found*)	**tu finis**	(*you finished*)
il trouva	(*he found*)	**il finit**	(*he finished*)
nous trouvâmes	(*we found*)	**nous finîmes**	(*we finished*)
vous trouvâtes	(*you found*)	**vous finîtes**	(*you finished*)
ils trouvèrent	(*they found*)	**ils finirent**	(*they finished*)

—re		*—ure*	
je vendis	(*I sold*)	**je conclus**	(*I concluded*)
tu vendis	(*you sold*)	**tu conclus**	(*you concluded*)
il vendit	(*he sold*)	**il conclut**	(*he concluded*)
nous vendîmes	(*we sold*)	**nous conclûmes**	(*we concluded*)
vous vendîtes	(*you sold*)	**vous conclûtes**	(*you concluded*)
ils vendirent	(*they sold*)	**ils conclurent**	(*they concluded*)

2. Unlike the Past Indefinite, this tense has no alternative translations. It is always translated by only one tense in English, that is, the English simple past.

Il traversa le Niger le 27 décembre.   *He crossed the Niger on December 27.*

3. The Present and Past Definite are the same for the **je, tu, il** forms of **–ir** and **–ure** verbs. The context must furnish the indication of time.

INSTRUCTIONS: *Can you give the meanings of the following tenses?*

	1. Je trouve le travail difficile. (*I find/I found*)
1. *I find*	**2.** Je trouvai le travail difficile. (*I find/I found*)
2. *I found*	**3.** Il quitta la ville. (*He is leaving/He left*)
3. *He left*	**4.** Ils quittent la ville. (*They are leaving/They left*)
4. *They are leaving*	**5.** Ils quittèrent le poste peu après. (*They are leaving/they left*)
5. *They left*	**6.** Il commence sa mission. (*He is beginning/he began*)
6. *He is beginning*	**7.** Il a quitté le poste. (*has left/left/either one*)

7. *either one*	**8.** Il quitta le poste. (*he left/he has left/either one*)
8. *he left*—the Past Definite has only one possible translation.	

INSTRUCTIONS: *The next exercises present the vocabulary and the forms necessary for understanding the reading at the end of the chapter. Work with your card, as usual.*

	1. Le sujet de ces remarques est une exploration du Niger.
1. The subject of these remarks is an exploration of the Niger.	**2.** Le Commandant Toutée commença sa mission le vingt–sept décembre, dix–huit cent quatre–vingt quinze.
2. Commandant Toutée started his mission on December 27, 1895. (**Commandant**=*commandant, major*, or *commander*)	**3.** Ses compagnons partirent en même temps.
3. His companions left at the same time.	**4.** **le bord**=*the bank* (*of a river*) Il traversa le Dahomey et arriva, en février, sur le bord du Niger.
4. He crossed the Dahomey and arrived on the bank of the Niger in February.	**5.** Ils traversèrent le Niger sans nulle difficulté.
5. They crossed the Niger without any difficulty.	**6.** Le Niger est un fleuve en Afrique centrale. (**fleuve** must mean _____)
6. *river* The Niger is a river in central Africa.	**7.** Dans cette région non–civilisée, il fonda un poste. (Did he *found* a post or *find* a post?)
7. In this uncivilized region, he *founded* a post.	**8.** Ils ne fondèrent pas un poste permanent.
8. They did not found a permanent post.	**9.** Il nomma le poste Arenberg.
9. He named the post Arenberg.	**10.** Ils nommèrent le poste Arenberg.
10. They named the post Arenberg.	**11.** Il réussit à descendre les rapides.
11. He succeeded in going down the rapids.	**12.** **davantage**=*more, further* Puis il descendit le fleuve davantage.
12. Then he went further down the river.	**13.** **monter**=*to go up* **remonter**=_____

13. to go back up	**14.** Puis il remonta les rapides non sans difficulté.
14. Then with some difficulty, he went back up the rapids (i.e. not without difficulty).	**15.** Il réussit à remonter les rapides non sans difficulté.
15. With some difficulty, he succeeded in going back up the rapids.	**16.** Ils réussirent à naviguer le fleuve sans aucune difficulté.
16. They succeeded in navigating the river without any difficulty.	**17.** Il démontra la navigabilité des rapides de Boussa.
17. He demonstrated the navigability of the Rapids of Boussa.	**18.** Il étudia les divers chenaux avec soin.
18. He studied the diverse channels with care.	**19.** Ils n'étudièrent que quelques chenaux avec soin.
19. They studied only a few channels with care.	**20.** Il n'étudia pas davantage la topographie de cette région peu civilisée.
20. He did not study any further the topography of this uncivilized region.	**21.** **un naufrage**=*a ship wreck* Il subit de fréquents naufrages.
21. He suffered frequent shipwrecks	**22.** Ils ne subirent que des naufrages infréquents.
22. They suffered only infrequent shipwrecks.	**23.** Ses compagnons ne subirent plus de naufrages.
23. His companions suffered no more shipwrecks.	**24.** **mener à bien**=*to complete successfully* Ils menèrent à bien leur mission.
24. They successfully completed their mission.	**25.** **d'ailleurs**=*moreover* D'ailleurs, ils ouvrirent une voie de communication avec le Soudan.
25. Moreover, they opened a line of communication with the Sudan.	**26.** D'ailleurs, ils n'ouvrirent une voie de communication qu'avec le Soudan.
26. Moreover, they opened a line of communication only with the Sudan.	**27.** D'ailleurs, ils n'ouvrirent qu'une voie de communication avec le Soudan.
27. Moreover, they opened only one line of communication with the Sudan.	**28.** **un poisson**=*fish* Ils rapportèrent d'intéressantes collections de roches et de poissons.
28. They brought some interesting collections of rocks and fish.	**29.** **subir**=*to suffer, to undergo* Il subit de fréquentes privations.

29. He suffered frequent hardships (privations).

---

66.   *Present and Past Definite Tense* —oir *verbs*

1.   The Present and Past Definite tense endings of most **—oir** verbs are as follows:

PRESENT		PAST DEFINITE	
Je reçois	(*I receive*)	**je reçus**	(*I received*)
tu reçois	(*you receive*)	**tu reçus**	(*you received*)
il reçoit	(*he receives*)	**il reçut**	(*he received*)
nous recevons	(*we receive*)	**nous reçûmes**	(*we received*)
vous recevez	(*you receive*)	**vous reçûtes**	(*you received*)
ils reçoivent	(*they receive*)	**ils reçurent**	(*they received*)

2.   **Pouvoir** (*to be able to*), **savoir** (*to know*), **connaître** (*to know*), **courir** (*to run*), **croire** (*to believe*) and **conclure** (*to conclude*) all follow this pattern in the Past Definite.

PAST DEFINITE	
je connus	*I knew*
il courut	*he ran*
ils crurent	*they believed*
elle conclut	*she concluded*
je pus	*I was able to*
vous sûtes	*you knew*

3.   Two exceptions are **voir** (*to see*) and **s'asseoir** (*to sit down*), which follow the **—ir** pattern (**je vis, je m'assis,** etc.)

INSTRUCTIONS: *Give the meanings of the following phrases and sentences. Cover the English with your card.*

		1.	Je pus
1.	I was able to	**2.**	Je sus
2.	I knew	**3.**	Nous pûmes
3.	we were able to	**4.**	Vous sûtes
4.	you knew	**5.**	Nous sûmes

5. we knew	**6.** Vous connûtes
6. you knew	**7.** Je reçus
7. I received	**8.** Ils reçurent
8. they received	**9.** Vous pûtes
9. you were able to	**10.** Vous crûtes
10. you believed	**11.** Nous crûmes
11. we believed	Which word goes with the verb form given?
	12. _____ pûtes (1) vous (2) nous (3) tu
12. (1)	**13.** _____ connus (1) nous (2) ils (3) je
13. (3)	**14.** _____ conclut (1) vous (2) il (3) tu
14. (2)	**15.** _____ reçûmes (1) vous (2) nous (3) ils
15. (2)	**16.** _____ crûtes (1) nous (2) vous (3) tu
16. (2)	**17.** _____ crurent (1) elles (2) vous (3) nous
17. (1)	

INSTRUCTIONS: *Give the meanings of the following sentences.*

	18. En 1895, le Commandant Toutée reçut la mission d'étudier l'hydrographie du Niger.
18. In 1895 Commandant Toutée received the mission of studying the hydrography of the Niger.	**19.** Il ne put partir qu'au mois de décembre.

19. He was not able to leave until the month of December.	**20.** Il crut à la navigabilité du fleuve.
20. He believed the river was navigable.	**21.** **courir**=*to run* Lui et ses compagnons coururent des dangers sérieux.
21. He and his companions were exposed to (ran) serious dangers.	**22.** **épreuves**=*trials, hardships* Ils connurent des épreuves terribles.
22. They experienced (knew) terrible hardships.	**23.** Il ne sut jamais sa destination exacte.
23. He never knew his exact destination.	**24.** Ils ne purent traverser le fleuve qu'à la baisse des eaux. (**baisser**=*to lower* **la baisse des eaux**=_____)
24. Literally, *the lowering of the water.* They could not cross the river except when the water was low.	**25.** Il conclut à la navigabilité du fleuve.
25. He concluded that the river was navigable.	**26.** La baisse des eaux le força à redescendre le fleuve.
26. The lowering of the waters forced him to go back down the river.	**27.** Après la dernière traversée du fleuve, il ne courut plus de grands dangers.
27. After the last crossing of the river, he faced no more great dangers.	**28.** **réunir**=*to reunite, to gather* Il put réunir des notions très utiles.
28. He was able to gather some very useful information.	**29.** Ils surent mener à bien leur mission.
29. They managed to complete their mission successfully. (Remember that **savoir** in addition to the meaning of *to know* may also carry the meaning of *ability.*)	**30.** **tant . . . que**=*as much . . . as* Ils purent réunir les notions les plus utiles, tant au point de vue hydrographique qu'au point de vue topographique.
30. They were able to gather the most useful information, as much from the hydrographical point of view as from the topographical point of view.	**31.** Le commandant reçut le prix Delalande-Guérineau tant pour ses observations météorologiques que pour les notions topographiques qu'il put réunir.
31. The commandant received the Delalande-Guérineau prize as much for his meteorological observations as for the topographical information which he was able to gather.	Review the items you have circled and then continue.

67.   *Past Definite Tense* —enir *verbs,* avoir, être, faire

1. The following forms indicate the Past Definite tense of **—enir** verbs:

venir

je vins	*I came*
tu vins	*you came*
il vint	*he came*
nous vînmes	*we came*
vous vîntes	*you came*
ils vinrent	*they came*

2. The following forms indicate the Past Definite tense of **être, avoir,** and **faire:**

être		avoir	
je fus	*(I was)*	j'eus	*(I had)*
tu fus	*(you were)*	tu eus	*(you had)*
il fut	*(he, it was)*	il eut	*(he, it had)*
nous fûmes	*(we were)*	nous eûmes	*(we had)*
vous fûtes	*(you were)*	vous eûtes	*(you had)*
ils furent	*(they were)*	ils eurent	*(they had)*

faire

je fis	*(I did)*
tu fis	*(you did)*
il fit	*(he did)*
nous fîmes	*(we did)*
vous fîtes	*(you did)*
ils firent	*(they did)*

READING PREPARATION

INSTRUCTIONS: *Indicate which pronoun goes with the verb form.*

1. (3)

2. (1)

3. (3)

1. _____ fus
   (1) vous   (2) il   (3) je

2. _____ fûmes
   (1) nous   (2) vous   (3) ils

3. _____ eurent
   (1) nous   (2) vous   (3) ils

4. _____ revinrent
   (1) vous   (2) ils   (3) elle

4. (2)	**5.** _____ devîntes (1) vous (2) nous (3) je
5. (1)	**6.** _____ vins (1) il (2) elles (3) je
6. (3)	**7.** _____ vint (1) il (2) elles (3) tu
7. (1)	

INSTRUCTIONS: _Which of these alternatives express the meanings of the verbs?_

	1. je fis (1) _I was_ (2) _I did_
1. (2)	**2.** je fus (1) _I was_ (2) _I did_
2. (1)	**3.** j'eus (1) _I was_ (2) _I had_
3. (2)	**4.** il eut (1) _he had_ (2) _there was_
4. (1)	**5.** il y eut (1) _he had_ (2) _there was_
5. (2) past definite of **il y a**	**6.** Il y eut de fréquentes épreuves à subir. (1) _there was_ (2) _there were_
6. (2)	**7.** Il eut de fréquentes épreuves à subir. (1) _he had_ (2) _there were_
7. (1)	

INSTRUCTIONS: _Express in English the meaning of the following sentences. Cover the English with your card, as usual._

	1. Il fut bientôt question d'étudier l'hydrographie du Moyen–Niger. (**moyen**=_average/middle_)
1. _middle_ It was soon a question of studying the hydrography of the middle Niger.	**2.** **étendre**=_to extend_ Il fut bientôt question d'étendre nos connaissances du Niger.

2. It was soon a question of extending our knowledge of the Niger.
(Notice that English usage determines whether to translate an infinitive by a present participle or another infinitive.)

3. **avoir lieu**=*to take place*
Le voyage eut lieu en 1895.

3. The voyage took place in 1895.

4. Il y eut de grands dangers à courir.

4. There were great dangers to run. (They were exposed to great dangers.)

5. **aussitôt**=*immédiatement*
Il y eut aussitôt de grands dangers à courir.

5. There were immediately great dangers to run.

6. Il fallut traverser le fleuve lors de la baisse des eaux.
(**fallut**=p.d. of **falloir,** *to be necessary*)

6. It was necessary to cross the river when the water was low.

7. Aux rapides de Boussa la navigation devint bientôt difficile.

7. At the rapids of Boussa navigation soon became difficult.

8. **avoir soin**=*to take care*
On eut grand soin de ne pas occasionner de naufrages.

8. They took much care not to cause shipwrecks.

9. **lutter**=*to struggle*
Ils eurent à lutter contre les plus grandes difficultés.

9. They had to struggle against the greatest difficulties.

10. Ils eurent soin d'observer exactement la topographie de cette région inconnue.

10. They took care to observe precisely the topography of this unknown region.

11. Aussitôt la situation redevint difficile.

11. Immediately the situation became difficult again.

12. Après quelques mois, ils revinrent en arrière.

12. After a few months, they retraced their steps (came back to the rear).

13. **bientôt**=*soon*
On eut bientôt à supporter les attaques continuelles des indigènes.

13. They soon had to endure the continual attacks of natives.

14. Ils eurent à lutter contre les indigènes.

14. They had to struggle against the natives.

15. Bientôt, de vives batailles eurent lieu avec les indigènes.

15. Soon, lively battles took place with the natives.

16. **être en butte à**=*to be exposed to*
Ils furent souvent en butte aux perfidies des indigènes.

---

16. They were often exposed to the treachery of the natives.

17. Il parut aussitôt que les indigènes étaient hostiles.
(Will **étaient** probably be a **past** or a **present** form?)

---

17. *past*
It immediately appeared that the natives were hostile.
(**parut** indicates the time)

18. On obtint des résultats utiles.

---

18. They obtained some useful results.

19. Ils parvinrent bientôt à mener à bien leur entreprise, tant au point de vue scientifique qu'au point de vue personnel.

---

19. They soon managed to lead their project to a successful conclusion as much from the scientific as from the personal point of view.

20. Cette mission eut l'effet d'étendre l'horizon de nos connaissances.

---

20. This mission had the effect of extending the horizon of our knowledge.

21. Le commandant parvint à obtenir les résultats voulus.

---

21. The commandant managed to obtain the desired results.

22. On voulut réunir des notions précises sur le Moyen-Niger.

---

22. They wanted to gather some precise information on the middle Niger.

23. Ils parvinrent en effet à faire une description détaillée de la région.

---

23. They indeed succeeded in making a detailed description of the region.

---

68. *Historical Present*

1. In French historical narrative, the Present tense is often used instead of (or in conjunction with) the regular past tenses. Usually the Historical Present will be better translated by an English past tense, but the context and English usage must govern.

Mais dès que Louis XVI s'applique à la politique intérieure, il ne voit plus clair.

But as soon as Louis XVI applied himself to domestic policy, he no longer saw clearly.

INSTRUCTIONS: *The following sentences concerning Louis XVI are in the Historical Present. Translate them into English.*

	1. Quand on annonce à Louis XVI la mort de Louis XV . . .
1. When they informed Louis XVI of the death of Louis XV . . .	2. **s'écrier**=*to cry out* . . . il s'écrie, "Quel fardeau!"
2. . . . he cried out, "What a burden!" (Are you circling unrecognized expressions?)	3. **la couronne**=*the crown* Quand il reçoit la couronne . . .
3. When he was crowned . . . (received the crown)	4. **le roi**=*the king* . . . le roi n'est pas heureux.
4. . . . the king was not happy.	5. La couronne est pour lui le plus grand des fardeaux.
5. The crown was for him the greatest of burdens.	6. Il croit à la bonté humaine . . .
6. He believed in human goodness . . .	7. **répugner à**=*to loathe, to abhor* . . . et il répugne donc aux moyens d'authorité. (**moyens** = *middle / average / some other meaning*)
7. *some other meaning* . . . and he therefore loathed authoritarian *means.* (Notice that here the context will not permit the same meaning of **moyen** which you met earlier—"**le Moyen-Niger.**" It is the context which sorts out unacceptable meanings.)	8. **avoir envie de**=*to desire* Il n'a aucune envie d'être roi.
8. He had no desire to be king.	9. Il répugne aux soins qu'impose la couronne.
9. He loathed the cares which the crown imposed.	

69. *Present Participles*

1. The Present Participle (in English the verbal *–ing* form) is recognized in French by **–ant** added to the stem of the verb. This stem for all regular verbs is the same as that of the **nous** form of the Present tense:

PRESENT TENSE		PRESENT PARTICIPLE	
Nous parlons	*we speak*	**parlant**	*speaking*
Nous finissons	*we finish*	**finissant**	*finishing*
Nous vendons	*we sell*	**vendant**	*selling*
Nous faisons	*we do*	**faisant**	*doing*

2. A few verbs have irregular stems. Learn the following:

avoir	*to have*	**ayant**	*having*
être	*to be*	**étant**	*being*
savoir	*to know*	**sachant**	*knowing*

3. The Present Participle is used in French as a verbal expression or as an adjective. In both cases it is translated by the English **–ing** form:

Sachant son affaire . . .	*Knowing his business* . . .
Répugnant aux moyens d'autorité . . .	*Loathing authoritarian means* . . .
C'est une femme charmante.	*She is a charming woman.*
Le vin a des qualités stimulantes.	*Wine has stimulating qualities.*

Notice that as an adjective the Present Participle agrees in gender and number with the noun it modifies.

4. Some Present Participles are also used as nouns, in which case they are immediately preceded by an article, an adjective, or a quantity word:

un suivant	*a follower, an attendant*
les survivants	*the survivors*
quelques croyants	*a few believers*
un croyant sincère	*a sincere believer*

Can you read the following without looking at the left-hand column?

1. **sot**=*stupid, foolish*
   N'étant point sot, Louis XVI profita des leçons du règne précédent.
   (Did he learn anything from the previous reign?)

---

1. *yes*
   Not being unintelligent (stupid), Louis XVI took advantage of the lessons of the preceding reign.

2. **la marine**=*the navy*
   Reconstituant la marine, il réussit à maintenir la paix sur le continent.
   (Does **maintenir** suggest that he *kept the peace* or *went to war*?)

2. *He kept the peace.*
Rebuilding the navy, he succeeded in maintaining peace on the continent.

3. **soustraire**=*to take away, to remove*
Ayant des connaissances, de la mémoire et du jugement, il eut la force de soustraire sa politique étrangère aux factions.

3. Possessing (having) knowledge, a good memory, and good judgment, he had the strength to remove his foreign policy from the factions.

4. Soustrayant sa politique étrangère aux factions, il s'appliqua à la politique intérieure.

4. Removing his foreign policy from the factions, he applied himself to domestic policy.

5. S'appliquant à la politique intérieure, il se montra inférieur à lui-même.

5. Applying himself to domestic policy, he showed himself inferior to his potential (to himself)

6. **se rendre compte de**=*to realize*
D'ailleurs, étant trop bon, presque sot, il ne se rendit pas compte des dangers menaçant son règne.

6. Moreover, being too good, almost foolish, he did not realize the dangers to his reign.

7. Etant pénétré de Fénelon, il s'affilia à une loge maçonnique de la cour.

7. Being imbued with Fénelon, he joined a Masonic lodge of the court.

8. **avoir recours à**=*to use, to have recourse to*
N'ayant aucune envie d'avoir recours à des moyens autoritaires, il fut presque trop bon.

8. Having no desire to use authoritarian means, he was almost too good.

9. Il répugna aux moyens d'autorité, croyant à la bonté humaine.

9. He loathed authoritarian means, believing in human goodness.

10. **se refuser à**=*to refuse*
D'ailleurs, ne sachant pas le danger, il se refusa à prévoir le pire.
(**prédire**=*to predict, foretell*
prévoir=_____)

10. *to foresee*
Moreover, not knowing the danger, he refused to foresee the worst.

11. Cependant, ne sachant nullement le pire, il ne se rendit jamais compte du danger.

11. However, not at all knowing the worst, he never realized the danger.

12. Ne se rendant plus compte du danger, il n'eut pas recours à la force.

12. No longer realizing the danger, he did not have recourse to force.

13. D'ailleurs, étant aveuglément optimiste, il ne crut point au pire.
(**aveugle**=*blind*
aveuglément=_____)

13. *blindly* Moreover, being blindly optimistic, he did not at all believe in the worst. (that the worst could happen)	**14.** S'aveuglant aux réalités politiques, il n'eut pas envie de commander.
14. Blinding himself to the political realities, he had no desire to command.	**15.** Dans son aveuglement il ne se rendit jamais compte de ses erreurs.
15. In his blindness, he never realized his errors.	

70.   *Present Participles with* en *and* tout

1. The Present Participle is often preceded by the preposition **en.** This may be translated as *while, in, on, by,* or *upon,* according to the context:

En faisant son devoir . . .	*While doing his duty* . . .
En connaissant les faits . . .	*By knowing the facts* . . .
En disant au revoir . . .	*On saying goodbye* . . .
En voyant le résultat . . .	*Upon seeing the result* . . .

2. The adverb **tout** is sometimes used before **en** + Present Participle. It acts to intensify the simultaneity of the actions (*while* or *although*) or to contrast them.

Tout en parlant je l'examinai de près.	*While speaking, I examined it closely.*
Tout en connaissant le jeu, il joue mal.	*Although knowing the game, he plays badly.*

INSTRUCTIONS: *Distinguish between the various meanings of* **en.**

	1. Tout en maintenant la paix sur le continent, il reconstitua la marine.
1. While maintaining peace on the continent, he rebuilt the navy.	**2.** Il se montra bien intentionné en profitant des leçons du règne précédent.
2. He showed himself to be well-intentioned by profiting from the lessons of the preceding reign.	**3.** En étant travailleur et consciencieux, il sut imposer sa volonté sur les factions.
3. By being industrious and conscientious, he was able to impose his will on the factions.	**4.** Tout en ayant des connaissances et du jugement, il ne montra jamais qu'une volonté faible.

4. While possessing knowledge and good judgment, he never showed any but a weak will.

5. He was able to maintain peace, all the while building up the navy.

6. Although filled with great qualities, he nonetheless showed an unjustified confidence in human goodness.

7. Although (while) filled with good ideas, he loathed the means necessary to implement them.

8. By refusing to realize the worst, he did great harm to the monarchy.

9. By persisting in his obstinate blindness, he was unable to become aware of these imminent dangers.

10. Although (while) well-intentioned, he blinded himself to the political realities.
(Note that here **politiques** is used as an adjective and conveys a different meaning than it did above as a noun—**"la politique intérieure,"** or *domestic policy*)

5. Il sut maintenir la paix, tout en reconstituant la marine.

6. **remplir**=*to fill*
Tout en étant rempli de grandes qualités, il montra cependant une confiance peu justifiée en la bonté humaine.

7. **réaliser**=*to fulfill, to implement*
Tout en étant rempli de bonnes idées, il répugne aux moyens nécessaires pour les réaliser.

8. En se refusant à se rendre compte du pire, il fait un mal énorme à la monarchie.

9. En persistant dans son aveuglement obstiné, il ne put se rendre compte de ces dangers imminents.

10. Tout en étant bien intentionné, il s'aveugla aux réalités politiques.

71. *Irregular verb*—voir

1. The Present tense of **voir** is as follows:

je vois	*I see*
tu vois	*you see*
il voit	*he sees*
nous voyons	*we see*
vous voyez	*you see*
ils voient	*they see*

Past Participle: **vu**   *seen*

Present Participle: **voyant**   *seeing*

Past Definite:

je vis	*I saw*
tu vis	*you saw*
il vit	*he saw*
nous vîmes	*we saw*
vous vîtes	*you saw*
ils virent	*they saw*

Note: Do not mistake the Past Definite of **voir** (**je vis, tu vis, il vit**) for the Present tense of **vivre,** which is conjugated the same way in the singular forms. (The Past Definite forms of **vivre** are: **je vécus,** etc.)

2.   An infinitive following **voir** is usually translated by a Present Participle:

Nous avons vu venir la guerre.   *We saw war coming.*
Il vit se former des nuages.   *He saw clouds being formed.*

INSTRUCTIONS: *Give the English for the following sentences. Work with your card as usual.*

---

1. Le roi ne voit plus clair.

1. The king no longer saw (sees) clearly.

2. **la cour**=*the court*
   Ceux de la cour de Louis XVI ne virent pas venir la Révolution.

2. Those of Louis XVI's court did not see the Revolution coming.

3. Ne voyant aucunement le danger, le roi ne se rendit pas compte de son imminence.

3. Not seeing the danger at all, the king did not realize its imminence.

4. Nous voyons cette époque comme une des plus intéressantes.

4. We see this period as one of the most interesting.

5. Pendant son voyage, le Commandant Toutée se vit en butte aux trahisons des indigènes.

5. During his voyage, Commandant Toutée found himself (saw himself) exposed to the betrayals of the natives.

6. On peut maintenant prévoir une voie de communication avec le Soudan français.

6. One can now foresee a line of communication with the French Sudan.

7. Le roi vit à Versailles.
   (Which does the context indicate? *lives/saw*)

7. *lives* The king lives at Versailles.	8. Le roi ne vit pas venir la fin de la monarchie. (**vit** = *lives/saw*)
8. *saw* The king did not see the end of the monarchy coming.	9. Le roi naquit, vécut, et mourut optimiste.
9. The king was born, lived, and died an optimist.	10. Il ne survécut pas à la Révolution.
10. He did not survive the Revolution.	

VOCABULARY DEVELOPMENT

INSTRUCTIONS: *Use the root word to determine the meaning of the related words.*

	1. **penser** = *to think* Les oeuvres de Voltaire sont remplies de **pensées** étincelantes.
1. The works of Voltaire are filled with sparkling *thoughts.*	2. C'est **la pensée** qui distingue l'homme des animaux.
2. It is *thought* that distinguishes man from animals.	3. Un philosophe est par définition **un penseur.**
3. A philosopher is by definition *a thinker.*	4. **une coutume** = *a custom* **J'ai coutume de** me reposer après dîner.
4. *I am accustomed to* relaxing after dinner.	5. **le droit** = *the law* **Le droit coutumier** n'est pas écrit, mais il est établi par l'usage.
5. *The common law* is unwritten but is established by usage.	6. On dit que les indigènes sont **coutumiers** des trahisons.
6. They say that the natives are *customarily* treacherous.	7. Quand on voyage, il faut **s'accoutumer à** des climats variés.
7. When one travels, it is necessary *to become accustomed* to various climates.	Now do the testing exercise to verify your mastery of these materials. Review the indicated sections if you miss any of the questions.

INSTRUCTIONS: *Choose the answer which best completes the sentence grammatically or which gives the best translation of the indicated words and phrases.*

1. Les historiens **ont soin** de vérifier leurs hypothèses.
A. need to   B. appear to   C. take care to   D. happen to

1. C (67)	**2.** Je **fus** fatigué. A. was B. had C. did
2. A (67)	**3.** _____ reçumes. A. ils B. vous C. nous D. on
3. C (66)	**4.** Je **sus** la nouvelle. A. had B. received C. knew D. believed in
4. C (66)	**5.** Dans **toute** entreprise nouvelle il y a des risques à courir. A. any B. all C. some
5. A (64)	**6.** **Tout le monde** est d'accord. A. anyone B. all the world C. everyone
6. C (64)	**7.** Il **finit** sa lecture le mois dernier. A. finished B. is finishing C. was finishing D. finishes
7. A (65)	**8.** Il **fonda** un poste permanent. A. founds B. found C. founded D. is founding
8. C (65)	**9.** En nous _____, il se rendit compte de son erreur. A. parlé B. parlons C. parler D. parlant
9. D (69)	**10.** Il fut réellement intelligent **tout en** ayant l'air d'être sot. A. by means of B. although C. upon D. omitted in translation
10. B (70)	**11.** Ordinairement **il vit** à Paris la plupart de l'année. A. He saw B. He lives C. He lived D. He sees
11. B (65)	**12.** Il **commence** sa mission le vingt–neuf décembre. A. started B. is starting C. has started
12. B (65)	

READING PASSAGE

As you read the following passage, write out the answers to these questions:

1. What is the region that Toutée was to explore?
2. How long did it take him to get to the future site of Arenberg?
3. What was his course after he left Arenberg?

4. What were his relations with the natives?
5. Why did he have to come back down the river?
6. What did he accomplish during his mission?

Prix Delalande-Guérineau

From *Comptes rendus de l'Académie des Sciences,*
(1896) pp. 1176-77.

Le Commandant d'artillerie Toutée a reçu, en 1895, la mission d'étudier l'hydrographie du Niger moyen [sic] entre Gaba, qui est le point **le plus septentrional** [1] des établissements anglais, et les environs de Tombouctou. Parti de Kotonou le 27 décembre 1894, il traversa le Dahomey et arriva, le
5   13 février 1895, sur le bord du Niger, où il fonda, à son confluent avec la Moussa, un poste qu'il nomma Arenberg; puis il descendit le fleuve jusqu'aux postes avancés de la Royal Niger Company, et, **revenant en arrière,** [2] il remonta les rapides réputés infranchissables de Boussa; pendant 47 kilomètres, il eut à lutter contre les plus grandes difficultés et courut des dangers
10   très sérieux, mais il n'en réussit pas moins dans son entreprise. **En amont,** [3] la navigation redevint facile, et la mission **atteignit** [4] le pays des Touareg, où elle fut en butte aux perfidies et aux trahisons **dont** [5] ces Berbères sont trop coutumiers. Le Commandant Toutée arriva néanmoins le 12 juin à Tibi–Farca, qui est placé sous l'autorité du gouverneur de Tombouctou. La baisse
15   des eaux, qui commençait à se faire sentir, le força à redescendre le fleuve, non sans avoir à supporter les attaques continuelles des Touareg et à subir de fréquents naufrages. Le 13 juillet, la mission rentra à Arenberg.

Dans cette importante et difficile expédition qu'il a menée avec une rapidité extraordinaire, le Commandant Toutée **a levé** [6] 650 kilomètres d'itinéraires
20   nouveaux et a navigué, pendant plus de 1.400 kilomètres, sur le Niger moyen, qui était encore inconnu, et **sur lequel** [7] il a réuni les plus utiles notions, tant au point de vue topographique et hydrographique qu'au point de vue de l'ethnographie des peuplades qu'il a traversées; il a démontré la navigabilité des rapides de Boussa, **dont** [8] il a étudié les divers chenaux avec soin, il a
25   fait de nombreuses observations météorologiques et il a formé d'intéressantes collections de poissons, de plantes et de roches.

Disons [9] enfin que cette expédition a beaucoup étendu notre horizon colonial vers le Niger et a ouvert une voie de communication facile entre le Soudan français et l'embouchure de ce fleuve.
30   En présence de ces résultats utiles à la Science et à la France, votre Commission **a décerné** [10] au commandant Toutée le prix Delalande-Guérineau.

---

1 *northern most*   **5** *of which*   **9** *let us say*
2 *retracing his steps*   **6** *surveyed*   **10** *awarded*
3 *upstream*   **7** *about which*
4 **atteindre**= *to reach* **8** *of which*

Write out the answers to these questions according to the following text:

1. What were the qualities of Louis XVI?
2. What were his accomplishments in foreign affairs?
3. How do we know that he did not enjoy being a king?
4. Why was he less capable in managing domestic affairs?
5. How does one recognize his liberalism?

Louis XVI

From Pierre Gaxotte, *La Révolution française,*
pp. 83–84. (Librairie Arthème Fayard)

Par malheur,[1] Louis XV mourut. Par malheur encore Louis XVI lui
succéda. Ce gros homme point sot était rempli de qualités **dont**[2] quelques-
unes au moins étaient d'un roi. Il était travailleur, attentif, consciencieux,
bien intentionné. Il avait des connaissances, de la mémoire, du jugement.

5 Ayant eu la force de soustraire sa politique étrangère aux factions, il trouva
l'homme **qu'il fallait**[3] **pour la réaliser,**[4] profita des leçons du règne
précédent, reconstitua la marine et réussit à maintenir la paix sur le continent
tout en **prenant** sur mer et aux colonies **la revanche**[5] du traité de Paris.

Mais dès qu'il s'applique à la politique intérieure, il est inférieur à lui-

10 même. Il ne voit plus clair, et ne sait plus **ce qu'**[6] il veut. Il a prononcé dans
sa vie quelques phrases qui **en disent long.**[7] Quand on lui annonce la mort
de Louis XV, il s'écrie: **"Quel fardeau!**[8] Et l'on ne m'a rien appris.
Il me semble que l'univers va tomber sur moi!" A Reims, quand il reçoit
la couronne: **"Elle me gêne!"**[9] En 1776, quand il reçoit la **démission**[10]

15 de Malesherbes: **"Que**[11] vous êtes heureux! **Que**[12] ne puis-je quitter ma
place!" **Au fond,**[13] c'est le roi du "Télémaque," un philosophe couronné
qui rougit de commander à des hommes libres. Il est si pénétré de Fénelon
et de Rousseau qu'un an après son **avènement,**[14] il s'affilie à une loge
maçonnique de la Cour. Il croit à la bonté humaine, et répugne aux moyens

20 d'autorité. Aveuglément optimiste, il s'obstine à penser que les choses
s'arrangeront d'elles-mêmes par le seul[15] jeu de la divine nature. Il se
refuse à prévoir le pire et à recourir à la force, au moment où il le peut
encore. Son libéralisme fit plus de mal à la monarchie que les maîtresses
de Louis XV et les banqueroutes de Terray.

1 *unfortunately*	6 *what*	12 *why*
2 *of which*	7 **en dire long**=*to say*	13 *at bottom*
3 *necessary to*	*much of him*	14 *accession to the throne*
4 *implement it*	8 *What a burden!*	15 *will take care of them-*
5 **Prendre la revanche** =	9 *It irks me!*	*selves by nothing more*
to take vengeance, to	10 *resignation*	*than the*
get even for	11 *How*	

Chapter Eleven

72. *The Imperfect Tense*

1. The stem for the Imperfect tense is the **nous** form of the present tense minus the ending —**ons,** e.g. **nous parlons—parl____; nous finissons— finiss_____.** The following verb endings attached to this stem tell you that the action is in past time (–ais, –ais, –ait, –ions, –iez, –aient) :

parler		**finir**	
je parlais	(*I spoke, I was*	**je finissais**	(*I finished, I was*
tu parlais	*speaking, I used*	**tu finissais**	*finishing, I used*
il parlait	*to speak*)	**il finissait**	*to finish*)
nous parlions		**nous finissions**	
vous parliez		**vous finissiez**	
ils parlaient		**ils finissaient**	

Since one group of –**ir** verbs does not take the –**issons, –issez, –issent** endings in the Present, you should not look for them to take this stem in the Imperfect. The Imperfect of **finir** is **je finissais,** etc. (*I was finishing*), but the Imperfect of **dormir** is **je dormais** (*I was sleeping*).

2. The only irregular stem is for **être:**

être	
j'étais	(*I was, I used to be*)
tu étais	
il était	
nous étions	
vous étiez	
ils étaient	

3.   The Imperfect has three possible meanings which are expressed in three different ways in English. The proper one must be established by the context.

(a)   Past description or characterization:

Sa maîtresse n'était pas une personne agréable.	*Her mistress was not a pleasant person.*
Sa maison se trouvait entre un passage et une ruelle.	*Her house was situated (found) between a passage way and an alley.*

(b)   Customary or habitual past action:

Elle se levait dès l'aube.	*She would (used to) get up at dawn.*
Elle faisait la cuisine et allait tous les jours à la messe.	*She did the cooking and went to Mass everyday.*
Elle travaillait jusqu'au soir sans interruption.	*She would (used to) work without interruption until evening.*

(c)   Actions incomplete (in progress) at a specified or implied moment in the past:

Alors qu'ils se promenaient, ils virent venir à eux des hommes armés.	*While they were strolling, they saw some armed men coming toward them.*
Tandis que Zadig défendait Sémire avec toute sa force, elle perçait le ciel de ses plaintes.	*While Zadig was defending Sémire with all his might, she was piercing the heavens with her cries.*

INSTRUCTIONS: *Before you can read accurately you must be able to identify the tenses of the verbs. Give the meaning and the tense of each phrase.*

	1. Nous prévoyons (*we foresee/we foresaw*)
1. *we foresee*—Present	**2.** nous prévoyions (*we foresee/we foresaw*)
2. *we foresaw*—Imperfect	**3.** il prévit (*he foresees/he foresaw*)
3. *he foresaw*—Past Definite	**4.** nous avons prévu (*we have foreseen/we used to foresee*)
4. *we have foreseen*—Past Indefinite Only the Imperfect can carry the meaning of "used to."	**5.** je viens (*I come/I came*)

5. *I come*—Present	**6.** je venais (*I was coming/I have come*)
6. *I was coming*—Imperfect	**7.** je vins (*I used to come/I came*)
7. *I came*—The Past Definite, which has only one possible translation.	**8.** je suis venu (*I am coming/I came*)
8. *I came*—Past Indefinite (If you said "*I am coming,*" review section 31 on the Past Indefinite of **être** verbs.)	**9.** je trouve (*I find/I found*)
9. *I find*—Present	**10.** je trouvai (*I find/I found*)
10. *I found*—Past Definite	**11.** je trouvais (*I find/I found*)
11. *I found*—Imperfect	**12.** il trouva (*he found/he is finding*)
12. *he found*—Past Definite	**13.** il trouvait (*he has found/he used to find*)
13. *he used to find*—Imperfect	

INSTRUCTIONS: *Pouvez-vous lire les phrases suivantes sans regarder la vérification?*

	1. **un conte** = *a story, a tale* Il s'agit d'un conte philosophique de Voltaire.
1. It concerns a philosophic tale by Voltaire.	**2.** Voltaire vivait au dix–huitième siècle.
2. Voltaire lived in the Eighteenth Century. (If you looked at this column, circle the word you did not recognize.)	**3.** Il pensait souvent à la question du bonheur.
3. He often thought of the question of happiness.	**4.** Où est le bonheur sur la terre?
4. Where is happiness on earth?	**5.** Il essayait d'approfondir cette question dans ses contes philosophiques.
5. He tried to go into the question deeply in his philosophic tales.	**6.** Il y avait à Babylone un jeune homme nommé Zadig.

6. There was in Babylon a young man named Zadig.	**7.** Il avait de grandes richesses.
7. He had great riches.	**8.** Il avait par conséquent des amis.
8. Consequently, he had friends.	**9.** Il possédait un esprit juste et modéré.
9. He possessed a fair, temperate mind. (Note that **esprit** has three meanings: *mind*, *spirit*, and *wit*.)	**10.** Il savait modérer ses passions.
10. He knew how to moderate his passions.	**11.** **affecter**=*to feign, to pretend* Il n'affectait rien.
11. He feigned nothing.	**12.** Il n'était pas affecté
12. He was not affected.	**13.** **le coeur**=*the heart* Son coeur était noble et sincère.
13. His heart was noble and sincere.	**14.** Il n'affectait pas les qualités qu'il ne possédait pas.
14. He did not feign to have the qualities which he did not have.	**15.** Il ne voulait point toujours avoir raison.
15. He did not always wish to be right.	**16.** **un parti**=*a party, a match* La beauté et la fortune de Sémire la rendaient le premier parti de Babylone. (**la** refers to _____)
16. *Sémire* The beauty and fortune of Sémire made her the most desirable match in Babylon.	**17.** La vue de cette dame était capable d'attendrir des tigres. (**tendre**=*soft, tender* **attendrir**=_____)
17. *to soften* The sight of this lady was capable of softening tigers.	**18.** **aimer**=*to love* Elle aimait Zadig avec passion.
18. She loved Zadig passionately.	**19.** Parce que Zadig aimait Sémire, il croyait qu'il pouvait être heureux.
19. Because Zadig loved Sémire, he believed that he could be happy.	**20.** Il voulait rendre Sémire heureuse.
20. He wanted to make Sémire happy.	**21.** Il croyait qu'il pouvait la rendre heureuse.
21. He believed that he could make her happy.	**22.** **alors que**=*while, just when* Alors qu'ils touchaient au moment de leur bonheur, un événement malheureux eut lieu.

22. Just when they were touching the moment of their happiness, an unfortunate event took place.	**23.** Le jeune Orcan n'avait aucune des vertus de Zadig.
23. Young Orcan had none of the virtues of Zadig.	**24.** **valoir mieux**=*to be better, to be worth more* Mais il croyait valoir beaucoup mieux que celui-ci.
24. But he believed himself to be much superior to the latter.	**25.** Alors qu'il n'avait aucune des vertus de Zadig, il croyait valoir beaucoup mieux.
25. While he had none of the virtues of Zadig, he believed himself much superior to him.	**26.** Par malheur, Orcan ne valait pas mieux que les autres.
26. Unfortunately, Orcan was not any better than the others.	**27.** Tout en affectant toutes sortes de vertus, il ne valait pas mieux que les autres.
27. Although feigning all kinds of virtues, he was not better than the others.	**28.** Son coeur était peu noble et sincère.
28. His heart was base (ignoble) and insincere.	**29.** D'ailleurs, il était jaloux et fort envieux.
29. Moreover, he was jealous and very envious.	**30.** Sa jalousie ne venait que de sa vanité. (Does **ne . . . que** signal *a negation* or *an exception to a negation?*)
30. *an exception* His jealousy came from nothing except his vanity or (his jealousy came only from his vanity).	**31.** Grâce à sa position, il croyait que tout lui était permis. (Does the phrase probably mean *he permitted everything/he was permitted to do anything.*)
31. He believed *he was permitted to do anything.* Because of his position he believed that he was permitted to do everything he pleased (everything was permitted to him).	**32.** Alors que Zadig se promenait avec Sémire, ils furent attaqués par des hommes armés.
32. While Zadig was taking a walk with Sémire, they were attacked by armed men.	**33.** **blesser**=*to wound* Tandis que (pendant que) Zadig défendait Sémire, leurs adversaires blessèrent celle-ci.
33. While Zadig was defending Sémire, their adversaries wounded the latter.	**34.** **se plaindre**=*to complain* **une plainte**=_____

34. *a complaint*

35. Tandis que Zadig défendait Sémire, celle-ci perçait le ciel de ses plaintes. (The fact that she was *"piercing the heavens"* suggests that her **plaintes** took the form of _____.)

35. *cries, screams, etc.*
While Zadig was defending Sémire, the latter was piercing the heavens with her cries.

36. **mettre en fuite**=*to put to flight*
Tandis que Sémire perçait le ciel de ses plaintes, Zadig mit les ravisseurs en fuite.

36. While Sémire was piercing the heavens with her cries, Zadig put the ravishers to flight.

37. Il nous faut laisser Zadig et Sémire pour le moment.

37. We must leave Zadig and Sémire for the moment.

38. Nous allons parler d'un personnage créé par Flaubert.

38. We are going to speak of a character created by Flaubert.

39. Flaubert était un des plus grands auteurs français au dix-neuvième siècle.

39. Flaubert was one of the greatest French authors in the nineteenth century.

40. Il s'agit d'un personnage dans un conte de Flaubert.

40. It concerns a character in a tale by Flaubert.

41. **s'appeler**=*to be named, to be called*
Elle s'appelait Félicité.

41. Her name was Félicité.

42. Elle était la domestique de Mme Aubain.
(**domestique—ami/servante**)

42. **servante**
She was the servant of Mme. Aubain.

43. **dès l'aube**=*at dawn*
Félicité se levait dès l'aube.

43. Félicité would get up at dawn.

44. Elle travaillait jusqu'au soir sans interruption.

44. She worked (would work) without interruption until evening.

45. Elle allait tous les matins à la messe.

45. She went to Mass every morning.

46. Après être rentrée de la messe, elle commençait son travail.

46. After having come back from Mass, she would start her work.

47. **marchander**=*to bargain, to haggle*
le marchandage=_____

47.	*bargaining, haggling*	**48.**	**l'entêtement** = *stubbornness* Elle montrait toujours un entêtement incroyable dans les marchandages.
48.	She would always show an unbelievable stubbornness in bargaining (at the market place).	**49.**	Personne ne montrait plus d'entêtement dans les marchandages.
49.	No one showed more stubbornness in bargaining and haggling.	**50.**	Son visage n'avait aucune beauté. (What part of the body does **visage** suggest?)
50.	It should suggest *visage* or *face.* Her face had no beauty.	**51.**	**maigre** × **gros** Son visage paraissait fort maigre.
51.	Her face appeared quite (very) thin.	**52.**	**aiguë** = *sharp, shrill* Sa voix était aiguë.
52.	Her voice was sharp.	**53.**	On n'aimait guère l'entendre parler parce que sa voix était si aiguë.
53.	One did not very much like to hear her speak because her voice was so sharp.	**54.**	**porter** = *to carry, to wear* Elle portait souvent une vieille robe toute noire.
54.	She often wore an old dress which was completely black.	**55.**	**un mouchoir d'indienne** = *a calico handkerchief* En toute saison elle portait un mouchoir d'indienne.
55.	In all seasons, she wore a calico handkerchief.	**56.**	La robe qu'elle portait n'était guère belle.
56.	The dress that she wore was scarcely beautiful.	**57.**	A vingt-cinq ans elle semblait déjà assez âgée. (**assez** = *quite/enough*)
57.	*quite* At 25, she already seemed quite old.	**58.**	Dès la cinquantaine, elle ne montra plus aucun âge.
58.	From fifty on, she no longer showed any age (she appeared ageless).	**59.**	**le bois** = *wood* Devenue maigre et silencieuse, elle semblait une femme en bois.
59.	Having become thin and silent, she seemed to be a woman made of wood.		

73. *The Past Perfect Tense*

1. Observe the verb forms in the following sentences:

Mme Aubin avait épousé un beau garçon sans fortune.	*Mme. Aubain had married a handsome but poor lad.*
Il était mort en 1809.	*He had died in 1809.*
Il lui avait laissé deux enfants très jeunes.	*He had left her two very young children.*
Elle s'était trouvée dans une situation désespérée.	*She had found herself in a desperate situation.*

2. The tense of the verb is the Past Perfect. It marks an action which took place before another past action or before a specified or implied past moment.

3. The Past Perfect tense is formed by the Imperfect of **avoir** or **être** plus the past participle. Remember that reflexive verbs are conjugated with **être** as are certain intransitive verbs of motion. **J'étais parti** is translated as *I had left*, not *I was left*.

INSTRUCTIONS: *As you read through the following exercises, circle the words which you do not recognize. Pay attention to the meanings of the verb tenses.*

	1. Il y avait eu à Babylone un jeune homme nommé Zadig.
1. There had been in Babylon a young man named Zadig.	**2.** Il avait cru pouvoir être heureux.
2. He had believed he could be happy (believed himself able).	**3.** La beauté et la fortune avaient rendu Sémire le premier parti de Babylone.
3. Beauty and wealth had made Sémire the best match in Babylone.	**4.** Les deux avaient touché au moment de leur bonheur.
4. The two had come to the moment of their happiness.	**5.** Ils avaient été attaqués.
5. They had been attacked.	**6.** Zadig avait défendu l'honneur de Sémire avec toute la force que donne l'amour.
6. Zadig had defended the honor of Sémire with all the force that love gives. (If you said "which gives love," make a note to review sec. 36.)	**7.** Sémire n'avait point été occupée de son danger.

7. Sémire had not been concerned (occupied) with her own danger.

8. She had thought only of Zadig.

9. The handsome young man whom Mme Aubain had married was poor.

10. He had died in 1809.

11. Before his death, he had accumulated nothing except a lot of debts.

12. He had left his wife two very young children.

13. Before her arrival in Pont-l'Evêque, she had sold all her real estate.

14. She had left her house at Saint-Melaine.

15. This house had belonged to her ancestors.

8. Elle n'avait pensé qu'à Zadig.

9. **un garçon**=*a boy, a young man*
Le beau garçon que Mme Aubain avait épousé était sans fortune.

10. Il était mort en 1809.

11. Avant sa mort, il n'avait amassé qu'une quantité de dettes.

12. Il avait laissé à sa femme deux enfants très jeunes.

13. **des immeubles** = *real estate, property*
Avant son arrivée à Pont–l'Evêque, Mme Aubain avait vendu tous ses immeubles.

14. **une maison**=*a house*
Elle avait quitté sa maison de Saint-Melaine.

15. **appartenir à**=*to belong to*
Cette maison avait appartenu à ses ancêtres.

Review the unfamiliar words until you can recognize them without difficulty.

74. *Past Anterior Tense*

1. Observe the following verb forms:

Aussitôt qu'il eut mis les ravisseurs en fuite, il ramena Sémire chez elle.

As soon as he had put the ravishers to flight, he took Sémire back to her house.

Dès qu'il fut revenu à lui-même . . .

As soon as he had regained consciousness . . .

2. The combination of the Past Definite of **avoir** or **être** plus the past participle forms the Past Anterior. It is a literary tense and is translated in the same way as the Past Perfect. It usually occurs after such expressions as **aussitôt que** (*as soon as*), **dès que** (*as soon as*), **après que** (*after*), and **quand** (*when*).

INSTRUCTIONS: *As you read through the following exercises, continue to pay special attention to the verb tenses.*

	1. Dès qu'ils eurent été attaqués, ils commencèrent à se défendre.
1. As soon as they had been attacked, they started to defend themselves.	**2.** **chez**=*to the house of, the home of* Après qu'il eut mis les ravisseurs en fuite, il ramena Sémire chez elle.
2. After he had put the ravishers to flight, he took Sémire back to her house.	**3.** **une nouvelle**=*a report, a bit of news* Aussitôt que le médecin eut vu l'abcès, il donna une mauvaise nouvelle.
3. As soon as the doctor had seen the abcess, he gave a bit of bad news.	**4.** **guérir**=*to heal, to get well* Dès que Zadig fut guéri, il alla rendre visite à Sémire.
4. As soon as Zadig had recovered, he went to visit Sémire.	**5.** Dès que le médecin eut guéri le malade, il demanda son argent.
5. As soon as the doctor had healed the sick person, he asked for his money.	**6.** Après que Mme Aubain eut vendu ses immeubles, elle vint à Pont–l'Evêque.
6. After Mme Aubain had sold her real estate, she came to Pont–l'Evêque.	**7.** Aussitôt qu'elle fut arrivée à Pont–l'Evêque, elle s'installa dans une maison qui avait appartenu à ses ancêtres. (Does **s'installer** mean *to move into* or *to move out of?*)
7. *to move into* As soon as she had arrived in Pont–l'Evêque, she moved into a house which had belonged to her ancestors.	

75.   *Infinitives After Prepositions*

1. Certain verbs, when followed by an infinitive, take a preposition, usually **à** or **de,** placed before the infinitive. In many cases you do not translate these prepositions (cf. section 10 and 11) :

Il commençait à étudier.	*He started to study.*
Nous tâchions de venir.	*We tried to come.*

2. Sometimes a better translation is obtained by using the *–ing* form of the English verb:

Ils cessaient de travailler.	*They stopped working.*
Vous aviez réussi à le faire.	*You had succeeded in doing it.*

3. After most other prepositions, translate the infinitive by the *–ing* form of the verb:

sans espérer	*without hoping*
avant d'aller	*before going*
après avoir montré	*after having shown*
après être sorti	*after having gone out*

4. The prepositions **pour** and **afin de** before an infinitive mean *in order to* and are in the nature of an intensifier of the verb. You may translate or not, according to the context:

Il est venu pour étudier (afin d'étudier).	*He came to study (in order to study).*
Pour expliquer cette affaire il nous faut du temps.	*To explain (in order to explain) this affair, we need some time.*
Pour ne pas manquer la messe	*In order not to miss Mass . . .*

5. Sometimes an infinitive by itself, with no preposition, when used as a subject or the object of a verb, will be translated by the *–ing* form of the verb:

Voir c'est croire.	*Seeing is believing.*
Ils voyaient venir à eux des hommes armés.	*They saw some armed men coming toward them.*

INSTRUCTIONS: *Translate the following sentences:*

	1. Nous tâchions de finir à temps.
1. We tried to finish on time.	**2.** Après s'être levé, on se lave. (Being the auxiliary of a reflexive verb, **être** is translated by *having/being*)
2. *having* After having gotten up, one washes up.	**3.** Après s'être couché, on s'endort.

3. After having gone to bed, one goes to sleep.	**4.** Elle s'était levée dès l'aube afin de partir.
4. She had gotten up at dawn in order to leave.	**5.** Nous n'avouons de petits défauts que pour persuader que nous n'en avons pas de grands. *La Rochefoucauld*
5. We admit to small defects only in order to persuade that we have no large ones.	**6.** **ce que**=*that (which)* La véritable éloquence consiste à dire tout ce qu'il faut, et à ne dire que ce qu'il faut. *La Rochefoucauld*
6. True eloquence consists in saying all that is necessary and in saying only that which is necessary.	**7.** Le désir de paraître habile empêche souvent de le devenir. *La Rochefoucauld*
7. The desire to appear clever often prevents becoming so. (**le** refers to the preceding idea)	**8.** C'est être bien habile que de savoir cacher son habileté. *La Rochefoucauld*
8. It is clever indeed to know how to conceal one's cleverness. (Notice that **que de** is not translated in this expression.)	**9.** **fou**=*mad, foolish* C'est être bien fou que de croire être sage tout seul. *La Rochefoucauld* (**sage**×**fou**)
9. It is to be foolish indeed to believe (oneself) to be wise all alone.	**10.** Pour être sage il faut l'aide d'autrui.
10. (In order) to be wise, the help of others is needed.	**11.** Partir c'est mourir un peu.
11. To take leave is to die a little bit.	**12.** Savoir c'est pouvoir.
12. Knowledge is power.	

76. *Review of* Faire

1. Some common **faire** idioms are:

Ils *font semblant* de travailler.	*They are pretending to work.*
Je *fais partie d'*un syndicat ouvrier.	*I belong to a labor union.*
On nous a *fait part de* votre maladie.	*We were informed of your illness.*

Nous ne désirons *faire de mal* à personne.	*We do not wish to harm anyone.*
Comment *se fait-il* que vous êtes ici?	*How does it happen that you are here?*
Elle *fait la cuisine*.	*She does the cooking.*
Elle *fait le ménage*.	*She does the housework.*

2. Remember that with **faire** expressions you may have to use several different English verbs to express your meaning.

INSTRUCTIONS: *What do the following sentences mean?*

		1.	Elle faisait la cuisine et le ménage.
1.	She did the cooking and the housework.	**2.**	Elle ne faisait que la cuisine et le ménage.
2.	She did only the cooking and the housework.	**3.**	Louis XVI fit un mal énorme à la monarchie.
3.	Louis XVI did an enormous amount of harm to the monarchy.	**4.**	**le pain**=*bread* On faisait exprès pour Félicité un gros pain de douze livres.
4.	They would make a big 12 pound loaf of bread especially for Félicité.	**5.**	Elle faisait l'impression d'une femme en bois.
5.	She gave the impression of a woman of wood.	**6.**	Son visage faisait l'impression d'être en bois.
6.	Her face gave the impression that it was made of wood.	**7.**	**son devoir**=*her duty* Faisant son devoir, elle travaillait sans plainte.
7.	Doing her duty, she worked without complaint.	**8.**	Ils ne font pas attention à vos plaintes.
8.	They do not pay any attention to your complaints.	**9.**	Au moment actuel, vous faites une étude de la langue française.
9.	At the present moment, you are making a study of the French language.	**10.**	La résonance magnétique fait l'objet d'un chapitre intéressant.
10.	Magnetic resonance is the subject of an interesting chapter.	**11.**	M. Aubain s'était fait une quantité de dettes.
11.	M. Aubain had accumulated a lot of debts.	**12.**	Quand il faisait beau, ils faisaient de longues promenades sous les palmiers.

12. When the weather was good, they would take long walks under the palm trees.	**13.** Quand il fait froid, on ne fait plus de promenades.
13. When it is cold, one no longer takes any walks.	**14.** Zadig ne désirait faire de mal à personne.
14. Zadig did not desire to harm anyone.	**15.** Zadig ne faisait pas semblant d'être malade.
15. Zadig was not pretending to be sick.	**16.** Il fit semblant de ne pas savoir la vérité.
16. He pretended not to know the truth.	**17.** Je ne savais pas la réponse, mais je faisais semblant de la savoir.
17. I did not know the answer, but I pretended to know it.	**18.** Roosevelt faisait partie du parti démocrate.
18. Roosevelt belonged to the Democratic party.	**19.** Orcan faisait partie de la conspiration.
19. Orcan was a part of the conspiracy.	**20.** On a fait part à Sémire de la blessure de Zadig. (**faire part de**=*inform of/belong to*)
20. *inform* Someone informed Sémire of Zadig's wound.	**21.** Comment se fait-il que vous ne faites plus de promenades?
21. Why is it that you no longer take any walks?	**22.** Félicité ne faisait que travailler.
22. Félicité did nothing but work.	**23.** Ils ne faisaient que se promener.
23. They did nothing but take walks.	**24.** Ils ne font que lire.
24. They do nothing but read.	**25.** Il semble que vous ne faites qu'apprendre à lire le français.
25. It seems that you are doing nothing but learning to read French.	**26.** Il s'ensuit que vous ne faites qu'étudier.
26. It follows that you do nothing but study.	

77. Faire *Followed by an Infinitive*

1. Faire followed by an infinitive expresses the meaning of *to cause*. Several different English constructions may be needed to make an adequate translation of its various meanings:

Il fait enregistrer ses bagages.	*He is having his baggage checked (is causing it to be checked).*
La baisse des eaux commençait à se faire sentir.	*The lowering of the water was beginning to make itself felt (to cause itself to be felt).*
C'est Louis XIV qui fit construire Versailles.	*It is Louis XIV who had Versailles built (caused to be built).*
Il fit partir l'ambassadeur.	*He sent the ambassador away (caused him to depart).*

2. Some of the common combinations of **faire** and infinitives are:

faire venir	*to send for (to cause to come)*
faire voir	*to show (to cause to be seen)*
faire savoir	*to inform (to cause to be known)*
faire remarquer	*to point out (to cause to be noticed)*

3. In the construction **faire faire quelque chose à quelqu'un** (to cause someone to do something) the **à** indicates the performer of the second action. The phrase may be translated by an active or a passive construction:

Le roi fit payer les impôts exacts aux privilégiés.	*The king obliged the privileged to pay the full taxes.* or *The king caused the full taxes to be paid by the privileged.*
La jalousie fit penser à Orcan qu'il aimait Sémire.	*Jealousy caused Orcan to think that he loved Sémire.*

INSTRUCTIONS: *What are the meanings of the following sentences? Remember that with* **faire** *expressions you may have to use several different English verbs to express your meanings.*

	1. La jalousie fit penser à Orcan qu'il aimait Sémire.
1. Jealousy caused Orcan to think that he loved Sémire.	**2.** accroire = *croire* Des courtisans avaient fait accroire à Orcan qu'il valait mieux que les autres.

2.	Courtiers had led Orcan to believe that he was superior to others (worth more).	**3.**	**envoyer**=*to send* Il fit envoyer des hommes armés pour saisir Sémire.
3.	He had some armed men sent to seize Sémire.	**4.**	**couler**=*to flow* Dans leur violence, ils firent couler le sang de cette dame innocente et pure.
4.	In their violence they caused the blood of this pure and innocent lady to flow.	**5.**	Zadig a fait voir son courage.
5.	Zadig showed his courage.	**6.**	C'est le roi qui fait envoyer des ambassadeurs à des pays étrangers.
6.	It is the king who has ambassadors sent to foreign countries.	**7.**	Il fit fuir les ravisseurs.
7.	He caused the abductors to flee.	**8.**	On fit venir le plus grand médecin du pays.
8.	They sent for the greatest doctor in the country.	**9.**	Le médecin fit aussitôt remarquer la gravité de la blessure.
9.	The doctor immediately pointed out the gravity of the wound.	**10.**	Elle faisait faire la cuisine à sa servante.
10.	She had her servant do the cooking. (She had the cooking done by her servant)	**11.**	C'est à sa servante qu'elle fait faire la cuisine.
11.	It is her servant that she has do the cooking.	**12.**	Elle n'a jamais su faire faire le ménage à son mari.
12.	She was never able to have her husband do the housework (to have the housework done by her husband).	**13.**	Le roi fit payer les impôts exacts aux aristocrates.
13.	The king made the aristocrats pay the full taxes (caused the full taxes to be paid by the aristocrats).	**14.**	Le roi ne faisait pas peur à ses courtisans.
14.	The king did not frighten his courtiers. (Notice that there is no infinitive following **faire**—therefore **à** does not refer to the performer of any action.)	**15.**	On faisait faire exprès pour elle un gros pain de douze livres.
15.	They would have a big twelve pound loaf of bread baked expressly for her.	**16.**	Je ne parviens pas à comprendre son raisonnement.

16. I cannot manage to understand his reasoning.	**17.** Il n'est pas parvenu à se faire comprendre.
17. He did not manage to make himself understood.	**18.** La baisse des eaux se faisait sentir.
18. The lowering of the water was making itself felt.	**19.** **enfin**=*finally, at last* Il est enfin parvenu à faire accepter son idée.
19. He at last managed to have his idea accepted.	**20.** Il parvint enfin à se faire accepter.
20. He at last managed to get himself accepted.	**21.** Son influence s'est enfin fait sentir.
21. His influence made itself felt at last.	**22.** Il a pu enfin faire accepter cette idée à ses confrères.
22. He was at last able to get this idea accepted by his colleagues.	**23.** Le poids de ses raisons s'était enfin fait sentir.
23. The weight of his reasons had at last made itself felt.	

VOCABULARY DEVELOPMENT

INSTRUCTIONS: *Part of the process of vocabulary development is the association of word families. Below the meaning of a root word is given to you. Try to arrive at the meanings of the related words.*

	1. **épouser**=*to marry* M. Aubain était l'époux de Mme Aubain. **l'époux**=_____ **l'épouse**=_____
1. *the husband* *the wife*	**2.** **blesser**=*to wound* (false cognate) Sa blessure à la tête n'était pas grave. **une blessure**=_____
2. *a wound*	**3.** Le blessé fut apporté à l'hôpital. **le blessé**=_____
3. *the wounded person*	**4.** Il a offensé tout le monde par ses remarques blessantes. **une remarque blessante**=_____

4. *an unkind or cutting remark*	**5.** **le sang**=*the blood* Après avoir été blessé, il saignait avec profusion. **saigner**=_____
5. *to bleed*	**6.** **un bifteck saignant**= _____
6. *a rare beefstake*	**7.** On le rapporta chez lui tout sanglant. **sanglant**=_____
7. *bleeding, bloody*	**8.** **ravir**=*to ravish, to abduct, to carry off; (fig.) to charm, to entrance* Il parvint à mettre les ravisseurs en fuite. **un ravisseur**=_____
8. *a ravisher, a kidnapper, an abductor*	**9.** **un ravissement**=_____
9. *a kidnapping, an abduction; rapture, delight*	**10.** Elle chante bien, et elle est très belle. C'est **une femme ravissante**= _____
10. *an entrancing, charming woman*	**11.** **un palmier**=*palm tree* **un pêcher**=_____
11. *peach tree*	**12.** **un oranger**=_____
12. *orange tree*	**13.** **un poirier**=_____
13. *pear tree*	**14.** **un cerisier**=_____
14. *cherry tree* (the ending **–er** or **–ier** affixed to the name of a fruit, as you have probably guessed, denotes the tree from which the fruit comes)	

TESTING EXERCISE

INSTRUCTIONS: *Circle the letter in the first frame which completes the sentence grammatically or which represents the best rendering in English.*

1. Tous les matins **elle se levait** dès l'aube.
A. was getting up   B. had gotten up   C. used to get up   D. gets up

1. C   **2.** **Tandis que** Zadig défendait Sémire, celle-ci perçait le ciel de ses plaintes.
(72)   A. while   B. although   C. after   D. before.

---

2. A (72)

3. Elle **était devenue** vieille et laide.
A. was becoming B. became C. had become D. would become.

3. C (73)

4. Elle **s'était trouvée** dans une situation désespérée.
A. found herself C. was finding herself
B. used to find herself D. had found herself.

4. D (73)

5. **Après être sorti,** il eut honte de ses actes.
A. without going out C. while going out
B. before going out D. after having gone out.

5. D (75)

6. Nous tâchions **de venir.**
A. to come B. from coming C. after coming D. without coming

6. A (75)

7. M. Aubain **s'était fait** une quantité de dettes.
A. did B. had accumulated C. had undertaken D. was making

7. B (73)

8. Le médecin **fit aussitôt remarquer la gravité de la blessure.**
A. also mentioned the seriousness of the wound.
B. immediately pointed out the seriousness of the wound.
C. caused another remark to be made about the seriousness of the wound.
D. again caused the wound to become worse.

8. B (76)

9. **Nous faisons semblant** de nous amuser.
A. we try to C. we always seemed
B. we are desirous of D. we pretend to

9. D (76)

10. Il paraît que **vous ne faites que lire.**
A. you cause (them) to read. C. you do nothing but read.
B. you have someone read to you. D. you do not read.

10. C (76)

Now review the section indicated for those you missed.

Zadig et les femmes

d'après *Zadig* par Voltaire

Du temps du roi Moabdar, il y avait à Babylone un jeune homme nommé Zadig, **né** [1] avec un beau **naturel** [2] fortifié par l'éducation. **Quoique** [3] riche et jeune, il savait modérer ses passions; il n'affectait rien, il ne voulait point toujours avoir raison, et savait respecter la faiblesse des hommes. Zadig,
5 avec de grandes richesses, et par conséquent avec des amis, avait de **la santé,** [4] **une figure** [5] aimable, un esprit juste et modéré, un cœur sincère et noble, et crut qu'il pouvait être heureux. Il **devait** [6] se marier à Sémire, **que** [7] sa

1 *born* 4 *health* 7 *whose*
2 *disposition* 5 *face*
3 *although* 6 *was to*

beauté, sa naissance et sa fortune rendaient le premier parti de Babylone. Il avait pour elle un attachement solide et vertueux, et Sémire aimait Zadig
10   avec passion.

Ils touchaient au moment fortuné qui devait les unir, lorsque se promenant **ensemble** [8] vers **une porte** [9] de Babylone, sous les palmiers qui ornaient les rivages (les bords) de l'Euphrate, ils virent venir à eux des hommes armés de sabres et **de flèches.** [10] C'étaient les satellites du jeune Orcan, neveu
15   d'un ministre, à qui les courtisans de son oncle avaient fait accroire que tout lui était permis. Il n'avait aucune des grâces ni des vertus de Zadig; mais croyant valoir beaucoup mieux, il était désespéré de n'être pas préféré. Cette jalousie, qui ne venait que de sa vanité, fit penser à Orcan qu'il aimait **éperduement** [11] Sémire. Les ravisseurs la saisirent, et dans **les emporte-**
20   **ments** [12] de leur violence ils la blessèrent, et firent couler le sang d'une personne **dont la vue** [13] était capable d'attendrir les tigres du mont Imaus.

Elle perçait le ciel de ses plaintes. Elle s'écriait: "Mon cher époux, on m'**arrache** [14] à celui que j'adore". Elle n'était point occupée de son danger, elle ne pensait qu'à son cher Zadig. Celui-ci, dans le même temps, **la** [15]
25   défendait avec toute la force que donnent la valeur et l'amour. Aidé seule- ment de deux **esclaves,** [16] il **mit** [17] les ravisseurs en fuite et ramena **chez elle** [18] Sémire, évanouie et sanglante, qui en ouvrant **les yeux,** [19] vit son libérateur. Elle **lui** [20] dit: "O Zadig! je vous aimais comme mon époux, je vous aime comme celui **à qui je dois** [21] l'honneur et la vie."
30   Jamais sentiments ne furent inspirés par une plus grande **reconnais- sance** [22] et un amour plus pur et légitime. Jamais il n'y eut un coeur plus pénétré que celui de Sémire. Jamais bouche plus ravissante n'exprima **des sentiments** [23] plus touchants. Sa blessure était légère. Elle guérit bientôt.

Zadig était blessé plus dangereusement: **une flèche** [24] reçue près de
35   **l'œil** [25] lui avait fait une blessure profonde. Un abcès forma. On fit venir le grand médecin Hermès, qui vint avec un grand nombre de suivants. Il visita le malade, et déclara que l'œil était irrévocablement perdu. Deux jours après l'abcès perça de lui-même et Zadig fut bientôt parfaitement guéri. Dès qu'il put sortir, il se prépara à rendre visite à Sémire, mais il
40   sut par un ami que cette belle dame, en apprenant la nouvelle du médecin, avait déclaré une aversion insurmontable pour **les borgnes** [26] et s'était mariée à Orcan lui-même.

A cette nouvelle Zadig tomba sans connaissance. Dès qu'il fut revenu à lui- même, il s'écria, "O vertu! **A quoi m'avez-vous servi?** [27] O fidélité! O
45   bonheur! Où êtes-vous dans ce monde?"

---

8 *together*
9 *gate*
10 *arrows*
11 *desperately*
12 *transport*
13 *the sight of whom*
14 *to tear away*

15 *her*
16 *slaves*
17 *put*
18 *to her house*
19 *eyes*
20 *to him*
21 *to whom I owe*

22 *gratitude*
23 *feelings*
24 *arrow*
25 *the eye*
26 *one-eyed men*
27 *What use have you been to me?*

1. In lines 1–4 the author states that Zadig
A. respected the weakness of others   C. lacked self-control
B. always wanted to have his own way   D. was young but poor

---

1. A

2. In lines 4–10 the author states that Zadig:
A. was in poor health
B. did not have many friends
C. was about to marry a beautiful but somewhat impoverished girl
D. was to marry the best catch in Babylon

---

2. D

3. In lines 11–19 the author states that:
A. while on a walk after their marriage Zadig and his wife met some armed men
B. Orcan had all the good qualities of Zadig
C. the minister's nephew was heartbroken not to be preferred
D. the followers of Orcan were armed with rifles and pistols

---

3. C

4. In lines 19–21 the author states that:
A. Orcan's men seized Sémire gently by the arm
B. they looked as fierce as the tigers of Mt. Imaus
C. in the struggle Sémire was wounded
D. Zadig became as vain as he was jealous

---

4. C

5. In lines 22–29 it is stated that:
A. Zadig rescued Sémire by himself
B. with the help of two slaves he put the abductors to flight
C. Sémire resisted her attackers with all her might
D. Zadig carried her unconscious but unscathed to her home

---

5. B

6. In lines 30–37 it is stated that:
A. Sémire secretly loved Orcan
B. the great doctor Hermès said that Zadig would unquestionably lose the sight of the eye
C. Zadig received a sabre cut over one eye
D. several attending doctors disagreed with this verdict

---

6. B

7. In lines 38–45 it is stated that:
A. when Sémire heard the doctor's pronouncement she said that she would only love Zadig the more
B. true to the doctor's prediction Zadig lost the sight of one eye
C. Orcan exclaimed: "Virtue and faithfulness will yet bring happiness in this world."
D. when Zadig heard that Sémire had married Orcan, he fainted

---

7. D

Un coeur simple

G. Flaubert—"Trois Contes" (1877)

Pendant un demi-siècle, les bourgeoises de Pont-l'Evêque envièrent à Mme Aubain sa servante Félicité.

Pour cent francs par an, elle faisait la cuisine et resta fidèle à sa maîtresse, qui cependant n'était pas une personne agréable.

5   Elle (Mme Aubain) avait épousé un beau garçon sans fortune, mort au commencement de 1809, **en lui laissant** [1] deux enfants très jeunes avec une quantité de dettes. Alors elle vendit tous ses immeubles, **sauf la ferme** [2] de Toucques et la ferme de Geffosses, et elle quitta sa maison de Saint-Melaine pour en habiter une autre moins **dispendieuse,** [3] ayant appartenu à ses
10   ancêtres et placée derrière les **halles** [4] . . . .

Félicité se levait dès l'aube, pour ne pas manquer la messe, et travaillait jusqu'au soir sans interruption; puis le dîner étant fini, **la vaisselle** [5] en ordre et la porte bien close, elle **enfouissait la bûche** [6] sous les cendres et s'endormait devant **l'âtre,** [7] son rosaire à la main. Personne dans les mar-
15   chandages ne montrait plus d'**entêtement.** [8] **Quant à** [9] la propreté, le poli de ses casseroles faisait le désespoir des autres servantes. Econome, elle mangeait avec lenteur, et **recueillait du doigt** [10] sur la table les **miettes** [11] de son pain, un de douze livres, **cuit** [12] exprès pour elle, et qui durait vingt jours.

20   En toute saison elle portait **un mouchoir d'indienne** [13] fixé **dans le dos** [14] par **une épingle.** [15]

Son visage était maigre et sa voix aiguë. A vingt-cinq ans, on **lui en donnait** [16] quarante. Dès la cinquantaine (50), elle ne montra plus aucun âge; et toujours silencieuse, **la taille droite** [17] et les gestes mesurés, elle
25   semblait une femme en bois, fonctionnant d'une manière automatique.

---

1. Lines 1–10 state that:
A. Mrs. Aubain's servant, Felicité, was a constant source of gossip to the townspeople of Pont-l'Evêque
B. Mrs. Aubain was a pleasant person who had no difficulty getting domestic help
C. she was widowed in 1809 and left with two young children and many debts
D. she sold all her property and with the money thus raised, moved to a more elaborate house, once owned by her ancestors.

---

1. C   **2.** Lines 11–25 state that:
A. Felicité was a hard worker and deeply religious

1 *leaving her with*	7 *hearth*	13 *calico handkerchief*
2 *except the farm*	8 *obstinacy*	14 *in the back*
3 *expensive*	9 *as for*	15 *pin*
4 *the market*	10 *gathered with her fingers*	16 *gave her*
5 *the dishes*	11 *crumbs*	17 *the figure erect*
6 *buried the log*	12 *baked (cooked)*	

B. she had a soft heart and often allowed herself to be bested in the bargaining of the market place

C. her housekeeping methods were the laughing stock of the town

D. at the age of fifty, she still retained some of the grace of youth and did her work with the energy of a person twenty-five years younger.

2. A

Chapter Twelve

REVIEW: All of the materials you have studied thus far are indispensable to your future progress. Reread the items you circled it Chapters Ten and Eleven before you start Chapter Twelve.

78. *The Subjunctive Mood—Present Tense*

1. In French you will meet a category of verbs which has no direct counterpart in English. This category is the Subjunctive mood. It has four tenses: the Present, the Imperfect, the Past Indefinite, and the Past Perfect. Although in theory the Subjunctive mood suggests that the action of the verb is viewed from a subjective point of view (as opposed to the objective, factual point of view of the Indicative), the Subjunctive forms do not differ basically in meaning from the Indicative forms you have already learned. The only difficulties they present are the recognition of another set of patterns and occasionally the finding of a different English structure to translate the accompanying conjunction or phrase (see below).

2. The Present Subjunctive endings for all verbs except **être** and **avoir** are —e, —es, —e, —ions, —iez, and —ent. The regular stem for the Subjunctive is the same as for the Imperfect (the **nous** form of the Present minus the Present ending—see section 72).

3.   Observe the following models of the Subjunctive as contrasted with the Indicative. Notice that the subjunctive forms of **–ir** and **–re** verbs differ in all except the **ils** form:

INDICATIVE	SUBJUNCTIVE	
je trouve (*I find*)	Il faut que je trouve	(*It is necessary for*
tu trouves	Il faut que tu trouves	*me to find*, etc.)
il trouve	Il faut qu'il trouve	
nous trouvons	Il faut que nous trouvions	
vous trouvez	Il faut que vous trouviez	
ils trouvent	Il faut qu'ils trouvent	
je finis (*I finish*)	Il se peut que je finisse	(*It is possible for*
tu finis	Il se peut que tu finisses	*me to finish*, etc.)
il finit	Il se peut qu'il finisse	
nous finissons	Il se peut que nous finissions	
vous finissez	Il se peut que vous finissiez	
ils finissent	Il se peut qu'ils finissent	
je vends (*I sell*)	Il vaut mieux que je vende	(*It is better for me*
tu vends	Il vaut mieux que tu vendes	*to sell*, etc.)
il vend	Il vaut mieux qu'il vende	
nous vendons	Il vaut mieux que nous vendions	
vous vendez	Il vaut mieux que vous vendiez	
ils vendent	Il vaut mieux qu'ils vendent	

4.   All present Subjunctive forms may be translated by the English present, future, or possible future, depending on the context:

Il est possible qu'il finisse sa lecture aujourd'hui.	*It is possible he is finishing his reading today*, or *He may finish his reading today.*
Il est possible qu'il finisse ses devoirs demain.	*It is possible he will finish his homework tomorrow*, or *He may finish his homework tomorrow.*

5.   You may expect to find the subjunctive in dependent clauses following verbs of *will* or *emotion:*

Je veux qu'il parte	*I want him to leave.*
Je suis heureux que vous veniez.	*I am happy that you are coming.*

READING PREPARATION

INSTRUCTIONS: *As you read the following French sentences, cover the English with your card. Continue to circle new or unfamiliar vocabulary.*

1. **un échec**=*a failure*
   Il se peut que nos chercheurs subissent d'abord des échecs.

1. It is possible that our researchers will at first suffer some failures.

2. Il se peut que vous subissiez d'abord quelques échecs.

2. -It is possible that you will suffer a few failures at first.

3. Je regrette qu'il subisse tant d'échecs.

3. I regret that he is suffering so many failures.

4. Il est nécessaire que l'on agisse prudemment dans ce domaine.

4. It is necessary to act prudently in this area.
   (remember that **l'** preceding **on** has no grammatical meaning)

5. **plein**=*full*
   Je suis heureux que vos travaux paraissent si pleins de promesses.

5. I am happy that your work appears so full of promise.
   (Notice that some plural French nouns may have to be translated by a singular English noun.)

6. **étendre**=*to extend*
   Pour faire des progrès futurs il faut que nous étendions nos connaissances des rayons X.

6. In order to make future progress, it is necessary for us to extend our knowledge of X-rays.

7. Pour lire couramment le français, il faut qu'on étende ses connaissances de la grammaire.

7. In order to read French fluently, one must extend one's knowledge of grammar.

8. Cependant, il ne faut pas que vous limitiez vos études à la grammaire.

8. However, you must not limit your studies to grammar.

9. Il se peut que l'évidence des progrès considérables apparaisse grâce à nos études.

9. It is possible that evidence of considerable progress will appear because of (thanks to) our studies.

10. **aboutir à**=*to lead to, to end up at*
    Il se peut qu'un effort collectif aboutisse à la mesure de la charge de l'électron.

10. It is possible that a collective effort may lead to the measuring of the electron charge.

11. Il est alors possible que nous aboutissions à des découvertes importantes.

11. It is then possible that we will end up by making some important discoveries.

12. **pousser**=*to push*
    Il faut que nous poussions plus avant dans la connaissance des phénomènes atomiques.

12. We must push further ahead in the knowledge of atomic phenomena.

13. Pour pousser plus avant, il faut que nous trouvions une aide matérielle à nos travaux.

13. In order to push further ahead, we must find some material support for our work.

14. Pour vous rendre compte des grands progrès que l'on a faits dernièrement dans ce domaine, il faut que vous lisiez tous les articles qui paraissent actuellement.

14. In order for you to realize the great progress that has been made lately in this area, you must read all the articles which are presently appearing.

15. **bouleverser**=*to overturn*
Il se peut que la science moderne aboutisse à un bouleversement à peu près complet des notions précédentes.

15. It is possible that modern science will (may) result in a nearly complete overturning of previous ideas.

16. Il faut qu'on rende plus accessibles aux chercheurs les données de la science moderne.

16. It is necessary to make the data of modern science more accessible to researchers.

17. Il faut également que l'on rende plus facile l'étude des langues.

17. It is also necessary to make the study of languages easier.

18. Il est possible que dans quelques années la science atteigne son développement essentiel.

18. It is possible that in a few years science will attain its essential development (will develop everything essential to it).

19. Il se peut, toutefois, que nous subissions des échecs en poussant plus avant.

19. We might, however, suffer some setbacks while pushing further ahead.

20. Je suis content que l'importance de cet effort collectif apparaisse clairement.

20. I am happy that the importance of this collective effort appears clearly.

21. **éclore**=*to appear, to blossom*
Il est possible que l'éclosion de la science moderne bouleverse la plupart des notions précédentes.

21. It is possible that the advent of modern science will overturn most previous ideas.

22. Il se peut que d'ici quelques années nous voyions la pleine éclosion d'une science nouvelle.

22. It is possible that a few years from now we will see the full flowering of a new science.

Review before continuing.

79.   *Present Subjunctive of* avoir *and* être *and Past Indefinite Tense*

1.   The Present Subjunctive forms of **avoir** and **être,** as might be expected, are completely irregular:

j'aie	(*I have, will have,*	**je sois**	(*I am, will be, may*
tu aies	*may have, etc.*)	**tu sois**	*be,*'etc.*)
il ait		**il soit**	
nous ayons		**nous soyons**	
vous ayez		**vous soyez**	
ils aient		**ils soient**	

2.   In the compound tenses of the Subjunctive the above forms of the auxiliaries are followed by the past participles. Do not forget that the forms of the verb **être** are to be translated as the comparable forms of the verb **avoir** when you are dealing with intransitive verbs (section 31):

Je doute qu'elles soient venues.	*I doubt that they have come.*
Il se peut qu'ils aient trouvé la solution.	*It is possible that they have found the solution.*

3.   Some impersonal expressions which are followed by the subjunctive are:

il convient que	*it is proper, fitting, advisable*
il est convenable que	*it is proper, fitting*
il faut que	*it is necessary*
il importe que	*it is important*
il semble que	*it seems*
il se peut que	*it is possible*
il est dommage que	*it is a shame*
il vaut mieux que	*it is better, preferable*
il est heureux que	*it is fortunate*
il est bon que	*it is good*
il est essentiel que	*it is essential*
il est faux que	*it is false*
il est impossible que	*it is impossible*
il est juste que	*it is just, right*
il est possible que	*it is possible*
il est rare que	*it is rare*
il est temps que	*it is time*

INSTRUCTIONS: *Continue to cover the English verification with your card while you read the French.*

1.   Je doute qu'ils soient d'accord.

1. I doubt they (will) agree (are in agreement.)

2. Il est possible cependant que vous soyez d'accord avec les projets du nouveau laboratoire.

2. It is possible, however, that you may agree with the projects (plans) of the new laboratory.

3. Il importe que nous soyons au courant de ces projets.

3. It is important for us to be aware of these projects.

4. Il se peut que je ne sois pas tout à fait au courant des développements les plus récents.

4. It is possible that I am not fully aware of the most recent developments.

5. **une équipe** = *a team*
Il est essentiel qu'une équipe de jeunes physiciens soit formée.

5. It is essential that a team of young physicists be formed (for a team to be formed).

6. **un outil** = *a tool*
Il faut de plus que l'outillage du nouveau laboratoire soit suffisant.

6. In addition, it is necessary that the tools (or equipment) of the new laboratory be adequate.

7. Il est heureux que nous ayons les moyens d'équiper un tel laboratoire.

7. It is fortunate that we have the means of equipping such a laboratory.

8. **dépenser** = *to spend*
les dépenses = _____

8. *The expenses,* or *expenditures*

9. Il est possible que vous n'ayez pas une idée exacte de l'étendue des dépenses que comporte un nouveau laboratoire.

9. It is possible that you do not have an exact (correct) idea of the extent of the expenditures that a new laboratory entails.

10. Il ne semble pas qu'ils aient raison de tant insister sur ces projets extravagants.

10. It doesn't seem that they are right in insisting so much on these extravagant projects.

11. Il faut naturellement que ces jeunes physiciens aient les moyens de vivre.

11. It is naturally necessary for these young physicists to have the means to live (to be able to live).

12. **se former** = *to be trained*
Il faut de plus qu'on ait le temps de se former aux disciplines sévères de la recherche expérimentale.

12. In addition, they must have the time to be trained in the severe disciplines of experimental research.
(Remember that reflexive verbs can often be translated by the passive.)

13. Le directeur du nouveau laboratoire exige qu'ils soient bien au courant des méthodes nouvelles.

13.	The director of the new laboratory requires that they be well informed of new methods.	**14.**	**un but** =*a purpose* Il est temps alors que nous précisions nos buts.
14.	It is time, then, for us to specify our purposes.	**15.**	Il convient toutefois que nous expliquions les détails de nos projets.
15.	It is advisable, however, for us to explain the details of our projects (plans).	**16.**	Il est peu probable d'ailleurs que j'aie les moyens d'effectuer cette oeuvre tout seul.
16.	It is unlikely, moreover, that I will have the means of effecting this work all alone.	**17.**	Je regrette toutefois que je n'aie pas le temps de m'expliquer davantage.
17.	I regret, however, that I do not have the time to explain myself more at length.	**18.**	Il est peu probable qu'ils aient eu les moyens d'effectuer ce travail tout seuls.
18.	It is unlikely that they (have) had the means of effecting this work all alone.	**19.**	Je regrette d'ailleurs que je n'aie pas eu le temps de m'expliquer davantage.
19.	I regret, moreover, that I did not have (have not had) the time to explain myself more at length.	**20.**	Il est dommage que je ne me sois pas expliqué davantage.
20.	It is a shame that I did not explain (have not explained) myself at greater length.	**21.**	Pour faire un travail sérieux, il faut qu'on soit formé aux disciplines de la recherche scientifique.
21.	In order to do serious work one must be trained in the discipline(s) of scientific research.	**22.**	Il faut d'ailleurs qu'on ait eu le temps de se former à ces disciplines.
22.	One must, moreover, have had the time to be trained in this (these) discipline(s).	**23.**	Il est dommage que vous ne vous soyez pas formé davantage aux disciplines de la recherche.
23.	It is a shame that you have not had (did not have) more training in the discipline(s) of research.	**24.**	Il est dommage que vous n'ayez pas pu vous expliquer davantage.
24.	It is a shame that you were not (have not been) able to explain yourself at greater length.	**25.**	Il est dommage, toutefois, qu'il n'ait pas voulu s'expliquer davantage.
25.	It is a shame, however, that he did not want to explain himself at greater length.		Review and then continue.

80.   *Conjunctions Occurring with the Subjunctive*

1.   The **nous** and **vous** forms of the Present Subjunctive and the Imperfect Indicative are sometimes confused, being spelled the same way for many verbs. To determine whether a verb is in the Imperfect Indicative or in the Present Subjunctive, look at the preceding clause or conjunction. If one of the impersonal expressions (section 79–3) or one of the following conjunctions precedes the verb, the verb is a Subjunctive form:

Vous soupçonniez l'existence des rayonnements cosmiques, mais vous n'aviez pas de preuves.	*You suspected the existence of cosmic radiation but you **had** no proof.*
Quoique (bien que) vous soupçonniez l'existence des rayonnements cosmiques, vous n'avez pas de preuves.	*Although you suspect the existence of cosmic radiation, you have no proof.*
A cette époque nous avancions plus vite que maintenant.	*At that time we were advancing more rapidly than now.*
Pour que (afin que) nous avancions dans les recherches expérimentales, il faut que nous ayons les moyens de vivre.	*In order for us to advance in experimental research, we must have the means to live.*
Nous trouvions ces procédés plus efficaces.	*We found these procedures more efficient.*
En attendant que (jusqu'à ce que) nous trouvions des procédés plus efficaces, les questions demeurent sans réponse.	*Until we find more efficient procedures, the questions remain unanswered.*

2.   Other conjunctions followed by the Subjunctive are:

sans que	*unless, without that*
au cas que	*in case that*
de sorte que	*so that, in such a way that*
nonobstant que	*in spite of the fact that*
pourvu que	*provided that*
supposé que	*supposing that*

3.   The following expressions are **not** followed by the Subjunctive:

après que	*after*
parce que	*because*
pendant que	*while*
tandis que	*while, whereas*

| **puisque** | since, because |
| **ainsi que** | just as, in the same way |

INSTRUCTIONS: *Can you distinguish the imperfect from the present subjunctive in these phrases?*

1. Afin que notre projet réussisse . . .

1. In order for our project to succeed . . .

2. Sans que notre projet réussisse . . .

2. Unless our project succeeds . . .

3. En attendant que notre projet réussisse . . .

3. Until our project succeeds . . .

4. Jusqu'à ce que notre hypothèse soit confirmée . . .

4. Until our hypothesis is confirmed . . .

5. Sans que notre hypothèse soit confirmée . . .

5. Unless our hypothesis is confirmed . . .

6. Pourvu que les faits confirment notre hypothèse . . .

6. Provided that the facts confirm our hypothesis . . .

7. Ils ont néanmoins continué le projet sans que leur hypothèse soit confirmée.

7. They nonetheless continued the project without their hypothesis being confirmed.

8. Au cas que cette première condition ne soit pas réalisée . . .

8. In case this initial condition is not fulfilled (met) . . .

9. Quoique cette première condition ne soit pas réalisée . . .

9. Although this first condition is not fulfilled . . .

10. Afin que le projet d'un laboratoire se réalise . . .

10. In order for the project of a laboratory to materialize . . .
   (Note that **se** is the reflexive verb employed here.)

11. Pendant que vous vous formiez aux disciplines attachantes de la recherche expérimentale . . .

11. While you were being trained in the fascinating discipline(s) of experimental research . . .

12. Sans que vous vous formiez aux disciplines sévères de la recherche expérimentale . . .

12. Unless you are trained in the strict discipline of experimental research . . .

13. **un appui**=support, aid
   Parce que vous donniez votre appui à cette oeuvre collective . . .

13. Because you gave your support to this collective work . . .

14. Sans que vous donniez votre appui à cette oeuvre . . .

14. Unless you give your support to this work . . .

15. rédiger=*to write up*
Pour que nous rédigions les résultats de nos travaux . . .
(**rédigions**—*imperfect/present subjunctive*)

15. *present subjunctive*—it follows **pour que**
In order for us to write up the results of our work . . .

16. Tandis que nous rédigions les résultats de nos travaux . . .
(**rédigions**—*imperfect/present subjunctive*)

16. *imperfect*—it follows **tandis que**
While we were writing up the results of our work . . .

17. Jusqu'à ce que nous poussions plus avant dans la connaissance des phénomènes atomiques . . .
(**poussions**=*imperfect/present subjunctive*)

17. *present subjunctive*—it follows **jusqu'à ce que**
Until we push further ahead in the knowledge of atomic phenomena . . .

18. Puisque nous poussions plus avant . . .
(**poussions**=*imperfect/present subjunctive*)

18. *imperfect*—it follows **puisque**
Since we were pushing further ahead . . .

19. Nonobstant que nous connaissions la plupart des découvertes modernes . . .

19. In spite of the fact that we know about most of the modern discoveries . . .

20. Puisque nous connaissions la plupart des découvertes modernes . . .

20. Since we knew about most of the modern discoveries . . .

21. Pour qu'on voie l'éclosion d'une nouvelle science, il faut des appuis matériels.

21. In order for us to see the advent of a new science, material support is needed.
(Note the translation of a French plural by an English singular.)

22. Quoiqu'on voie actuellement l'éclosion d'une nouvelle époque, il reste bien des obstacles à surmonter.

22. Although we presently are seeing the birth of a new epoch, many obstacles remain to overcome (surmount).

23. Jusqu'à ce que cette première condition soit réalisée, il ne peut rien sortir d'intéressant.

23. Until this first condition is met, nothing interesting can result.
(**Il** here is used impersonally.)

24. Nous ne pouvons rien faire d'intéressant sans que nous nous formions aux disciplines de la recherche expérimentale.

24.	We can do nothing interesting unless we are trained (without being trained) in the discipline(s) of experimental research.	**25.**	Il faut agir de sorte que nous réalisions toutes les conditions nécessaires.
25.	We must act in such a way that we fulfill all of the necessary conditions.	**26.**	Quoique vous donniez votre appui à cette oeuvre, elle ne peut guère réussir.
26.	Although you may give this work your support, it can scarcely succeed.	**27.**	Sans que nous rédigions les résultats de nos expériences de sorte qu'on puisse les étudier, notre travail va être inutile.
27.	Unless we write up the results of our experiments so that they may be studied, our work is going to be useless.	**28.**	Sans que nous nous formions aux disciplines de la recherche, nous ne pouvons rien faire d'important.
28.	Unless we are trained (without being trained) in the discipline(s) of research, we can do nothing important.		

81. *Pleonastic* ne

1. You have learned **ne** as an element of negation. There are certain French constructions, however, in which **ne** is pleonastic (superfluous). In these cases **ne** has no grammatical meaning and does not negate the verb.

2. Pleonastic **ne** is often found
   (1) in a clause following a comparison:

Il est plus riche que je *ne* croyais.	*He is richer than I believed.*
Il fait meilleur temps aujourd'hui qu'il *ne* faisait hier.	*The weather is better today than it was yesterday.*

   (2) in connection with the following conjunctions, which take the Subjunctive:

A moins que **vous *ne* rédigiez les résultats de vos travaux, personne ne peut les savoir.**	*Unless you write up the results of your work, no one can know about them.*
Avant que **vous *ne* rédigiez les résultats de vos recherches, il faut que vous finissiez vos expériences.**	*Before you write up the results of your research, you must finish your experiments.*

De crainte que (**de peur que**) vous *n*'**attendiez trop longtemps, il faut que vous rédigiez vos résultats dès maintenant.**	*For fear that* (*lest*) *you might wait too long, you must write up your results right now.*

(3)   with verbs of doubt used negatively or interrogatively:

Vous ne pouvez *nier* **qu'il n'ait raison.**	*You cannot deny that he is right.*
Niez-vous **qu'il n'ait raison?**	*Do you deny that he is right?*

3.   A second element of negation (**pas, point, plus, aucun,** etc.) will make the sentence negative.

A moins que vous ne trouviez *rien* . . .	*Unless you find **nothing** . . .*
De crainte que vous n'attendiez *pas* **assez longtemps** . . .	*Lest you **not** wait long enough . . .*

4.   Other expressions of fear follow the same pattern:

Je crains qu'il ne soit à l'heure.	*I am afraid he may be on time.*
Je crains qu'il ne soit *pas* **à l'heure.**	*I am afraid he may **not** be on time.*

INSTRUCTIONS: *Continue to cover the English verification with your card while you read the French.*

	1. Je ne le croyais pas riche.
1. I did not believe him rich.	2. Il est plus riche que je ne le croyais. (Is **plus** here a signal of *comparison* or *negation?*)
2. *comparison* He is richer than I believed him to be.	3. Je crains qu'il ne soit plus riche. (Is **plus** here a signal of *negation* or *comparison?*)
3. *negation* I fear that he is no longer rich.	4. Je crains qu'il ne soit très riche.
4. I am afraid that he is very rich.	5. Je crains qu'il ne soit pas très riche.
5. I am afraid that he is not very rich.	6. **attendre**=*to wait* De peur que nous n'attendions trop longtemps . . .

6. For fear that we might wait too long . . .	**7.** Avant que nous n'attendions trop longtemps . . .
7. Before we wait too long . . .	**8.** A moins que vous n'attendiez trop longtemps . . .
8. Unless you wait too long . . .	**9.** Pour que nous n'attendions pas trop longtemps . . .
9. In order that we not wait too long . . .	**10.** **le noyau**=*the nucleus* A moins que les recherches ne soient orientées vers la connaissance du noyau des atomes . . .
10. Unless research is oriented toward the knowledge of the nucleus of the atom . . .	**11.** A moins que les recherches ne soient plus orientées vers la connaissance du noyau des atomes . . .
11. Unless research is no longer oriented toward the knowledge of the nucleus of the atom . . .	**12.** **s'attendre à**=*to expect* A moins qu'on ne s'attende à des résultats plus décisifs . . .
12. Unless one expects more conclusive results . . .	**13.** De peur que vous ne vous attendiez à des résultats extraordinaires . . .
13. Lest you expect some extraordinary results . . .	**14.** Pour que nous ne nous attendions pas à quelque chose d'extraordinaire . . .
14. So that we will not expect anything extraordinary . . .	**15.** De peur que vous ne vous attendiez à rien de bon . . .
15. Lest you not expect anything good . . .	**16.** De peur que cet effort collectif n'aboutisse à un échec . . .
16. Lest this collective effort result (end up) in a failure . . .	**17.** De peur que notre entreprise ne se termine pas heureusement . . .
17. Lest our enterprise not end successfully (fortunately) . . .	**18.** A moins que cet effort n'aboutisse à un résultat insuffisant . . .
18. Unless this effort leads to an insufficient result . . .	**19.** A moins que cet effort n'aboutisse pas à une conclusion heureuse . . .
19. Unless this effort does not lead to a successful (fortunate) conclusion . . .	**20.** A moins que nous ne trouvions l'outillage du laboratoire insuffisant . . .
20. Unless we find the equipment of the laboratory inadequate . . .	**21.** A moins que nous ne trouvions pas l'outillage suffisant . . .

21. Unless we do not find the equipment adequate . . .	**22.** Il avait peur de ne pas réussir.
22. He was afraid of not succeeding.	**23.** Il craignait qu'il ne réussisse pas.
23. He was afraid that he would not succeed.	**24.** **rire**=*to laugh* Il faut rire avant d'être heureux, de peur de mourir sans avoir ri. La Bruyère
24. One must laugh before being happy for fear of dying without having laughed.	**Review!**

82. *Present Subjunctive of Irregular Verbs*—pouvoir, savoir, faire, aller, venir

1. You have already learned how to recognize the Present, Past Definite and Imperfect tenses of these verbs. Now learn them in the Present Subjunctive. **Pouvoir, savoir,** and **faire** have a completely irregular stem to which are added the regular Subjunctive endings:

IRREGULAR STEM PRESENT SUBJUNCTIVE

Pouvoir	**puiss**	**que je puiss**+**e**	*that I can, will be able, etc.*
savoir	sach	**que je sach**+**e**	*that I know, will know, etc.*
faire	fass	**que je fass**+**e**	*that I do, may do, will do*

2. **Aller** has a regular stem for the **nous** and **vous** forms and an irregular one for the others. A considerable number of irregular verbs, such as **venir,** follow this pattern:

que j'aill+e	*that I go, will*	que je vienn+e	*that I come,*
que tu aill+es	*go, may go, etc.*	que tu vienn+es	*will come, may*
qu'il aill+e		qu'il vienn+e	*come, etc.*
que nous all+ions		que nous ven+ions	
que vous all+iez		que vous ven+iez	
qu'ils aill+ent		qu'ils vienn+ent	

INSTRUCTIONS: *Pay special attention to the new verb forms.*

1. Il est essentiel qu'une équipe se fasse.

1. It is essential that a team be made up.	**2.** **le milieu**=*the environment* Pour que le milieu vital nécessaire puisse se développer heureusement, il faut de jeunes physiciens.
2. In order that the vital necessary environment be developed successfully, young physicists are required.	**3.** Il faut que ces physiciens puissent vivre.
3. It is necessary that these physicists be able to live.	**4.** Il importe que l'outillage soit suffisant.
4. It is important that the equipment be adequate.	**5.** Il vaut mieux que l'on soit assuré de la collaboration d'un personnel auxiliaire.
5. It is preferable to be assured of the collaboration of auxiliary personnel.	**6.** Il est convenable que la mise à exécution progressive des projets adoptés soit un problème des chercheurs.
6. It is appropriate that the progressive implementation of the projects adopted be a concern of the researchers.	**7.** Afin qu'ils sachent l'état présent de la connaissance des rayonnements cosmiques, il faut qu'ils fassent des études plus poussées.
7. In order for them to know the present status of knowledge of cosmic radiation, they must make more exhaustive studies.	**8.** **être en voie de**=**être en train de** A moins que nous ne puissions nous rendre compte des progrès des projets qui sont en voie de réalisation . . .
8. Unless we can realize the progress of projects which are now in the process of materializing . . .	**9.** A moins que nous ne puissions pas nous rendre compte des progrès faits dernièrement . . .
9. Unless we cannot realize the progress made lately . . .	**10.** Avant qu'on ne puisse s'appliquer à la recherche, il faut qu'on puisse vivre.
10. Before one can apply oneself to research, one must be able to live.	**11.** Avant qu'on ne soit plus capable de s'appliquer à la recherche . . .
11. Before one is no longer capable of applying oneself to research . . .	**12.** Sans que des organismes viennent en aide au nouveau laboratoire il ne peut rien sortir d'intéressant. (**Il** is used *personally/impersonally*)
12. *impersonally* Unless some organizations come to the aid of the new laboratory, nothing of interest can come out of it.	**13.** Pour qu'on puisse préciser la constitution des atomes, il est essentiel de faire des études minutieuses des spectres optiques.

13. In order for one to be able to describe the composition of atoms precisely, it is essential to make detailed studies of optical spectra.	**14.** Avant qu'on ne sache préciser la nature des rayons X, il faut faire des études plus poussées.
14. Before one can describe the nature of X-rays precisely, it is necessary to make more exhaustive studies.	**15.** Je crains que l'on ne fasse rien d'important.
15. I'm afraid nothing important will be done (is being done).	**16.** Pour que nous fassions un effort collectif et fructueux, il faut l'appui matériel des organismes scientifiques.
16. In order for us to make a collective, fruitful effort, the material support of scientific organizations (bodies) is needed.	**17.** Sans que ces travaux préliminaires se fassent, l'effort ne peut réussir.
17. Unless this preliminary work is done, the effort cannot succeed. (Remember that **pouvoir** is often accompanied by only one element of negation instead of two.)	

83. *Irregular Verb* mettre *and Compounds*

1. This verb is slightly irregular in the first three persons in the singular, in that it drops one *t* of the stem:

PRESENT TENSE

je mets	*I put, am putting*
tu mets	*you put, are putting*
il met	*he puts, is putting*
nous mettons	*we put, are putting*
vous mettez	*you put, are putting*
ils mettent	*they put, are putting*

2. The Imperfect tense is regular—**je mettais,** etc. *I was putting, used to put, etc.*

3. The present participle is regular—**mettant,** *putting.*

4. The past participle is irregular—**mis,** *put*

j'ai mis	*I have put, I put, etc.*
j'avais mis	*I had put, etc.*

5. The Past Definite forms are:

je mis (*I put*, etc)	**nous mîmes**
tu mis	**vous mîtes**
il mit	**ils mirent**

6. There are many compounds of **mettre,** but they all follow the same pattern. Notice how the affixing of the prefix affects the meaning. Following are some of the most common (which are also cognates):

admettre	(*to admit*)	**permettre**	(*to permit*)
commettre	(*to commit*)	**promettre**	(*to promise*)
émettre	(*to emit*)	**remettre**	(*to remit, postpone*)
omettre	(*to omit*)	**soumettre**	(*to submit*)
		transmettre	(*to transmit*)

What are the meanings and tenses of the French verbs?

	1. il met (*he puts/he put*)
1. *he puts—Present*	**2.** il mit (*he puts/he put*)
2. *he put—Past Definite*	**3.** je mis (*I put/I am putting*)
3. *I put—Past Definite*	**4.** je mets (*I am putting/I put—past*)
4. *I am putting—Present*	**5.** ils mirent (*they were putting/they put*)
5. *They put—Past Definite*	**6.** elle a mis (*she was putting/she has put*)
6. *She has put—Past Indefinite*	**7.** je mettais (*I used to put/I had put*)
7. *I used to put—Imperfect*	**8.** j'avais mis (*I was putting/I had put*)
8. *I had put—Past Perfect*	**9.** en mettant (*one used to put/while putting*)
9. *While putting—Present Participle*	**10.** vous mîtes (*you might/you used to put/you put*)

10.	*you put—Past Definite*	**11.**	ils avaient mis (*they were putting/they had put*)
11.	*They had put—Past Perfect* *Now read the following sentences.* *Continue to circle unrecognized vocabulary.*	**12.**	**une bouteille**=*a bottle* Pour commencer l'expérience je mis cent grammes d'eau de mer dans une bouteille.
12.	To begin the experiment, I put one hundred grams of sea water in a bottle.	**13.**	Au cours de l'expérience l'eau de mer émettait une odeur fort désagréable.
13.	During the experiment the sea water gave off a very disagreeable odor.	**14.**	Il ne faut pas que l'on omette de mettre une certaine quantité d'acide citrique dans la bouteille. (**Il ne faut pas**—*it is not necessary to/one must not*)
14.	*One must not* forget to put a certain quantity of citric acid in the bottle.	**15.**	Je soumis ma théorie à la vérification expérimentale. (**soumis**—*submit/submitted*)
15.	I *submitted* my theory to experimental verification.	**16.**	Les progrès que l'on a faits dernièrement en physique expérimentale promettent bien.
16.	The progress which has recently been made in experimental physics is promising.	**17.**	L'éclosion d'une nouvelle science permit aux chercheurs d'étendre leurs connaissances de la constitution des atomes. (**permit**—*permits/permitted*)
17.	The appearance of a new science *permitted* researchers to extend their knowledge of the composition of atoms.	**18.**	Plusieurs membres étant absents, on a remis la séance jusqu'à la semaine prochaine.
18.	Several members being absent, the session was postponed until the next week.	**19.**	Il s'est permis un cigare.
19.	He indulged in a cigar (allowed himself).	**20.**	Cet appareil promet d'éclipser tous les autres.
20.	This apparatus promises to outshine all the others.	**21.**	**un os**=*a bone* Je crains qu'il ne puisse remettre l'os.
21.	I am afraid that he cannot set the bone.	**22.**	Après que l'os fut remis, il se soumit à une opération chirurgicale.

22.	After the bone had been set he underwent a surgical operation.	**23.**	Il a remis la machine à neuf. (**neuf**=*new/nine*)
23.	He repaired the machine as good as *new*.	**24.**	Ils eurent soin de ne pas se commettre.
24.	They took care not to commit themselves.	**25.**	Nous nous sommes soumis à la volonté collective de la société.
25.	We submitted to the collective will of the society.	**26.**	Quand il commettait une erreur il était le premier à l'admettre.
26.	When he made a mistake he was the first to admit it.	**27.**	Admettons que j'aie tort.
27.	Let's admit that I may be wrong.	**28.**	Il fallait que l'on se soumette à la volonté royale.
28.	It was necessary to submit to the royal will.		

84. *Idioms with* mettre

1.   se mettre à=*to begin*

Il fallait se mettre au travail.   *It was necessary to begin the work.*
Elle s'est mise à chanter.   *She began to sing.*

2.   se mettre en route=*to start out on a trip*

Nous allons nous mettre en route   *We are going to start out at eleven*
à onze heures.   *o'clock.*

3.   mettre au point=*to perfect*

Ils ont mis l'appareil au point.   *They perfected the apparatus.*

4.   mettre au courant=*to inform, to bring up to date*

Il m'a mis au courant de la situa-   *He informed me about the situation.*
tion.

5.   mettre+*expression of time*=*to take time to do something*

Vous avez mis deux heures à le   *You took two hours to do it.*
faire.

	1. Avant qu'on ne se mette à se former aux disciplines de la recherche . . .
1. Before one starts to be trained in the disciplines of research . . .	2. Afin que nous mettions au point les travaux de nos prédécesseurs . . .
2. In order for us to perfect the work of our predecessors . . .	3. A moins que vous ne vous mettiez à travailler assidûment . . .
3. Unless you start to work assiduously . . .	4. En attendant qu'on me mette au courant des développements les plus récents . . .
4. Until someone brings me up to date on the most recent developments . . .	5. Afin de pouvoir mettre l'appareil au point . . .
5. In order to be able to perfect the apparatus . . .	6. A moins que nous ne nous mettions en route avant dix heures, nous ne pouvons pas arriver à temps.
6. Unless we get started before ten o'clock, we cannot arrive on time.	7. D'habitude nous mettons au moins deux heures à faire nos devoirs.
7. Ordinarily, we take at least two hours to do our homework.	8. Pour que vous puissiez vous mettre au courant des belles expériences de Perrin . . .
8. In order for you to be brought up to date on the splendid experiments of Perrin . . . (Notice the additional meaning of **beau–belle**.)	9. Ils se sont promis de se mettre en route à neuf heures. (**neuf**=*new/nine*)
9. They promised themselves to start out at *nine* o'clock.	10. Ils ont mis au moins **neuf** heures à faire le voyage.
10. They took at least *nine* hours to make the trip.	11. Il a mis au moins une heure à choisir un chapeau **neuf**.
11. He took at least one hour to choose a *new* hat.	

VOCABULARY DEVELOPMENT

INSTRUCTIONS: *Using the analogy of the information supplied, give the meaning of the other forms.*

	1. dix (10) une dizaine _____

1. about ten

2. le dixième _____

2. the tenth

3. dix pour cent

3. ten per cent

4. cent (100)
    cent pour cent _____

4. one hundred per cent

5. une centaine _____

5. about 100

6. le centième _____

6. the hundredth

7. des centaines _____

7. hundreds (of)

8. **le centenaire**=the *centenary* (hundredth anniversary)
    le cinquantenaire _____

8. the fiftieth anniversary

9. le cinquantième _____

9. the fiftieth

10. une cinquantaine _____

10. about fifty

11. cinquante pour cent _____

11. fifty per cent

12. quarante=40
    une quarantaine _____

12. about forty (Cf. "quarantine", the forty days a suspected victim of small pox was kept isolated.)

13. le quarantième _____

13. the fortieth

14. quarante pour cent _____

14. forty per cent

15. vingt=20
    vingt pour cent _____

15. twenty per cent

16. vingt-quatre _____

16. twenty-four

17. quatre-vingts _____

17. eighty

18. quatre-vingts pour cent
    _____

18. eighty per cent

19. le vingtième _____

19. the twentieth

20. le quatre-vingtième _____

20. the eightieth

21. quatre-vingt-dix _____

21. ninety

22. le quatre-vingt-dixième
    _____

22. the ninetieth

TESTING EXERCISE

INSTRUCTIONS: *Circle the letter which correctly completes the sentence or best expresses the meaning of the phrases indicated. Make a note to review those which you miss.*

    1. Il se peut que **je sois** en retard.
        A. I have   B. I am   C. I follow   D. I make

---

1. B   **2.** **Il vaut mieux que** l'équipe se forme tout de suite.
        A. It is fortunate that   C. It is preferable that
        B. It is necessary that   D. It is false that

---

2. C   **3.** **Quoique** vous donniez votre appui à ce projet . . .
        A. Although   B. While   C. In spite of the fact that   D. Unless

---

3. A   **4.** Tandis que nous **poursuivions** le but d'équiper notre laboratoire . . .
        A. pursue   B. were pursuing   C. may pursue   D. are pursued

---

4. B   **5.** **Pourvu que** nous voyions bientôt les résultats de nos recherches . . .
        A. in order that   B. although   C. in spite of the fact that   D. provided that

---

5. D   **6.** De peur que nous **n'attendions** trop longtemps . . .
        A. were not waiting   B. might wait   C. might not wait   D. were waiting

---

6. B   **7.** Match the following subjunctive forms with the infinitives:
        1. que je **puisse**   a. falloir
        2. que **j'aille**   b. perdre
        3. que nous **soyons**   c. être
        4. qu'il **fasse**   d. avoir
                          e. pouvoir
                          f. faire
                          g. savoir
                          h. aller
                          i. finir

---

7.   **8.** Nonobstant que vous **donniez** votre appui à projet . . .
1. e   A. were giving   B. had given   C. are giving
2. h
3. c
4. f

---

8. C   **9.** Afin que nous **mettions au point** les travaux préliminaires de ce projet . . .
        A. were perfecting   B. perfected   C. perfect

---

9. C   **10.** **Il convient que** nous nous mettions au courant de ses recherches.
        A. It is possible   C. It is advisable
        B. It is essential   D. It is improbable

---

10. C

READING PASSAGE

Une note sur la marche de la science

Extrait de Louis Leprince-Ringuet, "L'étude des
rayons cosmiques," *Journal de l'Ecole Polytechnique,*
IIIe série, no. 8 (octobre 1938), p. 294–296.

En 1938, un nouveau laboratoire de physique de l'Ecole Polytechnique
s'équipait pour les recherches sur la physique atomique et, plus spécialement,
sur les particules de très grande énergie et de très grand pouvoir pénétrant
appelées "rayons cosmiques." La réalisation d'un tel centre demandait,
5   surtout à cette époque, beaucoup de travail et la collaboration d'un nombre
important de personnes et d'organismes.

En effet, dans ces vastes domaines de la physique, où tant de difficultés
attendaient, et attendent, le chercheur il faut l'appui efficace **et** des organismes
officiels **et** [1] des organismes privés. Il est essentiel que se forme une équipe
10   de jeunes physiciens, travaillant avec un esprit de corps bien affirmé, pour que
le milieu vital nécessaire au travail de recherche puisse se développer heureusement. Il faut aussi que l'outillage soit suffisant et que l'on puisse être assuré
de la collaboration d'un personnel auxiliaire de mécaniciens et d'**aides** [2]
techniques et dévoués. Il faut que ces physiciens puissent vivre, ainsi que les
15   jeunes qui viennent se former aux disciplines sévères et attachantes de la
recherche expérimentale.

A l'occasion de la mise en marche de ce nouveau laboratoire, M. Louis
Leprince-Ringuet, professeur de physique à l'Ecole Polytechnique, a rédigé
quelques pages pour reconnaître l'appui matériel offert par le Ministère de la
20   Défense Nationale et de la Guerre, par la **Caisse** [3] Nationale de la Recherche
Scientifique, et par la Société des Amis de l'Ecole Polytechnique. En même
temps, il a fait les remarques suivantes sur les sujets de physique qui étaient
alors les plus "actuels":

"Chaque époque a vu l'éclosion et le développement de la connaissance de
25   branches diverses de la physique: au début du siècle dernier, ce furent les
merveilleuses découvertes de l'électromagnétisme et de l'électrodynamisme,
ce fut aussi la construction de la thermodynamique. Dans les années qui pré-
cédèrent 1900, les rayonnements de grande et de petite longueur d'**onde,** [4]
ondes électromagnétiques et rayons de Rœntgen furent spécialement étudiés.
30   Au début de ce siècle, la connaissance des rayons X s'est développée et a
permis de découvrir les grandes lois de la constitution des atomes, précisées
en même temps par l'étude minutieuse et patiente des spectres optiques.
Parallèlement d'ailleurs apparaissait l'évidence de la constitution granulaire
de l'électricité, et les belles expériences de Millikan, de Broglie, de Perrin
35   permettaient d'aboutir à la mesure de la charge de l'électron, qui est une des
constantes les plus sûres et les moins mises en doute de la physique. Poussant

1 *both . . . and*   **3** *fund*   **4** *wave*
2 *assistants*

plus avant dans la connaissance des phénomènes atomiques, les premières
découvertes de la radioactivité **dont l'honneur revient** [5] à Becquerel et à
Pierre et Marie Curie, ont montré que le noyau d'un atome, que l'on compare
souvent au soleil central d'un système dont les planètes sont les électrons
périphériques, pouvait exploser en projetant au loin certains produits de son
explosion.

Actuellement, on peut se demander quels sont les sujets de la physique en
cours de développement et de progrès rapides. Pour le voir, nous pouvons
agir de façon objective en ouvrant un des périodiques qui sont le reflet d'une
des activités scientifiques les plus vivantes, celle des Américains: **or,** [6] si nous
lisons les tables des matières du *Physical Review,* nous trouvons que la grande
majorité des articles se rapporte à deux sujets principaux: d'une part, à
l'étude de la constitution des noyaux d'atomes et de leur transmutation l'un
dans l'autre, d'autre part à l'étude de rayonnements d'un pouvoir de pénétra-
tion considérable et d'une énergie extrêmement grande que l'on nomme rayonnements cosmiques. En dehors de ces deux chapitres qui tiennent **la vedette,** [7]
il y a naturellement bien d'autres études, importantes elles aussi, sur la supra-
conductivité, le magnétisme, l'effet Zeemann, l'optique, le microscope à électrons, etc., mais, pour nous rapporter à une statistique des publications
américaines de physique, nous pouvons dire que près de 80 pour 100 des
recherches sont orientées vers la connaissance des atomes et spécialement de
leur noyau, ainsi que vers celle du rayonnement cosmique. Le développement
de ces deux sujets a commencé après la guerre et progresse d'une façon
extraordinaire **depuis** [8] quelques années, occupant maintenant l'activité de
centaines de chercheurs dans le monde. Cette science qui s'édifie est actuellement encore pleine de promesses: elle a complètement bouleversé les
notions que l'on pouvait avoir avant 1914 sur la constitution des éléments
simples, elle a permis la découverte de constituants élémentaires de la matière
que l'on ne soupçonnait pas: dans quelques dizaines d'années, cette partie de
la science **aura** [9] sans doute, comme cela s'est passé pour les autres, atteint son
développement essentiel: elle s'ajoutera au programme **dont pâtissent** [10] les
candidats aux grandes écoles ou simplement au baccalauréat, et n'offrira plus
l'intérêt de la recherche."

1. In lines 1–2 it is stated that the new laboratory:
   A. was soon to be equipped
   B. was then being equipped
   C. had already been equipped.

---

1. B   2. According to lines 8–16 an effective research center functions best:
   A. when it is under strictly private auspices
   B. when a very strict discipline is maintained over the younger members
      of the staff

---

5 *for which honor is due*   7 *the spotlight*   9 *will have*
6 *now*   8 *for*   10 *from which suffer*

C. when it provides a combination of material support and intellectual stimulation

D. when it is essentially supported from funds from the public sector.

---

2. C   **3.** Which discoveries are spoken of in lines 24–36 as having been made during the nineteenth century?

A. the granular nature of electricity

B. the nature of the atom

C. long and short wave lengths

D. the principles of aerodynamics.

---

3. C   **4.** The discoveries of radioactivity led people of that time to believe, according to lines 37–42 that:

A. the atom could explode

B. radioactive material had a solar origin

C. was a form of electrical charge

D. radioactive materials could have a medical value.

---

4. A   **5.** In lines 43–58 we learn that at that time:

A. there was only periodic interest in America in cosmic rays

B. the United States was one of the most active countries scientifically

C. two subjects dominated the field of physics exclusively

D. about 20% of the scientific articles written concerned atomic physics and cosmic rays.

---

5. B   **6.** Lines 61–69 tell us that the knowledge which was new for the author at that time:

A. had actually been discovered before World War I

B. would become commonplace in the future

C. had made physics the most advanced of the sciences

D. would probably contribute to a technological revolution.

---

6. B

Chapter Thirteen

REVIEW: Be sure that you are perfectly familiar with the new materials in Chapters Eleven and Twelve before beginning Chapter Thirteen.

85. *Pronouns—Direct and Indirect Objects*

1. Direct and indirect objects differ from each other in that the indirect object receives the action of the verb by means of a preposition, and the direct object receives the action without the means of a preposition. Since the usage of prepositions differs widely between languages, the meaning of a French direct object construction may be expressed in English by an indirect construction and vice-versa:

DIRECT OBJECT

Je cherche *les raisons* de sa conduite.	*I am looking for the reasons for his conduct.*
L'homme communique *sa pensée par* la parole.	*Man communicates his thought by speech.*

INDIRECT OBJECT

Il ressemble *à son frère*.	*He resembles his brother.*
Il parle franchement *à tout le monde*.	*He speaks frankly to everyone.*

243

2. The direct and indirect object pronouns refer to previously mentioned persons or things. They are as follows:

SUBJECT	DIRECT OBJECT		INDIRECT OBJECT
je	me	*me*	me
tu	te	*you*	te
il	l', le	*him, it*	lui
elle	l', la	*her, it*	lui
on	se	*oneself*	se
nous	nous	*us*	nous
vous	vous	*you*	vous
ils, elles	les	*them*	leur

The indirect object pronouns are often translated by *to me, to him,* etc., but in order to make an acceptable English translation, you must first choose an adequate English verb and then use the preposition which goes with it.

3. Notice that **nous, vous, me, te,** and **se** are both direct and indirect objects. **Les, lui, leur** may refer either to masculine or feminine antecedents.

4. In affirmative and negative statements the direct and indirect objects come immediately before the verb. This positioning helps you to distinguish the pronouns **le, la, les, l'** from the articles **le, la, les, l',** which precede a noun or an adjective+noun:

ARTICLE	PRONOUN	
Je connais *les* **hommes.**	**Je** *les* **connais.**	*I know them.*
Je dis *la* **vérité.**	**Je** *la* **dis.**	*I tell it.*
Cette théorie paraît étrange *aux* **anatomistes.**	**Elle** *leur* **paraît étrange.**	*It appears strange to them.*

In addition, since the articles are contracted with **à** and **de,** (and the object pronouns are not) **à le, à les, de le,** and **de les** are always recognizable as pronouns forms.

5. As you have noticed in the reading selections, **le** may refer not only to a previously mentioned person or thing, but also to a preceding idea. This type of construction may require several different means of expression in English:

Le désir de paraître habile empêche souvent de le devenir.	*The desire to appear clever often prevents one from becoming so.*
Le roi se refusa à recourir à la force au moment où il le pouvait encore.	*The king refused to have recourse to force while he still could.*

INSTRUCTIONS: *Remember to circle the difficult words and phrases as you read.*

	1. Vous me parlez.
1. You are speaking to me.	**2.** Je vous parle.
2. I am speaking to you.	**3.** Il nous parle.
3. He is speaking to us.	**4.** Vous parlez à Marie. Vous lui parlez. (**lui**—*to him/to her*)
4. You are speaking *to her.*	**5.** Vous parlez à Georges. Vous lui parlez. (**lui**—*to him/to her*)
5. You are speaking to *him.*	**6.** Il montre la lampe à Marie. Il la lui montre. (**lui** replaces _____)
6. *à Marie* He shows it to her.	**7.** Il nous montre la lampe. Il nous la montre. (*He shows it to her/He shows it to us*)
7. *He shows it to us.*	**8.** Il montre Marie à Georges. Il la lui montre. (**la** refers to _____)
8. *Marie* He shows her to him.	**9.** In the above frame **lui** replaces _____.
9. *à Georges*	**10.** **regarder**=*to look at* Nous vous regardons.
10. We look at you.	**11.** Vous nous regardez.
11. You look at us.	**12.** Nous nous regardons.
12. We look at each other.	**13.** Ils écrivent à leurs parents.
13. They write to their parents.	**14.** Ils leur écrivent.
14. They write to them.	**15.** Ils s'écrivent.
15. They write to each other.	**16.** Je vois l'importance de cette idée.
16. I see the importance of this idea.	**17.** Je la vois.
17. I see it.	**18.** Ils se voient.
18. They see each other.	**19.** Ils se parlent.

19. They speak to each other.	**20.** Il se parle.
20. He speaks to himself.	**21.** Il parle à Georges.
21. He speaks to George.	**22.** On se demande.
22. One wonders (asks oneself).	**23.** On vous demande de revenir.
23. One asks you to come back. (you are being asked to return.)	**24.** **un avis**=*an opinion* Je te donne mon avis.
24. I give you my opinion.	**25.** Je te le donne.
25. I give it to you.	**26.** Tu me donnes ton avis.
26. You give me your opinion.	**27.** Tu me le donnes.
27. You give it to me.	**28.** Je le donne à Georges. Je le lui donne.
28. I give it to him.	**29.** Je le leur donne.
29. I give it to them. (Notice that **lui** and **leur** follow the direct objects, whereas the other indirect objects precede them. The change of word order does not affect the meaning.)	**30.** Nous le lui avons expliqué.
30. We explained it to him.	**31.** Vous ne nous l'avez pas dit.
31. You did not tell it to us.	**32.** Ils vous l'ont écrit.
32. They wrote it to you.	**33.** **voici**=*here is, here are* Voici mes pensées.
33. Here are my thoughts.	**34.** Les voici.
34. Here they are.	**35.** Il a rédigé quelques pages au sujet du nouveau laboratoire. Les voici.
35. He has written up a few pages concerning the new laboratory. Here they are.	**36.** Voici mon opinion.
36. Here is my opinion.	**37.** Vous m'avez demandé mon opinion. La voici.
37. You have asked me for my opinion. Here it is.	**38.** **voilà**=*there is, there are* Voilà un beau sujet.

38. There is a fine subject.	**39.** Je cherchais mon livre. Le voilà.
39. I was looking for my book. There it is.	**40.** Voilà de belles pages.
40. There are some fine pages.	**41.** Les voilà.
41. There they are.	**42.** **bientôt**=*soon* Vous allez lire bientôt un passage de Rousseau.
42. You are soon going to read a passage from Rousseau.	**43.** Rousseau crut former une entreprise qui n'avait jamais eu d'exemple.
43. Rousseau believed he was undertaking something which had never had a precedent.	**44.** **nos semblables**=*our fellowmen* Il la forma pour montrer à ses semblables un homme dans la vérité de la nature.
44. He undertook it in order to show his fellowmen a man in all the truth of nature (as he actually was).	**45.** Dans ses *Confessions*, il veut leur montrer la vérité d'un homme unique, c'est-à-dire, lui-même.
45. In his *Confessions*, he wants to show them the truth about a unique man, that is, himself.	**46.** **le moule**=*the mold* Il nous dit que la nature l'avait jeté dans un moule unique.
46. He tells us that nature had cast him in a unique mold. (If the context did not give you the meaning of **jeter,** be sure to circle the word.)	**47.** Il veut la leur montrer, quoiqu'elle leur paraisse étrange.
47. He wants to show it (**la vérité**) to them, although it may appear strange to them.	**48.** C'est lui qui nous le dit.
48. It is he who tells us so.	**49.** **briser**=*to break* Il leur dit que la nature avait brisé le moule dans lequel elle l'avait jeté.
49. He said to them that nature had broken the mold in which she had cast him.	**50.** Il leur déclara que la nature l'avait brisé.
50. He declared to them that nature had broken it (the mold).	**51.** Il croyait connaître les hommes et se connaître.
51. He believed that he knew men (what men were) and that he knew himself.	**52.** Il croyait les connaître.

52. He believed he knew them.

53. Rousseau déclare qu'on ne peut le juger qu'après l'avoir lu.

---

53. Rousseau declares that one can judge him only after having read him.

54. **quant à**=*as for*
Quant à la vérité, il veut la dire à tout prix.
(**à tout prix**=at _____ price)

---

54. As for the truth, he desires to tell it at *any* price.
(Do not confuse **quant à**=*as for* with **quand**=*when*.)

55. Quant aux faits, il veut les montrer à ses semblables dans toute leur vérité.

---

55. As for the facts, he wishes to show them in all their truth to his fellowmen.

56. **la franchise**=*frankness*
Il veut les leur montrer en toute franchise, mais le peut-il?

---

56. He wishes to show them to them in all frankness, but can he (do it)?

57. Quand il s'adresse à ses contemporains, il leur parle en toute franchise.
(**quand**—*when/as for*)

---

57. *When* he addresses himself to his contemporaries, he speaks to them in all frankness.

58. Sa franchise étonnait à peu près tous ses contemporains.

---

58. His frankness astonished almost all of his contemporaries.

59. **méprisable**=*despicable*
Quant à ses défauts, il s'est montré vil et méprisable quand il l'a été.
(**l'** refers to _____)

---

59. *The condition of being vile and despicable.*
As for his defects, he has shown himself vile and despicable when he has been such.

60. **voiler**=*to veil, to cover*
dévoiler=_____

---

60. *to unveil, to reveal*

61. **tel que**=*such as, just as*
Quant à son intérieur, il croit l'avoir dévoilé tel que le Créateur lui-même l'a vu.

---

61. As for his inner self, he believes he has revealed (unveiled) it just as the Creator Himself has seen it.

62. Il n'hésite pas à se montrer méprisable.

---

62. He does not hesitate to show himself despicable.
(Circle **méprisable** if you did not remember it.)

63. Quant aux secrets de son coeur, il les découvre.

63. As for the secrets of his heart, he lays them bare (uncovers them).	**64.** **oser**=*to dare* Il invite tout homme à se déclarer son supérieur, s'il l'ose.
64. He invites any man to declare himself to be his superior, if he dares to do so.	**65.** Quand il a été méprisable, il a osé nous le dire.
65. When he was despicable, he dared to tell us so.	**66.** On a reproché à Rousseau son peu de modestie.
66. People have reproached Rousseau **for** his lack of modesty. (Notice that even though **à** is often translated as *to,* English usage must govern which preposition, if any, to choose.)	**67.** On le lui a reproché.
67. They have reproached him *for* it.	**68.** Certains lui disaient qu'il était peu modeste.
68. Certain people told him that he was not modest.	**69.** Il leur répondait que ce n'était pas sa faute si la nature l'avait jeté dans un moule unique.
69. He would answer them that it was not his fault if nature had cast him in the only mold of its kind.	**70.** On peut l'accuser de ne pas nous dire la vérité à tout instant, mais on ne peut pas lui reprocher le désir de nous la dire.
70. One can say to (accuse) him that he does not tell us the truth at every moment, but one cannot reproach him for his desire to tell it to us.	**71.** En tout cas, on ne peut juger son livre qu'après l'avoir lu.
71. In any case, one can judge his book only after having read it.	**72.** Voici quelques pensées des moralistes bien connus.
72. Here are a few thoughts from some well-known moralists.	**73.** **une larme**=*a tear* Il y a certaines larmes qui nous trompent souvent nous-mêmes après avoir trompé les autres. La Rochefoucauld
73. There are certain tears which often deceive us ourselves after having deceived others.	**74.** Nous sommes si accoutumés à nous déguiser aux autres qu'enfin nous nous déguisons à nous-mêmes. La Rochefoucauld
74. We are so accustomed to putting on a disguise (disguising ourselves) for	**75.** La mort n'arrive qu'une fois, et se fait sentir à tous les moments de la vie;

others that at last we put on a disguise for ourselves.

il est plus dur de l'appréhender que de la souffrir.

La Bruyère

(**appréhender**—*to apprehend/to fear*)

---

75. *to fear*
Death comes only one time and makes itself felt at every moment of life; it is harder to fear it than to suffer it.

---

86. *Agreement of Past Participle with Preceding Direct Object*

1. In the compound tenses the past participle of verbs conjugated with **avoir** agrees in gender and number with the direct object when the direct object precedes the verb. The agreement is made by adding –**e** (f.) and/or **s** (pl.) :

Nous avons fait cette expérience.
Nous l'avons faite.

We performed this experiment.
We performed it.

Nous avons fait ces expériences.
Nous les avons faites.

We have performed these experiments.
We have performed them.

ces expériences = *the direct object.* It can be replaced by the object pronoun **les.** If this is done, **les** will be placed in front of the verb (**avons fait**) and the past participle **fait** will have to agree in gender and number with what **les** represents, i.e., a feminine plural noun, hence **faites.** cf. :

J'ai vu les femmes.
Je *les* ai *vues*.

I saw the women.
I saw them.

2. The rule also applies to reflexive verbs, although they take **être** in the compound tenses :

Elles se sont écrit des lettres.

They wrote letters to each other.

(**se** = indirect object)

BUT :

Les lettres qu'elles se sont écrites sont courtes.

The letters which they wrote to each other are short.

(**Les lettres** = preceding direct object)

3. The utility of this point for a reading knowledge of French is that the agreement of the past participle may sometimes help you to identify the direct object. If the past participle has a feminine or plural form, look in front of the verb for a direct object (or for the subject, in the case of an intransitive verb conjugated with **être**).

READING PREPARATION

INSTRUCTIONS: *As you read the following sentences, notice the difference between the past participles which are preceded by a direct object and those which are not.*

	1. Pendant son expédition en Extrême-Orient, le professeur Charat a découvert une lampe préhistorique.
1. During his expedition in the Far East, Professor Charat discovered a prehistoric lamp.	**2.** Lors de sa conférence devant l'Académie, il a montré **une lampe** préhistorique qu'il avait découverte.
2. At the time of his lecture before the Academy, he showed a prehistoric lamp which he had discovered.	**3.** ⌐Il l'a montrée à ses confrères.
3. He showed it to his colleagues.	**4.** Il **la** leur a montrée.
4. He showed it to them.	**5.** **écouter**=*to listen to* Ses confrères ont poliment écouté sa conférence.
5. His colleagues politely listened to his lecture.	**6.** (a) Ils l'ont poliment écoutée. (b) Ils l'ont poliment écouté.
6. (a) They politely listened to *it*. (b) They politely listened to *him*.	**7.** Il paraît qu'il a appris l'Espéranto très facilement.
7. It appears that he learned Esperanto very easily.	**8.** Quant à l'Espéranto, c'est une langue qu'il a apprise facilement.
8. As for Esperanto, it is a language that he learned easily.	**9.** Je suis persuadé qu'il nous a dit la vérité.
9. I am persuaded that he told us the truth.	**10.** Quant à la vérité, il nous l'a dite.
10. As for the truth, he told it to us.	**11.** Il ne nous l'a pas dite tout à fait.
11. He did not tell it to us completely.	**12.** **s'asseoir**=*to sit down* Elle s'était assise.

12. She had sat down. (**se** here is the direct object)	**13.** Elles se sont assis**es**.
13. They (f.) sat down.	**14.** **s'endormir**=*to go to sleep* Il s'était endormi.
14. He had gone to sleep.	**15.** Elle **s'était** endorm**ie**.
15. She had gone to sleep.	**16.** Ils **se** sont endorm**is**.
16. They (masc.) went to sleep.	**17.** Elles **se** sont endorm**ies**.
17. They (fem.) went to sleep.	**18.** **Les lettres** qu'elles s'étaient écrites . . .
18. The letters that they had written each other . . .	

87. *Personal Pronouns with Impersonal Expressions*

1. When personal pronouns are used with the impersonal expressions **il faut** and **il reste,** the expression must be treated as an idiom and translated as a whole:

Il nous reste dix francs.	*We have ten francs left* *("ten francs remain to us").*
Il nous faut encore plusieurs semaines pour achever le projet.	*We need several more weeks to finish the project.*
Il m'est arrivé de me tromper.	*I have happened to be mistaken.*
Il vous importe de partir à temps.	*It is important for you to leave on time.*
Il lui convient de travailler davantage.	*It is advisable for him to work more.*

READING PREPARATION

INSTRUCTIONS: *Express the meanings of the following sentences. Cover the English with your card until you have worked out a meaning which you want to verify.*

	1. **la tâche**=the task Une fois que vous avez fait vos recherches, il ne vous reste que la tâche de rédiger vos résultats.
1. Once you have done your research, you have only to write up your results.	**2.** Il vous reste encore quelques pages à lire.

2. You have several pages yet to read.	**3.** Il nous suffit, pour effectuer l'expérience, d'ajouter une petite quantité d'acide citrique au liquide.
3. In order to perform the experiment, it is sufficient for us to add a small quantity of citric acid to the liquid.	**4.** **le soin**=*care* **soigneusement**=_____
4. *carefully*	**5.** Il nous importe d'observer soigneusement les résultats.
5. It is important for us to observe the results carefully.	**6.** Il nous est déjà arrivé plusieurs fois de nous tromper d'acide.
6. It has already happened several times for us to be mistaken about the acid (to choose the wrong acid).	**7.** Il nous convient de faire un examen soigneux de ses prétentions. (**prétentions**—*claims/pretenses*)
7. It behooves us (it is advisable for us) to make a careful examination of his *claims.*	**8.** Il lui faut reconnaître que ses prétentions sont presque incroyables.
8. He must (it is necessary for him to) recognize that his claims are almost unbelievable.	**9.** **apercevoir**=*to perceive, to notice* Il ne nous faut que peu de réflexion pour apercevoir la différence entre les hommes et les animaux.
9. We need to reflect only a short while to perceive the difference between men and the animals (only a little reflection is needed for us to. . .).	**10.** Pour que les singes puissent penser, il leur faut plus d'esprit qu'ils n'en ont maintenant.
10. In order for monkeys to be able to think, they need more intelligence (mind) than they now have.	**11.** **taire**=*to silence* or *suppress* Il ne nous faut rien taire.
11. We must suppress nothing.	**12.** Il leur reste la tâche de prouver leurs prétentions.
12. The task remains for them to prove their claims.	Review the new vocabulary items and then go on to the next section.

88. *Imperatives*—nous, vous, tu *Forms*

1. The imperative (request) patterns of the **tu, nous,** and **vous** forms consist of the verb without the subject pronouns. The **tu** form of the verb drops the final **s** after an **a** or an **e** (except when followed by **y** or **en**) :

Faites venir le médecin.	Send for the doctor. (Have the doctor come.)
Essayez de comprendre.	Try to understand.
Parlons franchement.	Let us speak frankly.
Sors à l'instant même.	Leave this very minute.
Avoue que tu as tort.	Admit you are wrong.
Ajoute que tu n'es pas au courant de la situation.	Add that you are not aware of the situation.
Manges—en.	Eat some.
Va te coucher.	Go to bed.
Vas–y!	Go there!

2. You will remember that reflexive verbs are conjugated with a subject and an object pronoun. The imperative of reflexive verbs retains the object pronoun but not the subject pronoun. Compare the following:

Vous vous amusez bien. (*indicative*)	*You are having a good time.*
Amusez-vous bien. (*imperative*)	*Have a good time.*
Nous nous levons. (*indicative*)	*We are getting up.*
Levons-nous. (*imperative*)	*Let's get up.*

3. The object pronouns *precede* the verb in *negative* requests. They follow the verb in affirmative requests, in which case **moi** and **toi** replace **me** and **te**:

Tais-toi.	*Be quiet.*
Taisez-vous.	*Be quiet.*
Donnez-le-moi.	*Give it to me.*
Ne me le donnez pas.	*Don't give it to me.*
Ne te tais pas.	*Don't be quiet.*
Ne vous taisez pas.	*Don't be quiet.*

READING PREPARATION

INSTRUCTIONS: *Notice the difference in word order between the affirmative and negative patterns.*

	1. Venez nous parler.
1. Come speak to us.	**2.** Parlez-nous franchement.
2. Speak to us frankly.	**3.** Faites-le maintenant.

3. Do it now.	**4.** Ne le faites pas maintenant.
4. Don't do it now.	**5.** Ecrivez-nous.
5. Write to us.	**6.** Ecrivons-leur.
6. Let's write to them.	**7.** Ne nous écrivez plus.
7. Don't write to us any more.	**8.** Ne leur écrivons plus.
8. Let's not write to them any more.	**9.** Donnez-le-moi.
9. Give it to me.	**10.** Ne me le donnez pas.
10. Don't give it to me.	**11.** Dites-lui tout.
11. Tell him (her) everything.	**12.** Ne lui dites rien.
12. Don't tell him (her) anything.	**13.** Montrez-les-lui.
13. Show them to him (her).	**14.** Ne lui montrez plus rien.
14. Don't show him (her) anything any more.	**15.** Croyez-moi . . .
15. Believe me . . .	**16.** Ne le croyez pas.
16. Don't believe him (it).	**17.** Nous nous écrivons.
17. We write to each other.	**18.** Ecrivons-nous.
18. Let's write to each other.	**19.** Nous ne nous écrivons plus.
19. We don't write to each other any more.	**20.** Ne nous écrivons plus.
20. Let's not write to each other any more.	**21.** Vous ne vous taisez pas.
21. You are not being quiet.	**22.** Ne vous taisez pas tout à fait.
22. Do not be completely quiet.	**23.** Amusez-vous bien.
23. Have a good time.	**24.** Il paraît que vous ne vous amusez pas trop.
24. It appears that you are not having too good a time.	**25.** Ne vous amusez pas trop.
25. Don't have too good a time.	**26.** Quant à Rousseau, ne le croyons pas littéralement.
26. As for Rousseau, let us not believe him literally.	**27.** Ne supposons pas que toutes ses confessions soient exactes.

			(**soient** is the subjunctive of **avoir/ être**)
27.	**être** Let us not suppose that all his confessions are correct.	**28.**	Ne disons pas cependant qu'il n'ait pas dit la vérité.
28.	Let us not say, however, that he did not tell the truth.	**29.**	Croyons plutôt qu'il s'est trompé quelquefois.
29.	Let us rather believe that he was sometimes mistaken.	**30.**	Permettons-lui de remplir parfois un vide occasionné par un défaut de mémoire. (**remplir un vide**=*to fill a* _____)
30.	Let us permit him sometimes to fill a *void* occasioned by a defect of memory.	**31.**	**ce que**=*that which* Permettons-lui de supposer vrai ce qu'il sait peut l'être. (**l'** refers to the idea of _____)
31.	*being true* Let us permit him to suppose to be true that which he knows may be true.	**32.**	Disons qu'il a quelquefois supposé vrai ce qu'il savait avoir pu l'être.
32.	Let us say that he sometimes supposed to be true that which he knew could have been true.		

89. *Third Person Imperatives*

1.   Que+the Present Subjunctive indicates a request or command concerning a third person:

Qu'il finisse sa leçon.	*Have him (let him) finish his lessons.*
Qu'ils viennent.	*Have them come (let them come.)*
Qu'elle fasse ses devoirs.	*Have her do (let her do) her homework.*

2.   Irregular imperatives of **avoir, être,** and **savoir** are:

avoir		être		savoir	
aie	*have*	**sois**	*be*	**sache**	*know*
ayons	*let's have*	**soyons**	*let's be*	**sachons**	*let us know*
ayez	*have*	**soyez**	*be*	**sachez**	*know*

N'ayez pas peur.   *Don't be afraid (have no fear).*
Soyons amis.   *Let's be friends.*
Sois sage.   *Be good.*

INSTRUCTIONS: *Remember to circle new and unrecognized vocabulary.*

		1.	Sachez obéir aux ordres.
1.	Know how to obey orders.	**2.**	Sachez que je suis à votre disposition.
2.	Know that I am at your disposal.	**3.**	Ayez soin de ne rien taire de mauvais.
3.	Take care not to suppress anything bad.	**4.**	Sache te taire.
4.	Know how to keep quiet.	**5.**	Ayons soin de dire toute la vérité.
5.	Let us take care to tell the whole truth.	**6.**	N'aie pas peur.
6.	Don't be afraid.	**7.**	**la franchise** = *frankness* **Soyons francs** = _____
7.	Let us be frank.	**8.**	Soyez assez franc pour ne dire que la vérité. (*Does* **que** *here signal an imperative or an exception to a negation?*)
8.	*An exception to a negation.* Be frank enough to tell only the truth.	**9.**	Qu'il apprenne à lire.
9.	Let him learn to read.	**10.**	Qu'ils travaillent avec un esprit d'équipe bien affirmé.
10.	Have them work with a strong team spirit.	**11.**	Que la mise à exécution soit logique.
11.	Let the implementation be logical.	**12.**	Qu'on accueille les élèves qui ont une vocation scientifique.
12.	Let them accept students with a scientific vocation.	**13.**	Que les élèves qui ont une vocation scientifique soient accueillis.
13.	Let students with a scientific vocation be accepted.	**14.**	Dieu dit, "Que la lumière soit!" et la lumière fut. Genèse 1:3
14.	God said, "Let there be light!" and the light was.	**15.**	Rousseau écrivit ses *Confessions* pour se justifier. (The tense of **écrivit** is *Present/Past definite?*)

15. Past Definite
Rousseau wrote his *Confessions* to justify himself.

16. S'imaginant devant le trône de l'Etre Suprême, il dit à Celui-ci . . .

16. Imagining himself before the throne of the Supreme Being, he says to Him . . .

17. **Rassembler**=*to assemble*
Rassemble devant Toi mes semblables.

17. Assemble my fellowmen before Thee.

18. **la foule**=*the crowd*
Rassemble devant Toi l'innombrable foule de mes semblables.

18. Assemble before Thee the innumerable crowd of my fellowmen.

19. **autour de**=*around*
Rassemble autour de moi l'innombrable foule de mes semblables.

19. Assemble around me the innumerable crowd of my fellowmen.

20. Rassemblés autour de moi, qu'ils écoutent mes confessions.

20. Being assembled around me, let them listen to my confessions.

21. **digne**=*worthy*
indigne=_____

21. *unworthy*

22. **gémir**=*to lament, to wail*
Qu'ils gémissent de mes indignités.

22. Let them lament my unworthiness.

23. **les misères**=*misfortunes, troubles*
Qu'ils rougissent de mes misères.

23. Let them blush over my misfortunes.

24. Et puis, que chacun d'eux se montre tel qu'il fut.

24. And then let each one of them show himself just as he was.

25. Que chacun découvre son coeur avec la même franchise que moi.
(**découvrir**—*to discover/to reveal*)

25. Let each one *reveal* his heart with the same frankness as I have.

26. Que chacun se découvre tel qu'il fut.

26. Let each one reveal himself such as he was.

27. **le pied**=*the foot*
Que chacun d'eux découvre son coeur au pied de Ton trône.

27. Let each one of them reveal his heart at the foot of Thy throne.

28. Et puis qu'un seul Te dise . . .

28. And then let a single one say to Thee . . .

29. Et puis qu'un seul ose dire, "Je valais mieux que cet homme-la."

29. And then let a single one dare to say, "I was better than that man."

90.   En—*Indirect Object and Preposition*

1.   En placed immediately before the verb usually stands as the replacement of an expression starting with **de**:

Nous avons besoin d'argent.	*We need some money.*
Nous *en* avons besoin.	*We need some.*
Les animaux n'ont pas de pensées.	*Animals have no thoughts.*
Ils n'*en* ont pas.	*They have none (they don't have any).*
Les animaux ne sont capables d'aucune espèce de progrès.	*Animals are not capable of any kind of progress.*
Ils n'*en* sont aucunement capables.	*They are not at all (in no way) capable of it.*
Buffon parle du rapport entre la parole et la pensée.	*Buffon speaks of the relation between speech and thought.*
Il *en* parle.	*He speaks about it.*

2.   En placed before a noun may usually be translated by (1) *in* or (2) *as*:

***En* France . . .**	*In France . . .*
***En* Angleterre . . .**	*In England . . .*
Il agit *en* philosophe.	*He acts as a philosopher.*
Il parle *en* professeur.	*He speaks as a professor.*

3.   En occurs with a number of idiomatic expressions, in which case it is the meaning of the entire phrase which must be expressed and not the individual word:

Il en est de ceci comme il en est de cela . . .	*It is the same with this as it is with that . . .*
En plus de ⎫ **En outre de** ⎬	*In addition to*
En qualité de ⎫ **En tant que** ⎬	*As (in the capacity of)*
En raison de	*Because of*
En face de	*Opposite, facing*

READING PREPARATION

INSTRUCTIONS: *As you read the following French sentences, cover the English with your card. Continue to check those sentences which contain new or unfamiliar vocabulary.*

Review them after you finish the exercise and again in a day or two, until you recognize them immediately.

	1. Les animaux ne sont capables d'aucune espèce de progrès.
1. The animals are not capable of any kind of progress.	**2.** Ils n'en sont pas capables.
2. They are not capable of it.	**3.** **l'abeille**=*the bee* On donne à l'abeille plus d'esprit que nous n'en avons. (*Here* **ne**—*negates/does not negate—the sentence.*)
3. *Does not negate—following a comparison it is superfluous without a second element of negation.* One grants (gives) the bee more intelligence than we have. (**En** refers to **esprit**.)	**4.** Il nous faut beaucoup de réflexion pour perfectionner nos arts.
4. Much reflection is necessary for us to perfect our arts (we need much reflection . . .).	**5.** Il en faut beaucoup pour les perfectionner.
5. Much of it is needed to perfect them.	**6.** **l'âme**=*the soul* Mais on peut voir d'autres preuves de l'immatérialité de notre âme.
6. But one can see other proofs of the immateriality of our soul.	**7.** Mais on peut en voir d'autres preuves.
7. But one can see other proofs of it.	**8.** Selon Buffon, il n'y a pas d'êtres intermédiaires entre l'homme et le singe.
8. According to Buffon, there are no intermediary beings between man and the monkey.	**9.** Selon lui, il n'y en a pas.
9. According to him, there are none (of them).	**10.** Le singe n'a aucun des pouvoirs de l'être pensant.
10. The monkey has none of the powers of the thinking being.	**11.** Il n'en a pas.
11. He has none of them.	**12.** Il faut beaucoup de raisons pour démontrer l'excellence de notre nature.

12.	Many reasons are necessary in order to demonstrate the excellence (superiority) of our nature.	**13.**	Il en faut beaucoup pour la démontrer.
13.	Many (of them) are necessary in order to demonstrate it.	**14.**	La pensée de Buffon se forma en France.
14.	The thought of Buffon was formed in France.	**15.**	Buffon parlait en philosophe.
15.	Buffon was speaking as a philosopher.	**16.**	Il parlait en tant que biologiste avant qu'il y ait eu une science de biologie.
16.	He spoke as a biologist before there was a science of biology.	**17.**	Rousseau parlait en qualité d'auteur.
17.	Rousseau was speaking as an author.	**18.**	En face des raisonnements de Buffon, on voit se former les théories évolutionnistes de Lamarck.
18.	Opposite (in constrast to) the reasonings of Buffon, one sees the evolutionist theories of Lamarck being formed.	**19.**	**la main**=*the hand* En face du trône de l'Etre suprême, Rousseau se voit, son livre à la main.
19.	Facing the throne of the Supreme Being, Rousseau sees himself with his book in his hand.	**20.**	En raison des vérités qu'il a dites, Rousseau se croit supérieur aux autres hommes.
20.	Because of the truths which he has told, Rousseau believes himself superior to other men.	**21.**	En plus de la pensée, l'homme possède la parole.
21.	In addition to thought, man possesses speech.	**22.**	En raison de la parole, il est supérieur aux bêtes.
22.	Because of speech, he is superior to animals.	**23.**	Il n'en est pas des hommes comme il en est des animaux.
22.	It is not the same with men as it is with animals.	**24.**	Il en est du singe comme il en est de l'abeille: ni l'un ni l'autre ne perfectionne jamais son ouvrage.
24.	It is the same with the monkey as it is with the bee: neither one ever perfects its work.	**25.**	**une suite**=*a sequence* Les animaux n'ont pas une suite de pensées, même à leur façon. (**même**—*even/the same*)
25.	The animals do not have a sequence of thoughts, *even* in their own way.	**26.**	Loin d'avoir des pensées comme nous, ils n'en ont même pas à leur façon.

26. Far from having thoughts as we do, they do not even have any in their own way.

27. **douer**=*to endow*
Ils ne sont pas doués de la puissance de la pensée.

27. They are not endowed with the power of thought.

28. Ils n'en sont pas doués.

28. They are not endowed with it.

29. Il en est du véritable amour comme il en est de l'apparition des esprits: tout le monde en parle, et peu de gens en ont vu.

La Rochefoucauld

29. It is with true love as it is with the apparition of spirits: everyone talks about both, and few people have seen either.

30. On aime mieux dire du mal de soi-même que de n'en point parler.

La Rochefoucauld

(**en** refers to _____)

30. **soi-même**
One prefers to speak ill of oneself rather than not to speak of oneself at all.

Can you read all of the above sentences easily? If so, go on to the next section.

91. *Indirect Object*—y

1.   Just as **en** replaces an expression starting with **de, y** replaces expressions starting with **à** or other prepositions. (**Lui** and **leur,** which also replace expressions starting with **à,** usually refer to persons and **y** to things.)

Elle est arrivée à Paris.	*She arrived in Paris.*
Elle y est arrivée.	*She arrived* **there.**
Ils faisaient de longues promenades au bord de la mer.	*They used to take long walks on the sea shore.*
Ils y faisaient de longues promenades.	*They used to take long walks* **there.**
Je me suis mis à travailler.	*I started to work.*
Je m'y suis mis.	*I started to do* **it.**

READING PREPARATION

INSTRUCTIONS: *As you read the following French sentences, cover the English with your card. Continue to check those sentences which contain new or unfamiliar vocabulary. Review them after you finish the exercise and again in a day or two, until you recognize them immediately.*

1. Buffon nous fait entendre qu'il arriva à l'idée d'une âme immatérielle. (**entendre**—*to hear/to understand*)

1. Buffon gives us to *understand* that he arrived at the idea of an immaterial soul.

2. Il y arriva.

2. He arrived at it.

3. **ce qui**=*that which, what* Il se demandait ce qui se passait au dedans de nous. (**se passer**=**avoir lieu**)

3. He wondered what went on within us.

4. Il se demandait ce qui s'y passait.

4. He wondered what went on there.

5. Une admirable clarté paraît dans sa prose.

5. An admirable clarity appears in his prose.

6. Une admirable clarté y paraît.

6. An admirable clarity appears there.

7. Il se mit à la tâche de prouver l'immatérialité de l'âme.

7. He began (set about) the task of proving the immateriality of the soul.

8. Il s'y mit.

8. He began (set about) it. (**mit** is the past definite of **mettre**)

9. Quant à l'immatérialité de l'âme, il y croyait.

9. As for the immateriality of the soul, he believed in it.

10. Aussi pensait-il à des arguments pour la prouver. (**Aussi** here means *also/therefore*)

10. *Therefore*—it comes at the beginning of the sentence. Therefore, he thought of arguments to prove it.

11. Aussi y pensait-il.

11. Therefore, he thought of them.

12. Quant à notre esprit, il est difficile de dire ce qui s'y passe.

12. As for our mind, it is difficult to say what goes on there.

13. Il mit des années à rédiger son oeuvre.

13. He spent years in composing (writing) his work.

14. Il y mit des années.

14. He spent years at it.

15. A propos de son livre, il y parle de la distance infinie entre les animaux et les hommes.

15. Speaking of his book, he speaks in it of the infinite distance between animals and men.

16. Buffon nous fait entendre qu'on peut voir une distance infinie entre les facultés de l'homme et celles du plus parfait animal.

16. Buffon gives us to understand that one can see an infinite distance between the faculties of man and those of the most perfect animal.

17. On peut y voir une distance infinie.

17. One can see an infinite distance between them.

18. D'après la pensée de Buffon, le Créateur a mis une distance infinie entre l'homme et la bête.

18. According to the thought of Buffon, the Creator has placed an infinite distance between men and the animals.

19. Le Créateur y a mis une distance infinie.

19. The Creator has placed an infinite distance between them.

20. Il ne se passe à leur intérieur rien de suivi.

20. Nothing coherent takes place within them.

21. Il ne s'y passe rien de suivi.

21. Nothing coherent takes place there.

22. Rousseau s'imaginait, son livre à la main, devant le trône du Souverain Juge.

22. Rousseau imagined himself, his book in his hand, before the throne of the Sovereign Judge.

23. Il s'y imaginait, son livre à la main.

23. He imagined himself there, his book in his hand.

24. La vérité ne fait pas autant de bien dans le monde que ses apparences y font de mal.
    La Rochefoucauld

24. The truth does not do as much good in the world as its appearances there do harm.

Y and **en** are extremely important function words. Go no further until you can recognize their various meanings easily.

92. *Irregular Verb*—aller

1. You have already met this verb in several of its forms. Now learn to recognize all its forms of the Present and Imperfect tenses:

PRESENT	IMPERFECT
Je vais *I go, am going*, etc.	**J'allais** *I went, was going*, etc.
Tu vas	**Tu allais**
Il, elle, on va	**Il, elle, on allait**
Nous allons	**Nous allions**
Vous allez	**Vous alliez**
Ils, elles vont	**Ils, elles allaient**

Past participle—**allé** (*gone*)

2. Notice that in the Present tense, the first three persons in the singular (**je, tu, il** forms) and the third person plural (**ils, elles** forms) are irregular, and that the first and second persons in the plural (**nous** and **vous** forms) are regular. This is a standard pattern for irregular verbs. It will help you to learn them if you will keep this fact in mind. Notice also above that in accordance with the rule for the formation of the Imperfect (Chapter Ten), the stem is taken from the first person plural (the **nous** form) of the Present tense to which are added the usual Imperfect endings.

3. **Aller** + infinitive is a common way of expressing a future:

Il va être question plus loin de ces résultats.	*It will be a question further on of these results.*

4. **Allons!** and **allez!** are commonly used as exclamations:

Allons! Vous n'êtes pas sérieux!	*Come now! You aren't serious!*
Allez! Vous plaisantez!	*Go on! You're joking!*

5. Some common **aller** idioms are:

S'en aller	*to leave, to go away*
Il y va de sa carrière.	*His career depends on it.*
Comment allez-vous?	*How are you?*
Je vais bien.	*I am well.*

READING PREPARATION

INSTRUCTIONS: *Give the meanings of the following sentences. Continue to make a check by the ones which contain new or unrecognized vocabulary. Review the checked sentences after you finish the exercise and again in a day or two.*

	1. Allons étudier.
1. Let's go study.	**2.** Allons! Soyez sérieux.

2. Come now! Be serious.	**3.** Ils vont partir à huit heures.
3. They are going to leave at eight o'clock.	**4.** Ils ne vont partir qu'après huit heures.
4. They are not going to leave until after eight o'clock.	**5.** Comment vont vos parents? Ils vont bien, merci.
5. How are your parents? They are well, thank you.	**6.** Et vous, comment allez-vous?
6. And you, how are you?	**7.** Je vais bien, merci.
7. I'm well, thank you.	**8.** Rousseau déclare qu'il va écrire un livre extraordinaire.
8. Rousseau declares that he is going to write an extraordinary book.	**9.** Il nous fait entendre qu'il ne va rien taire de mauvais.
9. He gives us to understand that he is not going to suppress anything bad.	**10.** Il ne va rien taire de bon.
10. He is going to suppress nothing good.	**11.** Il ne va pas se taire.
11. He is not going to remain silent.	**12.** Il suppose que ses semblables vont le croire sur sa parole.
12. He supposes that his fellowmen are going to believe him on his word.	**13.** Il s'imagine qu'ils vont croire une histoire semblable.
13. He imagines that they are going to believe a story like that.	**14.** Nous allons voir plus loin un plein développement de la pensée de Buffon.
14. We shall see further on a full development of the thought of Buffon.	**15.** Ses raisonnements vont peut-être nous convaincre.
15. His reasonings will perhaps convince us.	**16.** **une robe** = *a dress* Cette robe lui va très bien.
16. This dress suits her very well.	**17.** Cette robe ne lui va guère mieux que l'autre.
17. This dress hardly fits her better than the other one.	**18.** Ces robes ne vous vont pas du tout.
18. These dresses do not become you at all.	**19.** **un chapeau** = *a hat* Trouvez-vous que ce chapeau me va?
19. Do you think this hat looks nice on me? (**Trouver** often replaces **penser** in this sense.)	**20.** Je m'en vais.

20. I am leaving.	**21.** Il veut s'en aller.
21. He wants to leave.	**22.** Allons donc! Vous plaisantez!
22. Come now! You are joking!	**23.** Il faut que je m'en aille.
23. I must leave.	**24.** Je suis allé voir le match de tennis.
24. I went to see the tennis match.	**25.** Allons voir le match de tennis.
25. Let's go see the tennis match.	**26.** Nous sommes allés le voir.
26. We went to see it.	**27.** Il faut que j'aille le voir.
27. I must go see it.	**28.** Il faut qu'il s'en aille.
28. He has to leave.	**29.** Elle était déjà allée en France.
29. She had already gone to France.	**30.** Ils s'en étaient déjà allés.
30. They had already left.	**31.** Ils étaient déjà allés en France.
31. They had already gone to France.	

VOCABULARY DEVELOPMENT

INSTRUCTIONS: *The following groups of words suggest how a large recognition vocabulary may be built up from root words and words with associated meanings. The analogies are not perfectly consistent, naturally, but they help to develop a feel for anticipating a meaning. Cover the English verification with your card and try to arrive at the meaning of the French words by analogy with the model word.*

	1. **s'entretenir** = *to converse with* **un entretien** = _____
1. *a conversation*	**2.** **entretenir une maison** = *to keep up a house, to maintain a house* **l'entretien d'une maison** = _____
2. *the upkeep of a house*	**3.** **entendre** = *to hear, to understand* **s'entendre** = *to hear each other, to understand each other* **une expression à double entente** = _____
3. *an expression with a double meaning*	**4.** **une entente entre nations** = _____
4. *an understanding between nations*	**5.** **détendre** = *to relax, to ease tensions* **une détente internationale** = _____

5. *an international relaxing of tensions*	6. **exprimer**=*to express* **déprimer**=＿＿＿＿＿
6. *to depress*	7. **comprimer**=＿＿＿＿＿
7. *to compress*	8. **imprimer un livre**=＿＿＿＿
8. *to print a book*	9. **une imprimerie**=＿＿＿＿
9. *a printing house, printing press*	10. **un imprimeur**=＿＿＿＿
10. *a printer*	11. **imprimable**=＿＿＿＿
11. *printable*	12. **inimprimable**=＿＿＿＿
12. *unprintable*	13. **bâtir**=*to build* **un bâtiment**=＿＿＿＿
13. *a building*	14. **un bâtisseur**=＿＿＿＿
14. *a builder*	

TESTING EXERCISE

INSTRUCTIONS: *Choose the answer which best expresses the meaning of the indicated. If you miss any of them, review the section.*

1. Rousseau ne nous a peut-être pas dit tous les faits de sa vie, mais **il a au moins essayé de nous les dire.**
   A. tried to get us to tell them
   B. tried to tell them about us
   C. tried to tell them to us.

---

1. C
(85)

2. Jean se promenait dans le parc hier soir avec Marie. Je l'ai vue plus tard. In this sentence **l'** refers to:
   A. Marie   B. Jean   C. le parc

---

2. A
(85)

3. **Il nous faut** aller en ville.
   A. He needs us . . .   B. We need to . . .   C. We are needed . . .

---

3. B
(87)

4. **Il vous importe** de partir à temps.
   A. You are important . . .
   B. It is important for you . . .
   C. He finds it important for you . . .

---

4. B
(87)

5. **Elles se sont parlé.**
   A. They spoke to her
   B. They spoke about her.
   C. They spoke to each other.

5. C (86)	**6.**	**Amusez-vous bien.** A. Have a good time. B. You are having a good time. C. You had a good time.

6. A (88)	**7.**	**Qu'il parte** à l'instant. A. He is leaving. B. He left. C. Have him leave.

7. C (89)	**8.**	**Il parle en tant que professeur.** A. He speaks to many professors. B. He is talking of a professor. C. He is speaking as a professor.

8. C (90)	**9.**	Puisqu'elle avait beaucoup de travail, **elle s'y est mise** de bonne heure. A. put it off B. started C. went there

9. B (91)	**10.**	**Je m'en vais** à huit heures A. I am leaving B. I am taking it with me C. I am seeing about it

10. A
(92)

READING PASSAGES

INSTRUCTIONS: *Read the following passages and answer the questions at the end in order to verify your comprehension.*

Préambule des "Confessions"

Jean-Jacques Rousseau

Je forme une entreprise qui n'eut jamais d'exemple, et **dont** [1] l'exécution n'**aura** [2] point d'imitateur. Je veux montrer à mes semblables un homme dans toute la vérité de la nature, et cet homme, ce **sera** [3] moi.

Moi seul. Je sens mon coeur, et je connais les hommes. Je ne suis fait
5   comme aucun de ceux que j'ai vus; j'ose croire n'être fait comme aucun de ceux qui existent. Si je ne vaux pas mieux, au moins je suis autre. Si la nature a bien ou mal fait de briser le moule **dans lequel** [4] elle m'a jeté, c'est **ce dont** [5] on ne peut juger qu'après m'avoir lu.

Que la trompette du Jugement dernier sonne quand elle **voudra,** [6] je
10   **viendrai,** [7] ce livre à la main, me présenter devant le Souverain Juge. Je **dirai** [8] hautement: "Voilà ce que j'ai pensé, ce que je fus. J'ai dit le bien et le mal avec la même franchise. Je n'ai rien **tu** [9] de mauvais, rien ajouté de bon; et, s'il m'est arrivé d'employer quelque ornement indifférent, ce n'a

---

1 *whose*	**4** *in which*	**7** *future tense* **venir**
2 *will have*	**5** *something of which*	**8** *future tense* **dire**
3 *will be*	**6** *future tense* **vouloir**	**9** *past participle of* **taire**

jamais été que pour remplir un vide occasionné par mon défaut de mémoire.
15 J'ai pu supposer vrai ce que je savais avoir pu l'être, jamais ce que je savais
être faux. Je me suis montré tel que je fus, méprisable et vil quand je l'ai été,
bon, généreux, sublime, quand je l'ai été; j'ai dévoilé mon intérieur tel que
Tu l'as vu Toi-même, Etre éternel. Rassemble autour de moi l'innombrable
foule de mes semblables; qu'ils écoutent mes confessions, qu'ils gémissent de
20 mes indignités, qu'ils rougissent de mes misères. Que chacun d'eux découvre
à son tour son coeur au pied de ton trône avec la même sincérité; et puis,
qu'un seul te dise, s'il l'ose: Je fus meilleur que cet homme-là."

1. In lines 1–8 the author states that:
    A. he will attempt to imitate in his self-description the biographical revelations of the lives of the saints
    B. he considers himself superior to all men of his acquaintance
    C. after he was born, the mold in which he was cast, was broken
    D. fundamentally he is the same as any other man.

1. C   **2.** In lines 9–22 the author states that:
    A. in his book, he has reported the facts as he would have liked them to be
    B. he has spoken the truth as he saw it, neither adding nor deleting anything
    C. what he knew to be true he altered to fit the pattern he wished to present
    D. at the last judgment he will be prepared to point to his fellow men who surround the throne of the Eternal Being and say: "I was better than that man there."

2. B

La nature de l'homme

Buffon

L'homme rend par un signe extérieur ce qui se passe au dedans de lui, il
communique sa pensée par la parole: ce signe est commun à toute l'espèce
humaine; l'homme sauvage parle comme l'homme **policé,**[1] et tous deux
parlent naturellement, et parlent pour se faire entendre. Aucun des animaux
5 n'a ce signe de la pensée: ce n'est pas, comme on le croit communément,
faute[2] d'organisme; **la langue**[3] du singe a paru aux anatomistes aussi
parfaite que celle de l'homme. Le singe **parlerait**[4] donc, s'il pensait: si
l'ordre de ses pensées avait quelque chose de commun avec **les nôtres,**[5] il
parlerait notre langue; et, en supposant qu'il n'eût que des pensées de singe,
10 il parlerait aux autres singes: mais on ne les a jamais vus **s'entretenir**[6]
ou discourir ensemble. Ils n'ont donc pas même un ordre, une suite de
pensées à leur façon, bien loin d'en avoir de semblables aux nôtres; il ne se

1 *civilized*   3 *the tongue*   5 *ours*
2 *for lack of*   4 *would speak*   6 *converse*

passe à leur intérieur rien de **suivi,**[7] rien d'**ordonné,**[8] puisqu'ils n'expriment rien par des signes combinés et arrangés: ils n'ont donc pas la pensée, même
15   au plus petit degré.

    . . . C'est parce qu'ils ne peuvent joindre ensemble aucune idée, qu'ils ne pensent ni ne parlent; c'est par la même raison qu'ils n'inventent et ne perfectionnent rien. S'ils étaient doués de la puissance de réfléchir, même au plus petit degré, ils **seraient** [9] capables de quelque espèce de progrès, ils
20   **acquerraient** [10] plus d'industrie; les **castors** [11] aujourd'hui **bâtiraient** [12] avec plus d'art et de solidité que ne bâtissaient les premiers castors; l'abeille perfectionnerait **encore** [13] tous les jours la cellule qu'elle habite: car si on suppose que cette cellule est aussi parfaite qu'elle peut l'être, on donne à cet insecte plus d'esprit que nous n'en avons, on lui accorde une intelligence
25   supérieure à **la nôtre,**[14] **par laquelle il apercevrait** [15] tout d'un coup le dernier point de perfection auquel il doit porter son ouvrage, tandis que nous-mêmes ne voyons jamais clairement ce point, et qu'il nous faut beaucoup de réflexion, de temps et **d'habitude** [16] pour perfectionner le moindre de nos arts . . .
30   Mais ces preuves de l'immatérialité de notre âme peuvent s'étendre encore plus loin. Nous avons dit que la nature marche toujours et agit en tout par degrés imperceptibles et par **nuances:** [17] cette vérité qui **ailleurs** [18] ne souffre aucune exception, **se dément** [19] ici tout à fait. Il y a une distance infinie entre les facultés de l'homme et celles du plus parfait animal; preuve évidente
35   que l'homme est d'une différente nature, que seul il fait une classe à part, **de laquelle** [20] il faut descendre **en parcourant** [21] un espace infini, avant que d'arriver à celle des animaux: car si l'homme était de l'ordre des animaux, **il y aurait** [22] dans la nature un certain nombre d'êtres moins parfaits que l'homme et plus parfaits que les animaux **par lesquels** [23] on **descendrait** [24]
40   insensiblement et par nuances de l'homme au singe: mais cela n'est pas; on passe tout d'un coup de l'être pensant à l'être matériel, de la puissance intellectuelle à la force mécanique, de l'ordre et du dessein au mouvement aveugle, de la réflexion à l'appétit.

    Voilà plus qu'il n'en faut pour nous démontrer l'excellence de notre nature,
45   et la distance immense que la bonté du Créateur a mise entre l'homme et la bête. L'homme est un être raisonnable, l'animal est un être sans raison; et comme il n'y a point de milieu entre le positif et le négatif, comme il n'y a point d'êtres intermédiaires entre l'être raisonnable et l'être sans raison, il est évident que l'homme est d'une nature entièrement différente de celle de
50   l'animal, qu'il ne lui ressemble que par l'extérieur, et que le juger par cette ressemblance matérielle, c'est **se laisser tromper** [25] par l'apparence, et **fermer** [26] volontairement les yeux à la lumière qui doit nous la faire distinguer de la réalité.

---

7 *coherent*
8 *ordered*
9 *would be*
10 *would acquire*
11 *beavers*
12 *would build*
13 *still*

14 *ours*
15 *by which it would perceive*
16 *practice*
17 *shades of difference*
18 *elsewhere*
19 *contradicts itself*
20 *from which . . .*

21 *while covering*
22 *there would be*
23 *by which*
24 *would descend*
25 *to let oneself be deceived*
26 *to close*

1. Lines 1–7 state that:
A. man communicates his thoughts by gesture
B. both savage and civilized man use speech to make themselves understood
C. animals also communicate vocally
D. the tongue of the monkey is inferior automatically to that of man.

1. B   **2.** Lines 8–15 state that:
A. monkeys can speak to each other
B. they have been observed in groups carrying out what resembles human conversation
C. they have never been observed in what could be termed conversation
D. their expressed signs and ordered flow of action indicate some degree of rational communication.

2. C   **3.** Lines 16–29 state that:
A. if monkeys were endowed with the power of thought, they would be capable of progress
B. some progress in the cell of the bee has recently been observed
C. the beaver shows ability to improve the design of his building
D. man automatically improves in the manufacture of all he makes.

3. A   **4.** Lines 30–43 state that:
A. nature does not always effect her changes slowly
B. the difference in the nature of man and that of the higher animals is only one of degree
C. there is an infinite difference between the mind of man and that of the highest animal
D. there exist in the world beings less perfect than man but more perfect than animals.

4. C   **5.** Lines 44–53 state that:
A. the gradation between the thinking being and the material being is barely perceptible
B. man is capable of reflection, and the animal is not
C. there are numerous intermediate beings between man and the animal
D. exterior similarities indicate inner similarities.

5. B

Chapter Fourteen

93. *Relative Pronoun* dont

1. You have seen that one of the functions of **qui** and **que** is to join two phrases:

En raison de l'intérêt *qui* **s'attache à l'histoire des métaux** . . .	*Because of the interest which is connected with the history of metals* . . .
Les grès *que* **j'ai examinés** . . .	*The sandstones which I have examined* . . .

2. **Dont** has a like function, but it is used to replace expressions introduced by **de**. It may refer either to persons or things, and its meanings may be expressed in English by *whose, of which,* or simply *which,* depending on the English verb and its preposition:

L'histoire fait mention *de* **mines très anciennes au Sinaï.**	*History makes mention of very old mines in the Sinai region.*
Les mines les plus anciennes *dont* **l'histoire fasse mention sont au Sinaï.**	*The oldest mines* **of which** *history makes mention (or* **which** *history mentions) are in the Sinai region.*
On connaît la haute compétence *de* **M. de Morgan.**	*The great competence* **of** *M. de Morgan is well known.*
M. de Morgan, *dont* **on connaît la haute compétence, est présent.**	*M. de Morgan,* **whose** *great competence is well known, is present.*

INSTRUCTIONS: *Continue to circle the words which you do not recognize immediately.*

		1.	**le cuivre**=*copper* Les mines de cuivre du Sinaï sont les plus anciennes dont l'histoire fasse mention.
1.	The Sinai copper mines are the oldest of which history makes mention. (*Notice the subjunctive form, which usually appears in clauses following superlatives.*)	**2.**	L'auteur parle d'un sceptre en cuivre pur dont il a fait l'analyse.
2.	The author speaks of a sceptre of pure copper of which he has made an analysis (which he has analyzed).	**3.**	Il fait mention de M. de Morgan, dont on connaît les belles découvertes.
3.	He mentions M. de Morgan whose splendid discoveries are well known.	**4.**	Ce sont les résultats des études dont il va préciser les détails.
4.	These are the results of the studies the details of which he is going to specify.	**5.**	Il va être question plus loin des minerais de fer.
5.	It will be a question further on of iron ores.	**6.**	On trouve dans cette région les minerais dont il va être question plus loin.
6.	One finds in this region the ores of which it will be a question later on.	**7.**	Nous allons parler plus loin de plusieurs catégories de saints.
7.	Further on, we are going to speak of several categories of saints.	**8.**	Nous allons en parler.
8.	We are going to speak of them.	**9.**	Il existe dans l'Islam plusieurs catégories de personnes plus ou moins sacrées dont nous allons parler plus loin.
9.	There exist in Islam several categories of more or less sacred persons of whom we are going to speak later on.	**10.**	Mahomet fut l'objet d'une grande faveur divine.
10.	Mohammad was the recipient of a great divine favor.	**11.**	Mahomet, dont nous allons parler plus loin, fut l'objet d'une faveur divine.
11.	Mohammad, of whom we are going to speak further, was the recipient of a divine favor.	**12.**	. . . la grande faveur divine dont Mahomet fut l'objet . . .
12.	. . . the great divine favor of which Mohammad was the recipient . . .	**13.**	**autrement dit**=*that is to say, in other words* Il y a d'abord les descendants du Prophète, autrement dit les *chérifs*

	et les *sayyids* qui reçoivent héréditaire-ment une parcelle de la grande faveur divine dont Mahomet fut l'objet.
13. There are first of all the descendants of the Prophet, that is to say the *chérifs* and the *sayyids* who receive hereditarily a part of the great divine favor of which Mohammad was the recipient.	**14.** Il y a aussi les *majdzub,* dont les ravissements mystiques sont assez bien connus.
14. There are also the *majdzub* whose mystical ecstasies are quite well known.	**15.** Il faut faire mention d'une autre caté-gorie de saints.
15. We must make mention of another category of saints.	**16.** Il faut en faire mention.
16. We must make mention of it.	**17.** Il y a ensuite une autre catégorie dont il faut faire mention : les *wali,* ou saints officiels.
17. There is next another category of which we must make mention: the *wali,* or official saints.	**18.** Il y a enfin les fondateurs des con-fréries religieuses, dont les disciples sont les fameux derviches.
18. Finally, there are the founders of the religious brotherhoods, whose disciples are the famous dervishes.	**19.** **ailleurs** = *elsewhere* Il convient de préciser ailleurs les détails des actes rituels.
19. It is appropriate to specify elsewhere the details of the ritual acts.	**20.** Nous citons leurs actes rituels dont il convient de préciser les détails ailleurs.
20. We cite their ritual acts, the details of which it is appropriate to specify elsewhere.	**21.** Ces personnes sacrées sont plus ou moins ignorées du bédouin dont la ferveur va ailleurs.
21. These sacred persons are more or less unknown to the Bedouin whose fervor goes elsewhere (has other objects).	**22.** Il convient d'ailleurs de préciser ces détails. (**d'ailleurs**—*elsewhere/moreover*)
22. It is appropriate, *moreover,* to specify these details.	**23.** Le saint des bédouins ne répond pas nécessairement à la définition ordi-naire.
23. The Bedouin saint does not necessarily correspond to the ordinary definition.	**24.** Il s'agit ici des bédouins dont le saint ne répond nullement à la définition usuelle.

24.	It is here a question of the Bedouins whose saints do not correspond at all to the ordinary definition.	**25.**	Le commandant a démontré la navigabilité des rapides de Boussa, dont il a étudié les chenaux avec soin.
25.	The commandant demonstrated the navigability of the rapids of Boussa, the channels of which he studied carefully.	**26.**	Louis XVI était rempli de qualités dont quelques-unes étaient celles d'un roi.
26.	Louis XVI was filled with qualities, a few of which were befitting a king.	**27.**	Les ravisseurs firent couler le sang d'une personne dont la vue était capable d'attendrir des tigres.
27.	The abductors shed the blood of a person the sight of whom was capable of softening tigers.	**28.**	L'on compare souvent le noyau d'un atome au soleil central d'un système dont les planètes sont les électrons périphériques.
28.	The nucleus of an atom is often compared to the central sun of a system, the planets of which are the peripheral electrons.		

94. *Relative Pronoun* lequel

1. Lequel (*which, who, whom*) and its forms may signal either a question (see Chapter Fifteen) or the joining of two phrases. **Lequel** agrees with its antecedent in gender and number. It also contracts with **à** and **de**, giving the following forms:

MASC. SING.	MASC. PLURAL	FEM. SING.	FEM PLURAL
lequel	lesquels	laquelle	lesquelles
auquel	auxquels	à laquelle	auxquelles
duquel	desquels	de laquelle	desquelles

2. These relative pronouns may refer either to persons or things according to the context:

L'Islam ignore l'acte rituel *par lequel* **une personne devient définitivement sainte.**	*In Islam the ritual act **by which** a person becomes definitively holy is unknown.*
Chez tous les animaux *sur lesquels* **j'ai opéré . . .**	*In all the animals **upon which** I have operated . . .*

Il y a d'abord les descendants du prophète, *auxquels* se transmet une parcelle de la faveur divine.	*There are first of all the decendants of the prophet, **to whom** is transmitted a part of the divine favor.*

3. **Lequel** or one of its forms is sometimes used instead of **qui** or **que** in order to refer more precisely to the antecedent:

J'enlevai l'un des crochets à venin de la vipère, *lequel* n'avait pas moins de 9ᵐᵐ de longueur.	*I removed one of the venomous fangs of the viper, **which fang** was not less than 9ᵐᵐ long.*

Since **lequel** and its various forms agree in gender and number with their antecedents, **lequel** can in this sentence refer only to the fang (m.) which was removed.

INSTRUCTIONS: *Continue to circle the words which you do not recognize immediately.*

	1. L'Islam ignore, ou presque, l'acte rituel par lequel une personne cesse d'être profane.
1. In Islam the ritual act by which a person ceases to be unsanctified is unknown, or almost unknown.	2. L'Islam ignore presque totalement la consécration par laquelle une personne devient sainte.
2. In Islam the act of consecration by which a person becomes sanctified (holy) is almost totally unknown.	3. Par "agents du sacré", désignons des êtres doués d'un pouvoir surnaturel grâce auquel ils peuvent accomplir des choses merveilleuses.
3. By "agents of the holy" let us designate beings endowed with a supernatural power thanks to which they can accomplish marvelous things. (*Remember that the verb form without the subject pronoun signals the imperative.*)	4. **faire appel**=*to call upon, to appeal to* Le bédouin fait appel également aux saints officiels de son clan et au derviche, lequel parvient difficilement cependant à recruter des adeptes (des disciples) dans le désert.
4. The Bedouin appeals also to the official saints of his clan and to the dervish. The latter, however, manages with difficulty to recruit followers in the desert.	5. Il faut que nous précisions celui auquel le bédouin fait appel.
5. We must specify which one the Bedouin calls upon.	6. Il fait appel aux derviches et au *fakir*, lequel est réputé pour son pouvoir surnaturel.

6. He calls upon the dervishes and the *faqir,* who is reputed for his supernatural power.

7. **doit** = *must*
Pourtant, l'énergie occulte, à laquelle le bédouin fait appel, ne doit pas être trop forte.

7. However, the occult energy upon which the Bedouin calls must not be too strong.

8. L'énergie occulte, grâce à laquelle il accomplit des choses merveilleuses doit être assez faible pour qu'elle ne le sépare pas tout à fait du monde profane.

8. The occult energy, thanks to which he accomplishes marvelous things, must be sufficiently weak that it does not separate him completely from the secular world.

9. . . . les animaux sur lesquels j'ai opéré . . .

9. . . . the animals upon which I have operated . . .

10. Il est étonnant de noter la rapidité avec laquelle se coagule le sang des oiseaux.

10. It is astonishing to note the rapidity with which the blood of birds coagulates.

11. Pendant son expédition le commandant a navigué sur le Moyen–Niger, sur lequel il a réuni les notions les plus utiles.

11. During his expedition the commandant navigated upon the middle Niger, about which he gathered some extremely useful information.

12. L'homme fait une classe à part, de laquelle il faut descendre une distance infinie avant d'arriver à celle des animaux.
(Is **fait** here used as a verb or a noun?)

12. *a verb*
Man makes up a distinct class from which one must descend an infinite distance before reaching that of the animals.

13. Le fait de pouvoir penser distingue l'homme des animaux, lesquels ne possèdent pas ce don.
(Is **fait** here used as a verb or a noun?)

13. *a noun*
The fact of being able to think distinguishes man from the animals, which do not possess this gift.

14. Selon Buffon, il n'y a pas un grand nombre d'êtres moins parfaits que l'homme et plus parfaits que les animaux, par lesquels on peut descendre insensiblement de l'homme au singe.

14. According to Buffon, there is not a large number of beings less perfect than man and more perfect than the animals by which one may descend imperceptibly from man to the monkeys.

Re-read several times the words you have circled above, and then continue.

95. *Relative Pronouns* ce qui, ce que

1. The meanings of the compound relative pronouns **ce qui** (subject) and **ce que** (object) are usually expressed in English by *what, that which, which* or *the fact that.*

2. The pattern **ce que** (**ce qui**) + statement + **c'est** + statement is used to emphasize a certain part of the sentence:

Ce qui est évident c'est la fausseté de ces notions précédentes.	*What is evident is the falseness of these previous ideas.*
Ce que je prétends avoir établi c'est la fausseté de l'opinion généralement admise.	*What I claim to have established is the falseness of the generally accepted opinion.*

INSTRUCTIONS: *Continue to circle the words which you do not immediately recognize.*

---

1. Ce qui est remarquable, c'est que l'Islam ignore la consécration.

1. What is remarkable is that Islam is unaware of the (has no) act of consecration.

2. Ce que nous désignons par "agent du sacré", c'est un être touché par la faveur divine.

2. What we designate by an "agent of the holy" is a being touched by the divine favor.

3. On ne sait toujours ce qu'il faut entendre par le *wali.*

3. One does not always know what to understand by the word *wali.*

4. Il est rare que l'on sache exactement ce qui se passa dans l'Antiquité.

4. It is rare for one to know exactly what happened in ancient times.

5. Ce qui intéresse le conférencier, c'est la femelle nématode.

5. What interests the lecturer is the female of the nematode.

6. **auparavant** = *before, previously*
Ce fait confirme ce que je crois avoir établi auparavant.

6. This fact confirms what I believe to have established before.

7. **surtout** = *especially*
Ce qui me paraît surtout digne de remarque c'est que l'incubation était, dans ce cas, suspendue.

7. What appears to me to be especially worthy of remark (remarkable) is the fact that the incubation was in this case suspended.

8. Ce qui a empêché les larves de sortir de la femelle auparavant c'était la sécheresse prolongée de cette année.

8. What prevented the larva from coming out of the female previously was the prolonged drought of this summer.

9. **un oeuf** = *an egg*
Ce qui m'a fort étonné c'est le nombre de femelles brunes des nématodes que j'ai trouvées pleines d'oeufs.

9. What greatly surprised me is the number of brown females of the nematode which I found full of eggs.

10. Ce que je crois avoir établi auparavant, c'est la période de l'incubation des oeufs des nématodes.

10. What I believe to have established previously is the period of incubation of the nematode's eggs.

11. **autrefois** = *formerly*
Quoique disputées vivement autrefois, les mines de cuivre du Sinaï sont aujourd'hui tout à fait abandonnées, ce qui s'explique par la pauvreté de leurs minerais actuels.

11. Although vigorously contested formerly, the Sinai copper mines are now completely abandoned, a fact which is explained by the poor quality of their present ores.

12. Ce qui me paraît surtout étonnant, c'est que les mines disputées si vivement autrefois, sont maintenant abandonnées.

12. What appears especially surprising to me is that the mines contested so vigorously in former times are now abandoned.

13. La politesse est la fleur de l'humanité ; et ce qui n'est pas assez poli n'est pas assez humain.
                                                   Joubert

13. Politeness is the flower of humanity, and what is not polite enough is not human enough.

14. Ce qui nous empêche souvent de nous abandonner à un seul vice est que nous en avons plusieurs.
                                        La Rochefoucauld

14. That which often prevents us from abandoning ourselves to a single vice is that we have several of them.

15. M. de Morgan s'est mis à ma disposition, ce qui m'a aidé énormément.

15. Mr. de Morgan put himself at my disposal, which aided me enormously.

16. J'ai pu supposer vrai ce que je savais avoir pu l'être.

16. I may have supposed to be true that which I knew could have been so.

17. Je n'ai jamais supposé vrai ce que je savais être faux.

17. I have never supposed to be true that which I knew to be false.

18. L'homme rend par un signe extérieur ce qui se passe au dedans de lui.

18. Man expresses (renders) by an outward sign that which takes place within him.

19. Ce qui distingue l'homme des animaux, c'est la parole.
(Does **parole** here mean *word* or *language?*)

19. *Language* fits better in the context. What distinguishes man from the animals is language.

96. *Idioms*—soit . . . soit

1.   Soit is the subjunctive form of **est** (see Chapter Ten). It is used idiomatically to indicate alternatives and is translated by *either . . . or:*

. . . **des corps odorants placés *soit***   . . . *odorous bodies placed **either** in*
dans l'oxygène *soit* dans l'air.   *oxygen **or** in the open air . . .*

INSTRUCTIONS: *Continue to circle the words which you do not immediately recognize.*

	1. L'agent actif produit son effet maximum lorsque les tiges des fleurs sont plongées soit dans l'eau soit dans la mousse humide.
1. The active agent produces its maximum effect when the stems of the flowers are plunged either in water or in damp moss.	**2.** On peut faire varier les résultats en faisant varier les conditions soit de température soit d'humidité relative.
2. One can cause the results to vary by causing the conditions either of temperature or of relative humidity to vary.	**3.** Certaines plantes sont capables de produire une émission subite de parfum soit par suite du contact de la main soit par une brusque exposition aux radiations solaires.
3. Certain plants are capable of producing a sudden emission of fragrance either in consequence of a contact with the hand or by an abrupt exposure to the rays of the sun.	**4.** Suivant la température de l'atmosphère les nuages se voient soit sur les montagnes soit sur les prairies.
4. According to the temperature, clouds are seen either over the mountains or over the meadows.	

97. *Idioms with* venir

1. The meaning of **venir** followed by an infinitive construction varies according to the preposition used:

(A)   **venir**+**pour**+infinitive or simply **venir**+infinitive marks *intention:*

Il vient (pour) faire des remarques sur l'histoire des métaux.	*He is coming to make a few remarks on the history of metals.*
Le bédouin vient au fakir (pour) solliciter son aide.	*The Bedouin comes to the faqir to solicit his aid.*

(B)   **venir**+**de**+infinitive indicates a recent event and is translated by *has just* (present) or *had just* (imperfect):

Il *vient de* faire une conférence sur l'histoire des métaux.	*He **has just** given a lecture on the history of metals.*
Je *venais de* vous préciser le sujet de sa conférence.	*I **had just** specified to you the subject of his lecture.*

(C)   **venir**+**à**+infinitive means *to happen to:*

Si vous *venez à le* voir, dites-lui de venir me voir.	*If you **happen to** see him, tell him to come and see me.*

(D)   **en venir à**+infinitive means *to be reduced to, to come to:*

On *en vint à* abandonner les mines du Sinaï, les minerais étant épuisés.	*They **were reduced** to abandoning the Sinai mines, the ores being exhausted.*

READING PREPARATION

INSTRUCTIONS: *Continue to circle those sentences which contain new or unfamiliar vocabulary. Review them after you finish the exercise and again in a day or two, until you recognize them immediately.*

	1. Les bédouins viennent au tombeau de leur saint pour solliciter une faveur.
1. The Bedouins come to the tomb of their saint (in order) to solicit a favor.	2. Ils viennent de solliciter une faveur.
2. They have just solicited a favor.	3. On y vient implorer une guérison.
3. They come there to ask for a healing.	4. On vient d'y implorer une guérison.

4.	They have just asked for a healing at that place.	**5.**	On en venait à implorer une guérison.
5.	They came (were coming) to the point of asking for a healing.	**6.**	On venait à solliciter une faveur.
6.	They happened to ask for a favor.	**7.**	**prêter**=*to lend* **prêter serment**=*to take an oath* Ils vinrent au lieu de pèlerinage pour prêter serment.
7.	They came to the place of pilgrimage to take an oath.	**8.**	Ils venaient d'y prêter serment.
8.	They had just taken an oath there.	**9.**	Ils en sont venus à prêter serment.
9.	They were reduced to taking an oath.	**10.**	On venait à y prêter serment.
10.	They happened to take an oath there.	**11.**	**éloigner**=*to ward off* On y vient faire appel à une énergie occulte pour éloigner le mal.
11.	They come there to call upon an occult power to ward off evil.	**12.**	Cette étude qui vient d'être publiée, explique les usages religeux des bédouins.
12.	This study which has just been published, explains the religious practices of the Bedouins.	**13.**	Cette étude, qui venait d'être publiée faisait ressortir le caractère surnaturel des guérisons en question.
13.	This study which had just been published, brought out the supernatural character of the healings in question.		

VOCABULARY DEVELOPMENT

INSTRUCTIONS: *Try to associate the meaning of the words in each of the groups with the root word.*

		1.	**une guérison**=*a healing* **un guérisseur**=_____
1.	a healer	**2.**	Le malade est **guérissable.**
2.	The sick person is *curable.*	**3.**	La maladie est **inguérissable.** . .
3.	The disease is *incurable.*	**4.**	**loin**=*far away, far* Tout cela se passa dans un passé **lointain.**

4. All that happened in the *distant* past.	**5.** Après l'avoir attendu longtemps, on l'a aperçu dans le **lointain**.
5. After having waited for him a long time, they saw him in the *distance*	**6.** Ayant très peur de son neveu, elle voulait **l'éloigner**.
6. Being very afraid of her nephew, she wanted *to keep him at a distance*	**7.** Ces événements eurent lieu dans **un passé peu éloigné**.
7. Those events took place in *the recent past.*	**8.** **faible**=*weak* **la faiblesse**=_____
8. *the weakness*	**9.** La politique de Machiavel était d'aider **les faibles** et **d'affaiblir** les puissants.
9. The policy of Machiavelli was to aid *the weak* and *to weaken* the strong.	**10.** **Affaiblie** par la pluie, la maison s'écroula.
10. Weakened by the rain, the house collapsed.	**11.** **l'affaiblissement**= _____
11. *the weakening*	**12.** **un frère**=*a brother* Ses **confrères** de l'Académie l'ont chaleureusement applaudi.
12. His *colleagues* of the Academy applauded him warmly.	**13.** Dans la plupart des religions il y a des **confréries** religieuses.
13. In most religions, there are religious *brotherhoods.*	**14.** **témoigner**=*to witness, to testify* Ils furent des **témoins oculaires** de l'accident.
14. They were *eye witnesses* of the accident.	**15.** Le tribunal ne voulut pas accepter son **témoignage**.
15. The court did not wish to accept his *testimony.*	**16.** Pour que l'expérience réussisse, il faut qu'on ait **un échantillon témoin**.
16. In order for the experiment to succeed, one must have *a control sample* (one which witnesses to the validity of the experiment).	**17.** **porter**=*to carry, to bear* **un porte-bagages**= _____
17. *a luggage rack*	**18.** **un porte-bombes**=_____
18. *a bomb rack*	**19.** **un porte-cigares**=_____
19. *a cigar case*	**20.** **un porte-bonheur**=_____
20. *a good luck charm*	**21.** **un porte-malheur**=_____

21. *someone who brings bad luck, a jinx*	**22.** **un porte-parole**=_____
22. *a spokesman*	**23.** **sec, sèche**= *dry* Parce qu'il n'a guère plu cette année, nous connaissons une **sécheresse** extraordinaire.
23. Because it has hardly rained at all this year, we are experiencing an extraordinary *drought*.	**24.** une orange **desséchée**= _____
24. a *dried-out* orange	

INSTRUCTIONS: *Circle the letter which best completes the sentence or which best translates the indicated word or phrase.*

    1. C'est un conférencier *dont* le talent est connu.
       A. of which   B. that   C. from whom   D. whose

---

1. D
(93)
  2. Les feuilles dont l'arbre est couvert sont vertes.
     A. The leaves cover the green tree.
     B. The green leaves do not cover the tree.
     C. The leaves with which the tree is covered are green.
     D. The tree is therefore covered with green leaves.

---

2. C
(93)
  3. Les personnes *auxquelles* il fait appel sont les derviches et le fakir.
     A. to which   B. to what   C. to whom   D. at whom

---

3. C
(94)
  4. Il a réuni des notions utiles *desquelles* on a constaté la navigabilité du fleuve.
     A. of which   B. from whom   C. of whom   D. from which

---

4. D
(94)
  5. Mais il sut par un ami *auquel* il avait fait appel que la dame s'était mariée à un autre.
     A. at which   B. at whom   C. to whom   D. to which

---

5. C
(94)
  6. Il avait reçu une flèche dans l'oeil *duquel* il perdit la vue.
     A. from which   B. of whom   C. from whom   D. of which

---

6. D
(94)
  7. Ce qui était remarquable c'était qu'il n'y avait pas de consécration.
     A. It was remarkable that there was no act of consecration.
     B. What was remarkable was that there was no act of consecration.
     C. What was remarkable was that there would be no act of consecration.
     D. What was remarkable was that he was not consecrated.

---

7. B
(95)

READING PASSAGES

INSTRUCTIONS: *It is necessary to read accurately but also with at least moderate speed. Practice timing yourself. Take four minutes to read this passage of about 175 words. Circle but do not look up unfamiliar words the first time through. Then answer the questions at the end to determine your general comprehension. Then come back to the circled words and work out their meaning more precisely.*

Les nématodes de la betterave (*Heterodera Schachtii*)

Note de M. Willot, présentée par M. Wolf. (extrait).
Comptes rendus des séances de l'Académie des Sciences, Vol. 133, p. 703.

On trouve ordinairement vides, en juillet et août, toutes les femelles brunes du nématode de la **betterave;** [1] j'ai été fort étonné de les trouver, cette année, pleines d'œufs, d'embryons et de larves, même en septembre, et j'ai vu les larves s'agiter aussitôt que la femelle fut ouverte, ce qui n'a

5   généralement lieu que par une température chaude et dix minutes ou un quart d'heure après l'ouverture de la femelle.

Ce fait confirme, si je ne me trompe, ce que j'ai établi en 1890, **à savoir** [2] que c'est sous l'influence de la chaleur et de l'humidité que la femelle brune, qui est morte, **se gonfle,** [3] que le canal vulvaire s'ouvre mécaniquement et

10   permet aux larves de sortir. La sécheresse prolongée de cette année, loin de favoriser la dilatation des femelles et l'ouverture du canal, a produit un effet tout contraire. Ce qui me paraît surtout digne de remarque, c'est que l'incubation était suspendue, comme en hiver; on voyait, en effet, les œufs à tous les états de segmentation et tous les produits vivants . . .

1.   The first paragraph states that
    A. all females of the nematode are brown
    B. that the females of this species are usually empty during the summer months
    C. that during the summer months the females are usually vivid because of the mating season
    D. they are ordinarily full of eggs during the summer months.

---

1. B   2.   The author states in the first paragraph that
    A. he was mildly surprised at what he found
    B. he expected to find what he found.
    C. he was greatly surprised at his findings
    D. he waited until the temperature was warmer to make his observations.

---

2. C   3.   He states in the first paragraph that
    A. he noticed on this occasion that the larvae were moving before the female was opened.

---

1 *sugar beet*   2 *namely*   3 *swells up*

B. a warm temperature is usually necessary in order to induce movement among the larvae.
c. the females are generally full of eggs in September
D. the larvae do not generally move in a warm temperature.

3. B   **4.** In the second paragraph we learn that
A. the author had already reached a similar conclusion
B. the larvae leave the female shortly before her death
c. the female swells because of cold, damp weather
D. the female reproduces best in early spring.

4. A   **5.** In the second paragraph we learn that the condition described by the author in the first paragraph was due to
A. an early dilatation of the females
B. the swelling of the females
c. the unusual drought of this year
D. an early incubation.

5. C

INSTRUCTIONS: *Take twelve minutes to read this passage of about 600 words. Circle but do not look up unfamiliar words the first time through. Take the test to determine your general comprehension, and then come back to the circled words to work out their meaning more precisely.*

Surnaturel et guérison dans le Négueb

Joseph Chelhod, *Objets et Mondes*, Tome V (automne 1965), p. 158.

Dans cette thérapeutique qu'on pourrait qualifier de mystique, le bédouin du Négueb cherche donc la guérison en exploitant les ressources d'un sacré anonyme plus ou moins répandu dans la nature. Pourtant, cette énergie occulte, à laquelle il fait appel pour éloigner les *djinn* et chasser le mal, **doit** [1]
5   être suffisamment faible pour qu'elle ne fasse pas l'objet d'une séparation d'avec le monde profane. Pareille à une petite **pile** [2] électrique qu'on peut mettre sans inconvénient entre toutes les mains, l'amulette est exempte de **nocivité** [3] pour le porteur. Somme toute, le champ d'action de cette médecine "spirituelle", *tibb ruhâni*, comme on la désigne parfois, est limité par sa
10   faiblesse même: elle ne **serait** [4] agissante que dans les cas plus ou moins anodins et dans les maladies sans réelle gravité. C'est pourquoi, lorsque la puissance responsable des troubles se montre récalcitrante, les *Tiyâha* sollicitent l'intervention directe des agents du sacré, décédés ou vivants.
    Il convient de préciser ici que l'Islam ignore, ou presque, la consécration,
15   c'est-à-dire l'acte rituel par lequel une personne cesse d'être profane et devient

---

1 *must*
2 *battery;*
3 *harmfulness*
4 *conditional of* être

définitivement sainte parce qu'elle est **affectée** [5] au service divin. Par "agents du sacré", nous désignons donc non pas les membres d'un clergé—que cette religion ne connaît point—mais des êtres touchés par la faveur divine et doués d'un pouvoir surnaturel grâce auquel ils peuvent accomplir des choses
20 merveilleuses. Il existe dans l'Islam plusieurs catégories de personnes plus ou moins sacrées à qui on témoigne de la déférence parce qu'elles sont le réceptacle du surnaturel. Il y a d'abord les *chérifs* et les *sayyids*, autrement dit, les descendants de la famille du Prophète, les *'ahl al-bayt,* auxquels se transmet héréditairement une parcelle de la grande faveur divine dont
25 Mahomet fut l'objet; il y a aussi les *majdzub*, hommes sujets à des ravissements mystiques, que l'on croit possédés de l'esprit divin; il y a également les saints officiels, ou *wali;* il y a enfin les fondateurs des confréries religieuses et, à un moindre degré, leurs disciples, les fameux derviches. A vrai dire, ces personnes sacrées, très vénérées de l'Islam, sont plus ou moin ignorées
30 du bédouin dont la ferveur, notamment **en matière de** [6] guérison, va ailleurs. Sans doute, il respecte les *wali* et sollicite leur intervention. Mais les saints qu'il implore sont rarement ceux de la religion officielle: ses préférences vont surtout aux *wali* issus de son clan, qui **prennent figure** [7] d'ancêtres. Il fait également appel au derviche; mais celui-ci parvient difficilement à re-
35 cruter des adeptes dans le désert. En outre, le *fakir*, cet ami d'Allah réputé pour son pouvoir surnaturel, lui fait souvent **concurrence.** [8]

Le *wali* est généralement un homme qui a mené une vie pieuse et **a fait éclater,** [9] parfois de son vivant, ou après sa mort, la preuve de sa sainteté. Mais le saint des bédouins ne répond pas nécessairement à cette définition:
40 il **pourrait être** [10] un personnage mythique ou un ancêtre éponyme. En fait, chaque clan important ou du moins chaque tribu possède le sien propre. Son tombeau, marqué par un édifice surmonté d'une coupole, ou par une construction plus modeste, ou plus simplement par un monticule de pierres, est un lieu de pèlerinage. On s'y rend en groupe, à l'occasion des fêtes, pour
45 une action de grâce. Mais la visite pourrait avoir des motifs plus prosaïques: on vient pour prêter serment, solliciter une faveur ou implorer une guérison.

1. In lines 1–7, the author states that
   A. the Bedouin often invokes the *djinn* to protect him
   B. the spirit which he invokes wants to remain anonymous
   C. that the power he invokes permeates all nature
   D. not everyone is qualified to call upon these spiritual forces.

---

1. C   **2.** In lines 7–11 we learn that
   A. the battery and the amulet are alike
   B. the amulet is unlike the battery completely
   C. one is ineffective without the other
   D. neither is without inconvenience.

---

5 *assigned*   **7** *take the shape*   **9** *has made obvious*
6 *in questions of*   **8** *competition*   **10** *could be*

2. A **3.** The spiritual medicine spoken of in lines 8–13.
   A. is far from being harmless
   B. is often reputed effective against the most stubborn diseases
   C. is effective only in minor cases
   D. comes from the *djinn*.

---

3. C **4.** In lines 14–20 we learn that in Islam
   A. saints are usually ignored
   B. the clergy is composed of saintly beings
   C. there is no rite of sanctification
   D. some of the clergy do not know much about this religion.

---

4. C **5.** Lines 20–36 state that
   A. the deity most favorable to the Bedouins is the one invoked by Mohammad
   B. the dervishes are more numerous than the other holy persons
   C. some Bedouins suppose divine power to be transmitted from father to son in spite of Mohammad's objection to the belief
   D. some holy persons have achieved an official status.

---

5. D **6.** The dervish (lines 28–36)
   A. is very popular among the Bedouins
   B. is a descendant of Mohammad
   C. does not find many followers among the desert people
   D. works closely with the *faqîr*.

---

6. C **7.** Lines 37–46 state that
   A. the *wali* and the Bedouin saint are practically synonymous
   B. the saint's tomb is sometimes visited for mundane reasons
   C. some saints are accepted by all the Bedouins
   D. the office of *wali* is held hereditarily.

---

7. B

Chapter Fifteen

98. *Interrogative Forms—Inversion and* est-ce que

1. In French, questions are often introduced by simply putting the subject pronoun after the verb:

> **Parlez-vous français?**   *Do you speak French?*

If the subject is a noun rather than a pronoun, a pronoun is often supplied in addition to the noun. This pronoun is not translated:

> **Jean vient-il?**   *Is John coming?*

2. The same interrogative effect can be obtained by using the interrogative formula **est-ce que** and not inverting the word order:

> **Est-ce que vous parlez français?**   *Do you speak French?*
> **Est-ce que Jean vient?**   *Is John coming?*

The formula **est-ce que** is not translated; it is merely a device used to introduce a question.

READING PREPARATION

INSTRUCTIONS: *Practice reading the following sentences until you can recognize all of the question forms. The new vocabulary comes from one of the reading passages of this chapter.*

1. un orage = *a storm*
Le nombre et l'intensité des orages semblent avoir augmenté dernièrement. Cette augmentation est-elle réelle?

1. The number and the intensity of storms seem to have increased lately. Is this increase actual?

2. l'accroissement = *the growth*
Est-elle le résultat du rapide accroissement des organes de publicité?

2. Is it the result of the rapid growth of organs of publicity? (news media)

3. Est-ce qu'elle est le résultat de l'accroissement des stations météorologiques?

3. Is it the result of the increase of meteorological stations?

4. le peuplier = *the poplar*
Le peuplier était-il grand?

4. Was the poplar large?

5. Etait-il isolé?

5. Was it isolated?

6. entourer = *to surround*
Etait-il entouré d'autres arbres de même hauteur?

6. Was it surrounded by other trees of the same height?

7. la taille = *the size*
Est-ce qu'il était de grande taille?

7. Was it of great size?

8. un ruisseau = *a stream*
Est-ce qu'il était près d'un ruisseau?

8. Was it near a stream?

9. le pied = *the foot, the bottom of*
Son pied était-il près d'un ruisseau?

9. Was its foot (the bottom of it) near a stream?

10. Avez-vous pris le récit au pied de la lettre?

10. Did you take the account literally?

11. la foudre = *the lightning*
Le coup de foudre avait-il été précédé d'une forte averse?

11. Had the lightning bolt been preceded by a hard downpour?

12. Le coup de foudre a-t-il frappé le peuplier ou le pommier?
(**une pomme** = *an apple*)

12. Did the lightning bolt strike the poplar or the apple tree?

13. Y avait-il des habitations près de l'arbre foudroyé?

13. Were there any houses near the tree which was struck by lightning?
(Notice that a phrase is sometimes needed to translate a word.)

14. L'oranger était-il près d'un ruisseau?

14. Was the orange tree near a stream?	15. Y avait-il des témoins capables?
15. Were there capable witnesses?	16. Y a-t-il eu des témoins oculaires du coup de foudre?
16. Were there eye witnesses of the lightning bolt?	

99. *Interrogative adverbs*—quand, combien, *etc.*

1. The following words are often encountered in question patterns. The inverted form and the **est-ce que** form are both translated in the same way:

Où allez-vous?
Où est-ce que vous allez? } *Where are you going?*

Quand allez-vous revenir?
Quand est-ce que vous allez revenir? } *When are you going to come back?*

Pourquoi vous en allez-vous?
Pourquoi est-ce que vous vous en allez? } *Why are you leaving?*

Comment dit-on cela?
*Comment est-ce qu'*on dit cela? } *How does one say that?*

Combien de pages avez-vous lues?
Combien de pages *est-ce que* vous avez lues? } *How many pages have you read?*

INSTRUCTIONS: *Continue to circle the words which you do not recognize immediately.*

	1. **à votre avis**=*in your opinion* Pourquoi, à votre avis, ces faits méritent-ils d'être étudiés?
1. Why in your opinion do these facts merit being studied?	**2.** **encore**=*yet, still, again* Pourquoi faut-il encore étudier la question?
2. Why is it still necessary to study the question?	**3.** **un journal**=*a newspaper* Combien de détails furent publiés par les journaux?
3. How many details were published by the newspapers?	**4.** Quand l'orage a-t-il eu lieu?
4. When did the storm take place?	**5.** **durer**=*to last* Combien de temps l'orage a-t-il duré?

5. How long did the storm last?	**6.** **à peu près**=*approximately* A peu près combien de temps l'orage a-t-il duré?
6. Approximately how long did the storm last?	**7.** **frapper**=*to strike, to hit* Quand est-ce que le coup de foudre a frappé, à peu près?
7. When did the lightning bolt strike, approximately?	**8.** Où se trouvait le ruisseau?
8. Where was the stream?	**9.** **une fenêtre**=*a window* Combien de fenêtres furent brisées?
9. How many windows were broken?	**10.** Quand est-ce que les fenêtres furent brisées?
10. When were the windows broken?	**11.** La foudre a-t-elle encore frappé?
11. Did the lightning strike again?	**12.** Où est-ce que le coup de foudre a frappé?
12. Where did the lightning strike?	**13.** Quand l'événement se passa-t-il, à peu près?
13. When did the event take place, approximately?	**14.** Pourquoi l'auteur voulait-il savoir les réponses à une série de questions?
14. Why did the author want to know the answers to a series of questions?	**15.** Pourquoi est-ce qu'il voulait encore étudier la foudre?
15. Why did he still want to study lightning?	**16.** Pourquoi, à votre avis, la foudre a-t-elle frappé un arbre de grande taille?
16. Why, in your opinion, did lightning strike a tree of great size?	**17.** Comment, à votre avis, peut-on étudier la foudre?
17. How, in your opinion, can one study lightning?	**18.** Comment est-ce que l'auteur a su encore d'autres détails de l'événement?
18. How did the author learn still other details of the event?	**19.** Combien de témoins a-t-il encore consultés, à peu près?
19. How many more witnesses did he consult, approximately?	**20.** A peu près combien de temps mit-il à rédiger ses conclusions?
20. About how much time did he take to write up his conclusions?	**21.** Où est-ce que ces faits furent publiés?
21. Where were these facts published?	**22.** Où peut-on encore les trouver?

22. Where can one still find them?	**23.** **ébranler**=*to shake, to weaken* Combien d'habitations le coup de foudre a-t-il ébranlées?
23. How many dwellings did the lightning shake (weaken)?	

100. *Interrogative Pronouns*—qui *and* que

1. You have learned **qui** and **que** as pronouns which join two clauses. They are also question words. **Qui** asks *who?* or *whom?* and **que** asks *what?*. As relative pronouns both **qui** and **que** may refer either to things or persons. In question forms **qui** refers only to *persons* and **que** only to *things:*

Qui **est là?**	*Who* is there?
Qui **voyez-vous?**	*Whom* do you see?
Que **faites-vous?**	*What* are you doing?
Que **se passe-t-il?**	*What* is going on?

2. When you see **qui** or **que** followed by **est-ce que** or **est-ce qui,** remember that these last two phrases are only the signals of a question and are not to be translated:

Qui *est-ce qui* **est là?**	*Who* is there?
Qui *est-ce que* **vous voyez?**	*Whom* do you see?
Qu'est-ce que **vous faites?**	*What* are you doing?
Qu'est-ce qui **se passe?**	*What* is going on?

3. **Qu'est-ce que c'est?** and **Qu'est-ce que c'est que cela?** mean "What is it?" or "What is that?"

INSTRUCTIONS: *Continue to circle the words which you do not immediately recognize.*

	1. Qui étudie cette question?
1. Who is studying this question?	**2.** Qui est-ce qui étudie cette question?
2. Who is studying this question?	**3.** **résoudre**=*to resolve, to solve* Que faut-il faire pour résoudre la question?
3. What must be done in order to resolve the question?	**4.** Qu'est-ce qu'il faut faire pour résoudre la question?
4. What must be done in order to resolve the question?	**5.** Qui a résolu le problème?

5. Who solved the problem?	6. Qu'est-ce qui vous a permis de le résoudre?
6. What permitted you to solve it?	7. *Parlons du rapport entre l'art et science.* **lier**=*to bind, to relate* Qu'est-ce qui lie l'art à la science?
7. What relates art to science?	8. Qui est-ce qui a traité cette question?
8. Who has treated this question?	9. **emprunter à**=*to borrow from* Qu'est-ce que l'art emprunte aux sciences naturelles?
9. What does art borrow from the natural sciences? (*Notice that* **aux** *must be translated as* **from the** *and not* **to the,** *because of English usage.*)	10. Qui a emprunté une méthode aux sciences naturelles?
10. Who has borrowed a method from the natural sciences?	11. Qu'emprunte l'art aux sciences naturelles?
11. What does art borrow from the natural sciences?	12. **une règle**=*a rule* Qui est-ce qui emprunta des règles aux sciences naturelles?
12. Who borrowed rules from the natural sciences?	13. Qu'est-ce qui a prouvé l'importance de ces règles?
13. What proved the importance of these rules?	14. Qui est-ce qui a prouvé l'importance de ces règles?
14. Who proved the importance of these rules?	15. Qu'est-ce que c'est?
15. What is it?	16. Qu'est-ce que c'est que cela?
16. What is that?	17. Qu'est-ce que c'est qu'un cheval?
17. What is a horse?	18. Qu'est-ce que c'est que la foudre?
18. What is lightning?	19. **un caractère**=*a characteristic* Qu'est-ce donc qu'un caractère notable?
19. What then is a notable characteristic?	20. Qu'est-ce donc qu'un tremblement de terre?
20. What then is an earthquake?	21. Qu'est-ce qui a rendu la tâche difficile?

21. What made the task difficult?	**22.** Qui est-ce qui a rendu la tâche difficile?
22. Who made the task difficult?	**23.** Qu'est-ce qu'un linguiste?
23. What is a linguist?	**24.** Qui est-ce qui est linguiste?
24. Who is a linguist?	

101. *Questions with Prepositions*

1. When the question begins with a preposition, you will often find **qui** (for persons) but **quoi** (not **que**) for things:

De *quoi* **avez-vous besoin?**	*What do you need?*
De *qui* **parlez-vous?**	*About **whom** are you speaking?*
A *qui* **parlez-vous?**	*To **whom** are you speaking?*
A *quoi* **vous intéressez–vous?**	*What are you interested in?*

INSTRUCTIONS: *Pay special attention to the difference between* **qui** *and* **quoi**.

	1. De quoi s'agit-il?
1. What does it concern?	**2.** De qui s'agit-il?
2. Whom does it concern?	**3.** De quoi est-il question?
3. What does it concern?	**4.** De quoi avons-nous besoin?
4. What do we need?	**5.** De qui avez-vous besoin?
5. Whom do you need?	**6.** De quoi a-t-il honte?
6. What is he ashamed of?	**7.** **appuyer**=*to support* **s'appuyer**=*to be based on* Sur quoi s'appuie la théorie de Taine?
7. On what is Taine's theory based?	**8.** A qui pensez-vous?
8. About (of) whom are you thinking? (Notice that English usage requires the preposition *of* or *about*, not *to*.)	**9.** A quoi pensez-vous?
9. What are you thinking about (of)?	**10.** A quoi vont aboutir toutes vos recherches?

10. What will be the result of all your research? ("What is it going to end up at?")	**11.** A quoi peut-on reconnaître un véritable linguiste?
11. By what can one recognize a true linguist?	**12.** **un chien**=*a dog* A quoi peut-on reconnaître une parenté entre le chien et le cheval?
12. By what may one recognize a relationship between the dog and the horse?	**13.** A quoi faut-il avoir recours pour savoir si, de deux caractères, l'un est plus important que l'autre?
13. To what must one have recourse in order to know whether, of two characteristics, one is more important than the other?	**14.** **apprécier**=*to evaluate* A quoi peut-on avoir recours pour apprécier une œuvre d'art à sa juste valeur?
14. To what may one have recourse in order to evaluate a work of art at its true worth?	**15.** A qui faut-il s'adresser pour avoir une appréciation juste de cette œuvre d'art?
15. To whom must one address oneself in order to have an accurate evaluation of this work of art?	

102. *Interrogative Forms*—quel, lequel, *etc.*

1.   Quel is an interrogative adjective translated by *which* or *what*. Like all adjectives, it agrees in gender and number with the noun it modifies:

Quel journal lisez-vous? (m. sing.)	*What* (*which*) *newspaper do you read?*
Quels journaux lisez-vous? (m. plural)	*What* (*which*) *newspapers do you read?*
Quelle est la règle dont vous parlez? (f. sing.)	*What is the rule you are talking about?*
Quelles sont les règles empruntées aux sciences naturelles? (f. pl.)	*What are the rules borrowed from the natural sciences?*

2.   Quel also serves to mark an exclamation:

"Quel fardeau!" s'écria-t-il.	*"What a burden!" he cried out.*
Quelle bonne surprise!	*What a nice surprise!*
Quelles belles fleurs!	*What beautiful flowers!*
Quels grands arbres!	*What large trees!*

3. You have learned **lequel** and its various forms as connecting words (relative pronouns.) They are also used as interrogative pronouns and, as usual, take the number and gender of the nouns they replace. They may refer either to persons or things and are translated by *which one, which ones, of which ones,* etc., depending on the form used:

MASCULINE SING.	FEMININE SING.	MASCULINE PL.	FEMININE PL.
lequel	**laquelle**	**lesquels**	**lesquelles**
auquel	**à laquelle**	**auxquels**	**auxquelles**
duquel	**de laquelle**	**desquels**	**desquelles**

Lequel voyez-vous? — *Which one do you see?*
Auquel pensez-vous? — *Which one are you thinking about?*
Auxquels pensez-vous? — *Which ones are you thinking about?*
De laquelle parlez-vous? }
Duquel parlez-vous? } — *Which one are you talking about?*
Desquelles parlez-vous? }
Desquels parlez-vous? } — *Which ones are you talking about?*

INSTRUCTIONS: *Continue to circle the words which you do not recognize immediately.*

		1.	Quelle est la parenté qui règne entre l'art et les sciences?
1.	What is the relation which reigns between art and the sciences?	**2.**	Quelle parenté a-t-on établi entre l'art et les sciences?
2.	What relationship has been established between art and the sciences?	**3.**	A quels observateurs l'auteur a-t-il enfin écrit?
3.	To which observers did the author finally write?	**4.**	Auxquels a-t-il enfin écrit?
4.	To which ones did he finally write?	**5.**	Quelles réponses ont-ils pu donner?
5.	What answers were they able to give?	**6.**	Lesquelles ont-ils enfin pu donner?
6.	Which ones (answers) were they finally able to give?	**7.**	Quel arbre la foudre a-t-elle frappé?
7.	Which tree did (the) lightning strike?	**8.**	Lequel a-t-elle frappé?
8.	Which one did it strike?	**9.**	**environ**=*about, approximately* **les environs**=*the surrounding area, neighborhood* Quelle était la hauteur de l'arbre, environ?
9.	What was the height of the tree, approximately?	**10.**	Quelle en était la hauteur, environ? (Which words of #9 does **en** replace?)

10.	*de l'arbre* What was the height of it, approximately?	**11.**	**les dégâts**=*damage* Quels dégâts a-t-on observés dans les environs?
11.	What damage did they observe in the surrounding area (neighborhood)?	**12.**	Quels dégâts résultent ordinairement de la foudre?
12.	What damage usually results from lightning?	**13.**	Lesquels résultent d'habitude (ordinairement) de la foudre?
13.	Which ones usually result from lightning?	**14.**	De quel arbre s'agissait-il?
14.	Which tree did it concern?	**15.**	Duquel s'agissait-il?
15.	Which one did it concern?	**16.**	Quelle fut la durée de l'orage?
16.	What was the duration of the storm? (How long did the storm last?)	**17.**	Quelle règle difficile!
17.	What a difficult rule!	**18.**	**une averse**=*a downpour* Quelle averse!
18.	What a downpour!	**19.**	Quel dommage!
19.	What a pity!	**20.**	Quel homme!
20.	What a man!	**21.**	Quel habile homme!
21.	What a clever man!	**22.**	Quelles belles femmes!
22.	What beautiful women!	**23.**	Quel orage!
23.	What a storm!		

103. *Review of Inverted Word Order*

1. The following constructions should tell you to anticipate the possibility of the subject following the verb:

(a)   a question

> **Que faut-il faire?**   *What must be done?*

(b)   a sentence beginning with **aussi, ainsi, peut-être,** or **sans doute**

Aussi nous trouvons-nous reportés   *Therefore, we find ourselves carried*
dans le domaine des sciences.   *back into the domain of science.*

Ainsi la matière peut-elle paraître sèche et abstraite.	*Thus the material may appear dry and abstract.*
Sans doute la matière est-elle sèche.	*The material is no doubt dry.*

(c)   a clause following an object relative pronoun

C'est le sujet que traite Taine.	*This is the subject which Taine treats.*
C'est le sujet dont parle Taine.	*This is the subject of which Taine speaks.*
Ce sont les principes sur lesquels insiste Taine.	*These are the principles upon which Taine insists.*

INSTRUCTIONS: *In the following sentences identify those subjects which follow a verb.*

1.   Le vertébré peut subir tous les changements que comporte le changement d'habitation.

1. *le changement*
The vertebrate is able to undergo all the changes that a change in habitat entails.

2.   Il s'agit du thème que traite Taine.

2. *Taine*
It concerns the theme which Taine treats.

3.   Lisez les livres qu'écrivent nos auteurs modernes.

3. *auteurs*
Read the books that our modern authors are writing.

4.   Sa conférence traitait des romans d'aventure que composa A. Dumas.

4. *A. Dumas*
His lecture treated the adventure novels that A. Dumas wrote.

5.   Ainsi s'accroît le potentiel scientifique de l'école.

5. *le potentiel*
Thus the scientific potential of the school is increased.
(Are you circling unfamiliar words for future review?)

6.   Peut-être la lecture devient-elle plus facile maintenant.

6. *elle*
Perhaps reading is becoming easier now.

7.   Ainsi apparaît l'utilité de l'électro–aimant.

7. *l'utilité*
Thus the usefulness of the electro-magnet is seen (appears).

8.   Aussi peut-on utiliser le fleuve pour produire de l'électricité.

8. *on*
Therefore the river can be used to produce electricity.

9. Peut-être les choses se passent-elles de la sorte pour certaines espèces.

9. *elles*
Perhaps things happen this way for certain species.

10. Ainsi ne faut-il pas s'étonner que ces méthodes ne soient pas spécifiques.

10. *il*
Thus one must not be surprised that these methods are not specific.

104. *Use of* n'est-ce pas

1. *N'est-ce pas* is a very common expression which asks the listener or reader to agree with or confirm the speaker's statement. It is translated by the "tag question" which English usage requires:

C'était un orage terrible, n'est-ce pas?   *It was a terrible storm **wasn't it?***

Il parle bien, n'est-ce pas?   *He speaks well, **doesn't he?***

INSTRUCTIONS: *Translate* **n'est-ce pas** *into the tag question required by English usage.*

1. L'orage n'était pas inattendu, n'est-ce pas?

1. The storm was not unexpected, *was it?*

2. La foudre est tombée sur quelques habitations, n'est-ce pas?

2. The lightning struck (fell on) a few dwellings, *didn't it?*

3. La foudre n'a pas fait de dégâts, n'est-ce pas?

3. The lightning didn't do any damage, *did it?*

4. Pour savoir si de deux caractères l'un est plus important que l'autre, il faut faire appel aux règles d'évaluation, n'est-ce pas?

4. In order to know whether of two characteristics one is more important than the other, it is necessary to call upon the rules of evaluation, *isn't it?*

5. Pour savoir quelles sont ces règles, il nous faut faire une excursion dans l'histoire naturelle, n'est-ce pas?

5. In order to know what these rules are, it is necessary for us to make an excursion into natural history, *isn't it?*

6. La parenté qui lie l'art à la science n'apparaît pas tout de suite, n'est-ce pas?

6. The relationship which links art to science does not appear right away (immediately), *does it?*

7. A neighbor is a person who lives near you, *isn't he?*

8. The pea and the acacia (locust tree) are related plants, *aren't they?*

9. The mammals which fly are not very closely related to the mammals which swim, *are they?*

10. We have seen a great increase of mass media lately, *haven't we?*

11. The newspapers did not publish many details of this famous storm, *did they?*

12. *Is it not* the business of the sciences to evaluate the character of it?

7. Un voisin est une personne qui habite près de vous, n'est-ce pas?

8. **le pois**=*the pea*
Le pois et l'acacia sont des plantes voisines, n'est-ce pas?

9. **voler**=*to fly, to steal*
nager=*to swim*
Les mammifères volants ne sont pas très voisins des mammifères nageants, n'est-ce pas?

10. Nous avons vu dernièrement un grand accroissement des organes de publicité, n'est-ce pas?

11. Les journaux n'ont pas publié beaucoup de détails sur ce célèbre orage, n'est-ce pas?

12. N'est-ce pas l'affaire des sciences que d'en évaluer le caractère?

REVIEW SECTION

INSTRUCTIONS: *Distinguish between the different meanings of* **encore** *in the following sentences.*

1. Was the tree *still* there yesterday?

2. It had not *yet* been struck by lightning.

3. It had been struck by lightning *again*.

4. *Even though* it was struck by lightning, three-fourths of it remained standing.

1. L'arbre était-il encore là hier?
(**encore**=*still/again*)

2. Il n'avait pas encore été foudroyé.
(**encore**=*yet/again*)

3. Il avait été foudroyé encore une fois.
(**encore**=*still/again*)

4. Encore qu'il ait été foudroyé, il en resta les trois quarts debout.
(**encore que**=*again/even though*)

5. Il n'y avait qu'un seul arbre et **encore** était-il fendu en deux parties.

5. There was only one tree, and *even* it was split into two parts.	**6.** En voulez-vous encore?
6. Do you want some more?	**7.** *Can you recognize the meanings of these conjunctions?* **Sans que** vous ayez recours à de bons observateurs, vous ne connaîtrez pas de détails.
7. *Without* having recourse to good observers you will not know any details.	**8.** **Sans que** vous sachiez la taille de l'arbre, il vous est difficile d'imaginer la force de l'orage.
8. *Without* knowing the size of the tree, it is difficult for you to imagine the force of the storm.	**9.** se rendre=aller **A moins que** vous ne puissiez vous rendre sur place vous-même, faites venir des hommes qualifiés pour vérifier l'explosion.
9. *Unless* you can go to the spot yourself, send for some men qualified to verify the explosion.	**10.** **A moins que** les détails ne soient publiés dans les journaux, il nous est impossible de les savoir.
10. *Unless* the details are published in the newspapers, it is impossible for us to know them.	**11.** **Quoique** l'arbre ait été fendu en deux parties, il en restait le tiers debout.
11. *Although* the tree was split into two pieces, one-third of it remained standing.	**12.** **Quoique** les témoins aient décrit les détails du foudroiement, les descriptions en semblèrent peu croyables.
12. *Although* witnesses described the details of the blast, the descriptions of it did not appear credible.	**13.** **Pourvu que** la matière ne paraisse pas sèche, le style importe peu.
13. *Provided* the material does not appear dry, the style does not matter very much.	**14.** **Pourvu que** la méthode soit bonne, la résultat est assurée.
14. *Provided* the method is sound, the result is sure.	**15.** **Avant d'**essayer d'évaluer deux caractères notables, ayons recours à la science.
15. *Before* trying to evaluate two important characteristics, let us have recourse to science.	**16.** **Avant que** vous n'en fassiez une évaluation, consultez l'histoire naturelle.
16. *Before* you make an evaluation of it, consult natural history.	**17.** If you miss any of these next exercises on pronouns, review Chapter Thirteen. Il nous faut **y** faire une excursion.

17. We must make an excursion *there*.

18. La taille et la grandeur **y** sont moins importantes que la structure.

18. The size and height are *here* less important than the structure.

19. La lettre était tout à fait inattendue, mais tous trois **y** ont répondu avec obligeance.

19. The letter was completely unexpected, but all three obligingly replied to *it*.

20. Ce qu'il **en** disait était aussi inattendu que profond.

20. What he said *about it* was as unexpected as it was profound.

21. le bilan=*the balance sheet*
Lorsqu'on **en** fait le bilan, on s'aperçoit de l'intensité de l'orage.

21. When the balance-sheet is drawn up, the intensity of the storm is perceived.

22. Tous trois **les lui** ont envoyées.

22. All three sent *them to him*.

23. Je **les leur** ai demandés.

23. I asked *them for them*.

24. Il **nous les** a montrés.

24. He showed *them to us*.

25. Les mesures **dont** il avait parlé n'étaient qu'approximatives.

25. The measurements *about which* he had spoken were only approximate.

26. Ils m'envoyèrent les détails **dont** j'avais besoin.

26. They sent me the details *of which* I had need.

27. Le peuplier **dont** il s'agissait avait été fendu en deux parties.

27. The poplar *of which* it was a question had been split into two parts.

28. Ce n'est pas **ce qu'**on dit, mais **ce qu'**on fait entendre; ce n'est pas **ce qu'**on peint, mais **ce qu'**on fait imaginer qui est important dans l'éloquence et les arts.

Joubert

28. It is not *what* one says but *what* one causes to be understood; it is not *what* one paints but *what* one causes to be imagined that is important in eloquence and the arts.

29. Il est quelquefois agréable à un mari d'avoir une femme jalouse; il entend toujours parler **de ce** qu'il aime.

La Rochefoucauld

29. It is sometimes pleasant for a husband to have a jealous wife; he always hears remarks about *that which* he loves.

30. ennuyer=*to bore*
Nous pardonnons souvent à **ceux qui** nous ennuient, mais nous ne pouvons pardonner à **ceux que** nous ennuyons.

La Rochefoucauld

30. We often pardon *those who* bore us, but we cannot pardon *those whom* we bore.

31. ensemble=*together*
Ce qui fait que les amants et les maîtresses ne s'ennuient point d'être ensemble, c'est qu'ils parlent toujours d'eux-mêmes.

La Rochefoucauld

31. *What* causes lovers and mistresses not to be bored at being together is that they are always talking about themselves.

VOCABULARY DEVELOPMENT

INSTRUCTIONS: *Give the meanings of the indicated words. Associate them with the other words of the same family.*

1. une remarque révélatrice=*a revealing remark*
une tempête dévastatrice=_____
_____

1. *a devastating storm*

2. une puissance formatrice=_____
_____

2. *a formative power*

3. une force destructrice=_____
_____

3. *a destructive or destroying power*

4. une force motrice=_____
_____

4. *a moving power*

5. faire=*to do, to make*
Les obstacles étaient insurmontables; le projet n'était donc pas faisable.

5. *feasible*

6. L'armée n'avait plus d'armes, ce qui a contribué à sa défaite.

6. *defeat*

7. Il arrive souvent que le singe contrefasse les gestes des hommes.

7. *mimics, imitates (counterfeits)*

8. Les dégâts occasionnés par l'orage ont défait les travaux des années.

8. *undone, destroyed*

9. court=*short*
N'ayant plus de temps, il se trouvait obligé de raccourcir ses remarques.

9. *to shorten*

10. On ne possède pas la totalité de ses remarques, il n'en reste qu'**un récit raccourci.**

10. *a shortened version*

11. **le lait**=*the milk*
Tout mammifère est capable d'**allaiter.**

11. Any mammal is capable of *giving milk.*

12. La nuit, si on regarde le ciel, on peut voir **la voie lactée.**

12. *the Milky Way*

13. **un coup**=*a blow*
un coup de pied=*a kick*
(In English we distinguish the different kinds of blows by a different word. The French make the same distinction by **coup**+the means of striking.)
une main=*a hand*
J'avais besoin de son aide; il m'a donc donné **un coup de main.**

13. I needed his help; he therefore gave me a *helping hand.*

14. **l'œil**=*the eye*
Puisque le livre paraissait intéressant, j'y ai jeté un **coup d'œil.**

14. Since the book appeared interesting, I glanced at it (cast upon it a *glance*).

15. **le poing**=*the fist*
Etant furieux, il m'a donné **un coup de pied,** et puis quelques **coups de poing.**

15. Being furious, he *kicked* me and then *hit* me several times *with his fist.*

16. Voulant parler à Marie, je lui ai donné un **coup de téléphone.**

16. Wishing to speak to Mary, *I called her on the phone.*

17. **un fer**=*an iron*
Voulant aller au bal, **elle a donné un coup de fer à sa robe.**

17. Wishing to go to the dance, *she ironed her dress.*

18. Parce qu'il faisait très chaud, on courait le risque d'**un coup de soleil.**

18. Because it was very hot, one ran the risk of *sunstroke,* or *sunburn.*

19. **les dents**=*the teeth*
Il a mangé son dîner très vite **sans perdre un coup de dent.**

19. He ate his dinner very quickly *without missing (losing) a bite.*

TESTING EXERCISE

INSTRUCTIONS: *Circle the letter which gives the best translation of the italicized word, or which best completes the sentence grammatically. If you miss any of the questions, go back over the section indicated. Then go on to the reading passage.*

1. *Auquel* pensez-vous?
A. At which one   B. Of which one   C. In which one   D. On which one

---

1. B
(102)

2. On n'a pas dit *quelle fut la durée de l'orage.*
A. what a long storm it was   C. how hard the rain was
B. how long the storm lasted   D. how intense the thunder was

---

2. B
(102)

3. *Que* voyez-vous?
A. What   B. Who   C. When   D. Why

---

3. A
(100)

4. *Qu'est-ce qui* a rendu la tâche difficile?
A. Who   B. What   C. Which one   D. Whom

---

4. B
(100)

5. *Qui est-ce que Marie a vu?*
A. Whom did Marie see?   B. Who saw Marie?   C. What did Marie see?

---

5. A
(100)

6. *Qui est-ce qui a vu Marie?*
A. Whom did Marie see?   B. What did Marie see?   C. Who saw Marie?

---

6. C
(100)

7. Qui sont les amis *qu'a visités Marie?*
A. who visited Marie   B. whom Marie visited

---

7. B
(103)

8. Les journaux n'ont pas publié beaucoup de détails, *n'est-ce pas?*
A. is it?   B. are they?   C. did they?   D. aren't they?

---

8. C
(104)

9. Le conférencier a parlé des œuvres publiées dernièrement. _____
a-t-il parlé le plus favorablement?
A. Duquel   B. A laquelle   C. Desquels   D. Desquelles

---

9. D
(102)

10. *Quand* l'événement se passa-t-il?
A. Why   B. How long   C. How   D. When

---

10. D
(99)

11. *Pourquoi* vous en allez-vous?
A. Where   B. Why   C. How long   D. When

---

11. B
(99)

READING PASSAGES

INSTRUCTIONS: *Read through these exercises with a pencil in hand. Circle the vocabulary items that are not immediately familiar to you. Continue to review them until they are perfectly familiar.*

Le Degré d'importance du caractère.

H. Taine, *Philosophie de l'art.*

Qu'est-ce donc qu'un caractère notable, et d'abord comment savoir, deux caractères étant donnés, si l'un est plus important que l'autre? Nous nous trouvons reportés par cette question dans le domaine des sciences; car il s'agit ici des êtres en **eux-mêmes,**[1] et c'est justement l'affaire des sciences
5 que d'évaluer les caractères dont les êtres sont composés. Il nous faut faire une excursion dans l'histoire naturelle; je ne m'en excuse pas **auprès de**[2] vous; si la matière paraît d'abord sèche et abstraite, il n'importe; la parenté qui lie l'art à la science est un honneur pour lui comme pour elle; c'est une gloire pour elle de fournir à la beauté ses principaux supports; c'est une
10 gloire pour lui que d'appuyer ses plus hautes constructions sur la vérité.

Il y a cent ans[3] environ que les sciences naturelles ont découvert la règle d'évaluation que nous allons leur emprunter; c'est le principe de la subordination des caractères; toutes les classifications de la botanique et de la zoologie ont été construites d'après **lui,**[4] et son importance a été prouvée
15 par des découvertes aussi inattendues que profondes. Dans une plante et dans un animal, certains caractères ont été reconnus comme plus importants que les autres; ce sont les moins variables; **à ce titre,**[5] ils possèdent une force plus grande que celle des autres; car ils résistent **mieux**[6] à l'attaque de toutes les circonstances intérieures ou extérieures qui peuvent les défaire
20 ou les altérer. Par exemple, dans une plante, la taille et la grandeur sont moins importantes que la structure; car, à l'extérieur, certains caractères accessoires font varier la grandeur et la taille sans altérer la structure. Le pois qui **rampe**[7] à terre et l'acacia qui monte dans l'air sont des **légumineuses**[8] très voisines; **une tige de blé**[9] haute de trois pieds et un bambou
25 haut de trente pieds sont des **graminées**[10] parentes; **la fougère,**[11] si petite en nos climats, devient un grand arbre sous les tropiques. Pareillement encore, dans un vertébré, le nombre, la disposition et l'emploi des membres sont moins importants que la possession des **mamelles.**[12] Il peut être aquatique, terrestre, aérien, subir tous les changements que comporte le
30 changement d'habitation, sans que pour cela la structure qui le rend capable d'allaiter soit altérée ou détruite. La **chauve-souris**[13] et la **baleine**[14] sont des mammifères comme le chien, le cheval et l'homme. Les puissances formatrices qui ont **effilé**[15] les membres de la chauve-souris et changé ses mains en **ailes,**[16] qui ont **soudé,**[17] raccourci et presque **effacé**[18] les membres
35 postérieurs de la baleine, n'ont point eu de **prise chez** l'une ni **chez**[19] l'autre sur l'organe qui donne au petit son aliment, et le mammifère volant, comme le mammifère nageant, restent frères du mammifère qui marche. Il en est

1 *themselves*	8 *legumenous plants*	15 *tapered*
2 *to*	9 *stalk of wheat*	16 *wings*
3 *one hundred years ago*	10 *graminaceae*	17 *joined*
4 *it (refers to* le principe)	11 *the fern*	18 *obliterated*
5 *as such*	12 *mammae* (Zool.)	19 *effect on*
6 *better*	13 *bat*	
7 *creeps*	14 *whale*	

ainsi dans toute l'**échelle** [20] des êtres et sur toute l'échelle des caractères. Telle
disposition organique est un **poids** [21] si lourd que les forces capables
40 d'ébranler des poids moindres ne parviennent pas à l'ébranler.

1. The first ten lines state that:
   A. there is little relation between the methods of art and science
   B. it is the function of science to determine the value of given characteristics
   C. art and science are mutually independent of natural history
   D. to determine the relative merits of art and science a detailed study of
      notable characteristics is necessary.

---

1. B   **2.** Lines 11–20 state that:
   A. the principle of the subordination of characteristics was discovered about
      one hundred years ago
   B. in plants, as in animals, variable characteristics are important in deter-
      mining structure
   C. exterior circumstances affect internal structure
   D. size is directly related to internal structure.

---

2. A   **3.** Lines 20–28 state that:
   A. the creeping pea vine is related to the bamboo
   B. the climbing acacia is fundamentally not of the same family as a stalk
      of wheat
   C. among the vertebrates, the number and disposition of the limbs deter-
      mine classification
   D. the ability to breast feed its young is the most important classification
      characteristic among the vertebrates.

---

3. D   **4.** Lines 28–38 state that:
   A. the bat and the whale have more in common structurally than the dog,
      the horse and man
   B. structurally speaking the horse and the dog are dissimilar
   C. environmental circumstances changed the outward forms of the bat
      and the whale without affecting their ability to suckle their young
   D. because man is also a mammal, he is irresistibly drawn to extend his
      dominion to the air like the bat and to the sea like the whale.

---

4. C

"Renseignements sur un coup de foudre d'une intensité très exceptionnelle"

Daniel Calladon, "Physique du Globe," *Comptes
rendus de l'Académie des sciences.*

Lorsqu'on essaye de faire les **bilans** [1] annuels des grandes **perturbations,** [2] soit de l'atmosphère, soit de l'**écorce** [3] du globe, pendant la durée

---

20 *scale*   **21** *a weight*

1 *balance sheet*   **2** *disturbances*   **3** *crust*

des vingt dernières années, pour les comparer avec ceux des vingt années antérieures, il semble que nous sommes comparativement dans une époque
5   où ces phénomènes ont atteint, ou approchent d'un maximum d'intensité.

Cette augmentation est-elle réelle ou apparente? Est-elle seulement le résultat du rapide accroissement des organes de publicité et du plus grand nombre des stations météorologiques? C'est ce qu'il est difficile d'apprécier; mais on peut admettre que, **depuis** [4] quelques années, le nombre des dévas-
10   tations cycloniques, celui des orages dévastateurs, de fortes **chutes de grêle** [5] et des tremblements de terre, a subi en réalité une augmentation notable.

J'ai à décrire un coup de foudre qui a frappé le 7 du courant, un grand peuplier à Schoren, village bernois, à 1^{km} de la ville de Langenthal, et qui
15   a produit dans ce village et dans les environs, jusqu'à quelques centaines de mètres, des dégâts qui **pourraient être** [6] comparés à ceux produits par l'explosion d'une **poudrière.**[7]

Ces faits méritent d'être étudiés, soit dans un but scientifique, soit en vue de la sécurité des bâtiments qu'on désire préserver des effets de la foudre.
20   Les détails publiés par quelques journaux sur ce foudroiement paraissaient si anormaux que, ne pouvant me rendre sur place et désirant les faire vérifier avec soin, j'ai eu recours à trois bons observateurs, qualifiés pour cette étude: M. Ziegler, forestier en chef du district de Langenthal, M. W. Sahli, docteur-médecin à Langenthal, et M. F. Kronaeur, recteur du **progymnase** [8] de la
25   même ville, auxquels j'ai adressé une série de questions à examiner sur place. Tous trois y ont répondu avec une grande obligeance.

Dans mon questionnaire, j'insistais, entre autres détails, sur les points suivants que des études précédentes m'ont appris avoir une notable importance: le peuplier était-il de grande taille et isolé ou entouré d'autres arbres
30   de même hauteur? Son pied était-il très voisin d'un ruisseau ou d'**une pièce d'eau?** [9] Le coup de foudre avait-il été précédé, accompagné ou seulement suivi d'une très forte averse? Je demandais enfin des mesures très approximatives des plus grandes distances auxquelles quelques gros éclats avaient été projetés, et des fenêtres endommagées ou brisées par la
35   commotion.

Ces messieurs, ayant visité Schoren à des jours différents, m'ont envoyé séparément des lettres, dont les récits fort détaillés concordent bien sur tous les points essentiels. J'en extrais les renseignements suivants:

Le peuplier frappé était un arbre **sain,**[10] de $0^m,90$ de diamètre et 20^m,
40   25 de hauteur, isolé au milieu du village de Schoren, sur une grande place, entouré, à 20^m ou 40^m, d'habitations séparées les unes des autres. Une seule de ces maisons est placée près de l'arbre, à 6^m de distance; un petit ruisseau les sépare et traverse la place; il passe à 1^m du pied du peuplier.

Cet arbre a été fendu en deux parties; celle restant sur place équivaut
45   au tiers du tout: elle est à demi renversée et s'appuie contre la maison.

---

4 *for*   7 *powder-magazine*   9 *a body of water*
5 *hail storms*   8 *school*   10 *healthy*
6 *could be* (*cond.*)

1. In the first paragraph the author indicates that there seems to have been a recent increase in disturbances of
   A. the atmosphere but not the earth's surface
   B. the earth's surface but not the atmosphere
   C. both the earth's surface and the atmosphere

1. C

2. In lines 6–12 he implies that
   A. the increase is only apparent
   B. several factors make a definitive answer impossible
   C. hailstorms are really more devastating than cyclones
   D. a better comparison with former years will be possible as more weather stations are established

2. B

3. In lines 13–17 he states that during a recent storm lightning struck
   A. a powder magazine, causing considerable damage
   B. a large number of people in the village of Schoren
   C. a tree
   D. several houses

3. C

4. In lines 20–27 the author states that
   A. his information comes from personal observation
   B. it was extremely difficult to find capable witnesses
   C. his informants were slow in answering
   D. he endeavored to choose capable observers

4. D

5. In lines 27–35 he asked about
   A. the number of people killed
   B. the value of the property destroyed
   C. the location of the church relative to the damaged area
   D. the number of windows damaged or broken

5. D

6. In lines 36–38 we learn that the accounts furnished to the author were
   A. sparse
   B. detailed
   C. in contradiction with each other
   D. written after the observers had compared notes

6. B

7. Lines 39–45 tell us that the tree in question was
   A. about three times the height of an average man
   B. at a considerable distance from any water
   C. located on the outskirts of the village
   D. located quite near a house

7. D

Chapter Sixteen

REVIEW: Before you begin Chapter Sixteen review the items you circled in Chapters Fourteen and Fifteen.

105. *The Future Tense*

1. Action in future time is signaled by the presence of the following endings: **–ai, –as, –a, –ons, –ez, –ont.** They are added to the infinitive of regular verbs (for **–re** verbs the final **–e** is dropped before the endings):

je parler*ai*	*I will speak*
tu trouver*as*	*you will find*
il finir*a*	*he will finish*
nous agir*ons*	*we will act*
vous mettr*ez*	*you will put*
ils se rendr*ont* compte	*they will realize*
je vendrai	*I will sell*
tu vendras	*you will sell*
il vendra	*he will sell*
nous vendrons	*we will sell*
vous vendrez	*you will sell*
ils vendront	*they will sell*

(A few verbs have irregular future stems—see section 108.)

312

2. You will notice that the endings of the **je, tu, il** forms are the same as for the Past Definite of **–er** verbs. To avoid confusing the two tenses, look at the stem. If the stem is an infinitive (or an irregular future), the tense is the future and not the past definite.

j'empruntai	*I borrowed*	**j'emprunterai**	*I will borrow*
il désira	*he desired*	**il désirera**	*he will desire*
tu demandas	*you asked*	**tu demanderas**	*you will ask*

READING PREPARATION

INSTRUCTIONS: *Select the meanings indicated by these verbs and identify the tenses.*

	1. **Je commence** à vous comprendre. (*I am starting/I started*)
1. *present—I am starting* to understand you.	**2.** **Je commençai** à vous comprendre. (*I start/I started*)
2. *past definite—I started* to understand you.	**3.** **Je commencerai** peut-être à vous comprendre. (*I started/I will start*)
3. *future—I will* perhaps *start* to understand you.	**4.** **J'ai commencé** à te comprendre. (*I am starting/I have started*)
4. *past indefinite—I have started* to understand you.	**5.** **Il traversa** le Mississippi en avril. (*He crosses/He crossed/He has crossed*)
5. *past definite—He crossed* the Mississippi in April. (**Traversa** never means *has crossed*.)	**6.** **Il traversera** le Niger en février. (*He will cross/He crossed*)
6. *future—He will cross* the Niger in February.	**7.** **Il traverse** le Niger. (*He is crossing/He crossed*)
7. *present—He is crossing* the Niger.	**8.** **Il quitta** sa ville natale. (*He left/He will leave*)
8. *He left* his native city.	**9.** **Il quittera** sa ville natale. (*He left/He will leave*)
9. *He will leave* his native city.	**10.** **Je comptai** vous voir. (*I counted on/I will count on*)
10. *I counted on* seeing you.	**11.** **Je compterai** vous voir. (*I counted on/I will count on*)

11. *I will count on* seeing you.	**12.** **aborder**=*to take up* (*a subject*), *to reach* (*a place*) Le conférencier aborda une nouvelle question.
12. The lecturer took up a new question.	**13.** Le conférencier abordera une nouvelle question.
13. The lecturer will take up a new question.	**14.** Dans ce chapitre vous lirez un essai de Victor Hugo.
14. In this chapter you will read an essay by Victor Hugo.	**15.** **du moins**=*at least* Vous lirez du moins quelques pensées de Victor Hugo sur le drame et la poésie.
15. At least you will read a few of Victor Hugo's thoughts about drama and poetry.	**16.** Il abordera la question de l'imitation de la nature dans la poésie.
16. He will take up the question of the imitation of nature in poetry.	**17.** **laid**=*ugly* Il demandera si le poète peut mettre le laid dans sa poésie aussi bien que le beau.
17. He will ask whether (if) the poet may put the ugly in his poetry as well as the beautiful.	**18.** Il demandera s'il faut éliminer le grotesque dans la poésie pour faire comme la nature.
18. He will ask whether (if) it is necessary to eliminate the grotesque in poetry in order to do as nature does.	**19.** Les poètes classiques éliminèrent le grotesque pour atteindre au sublime.
19. The classical poets eliminated the grotesque in order to attain to the sublime. (Did you translate **éliminèrent** by the future? If you did, pay extra attention to the ending in the next frame.)	**20.** **pourtant**=*however* Pourtant, les grands poètes, selon Hugo, ne l'élimineront pas.
20. However, the great poets, according to Hugo, *will not* eliminate it.	**21.** **mêler**=*to mix, to mingle* Ils mêleront le grotesque au sublime.
21. They will mingle the grotesque with the sublime.	**22.** Ils mêleront l'ombre à la lumière. (*Being contrasted with* **la lumière**, **l'ombre** *must mean* _____.)
22. *darkness, shadow* They will mingle darkness with light.	**23.** **le corps**=*the body* Ils mêleront dans leur art le corps à l'âme.

(*Being contrasted with body,* **l'âme** *must refer to* _____.)

---

23. *the soul*
In their art they will combine the body with the soul.

24. Pourtant, la véritable poésie s'imposera rien que par la force de sa beauté.

---

24. However, true poetry will impose itself by nothing more than (merely by) the force of its beauty.

25. **confondre**=*to confuse*
Pourtant, le vrai poète ne confondra pas la laideur et la beauté, mais il mettra toutes les deux dans sa poésie.

---

25. However, the true poet will not confuse ugliness with beauty, but he will put both of them in his poetry.

26. Victor Hugo emprunta ses matières à la nature même.

---

26. Victor Hugo borrowed his material from nature itself.
(If you confused **emprunta** with the future, look at the stem ending again.)

27. Le grand poète empruntera ses matières à la nature même.

---

27. The great poet will borrow his material from Nature itself.

28. **prétendre**=*to claim, to maintain*
Il ne quittera pas le domaine de la nature pour donner à son art une prétendue vérité.
(English usage requires a different expression for the adjective than it does for the verb. **Prétendue** here must mean _____.)

---

28. *so-called* or *supposed* (what is claimed by others)
He will not leave the domain of nature to give his art a so-called truth.

29. La question nous intéresse; pourtant, nous en aborderons une autre.
(**en** refers to _____)

---

29. *la question*
The question interests us; however, we will take up another one (of them).

30. Nous étudierons un autre aspect du futur pour que vous ne confondiez pas les temps des verbes.
(Is **confondiez** the subjunctive or the imperfect?)

---

30. *subjunctive—it follows* **pour que**
We will study another aspect of the future so that you will not confuse the tenses of the verbs.

106. *The Historical Future*

1. As a matter of style, many French historians use the Historical Future as a means of looking forward from a moment in the past. This point of view may be understood without translating, but if the sentence must be translated, the Past or *was* + infinitive are usually adequate:

Il quitta (past def.) **sa ville natale en 1165.**	*He left his native city in 1165.*
Il s'installera bientôt en Egypte.	*He was soon to settle in Egypt* (or *soon settled*).
Il y restera presque quarante ans.	*He was to remain there for almost forty years* (or *remained there*).

READING PREPARATION

INSTRUCTIONS: *Translate the following phrases into smooth, narrative English.*

	1. Nous parlerons maintenant du grand philosophe juif, Moïse Maïmonide, qui vivait au Moyen Age.
1. We will now speak of the great Jewish philosopher Moses Maimonides who lived in the Middle Ages.	**2.** **sa formation**=*his education, training* Il naquit en Espagne en 1135 et y reçut sa première formation.
2. He was born in Spain in 1135 and there received his early education.	**3.** Cependant, sa famille quittera bientôt Cordoue.
3. However, his family was soon to leave Cordova (or *soon left*—in the following statements the simple past may be used interchangeably with *was to* + infinitive).	**4.** Nos émigrés abordèrent Saint-Jean-d'Acre quatre ou cinq années plus tard. (**abordèrent**=*reached/took up*)
4. Our emigrants *reached* Saint-Jean-d'Acre four or five years later.	**5.** Le père mourra peu de temps après.
5. The father was to die shortly after. (**mourra**=*future*, **mourut**=*past definite*)	**6.** **tarder**=*to delay, to be long in* La famille ne tarda pas à s'installer en Egypte.
6. The family was not long in settling in Egypt.	**7.** Ils y vivront quarante ans.

7. They were to live there for forty years.	8. Son frère, le soutien de la famille, disparaîtra dans un naufrage.
8. His brother, the support of the family, was to disappear in a shipwreck.	9. **perdre**=*to lose* Après la perte de son frère Moïse gagnera sa vie par l'art de guérir. (**la perte**=_____)
9. After *the loss* of his brother, Moses was to earn his living by the art of healing.	10. Il s'imposa aussi devant les autorités musulmanes comme chef et porte-parole de la confession juive.
10. He also became (imposed himself as) the chief of and the spokesman for the Jewish faith before the Moslem authorities.	11. **cette dignité**=*this office* Cette dignité restera dans sa famille jusqu'au XIVéme siècle.
11. This office was to remain in his family until the fourteenth century.	12. La famille ne perdra cette dignité qu'au XIVéme siècle.
12. The family was not to lose this office until the fourteenth century.	13. Moïse Maïmonide quittera ce bas monde en 1204.
13. Moses Maimonides was to leave this lower world in 1204.	

107. *The Conditional*

1. The Conditional form of the verb expresses an action which depends on another action. It expresses hypothesis, or a condition contrary to present fact:

Si la poésie suivait vraiment la nature, elle changerait la face du monde intellectuel.	*If poetry truly followed nature, it* ***would change*** *the face of the intellectual world.*
Si la poésie était réellement "vraie", elle imiterait la nature dans sa complexité.	*If poetry were really "true," it* ***would imitate*** *nature in its complexity.*

2. The conditional uses the same stem as the future—it is thus identified by the following endings attached to the infinitive (**–re** infinitives without the final **–e**) :

je réussir*ais*	*I would succeed*
tu finir*ais*	*you would finish*
il trouver*ait*	*he would find*
nous parler*ions*	*we would speak*
vous mettr*iez*	*you would put*
ils se rendr*aient* compte	*they would realize*

je prendr*ais*	*I would take*
tu prendr*ais*	*you would take*
il prendr*ait*	*he would take*
nous prendr*ions*	*we would take*
vous prendr*iez*	*you would take*
ils prendr*aient*	*they would take*

Notice that these endings are the same as for the Imperfect. To avoid confusing the two forms, look at the stem. If it is an infinitive, the verb is conditional and not imperfect.

READING PREPARATION

INSTRUCTIONS: *What is the tense of the verbs in the following phrases?*

	1. **Je désirais** vous parler. (*imperfect/conditional*)
1. *imperfect* *I wanted* to speak to you.	2. **Je désirerais** vous parler. (*imperfect/conditional*)
2. *conditional* *I would like* to speak to you.	3. **Nous nous mettions** à travailler. (*imperfect/conditional*)
3. *imperfect* *We started* to work.	4. **Nous nous mettrions** à travailler. (*imperfect/conditional*)
4. *conditional* *We would start* to work.	5. **Vous suivriez** un cours de chimie. (*imperfect/conditional*)
5. *conditional*—If you said "imperfect," examine the stem again. *You would follow* a course of chemistry.	6. **Vous suiviez** un cours de chimie. (*imperfect/conditional*)
6. *imperfect* *You followed* a course in chemistry.	7. Maintenant lisons quelques phrases et faisons une révision.
7. Now let us read a few phrases and make a review.	8. Si nous savions lire plus vite, nous apprendrions plus rapidement.
8. If we knew how (were able) to read quicker, we would learn more rapidly.	9. Vous n'apprendriez jamais à lire si vous n'étudiiez pas.

9.	You would never learn to read if you didn't study.	10.	Le malade vivrait toujours si on avait fait venir le médecin à temps.
10.	The sick person would still be alive if one had sent for the doctor in time.	11.	**demeurer**=*to live, to remain* Si l'on n'abordait jamais la question, elle demeurerait sans réponse.
11.	If one never took up the question, it would remain unanswered.	12.	Si l'art n'empruntait rien aux sciences, sa base, selon Taine, demeurerait peu solide.
12.	If art borrowed nothing from the sciences, its foundation, according to Taine, would remain weak.	13.	En parlant des singes, Buffon en vient à dire que s'ils pensaient, ils parleraient.
13.	While speaking of monkeys, Buffon goes so far as to say (comes to the point of saying) that if they thought, they would speak.	14.	Si les singes avaient même des pensées de singes, ils parleraient aux autres singes.
14.	If monkeys even had monkey thoughts, they would speak to the other monkeys.	15.	S'ils étaient doués de la puissance de réfléchir, ils perfectionneraient toujours leurs arts.
15.	If they were gifted (endowed) with the power of reflection, they would constantly (always) perfect their arts.	16.	Si les animaux en étaient doués, ils se mettraient à perfectionner leurs ouvrages.
16.	If the animals were endowed with it, they would begin to perfect their works.	17.	Parlons de nouveau de Victor Hugo et de ses pensées sur la poésie.
17.	Let us speak again of Victor Hugo and his thoughts on poetry.	18.	Selon lui, si les poètes modernes voyaient la nature telle qu'elle est, ils suivraient d'autres principes poétiques.
18.	According to him, if modern poets saw nature such as it is, they would follow other poetic principles.	19.	**sentir**=*to feel, to smell* Ils sentiraient que le laid y existe à côté du beau.
19.	They would feel (sense) that the ugly exists there (in nature) beside the beautiful.	20.	Ils abandonneraient l'idée classique qu'il faut éliminer l'ombre pour mieux voir la lumière.
20.	They would abandon the classical idea that one must eliminate the shadow in order to see the light.	21.	**amener**=*to lead* Ils amèneraient la poésie à la vérité.
21.	They would lead poetry to truth.	22.	Ce principe nous amènerait à une idée nouvelle de la poésie, n'est-ce pas?

22. This principle would lead us to a new idea of poetry, wouldn't it?	**23.** On se demanderait si une nature mutilée en serait plus belle.
23. One would wonder if a disfigured nature would be more beautiful because of it. (**En** refers to a previous idea, i.e. *for having been disfigured*.)	

108. *Future and Conditional of Irregular Verbs*

1. A number of irregular verbs do not use the infinitive as a stem for the Future and Conditional. Instead they have a special stem to which the usual endings are added:

INFINITIVE	FUTURE—CONDITIONAL STEM	
avoir	aur–	*will, would have*
être	ser–	*will, would be*
aller	ir–	*will, would go*
faire	fer–	*will, would do*
pouvoir	pourr–	*will, would be able*
vouloir	voudr–	*will, would want, like*
falloir	il faudr–	*will, would be necessary*
voir	verr–	*will, would see*
recevoir	recevr–	*will, would receive*
mourir	mourr–	*will, would die*
savoir	saur–	*will, would know*
tenir	tiendr–	*will, would hold*
venir	viendr–	*will, would come*

READING PREPARATION

INSTRUCTIONS: *Read the following phrases, paying special attention to the verb endings of these phrases drawn from previous readings.*

	1. Il ne pourrait rien en sortir d'intéressant.
1. Nothing of interest could result from it.	**2.** Il ne pourra rien en sortir d'important.
2. Nothing of importance can result from it (will be able to come out of it).	**3.** Les jeunes viendront se former aux disciplines de la recherche expérimentale.

3. The young people will come to be trained in the disciplines of experimental research.

4. Ils pourraient mieux travailler, s'ils étaient mieux équipés.

4. They would be able to work better if they were better equipped.

5. Ils pourront le faire mieux s'ils sont mieux équipés.

5. They will be able to do it better if they are better equipped.

6. La poésie fera un grand pas qui changera toute la face du monde intellectuel.
(*Here* **pas** *means—not/step*)

6. *step*
Poetry will take a great step which will change the entire face of the intellectual world.

7. La poésie ferait un grand pas qui changerait toute la face du monde intellectuel.

7. Poetry would take a great step which would change the entire face of the intellectual world.

8. Si l'on connaissait bien la race physiologiquement on aurait un grand jour sur la qualité secrète des esprits.

8. If one knew the race well physiologically one would have a great insight into the secret quality of the minds.

9. Je n'aurai à faire ici qu'un travail d'adaptation.

9. I will have to do only a work of adaptation here.

10. Je n'aurais à faire ici qu'un travail de révision.

10. I would have to do only a work of revision here.

11. Je trouverai là toute la question traitée, et je me bornerai à donner les citations qui me seront nécessaires.

11. I will find the whole question treated there, and I will restrict myself to supplying the quotations which will be necessary for me.

12. Si je trouvais là toute la question traitée, je me bornerais à donner les citations qui me seraient nécessaires.

12. If I found the whole question treated there, I would restrict myself to supplying the quotations which would be necessary for me.

13. Ce ne sera donc qu'une compilation de textes.

13. It will therefore be only a compilation of texts.

14. Ce ne serait donc qu'une compilation de textes.

14. It would therefore be only a compilation of texts.
(Comprenez-vous ce que vous lisez? Oui? Fort bien! Regardez maintenant les phases suivantes.)

15. Il mourait lentement.
(*Est-ce que le verbe est à l'imparfait ou au conditionel?*)

15. *The Imperfect.* Remember that these **–rir** verbs have an **–rr–** stem for the Conditional and a single **–r** for the Imperfect.
He was slowly dying.

16. *Conditional*
He would die slowly.

17. *The Imperfect*
By working more, he was acquiring a considerable sum of money.

18. By working more he would acquire a considerable sum of money.

19. If the bedouin falls sick, he will go to a place of pilgrimage to ask for a healing.

20. If he fell seriously ill, he would not go to the dervish.

21. If he went on (made) a pilgrimage he would no doubt be cured.

22. A little while ago, we saw a few biographical facts concerning Maimonides.

23. In a little while we will see some more (of them).

24. In a little while, we (one) will see several interesting questions treated by his biographers.

25. If we went deeply into his writings, we would see, if not an easy work, at least a work which reveals much about the Middle Ages.

26. We would see at the same time a lucid mind and a difficult work.

16. Il mourrait lentement.
(*L'imparfait ou le conditionnel?*)

17. En travaillant davantage, il acquérait une somme considérable d'argent.
(*L'imparfait ou le conditionnel?*)

18. En travaillant davantage, il acquerrait une somme considérable d'argent.

19. Si le bédouin tombe malade, il ira à un lieu de pèlerinage solliciter une guérison.

20. S'il tombait gravement malade, il n'irait pas au derviche.

21. S'il faisait un pèlerinage, sans doute recevrait-il une guérison.

22. Nous avons vu tout à l'heure quelques faits biographiques à propos de Maïmonide.

23. Nous en verrons d'autres tout à l'heure.

24. On verra tout à l'heure quelques questions intéressantes traitées par ses biographes.

25. **sinon**=*if not*
Si nous approfondissions ses écrits, nous verrions, sinon une oeuvre facile, du moins une œuvre révélatrice du moyen age.

26. **tout à la fois**= *at the same time, both*
Nous verrions tout à la fois un esprit lucide et une œuvre résistante.

27. Si on lisait quelques-uns de ses écrits, on voudrait peut-être en connaître davantage.

27. If one read a few of his writings, one would perhaps want to know more of them.

28. In order to go into them deeply, however, it would be necessary to know both Hebrew and the intellectual history of the Middle Ages.

29. In order to read them in a modern language, it would be necessary to look for a translation which would be at the same time clear and correct.

30. One would perhaps come to the point of liking them.

31. If you studied them long enough, you would perhaps come to the point of understanding them.

32. No doubt you would not be able to read them without a translation.

28. Pour les approfondir, cependant, il faudrait savoir à la fois l'hébreu et l'histoire intellectuelle du moyen age.

29. traduire=*to translate*
Pour les lire en langue moderne, il faudrait chercher une traduction qui soit à la fois claire et exacte.

30. On en viendrait peut-être à les aimer.

31. Si vous les étudiiez assez longtemps, vous en viendriez peut-être à les comprendre.

32. Sans doute ne sauriez-vous les lire sans traduction.

109. *Use of Future After* quand, lorsque, aussitôt que, *and* dès que

1. In English, we sometimes use the present tense even though future action is implied. The French use the future under these circumstances. Let English usage govern your translation:

Venez me voir quand vous *aurez* le temps. Come see me when you **have** time.

Aussitôt que j'*aurai* fini, je vous téléphonerai. As soon as I **finish**, I *will* phone you.

Dès que je *serai* prêt, je vous le dirai. As soon as I **am** ready, I *will* tell you.

READING PREPARATION

INSTRUCTIONS: *Translate these sentences into smooth, current English. Continue to circle the words you do not recognize.*

		1. Dès que vous ferez des recherches sérieuses, peut-être aurez-vous besoin de plusieurs langues.
1.	As soon as you do serious research, you will perhaps need several languages.	**2.** Aussitôt que vous acquerrez un vocabulaire suffisant, le français deviendra plus facile.
2.	As soon as you acquire a sufficient vocabulary, French will become easier.	**3.** Quand vous saurez lire facilement le français, vous aurez à votre disposition un bon outil de recherche.
3.	When you (will) know how to read French easily, you will have a good research tool at your disposal.	**4.** Lorsque nous aurons le temps, nous nous y mettrons.
4.	When we have the time, we will set about to do it (start to do it).	

110. *Additional Conditional Patterns*

1.   There are two patterns in which the verbs of both the conditional and the result clauses are in the Conditional. They are translated as follows:

Quand (bien) même l'artiste *essaierait* d'imiter toute la nature, il n'y *réussirait* pas.	*Even if the artist **tried** to imitate all of nature, he **would** not **succeed** in doing so.*
Il y *penserait* toute la journée qu'il n'y *comprendrait* rien.	*(Even) if he **thought** about it all day long, he **would understand** nothing about it.*

2.   Another meaning conveyed by the Conditional is that of *supposition*. A translation which is usually adequate is *supposed* + infinitive.

Selon certains, le français *serait* une langue facile.	*According to some, French **is supposed to be** an easy language or Some **suppose** French **to be** an easy language.*

READING PREPARATION

INSTRUCTIONS: *Express the meanings of the following French sentences. Remember that any translation which expresses the meaning is satisfactory even if it is not exactly like the one given here.*

		1.	Selon certains historiens, Maïmonide serait un des plus grands philosophes du moyen age.
1.	According to certain historians, Maimonides is supposed to be one of the greatest philosophers of the Middle Ages.	**2.**	Selon Hugo, le poète ressemblerait au prophète.
2.	According to Hugo, the poet is supposed to resemble the prophet.	**3.**	D'après lui, la poésie serait capable de changer la face du monde intellectuel.
3.	According to him, poetry is supposed to be capable of changing the face of the intellectual world.	**4.**	Selon certains linguistes, le chinois serait la langue la plus connue.
4.	According to certain linguists, Chinese is supposed to be the most (widely) known language.	**5.**	Cependant, je passerais bien des années à étudier le chinois que je ne le comprendrais pas.
5.	However, even if I spent many years studying Chinese, I would not understand it.	**6.**	Quand on passerait des années à l'étudier, on ne le saurait toujours pas.
6.	If one spent years studying it, one would still not know it.	**7.**	Quand on mettrait tout son temps à étudier cette philosophie, elle ne serait toujours pas tout à fait claire.
7.	If one spent all his time studying this philosophy, it would still not be entirely clear.	**8.**	On passerait tout son temps à étudier la philosophie qu'on n'en finirait jamais.
8.	(Even) if one spent all his time studying philosophy, he would (still) never finish with it.		

111. *Review Section*

		1.	Faisons maintenant une révision des conjonctions, des pronoms, et du subjonctif.
1.	Now let us review conjunctions, pronouns, and the subjunctive.	**2.**	L'événement a eu lieu ainsi que nous le disions. (*Is **disions** an imperfect or subjunctive form in this sentence?*)

2. *Imperfect*—**ainsi que** *is not followed by the subjunctive.*
The event took place just as we said (it would).

3. *In the above sentence,* **le** *refers to the previously mentioned idea of* _____.

3. *The action taking place.*

4. Si l'événement a lieu, il faut que nous le disions.
(*Is* **disions** *an imperfect or a subjunctive form?*)

4. *Subjunctive*—*it is preceded by* **il faut.**
If the event takes place, we will have to tell about it (or say so).

5. Il faut que vous trouviez les moyens de vivre, comme les autres physiciens.

5. You have to find the means to live, just as the other physicists do.

6. Pour bien lire le français il faut que vous appreniez les verbes ainsi que les pronoms et les adjectifs.

6. In order to read French well you must learn the verbs just as you do the pronouns and the adjectives.

7. Avant que vous ne vous fassiez poète, étudiez la nature.

7. Before you become a poet, study Nature.

8. La poésie complète n'existe pas sans que l'ombre se mêle avec la lumière.

8. Complete poetry does not exist without shadow being mixed with light.

9. Selon Hugo, la vraie poésie n'existe pas sans qu'il y ait des contraires harmonieux.

9. According to Hugo, true poetry does not exist without including harmonious contrasts.

10. A moins qu'une œuvre ne soit complète, elle ne peut être harmonieuse.

10. Unless a work is complete, it cannot be harmonious.

11. Quoique cette œuvre soit belle, elle n'est pas moderne.

11. Although this work is beautiful, it is not modern.

12. Pourvu que le poète fasse comme la nature et mêle, sans pourtant les confondre, la bête à l'esprit, il sera considéré comme moderne.

12. Provided the poet does as Nature and mixes the animal and the spiritual, without, however, confusing them, he will be considered modern.

13. **vraisemblable**=*likely*
Ce que vous dites à propos de sa vie est fort vraisemblable.

13. What you say concerning his life is very likely.

14. Ce qui nous intéresse, ce sont les faits biographiques.

14. What interests us are the biographical facts.

15. Les faits biographiques dont nous avons parlé sont pourtant peu vraisemblables.

15. The biographical facts about which we have spoken are, however, very unlikely.

16. Je me bornerai à vous les raconter.

16. I will confine myself to relating them to you.

17. Les persécutions religieuses dont sa famille fut l'objet lui firent quitter le pays.

17. The religious persecutions from which his family suffered made them (the family) leave the country.

18. **faire preuve de**=*to manifest, to give proof of*
La grande intelligence dont il fit preuve l'assura du respect de ses chefs.

18. The great intelligence of which he gave proof assured him of the respect of his superiors.

19. Sa famille fut la victime du zèle réformateur des Almohades, lesquels en vinrent à bouleverser les communautés juives de l'Espagne.

19. His family was the victim of the reforming zeal of the Almohades, who went so far as to overturn the Jewish communities of Spain.

20. La famille forma le projet de s'installer en Egypte, ce qu'elle ne tarda pas à faire.

20. The family made plans to settle in Egypt, which they did not delay in doing.

21. Cependant, il y perdit son frère.

21. However, he lost his brother there.

22. Les qualités d'homme d'état dont il fit preuve le firent choisir comme porte-parole de la communauté juive.

22. The qualities of a statesman which he displayed caused him to be elected as spokesman for the Jewish community.

23. **acharnement**=*tenacity, fury*
Il fit une carrière brillante parce qu'il continua à travailler avec acharnement.

23. He had a brilliant career because he continued to work with tenacity.

112. *Irregular Verb* devoir

1. The forms of **devoir** are as follows:

PRESENT	IMPERFECT	PRESENT SUBJUNCTIVE
je dois	je devais	je doive
tu dois	tu devais	tu doives
il doit	il devait	il doive
nous devons	nous devions	nous devions
vous devez	vous deviez	vous deviez
ils doivent	ils devaient	ils doivent

Past participle—**dû**

Present participle—**devant** (to avoid confusing this form of the verb with the preposition **devant,** consult the context.)

The future—conditional stem is **devr–** (**il devra, il devrait,** etc.)

PAST DEFINITE	
je dus	nous dûmes
tu dus	vous dûtes
il dut	ils durent

2. The meaning of **devoir**+noun is expressed by *to owe:*

Il me doit cinq francs.   *He owes me five francs.*

3. **Devoir**+infinitive may express conjecture, obligation, or intent. Become familiar with the following meanings:

(A)   the conditional—*ought to*

Je devrais partir.   *I ought to leave.*
Vous devriez étudier davantage.   *You ought to study more.*

(B)   the present—*must* or *is* (*am, are*) *to*

Je n'ai pas réussi au dernier examen. Je dois étudier davantage.   *I did not pass the last test. I must study more.* (obligation)

Personne ne l'a vu récemment. Il doit être malade.   *No one has seen him recently. He must be sick.* (conjecture)

| Il nous a fait part de son iti-néraire. Il doit arriver demain. | He informed us of his itinerary. He is to arrive tomorrow. (intention) |

(C)   the imperfect—was (were) to, must have

| Il devait arriver à cinq heures, mais on ne l'a pas encore vu. | He was to arrive at five o'clock, but no one has seen him yet. (intent) |
| Il avait l'air agité. Il devait être en colère. | He looked agitated. He must have been angry. (conjecture) |

(D)   the past indefinite or past definite—had to or must have

| Personne ne l'a vu la semaine passée—il a dû être malade (il dut être malade.) | No one saw him last week—he must have been sick. (conjecture) |
| Il était si malade qu'il a dû consulter de médecin (il dut consulter le médecin). | He was so sick that he had to consult the doctor. (obligation) |

READING PREPARATION

INSTRUCTIONS: *Distinguish between the various meanings of* **devoir** *in the following sentences.*

1. In order to understand the thought of Maimonides, one must take a step into intellectual history.

2. One must consult, if not the primary sources, at least some capable historians.

3. In order for you not to be unaware (so that you will not be unaware) of the details of his life, I must give you a short biographical sketch.

4. Born in 1135, he was to receive his early education in a Jewish community.

1. Pour comprendre la pensée de Maïmonide, on doit faire un pas dans l'histoire intellectuelle.

2. On doit consulter, sinon les sources primaires, du moins des historiens capables.

3. Pour que vous n'ignoriez pas les détails de sa vie, je dois vous faire un court exposé biographique.

4. Né en 1135, il devait recevoir sa première formation dans une communauté juive.

5. **à peine**=*scarcely, hardly*
A peine sorti de l'enfance, il subit les conséquences d'une calamité qui devait bouleverser son existence.

5. (When) scarcely out of childhood, he suffered the consequences of a calamity which was to disrupt his existence.

6. The Jewish and Christian minorities were to feel keenly the reforming zeal of the Moslems.

7. Judged by the results, the persecutions must have been severe.

8. After having left their native country, the emigrants must have been quite unhappy.

9. Because of religious persecutions, his family had to settle in Egypt.

10. Having had to leave their native country because of persecutions, the emigrants settled in Egypt.

11. These years must have been difficult.

12. Because of the loss of his brother, Moses had to earn his living by the art of healing.

13. In order to become a court doctor he must have made a great impression on the dignitaries.

14. *owed*
He owed his position to his personal qualities.

15. *position*
His family owed to him its position as spokesman for the Jewish community before the Moslem authorities.

6. **ressentir**=*to feel, to experience*
Les minorités juive et chrétienne devaient ressentir vivement le zèle réformateur des Musulmans.

7. Jugées d'après les résultats, les persécutions ont dû être sévères.

8. Après avoir quitté leur pays natal, les émigrés devaient être assez malheureux.

9. **par suite de**=*because of, as a result of*
Par suite des persécutions religieuses, sa famille a dû (dut) s'installer en Egypte.

10. Ayant dû quitter leur pays natal par suite des persécutions, les émigrées s'installèrent en Egypte.

11. Ces années durent être difficiles.

12. Par suite de la perte de son frère, Moïse a dû (dut) gagner sa vie par l'art de guérir.

13. Pour devenir médecin de cour, il a dû faire une grande impression sur les dignitaires.

14. Il devait sa position à ses qualités personnelles.
(**Devait** is followed by a noun. It must therefore mean—*was to/owed*)

15. Sa famille lui devait sa qualité de porte-parole de la communauté juive devant les autorités musulmanes.
(**Qualité** here must mean *quality/position*)

16. Devant sa qualité de médecin de cour à ses qualités personnelles, il fit une carrière brillante.
(**Devant** here must mean *owing/before*)

16. *owing*
Owing his position of court doctor to his personal qualities, he had a brilliant career.

17. This is a subject to which we shall have to return later.

18. What ought to interest us for the time being is the reading.

19. What we ought to do now is to go on to the reading.

20. However, you will first have to glance at the vocabulary section.

21. You even ought to go into that section deeply.

22. If you no longer make many mistakes, you must read quite fluently.

23. However, if you still make a few, you must correct them.

24. Indeed, if you succeed in reading French fluently, you will owe this skill (facility) to your assiduous work.

17. C'est un sujet sur lequel nous devrons revenir plus tard.

18. Ce qui devrait nous intéresser pour le moment, c'est la lecture.

19. Ce que nous devrions faire maintenant, c'est passer à la lecture.

20. Pourtant, vous devrez d'abord jeter un coup d'œil sur la section de vocabulaire.

21. Vous devriez même approfondir cette section-là.

22. Si vous ne faites plus beaucoup de fautes, vous devez lire assez couramment.

23. Pourtant, si vous en faites encore quelques unes, vous devez les corriger.

24. En effet, si vous arrivez à lire couramment le français, vous devrez cette facilité à votre travail assidu.

Review the circled words before continuing.

VOCABULARY DEVELOPMENT

INSTRUCTIONS: *Using the analogy of the words given, try to anticipate the meanings of the related words.*

1. **enseigner**=*to teach*
renseigner=*to inform*
Pour **enseigner** la physique atomique de nos jours, il faut qu'on **se renseigne** bien sur les structures atomiques.

1. *to teach . . .*
inform oneself (or) *be informed*

2. Le disciple suit toujours les **enseignements** de son maître.

2. *teachings*	**3.** Pouvez-vous me donner des **renseignements** sur votre formation?
3. *information*	**4.** Il a répondu à toutes les questions—il doit être **bien renseigné.**
4. *well informed*	**5.** **la chute** = *the fall* **le parachute** = _____
5. *the parachute (that which protects from a fall)*	**6.** **la pluie** = *the rain* **le parapluie** = _____
6. *the umbrella*	**7.** Quand on fait une promenade en été, on se sert souvent d'un **parasol.**
7. *a parasol*	**8.** Lors d'un orage, on est content d'avoir la protection d'un **paratonnerre.**
8. *a lightning rod*	**9.** **la boue** = *the mud* **le pare-boue** d'une automobile
9. *the mudguard*	**10.** **le pare-brise** d'une automobile
10. *the windshield*	**11.** **des soucis** = *cares, worries, anxieties* Etant riche et beau, il ne **se souciait de rien.**
11. *didn't worry about anything*	**12.** Il avait l'air **peu soucieux.**
12. *carefree*	**13.** Quand on doit beaucoup d'argent, **on a souvent l'air soucieux.**
13. *one often looks worried.*	**14.** **Ne vous souciez** de rien.
14. *Don't worry about anything.*	**15.** On doit être **soucieux de** ne pas trop étudier, n'est-ce pas?
15. *careful*	

TESTING EXERCISE

INSTRUCTIONS: *Before continuing, take the following test. Circle the answer which most nearly expresses the meaning of the indicated word or which represents the best translation. Mark the points you miss, and review the section indicated.*

    1. Cette dignité **restera** longtemps dans la famille.
       A. had remained   B. will remain   C. would remain   D. was remaining

1. B   **2.** Nous **désirerions** vous parler.
(106)   A. would like   B. used to like   C. liked   D. will like

2. A (107)	**3.**	Je **ressentis** vivement le ridicule de la situation. A. would feel B. felt C. will feel D. used to feel
3. B (105)	**4.**	Il **mourait** lentement. A. will die B. would die C. was dying D. had died
4. C (108)	**5.**	Lorsque nous **saurons** les matières de notre cours, nous pourrons passer l'examen. A. used to know B. know C. knew D. would know
5. B (109)	**6.**	Je **passerais** bien des années à étudier la zoologie que je n'y comprendrais rien. A. I will spend B. I would spend C. If I spent D. I spent
6. C (110)	**7.**	Il me **devait** une somme considérable d'argent. A. will owe B. owed C. should owe D. probably owes
7. B (112)	**8.**	Vous **devriez** étudier davantage. A. were to study B. should study C. must study D. had to study
8. B (112)	**9.**	C'est un homme très **laid**. A. clever B. lazy C. obscure D. ugly
9. D	**10.**	On doit apprendre à bien **traduire** le français. A. read B. appreciate C. understand D. translate
10. D	**11.**	Il a **mêlé** les faits à des fables. A. mistook B. recounted C. mixed D. eliminated
11. C		

READING PASSAGES

INSTRUCTIONS: *In the following passage of about 400 words, Victor Hugo speaks of the nature of the "new" (1827) poetry. Take eight minutes to read the passage, circling unrecognized words, and then answer the multiple choice questions to verify your comprehension. If you cannot read the passage in eight minutes, work out the meanings of the unfamiliar words and practice the passage until you can.*

La poésie moderne

Victor Hugo, Préface de *Cromwell*, 1827

. . . Voilà donc une nouvelle religion, une société nouvelle; sur cette double base, il faut que nous voyions grandir une nouvelle poésie . . . Le christianisme amène la poésie à la vérité. Comme lui, la muse moderne verra les choses d'un coup d'œil plus haut et plus large. Elle sentira que

5   tout dans la création n'est pas humainement beau, que le laid y existe à

côté du beau, le difforme près du gracieux, le grotesque **au revers** [1] du
sublime, le mal avec le bien, l'ombre avec la lumière. Elle se demandera
si la raison étroite et relative de l'artiste doit **avoir gain de cause sur** [2]
la raison infinie, absolue, du Créateur; si c'est à l'homme de rectifier Dieu;
10   si une nature mutilée en sera plus belle; si l'art a le droit de dédoubler,
pour ainsi dire, l'homme, la vie, la création; si chaque chose marchera mieux
quand on lui aura ôté son muscle et son ressort; si, enfin, c'est le moyen
d'être harmonieux que d'être incomplet. C'est alors que, l'œil fixé sur des
événements tout à la fois risibles et formidables, et sous l'influence de cet
15   esprit de mélancolie chrétienne et de critique philosophique que nous ob-
servions tout à l'heure, la poésie fera un grand pas, un pas décisif, un pas
qui, **pareil à** [3] la secousse d'un tremblement de terre, changera toute la
face du monde intellectuel. Elle se mettra à faire comme la nature, à mêler
dans ses créations, sans pourtant les confondre, l'ombre à la lumière, le
20   grotesque au sublime, en d'autres termes, le corps à l'âme, la bête à l'esprit;
car le point de départ de la religion est toujours le point de départ de la
poésie . . .
    La poésie née du christianisme, la poésie de notre temps est donc le
drame, le caractère du drame est le réel, le réel résulte de la combinaison toute
25   naturelle de deux types, le sublime et le grotesque qui se croisent dans le
drame, comme ils se croisent dans la vie et dans la création. Car la poésie
vraie, la poésie complète, est dans l'harmonie des contraires. Puis, il est
temps de le dire hautement, et c'est ici surtout que les exceptions confir-
meraient la règle, tout ce qui est dans la nature est dans l'art.

1.   La poésie dont parle l'auteur (lignes 1–7) doit être fondée sur
    A. la beauté du Christianisme
    B. la laideur de la nature
    C. la vérité que l'on trouve grâce au Christianisme
    D. la raison de l'artiste

1. C   **2.**   Le premier paragraphe nous permet de penser que les poètes avant Hugo
    A. avait mis des objets laids dans leur poésie
    B. avaient désiré suivre la raison infinie du Créateur
    C. s'étaient inspirés de la mélancolie chrétienne
    D. avaient imité le beau en rejetant le laid

2. D   **3.**   Selon Hugo, la nouvelle poésie
    A. sera ébranlée comme par un tremblement de terre
    B. exercera une influence énorme sur le monde intellectuel
    C. ne sera pas du tout décisive
    D. doit confondre les qualités contraires, telles que le corps et l'âme

---

1 *on the other side*   **2** *prevail against*   **3** *similar to*

3. B   **4.** Dans le dernier paragraphe nous apprenons que
      A. le résultat réel de la poésie est dramatique
      B. c'est au théâtre que l'on doit chercher la poésie moderne
      C. la règle de la poésie moderne est universelle
      D. le drame ne saurait exprimer les profondeurs de la vie et de la création

4. B

Un Penseur du Moyen Age

Extrait de Georges Vajda, "La Pensée religieuse de
Moïse Maïmonide: unité ou dualité?" *Cahiers de
civilisation médiévale*, IX (1966), 29–30.

Moïse, fils de Maïmoun . . . naquit à Cordoue, le 30 mars 1135, d'une
famille établie depuis de nombreuses générations dans l'Espagne musulmane;
son père était un savant rabbin, sinon du tout premier rang, du moins d'une
certaine notoriété. Le jeune garçon reçut ainsi sa première formation **au**
5   **sein** [1] d'une communauté juive florissante qui comptait parmi ses membres
des personnalités fort en vue dans le judaïsme d'Espagne, communauté très
ouverte **au surplus,** [2] dans ses couches supérieures, à la culture arabe, litté-
raire ou philosophique. Mais, à peine sorti de l'enfance, il subit les conséquences d'une calamité publique qui devait bouleverser, sans le changer
10   pourtant radicalement, le cours de son existence. L'invasion de la Péninsule
par les Almohades, dont le zèle réformateur n'épargna point leurs **propres** [3]
coreligionnaires, et encore moins les minorités juive et chrétienne, détruisit,
ou tout au moins désorganisa profondément, pour de longues années, les
communautés juives de la partie de l'Espagne et du Portugal actuels dominée
15   alors par les Musulmans. Des deux voies de fuite ouvertes aux survivants,
l'Espagne chrétienne et le Maroc, la famille de Moïse Maïmonide choisit, pour
des raisons qui nous **échappent,** [4] la seconde; elle quitta Cordoue vers 1149
et alla s'installer à Fès, où nous la trouvons encore en 1159/60.

On a passionnément discuté sur la question de savoir si, pendant cette
20   période difficile, Moïse Maïmonide et sa famille se résignèrent ou non à une
conversion forcée à l'Islam, tout en vivant secrètement comme Juifs. Beaucoup de leurs amis y furent certainement contraints et Maïmonide lui-même
fut accusé, bien des années plus tard, en Égypte, par un musulman qui ne lui
voulait pas de bien, d'avoir renié l'Islam après l'avoir professé naguère au
25   Maghreb, incrimination qui eût pu avoir des conséquences tragiques,
n'étaient [5] les hautes protections dont il était entouré. Le problème n'a pas
reçu de solution définitive, mais ce qui est indubitable c'est que, Juif avoué
ou musulman crypto-juif, Maïmonide paracheva sa formation sacrée, dans la
loi juive, et sa formation profane, philosophie et médecine, en la docte cité
30   de Fès; c'est peut-être encore au Maghreb qu'il composa son petit *Art de la*

1 *within*   **3** *own*   **5** *if it were not for*
2 *moreover*   **4** *escape*

logique, coup d'essai remarquable qui faisait bien augurer de sa grandeur future.

35   Peu après 1160, la famille de Maïmonide (son père était encore en vie) réussit à quitter pour toujours l'Occident musulman rendu si inhospitalier aux minorités religieuses par la première domination almohade. Si nous sommes mal renseignés sur les pérégrinations de nos émigrés pendant les quatre ou cinq années qui suivent, nous savons qu'ils abordèrent à Saint-Jean d'Acre le 12 octobre 1165. Le père mourra peu de temps après et la famille ne tardera pas à s'installer en Égypte, exactement à Fostat (ou
40   Vieux-Caire), siège de l'une des communautés juives les plus considérables à cette époque.

        Moïse Maïmonide vivra presque quarante ans en Égypte, toujours soucieux de ne pas monnayer sa science sacrée, autrement dit, de ne pas se mettre au service rémunéré de ses coreligionnaires. Sa subsistance sera assurée tout
45   d'abord par son association sédentaire au commerce de pierres précieuses où ses frères, comme beaucoup de Juifs d'Égypte au XIIᵉ siècle, avaient des intérêts. Ce négoce **périclita** ⁶ cependant lorsque son frère, **cheville ouvrière** ⁷ de l'affaire, disparut dans un naufrage. Il gagna alors sa vie par l'art de guérir; devenu après la chute de la dynastie fatimide, en 1171, le
50   protégé d'un des grands dignitaires de la dynastie ayyoubide, il fit une carrière brillante en qualité de médecin de cour, non certes de Saladin, comme on peut le lire dans divers ouvrages de vulgarisation, et déjà chez l'un de ses premiers biographes musulmans, mais de son successeur al-Malik al-Afdal. A la faveur de cette position privilégiée, il s'imposa aussi comme chef et
55   porte-parole officiel de sa confession devant les autorités musulmanes — cette dignité restera dans sa famille jusqu'au XIVᵉ siècle, — tandis que sa réputation de maître en sciences religieuses gagnera les régions éloignées de la **diaspora** ⁸ juive, du Yémen jusqu'au Languedoc. **Valétudinaire** ⁹ pendant bien des années, mais travaillant avec acharnement jusqu'à ses derniers
60   jours, Moïse Maïmonide quittera ce bas monde le 13 décembre 1204.

INSTRUCTIONS: *Circle the answer which most accurately paraphrases the meaning of the reading passage.*

   1.   Son père (lignes 1–4) était
           A. peu connu
           B. parmi les plus célèbres des rabbins
           C. assez bien connu
           D. chef du synagogue

---

1. C   **2.**   Il paraît que le communauté juive (lignes 4–8)
                     A. détestait les arabes
                     B. se croyait supérieure à la culture arabe

---

6 *was jeopardized*   **8** *dispersion*   **9** *an invalid*
7 *king-pin*

c. était très fermée

d. était en contact avec la pensée arabe

---

2. D   **3.** Le résultat de l'invasion de la Péninsule (lignes 8–15) fut

A. le bouleversement temporaire des communautés juives

B. la destruction permanente d'une partie de l'Espagne

c. de forcer les juifs à quitter l'Espagne pour le Portugal

D. la destruction permanente des communautés juives en Espagne

---

3. A   **4.** Les envahisseurs (lignes 11–18)

A. s'attaquèrent à des musulmans

B. croyaient que les chrétiens n'étaient pas aussi importants que les musulmans

c. détruisirent tout culte religieux en Espagne

D. échappent à toute explication rationnelle

---

4. A   **5.** L'auteur affirme (lignes 19–32)

A. que Moïse résista à tous les efforts faits pour le convertir

B. qu'il avait de puissants amis musulmans

c. que sa conversion à l'Islam n'était pas sincère

D. que son *Art de la logique* était la plus grande de ses œuvres

---

5. B   **6.** Ensuite nous apprenons (lignes 33–42)

A. qu'il n'y avait plus beaucoup d'hôpitaux dans l'Occident musulman

B. que l'auteur ne sait pas très bien ce que firent les émigrés pendant leurs voyages

c. que le père mourut de chagrin

D. que la famille fut chassée d'Egypte

---

6. B   **7.** La mort de son frère (lignes 47–48) eu lieu

A. dans le désert   B. en ville   c. sur l'océan   D. lors d'une bataille

---

7. C   **8.** Pour gagner sa vie en Egypte, Maïmonide a dû

A. accepter des dons des autres juifs

B. diriger le commerce de son frère après la mort de celui-ci

c. devenir médecin

D. écrire des livres de vulgarisation

---

8. C   **9.** Il devait sa qualité de porte–parole de la communauté juive (lignes 51–58) à

A. sa réputation mondiale

B. ses œuvres de philosophie

c. son travail acharné

D. sa position à la cour

---

9. D

Chapter Seventeen

113. *Future Perfect and Conditional Perfect*

1. The usual meanings of the Future or Conditional+past participle (the Future or Conditional Perfect) are translated by the corresponding English tenses as follows:

Il sera arrivé avant cinq heures.	*He will have arrived before five o'clock.*
Il serait arrivé avant cinq heures.	*He would have arrived before five o'clock.*

2. The meanings of the Past Conditional of **pouvoir, devoir, vouloir,** etc.+infinitive are expressed as follows:

J'aurais dû venir.	*I should have come (ought to have come).*
J'aurais pu venir.	*I could have come (would have been able to come).*
J'aurais voulu venir.	*I would have liked to come.*

3. The Future and the Future Perfect, in addition to their other meanings, may express *probability:*

On n'a pas vu Jean dernièrement —il *sera* malade.	*We haven't seen John lately—he **must** be sick.*
Personne ne l'attendait à la gare— il *sera* arrivé en avance.	*No one was waiting for him at the station—he **must have** arrived early.*

338

4. The Conditional and the Conditional Perfect may express hypothesis:

Les anthropologistes parlent d'une "mentalité primitive" qui *serait* celle des races inférieures.	*The anthropologists speak of a "primitive mind" which they* **suppose** *(is* **supposed***) to be that of inferior races.*
Cette "mentalité primitive" *aurait* jadis *été* celle de l'humanité en général.	*This "primitive mind"* **is supposed to have** *been formerly that of humanity in general.*

READING PREPARATION

INSTRUCTIONS: *As you read the following French sentences, cover the English with your card. Continue to circle those sentences which contain new or unfamiliar vocabulary.*

1. D'ici un mois vous aurez fait un grand pas dans la connaissance du français.

1. A month from now you will have taken a great step in the knowledge of French.

2. Vous aurez enfin appris tous les temps des verbes.

2. You will finally have learned all the tenses of the verbs.

3. Vous aurez passé quelques heures à lire des auteurs français.

3. You will have spent a few hours reading French authors.

4. Selon certains anthropologistes, la "mentalité primitive" correspondrait à une structure fondamentale différente.

4. According to certain anthropologists, the "primitive mind" is supposed to correspond to a different fundamental structure.

5. La race aurait évolué.

5. It is supposed that the race evolved.

6. Ce sont les anthropologistes qui auront formulé la théorie.

6. It is the anthropologists who must have formulated the theory.

7. **mettre sur le compte de** = *to attribute (put on the account of)*
On mettrait la superstition sur le compte de la mentalité primitive.

7. Superstition is supposed to be attributable to the primitive mind.

8. La théorie sera basée sur des croyances et des pratiques constatées dans une humanité peu civilisée.

8. The theory must be based on beliefs and practices ascertained in a people only slightly civilized.

9. Les partisans de cette théorie mettent la superstition sur le compte de la mentalité primitive.

9.	Those who favor this theory attribute superstition to the primitive mind.	**10.**	Notre mentalité moderne aura supplanté la mentalité primitive.
10.	Our modern mind must have supplanted (replaced) the primitive mind.	**11.**	Celle-là aurait supplanté celle-ci.
11.	One supposes that the former supplanted the latter.	**12.**	Basée comme elle l'est sur de très bonnes preuves, cette hypothèse sera sans doute la meilleure.
12.	Based as it is on very good proofs, this hypothesis is no doubt the best.	**13.**	Selon certains, Maïmonide se sera résigné à une conversion forcée.
13.	According to some, Maimonides probably (or must have) resigned himself to a forced conversion.	**14.**	Il aurait gagné sa vie par l'art de guérir.
14.	He is purported to have earned his living by the art of healing.	**15.**	Il aurait été un des plus grands philosophes du moyen age.
15.	He is supposed to have been one of the greatest philosophers of the Middle Ages.	**16.**	Sa philosophie sera, dit-on, la plus pénétrante de l'époque.
16.	It is said that his philosophy is probably the most penetrating of the time.	**17.**	S'il n'avait insisté que sur les points principaux, il aurait beaucoup raccourci son récit.
17.	If he had insisted only on the main points, he would have greatly shortened his account.	**18.**	Il aurait voulu le raccourcir.
18.	He would have liked to shorten it.	**19.**	Il aurait pu le raccourcir beaucoup.
19.	He could have shortened it a great deal.	**20.**	En effet, il paraît qu'il aurait dû le raccourcir.
20.	Indeed, it appears that he should have shortened it.	**21.**	Si vous aviez étudié davantage, vous auriez réussi à l'examen.
21.	If you had studied more, you would have passed the test.	**22.**	Je sais que vous auriez voulu y réussir.
22.	I know that you would have liked to pass it.	**23.**	Vous auriez sans doute pu y réussir.
23.	You no doubt could have passed it.	**24.**	Tout le monde aurait dû y réussir.
24.	Everyone should have passed it.	**25.**	S'ils avaient fait attention à la lecture, ils l'auraient mieux comprise.

25. If they had paid attention to the reading, they would have understood it better.	**26.** Ils auraient pu facilement y faire attention.
26. They could easily have paid attention to it.	**27.** Ils auraient dû y faire attention.
27. They should have paid attention to it.	**28.** Si nous avions analysé l'examen plus soigneusement, nous nous serions rendus plus vite compte de nos erreurs.
28. If we had analyzed the test more carefully, we would have realized our errors more quickly.	**29.** Nous aurions pu nous en rendre compte.
29. We could have realized them.	**30.** Nous aurions dû nous en rendre compte.
30. We should have realized them.	**31.** Nous aurions voulu l'analyser plus soigneusement, si nous avions eu le temps.
31. We would have liked to analyze it more carefully, if we had had the time.	**32.** D'ici peu vous aurez achevé la lecture de la première partie du texte.
32. In a little while, you will have finished the reading of the first part of the text.	**33.** D'ici un mois vous vous y serez mis, du moins.
33. A month from now, you will have started it, at least.	**34.** **plus tôt**=*sooner* Vous l'auriez déjà achevé si vous vous y étiez mis plus tôt.
34. You would already have finished it if you had started it sooner.	**35.** **l'orgueil**=*pride* Si nous n'avions point d'orgueil, nous ne nous plaindrions pas de celui des autres. La Rochefoucauld
35. If we had no pride, we would not complain about that of others.	**36.** Il y a des gens qui n'auraient jamais été amoureux s'ils n'avaient jamais entendu parler de l'amour. La Rouchefoucauld
36. There are people who would never have fallen in love if no one had ever spoken to them about love.	

114. *Past Indefinite of the Subjunctive*

1. The Present Subjunctive of **avoir** and **être** (**j'aie, je sois,** etc.) +the past participle are translated like the regular Past Indefinite:

Il a eu tort.	*He was (has been) wrong.*
Il se peut qu'il *ait eu* tort.	*It is possible he **was** (**has been**) wrong.*
Il s'est déjà rendu compte de son erreur.	*He has already realized his error.*
Il se peut qu'il se *soit* déjà rendu compte de son erreur.	*It is possible that he **has** already **realized** his error.*

READING PREPARATION

INSTRUCTIONS: *As you read the following French sentences, cover the English with your card. Continue to check those sentences which contain new or unfamiliar vocabulary. Review them after you finish the exercise and again in a day or two, until you recognize them immediately.*

1. Pour savoir lire si bien il faut qu'il ait bien travaillé.

1. In order to know how to read so well, he must have worked hard.

2. Il est faux que nous ayons mis au point notre connaissance du français.

2. It is false that we have perfected our knowledge of French.

3. Il est possible que nous nous y soyons mis trop tard.

3. It is possible we started it too late (or "started to do it too late").

4. Est-il vrai qu'il soit déjà arrivé?

4. Is it true that he has already arrived?

5. **songer à**=*to think about, to dream* Est-il possible que vous n'ayez pas songé à votre avenir?

5. Is it possible that you have not thought of your future?

6. Je ne dis pas que je n'y aie pas songé.

6. I don't say that I haven't thought about it.

7. **réfléchir à**=*to reflect upon, to think about* Il est douteux que beaucoup de monde y ait réfléchi.

7. It is doubtful that many people have thought about it.

8. Il est possible qu'on y ait déjà réfléchi.

8. It is possible that one has already thought about it.

---

115. *Imperfect of the Subjunctive*

1. The following endings are the sign of the Imperfect of the Subjunctive:

aimer	rendre	croire
j'aim*asse*	je rend*isse*	je cr*usse*
tu aim*asses*	tu rend*isses*	tu cr*usses*
il aim*ât*	il rend*ît*	il cr*ût*
nous aim*assions*	nous rend*issions*	nous cr*ussions*
vous aim*assiez*	vous rend*issiez*	vous cr*ussiez*
ils aim*assent*	ils rend*issent*	ils cr*ussent*

2. Some **–ir** verbs have the same endings for the Imperfect of the Subjunctive as for the Present of the Subjunctive, except for the **il** form, which ends in **–ât, –ît** or **–ût.** The tense must be determined by the context:

Il faut que nous finissions (Present).   *We have to finish.*
Il fallait que nous finissions (Imperfect).   *We had to finish.*

3. The Past Definite of irregular verbs will suggest the Imperfect forms. The third person singular of the Imperfect Subjunctive is distinguished from the Past Definite by the circumflex accent:

PAST DEFINITE		IMPERFECT SUBJUNCTIVE
il eut	(*he had*)	**il eût**
il fut	(*he was*)	**il fût**
il put	(*he could*)	**il pût**

4. For practical purposes the Imperfect of the Subjunctive has all of the meanings of the Imperfect of the Indicative and can often be translated the same way:

Il travaillait avec acharnement.   *He was working (or worked) furiously.*

**Bien qu'il travaillât avec acharne-
ment, il n'arrivait pas à achever
son ouvrage.**
*Although he was working (or worked)
furiously, he did not manage to complete his work.*

Il était consciencieux.	*He was conscientious.*
Quoiqu'il fût consciencieux, il fut également sot.	*Although he was conscientious, he was also foolish.*

However, because of the expressions and conjunctions which accompany the subjunctive, the phrase must sometimes be turned in a different way:

Pour qu'il achevât son ouvrage, il avait besoin d'un grand appui matériel.	*In order that he might finish his work, he needed great material support.*
Pour achever son ouvrage à temps, il fallait qu'il passât tout son temps à y travailler.	*In order for him to finish his work on time, it was necessary for him to spend (or that he spend) all his time working on it.*

READING PREPARATION

INSTRUCTIONS: *Tell whether the following forms are Past Definite or the Imperfect of the Subjunctive.*

		1.	il fut
1.	*Past Definite*	**2.**	il fût
2.	*Imperfect of the Subjunctive*	**3.**	il marcha
3.	*Past Definite*	**4.**	il marchât
4.	*Imperfect of the Subjunctive*	**5.**	je dus (**devoir**)
5.	*Past Definite*	**6.**	je dusse
6.	*Imperfect of the Subjunctive*	**7.**	ils firent (**faire**)
7.	*Past Definite*	**8.**	ils fissent
8.	*Imperfect of the Subjunctive*	**9.**	ils fussent (**être**)
9.	*Imperfect of the Subjunctive*	**10.**	ils furent
10.	*Past Definite*	**11.**	nous donnassions
11.	*Imperfect of the Subjunctive*	**12.**	nous donnâmes
12.	*Past Definite*	**13.**	nous lûmes (**lire**)
13.	*Past Definite*	**14.**	nous lussions

14. *Imperfect of the Subjunctive*	**15.**	il sût (**savoir**)
15. *Imperfect of the Subjunctive*	**16.**	il sut
16. *Past Definite*	**17.**	elle put
17. *Past Definite*	**18.**	elle pût
18. *Imperfect of the Subjunctive*	**19.**	nous attendîmes
19. *Past Definite*	**20.**	nous attendissions
20. *Imperfect of the Subjunctive*	**21.**	on fît
21. *Imperfect of the Subjunctive*	**22.**	on fit
22. *Past Definite*		

INSTRUCTIONS: *Read the right-hand column. Look at the left-hand column only when you feel you need to verify the meaning you get from the French.*

	1. Vous souvenez-vous de Louis XVI?
1. Do you remember Louis XVI?	**2.** Quoiqu'il fût trop optimiste, il n'était point sot.
2. Although he was too optimistic, he was not unintelligent (or foolish).	**3.** Bien qu'il se souvînt des leçons de ses prédécesseurs, il ne survécut pas à la Révolution.
3. Although he remembered the lessons of his predecessors, he did not survive the Revolution.	**4.** Vous souvenez-vous de Sémire?
4. Do you remember Sémire?	**5.** Quoiqu'elle fût belle, on pouvait la croire peu sincère.
5. Although she was beautiful, one could believe her insincere.	**6.** Nonobstant qu'elle eût toutes les raisons du monde d'être reconnaissante envers Zadig, elle épousa Orcan.
6. Notwithstanding that she had every reason in the world to be grateful to Zadig, she married Orcan.	**7.** Jusqu'à ce qu'elle épousât celui-ci, elle aimait celui-là avec passion.
7. Until she married the latter, she loved the former passionately.	**8.** Bien qu'elle ne se souvînt pas de son bienfaiteur, elle lui devait quand même la vie et l'honneur.

8. Although she did not remember her benefactor, she owed him her life and her honor just the same.

9. **plaire à**=*to please*
Avant que Zadig ne perdît son œil, il plaisait à Sémire.

9. Before Zadig lost his eye, he was pleasing to Sémire.

10. Quoiqu' Orcan ne lui plût nullement auparavant, elle l'épousa par la suite.

10. Although Orcan did not please her at all before, she married him afterwards.

11. Il se peut que vous vous soyez souvenu de Victor Hugo.

11. It is possible that you (have) remembered Victor Hugo.

12. Sans qu'il voulût paraître immodeste, il se crut un des plus grands poètes français.

12. Without wishing to appear immodest, he believed himself to be one of the greatest French poets.

13. Nonobstant qu'il parût peu modeste, il eut peut-être raison de croire à son génie.

13. Notwithstanding that he appeared immodest, he was perhaps right in believing in his genius.

14. Pour qu'il pût s'imposer comme autorité en matière de poésie il fallait qu'il eût un talent immense.

14. In order that he might be able to become prominent as an authority on poetry, he had to have an immense talent.

15. Avant que Maïmonide ne devînt porte-parole officiel de la communauté juive, il fut médecin de cour.

15. Before Maimonides became official spokesman of the Jewish community, he was court physician.

16. Quoiqu'il fût médecin, il devint le porte-parole officiel.

16. Although he was a doctor, he became the official spokesman.

17. Quoique le père mourût peu après 1165, la famille ne tarda pas à s'installer en Égypte.

17. Although the father died shortly after 1165, the family lost no time in settling in Egypt.

Before continuing, review the words you circled in the above exercises.

116. *Imperfect Subjunctive—Conditional Meanings*

1. The imperfect of the Subjunctive may also express the meaning of *even if* or *if only*, as in the following phrases:

Fût-elle la plus belle femme du monde . . .   *Even if she were the most beautiful woman in the world . . .*

Elle a bien voulu nous inviter, _ne fût-ce que_ par politesse.	_She was indeed willing to invite us, **if only** out of politeness._

2. The Subjunctive + past participle may express the meaning of the Past Conditional. Because this meaning makes a vital difference to the sentence, you should be alert to it:

Il partit après qu'il eut détruit la machine (Past ant.).	_He left after he had destroyed the machine._
Sans notre intervention, il eût détruit la machine (Past cond.).	_Without our intervention, he **would have destroyed** the machine._

READING PREPARATION

INSTRUCTIONS: _As you read the following French sentences, cover the English with your card. Continue to check those sentences that contain new or unfamiliar vocabulary._

		1.	Nous devrions lui rendre visite, ne fût—ce que par devoir.
1.	We ought to pay him (her) a visit, if only out of duty.	**2.**	Fussent-ils les témoins les plus sûrs, je ne les croirais pas.
2.	Even if they were the surest witnesses, I would not believe them.	**3.**	Qui fut venu?
3.	Who had come?	**4.**	Qui fût venu?
4.	Who would have come?	**5.**	Il eût certainement regretté ses mots.
5.	He would certainly have regretted his words.	**6.**	Il regretta ses mots aussitôt qu'il les eut dits.
6.	He regretted his words as soon as he had said them.	**7.**	Qui l'eût dit?
7.	Who would have said it?	**8.**	Qui l'eût cru?
8.	Who would have believed it? (or _him_)	**9.**	L'événement eût pu avoir des conséquences tragiques.
9.	The event could have had tragic consequences.	**10.**	Les observateurs rédigèrent leurs récits aussitôt que l'orage eut fini.
10.	The observers wrote up their accounts as soon as the storm had ended.	**11.**	Sans le témoignage d'observateurs qualifiés, on n'eût jamais su les conséquences de l'orage.

11. Without the testimony of qualified observers, one would never have known the consequences of the storm.	Review the phrases you have circled until you can recognize them immediately.

117. Review of All Verb Forms

INSTRUCTIONS: *The following exercise is a review of all the tenses of French. Circle the ones you do not immediately recognize and when you finish the exercise, review the sections of the text which treat them.*

1. "You are right," he answers me. (*Notice the inversion of subject and verb in this pattern.*)

2. "You are right," he was saying to me when the telephone rang.

3. "You are indubitably right," he would answer me if I consulted him.

4. "You will be wrong," he had answered me.

5. "You are wrong," he answered me.

6. "You are wrong," he will answer me.

7. "You look tired," he would have answered me.

8. *Conditional meaning—none of the phrases which introduce the Subjunctive are present* (**bien que,** etc.) "Perhaps you are wrong," he would have answered me.

9. "You are right," he should have answered me.

10. "You look tired," he had already answered me.

11. "You are wrong," he will quickly have answered me.

1. "Vous avez raison", me répond-il.

2. "Vous avez raison", me disait-il quand le téléphone a sonné.

3. "Vous avez indubitablement raison", me répondrait-il si je le consultais.

4. "Vous aurez tort", m'avait-il répondu.

5. "Vous avez tort", me répondit-il.

6. "Vous avez tort", me répondra-t-il.

7. "Vous avez l'air fatigué", m'aurait-il répondu.

8. "Vous avez peut-être tort", m'eût-il répondu. (Here the Imperfect Subjunctive form has the *Imperfect meaning/Conditional meaning.*)

9. "Vous avez raison", aurait-il dû me répondre.

10. "Vous avez l'air fatigué", m'avait-il déjà répondu.

11. "Vous avez tort", m'aura-t-il vite répondu.

12. Il répond savamment, mais même ses amis n'en croient rien. (**en** refers to _____)

12.	what he says He answers learnedly, but even his friends do not believe anything about it.	13.	Je suis sûr de répondre savamment, mais même mes amis n'en croiront rien.
13.	I am sure of answering learnedly, but even my friends will believe nothing of it.	14.	Il ignore ma réponse. (**ignore**=*ignores/is unaware of*)
14.	He is unaware of my answer.	15.	Il ignora ma réponse.
15.	He was unaware of my answer.	16.	Il ignorera apparemment toujours ma réponse.
16.	He apparently will always be unaware of my answer.	17.	Je me trompai, sans doute.
17.	I was mistaken, no doubt.	18.	Je me tromperai, sans doute.
18.	I will be mistaken, no doubt.	19.	Ils se trompaient souvent de chemin.
19.	They would (used to) often take the wrong road.	20.	S'ils n'avaient pas de carte, ils se tromperaient de chemin.
20.	If they had no map, they would take the wrong road. (*Notice the two different meanings of* **would**—*habitual action and conditional statement.*)	21.	Je m'étais fort trompé.
21.	I had been very mistaken.	22.	Je me serais bien trompé.
22.	I would have been very mistaken.	23.	A moins que je ne me trompe . . .
23.	Unless I am mistaken . . . (Remember that with **à moins que, ne** alone does not negate.)	24.	A moins que je ne me sois trompé
24.	Unless I was (*or* have been) mistaken	25.	Il était sûr d'avoir raison, pourvu qu'il ne se trompât pas de chiffres.
25.	He was sure of being right, provided that he was not mistaken in his figures.	26.	. . . pourvu qu'il ne se fût pas trompé.
26.	. . . provided that he had not been mistaken.	27.	**avertir**=*to warn* "Vous devriez les avertir", a-t-il dit.
27.	"You ought to warn them," he said.	28.	"Vous devrez les avertir", a-t-elle dit.

28. "You will have to warn them," she said.	**29.** "Vous auriez dû m'en faire part", a-t-elle dit.
29. "You ought to have told me about it," she said.	**30.** "Vous auriez bien pu m'en faire part", a-t-elle dit.
30. "You could well have told me about it," she said.	**31.** "Vous auriez pu les avertir", a-t-elle insisté.
31. "You could have warned them," she insisted.	**32.** Il partit aussitôt que je l'eus averti.
32. He left as soon as I had warned him.	**33.** Il partira sans doute avant que vous ne l'avertissiez. (**Avertissiez** is *subjunctive/imperfect?*)
33. *subjunctive—it follows* **avant que** He will no doubt leave before you warn him.	**34.** "Il vaudrait mieux leur en faire part", a-t-elle dit.
34. "It would be better to tell them about it," she said.	**35.** "Il valait mieux nous en faire part", a-t-elle répété.
35. "It was better to tell us about it," she repeated.	**36.** "Il valait mieux qu'il m'en fît part", a-t-elle dit. (**Fît** is the *past indefinite/imperfect subjunctive* of **faire?**)
36. *imperfect subjunctive* "It was better for him to tell me about it," she said.	**37.** "Il vaudrait mieux qu'il m'en fasse part", a-t-elle dit.
37. "It would be better for him to tell me about it," she said.	**38.** "Il faudrait trop de temps", ai-je répondu.
38. "It would take too much time," I answered ("too much time would be necessary").	**39.** "Il aurait fallu trop de temps", a-t-il répondu.
39. "It would have taken too much time," he answered.	**40.** "Il avait déjà fallu trop de temps", ai-je répondu.
40. "It had already taken too much time," I answered.	**41.** "Quand arrive-t-il?", se demande-t-on.
41. "When is he arriving?" one wonders.	**42.** "Quand arrivera-t-il?", se demanda-t-elle.
42. "When will he arrive?" she wondered.	**43.** Quand arriva-t-il?

43.	When did he arrive?	**44.**	Quand serait-il arrivé, à votre avis?
44.	When would he have arrived, in your opinion?	**45.**	On eût bien fait d'arriver à temps.
45.	One would have done well to arrive on time.	**46.**	Qui était arrivé à temps?
46.	Who had arrived on time?	**47.**	Qu'est-ce qui arriverait pendant votre absence, à votre avis?
47.	What would happen during your absence, in your opinion?	**48.**	Qu'est-ce qui était arrivé pendant mon absence?
48.	What had happened during my absence?	**49.**	Qui était arrivé avant qu'elle partît?
49.	Who had arrived before she left? (Notice that **avant que** is not always followed by **ne.**)	**50.**	Avant qu'elle arrivât . . .
50.	Before she arrived . . .	**51.**	Avant qu'elle fût arrivée . . .
51.	Before she had arrived . . .	**52.**	Avant qu'elle ne soit arrivée . . .
52.	Before she arrived . . .	**53.**	Aussitôt qu'elle fut arrivée . . .
53.	As soon as she had arrived . . .	**54.**	Dès qu'elle arrivera . . .
54.	As soon as she arrives . . .	**55.**	**se moquer de**=*to laugh at, to make fun of* Vous ne vous moquez pas de moi.
55.	You are not making fun of me.	**56.**	Ne vous moquez pas de moi.
56.	Don't make fun of me.	**57.**	Se moque-t-il aussi de moi?
57.	Is he making fun of me, too?	**58.**	Aussi se moque-t-il de moi.
58.	Therefore, he is making fun of me.	**59.**	Ne nous trompons pas.
59.	Let us make no mistake.	**60.**	Nous ne nous trompons pas.
60.	We are not mistaken.	**61.**	**quand même**=*anyway, just the same* Faites ce que vous voudrez, quand même.
61.	Do what you want to, anyway.	**62.**	Vous ferez quand même ce que vous voudrez.

62. You will do what you want to anyway.

63. Vous en allez-vous quand même?

63. Are you leaving, anyway?

64. Allez-vous-en quand même.

64. Go away (leave), anyway.

65. Ne vous en allez pas quand même.

65. Don't leave, anyway.

66. **en dedans** = *within*
L'homme ne peut communiquer sans qu'il rende par un signe extérieur ce qui se passe en dedans de lui.

66. Man cannot communicate without indicating by some exterior sign that which is taking place within himself.

67. Sans que vous étudiiez la nature, vous ne comprendrez pas l'homme.

67. Without studying nature you will not understand man.

68. Quant à leurs livres, nous les leur enverrons.

68. As for their books, we will send them to them.

69. Elle a acheté les pommes vingt centimes la livre et les lui a données.

69. She bought the apples for twenty centimes a pound and gave them to him.

70. Je le leur ai donné.

70. I gave it (m.) to them.

71. Je la leur ai donnée.

71. I gave it (f.) to them.

72. Sans qu'on en fasse l'étude, l'antiquité est difficile à connaître.

72. Unless one studies about it, antiquity is difficult to know.

73. Vous ne saurez distinguer entre ces deux personnes sans que vous leur posiez des questions.

73. You will not be able to differentiate between these two persons without questioning them.

74. A moins que vous ne leur posiez des questions pénétrantes, vous n'en saurez rien.

74. Unless you ask them penetrating questions, you won't find out anything about it.

75. Quoique les mines fussent vivement disputées autrefois, elles sont abandonnées aujourd'hui.

75. Although the mines were formerly vigorously disputed, they are abandoned today.

76. Quoique le nombre de femelles brunes pleines d'œufs m'ait étonné, il aurait pu y en avoir davantage.

76. Although the number of brown females filled with eggs surprised me, there could have been more of them.

77. Avant que vous ne parliez trop de ce fait, il vaudrait mieux le confirmer.

77. Before you speak too much about this fact, it would be better to confirm it.	**78.** Avant que vous ne fassiez appel à moi, tâchez d'y répondre vous-même.
78. Before you call on me, try to answer it yourself.	**79.** On lui en donne plus qu'il ne mérite.
79. He is given more than he deserves.	**80.** Je vous reverrai avant que vous ne vous en alliez.
80. I will see you again before you leave.	**81.** Donnez-lui son argent avant qu'il ne s'en aille.
81. Give him his money before he leaves.	**82.** Avant que nous ne nous en allions, il nous faut dire bonsoir aux autres.
82. Before we leave, we must say good evening to the others.	**83.** Avant qu'il ne mourût, Rousseau écrivit ses *Confessions*.
83. Before he died, Rousseau wrote his *Confessions*.	**84.** "Quoique je sois homme, j'ose croire être différent des autres", dit Rousseau.
84. "Although I am a man, I dare to believe myself different from the others," Rousseau said.	**85.** "Quoique j'aie dit du mal, j'ai dit du bien avec la même franchise", avait-il dit.
85. "Although I have spoken evil, I have spoken good with equal frankness," he had said.	**86.** Le malade serait encore vivant si l'on avait fait chercher le médecin plus tôt.
86. The sick person would still be alive if one had sent for the doctor sooner.	**87.** Encore si j'étais sûr!
87. And if only I were sure!	**88.** Si les animaux étaient encore mieux doués, ils pourraient peut-être réfléchir.
88. If the animals were still more gifted, they would be able perhaps to reflect.	**89.** Pendant trois mois encore ils restèrent en Egypte.
89. They remained in Egypt for three months more.	**90.** Il tombait encore gravement malade.
90. Again he fell seriously ill.	**91.** On en est venu à les aimer encore.
91. We got to like them again.	**92.** On est arrivé à les aimer encore davantage.
92. We came to like them still more.	**93.** Pourvu qu'on soit doué de la puissance de réfléchir, on est capable de faire des progrès.

93. Provided that one be gifted with the power of reflection, one is capable of making progress.	**94.** Pourvu qu'on se taise quand on n'a rien à dire, on passe pour sage.
94. Provided that one keeps quiet when one has nothing to say, one is considered wise.	**95.** Avant que nous ne disions que le singe est un être raisonnable, regardons la question de plus près.
95. Before we say that the monkey is a reasonable being, let us look at the question more closely.	**96.** Si les hommes ne se flattaient pas les uns les autres, il n'y aurait guère de société. Vauvenargues
96. If men did not flatter each other, there would be scarcely any society.	**97.** Pour exécuter de grandes choses, il faut vivre comme si on ne devait jamais mourir. Vauvenargues
97. In order to do great things one must live as if one were never to die.	**98.** **rencontrer**=*to meet* Voltaire prétend avoir rencontré dans ses voyages un homme fort sage.
98. Voltaire claims to have met in his travels a very wise man. (Remember that **prétendre** is a deceptive cognate.)	**99.** Il rencontra cet homme aux Indes.
99. He met this man in India. (Note the plural form translated by the singular.)	**100.** On rencontrera bien des personnages semblables dans les œuvres de Voltaire.
100. One will meet many similar personages in the works of Voltaire.	**101.** **manquer**=*to miss, to lack, to fail* Etant riche, ce sage ne manquait de rien.
101. Being rich, this wise man lacked nothing.	**102.** S'il est riche, un sage ne manquera jamais de rien.
102. If he is rich, a wise man will never lack anything.	**103.** Ne manquant de rien, il n'avait besoin de tromper personne.
103. Lacking nothing, he didn't need to deceive anyone.	**104.** Encore s'amusait-il à philosopher.
104. Furthermore, he amused himself by philosophizing.	**105.** Il ne nous trompera pas—il nous dira la vérité.
105. He will not deceive us—he will tell us the truth.	**106.** **jouir de**=*to enjoy* N'ayant jamais trompé personne, il jouissait du respect de tout le monde.

106. Having never deceived anyone, he enjoyed everyone's respect.	**107.** L'homme sage ne manque jamais d'être heureux, dit-on.
107. The wise man never fails to be happy, it is said.	**108.** Néanmoins, ce sage-là manqua de l'être. (Here **l'** refers to the condition of being _____.)
108. *happy* Nonetheless, that wise man did fail to be happy.	**109.** Quoique le sage fût riche, il n'était pas heureux.
109. Although the wise man was rich, he was not happy.	**110.** **des soucis** (m.) = *worries, troubles* Il ne jouissait pas d'une existence sans soucis.
110. He did not enjoy an untroubled existence.	**111.** Il dit un jour: "Je voudrais n'être jamais né".
111. He said one day: "I wish I had never been born." ("I would wish never to have been born.")	**112.** Bien qu'il enseignât les autres, il se croyait fort ignorant.
112. Although he taught others, he believed himself to be very ignorant.	**113.** **instruire** = *to inform of, to educate* Quoiqu'il fût bien instruit, il se reconnut fort ignorant.
113. Although he was well educated, he recognized himself as being very ignorant.	**114.** Il dit: "Les quarante années que j'ai étudié sont autant d'années de perdues".
114. He said: "The forty years I have studied are so many years wasted (lost)." (Notice that the **de** introducing the adjective has no counterpart in English).	**115.** Il croyait que les quarante années qu'il avait passées à étudier étaient quarante années de perdues.
115. He believed that the forty years he had spent studying were forty years wasted.	**116.** Ce qu'il avait enseigné aux autres était fort incertain.
116. That which he had taught to others was very uncertain.	**117.** C'était encore pis quand on lui posait des questions.
117. It was still worse when they asked him questions.	**118.** **dégoûter** = *to disgust* (*fill with distaste*) Ses études l'avaient dégoûté.

118. His studies had disgusted him. (He was filled with distaste for them.)

119. **éprouver**=*to feel, to experience* Pourquoi éprouvait-il tant de dégoût?

119. Why did he feel so much distaste?

120. Pourquoi éprouverait-on un tel dégoût?

120. Why would anyone feel such a distaste?

121. Ses études le dégoûtaient parce qu'il n'avait jamais pu trouver les réponses à ses questions.

121. His studies filled him with distaste because he had never been able to find the answers to his questions.

122. La sagesse dont il jouissait ne le rendait point heureux.

122. The wisdom which he enjoyed did not make him at all happy.

123. Il passait son temps à penser, et il n'avait jamais pu s'instruire de ce qui produit la pensée.

123. He spent (would spend) his time thinking, and he had never been able to learn what produces thought.

124. Saurons-nous jamais nous instruire de ce qui produit la pensée?

124. Will we ever be able to learn what produces thought?

125. Il ressentait le passage du temps, et il n'avait jamais su ce que c'est que le temps. (**ressentait**—*felt/resented*)

125. He *felt* the passing of time and he had never known (learned) what time is.

126. Personne ne saurait dire ce que c'est que le temps.

126. No one can say what time is.

127. Il ignorait ce que c'est que le temps. (**ignorait**—*ignored/did not know*)

127. *did not know, was unaware* He did not know what time was.

128. Il ne saura apparemment jamais ce que c'est que le temps.

128. He will apparently never know what time is.

129. Si ce pauvre homme ne pensait pas tant, il serait plus heureux.

129. If this poor man didn't think so much, he would be happier.

130. **s'occuper de**=*to be concerned with* S'il ne s'occupait pas tant de la pensée, il jouirait davantage de la vie.

130. If he were not so concerned with thought, he would enjoy life more.

131. S'il s'en occupait moins, il ne manquerait pas d'être heureux.

131. If he were less concerned with it, he would not fail to be happy.

132. S'il ne s'en était pas tant occupé, il n'aurait pas éprouvé tant de dégoût de la vie.

132. If he had not been so concerned with it, he would not have felt so much distaste for life.

133. **plus . . . plus**=*the more . . . the more*
Plus il jouissait de lumières, plus il était malheureux.

133. The more enlightenment he enjoyed, the more unhappy he was.

134. La voisine du bramin, une vieille femme ignorante et superstitieuse, vivait heureuse.

134. The neighbor of the Brahman, an ignorant and superstitious old woman, lived happily.

135. Simple, sotte, et superstitieuse, cette vieille femme menait une vie sans soucis.

135. Simple, stupid, and superstitious, this old woman led an untroubled life.

136. Elle ne s'était jamais souciée d'aucune question à propos de son âme.

136. She had never worried about any question concerning her soul.

137. **affliger**=*to afflict*
s'affliger=*to be troubled*
Elle ne s'était jamais affligée de ne pas savoir comment son âme était faite.

137. She had never been troubled for not knowing (because she did not know) how her soul was made.

138. Les questions qui affligeaient son voisin ne l'avaient jamais affligée.

138. The questions which had afflicted her neighbor had never afflicted her.

139. Il vit encore la vieille femme.

139. He saw the old woman again.

140. Moins elle pensait, plus elle était heureuse.

140. The less she thought, the happier she was.

141. Nous ferions tous bien de lui ressembler, n'est-ce pas?

141. We would all do well to resemble her, wouldn't we?

142. Car plus on pense à la question, plus elle devient obscure.

142. For the more one thinks about the question, the more obscure it becomes.

143. Moins on pense à la vie, moins on est malheureux.

143. The less one thinks about life, the less unhappy one is.

144. Quand on se moque un peu de ses études, on vit plus content.

144. When one laughs a little at one's studies, one lives more contentedly.

145. **la peine**=*pain*
une question pénible=_____

145. a painful question

146. Si le bramin se moquait du monde, il ne se perdrait pas dans ces questions pénibles.

146. If the Brahman laughed at the world, he would not get lost (lose himself) in these painful questions.

147. S'il s'en était moqué davantage, il ne s'y serait pas perdu.
(With reference to # 146 **en** refers to _____; **y** refers to _____)

147. *the world*
the questions
If he had laughed at it more, he would not have gotten lost in them.

148. Lequel devrions-nous choisir, à votre avis—la connaissance ou le bonheur?

148. Which ought we to choose, in your opinion—knowledge or happiness?

149. **une réponse sensée**=*a sensible (or sane) answer*
une réponse insensée=_____

149. *a mad (or foolish) answer*

150. **un parti**=*a decision*
N'est-ce pas un parti insensé que de choisir le malheur au lieu du bonheur?

150. Is it not a mad decision to choose unhappiness instead of happiness?

151. **faire cas de**=*to value*
N'est-ce pas un parti très insensé que de faire trop grand cas de la raison?

151. Is it not a very mad (foolish) decision to value reason too highly?

152. Si l'on fait cas du bonheur, on fait encore plus de cas de la raison.

152. If we value happiness, we value reason still more.

153. Je me demande encore lequel des deux avait raison.

153. I still wonder which one of the two was right.

154. Que faut-il en penser?

154. What should (must) one think of it?

VOCABULARY DEVELOPMENT

INSTRUCTIONS: *Building from the meaning of the first word, give the meanings of the indicated words.*

1. **entendre**=*to understand* (also=*to hear*)

	Est-ce que **l'entendement** produit la pensée?
1. Does the *understanding* produce thought?	**2.** Les grands pouvoirs sont arrivés à **une entente.**
2. The great powers arrived at *an understanding.*	**3.** **supporter**=*to endure, to bear* La vie m'est **insupportable.**
3. Life is *unendurable* for me.	**4.** **inonder**=*to flood* La région est sujette à de fréquentes **inondations.**
4. The region is subject to frequent *floods.*	**5.** **dégoûter**=*to disgust, to fill with distaste* On voit à ses robes que c'est une femme **de bon goût.**
5. One sees by her dresses that she is a woman *of good taste.*	**6.** **Goûtez un peu** de ce chocolat.
6. *Take a little taste* of this chocolate.	

TESTING EXERCISE

INSTRUCTIONS: *Test yourself on your ability to distinguish the tenses of French. Circle the answer which best expresses the meaning of the indicated words. When you can recognize them all, you will have made a major breakthrough. Review the section indicated if you miss any.*

1. Vous auriez dû y faire attention.
A. You should pay attention to it.
B. You will have paid attention to it.
C. You must pay attention to it.
D. You should have paid attention to it.

1. D
(113)

2. Nous **aurons abordé** un nouveau sujet.
A. should have taken up   C. will have taken up
B. will take up   D. should take up

2. C
(113)

3. Il abandonna son travail avant qu'**il n'achevât** son projet.
A. he finishes   C. he didn't finish
B. he finished   D. he may have finished

3. B
(115)

4. **Fût-il** le témoin le plus sûr, je ne le croirais pas.
A. Even if he were   C. He might have been
B. He was   D. He may be

4. A (116)	5.	L'événement **eût pu avoir** des conséquences fâcheuses. A. could have had c. may yet have B. will probably have D. probably had
5. A (116)	6.	**Il faudra** trop de temps. A. It will take c. It would take B. It took D. It is taking
6. A (117)	7.	**Il demeura** honteux et confus. A. He will remain c. He would remain B. He remained D. He remains
7. B (117)	8.	Il ne sait pas **ce que c'est que le temps.** A. what time it is c. what time is B. what these times are D. only what time is
8. C (117)	9.	La voisine du bramin **ne s'était jamais posé de questions** à propos de son âme. A. never asked herself any questions B. had never asked herself any questions C. was never asked any questions D. had never been asked any questions
9. B (117)	10.	**Ne vous moquez pas de moi.** A. You are not making fun of me. B. You should not make fun of me. C. Do not make fun of me.
10. C (117)		

READING PASSAGE

INSTRUCTIONS: *Give yourself sixteen minutes to read through the following story by Voltaire. Circle the words which you do not immediately recognize, but do not stop to look them up the first time through. When you finish, answer the questions at the end to verify your comprehension. Then return to the difficult structures and work out their meaning more precisely. Practice reading the story until you can read it in the time allotted.*

Histoire d'un bon bramin

Voltaire

Je rencontrai dans mes voyages un vieux bramin, homme fort sage, plein d'esprit, et très savant; de plus, il était riche, et, **partant,**[1] il en était plus sage encore: car, ne manquant de rien, il n'avait besoin de tromper personne. Sa

---

1 *consequently*

famille était très bien gouvernée par trois belles femmes qui s'étudiaient à
5 lui plaire; et, quand il ne s'amusait pas avec ses femmes, il s'occupait à
philosopher.

Près de sa maison, qui était belle, ornée et accompagnée de jardins
charmants, demeurait une vieille indienne, bigote, imbécile, et assez pauvre.

Le bramin me dit un jour: "Je voudrais n'être jamais né". Je lui
10 demandai pourquoi. Il me répondit: **"J'étudie depuis** [2] quarante ans, ce
sont quarante années de perdues; j'enseigne les autres, et j'ignore tout: cet
état porte dans mon âme tant d'humiliation et de dégoût que la vie m'est
insupportable. Je suis né, je vis dans le temps, et je ne sais pas ce que c'est
que le temps; je me trouve dans un point entre deux éternités, comme disent
15 nos sages, et je n'ai nulle idée de l'éternité. Je suis composé de matière; je
pense, je n'ai jamais pu m'instruire de ce qui produit la pensée; j'ignore si
mon entendement est en moi une simple faculté, comme celle de marcher,
de digérer, et si je pense avec ma tête comme je prends avec mes mains. Non
seulement le principe de ma pensée m'est inconnu, mais le principe de mes
20 mouvements m'est également **caché:** [3] je ne sais pourquoi j'existe. Cependant
on me fait chaque jour des questions sur tous ces points: il faut répondre;
je n'ai rien de bon à dire; je parle beaucoup, et je demeure confus et honteux
de moi–même après avoir parlé.

C'est **bien pis** [4] quand on me demande si Brahma a été produit par
25 Vichnou, ou s'ils sont tous deux éternels. Dieu m'est témoin que je n'en sais
pas un mot, et **il y paraît bien à** [5] mes réponses. "Ah! mon révérend père,
me dit-on, apprenez-nous comment le mal inonde toute la terre". Je suis aussi
en peine [6] que ceux qui me font cette question: je leur dis quelquefois que
tout est le mieux du monde; mais ceux qui ont été ruinés et mutilés à la
30 guerre n'en croient rien, ni moi **non plus;** [7] je me retire chez moi **accablé
de** [8] ma curiosité et de mon ignorance. Je lis nos anciens livres, et ils
redoublent mes ténèbres. Je parle à mes compagnons: les uns me répondent
qu'il faut jouir de la vie, et se moquer des hommes; les autres croient savoir
quelque chose, et se perdent dans des idées extravagantes; tout augmente le
35 sentiment douloureux que j'éprouve. Je suis prêt quelquefois de tomber dans
le désespoir, quand je **songe** [9] qu'après toutes mes recherches je ne sais ni
d'où je viens, ni ce que je suis, ni où j'irai, ni ce que je deviendrai".

L'état de ce bon homme me fit une vraie peine: personne n'était ni plus
raisonnable ni de meilleure foi que lui. Je **conçus** [10] que plus il avait de
40 lumières dans son entendement et de sensibilité dans son cœur, plus il était
malheureux.

Je vis le même jour la vieille femme qui demeurait dans son voisinage: je
lui demandai si elle avait jamais été affligée de ne savoir pas comment son
âme était faite. Elle ne comprit seulement pas ma question: elle n'avait
45 jamais réfléchi un seul moment de sa vie sur un seul des points qui tour-

---

2 *I have been studying for...*	**5** *this appears clearly from*	**8** *overwhelmed by*
3 *hidden*	**6** *in difficulty*	**9** *think*
4 *much worse*	**7** *either*	**10** *from concevoir*

mentaient le bramin; elle croyait aux métamorphoses de Vichnou de tout son
cœur, et pourvu qu'elle pût avoir quelquefois de l'eau du Gange pour se laver,
elle se croyait la plus heureuse des femmes.

50   Frappé du bonheur de cette pauvre créature, je revins à mon philosophe,
et je lui dis: "N'êtes-vous pas honteux d'être malheureux, dans le temps qu'à
votre porte il y a un vieil automate qui ne pense à rien, et qui vit content?
—Vous avez raison, me répondit-il; je me suis dit cent fois que je serais
heureux si j'étais aussi sot que ma voisine, et cependant je ne voudrais pas
d'un tel bonheur".

55   Cette réponse de mon bramin me fit une plus grande impression que tout
le reste; je m'examinai moi-même, et je vis qu'en effet je n'aurais pas voulu
être heureux à condition d'être imbécile.

Je proposai la chose à des philosophes, et ils furent de mon avis. "Il y a
pourtant, disais-je, une furieuse contradiction dans cette façon de penser:
60   car enfin de quoi s'agit-il? D'être heureux. **Qu'importe** [11] d'avoir de
l'esprit ou d'être sot? Il y a bien plus: ceux qui sont contents de leur être
sont bien sûrs d'être contents; ceux qui raisonnent ne sont pas si sûrs de bien
raisonner. Il est donc clair, disais-je, qu'il faudrait choisir de n'avoir pas le
sens commun, **pour peu que** [12] ce sens commun contribue à notre **mal-**
65   **être".** [13] Tout le monde fut de mon avis, et cependant je ne trouvai personne
qui voulût accepter **le marché** [14] de devenir imbécile pour devenir content.
De là je conclus que, si nous faisons cas du bonheur, nous faisons encore
plus de cas de la raison.

Mais, après y avoir réfléchi, il paraît que de préférer la raison à la félicité,
70   c'est être très insensé. Comment donc cette contradiction peut-elle s'expliquer?
Comme toutes les autres. Il y a là de quoi parler beaucoup.

1. In the first paragraph, we learn that the Brahman:
    A. was rich but that he wanted still greater wealth
    B. had a weakness for beautiful women
    C. liked to deceive people
    D. was highly learned

---

1. D   2. The second paragraph states that:
    A. the Brahman's house was plain but comfortable
    B. it was surrounded by beautiful fountains
    C. an old woman lived close by
    D. she used to talk philosophy with the Brahman

---

2. C   3. The third paragraph states that the Brahman:
    A. had been studying for fourteen years in order to find the answer to the
       problems of life
    B. had discovered the nature of thought

---

11 *what does it matter*   **13** *misfortune*   **14** *the bargain*
12 *if ever*

c. had finally found the reason for existence

d. was ashamed of his lack of knowledge

---

3. D   **4.** Lines 24–37 state that the Brahman:

A. would sometimes reply, when questioned, that everything in the world was for the best

B. gained much valuable knowledge from ancient books

C. found consolation in talking with his colleagues

D. still felt himself to be wiser than those who questioned him

---

4. A   **5.** In lines 41–48 it is stated that:

A. the author concludes that a man becomes happier as he gains more knowledge

B. the old woman was concerned with the state of her soul

C. what made her the happiest was to be able to wash in water from the river Ganges

D. the more ignorant a person is, the more unhappy he is.

---

5. C   **6.** Lines 49–57 tell us that:

A. the Brahman and his neighbor were equally happy

B. the Brahman would willingly exchange his happiness for hers

C. the Brahman would not wish to be happy on condition of being stupid

D. happiness in life is more important than knowledge.

---

6. C   **7.** The last two paragraphs state that:

A. those who are content with themselves are sure to be reasonable

B. nothing is worth the sacrifice of our common sense

C. happiness is prized above reason among the poor

D. the question of the relative value of happiness and reason can be the subject of endless discussion.

---

7. D

Chapter Eighteen

REVIEW: The words circled in previous Chapters before going on to this one.

118. Prendre—*Compounds and Idioms*

1. Some common idioms formed with the verb **prendre** are as follows:

prendre à	*to take (something) from*
prendre figure de	*to take the form of*
prendre congé de quelqu'un	*to take leave of someone*
prendre garde à	*to take care to*
prendre garde de	*to take care not to*
prendre part à	*to take part in*
prendre un parti	*to come to a decision*
en prendre son parti	*to resign oneself to*
s'en prendre à	*to find fault with, to blame*
s'y prendre	*to go about something*

READING PREPARATION

INSTRUCTIONS: *After familiarizing yourself with the above idioms, read through the following exercise. Circle the phrases you do not recognize.*

1. Les *wali* prennent figure d'ancêtres.

1. The *wali* take the form of ancestors.

2. **force nous est**=*we are obliged to, we must*
Force nous est de prendre congé de nos amis.

2. We are obliged to take leave of our friends.	**3.** Force me fut de prendre part aux cérémonies.
3. I was obliged to take part in the ceremonies.	**4.** Force nous est donc d'en prendre notre parti.
4. We must therefore resign ourselves to it.	**5.** Le roi sut maintenir la paix, tout en prenant revanche du traité de Paris.
5. The king was able to maintain the peace, all the while taking revenge for the Treaty of Paris.	**6.** Je sais comment il faut m'y prendre.
6. I know how I must go about it.	**7.** Il n'a pas réussi à l'examen, n'ayant pas su comment s'y prendre.
7. He did not pass the examination, not having known how to go about it.	**8.** La mort lui a pris sa fille.
8. Death took his daughter from him.	**9.** Il est vrai qu'il avait subi des pertes très grandes, mais il n'aurait pas dû s'en prendre à ses amis.
9. It is true he had suffered very great losses, but he should not have found fault with his friends.	**10.** Au contraire, qu'il s'en prenne à lui-même.
10. To the contrary, let him blame himself.	**11.** Qu'il ne s'en prenne qu'à lui-même.
11. Let him blame only himself.	**12.** C'est à prendre ou à laisser.
12. Take it or leave it.	**13.** Il a pris le parti de se taire.
13. He chose to remain silent.	**14.** La maison avait pris feu.
14. The house had caught on fire.	**15.** Prenons garde à travailler assidûment.
15. Let us take care to work assiduously.	**16.** Prenons garde de travailler trop.
16. Let us be careful not to work too much.	**17.** Prenez garde à arriver à l'heure.
17. Take care to arrive on time.	**18.** Prenez garde d'arriver en retard.
18. Be careful not to arrive late.	**19.** **comprendre**=*to understand, to include* Ils nous ont fait comprendre que . . .
19. They gave us to understand that . . .	**20.** Il n'y comprend rien.

20. He understands nothing about it.	**21.** Cela se comprend qu'il ait été en retard.
21. It is understandable that he was late.	**22.** Le dîner est à cinquante francs, vin compris. (Here **compris** must mean *understood/included*)
22. The dinner is fifty francs, wine *included*.	**23.** Nous avons **entrepris** l'étude des . . .
23. We *undertook* the study of the . . .	**24.** Après de grands efforts il reprit le dessus.
24. After great effort he got the upper hand again.	**25.** Les affaires reprirent vivement, grâce à l'intervention du président.
25. Business picked up sharply, thanks to the intervention of the president.	**26.** Cela me surprendrait qu'il revienne.
26. It would surprise me if he came back.	**27.** Il a pris congé de son ami à la Gare de Lyon.
27. He took leave of his friend at the Gare de Lyon.	**28.** Prenez garde de tomber.
28. Be careful not to fall.	**29.** Il faut en prendre un parti.
29. One has to make up one's mind about it.	**30.** Ils prirent conscience de leurs intérêts propres.
30. They took their own interests into account.	Review the circled words and then continue.

119. *Idioms with* tenir

1. Some common idioms formed with **tenir** are as follows:

(A) **tenir à** = (1) *to desire, to insist on,* (2) *to depend on.*

Je *tiens à* **le mettre au courant de mes intentions.**	*I desire* to make him aware of my intentions.
Cela ne *tient* **qu'à vous.**	*That depends only on you.*

(B) **tenir de** = *to take after, to resemble, to result*

Il tient de son père.   *He takes after (resembles) his father.*

(C) **se tenir debout** = *to stand up*

Il ne pouvait plus se tenir debout, tant il était fatigué.   *He was so tired he could no longer stand up.*

(D) **se tenir à** = *to keep at, to remain*

Malgré sa maladie, il se tenait à son travail.   *In spite of his sickness, he kept at his work.*

(E) **tenir pour** = *to be in favor of, to consider as*

Il tient pour la paix.   *He is in favor of peace.*
Je le tiens pour un honnête homme.   *I consider him an honest man.*

(F) **s'en tenir à** = *to be satisfied with, to confine oneself to*

Je m'en tiens à des conclusions vérifiées empiriquement.   *I am confining myself to conclusions verified empirically.*

READING PREPARATION

INSTRUCTIONS: *Distinguish between the various meanings of* **tenir**. *Continue to circle new or unrecognized words.*

1. Let's talk about the philosopher Bergson.

2. He desires to explain the religious phenomenon in the rational (reasonable) being.

3. He states first of all that religion has always held and still holds a great place in the life of all peoples.

1. Parlons du philosophe Bergson.

2. Il tient à expliquer le phénomène religieux chez l'être raisonnable.

3. Il constate d'abord que la religion a toujours tenu et tient encore une grande place dans la vie de tous les peuples.

4. **quelquefois** = *sometimes*
Il constate également que la religion est quelquefois grossière.
(**grossière** suggests the idea of *crudeness/refinement*)

4. *crudeness*
He also states that religion is sometimes crude.

5. Plus elle est grossière, plus elle tient de place dans la vie d'un peuple.

5. The cruder (or grosser) it is, the more place it holds in the life of a people.

6. A première vue, la religion semble tenir de la superstition.

6. At first glance, religion seems to resemble superstition.

7. Et encore si elle s'en tenait là!

7. And still if it only stopped there! (confined itself simply to being crude and superstitious)

8. **prescrire**=*to prescribe, to command*
Mais quelquefois elle a même prescrit des crimes.

8. But it has sometimes even commanded crimes.

9. C'est un phénomène dont il faut tenir compte.

9. It is a phenomenon which must be taken into account.

10. **soi-disant**=*so called*
Ce phénomène chez un soi-disant être raisonnable tient du prodige.

10. This phenomenon in a so-called reasonable being has a touch of the marvelous.

11. Comment la religion parvient-elle à prescrire chez un soi-disant être raisonnable une croyance si peu raisonnable?

11. How does religion manage to prescribe so unreasonable a belief in a so-called reasonable being?

12. Mais pour résoudre ce problème il ne faut pas s'en tenir aux critiques précédents.

12. But in order to solve this problem one must not confine oneself to the previous critics.
(Remember that **il ne faut pas** means *It is necessary not to* and not *it is not necessary to*.)

13. Ceux-ci s'en sont tenus à des descriptions des soi-disant sociétés primitives, laissant intacte la question principale.

13. The latter have restricted themselves to descriptions of so-called primitive societies, leaving the main question intact.

14. Si l'on tient à éclaircir la question, on ne doit pas s'en tenir aux raisons apparentes.

14. If one desires to clarify the question, one must not stop at the apparent reasons.

15. Quelquefois les soi-disant raisons apparentes n'expliquent pas les faits.

15. Sometimes the so-called apparent (or evident) reasons do not explain the facts.

16. Personne ne tient la question pour résolue.

16. No one considers the question as solved.	**17. tenir compte de**=*to take into account* Pour la résoudre, il faut qu'on tienne compte de toutes les données.
17. To solve it, one must take all the data into account.	**18.** Bergson ne tient pas beaucoup aux explications de ses confrères.
18. Bergson is not very keen about his colleagues' explanations.	**19.** Il ne les tient pas pour suffisantes.
19. He does not consider them (to be) sufficient.	**20.** Il veut s'en tenir aux faits.
20. He wants to confine himself to the facts.	**21.** Plus il tient à la résoudre, plus elle tient de place dans son œuvre.
21. The more he desires to solve it, the greater the place it occupies in his work.	**22.** Tenez-vous à apprendre à lire le français?
22. Do you want to learn how to read French?	**23.** Le résultat ne tient qu'à vous.
23. The result depends only on you.	**24.** Il ne faut que vous tenir tous les jours à votre travail.
24. All that is necessary is to keep to your work every day.	Do not continue until you can recognize the above idioms immediately.

120. *Possessive Pronouns*

1. In Chapter Three you learned the possessive adjectives (**mon, ma, mes,** etc.). Compare these now with the possessive pronouns:

SINGULAR		PLURAL		
Masc.	Fem.	Masc.	Fem.	
le mien	**la mienne**	**les miens**	**les miennes**	*mine*
le tien	**la tienne**	**les tiens**	**les tiennes**	*yours*
le sien	**la sienne**	**les siens**	**les siennes**	*his, hers*
le nôtre	**la nôtre**	**les nôtres**	**les nôtres**	*ours*
le vôtre	**la vôtre**	**les vôtres**	**les vôtres**	*yours*
le leur	**la leur**	**les leurs**	**les leurs**	*theirs*

2. The possessive pronouns stands for and takes the gender and number of the thing possessed:

Tel est *mon désir*. Tel est *le mien*.	*Such is mine.*
Tels sont *mes désirs*. Tels sont *les miens*.	*Such are mine.*
Telle est *ma conclusion*.	
Telle est *la mienne*.	*Such is mine.*
Telles sont *mes conclusions*.	
Telles sont *les miennes*.	*Such are mine.*

3. In cases of ambiguity, the disjunctive pronoun (**moi, lui, elle,** etc.) is added for clarification:

Ma mère et la sienne.	*My mother and his,* or *hers,* or *its.*
Ma mère et la sienne à elle.	*My mother and hers.*
Ma mère et la sienne à lui.	*My mother and his.*

4. The article (**le, la, les**) contracts with **à** and **de:**

Je vais prendre congé *de mes amis*.	*I am going to take leave of my friends.*
Je vais prendre congé *des miens*.	*I am going to take leave of mine.*
Je m'en tiens *à mes idées person-* **nelles.**	*I confine myself to my personal ideas.*
Je m'en tiens *aux miennes*.	*I confine myself to mine.*

5. When the possessive pronoun is used without an antecedent it indicates relatives or friends:

Il est *des nôtres*.	*He is one of us (a friend of ours).*
Rappelez-moi au bon souvenir *des* **vôtres.**	*Remember me to your family.*

READING PREPARATION

INSTRUCTIONS: *As you read through the following French sentences, cover the English with your card. Check those sentences which contain new or unfamiliar vocabulary.*

	1. Il s'y prend d'une façon inattendue en comparant les religions primitives aux nôtres.
1. He goes about it in an unexpected way by comparing primitive religions to ours.	2. Celles-ci ne sont guère plus élevées que celles-là.

2. The latter are scarcely more elevated than the former.

3. Next he talks about the ideas of Mr. Lévy-Bruhl as well as of his own.

4. He seems to give his preference to his own.

5. The anthropologists indeed speak of a "primitive mind" which is supposed to be fundamentally different from ours. (Notice the meaning of **bien** in this context.)

6. Indeed, ours does seem different from theirs.

7. If there exists a fundamental difference between theirs and ours, we are obliged to believe in an evolution of the species.

8. Whether we like it or not, we have to draw from these facts the conclusion that the human intelligence has evolved, don't we?

9. If one admits a "mind" of primitive races, one must admit that ours must have replaced it.

10. However, do not certain of our present beliefs resemble theirs?

11. But even in admitting that we do not think like the non-civilized person, is it not true that our mind still resembles his?

3. **aussi bien que**=*as well as*
Ensuite il parle des idées de M. Lévy-Bruhl aussi bien que des siennes.

4. Il semble donner sa préférence aux siennes à lui.

5. **foncièrement**=*essentially, fundamentally*
Les anthropologistes parlent bien d'une "mentalité primitive" des races inférieures qui serait foncièrement différente de la nôtre.

6. En effet, la nôtre semble différente de la leur.

7. S'il existe une différence foncière entre les leurs et les nôtres, force nous est de croire à une évolution de l'espèce.

8. **Bon gré mal gré**=*whether one likes it or not*
Bon gré mal gré, nous devons tirer de ces faits la conclusion que l'intelligence humaine a évolué, n'est-ce pas?

9. Si l'on admet une "mentalité" des races primitives, on doit admettre que la nôtre a dû supplanter la leur.

10. Cependant, certaines de nos croyances actuelles ne ressemblent-elles pas aux leurs?

11. Mais même en admettant que nous ne pensions pas comme le non-civilisé, n'est-il pas vrai que notre esprit ressemble toujours au sien?

12. **vu**=*because of, in view of*
Vu les ressemblances, ne devons-nous pas admettre bon gré mal gré que le sien fonctionne de la même façon que le nôtre?

12. In view of the resemblances, must we not admit, whether we like it or not, that his functions in the same way as ours?

13. Vu la difficulté à transmettre héréditairement une habitude contractée par les parents, n'est-il pas difficile d'admettre que notre esprit diffère foncièrement du sien?

13. In view of the difficulty in transmitting hereditarily a habit contracted by the parents, is it not difficult to admit that our mind differs fundamentally from his?

14. Est-ce que les idées de Bergson diffèrent des vôtres?

14. Do the ideas of Bergson differ from yours?

15. Aimez-vous mieux les siennes ou les vôtres?

15. Do you like his better or yours?

16. **à tout prendre** = *everything considered*
A tout prendre, je tiens plutôt pour les siennes que pour les miennes.

16. Everything considered, I rather favor his more than mine.

17. Bon gré mal gré je devrai sans doute accorder ma préférence aux siennes.

17. Whether I like it or not, I will no doubt have to grant my preference to his.

18. A tout prendre, on peut tenir la question pour difficile.

18. Everything considered, one may consider the question as difficult.

After you can determine the meaning of the phrases circled above, go on to the next section.

121. *Conjunctions Which Take the Indicative*

1. In Chapter Eleven you learned a group of conjunctions which are followed by the Subjunctive. The following ordinarily take the indicative. Therefore, an —**iez** verb-ending after one of the below indicates the Imperfect and not the Subjunctive:

alors que = *at the time when, while*

Alors que le bramin se tourmentait, sa voisine vivait heureuse.   *While the Brahman was tormenting himself, his neighbor was living happily.*

maintenant que = *now that*

Maintenant qu'on comprend les questions, les réponses sont faciles.   *Now that one understands the questions, the answers are easy.*

tant que = *as long as*

Tant qu'on ne saura pas les verbes, la lecture sera difficile.   *As long as one does not know the verbs, the reading will be difficult.*

attendu que
vu que } = *seeing that, whereas*

Vu que (attendu que) les ressemblances sont si frappantes, on doit soupçonner une parenté étroite.   *Seeing that the resemblances are so striking, one must suspect a close relationship.*

selon que
suivant que } = *according to whether*

Selon que (suivant que) vous lisez beaucoup ou peu, la lecture sera facile ou difficile.   *According to whether you read much or little, reading will be easy or difficult.*

à mesure que = *in proportion as, as*

A mesure que l'atmosphère se refroidit, les nuages se forment.   *As the atmosphere cools, clouds are formed.*

de même que . . . de même = *just as . . . so*

De même que la nature est variée, de même la poésie doit l'être également.   *Just as nature is varied, so must poetry be varied as well.*

2. The following conjunctions may be followed either by the Indicative or the Subjunctive:

de sorte que
de façon que
de manière que } = *in such a way that, so that*
en sorte que

si + adjective or adverb + **que**
tellement + adjective or adverb + **que** } *so* + adjective or adverb + *that*

Il a fait sa composition de telle manière (telle façon) qu'il n'y avait pas de fautes.	*He did his composition in such a way that there were no mistakes.*
Elle avait si (tellement) bien chanté qu'on l'applaudissait chaleureusement.	*She had sung so well that she was warmly applauded.*
BUT **Faites votre composition de manière qu'il n'y ait pas de fautes.**	*Do your composition so that there will be no mistakes.*

3. You have already met the following which are followed by the Indicative:

après que = *after*
dès que = *as soon as, when*
depuis que = *since*
lorsque
quand } = *when*
jusqu'au moment où = *until*
pendant que = *while*
tandis que = *while, whereas*
comme = *as*
parce que = *because*
puisque = *since, because*
si = *whether.*

READING PREPARATION

INSTRUCTIONS: *Make a special note of the conjunctions which you do not recognize.* . . . .

	1. Il s'en souviendra tant qu'il vivra.
1. He will remember it as long as he lives.	**2.** Dès que vous aurez fini, venez me voir.
2. As soon as you have finished, come see me.	**3.** Puisque vous y tenez, soyez des leurs.
3. Since you set store by it, join them (be one of them).	**4.** Il faisait noir quand il a pris congé du général.
4. It was dark when he took his leave of the general.	**5.** Aussitôt que vous aurez pris un parti, faites-le-moi savoir.
5. As soon as you arrive at a decision, let me know about it.	**6.** Il prit part à la célébration, tandis qu'elle se tenait à l'écart.

6. He took part in the celebration, whereas she kept herself aloof.

7. As soon as he applies himself to politics, he takes after his predecessor.

8. As he learns himself, he teaches his successor.

9. I'll be there up to the time you arrive.

10. As the atmosphere cools, clouds are formed.

11. While we were spending long hours in studying, you were amusing yourself, so it seems.

12. *Subjunctive*—they follow **sans que** and **il est douteux.**
Unless we spend (without spending) long hours in studying, it is doubtful that we will pass the exam.

13. While men are capable of expressing (translating) their thoughts by words, animals are not.

14. As (because) religious states are made known by attitudes, we would be made aware by some sign if animals were capable of religious feeling.

15. Seeing that man is the only being endowed with reason, it is very astonishing that he is the only being capable of pinning (suspending) his judgment to unreasonable things.

16. Seeing that there are so many differences between the primitive mind and

7. Dès qu'il s'applique à la politique, il tient de son prédécesseur.

8. A mesure qu'il apprend lui-même, il apprend à son successeur.

9. Je serai là jusqu'au moment où vous arriverez.

10. A mesure que l'atmosphère se refroidit, des nuages se forment.

11. Alors que nous passions de longues heures à étudier, vous vous amusiez, à ce qu'il paraît.
(**à ce qu'il paraît**—*he appears/so it seems*)

12. Sans que nous passions de longues heures à étudier, il est douteux que nous réussissions à l'examen.
(Are **passions** and **réussissions** in the Indicative or Subjunctive?)

13. **traduire**=*to translate, to express*
Alors que les hommes sont capables de traduire leurs pensées par des paroles, les animaux ne le sont pas.

14. Comme les états religieux se traduisent par des attitudes, nous serions avertis par quelque signe si l'animal était capable de religiosité.

15. Attendu que l'homme est le seul être doué de raison, il est fort étonnant qu'il soit le seul être capable de suspendre son jugement à des choses déraisonnables.

16. Vu qu'il y a tant de différences entre la mentalité primitive et la nôtre, on ne peut pas s'empêcher d'en chercher les raisons.

17. **l'étendue** (f.) =*the extent*
A mesure que nous voyions l'étendue

our own, one cannot keep from looking for the reason for it.

de la superstition, notre étonnement grandissait.
(Is **voyions** in the Imperfect or Present Subjunctive?)

17. *Imperfect*—**à mesure que** is not followed by the subjunctive.
As we saw the extent of superstition, our astonishment increased.

18. A moins que nous ne nous rendions compte de l'étendue de la superstition, nous ignorerons toujours son caractère essentiel.
(Is **rendions** in the Imperfect or the Present Subjunctive?

18. *Present Subjunctive*—**à moins que** is followed by the Subjunctive.
Unless we realize the extent of superstition, we will always remain unaware of its essential characteristic(s).

19. Attendu que l'homme est un soi-disant être intelligent, le spectacle de sa superstition est d'autant plus surprenant.

19. Seeing that man is a supposedly intelligent being, the spectacle of his superstition is all the more surprising.

20. **les gens**=*people*
Tant qu'il y aura des gens au monde, il y aura apparemment de la superstition.

20. As long as there are people in the world, there will apparently be superstition.

21. **avoir beau faire (dire)**=*to do (say) something in vain*
Tant qu'il y aura des gens au monde, l'esprit aura beau combattre la superstition—on y croira quand même.

21. As long as there are people in the world, the mind will combat superstition in vain—people will nonetheless believe in it (or "it is useless for the mind to combat superstition").

22. La raison a beau dire "La superstition est absurde"—l'humanité s'y attache d'autant plus fort.

22. Reason says in vain "Superstition is absurd"—humanity becomes all the more strongly attached to it (or "no matter how much reason says . . .").

23. Vu que l'humanité ne s'y attache que davantage, on a beau s'y opposer.

23. Seeing that humanity only attaches itself more firmly to it, it is useless to oppose it.

24. Selon que nos observations seront plus ou moins justes, nos conclusions seront plus ou moins solides.

24. According to whether our observations are more or less accurate, our conclusions will be more or less sound.

25. **remercier**=*to thank*
"Je vous remercie beaucoup de votre aide".
"Il n'y a pas de quoi".
(Being a response to an expression of

	thanks, the second phrase probably means _____.)
25. *You're welcome—literally, "There is nothing (to thank me for").*	**26.** La situation est grave—il n'y a pas de quoi rire.
26. The situation is serious—there is nothing to laugh at (*or* it is no laughing matter).	**27.** Il n'y a pas de quoi se surprendre—tout le monde s'y attendait.
27. There is nothing to be surprised at—everyone expected it.	**28.** Il y a de quoi rire.
28. It is laughable (there is cause for laughing).	**29.** Il y a là de quoi se surprendre.
29. This is surprising (there is cause in this subject for surprise).	**30.** Il s'y prenait de façon qu'il nous donna bientôt de quoi rire.
30. He went about it in such a way that he soon gave us something to laugh about.	**31.** Nous y travaillions de sorte que l'entreprise fut bientôt achevée.
31. We worked on it in such a way that the enterprise was soon completed.	**32.** Vous auriez dû travailler de manière à achever votre lecture hier soir.
32. You should have worked in such a way as to complete your reading last night.	*In the following phrases, review the meanings of the object pronouns and* **encore.**
	1. Ils ne s'en souviennent plus.
1. They do not remember it anymore.	**2.** Il semble qu'il n'y réfléchit plus.
2. It appears that he is no longer thinking about it.	**3.** Plus on y pense, moins on y comprend.
3. The more one thinks about it, the less one understands about it.	**4.** Nous ne savons guère ce qui s'y passe.
4. We hardly know what is going on there.	**5.** Le roi, dont on disait du bien, savait maintenir la paix.
5. The king, who was well spoken of, knew how to maintain peace.	**6.** La façon dont il se conduisait lui fit grand honneur.
6. The manner in which he conducted himself reflected great credit upon him.	**7.** Il ne savait pas ce dont il était capable.
7. He did not know what he was capable of.	**8.** Les leur ont-ils montrés?
8. Did they show them to them?	**9.** Demandez-les-lui.

9. Ask him for them.	**10.** Force lui était donc de le lui rendre.
10. He was therefore forced to give it back to him.	**11.** Et encore si vous vous en teniez là.
11. And even if you confined yourself to that.	**12.** Des croyances peu raisonnables sont encore acceptées par des êtres intelligents.
12. Irrational beliefs are still accepted by intelligent beings.	**13.** Il me remercia encore de l'aide que j'avais pu lui rendre.
13. He thanked me again for the help that I had been able to give him.	**14.** La superstition est encore plus déraisonnable, mais on s'y attache quand même.
14. Superstition is even more unreasonable, but we cling to it nevertheless.	**15.** La situation est encore grave.
15. The situation is still serious.	**16.** Il n'était encore que jeune homme.
16. He was yet only a young man.	**17.** Et encore les gens venaient le voir.
17. And yet people came to see him.	**18.** Non seulement était-il philosophe, mais encore il était sage.
18. Not only was he a philosopher, but yet (in addition) he was wise.	

INSTRUCTIONS: *Identify the subject in the following sentences.*

	1. Quelle ne devrait pas être notre confusion maintenant! (The subject is _____)
1. *confusion* How great ought now to be our confusion! (The sentence is an exclamation and the meaning can be better rendered by a paraphrase in the affirmative.)	**2.** Là semble d'ailleurs s'en être tenu l'auteur.
2. *l'auteur* is the subject The author seems to have restricted himself to that point (*là*).	**3.** Là semble être le sens de ses remarques.
3. *le sens* is the subject That seems to be the meaning of his remarks.	**4.** Quel ne devrait pas être notre étonnement si nous nous comparions à l'animal sur ce point.

4. *étonnement* is the subject of the first clause. How great should be our surprise (what should not be our surprise) if we were to compare ourselves to animals on this point.	**5.** Rien de plus douteux.
5. *Rien* is the subject, but the verb in this common elliptical pattern is missing. Nothing is more doubtful.	**6.** Rien de plus indubitable.
6. Nothing is more indubitable.	

INSTRUCTIONS: *How is* **que** *used in the following sentences?*

	1. La "mentalité primitive" correspondrait à une structure fondamentale différente que la nôtre aurait supplanté. (**que** = *which/than*)
1. The "primitive mind" is supposed to correspond to a different fundamental structure *which* ours is supposed to have supplanted.	**2.** La "mentalité primitive" ne se rencontre aujourd'hui que chez des retardataires. (**que** = *which/except*)
2. The "primitive mind" is not encountered today *except* among backward peoples.	**3.** **décrire** = *to describe* **circonscrire** = _____
3. to circumscribe.	**4.** En circonscrivant ainsi le champ d'études, on ne fait que constater l'existence de certains croyances chez des retardataires. (**que** = *than/except*)
4. By thus circumscribing the field of studies, one does nothing *except* to ascertain the existence of certain beliefs among backward peoples.	**5.** Rien de plus facile que de circonscrire ainsi le champ d'études. (**que** = *which/than*)
5. Nothing is easier *than* thus circumscribing the field of studies.	

TESTING EXERCISE

INSTRUCTIONS: *Keep your card over the left-hand column while you do the testing exercises. Circle the letter of the best translation of the words indicated. Then verify your answer, and review the sections indicated for those you missed.*

1. **Prenez garde à** choisir la bonne réponse.
    A. Take care to   B. Take care not to   C. Take a guard to

---

1. A
(118)

2. Il **a pris congé** de ses amis.
    A. took leave   B. looked like   C. blamed   D. described

---

2. A
(118)

3. Il tient **à lui parler à elle de sa maison à elle.**
    A. to speak to him about his house
    B. to speak to her about his house
    C. to speak to him about her house
    D. to speak to her about her house

---

3. D
(120)

4. Je m'en tiendrai à **son opinion** à lui.
    A. sound opinion   B. his opinion   C. her opinion

---

4. B
(120)

5. Ma vue à moi et **la vôtre** sont toutes les deux correctes.
    A. your   B. yours   C. you   D. the vote

---

5. B
(120)

6. **Attendu que** vos amis sont absents . . .
    A. While waiting   B. While   C. Seeing that   D. According to whether

---

6. C
(121)

7. Il **prit part** au conflit.
    A. took leave of   C. found fault with
    B. made a decision about   D. participated in

---

7. D
(118)

8. Dès qu'il viendra, il **tiendra à** vous en faire part.
    A. will desire   B. will keep at   C. will be satisfied to   D. will resemble

---

8. A
(119)

9. **Tant qu'**ils sont là, donnez-leur les leurs.
    A. After   B. As soon as   C. Until   D. As long as

---

9. D
(121)

10. Maintenant que vous les avez vues, rendez-lui **les siennes** à lui.
    A. his   B. hers   C. theirs   D. mine

---

10. A
(120)

READING PASSAGE

INSTRUCTIONS: *Give yourself fifteen minutes to read the following paragraph of about 700 words. Circle the words which you do not immediately recognize, but do not look them up the first time through. Verify your comprehension of the passage by answering the questions at the end. Then come back to the circled words and work out their meanings more precisely. Practice reading the passage until you can do it in the time allowed.*

Le phénomène religieux

From Henri Bergson, *Les deux sources de la morale et de la religion.* Used by permission of Librairie Félix Alcan, Paris.

Le spectacle de ce que furent les religions, et de ce que certaines sont encore, est bien humiliant pour l'intelligence humaine. Quel tissu d'aberrations! L'expérience a beau dire « c'est faux » et le raisonnement « c'est absurde », l'humanité ne **s'en cramponne** [1] que davantage à l'absurdité et
5 à l'erreur. Encore si elle s'en tenait là! Mais on a vu la religion prescrire l'immoralité, imposer des crimes. Plus elle est grossière, plus elle tient matériellement de place dans la vie d'un peuple. Ce qu'elle devra **partager** [2] plus tard avec la science, l'art, la philosophie, elle le demande et l'obtient d'abord pour elle seule. Il y a là de quoi surprendre, quand on a commencé
10 par définir l'homme un être intelligent.

Notre étonnement grandit, quand nous voyons que la superstition la plus basse a été pendant si longtemps un fait universel. Elle subsiste d'ailleurs encore. On trouve dans le passé, on trouverait même aujourd'hui des sociétés humaines qui n'ont ni science, ni art, ni philosophie. Mais il n'y a jamais
15 eu de société sans religion.

Quelle ne devrait pas être notre confusion, maintenant, si nous nous comparions à l'animal sur ce point! Très probablement l'animal ignore la superstition. Nous ne savons guère ce qui se passe dans des consciences autres que la nôtre; mais comme les états religieux se traduisent d'ordinaire par
20 des attitudes et par des actes, nous serions bien avertis par quelque signe si l'animal était capable de religiosité. Force nous est donc d'en prendre notre parti. L'*homo sapiens*, seul être doué de raison, est le seul aussi qui puisse suspendre son existence à des choses déraisonnables.

On parle bien d'une « mentalité primitive » qui serait aujourd'hui celle
25 des races inférieures, qui aurait **jadis** [3] été celle de l'humanité en général, et sur le compte de laquelle il faudrait mettre la superstition. Si l'on se borne ainsi à grouper certaines manières de penser sous une dénomination commune et à relever certains rapports entre elles, on fait œuvre utile et inattaquable: utile, en ce que l'on circonscrit un champ d'études ethnologiques et psy-
30 chologiques qui est du plus haut intérêt; inattaquable, puisque l'on ne fait que constater l'existence de certaines croyances et de certaines pratiques dans une humanité moins civilisée que la nôtre. Là semble d'ailleurs s'en être tenu M. Lévy-Bruhl dans ses remarquables ouvrages, surtout dans les derniers. Mais on laisse alors intacte la question de savoir comment des croyances ou
35 des pratiques aussi peu raisonnables ont pu et peuvent encore être acceptées par des êtres intelligents. A cette question nous ne pouvons pas nous empêcher de chercher une réponse. Bon gré mal gré, le lecteur des beaux livres de M. Lévy-Bruhl tirera d'eux la conclusion que l'intelligence humaine a évolué; la logique naturelle n'aurait pas toujours été la même; la « mentalité primi-

---

1 *clings*   **2** *share*   **3** *formerly*

⁴⁰ tive » correspondrait à une structure fondamentale différente, que la nôtre aurait supplantée et qui ne se rencontre aujourd'hui que **chez** ⁴ des retardataires. Mais on admet alors que les habitudes d'esprit acquises par les individus au cours des siècles ont pu devenir héréditaires, modifier la nature et donner une nouvelle mentalité à l'espèce. Rien de plus douteux. A supposer qu'une

⁴⁵ habitude contractée par les parents se transmette jamais à l'enfant, c'est un fait rare, dû à tout un **concours** ⁵ de circonstances accidentellement réunies: aucune modification de l'espèce ne sortira de là. Mais alors, la structure de l'esprit restant la même, l'expérience acquise par les générations successives, déposée dans le milieu social et restituée par ce milieu à chacun de nous,

⁵⁰ doit suffire à expliquer pourquoi nous ne pensons pas comme le non-civilisé, pourquoi l'homme d'autrefois différait de l'homme actuel. L'esprit fonctionne de même dans les deux cas, mais il ne s'applique peut-être pas à la même matière, probablement parce que la société n'a pas, ici et là, les mêmes besoins. Telle sera bien la conclusion de nos recherches. Sans anticiper sur elle,

⁵⁵ bornons-nous à dire que l'observation des « primitifs » pose inévitablement la question des origines psychologiques de la superstition, et que la structure générale de l'esprit humain — l'observation par conséquent de l'homme actuel et civilisé — nous paraîtra fournir des éléments suffisants à la solution du problème.

INSTRUCTIONS: *In the following exercise you may find two or more alternatives which seem possible. Choose the one which best expresses the meaning of the text.*

1. Lines 1–10 state that
    A. reason has never really demonstrated the falseness of religions
    B. in spite of their absurdity religions have generally opposed crimes
    C. it is the religious phenomenon which led to the definition of man as a religious being
    D. human kind clings to false ideas even when reason says they are false

---

1. D   2. Lines 11–15 state that
    A. all societies have had a religion.
    B. superstition was limited to a pre-scientific age
    C. the extent of superstition is not surprising

---

2. A   3. Lines 16–23 state that
    A. animals possibly have some form of religious instinct
    B. if animals were religious, we would know it
    C. man as a rational being should seek the most rational religion
    D. with respect to the religious phenomenon, man is much like the animals

---

3. B   4. The verb tenses of lines 24–26 in the fourth paragraph indicate that the idea of a "primitive mind"
    A. was definitely established
    B. would be definitely established if enough data were available

---

4 *among*   5 *combination*

C. is supposed by some people to be established
D. will likely be established in the future

4. C   **5.** Lines 26–38 state that
A. the works of Lévy-Bruhl have established the origins of the religious phenomena fairly well
B. Lévy-Bruhl does not deal with the real problem
C. the reader will probably not draw an evolutionary concept from Lévy-Bruhl's work, even though the concept is implicit in the work
D. the work of Lévy-Bruhl is of practically no value.

5. B   **6.** Lines 42–54 state that the evolutionary theory of Lévy-Bruhl is
A. somewhat doubtful   C. fairly well established
B. extremely doubtful   D. not at all doubtful

6. B

Chapter Nineteen

REVIEW: Make sure that you can easily recognize the structures and vocabulary of the previous two lessons before beginning this one.

122. *Expressions of Time*—il y a, voici, voila

1. The phrase **il y a** is used idiomatically as an indicator of time. Followed immediately by a period of time, it expresses the idea of *ago:*

Cela s'est passé il y a cinq ans.	*That happened five years ago.*
Il est mort il y a deux semaines.	*He died two weeks ago.*

2. Followed by a period of time and a Present tense clause, **il y a . . . que** is translated by the Present Perfect tense as follows:

Il y a trois ans que nous étudions le français.	*We **have been studying** French **for** three years.*
Combien de temps y a-t-il que vous étudiez cette question?	*How long **have you been studying** this question?*
Il y a un an que vous êtes à cette université.	*You **have been** at this university **for** one year.*

3.   The same construction occurs with the expression **voilà** or **voici**+*time* +**que.** Translate **voilà (voici)** as *for* and use the Present Perfect form of the verb:

Voilà douze ans qu'elle joue du piano.	She *has been playing* the piano *for twelve years.*
Voici une semaine qu'il fait beau temps.	It *has been* good weather *for a week.*

4. If the French verb is in the Imperfect, use the Past Perfect form, as follows:

Il y avait un quart d'heure que je les attendais.	I *had been waiting* for them *for a quarter of an hour.*
Y avait-il longtemps que vous les attendiez?	Had *you been waiting* for them *for a long time?*
Voilà deux heures qu'il dormait.	He *had been sleeping for* two hours.

READING PREPARATION

INSTRUCTIONS: *Express the meanings of the following sentences. Pay special attention to the tenses required for the various constructions.*

	1. Il y a plus de cent ans, Alexis de Tocqueville visita le Nouveau Monde.
1. More than a hundred years ago, Alexis de Tocqueville visited the New World.	2. Il écrivit, il y a une centaine d'années, des réflexions perspicaces sur cette nouvelle nation.
2. He wrote, about a hundred years ago, some perspicacious reflections about this new nation. (Remember that the suffix . . . **aine** indicates an approximate number).	3. Il publia ses œuvres il y a cent ans, à peu près.
3. He published his works about a hundred years ago. (Remember to circle unfamiliar words.)	4. Il y a dans son œuvre des réflexions perspicaces sur l'avenir des Etats–Unis.
4. There are in his work some perspicacious reflections on the future of the United States.	5. Il y a longtemps que l'on parle de ses observations.

5. People have been talking about his observations for a long time.

6. Il y a bien des siècles, dit-il, au moyen age, l'Europe vivait une époque de fractionnement.
(Does **fractionnement** suggest that Europe was *divided* or *united?*)

6. *divided*
Many centuries ago, he said, in the Middle Ages, Europe was living through a period of divisions (fractionation).

7. Il y avait longtemps que chaque groupe de la société tendait à s'individualiser.

7. For a long time, each group of society had been tending to become individualized.

8. **à tout prendre** = *everything considered, taken as a whole*
A tout prendre, l'Europe était plus divisée il y a cinq cents ans que maintenant.

8. Everything considered, Europe was more divided 500 years ago than now.

9. A tout prendre, l'Europe est plus unie aujourd'hui qu'au moyen age.

9. Everything considered, Europe is more united today than in the Middle Ages.

10. A tout prendre, les conditions qui divisaient l'Europe il y a sept cents ans sont disparues.

10. Everything considered, the conditions which divided Europe 700 years ago have disappeared.

11. **appartenir** = *to belong to*
Il y a à peu près huit cents ans, l'individu croyait appartenir à une famille ou à une cité, plutôt qu'à une nation.

11. About eight hundred years ago, the individual believed he belonged to a family or to a city, rather than to a nation.

12. Il y avait apparemment des siècles que l'on appartenait à des groupes fractionnés plutôt qu'à une nation.

12. For centuries, apparently, people had belonged to divided groups rather than to a nation.

13. Il y avait des siècles que cette tendance se faisait sentir.

13. This tendency had been making itself felt for centuries.

14. Il y a plus d'une centaine d'années, la tendance contraire s'est faite sentir.

14. More than a hundred years ago, the opposite tendency made itself felt.

15. Il y a peu de temps que l'on appartient à une nation plutôt qu'à une province.

15. For only a short while have people belonged to a nation rather than to a province.

16. Il y a quelque temps que la tendance contraire se fait sentir.

16. For some time the contrary tendency has been making itself felt.	17. **partager**=*to share* Voilà longtemps que les Européens partagent les mêmes idées.
17. For a long time the Europeans have shared the same ideas.	18. Voilà longtemps que les Européens partageaient la même religion.
18. For a long time, the Europeans had shared the same religion.	19. Voilà bien des siècles qu'ils appartiennent à la même famille.
19. For many centuries they have belonged to the same family.	20. Voilà cependant longtemps qu'une religion commune unissait l'Europe.
20. For a long time, however, a common religion had united Europe.	21. Voilà quelque temps que cette marche vers l'unité ne se fait plus sentir.
21. For some time this march (progress) toward unity has no longer made itself felt.	Review the words circled above and then continue.

123. *Expression of Time with* depuis

1. If the word **depuis** is used with the Past Indefinite tense + a quantity of time, use *for* to express its meaning:

Je ne vous ai pas vu depuis un mois.   *I have not seen you **for** a month.*

2. If **depuis** is used with a Present Tense verb, translate the verb by the English Present Perfect, as with **il y a, voilà,** and **voici.** If the French verb is in the Imperfect, use the English Past Perfect:

Nous parlons de cette affaire depuis une semaine.	*We **have been talking** about this matter **for** a week.*
Depuis quand parle-t-on de cette affaire?	*How long **have** they **been talking** about this matter?*
Nous parlons de cette affaire depuis quelques jours.	*We **had been talking** about this matter **for** several days.*
Depuis combien de temps en parlaient-ils?	*How long **had** they **been talking** about it?*

3. If **depuis** is not followed by a quantity of time, use *since* to translate it:

Je ne l'ai pas vu depuis hier.	*I **have not seen** him (it) **since** yesterday.*
Il travaille depuis ce matin.	*He **has been working since** this morning.*

READING PREPARATION

INSTRUCTIONS: *As you read the following sentences, give special attention to the phrases required to translate the various patterns.*

	1. Depuis quand apprenez-vous le français?
1. How long (since when) have you been learning French?	2. Il apprenait le français depuis un mois, n'est-ce pas?
2. He had been learning French for a month, hadn't he?	3. Il y avait un mois qu'il apprenait le français, n'est-ce pas?
3. He had been learning French for a month, hadn't he?	4. Ils parlaient de cette affaire depuis quinze jours.
4. They had been talking about this matter for two weeks. (Notice that "fifteen days" is "two weeks".)	5. Je ne l'ai pas vue depuis une semaine.
5. I have not seen her for a week.	6. Elle est à Paris depuis deux jours.
6. She has been in Paris for two days.	7. Depuis ce jour-là je n'en ai plus entendu parler.
7. Since that day I have heard nothing more of it (heard nothing more spoken of it).	8. Vous faites bien des progrès depuis que vous êtes à l'université.
8. You have been making much progress since you have been at the university.	9. Il y a longtemps de cela.
9. That was a long time ago.	10. Voilà six ans que je le connais.
10. I have known him for six years.	11. Reprenons le thème de notre auteur Tocqueville.
11. Let us take up again the theme of our author, Tocqueville.	12. **apercevoir**=*to perceive* Depuis plusieurs années il apercevait une grandeur future du Nouveau Monde.
12. For several years, he had perceived a future greatness of the New World.	13. Depuis plus de cinquante ans, on peut vérifier ses prédictions.
13. For more than fifty years one has been able to verify his predictions.	14. Depuis plus d'un demi-siècle ses prédictions sur la Russie se réalisent.

14. For more than half a century his predictions about Russia have been in the process of fulfillment.

15. **saisir la portée de**=*to grasp the import of, significance of*
Depuis ce temps-là, le public a mieux saisi la portée de ses analyses.

15. Since that time, the public has better grasped the import of his analyses.

16. Sans approfondir l'histoire des deux nations vous ne sauriez saisir la portée de ses prédictions.

16. Without thoroughly examining the history of the two nations you cannot grasp the import of his predictions. (Remember that **savoir** sometimes appears with only one element of the negation.)

17. **les mœurs**=*morals, customs*
Depuis longtemps nous pouvons constater cette uniformité de pensée et de mœurs dont parlait Tocqueville.

17. For a long time, we have been able to observe that uniformity of thought and customs of which Tocqueville was speaking.

18. On peut mieux apercevoir la portée de ses prédictions depuis leur accomplissement.

18. One can better perceive the import of his predictions since their fulfillment.

19. **à travers**=*through, across*
A travers cette uniformité de mœurs on voit mieux la portée de ses remarques.

19. Through this uniformity of customs, one sees better the import of his remarks.

20. On ne saurait nier sa perspicacité—ses prédictions se sont réalisées depuis.

20. One cannot (It would be impossible to) deny his perspicacity—his predictions have since been fulfilled.

21. A travers les années depuis sa mort, ces prédictions se sont accomplies.

21. Throughout the years since his death, these predictions have been fulfilled.

22. L'Europe a traversé des siècles de guerres.

22. Europe has passed through centuries of wars.

23. L'Europe a traversé des siècles de guerres sans cesse renaissantes.

23. Europe has passed through centuries of continually recurring wars.

24. **une lieue**=*a league*
L'Europe, à travers les guerres sans cesse renaissantes, est parvenue à avoir de quatre cents à cinq cents habitants par lieue carrée.

24. Europe, in spite of (having passed through) continually recurring wars, has succeeded in having from 400 to 500 inhabitants per square league.

Do not go on until you can read the above sentences easily.

124.   *Adjectives which Change Meaning with Position*

1.   There are a few adjectives whose meanings may vary depending on their position.

ADJECTIVE	BEFORE NOUN	AFTER NOUN
ancien, –ne	*former*	*ancient, old*
bon, –ne	*simple or good*	*good*
brave	*worthy*	*brave*
certain, –e	*particular*	*sure*
cher, chère	*dear*	*expensive*
grand, –e	*great* or *big*	*tall, big*
pauvre	*unfortunate*	*poor, needy*
propre	*own*	*clean, proper*
seul, –e	*only, the mere fact of*	*alone*

READING PREPARATION

INSTRUCTIONS: *In the following phrases notice how the meaning of the phrases changes with the position of the adjective.*

	1. mon ancien professeur
1. my former teacher	2. l'histoire ancienne
2. ancient history	3. un bon homme
3. a simple man, a guy	4. un homme bon
4. a good man	5. une brave femme
5. a worthy woman	6. une femme brave
6. a brave woman	7. un certain fait
7. a particular (certain) fact	8. un fait certain
8. a sure fact	9. un grand homme
9. a great man	10. un homme grand
10. a tall man	11. la même vertu
11. the same virtue	12. la vertu même
12. virtue itself	13. un pauvre homme
13. a poor man (a man to be pitied)	14. un homme pauvre

14. a poor man (in need of money)		**15.** ses propres mains
15. his own hands		**16.** ses mains propres
16. his clean hands		

125. *Idioms*—servir, sentir

1. The verb **servir,** like **venir,** changes meaning according to the preposition used with it:

servir = *to serve*

On sert le dîner à sept heures.	*Dinner is served at seven o'clock.*

servir à = *to be used for, to be good for*

A quoi cela sert-il?	*What is that good for?*
A quoi sert un couteau?	*What is a knife used for?*
O vertu! A quoi m'avez-vous servi?	*Oh virtue! What good have you done me?*

servir de = *to be used as, to serve as*

Les pupitres servent de tables.	*The desks are used as tables.*

se servir de = *to use, to make use of*

Vous servez-vous de votre auto?	*Are you using your car?*
Vous servez-vous souvent du dictionnaire?	*Do you often make use of the dictionary?*

2. The meaning of **sentir** must be established by the context.

sentir = *to feel (to sense), to smell, to smell of*

Je sentis trembler la maison.	*I felt the house tremble.*
Il y a des fleurs qui sentent bon.	*There are sweet-smelling flowers (which smell good).*
La maison sent le tabac.	*The house smells of tobacco.*

se sentir = *to feel*

Je me sens fatigué.	*I feel tired.*

READING PREPARATION

INSTRUCTIONS: *Continue to circle unfamiliar vocabulary.*

	1. Faisons une révision des matières des leçons précédentes.
1. Let us review material of the previous lessons.	**2.** Une analyse du phénomène religieux sert à nous éclaircir sur ses origines.
2. An analysis of the religious phenomenon is useful in enlightening us concerning its origins.	**3.** **ce genre**=*this kind* Ce genre d'analyse sert de point de départ à Bergson.
3. This kind of analysis serves as a point of departure for Bergson.	**4.** Celui-ci se sert des données d'une analyse empirique comme point de départ.
4. The latter uses the data of an empirical analysis as a point of departure.	**5.** A quoi cette analyse sert-elle?
5. What is this analysis good for?	**6.** De quels moyens devra-t-on se servir pour mener cette entreprise à bien?
6. What means will one have to use in order to lead this enterprise to a successful conclusion?	**7.** Les écrits de M. Lévy-Bruhl nous serviront de point de comparaison.
7. The writings of Mr. Lévy-Bruhl will serve us as a point of comparison.	**8.** On sent une certaine hésitation de la part de Bergson à accepter les conclusions de Lévy-Bruhl.
8. One senses a certain hesitation on Bergson's part to accept the conclusions of Lévy-Bruhl.	**9.** Le bon bramin se sentait prêt à tomber dans le désespoir.
9. The good Brahman felt ready to fall into despair.	**10.** Quoiqu'il fût bien instruit, il se sentait fort ignorant.
10. Although he was well educated, he felt very ignorant.	**11.** **le poids**=*the weight* Bien qu'il eût fait de belles études, il sentait vivement tout le poids de son ignorance.
11. Although he had studied very well, he felt keenly all the weight of his ignorance.	**12.** Parlons de votre auto. Vous en servez-vous ce soir?
12. Let's talk about your car. Are you using it tonight?	**13.** Voulez-vous vous servir de la mienne?

13. Do you want to use mine?	**14.** La mienne sent le tabac. Qui s'en est servi la dernière fois?
14. Mine smells of tobacco. Who used it the last time?	**15.** **une panne**=*a breakdown, a stoppage* Est-ce qu'elle est en panne?
15. Is it broken down?	**16.** Si elle est toujours en panne, à quoi sert-elle?
16. If it is always broken down, what is it good for?	**17.** **conduire une auto**=*to drive*, or *steer a car* Vous sentez-vous capable de la conduire?
17. Do you feel yourself capable of driving it?	**18.** Le volant sert à conduire (ou à diriger) l'auto. (**Le volant** must be the _____.)
18. *steering wheel* The steering wheel is used to steer the car.	When you can readily distinguish the meanings of the above verbs, go on to the next section.

126. *Indefinite Pronouns and Adjectives*

1. A number of indefinite adjectives are encountered as pronouns also:

Il y a d'autres raisons à ajouter.	*There are other reasons to be added.*
Il y en a *d'autres* à ajouter.	*There are **others** to be added.*
Chaque raison a sa valeur.	*Each reason has its value.*
Chacune a sa valeur.	***Each one** has its value.*
Plusieurs raisons sont possibles.	*Several reasons are possible.*
Plusieurs sont possibles.	***Several** are possible.*
Il nous a expliqué toutes les raisons.	*He explained all the reasons to us.*
Il nous les a expliquées *toutes*.	*He explained **all** of them to us.*
Il les a expliquées à tous ses auditeurs.	*He explained them to all his listeners.*
Il les a expliquées à *tous*.	*He explained them to **all**.*
Il nous a *tout* expliqué.	*He explained **everything** to us.*
Comment a-t-il pu arriver à une telle conclusion?	*How could he have arrived at such a conclusion?*
Telle était sa conclusion.	***Such** was his conclusion.*

2. Other indefinite expressions are:

Quiconque veut venir, peut venir.	***Whoever** desires to come can come.*

N'importe quel livre peut servir dans ce cas.	*Any (no matter what) book can serve in this case.*
N'importe qui peut dire cela.	*Anyone (no matter who) may say that.*
Donnez-moi un livre *quelconque.*	*Give me just any book.*
On a dû fixer une date *quelconque.*	*One had to fix a date at random.*
Baudelaire n'était pas un auteur *quelconque.*	*Baudelaire was not just any author.*

READING PREPARATION

INSTRUCTIONS: *Continue to circle unfamiliar words for future review.*

1. **réunir**=*to unite, to reunite*
   Au moyen age le seul lien de la religion suffisait à tout réunir.

1. In the Middle Ages the single bond of religion sufficed to unite everything.

2. Les Anglais, les Français, les Allemands, tous étaient réunis par le lien d'une seule religion.

2. The English, the French, the Germans, all were united by the bond of a single religion.

3. **fortement**=*strongly*
   Cependant chaque peuple tendait alors fortement à s'individualiser.

3. However, each people at that time strongly tended to become individualized.

4. Chacun tendait fortement à s'individualiser.

4. Each one tended strongly to become individualized.

5. Chacun croyait appartenir à une cité plutôt qu'à une nation.

5. Each one believed he belonged to a city rather than to a nation.

6. On parvient difficilement à comprendre une telle situation.

6. One manages with difficulty to understand such a situation.

7. Telle fut la situation.

7. Such was the situation.

8. Aujourd'hui toutes ces conditions ont changé.

8. Today, all of these conditions have changed.

9. De nos jours toutes ont changé.

9. In our time all of them have changed.

10. De nos jours tout a changé.

10. In our time everything has changed.

11. De nos jours plusieurs liens unissent entre elles les parties les plus éloignées de la terre.

11.	Today several bonds unite (to each other) the most distant parts of the earth.	**12.**	A l'époque actuelle, plusieurs unissent les parties les plus diverses de la terre.
12.	At the present time, several (of these bonds) unite the most diverse parts of the earth.	**13.**	Plusieurs liens les réunissent, tels que les mêmes mœurs et les mêmes besoins.
13.	Several bonds unite them, such as the same customs and the same needs.	**14.**	Tels sont les facteurs qui les réunissent.
14.	Such are the factors which unite them.	**15.**	On pourrait citer d'autres exemples.
15.	One could cite other examples.	**16.**	On pourrait en citer d'autres.
16.	One could cite others (of them).	**17.**	**prêter**=*to lend* **prêter attention**=*to pay attention* Quiconque veut y prêter attention s'en rendra compte.
17.	Whoever wishes to pay attention to it will realize it.	**18.**	N'importe quel observateur peut s'en rendre compte, s'il y prête son attention.
18.	Any (no matter which) observer can be informed of it if he gives his attention to it.	**19.**	N'importe qui peut en dire autant.
19.	Anyone can say as much about it.	**20.**	Tocqueville prévoyait une grande population aux Etats-Unis partageant la même langue, les mêmes habitudes et les mêmes mœurs.
20.	Tocqueville foresaw a great population in the United States sharing the same language, the same habits and the same morals (or customs).	**21.**	Il prévoyait le jour où cette nouvelle nation ne serait plus une nation quelconque.
21.	He foresaw the day when this new nation would no longer be an ordinary nation. (Notice that when **où** is used to indicate time, it is translated as *when*.)	**22.**	Il prédit le jour où les Etats-Unis et la Russie se confronteraient.
22.	He predicted the day when the United States and Russia would confront each other.	**23.**	Chacun de ces peuples semblait s'avancer vers le même but.
23.	Each one of these peoples seemed to be advancing toward the same goal.	**24.**	N'importe qui à l'époque actuelle peut en dire autant.

24. Anyone at the present time can say as much about it.

25. Est-ce qu'un observateur quelconque aurait pu en dire autant?

25. Would an ordinary observer have been able to say as much about it?

26. Est-ce que n'importe quel historien aurait pu en dire autant?

26. Would any historian have been able to say as much about it?

27. Si vous y prêtez attention vous verrez ce qu'il a dit de vrai.

27. If you pay attention to it, you will see what truth he has told.

28. Quiconque vient à approfondir la question trouvera de quoi parler beaucoup.

28. Whoever happens to go into the question deeply will find enough to talk about at length.

29. Quiconque veut être l'égal d'un autre doit prouver son égalité.

29. Whoever wants to be the equal of another person must prove his equality.

30. Quiconque veut être libre doit savoir conquérir sa liberté.

30. Whoever wants to be free must be able to win his liberty.

31. Chacun en tirera les conclusions qu'il voudra.

31. Each one will draw from it the conclusions that he wishes.

32. Faisons une courte révision de quelques pronoms.

32. Let us make a short review of a few pronouns.

33. Il y a longtemps que je ne lui en parle plus.

33. I have not spoken to him about it for a long time.

34. On ne saurait les lui nier.

34. One could not deny them to him.

35. On parvint difficilement à le lui expliquer.

35. One succeeded with difficulty in explaining it to him.

36. C'est un fait dont l'imagination ne saurait saisir la portée.

36. It is a fact of which the imagination cannot grasp the significance.

37. Les deux puissances dont il parle sont l'Amérique et la Russie.

37. The two powers of which he is talking are America and Russia.

38. Je vous prêterai l'argent dont vous avez besoin.

38. I will lend you the money which you need.

39. Nous pouvons constater cette uniformité dont il fit mention.

39. We can certify to this uniformity which he mentioned.

40. La crainte a toujours ses yeux ouverts; l'amour aime à fermer les siens.

Joubert

40. Fear always has its eyes open; love likes to close its own (eyes).	**41.** Chacun dit du bien de son cœur, et personne n'ose en dire de son esprit. La Rochefoucauld
41. Each person says good things about his heart, and no one dares to say the same of his mind.	

127. *Indefinite Expressions Followed by Subjunctive*

1. A number of indefinite expressions take the Subjunctive and are translated as follows:

Quelque malin que vous soyez, vous ne réussirez pas.	***However clever you might be,*** *you will not succeed.*
Quelque effort que vous fassiez vous ne mènerez rien à bien.	***Whatever effort you might make,*** *you will succeed in nothing.*
Quelque bonnes que soient vos raisons, vous n'avez pas raison.	***However good your reasons might be,*** *you are not right.*
Quelles que soient vos raisons, vous avez tort.	***Whatever your reasons might be,*** *you are wrong.*
Qui que vous soyez, personne ne vous croira.	***Whoever you might be,*** *no one will believe you.*
Quoi que vous fassiez, vos efforts sont en vain.	***Whatever (no matter what) you might do,*** *your efforts are in vain.*
Si (tout) éloquent que vous soyez, vous ne convaincrez personne.	***However eloquent you might be,*** *you will convince no one.*

READING PREPARATION

INSTRUCTIONS: *Make yourself thoroughly familiar with the following expressions.*

	1. Quelque bien que l'on dise de nous, on ne nous apprend rien de nouveau. La Rochefoucauld
1. Whatever good people say about us, they teach us nothing new.	**2.** Le beau n'est pas distinct de l'utile, quoi qu'en pensent les ignorants. Rodin
2. The beautiful is not distinct from the useful whatever the ignorant may think about it.	**3.** **aussi bien que**=*as well as* Baudelaire, dont vous lirez un poème en prose tout a l'heure, était un grand philosophe morale aussi bien qu'un poète.

3. Baudelaire, one of whose prose poems you will read shortly, was a great moral philosopher as well as a poet.

4. He wrote in prose as well as in verse.

5. He offered his readers observations on ethics as well as very beautiful verses. (Notice that French has different words for male and female readers.)

6. I mean that he proposed some unusual lessons of morality (ethics) from time to time.

7. I mean that he proposed a few lessons of an unusual morality.

8. les leçons
I wonder if there are a few (some) of them (which are) true.

9. However, one could not reject all of them.

10. You could not reject all of them.

11. les leçons d'une morale singulière
Whatever might be your ideas on ethics, you will find in them (these lessons) something surprising.

12. For it is not a question of just any morality.

13. For Baudelaire was not just any author.

4. Il écrivait en prose aussi bien qu'en vers.

5. Il offrait à ses lecteurs et lectrices des observations morales aussi bien que des vers très beaux.

6. vouloir dire = *to mean*
Je veux dire qu'il proposait de temps en temps quelques singulières leçons de moralité.

7. Je veux dire qu'il proposait quelques leçons d'une moralité singulière.

8. Je me demande s'il y en a quelques-unes de vraies.
(To which word in the previous sentence does **en** refer?)

9. Cependant, on ne saurait les rejeter toutes.

10. Vous ne sauriez les rejeter toutes.

11. Quelles que soient vos idées sur l'éthique, vous y trouverez quelque chose de surprenant.
(**Y** refers to what idea in the previous sentences?)

12. Car il ne s'agit pas d'une moralité quelconque.

13. Car Baudelaire n'était pas un auteur quelconque.

14. à plus forte raison = *for still greater reason*
A plus forte raison faut-il avoir soin de bien saisir la portée de ses idées.

14. For still greater reason must one be careful to grasp well the import of his ideas.

15. **hors de portée de** = *out of the reach of*
Néanmoins quelque étrange qu'elle paraisse, elle n'est pas hors de la portée de tout le monde.

15. Nonetheless, however strange it might appear, it is not out of reach of everyone.

16. Quiconque veut la comprendre ne manquera pas de la comprendre.

16. Whoever wants to understand it will not fail to understand it.

17. Elle est à la portée de quiconque veut en saisir les principes.
(To which preceding idea does **en** refer?)

17. **la morale**
It is within the grasp of whoever wishes to grasp the principles of it.

18. **battre** = *to beat*
Ce qu'il propose, c'est que nous battions les pauvres.

18. What he proposes is that we beat the poor.

19. Propose-t-il vraiment que nous les battions tous?

19. Does he really propose that we beat all of them?

20. **l'aumône** = *alms*
Non, il ne faut battre que ceux qui nous demandent l'aumône.

20. No, we must beat only those who ask alms of us.

21. Faut-il battre quiconque nous demandera l'aumône?

21. Must we beat whoever asks alms of us? (Notice that the English present is used here instead of the future, to conform to English usage.)

22. Oui, à d'autant plus forte raison faut-il battre celui-là.

22. Yes, for still greater reason must we beat that one (who asks alms of us).

23. **assommer** = *to fell, to knock down*
Qui qu'il soit, quelque digne qu'il paraisse, il faut l'assommer.

23. Whoever it might be, however worthy he might appear, you must knock him down.

24. Comment Baudelaire a-t-il jamais pu avancer une telle idée?

24. How could Baudelaire ever advance such an idea?

25. **c'est que** = *the fact is that*
C'est que cette idée s'est engendrée dans son esprit par suite de quelques lectures qu'il avait faites.

25. The fact is that this idea came to his mind (was engendered in his mind) in consequence of some reading he had done.

26. Quelques livres qu'il ait lus, ils ont dû être étranges.

26. Whatever books he might have read, they must have been strange.

27. **parcourir**=*to travel over, to read through rapidly*
Il y avait quelque temps qu'il parcourait quelques livres à la mode.

27. For some time he had been reading a few popular books.

28. Quant aux formules destinées à rendre les peuples heureux, il les y avait trouvées toutes.

28. As for the formulas (platitudes, set forms) intended to make the public happy, he had found all of them there.

29. Plus il parcourait ces livres, moins il croyait à leur sagacité.

29. The more he read through these books, the less he believed in their wisdom.

30. **s'apercevoir de**=*to notice, to discover*
Il croyait s'apercevoir d'une idée supérieure.

30. He believed he had discovered a superior idea.

31. Il croyait s'en apercevoir grâce à ses lectures.

31. He believed he had discovered it because of his readings.

32. Il se croyait le premier à s'en apercevoir.

32. He believed himself the first to notice (discover) it.

33. **au fond de**=*at the bottom of*
Il croyait s'apercevoir d'une idée supérieure au fond de son intellect.

33. He believed he discovered a superior idea at the bottom of his intellect.

34. Ce n'était encore que l'idée d'une idée, quelque chose de très vague.

34. It was as yet only the idea of an idea, something very vague.

35. **mendier**=*to beg*
C'est à d'autant plus forte raison qu'il croyait à la supériorité de son idée qu'il faut battre les mendiants.

35. It is with all the greater reason that he believed in the superiority of his idea that one must beat the beggars.

36. **sauter**=*to jump*
Quand un pauvre vous demande l'aumône, il faut que vous lui sautiez dessus.
(Since we are talking about **un pauvre, dessus** must mean *above him/on him*)

36. When a poor man asks alms of you, you must jump *on* him.

37. **casser**=*to break*
Après avoir sauté sur votre mendiant, il faut lui casser les dents.

37. After having jumped on your beggar, you must break his teeth.

38. **secouer**=*to shake*
Vous devriez le secouer.

38. You ought to shake him.	**39.** Vous devez lui secouer la tête contre le mur.
39. You must shake his head against the wall.	**40.** **le dos**=*the back* Quoi qu'il fasse, vous devez essayer de lui lancer des coups de pied dans le dos.
40. Whatever he does, you must try to kick him in the back.	**41.** Quoiqu'il fasse grande résistance, il faut tâcher de lui donner au moins des coups de pied.
41. Although he may make great resistance, you must try at least to kick him. (Remember the difference between **quoique**=*although* and **quoi que**= *whatever*.)	**42.** Quoi que vous fassiez d'autre, il faut essayer de lui donner de grands coups de pied.
42. Whatever else you might do, you must try to give him several good kicks.	**43.** Quoique vous lui fassiez l'aumône, il a encore besoin de quelque chose d'autre.
43. Although you give him alms, he still needs something else.	**44.** Qui que vous battiez ainsi vous sera certainement reconnaissant.
44. Whomever you beat thus, will certainly be grateful to you.	**45.** Si vastes que soient mes lectures je n'ai jamais rencontré une telle éthique.
45. As extensive as (however extensive) my reading has been, I have never encountered such an ethic.	**46.** Tout habile qu'il soit, l'auteur doit se moquer de nous. (Does **doit** here indicate *obligation* or *conjecture?*)
46. *conjecture* As clever as (however clever) he might be, the author must be making fun of us.	**47.** Qui qu'il soit, l'auteur doit certainement se moquer de nous.
47. Whoever he might be, the author certainly must be making fun of us.	**48.** Pourquoi faut-il sauter sur quiconque nous demande l'aumône et lui donner des coups de poing?
48. Why must we jump on whoever asks us for charity and strike him with our fists?	**49.** **l'orgueil**=*pride* C'est, au fond, qu'il faut lui rendre l'orgueil.
49. Because, after all, we must give him back his pride.	**50.** Tout orgueilleux qu'il soit, il ne l'est jamais assez s'il doit mendier.

50. However proud he might be, he is never proud enough if he must beg.	**51.** Mais, au fond, c'est Baudelaire qui doit vous l'expliquer.
51. But after all, it is Baudelaire who must explain it to you.	When all of the material in this section is familiar to you, go on to the following part.

TESTING EXERCISE

INSTRUCTIONS: *Circle in the margin the number which corresponds to the best rendering of the indicated words. For those which you miss, review the appropriate sections.*

1. **Il y a longtemps que** l'on parle de ses observations.
   A. They talked about them a long time ago.
   B. They used to talk about them at length.
   C. They have been talking about them for a long time.

1. C
(122)

2. Cela se faisait **il y a** des siècles.
   A. That has been done for centuries.
   B. That was done centuries ago.
   C. There are centuries in which that was done.

2. B
(122)

3. Il apprenait le français **depuis** un mois.
   A. since   B. for   C. ago

3. B
(123)

4. Il **attendait** l'autobus depuis un quart d'heure.
   A. He has been waiting   B. He is waiting   C. He had been waiting

4. C
(123)

5. Il s'agit d'un incident de l'histoire **ancienne.**
   A. ancient   B. former   C. antiquated

5. A
(124)

6. On a bien du plaisir à **sentir** une fleur.
   A. to feel   B. to smell   C. to sense

6. B
(125)

7. Vos protestations ne **servent à** rien.
   A. are used   B. are good for   C. serve

7. B
(126)

8. **Quiconque** veut venir sera accueilli avec plaisir.
   A. Whatever   B. Whoever   C. No matter what

8. B
(127)

9. **Tout** éloquent que vous soyez, vous ne convaincrez personne.
   A. Completely   B. Even if   C. However

9. C
(127)

10. C'est notre devoir de lui rendre son **orgueil.**
    A. organ   B. jacket   C. pride

10. C

READING PASSAGES

INSTRUCTIONS: *The following passage contains a lesson of "moral philosophy" by the nineteenth-century author Charles Baudelaire. As you read the passage look for the main ideas, and circle the phrases which you do not immediately recognize. Take ten minutes to read the passage. Then answer the questions at the end in order to verify your comprehension, and come back to the more difficult parts to work out their precise meanings.*

Assommons les pauvres

Baudelaire—Poèmes en prose

Pendant quinze jours je m'étais confiné dans ma chambre et je m'étais entouré des livres à la mode dans ce temps-là (il y a seize ou dix-sept ans) : je veux parler des livres où il est traité de l'art de rendre les peuples heureux, sages et riches, en vingt-quatre heures. J'avais donc digéré—avalé, veux-je

5   dire—toutes les **élucubrations** [1] de tous ces entrepreneurs de bonheur public —de ceux qui conseillent à tous les pauvres de se faire esclaves, et de ceux qui leur persuadent qu'ils sont tous des rois détrônés. On ne trouvera pas surprenant que je fusse alors dans un état d'esprit avoisinant **le vertige** [2] ou la stupidité.

10   Il m'avait semblé seulement que je sentais, confiné au fond de mon intellect, le germe obscur d'une idée supérieure à toutes **les formules de bonne femme** [3] dont j'avais récemment parcouru le dictionnaire. Mais ce n'était que l'idée d'une idée, quelque chose d'infiniment vague.

Et je sortis avec une grande soif. Car le goût passionné des mauvaises
15   lectures engendre un besoin proportionnel du **grand air.** [4]

Comme j'allais entrer dans un cabaret, un mendiant me tendit son chapeau, avec un de ces regards inoubliables qui **culbuteraient** [5] les trônes, si l'esprit **remuait** [6] la matière.

En même temps, j'entendis une voix qui **chuchotait** [7] à mon oreille, une
20   voix que je reconnus bien; c'était d'un bon Ange, ou d'un bon Démon, qui m'accompagne partout.

Or, [8] sa voix me chuchotait ceci: "Celui-là seul est l'égal d'un autre, qui le prouve, et celui-là seul est digne de la liberté, qui sait la conquérir".

Immédiatement, je sautai sur mon mendiant. D'un seul coup de poing,
25   je lui bouchai un œil, qui devint, en une seconde, gros comme une balle. Je cassai un de mes **ongles** [9] à lui briser deux dents, et comme je ne me sentais pas assez fort, étant né délicat et m'étant peu exercé à la boxe, pour assommer rapidement ce vieillard, je le saisis d'une main par le collet de son habit, de l'autre je **l'empoignai à la gorge,** [10] et je me mis à lui secouer vigoureuse-
30   ment la tête contre un mur. Je dois avouer que j'avais **préalablement** [11]

---

1 *great learning*
2 *vertigo*
3 *platitudes*
4 *open air*

5 *would topple*
6 *moved*
7 *whispered*
8 *now*

9 *nails*
10 *put my hand around his throat*
11 *previously*

inspecté les environs d'un coup d'œil, et que j'avais vérifié que dans cette **banlieue** ¹² déserte je me trouvais, pour un assez long temps, hors de la portée de tout agent de police.

⁣⁣⁣⁣ Ayant ensuite, par un coup de pied lancé dans le dos, assez énergique pour
35 briser les **omoplates,**¹³ terrassé ce sexagénaire affaibli, je me saisis d'une grosse branche d'arbre qui **traînait** ¹⁴ à terre, et je le battis avec l'énergie obstinée des cuisiniers qui veulent attendrir un bifteck.

⁣⁣⁣⁣ Tout à coup—O miracle! O jouissance du philosophe qui vérifie l'excellence de sa théorie!—je vis cette antique carcasse se retourner, **se redresser** ¹⁵
40 avec une énergie que je n'aurais jamais soupçonnée dans une machine si singulièrement **détraquée,** ¹⁶ et, avec un regard de haine qui me parut de bon augure, le **malandrin** ¹⁷ décrépit se jeta sur moi, me pocha les deux yeux, me cassa quatre dents, et avec la même branche d'arbre me battit **dru comme plâtre.**¹⁸ Par mon énergique médication, je lui avais donc
45 rendu l'orgueil et la vie.

⁣⁣⁣⁣ Alors, je lui fis **force** ¹⁹ signes pour lui faire comprendre que je considérais la discussion comme finie, et je lui dis: "Monsieur, vous êtes mon égal! **veuillez** ²⁰ me faire l'honneur de partager avec moi ma **bourse:** ²¹ et souvenez-vous, si vous êtes réellement philanthrope, qu'il faut appliquer
50 à tous vos confrères, quand ils vous demandent l'aumône, la théorie que j'ai eu la douleur d'essayer sur votre dos".

⁣⁣⁣⁣ Il m'a bien **juré** ²² qu'il avait compris ma théorie, et qu'il obéirait à mes conseils.

INSTRUCTIONS: *Circle the answer which is most nearly correct according to the reading passage.*

1. Dans le premier paragraphe nous apprenons que Baudelaire
A. avait été gravement malade
B. écrivait une thèse sur la littérature populaire
C. avait lu un assez grand nombre de livres superficiels
D. était adolescent a ce temps-là.

---

1. C   **2.** Les livres en question (lignes 1–9)
A. plaisaient à Baudelaire à cause de leur finesse
B. conseillaient l'orgueil aux pauvres
C. s'adressaient à l'aristocratie
D. rendaient Baudelaire un peu stupide.

---

2. D   **3.** Le mendiant que Baudelaire rencontra lui paraissait d'abord (lignes 16–18)
A. humble
B. orgueilleux

---

12 *suburb*   16 *broken down*   20 *imperative* of **vouloir**
13 *shoulder-blades*   17 *highwayman*   21 *purse*
14 *was dragging*   18 *black and blue*   22 *swore*
15 *straighten up*   19 *many*

c. féroce

d. impressionant par la force de son caractère.

---

3. A   **4.** Le seul être qui ait droit à la liberté est (lignes 19–23)

A. un bon ange.

B. celui qui l'obtient par ses pouvoirs.

c. celui qui la tient de quelqu'un de plus grand que lui.

D. un bon démon.

---

4. B   **5.** Ensuite nous apprenons (lignes 24–37)

A. que Baudelaire était d'une constitution robuste.

B. qu'il a voulu faire venir la police.

c. que Baudelaire a fini par offrir un bifteck au mediant.

D. qu'il battit le mendiant vigoureusement.

---

5. D   **6.** Le mendiant a (lignes 38–45)

A. lancé un regard haineux.

B. fait venir la police.

c. volé la bourse de l'auteur.

D. donné de grands coups de pied.

---

6. A   **7.** Par cette leçon, le mendiant a appris (lignes 46–54)

A. qu'il faut d'abord faire venir la police.

B. que tous ses confrères vont lui appliquer la même leçon.

c. qu'il faut prouver son égalité.

D. qu'il ne faut pas être philanthrope.

---

7. C

READING PASSAGE

INSTRUCTIONS: *Give yourself fifteen minutes to read the following passage by Alexis de Tocqueville (ca. 750 words). Circle the words you do not recognize, but do not look them up at first. Finish the passage and verify your comprehension by taking the reading test at the end of the chapter. Then come back and work out a more exact reading of the circled words. When you have done so, practice reading the passage until you can read it in the time allotted.*

De la démocratie en Amérique

Alexis de Tocqueville

Je pense que le territoire sur lequel la race anglo-américaine doit un jour s'étendre égale les trois quarts de l'Europe. Le climat de l'Union est, à tout prendre, préférable à celui de l'Europe; ses avantages naturels sont aussi grands, il est évident que sa population ne saurait manquer d'être un jour proportionelle à la nôtre.

5

L'Europe divisée entre tant de peuples divers; l'Europe à travers les guerres sans cesse renaissantes et la barbarie du moyen âge, est parvenue à avoir quatre cent dix habitants par lieue carrée. Quelle cause si puissante pourrait empêcher les Etats-Unis d'en avoir autant un jour?

Il se passera bien des siècles avant que les divers rejetons de la race anglaise d'Amérique cessent de présenter une physionomie commune. On ne peut prévoir l'époque où l'homme pourra établir dans le Nouveau Monde l'inégalité permanente des conditions.

Quelles que soient donc les différences que la paix ou la guerre, la liberté ou la tyrannie, la prospérité ou la misère, mettent un jour dans la destinée des divers rejetons de la grande famille anglo-américaine, ils conserveront tous du moins un état social analogue et auront de commun les usages et les idées qui **découlent** [1] de l'état social.

Le seul lien de la religion a suffi au moyen age pour réunir dans une même civilisation les races diverses qui peuplèrent l'Europe. Les Anglais du Nouveau Monde ont entre eux mille autres liens, et ils vivent dans un siècle où tout cherche à s'égaliser parmi les hommes.

Le moyen âge était une époque de fractionnement. Chaque peuple, chaque province, chaque cité, chaque famille, tendait alors fortement à s'individualiser. De nos jours, un mouvement contraire se fait sentir, les peuples semblent marcher vers l'unité. Des liens intellectuels unissent entre elles les parties les plus éloignées de la terre, et les hommes ne sauraient rester un seul jour étrangers les uns aux autres, ou ignorants de ce qui se passe dans un coin quelconque de l'univers; aussi remarque-t-on aujourd'hui moins de différence entre les Européens et leurs descendants du Nouveau Monde, malgré l'océan qui les divise, qu'entre certaines villes du XIIIème siècle qui n'étaient séparées que par une rivière. . .

Si ce mouvement d'assimilation rapproche des peuples étrangers, il s'oppose à plus forte raison à ce que les rejetons du même peuple deviennent étrangers les uns aux autres.

Il arrivera donc un temps où l'on pourra voir dans l'Amérique du Nord cent cinquante millions d'hommes égaux entre eux, qui tous appartiendront à la même famille, qui auront le même point de départ, la même civilisation, la même langue, la même religion, les mêmes habitudes, les mêmes mœurs, et à travers lesquels la pensée circulera sous la même forme et se peindra des mêmes couleurs. Tout le reste est douteux, mais ceci est certain. Or, voici un fait entièrement nouveau dans le monde, et dont l'imagination elle-même ne saurait saisir la portée.

Il y a aujourd'hui sur la terre deux grands peuples qui, partis de points différents, semblent s'avancer vers le même but: ce sont les Russes et les Anglo-Américains.

Tous deux ont grandi dans l'obscurité; et tandis que les regards des hommes étaient occupés ailleurs, ils se sont placés tout à coup au premier rang des nations, et le monde a appris presque en même temps leur naissance et leur grandeur.

---

1 *derive*

Tous les autres peuples paraissent avoir atteint à peu près les limites qu'a tracées la nature, et n'avoir plus qu'à se conserver; mais eux sont en croissance: tous les autres sont arrêtés ou n'avancent qu'avec mille efforts; eux seuls marchent d'un pas aisé et rapide **dans une carrière** [2] dont l'œil ne
55 saurait encore apercevoir la borne.

L'Américain lutte contre les obstacles que lui oppose la nature, le Russe est **aux prises avec** [3] les hommes. L'un combat le désert et la barbarie, l'autre la civilisation **revêtue** [4] de toutes ses armes: aussi les conquêtes de l'Américain se font-elles avec le **soc** [5] du **laboureur,** [6] celles du Russe avec
60 **l'épée** [7] du soldat.

Pour atteindre son but, le premier **s'en repose sur** [8] l'intérêt personnel, et laisse agir, sans les diriger, la force et la raison des individus.

Le second concentre en quelque sorte dans un homme toute la puissance de la société.

65 L'un a pour principal moyen d'action la liberté; l'autre, la servitude.

Leur point de départ est différent, leurs voies sont diverses; néanmoins, chacun d'eux semble appelé par un dessein secret de la Providence à tenir un jour dans ses mains les destinées de la moitié du monde.

INSTRUCTIONS: *Circle the phrase which most nearly expresses the meaning of the text.*

1. Le premier et le deuxième paragraphes nous apprennent
A. que le territoire des Etats-Unis est plus grand que celui de l'Europe
B. que la population des Etats-Unis égalait en ce temps-là celle de l'Europe
C. que le climat du Nouveau Monde n'était pas meilleur que celui des pays européens
D. que, selon toutes les apparences, rien ne pouvait empêcher la nouvelle nation d'égaler les nations européennes.

1. D   **2.** Selon le troisième et le quatrième paragraphes, l'auteur était de l'opinion
A. que les Anglo-Américains devaient conserver encore longtemps les mêmes mœurs.
B. que l'inégalité commençait déjà à s'établir en Amérique du vivant de l'auteur.
C. que les diverses branches de la race ne se ressemblaient plus guère à cette époque.
D. que les guerres, la misère, la prospérité, etc., étaient capables de changer le caractère fondamental de la race.

2. A   **3.** Le cinquième et le sixième paragraphes nous disent
A. que les hommes au moyen age étaient plus divisés que maintenant
B. que les mêmes liens qui unissent les peuples aujourd'hui les unissaient autrefois
C. qu'à l'heure actuelle, les liens intellectuels entre les diverses parties de la terre s'affaiblissent.

2 *on a course*	**5** *plowshare*	**7** *the sword*
3 *at grips with*	**6** *plowman*	**8** *relies on*
4 *clad*		

3. A   **4.** Dans le huitième paragraphe, l'auteur prévoit pour l'Amérique
             A. une société complètement égalitaire.
             B. un avenir douteux.
             C. une Utopie imaginaire.
             D. une uniformité de mœurs mais non pas de vie intellectuelle.

4. A   **5.** Quand l'auteur regarde les Russes et les Anglo-Américains, il s'étonne de (lignes 44–50)
             A. leur origine commune.
             B. la vitesse de leur ascension au rang des plus grandes nations.
             C. leur obscurité actuelle.
             D. la restitution de leur grandeur primitive.

5. B   **6.** L'Américain (lignes 56–60) diffère du Russe en ce que celui-ci
             A. est agriculteur.
             B. poursuit son dessein à force d'armes.
             C. ne jouit pas d'un climat aussi favorable que celui-là.
             D. n'avance pas aussi rapidement que celui-là.

6. B   **7.** Les deux nations (lignes 66–68) semblent appelées à une même destinée
             A. à cause de la vigueur économique de chacune d'elles.
             B. quoiqu'elles fussent d'origines et de mœurs différentes.
             C. parce que toutes les deux ont su concentrer les pouvoirs du gouvernement dans les hommes plus capables.

7. B

Chapter Twenty

128. *Use of* chez

1. The preposition **chez** carries many different meanings according to the context. Its original meaning was *in the dwelling of* and since has acquired the extended meanings of *at the house of, at the place of,* or *business of, in the country of, in the case of, in the work,* or *thought of.* It is used with nouns or disjunctive pronouns (**moi, elle, eux,** etc.). Its translation may even require a totally different structure in English than in French:

Je vous attendrai *chez moi.*	*I will wait for you* **at my place.**
Il se fait tard—je devrais rentrer *chez moi.*	*It is getting late—I ought to go* **home.**

READING PREPARATION

INSTRUCTIONS: *Distinguish between the different meanings of* **chez.**

		1.	Tu nous attendras **chez toi,** n'est-ce pas?
1.	You will wait for us *at your place,* won't you?	**2.**	Nos amis nous attendent **chez eux.**
2.	Our friends are waiting for us *at their place.*	**3.**	Faites comme **chez vous.**
3.	Make yourself *at home.*	**4.**	Est-ce que tu vas passer le week-end **chez toi?**
4.	Are you going to spend the weekend *at your place* (*at home*)?	**5.**	Qu'est-ce que Jean fait tout seul **chez lui** tous les jours?
5.	What does John do all alone *at his place* (*house*) every day?	**6.**	Il faut que j'aille **chez le dentiste.**

6. I have to go *to the dentist.*

7. Go quickly *to the doctor's* and get me some medicine.

8. The customs *among the Eskimos* are different from *ours* (than *among us*).

9. *At my grandfather's* one makes oneself *at home.*

10. Eisenhower is the one who carried the war *to the German homeland.*

11. You should have waited for us *at your place.*

12. *In Tocqueville's works* (or *thought*, etc.) one finds a keen interest in the spirit of nations.

13. He points out ("causes to be noticed") some unexpected contradictions *among the French.*

14. *Among the latter*, one may notice the tendency to be carried to extreme acts, sometimes below the level of humanity, sometimes above.

15. One finds *among the French* sometimes a keen hatred of servitude and sometimes a passion for submission to any prince whatever.

16. One may expect to see *among the French* that their masters sometimes fear them too much and sometimes too little.

17. *In Tocqueville's works* (*writings, thought*, etc.) one may expect to find very perspicacious insights either of the spirit of diverse peoples or of their future.

---

7. Allez vite **chez le médecin** me chercher des médicaments.

8. Les coutumes **chez les Esquimaux** sont autres que **chez nous.**

9. **Chez mon grand-père** on fait comme **chez soi.**

10. C'est Eisenhower qui porta la guerre **chez les Allemands.**

11. Vous auriez dû nous attendre **chez vous.**

12. **Chez Tocqueville** on trouve un vif intérêt à l'esprit des nations.

13. Il fait remarquer des contradictions inattendues **chez les Français.**

14. **tantôt . . . tantôt**=sometimes this . . . sometimes that
Chez ceux-ci, on peut remarquer la tendance à se porter à des actes extrêmes, tantôt au–dessous du niveau de l'humanité, tantôt au–dessus.

15. On trouve **chez les Français** tantôt une haine vive de la servitude, tantôt une passion de s'asservir à un prince quelconque.

16. **s'attendre à**=to expect
On peut s'attendre à voir **chez les Français** que leurs maîtres les craignent tantôt trop tantôt trop peu.

17. **un aperçu**=an insight, a glimpse
Chez Tocqueville on peut s'attendre à trouver des aperçus très perspicaces soit de l'esprit des divers peuples soit de leur avenir.

18. **Chez lui** on devrait s'attendre à des aperçus tantôt de la vie nationale d'un peuple tantôt des forces motrices d'un pays.

18. *In his writings* one ought to expect insights sometimes into the national life of a people and sometimes into the moving forces of a country.

19. *In Bergson's works* one sometimes finds remarks on the religious phenomenon among backward peoples and sometimes among more civilized peoples.

20. *In the mind of certain people,* the work of Bergson is definitive.

21. *In the mind of others,* it is capable of improvement.

19. **Chez Bergson** on trouve des remarques sur le phénomène religieux tantôt chez les retardataires tantôt chez les peuples plus civilisés.

20. **Chez certains,** l'œuvre de Bergson est définitive.

21. **Chez d'autres,** elle est capable d'amélioration.

Before going on, review the phrases circled above.

129. *Prepositional Modifiers*

1. Prepositional phrases introduced by **en, à,** or **de** (or a contraction of these last two) are often used as modifiers. In modifiers with **à,** the sense can often be obtained by translating the **à** as *with.* If the **à** is followed by an infinitive, try *for* with the *–ing* form of the verb.

INSTRUCTIONS: *Respond to the following exercises.*

1. **une salle** = *a room*
D'ordinaire on sert le dîner dans la salle à manger.
(**La salle à manger** must be the _____.)

1. *The room for eating,* or *the dining room*
Ordinarily, one serves dinner in the dining room.

2. Une bonne dactylo doit savoir se servir d'une machine à écrire.
(**Une machine à écrire** is a _____.
One person who must know how to use one is a _____.)

2. *A machine for writing,* or *a typewriter*
Secretary, typist

3. Pour faire des vêtements un tailleur doit savoir se servir d'une machine à coudre.
(Because he makes clothes, **un tailleur** must be a _____.
The machine he uses must be _____.)

3. *a tailor*
a sewing machine (machine for sewing)
In order to make clothes a tailor must know how to use a sewing machine.

4. A mercury thermometer is used to indicate the temperature.

5. *feet*
The cat is a four-footed animal (with four feet)

6. *hair*
It is precisely at that moment that we met a very weak old man with white hair.

7. *ice cream*
Since it was excessively warm, they ended up by buying a little chocolate ice cream.

8. *tea*
tea cup
What very much distressed me was that after having spilled my tea on her new dress, I broke the tea cup.

9. *mill*
In a country like Holland where it is very windy, one could expect to see numerous wind mills.

4. Un thermomètre à mercure sert à indiquer la température.

5. Le chat est un animal à quatre pattes. (To find the meaning of **pattes** look at the context. What do animals have four of?)

6. C'est précisément à ce moment-là que nous avons rencontré un vieil homme très faible et aux cheveux blancs. (If you do not remember the meaning of **cheveux,** scrutinize the context.)

7. **finir par**=*to end up by, to do something at last*
Parce qu'il faisait excessivement chaud, ils finirent par acheter un peu de **glace au chocolat.**
(In this context **glace** must mean _____.)

8. **renverser**=*to tip over, to spill*
Ce qui m'a fort désolé c'est qu'après avoir renversé mon thé sur sa nouvelle robe, j'ai brisé **la tasse à thé.**
(The idea of spilling suggests that **thé** might have a cognate _____.
The idea of breaking suggests that **une tasse à thé** might well be a _____.)

9. **le vent**=*the wind*
Dans un pays comme la Hollande où il fait beaucoup de vent, on pourrait très bien s'attendre à voir de nombreux moulins à vent.
(**Moulin** in this context must mean _____.)

10. Les locomotives à vapeur ont été remplacées de nos jours par les trains électriques.
(Being contrasted with modern electric trains, **les locomotives à vapeur** must be _____.)

10. *steam engines*
Steam engines have been replaced nowadays by electric trains.

11. D'habitude c'est dans la salle de bain qu'on se lave.
(The reference to washing oneself suggests that the **salle de bain** is the _____.)

11. *bathroom*
Usually, one washes oneself in the bathroom.

12. On s'attendrait à voir la Joconde (Mona Lisa) dans une galerie de peinture.
(**Une galerie de peinture** must be a _____.)

12. *picture* or *art gallery*
One would expect to see the Mona Lisa in an art gallery.

13. Heureusement, sa nouvelle robe, sur laquelle je viens de renverser ma tasse de thé, est en coton.

13. Fortunately her new dress on which I have just spilled my cup of tea is cotton.
(Notice that **en** here indicates the material out of which the dress is made.)

14. J'ai eu le malheur de briser cette tasse à thé en la laissant tomber sur une table en métal.

14. I had the misfortune of breaking this tea cup by dropping it (letting it fall) on a metal table.

15. La montre en or, qui appartenait à mon ancien professeur, est disparu.

15. The gold watch, which used to belong to my former professor, has disappeared.

16. **un étage**=*a story (floor) of a house*
La maison doit être ancienne—on monte au troisième étage par un escalier en colimaçon.
(Un **escalier en colimaçon** must be a _____.)

16. *spiral stair case*
The house must be very old—one goes up to the fourth floor by a spiral stair case. (The French start numbering the floors with the first one above the ground floor, whereas the Americans start with the ground floor.)

17. Elle porte des vêtements tout noirs. Elle doit être en deuil.
(The reference to black clothes suggests that **en deuil** must mean _____.)

17. *in mourning*
She is wearing completely black clothes. She must be in mourning.
(Notice that **en** here indicates a condition.)

18. La France et l'Allemagne ont souvent été en guerre.

18. France and Germany have often been at war.

19. Un soldat peut rentrer chez lui quand il est en congé.
(**En congé** probably means _____.)

19. *on leave,* or *furlough*
A soldier can return to his home when he is on leave.

20. **le veston**=*the suit coat*
Quand il fait très chaud, on aime ôter son veston pour travailler en bras de chemise.
(Since one is **en bras de chemise** after taking off one's suit coat, **en bras de chemise** probably means _____.)

20. *in one's shirt sleeves*
When it is very warm, one likes to take off one's suit coat in order to work in one's shirt sleeves.

21. Parce qu'il paraissait toujours peureux, il fut traité de lâche.
(**lâche,** being associated with **peureux,** must mean _____.)

21. *cowardly*
Because he always appeared to be fearful, he was treated as a coward.

22. Les batailles sont toujours inattendues —c'est une drôle de guerre.

22. The battles are always unexpected— it's a funny war. (Notice that it is the meaning of the expression, and not the individual words, which is translated, and the English phrase has no preposition.)

23. Il partit de nuit.

23. He left by night.

24. Moïse était âgé de cent vingt ans, dit-on, quand il mourut.

24. Moses was a hundred and twenty years old, it is said, when he died.

130. *Review Section*

INSTRUCTIONS: *Re-read the sections on relative pronouns (Ch. Fourteen) and interrogatives (Ch. Fifteen). Then read the following exercises, marking for future review the words you do not recognize.*

1. **à propos de**=*concerning, with regard to*
Vous lisiez tout à l'heure des pensées à propos de l'esprit d'une nation.

1. A little while ago you were reading some thoughts concerning the spirit of a nation.	**2.** **soulever une question**=*to raise a question* Renan soulève quelques questions à propos de l'esprit d'une nation.
2. Renan raises a few questions concerning the spirit of a nation.	**3.** Voici quelques-unes des questions qu'il soulève et auxquelles il répond.
3. Here are a few of the questions that he raises and which he answers.	**4.** A vrai dire, il ne pose pas les questions d'une façon directe.
4. To tell the truth, he does not pose the questions directly (in a direct way).	**5.** A vrai dire, il les suggère plutôt.
5. To tell the truth, he rather suggests them.	**6.** En voici quelques-unes.
6. Here are a few of them.	**7.** Qu'est-ce qu'une nation?
7. What is a nation?	**8.** Qu'est-ce qui constitue l'âme d'une nation?
8. What constitutes the soul of a nation? (Remember that **est-ce que** and **est-ce qui** are simply question signals— it is the first **qui** or **que** which asks *who* or *what*.)	**9.** Qui est-ce qui constitue la nation?
9. Who constitutes the nation?	**10.** De quoi cette âme est-elle composée?
10. Of what does this soul consist?	**11.** A quoi la nation doit-elle son âme?
11. To what does the nation owe its soul?	**12.** Est-ce que la nation est l'aboutissement d'un long passé de sacrifices et de dévouements ou est-ce que l'homme s'improvise?
12. Is the nation the end result of a long past of sacrifices and devotion or is man improvised (formed by the needs of the moment?)	**13.** **le legs**=*the legacy* Lequel des deux est le plus important dans l'esprit d'une nation—le consentement actuel de vivre ensemble ou le legs du passé?
13. Which is more important in the spirit of a nation—the present consent to live together or the legacy of the past?	**14.** D'où vient le legs dont nous sommes les héritiers? (The association with **legs** suggests that **héritiers** indicates _____.)
14. *heirs* Where does the legacy of which we are the heirs come from?	**15.** Pourquoi sommes-nous ce que nous sommes?

15. Why are we what we are?

16. Qu'est-ce qui nous a faits ce que nous sommes?

16. What has made us what we are?

17. Qui est-ce qui nous a faits ce que nous sommes?

17. Who has made us what we are?

18. Qui est-ce qui nous a légué notre héritage?

18. Who has bequeathed to us our inheritance?

19. Quel est le capital social sur lequel on assied une idée nationale?
(If you remember that one meaning of **asseoir** is *to seat,* what might the context suggest as another meaning?)

19. *To base, to found* (or *to lay the foundation,* etc.)
What is the social capital upon which one founds (or bases) a national idea?

20. **les douanes**=*the customs* (*offices*)
Lesquelles sont plus importantes à une nation—les frontières et les douanes communes ou les espérances que les citoyens possèdent en commun?
(Being associated with **douanes**, **frontières** will probably not be "frontiers" but _____.)

20. *borders*
Which are more important to a nation—common borders and customs offices or the hopes which the citizens possess in common?

21. A-t-on raison de dire à ses ancêtres, "Nous sommes ce que vous fûtes"?
(Is **fûtes** the Imperfect Subjunctive or Past Definite of **être?**)

21. *Past Definite*—the Imperfect Subjunctive is **"vous fussiez"** (but **il fût**).
Is one right in saying to one's ancestors, "We are what you were"?

22. N'est-ce pas que nous serons ce que vous êtes?

22. Is it not true that we will be what you are?

23. **la patrie**=*the country, the homeland*
N'est-ce pas là l'hymne abrégé de toute patrie?

23. Is this not the anthem in short of any country?

24. **malgré**=*in spite of*
Qu'est-ce qui unit la patrie malgré les diversités de langue et de race?

24. What unites the country in spite of the diversities of language and race?

25. **à cause de**=*because of*
Est-ce qu'une patrie devient prospère malgré ou à cause des diversités de ses citoyens?

25. Does a country become prosperous in spite of or because of the diversities of its citizens?

26. **en fait de** = *with regard to*
N'est-ce pas, en fait de souvenirs nationaux, que les deuils valent mieux que les triomphes?

26. Is it not true, with regard to national memories, that times of mourning are better (worth more) than times of triumph?

27. De quoi dépend l'existence d'une nation?

27. Upon what does the existence of a nation depend?

28. Est-ce que les nations sont quelque chose d'éternel?

28. Are nations something eternal? (Notice that **d'** has no corresponding word in the English translation of this French pattern.)

29. **remplacer** = *to replace*
Qu'est-ce qui les remplacera?

29. What will replace them?

30. Quels sont les droits des populations en fait de ces questions diplomatiques?

30. What are the rights of the populations with regard to these diplomatic questions?

31. **jouir** = *to enjoy*
De quels droits jouissent les populations en fait de ces questions diplomatiques?

31. What rights do the populations enjoy with regard to these diplomatic questions?

32. Desquels jouissent-ils?

32. Which ones do they enjoy?

33. Rien ne peut remplacer les droits des gens.

33. Nothing can replace the rights of people.

34. De quelque nation que nous soyons, nous devons quand même le présent au passé.
(Since **devons** is not followed by an infinitive, does it mean *owe* or *must?*)

34. *owe*
Of whatever nation we might be, we still owe the present to the past.

35. Qu'il s'agisse de frontières disputées ou d'autres questions diplomatiques, consultons quand même les populations en question.

35. Whether it concerns disputed borders or other diplomatic questions, let us, nonetheless, consult the populations in question.

36. Avoir souffert, joui, espéré ensemble, voilà ce qui vaut mieux que des douanes communes pour unifier la patrie.
(Here, does **voilà** serve to indicate time or to point out?)

36. *to point out*
To have suffered, enjoyed, and hoped together, that is what is worth more for unifying the country than having the same customs offices.

37. Voilà de longues années que nous souffrons, jouissons, et espérons ensemble malgré la diversité de la nation.
(In this sentence does **voilà** indicate time or point out?)

---

37. *It indicates time.*
For (many) long years we have suffered, enjoyed, and hoped together in spite of the diversity of the nation.

38. Voilà de nombreuses années qu'on ne consultait pas les habitants des régions disputées malgré le droit de ceux-ci de donner leur avis là-dessus.
(**Ceux-ci,** being masculine and plural can refer only to _____.)

---

38. **les habitants**
For many years no one had consulted the inhabitants of the disputed regions in spite of their right to give their opinion about it.

39. Prétendez-vous remplacer la guerre et la diplomatie par des moyens d'une simplicité enfantine?
(Since the cognate meaning of "*pretend*" does not fit the situation, which of these two expresses the meaning? 1) *to claim* 2) *to require*)

---

39. *to claim*
Do you claim that you will replace war and diplomacy with childishly simple methods?

40. **rire**=*to laugh*
Ce que l'auteur vient d'en dire fera rire les gens.

---

40. What the author just said about it will make people laugh.

41. Ce que l'on vient de dire là-dessus me fait sourire.
(The combination of **sou(s)** and **rire** suggests _____.)

---

41. *to smile*
What has just been said about it makes me smile.

42. Voilà qui me fait sourire.

---

42. Now that's what makes me smile.

Review, and then go on to the vocabulary section.

VOCABULARY SECTION

INSTRUCTIONS: *Associate the meaning of the indicated word with other words of the same family.*

1. **tâtonner**=*to grope, to feel one's way*
L'aveugle a cherché son chemin **en tâtonnant**.

1. The blind man tried to find his way *by groping*.	**2.** Il n'y avait pas de lumière, mais après bien des **tâtonnements** il a réussi à trouver la porte.
2. There was no light, but after many *gropings* he succeeded in finding the door.	**3.** Ne pouvant plus voir, il cherchait son chemin **à tâtons**.
3. Not being able to see any longer, he tried to find his way *gropingly*, (or *by groping*).	**4.** **le fruit**=*the fruit* L'année passée avait été **fructueuse**.
4. The past year had been *fruitful*.	**5.** N'ayant pas réussi à ramasser les renseignements nécessaires, il tenait l'entreprise pour **infructueuse**.
5. Not having succeeded in gathering the necessary information, he held the undertaking to be *unfruitful*.	**6.** Il a coupé ses pommiers parce qu'ils n'avaient pas **fructifié**.
6. He cut down his apple trees because they *had not borne fruit*.	**7.** **obéir**=*to obey* Il a fini par **obéir** aux ordres de son père.
7. He ended up by *obeying* the orders of his father.	**8.** Il a fini par **désobéir** aux ordres de son père.
8. He ended up by *disobeying* the orders of his father.	**9.** Cette nation française est tantôt l'ennemi déclaré de toute **obéissance**, tantôt une nation qui semble douée pour la servitude.
9. This French nation is sometimes the declared enemy of all *obedience* and sometimes a nation which seems gifted for servitude.	**10.** Elle fait voir une passion pour la **désobéissance**.
10. It manifests a passion for *disobedience*.	**11.** **la mode**=*the fashion* Elle s'adonne à tout ce qui est **à la mode**.
11. It gives itself to everything that is *in fashion*.	**12.** Cependant, selon Renan, le plus sûr moyen d'avoir raison dans l'avenir est, à certaines heures, de savoir se résigner à être **démodé**.
12. However, according to Renan, the surest way to be right in the future is to know how, at certain times, to resign oneself to being *out of fashion* (or obsolete).	

TESTING EXERCISE

INSTRUCTIONS: *Circle the letter which gives the best translation of the word indicated.*

1. La poésie **chez** Lamartine n'est pas la même que **chez** Vigny.
   A. at the home of   B. in the work of   C. at the place of business of

---

1. B   2. **Chez les Américains** on ne peut se passer de l'automobile.
   A. In American homes   B. Among Americans   C. In American offices

---

2. B   3. On aime se croire maître **chez soi.**
   A. in one's thoughts   B. in one's home   C. in one's work

---

3. B   4. **Chez les Français** il n'y a pas d'équivalent du football américain.
   A. In French homes   B. In French offices   C. Among the French

---

4. C   5. Si vous avez mal aux dents, vous allez **chez** le dentiste.
   A. to the office of   B. to the home of   C. in the thought of

---

5. A   6. Si vous ne faites pas attention, vous ne devez pas **vous attendre à** comprendre la pensée de Pascal.
   A. wait for   B. hear about   C. expect to

---

6. C   7. **Tantôt** on pouvait le suivre **tantôt** on ne pouvait rien comprendre.
   A. As soon as   B. As much . . . as   C. Sometimes . . . sometimes

---

7. C   8. Il a fait la sottise de briser **sa tasse à thé.**
   A. his cup of tea   B. his tea cup

---

8. B   9. **Qui est-ce que vous avez vu?**
   A. Who saw you?   B. What did you see?   C. Whom did you see?

---

9. C

READING PASSAGES

INSTRUCTIONS: *Give yourself twelve minutes to read the first passage of 650 words and seven minutes for the second. Circle the words which you do not immediately recognize, but do not look them up the first time through. Verify your comprehension of the passage by answering the questions at the end, and then come back to the circled words and work out their meanings more precisely. Then practice reading the passages until you can read them in the time allowed. The two reading passages in this chapter give analyses of the French nation and spirit by two noted French authors.*

Qu'est-ce qu'une nation?

D'après E. Renan
Conférence faite en Sorbonne, le 11 mars 1882

Une nation est une âme, un principe spirituel. Deux choses qui, à vrai dire, n'en font qu'une, constituent cette âme, ce principe spirituel. L'une est dans le passé, l'autre dans le présent. L'une est la possession en commun d'un riche legs de souvenirs; l'autre est le consentement actuel, le désir de
5   vivre ensemble, la volonté de continuer **à faire valoir** [1] l'héritage qu'on a reçu indivis. L'homme ne s'improvise pas. La nation, comme l'individu, est **l'aboutissement** [2] d'un long passé d'efforts, de sacrifices et de dévouements. Le culte des ancêtres est de tous le plus légitime; les ancêtres nous ont faits ce que nous sommes. Un passé héroïque, de grands hommes, de la gloire
10   (j'entends de la véritable), voilà le capital social sur lequel on assied une idée nationale. Avoir des gloires communes dans le passé, une volonté commune dans le présent; avoir fait de grandes choses ensemble, vouloir en faire encore, voilà les conditions essentielles pour être un peuple. On aime en proportion des sacrifices qu'on a **consentis,** [3] des maux qu'on a soufferts.
15   On aime la maison qu'on a bâtie et qu'on transmet. Le chant spartiate: "Nous sommes ce que vous fûtes; nous serons ce que vous êtes", est dans sa simplicité l'hymne abrégé de toute patrie.

Dans le passé, un héritage de gloire et de regrets à partager, dans l'avenir un même programme à réaliser; avoir souffert, joui, espéré ensemble, voilà
20   ce qui vaut mieux que des douanes communes et des frontières conformes aux idées stratégiques; voilà ce que l'on comprend malgré les diversités de race et de langue. Je disais tout à l'heure: "avoir souffert ensemble"; oui, la souffrance en commun unit plus que la joie. En fait de souvenirs nationaux, les deuils valent mieux que les triomphes; car ils imposent des devoirs; ils
25   commandent l'effort en commun.

Une nation est donc une grande solidarité, constituée par le sentiment des sacrifices qu'on a faits et de ceux qu'on est disposé à faire encore. Elle suppose un passé; elle se résume pourtant dans le présent par un fait tangible: le consentement, le désir clairement exprimé de continuer la vie commune.
30   L'existence d'une nation est un plébiscite de tous les jours, comme l'existence de l'individu est une affirmation perpétuelle de la vie. . .

Il est clair qu'en pareille matière aucun principe ne doit être poussé à l'excès. Les vérités de cet ordre ne sont applicables que dans leur ensemble et d'une façon très générale. Les volontés humaines changent; mais qu'est-ce
35   qui ne change pas ici-bas? Les nations ne sont pas quelque chose d'éternel. Elles ont commencé, elles finiront. La confédération européenne, probablement les remplacera. . .

Je me résume. L'homme n'est esclave ni de sa race, ni de sa langue, ni de sa religion, ni du cours des fleuves, ni de la direction des chaînes de

---

1 *to preserve*   **2** *the end result*   **3** *authorized*

40 montagnes. Une grande agrégation d'hommes, saine d'esprit et chaude de
cœur, crée une conscience morale qui s'appelle une nation. Tant que cette
conscience morale prouve sa force par les sacrifices qu'exige l'abdication de
l'individu au profit d'une communauté, elle est légitime, elle a le droit d'exister.
Si des doutes s'élèvent sur ses frontières, consultez les populations disputées.

45 Elles ont bien le droit d'avoir un avis sur la question. Voilà qui fera sourire
les **transcendants** [4] de la politique, ces infaillibles qui passent leur vie à
se tromper et qui, du haut de leurs principes supérieurs, prennent en pitié
notre **terre-à-terre.** [5] "Consulter les populations, fi donc! quelle naïveté!
Voilà bien ces chétives idées françaises qui prétendent remplacer la diplomatie

50 et la guerre par des moyens d'une simplicité enfantine". Attendons, Messieurs;
laissons passer le règne des transcendants; sachons subir le dédain des forts.
Peut-être, après bien des tâtonnements infructueux, reviendra-t-on à nos
modestes solutions empiriques. Le moyen d'avoir raison dans l'avenir est,
à certaines heures, de savoir se résigner à être démodé.

   1. A nation derives its spiritual existence from (lines 1–6) :
      A. the present aspirations of its inhabitants
      B. its past efforts
      C. both the present and the past

---

1. C   **2.** Lines 6–11 state that the capital of a national spirit is:
      A. a heroic past   C. the desire to surpass one's ancestors
      B. a great leader   D. a sense of being superior to other nations.

---

2. A   **3.** The most unifying force of a nation is (lines 18–25) :
      A. the geography of the country
      B. the remembrance of suffering endured in common
      C. the great national triumphs
      D. the desire for the future progress of the nation.

---

3. B   **4.** Lines 32–38 suggest that the idea of a European confederation is:
      A. highly improbable because of the nationalistic spirit of each nation
      B. likely, because of the present decadent state of Europe
      C. probable, because nations evolve
      D. unlikely, because this principle cannot be pushed too far.

---

4. C   **5.** Lines 40–46 express the idea that:
      A. the question of national borders should be decided by principles, not
         conscience
      B. the sense of nationhood is legitimate as long as the people involved still
         consent to sacrifice for it
      C. no individual good should be sacrificed for a nebulous common good
      D. it is of doubtful value to decide momentous national questions by con-
         sulting the populace

---

4 *superior beings*   **5** *common placeness*

5. B   **6.** Renan senses that the immediate attitude toward his proposal will be (lines 45–50) :

                    A. enthusiastic   C. moderately favorable
                    B. violently divided   D. disdainful

---

6. D

INSTRUCTIONS: *The next passage contains about 360 words. Follow the same procedure as above, giving yourself seven minutes for the reading.*

La nation française

From Alexis de Tocqueville, *L'Ancien régime et la Révolution*

Quand je considère cette nation en elle-même, je la trouve plus extra-ordinaire qu'aucun des événements de son histoire. En a-t-il paru sur la terre une seule qui fût si remplie de contrastes et si extrême dans chacun de ses actes; plus conduite par des sensations, moins par des principes; faisant
5 ainsi toujours plus mal ou mieux qu'on ne s'y attendait, tantôt au-dessous du niveau commun de l'humanité, tantôt fort au-dessus; un peuple telle-ment **inaltérable** [1] dans ses principaux instincts, qu'on le reconnaît encore dans des portraits qui ont été faits de lui il y a deux ou trois mille ans, et en même temps tellement mobile dans ses pensées journalières et dans
10 ses goûts, qu'il finit par devenir un spectacle inattendu à lui-même, et demeure souvent aussi surpris que les étrangers à la vue de ce qu'il vient de faire; le plus **casanier** [2] et le plus routinier de tous quand on l'abandonne à lui-même, et lorsqu'une fois on l'a **arraché** [3] malgré lui à son logis et à ses habitudes, prêt à pousser jusqu'au bout du monde et à tout oser; indocile par tempéra-
15 ment, et s'accommodant mieux toutefois de l'empire arbitraire et même violent d'un prince que du gouvernement régulier et libre des principaux citoyens; aujourd'hui l'ennemi déclaré de toute obéissance, demain mettant à servir une sorte de passion que les nations les mieux douées pour la servitude ne peuvent atteindre; conduit par **un fil** [4] tant que personne ne résiste,
20 ingouvernable dès que l'exemple de la résistance est donné quelque part; trompant toujours ainsi ses maîtres, qui le craignent trop ou trop peu; jamais si libre **qu'il faille** [5] désespérer de **l'asservir,** [6] ni si asservi qu'il ne puisse encore briser **le joug;** [7] apte à tout, mais n'excellant que dans la guerre; adorateur du **hasard,** [8] de la force, du succès, de l'éclat et du bruit plus que
25 de la vraie gloire; plus capable d'héroïsme que de vertu, de génie que de bon sens, propre à concevoir d'immenses desseins plutôt qu'à **parachever** [9] d'immenses entreprises; la plus brillante et la plus dangereuse des nations de

---

1 *unvarying*   4 *a thread*   7 *the yoke*
2 *home-loving*   5 *that it is necessary*   8 *chance*
3 *torn away*   6 *to enslave*   9 *to carry out*

l'Europe et la mieux faite pour y devenir **tour à tour** [10] un objet d'admiration, de haine, de pitié, de terreur, mais jamais d'indifférence.

1. In lines 1–4 the author states that the French nation:
   A. is governed by principles
   B. reacts in a predictable manner
   C. is more astonishing than any of its historical events

1. C   2. In lines 5–13 he goes on to say that the French nation:
   A. has undergone profound and fundamental changes during the past few generations
   B. surprises itself with its occasional lack of stability
   C. is almost never homeloving and lethargic
   D. even when once aroused is unimaginative in its reactions

2. B   3. In lines 14–18 he states that the French
   A. adapt more easily to a government made up of its principal citizens
   B. are sometimes more suited by temperament to an arbitrary and even violent form of government
   C. are law-abiding and predictable in their political reactions
   D. are always less docile, however, than other nations accustomed to greater social controls.

3. B   4. In lines 19–23 the author states that the French:
   A. do not excel in war
   B. are viewed with little concern by the other countries of Europe
   C. prefer solid success to superficial finery
   D. have more genius than common sense.

4. D

---

10 *alternately*

Chapter Twenty-One

131. *Review of* que

1. The word **que,** as you have learned, has many uses and meanings in French. Here is a summary and a review of the more common ones:

(1) **Que** as a pronoun

Que regardez–vous?	*What are you looking at?*
Le livre *que* vous avez lu est le sien.	*The book **which** you have read is his.*
L'auteur *que* nous lisons est assez médiocre.	*The author **whom** we are reading is quite mediocre.*

(2) **Que** as a conjunction

The most common meaning of **que** as a conjunction is *that,* but it may sometimes replace such compound conjunctions as **afin que, à moins que, avant que, depuis que, lorsque, sans que:**

Il a dit *qu'*il allait venir.	*He said **that** he was going to come.*
Venez *que* (afin que) je vous parle.	*Come here **so that** I may talk to you.*
Il ne peut rien faire *que* (sans que) je ne le lui dise.	*He can't do anything **unless** I tell him.*
Un jour *qu'*il faisait beau . . .	*A day **when** the weather was fine . . .*

(3) **Que** as the replacement of an initial adverb or conjunction

In this case **que** is translated in the same way as the initial conjunction:

Quand on est jeune et *qu'*on se porte bien, on doit travailler.	*When one is young and **when** one is in good health, one must work.*
Si j'ai le temps et *que* j'aie l'argent, je le ferai.	*If I have time and **if** I have the money, I'll do it.*
Comme il faisait nuit et *que* nous ne pouvions voir, nous sommes rentrés.	*As it was dark and **as** we were unable to see, we returned home.*

(4) **Que** as a term of comparison:

Elle est aussi grande *que* sa sœur.	*She is as big **as** her sister.*
Il est moins âgé *que* son frère.	*He is younger **than** his brother.*
C'est le plus grand que j'aie vu.	*It is the largest **that** I have seen.*

(5) **Que** as an indicator of an alternative:

*Qu'*il le fasse ou non . . .	***Whether** he does it or not . . .*
*Qu'*il fasse beau, qu'il fasse mauvais, j'aime sortir.	***Whether** it is good or bad weather, I like to go out.*
*Qu'*elle joue ou qu'elle chante, elle est toujours vedette.	***Whether** she plays or sings, she is always a star.*

(6) **Que** as the sign of the third person imperative:

*Qu'*il nous dise la vérité!	***Let** him tell us the truth!*
Que les autres s'approchent.	***Have** the others come forward.*
*Qu'*on nous amène les prisonniers.	***Let** the prisoners be brought to us.*

(7) **Que** as introducing an exclamatory statement:

Que de monde!	***What** a lot of people!*
Que vous me semblez beau!	***How** handsome you seem to me!*
*Qu'*elle est belle!	***How** beautiful she is!*

(8) **Que** is used in various expressions as an expletive or intensifier:

Pensez-vous qu'il vienne? ***Que** si, il viendra.	*Do you think that he will come? **Certainly**, he'll come.*
Je pense *que oui.*	*I think **so**.*
Il dit *que non.*	*He says **not**.*
C'est un beau cheval *que* le vôtre.	*That's a fine horse **of** yours.*

(9) **Que** as the indicator of an exception to a negation:

Elle ne fait *que* pleurer. — *She does nothing **but** weep.*
On n'a *qu'*une vie. — *One has **only** one life.*

(10) **Que** meaning *why:*

Que ne le disiez-vous? — ***Why** didn't you say so?*

(11) **Que** in expressions of time:

Il y a dix ans *qu'*il est absent. — *He has been absent **for** ten years.*

(12) **Que** in indefinite expressions:

Quoi que vous ayez dit, il ne vous a pas cru. — ***Whatever** you might have said, he did not believe you.*
Si intelligent *qu'*il soit, il n'a pas compris. — ***However** intelligent he might be, he did not understand.*

READING PREPARATION

INSTRUCTIONS: *Give the meaning of* **que** *in each of the following sentences. Continue to circle the words which you do not immediately recognize.*

	1. Approchez, que je vous regarde.
1. Come closer so that I may look at you.	2. Qu'il vienne, puisqu'il veut me parler.
2. Let him come, since he wants to speak to me.	3. Sortons des ténèbres que nous puissions voir clair.
3. Let us go out of the darkness so that we may see clearly.	4. Il est aussi intelligent que son ami.
4. He is as intelligent as his friend.	5. Elle est plus jeune que sa sœur.
5. She is younger than her sister.	6. Cette conférence était moins intéressante que celle de l'autre soir.
6. This lecture was less interesting than that of the other evening.	7. Quoi qu'il dise, on ne le croira pas.
7. Whatever he says, they will not believe him.	8. Quoi que vous cherchiez, vous ne le trouverez point. (**Quoi que**—*whatever/although*)

8. *Whatever* you are looking for, you will not find it.	**9.** Quoique vous le cherchiez, vous ne le trouverez jamais. (**Quoique**=*whatever/although*)
9. *Although* you might look for it, you will never find it.	**10.** Quoi qu'il arrive, il ne pourra en tirer aucun avantage.
10. Whatever happens, he will not be able to gain any advantage from it.	**11.** Quoi qu'il en soit, vous le verrez à découvert. (**à découvert**—*vaguely/plainly*)
11. Be that as it may, you will see it *plainly*.	**12.** **se vanter de**=*to boast of* S'est-il vanté de quoi que ce soit?
12. Did he boast of anything at all?	**13.** La fortune ne paraît jamais si aveugle qu'à ceux à qui elle ne fait pas de bien. La Rochefoucauld
13. Fortune never appears so blind as to those to whom it does no good.	**14.** Que dites-vous?
14. What are you saying?	**15.** Que ne le disait-il?
15. Why didn't he say so?	**16.** Nous ne savions que faire ni où chercher.
16. We didn't know what to do nor where to look.	**17.** Cette femme est moins heureuse qu'elle n'en a l'air.
17. That woman is less happy than she seems.	**18.** Faites ce que je vous dis.
18. Do what I tell you.	**19.** Ce que vous faites est peu louable.
19. What you are doing is to be blamed.	**20.** Il ne savait plus ce qu'il fallait faire.
20. He no longer knew what had to be done.	**21.** Dites ce qui bon vous semble.
21. Say what you think best.	**22.** Que vous ayez tort ou que vous ayez raison, c'est égal.
22. Whether you are right or wrong, it is all the same.	**23.** Qu'il pleuve ou qu'il fasse beau, je viendrai.
23. Whether it rains or shines, I will come.	**24.** Que tu le veuilles ou non, il n'a pas l'âme fort élevée.
24. Whether you like it or not, he doesn't have a very elevated mind (soul).	**25.** Que ne vient-il nous voir lui-même?

25. Why doesn't he come to see us himself?	**26.** Imbécile que vous êtes!
26. You imbecile!	**27.** Pauvre malheureux que tu es!
27. Poor wretch that you are!	**28.** Que de gens! Je n'ai jamais vu une telle foule.
28. So many people! I have never seen such a crowd.	**29.** Que de déceptions, que de maux!
29. What disappointments, what troubles!	**30.** Que c'est bien vrai!
30. How true it is!	**31.** C'est se tromper que de croire qu'il n'y ait que de violentes passions. La Rochefoucauld
31. It is to be mistaken to think that there are only violent passions.	**32.** Couvert de sang qu'il était, on ne le reconnaissait plus.
32. Covered with blood as he was, he was no longer recognizable.	**33.** Si nous résistons à nos passions, c'est plus par leur faiblesse que par notre force. La Rochefoucauld
33. If we resist our passions, it is more because of their weakness than our strength.	**34.** On ne loue d'ordinaire que pour être loué. La Rochefoucauld
34. One usually praises only to be praised.	**35.** Il n'y a que lui qui sache ce qui en est.
35. He is the only one who knows what has happened to it.	**36.** Qu'il sorte à l'instant.
36. Have him leave immediately!	**37.** Il n'a fait qu'entrer et sortir.
37. He did nothing more than to go in and out.	**38.** Il n'y a pour l'homme que trois événements: naître, vivre, et mourir. Il ne se sent pas naître, il souffre à mourir et il oublie de vivre. La Bruyère
38. There are only three events for man: to be born, to live, and to die. He is not aware of being born, he suffers in dying, and he forgets to live.	**39.** Qu'il espère tant qu'il voudra, cela ne changera rien.
39. Let him hope as much as he wants, it won't change anything.	**40.** Qu'elle se fatigue le moins possible quand elle rentrera chez elle.

40.	Let her tire herself the least possible when she returns home.	**41.**	Que nous nous éclaircissions sur ce sujet.
41.	Let us inform ourselves on this matter.	**42.**	Que celui qui est satisfait en fasse profession.
42.	Let him who is satisfied say so.	**43.**	Qu'on soulève la question à la prochaine conférence.
43.	Let the question be raised at the next meeting.	**44.**	Comprenez-vous ce que c'est que l'âme d'un peuple?
44.	Do you understand what the soul of a people is?	**45.**	Malgré une fortune considérable il ne sait ce que c'est que de rire.
45.	In spite of a considerable fortune he does not know what it is to laugh.	**46.**	Mais ce qu'il aimait le plus, c'étaient les batailles inattendues.
46.	The unexpected battles were what he liked the best.	**47.**	Ce qui lui plaît le moins, ce sont les visites chez le dentiste.
47.	The trips to the dentist are what pleases him the least.	**48.**	Ce que je veux apprendre, c'est l'espagnol.
48.	What I wish to learn is Spanish.	**49.**	Comme il avait fini son travail et qu'il lui restait encore du temps, il fuma une cigarette.
49.	As he had finished his work and some time remained, he smoked a cigarette.	**50.**	Lorsqu'on est en congé et qu'on n'a pas d'argent, on doit rester chez soi.
50.	When one is on vacation (leave) and when one has no money, it is necessary to stay home.	**51.**	Si on vient et qu'on veuille me parler, je serai chez moi.
51.	If somebody comes and wishes to speak with me, I will be at home.	**52.**	Il ne se passe jamais une semaine qu'il ne vienne chez nous.
52.	Never a week passes that he does not come to our place.	**53.**	Quand il viendra et qu'il vous trouvera ici, il se mettra en colère.
53.	When he comes and finds you here, he will be angry.	**54.**	Puisque vous avez fini et que vous avez le temps, venez voir le jardin.
54.	Since you have finished and you have the time, come see the garden.	**55.**	Qu'il s'agisse du rouge ou du noir, vous n'avez qu'à choisir.
55.	Whether it be a question of the red or the black, you have only to choose.	**56.**	Il ne peut faire un pas que son frère ne le suive.

56. He cannot take a step without his brother following him.

57. In a little while you will read some pages that Pascal addressed to some libertine friends in the seventeenth century.

58. The idea of believing suggests he was *religious*.
It must be explained that Pascal was a convinced believer.

59. He was addressing himself to freethinkers whom he wished to convert.

60. Unbelieving though his friends were, Pascal wanted to have them examine the Christian religion.

61. He advanced all kinds of reasonings which he believed capable of shaking them and causing them to come out of their indifference.

62. In a little while you will be able to give your opinion about the matter.

63. Let them learn at least what the religion is that they are attacking, before they attack it.

64. Let them reflect on the human condition.

65. The ultimate ends of life are hidden from us, he says.

66. I don't know what my body is, nor my senses, nor my soul—nor who placed me in the world.

67. But that which I know the least about is that very death which I cannot escape.

57. **sous peu**=*in a little while*
Vous lirez sous peu des pages que Pascal adressait à des amis libertins au dix-septième siècle.

58. Il faut expliquer que Pascal était un croyant convaincu.
(Etait-il **religieux** ou **irréligieux?**)

59. Il s'adressait à des libres penseurs qu'il voulait convertir.

60. Tout incrédules que fussent ses amis, Pascal voulait leur faire examiner la religion chrétienne.

61. Il avança toutes sortes de raisonnements qu'il croyait capables de les secouer et de les faire sortir de leur indifférence.

62. Vous pourrez sous peu donner votre avis là-dessus.

63. Qu'ils apprennent au moins, dit-il, quelle est la religion qu'ils combattent, avant que de la combattre.

64. Qu'on fasse réflexion sur la condition humaine.

65. Les fins de la vie nous sont cachées, dit-il.

66. Je ne sais ce que c'est que mon corps, que mes sens, que mon âme–ni qui m'a mis au monde.

67. Mais ce que j'ignore le plus est cette mort même que je ne saurais éviter.

68. Qu'on s'imagine un nombre d'hommes dans les chaînes et qui attendent la mort.

68.	Let us imagine a number of men in chains who are awaiting death.	69.	Voilà ce que c'est que la condition humaine.
69.	That is what the human condition is.		

TESTING EXERCISE

INSTRUCTIONS: *Choose the answer corresponding to the best translation of the indicated words. The numbers refer to Section 131.*

1. Je ne sais ce que c'est que le monde ni **que** moi-même ni **que** mon corps.
   A. which   B. than   C. that   D. not translated

1. D
(8)

2. Je me trouve attaché à un coin sans que je sache pourquoi je suis placé en ce lieu plûtot **qu'**en un autre.
   A. which   B. that   C. what   D. than

2. D
(2)

3. Tout ce que je sais est **que** je dois bientôt mourir.
   A. what   B. than   C. that   D. which

3. C
(2)

4. **Qu'**on s'imagine un nombre d'hommes dans les chaînes.
   A. which   B. that   C. what   D. let

4. D
(6)

5. Il ne jouera plus **que** je ne le lui dise.
   A. let   B. what   C. than   D. unless

5. D
(3)

6. Quand on a faim et **qu'**on n'a pas d'argent on se passe de manger.
   A. when   B. that   C. only   D. let

6. A
(3)

7. Elle est moins jeune **qu'**elle n'en a l'air.
   A. which   B. than   C. that   D. what

7. B
(4)

8. **Qu'**il y avait de gens!
   A. let   B. that   C. what a lot   D. which

8. C
(7)

9. Pensez-vous qu'il ait raison? **Que** si, il a raison.
   A. which   B. than   C. certainly   D. that

9. C
(8)

10. Il **n'**en a dit **que** quelques mots.
    A. which   B. than   C. only   D. that

10. C
(9)

11. Voilà deux mois **que** vous étudiez
    A. which   B. for   C. than   D. unless

11. B
(11)

READING PASSAGE

INSTRUCTIONS: *Read the following passage from Pascal and verify your comprehension by taking the test at the end of the chapter.*

Dialogue avec les libertins

Pascal

Qu'**ils** [1] apprennent au moins quelle est la religion qu'ils combattent, avant que de la combattre. Si cette religion se vantait d'avoir une vue claire de Dieu, et de la posséder à découvert et **sans voile,**[2] ce serait la combattre que de dire qu'on ne voit rien dans le monde qui la montre avec cette
5 évidence. Mais puisqu'elle dit, au contraire, que les hommes sont dans les ténèbres et dans l'éloignement de Dieu, qu'Il s'est caché à leur connaissance, que c'est même le nom qu'il se donne dans les Ecritures, "Deus absconditus"; et, enfin, si elle travaille également à établir ces deux choses: que Dieu a établi des marques sensibles dans l'Eglise pour se faire
10 reconnaître à ceux qui le chercheraient sincèrement; et qu'il les a couvertes néanmoins de telle sorte qu'il ne sera aperçu que de ceux qui le cherchent de tout leur cœur, quel avantage peuvent-ils tirer, lorsque dans **la négligence** [3] (où ils font profession d'être) de chercher la vérité, ils crient que rien ne la leur montre puisque cette obscurité où ils sont, et qu'ils objectent à l'Eglise,
15 ne fait qu'établir une des choses qu'elle soutient sans toucher à l'autre, et établit sa doctrine, bien loin de la ruiner?

L'immortalité de l'âme est une chose qui nous importe si fort, qui nous touche si profondément, qu'il faut avoir perdu tout sentiment pour être dans l'indifférence de savoir ce qui en est. Toutes nos actions et nos pensées
20 doivent prendre des routes si différentes, selon qu'il y aura des biens éternels à espérer ou non, qu'il est impossible de faire une **démarche** [4] avec sens et jugement, qu'en la réglant par la vue de ce point, qui doit être notre dernier objet.

Ainsi notre premier intérêt et notre premier devoir est de nous éclaircir
25 sur ce sujet, d'où dépend toute notre conduite. Et c'est pourquoi, entre ceux qui n'en sont pas persuadés, je fais une extrême différence de ceux qui travaillent de toutes leurs forces à s'en instruire, à ceux qui vivent sans s'en mettre en peine et sans y penser . . .

Cette négligence en une affaire où il s'agit d'eux-mêmes, de leur éternité,
30 de leur tout, m'irrite plus qu'elle ne m'attendrit; elle m'étonne et m'**épouvante:**[5] c'est un **monstre** [6] pour moi. Je ne dis pas ceci par le zèle pieux d'une dévotion spirituelle. J'entends au contraire qu'on doit avoir ce sentiment par un principe d'intérêt humain et par intérêt d'amourpropre: il ne faut pour cela que voir ce que voient les personnes les moins éclairées.

---

1 *Pascal is speaking of the*	**3** *indifference*	**5** *appalls*
libertines	**4** *step*	**6** *intellectual monstrosity.*
2 *unveiled*		

35 **Il ne faut pas** [7] avoir l'âme fort élevée pour comprendre qu'il n'y a point ici de satisfaction véritable et solide, que tous nos plaisirs ne sont que vanité, que nos maux sont infinis, et qu'enfin la mort, qui nous menace à chaque instant, doit infailliblement nous mettre, dans peu d'années, dans l'horrible nécessité d'être éternellement ou **anéantis** [8] ou malheureux.

40 Il n'y a rien de plus réel que cela, ni de plus terrible. Faisons tant que nous voudrons les braves: voilà la fin qui attend la plus belle vie du monde. Qu'on fasse réflexion là-dessus, et qu'on dise ensuite s'il n'est pas indubitable qu'il n'y a de bien en cette vie qu'en l'espérance d'une autre vie, qu'on n'est heureux qu'à mesure qu'on s'en approche, et que, comme il n'y aura plus de 45 malheurs pour ceux qui avaient une entière assurance de l'éternité, il n'y a point de bonheur pour ceux qui n'en ont aucune lumière.

C'est donc assurément un grand mal que d'être dans ce doute; mais c'est au moins un devoir indispensable de chercher, quand on est dans ce doute; et ainsi celui qui doute et qui ne cherche pas est tout ensemble et bien mal- 50 heureux et bien injuste. Que s'il est avec cela tranquille et satisfait, qu'il en fasse profession, et enfin, qu'il en fasse vanité, et que ce soit de cet état même qu'il fasse le sujet de sa joie et de sa vanité, je n'ai pas de termes pour qualifier une si extravagante créature.

Où peut-on prendre ces sentiments? Quel sujet de joie trouve-t-on à 55 n'attendre plus que des misères sans ressources? Quel sujet de vanité de se voir dans des obscurités impénétrables, et comment se peut-il faire que ce raisonnement se passe dans un homme raisonnable?

Je ne sais qui m'a mis au monde, ni ce que c'est que le monde, ni que moi-même; je suis dans une ignorance terrible de toutes choses; je ne sais ce 60 que c'est que mon corps, que mes sens, que mon âme et cette partie même de moi qui pense ce que je dis, qui fait réflexion sur tout et sur elle-même, et ne se connaît non plus que le reste. Je vois ces effroyables espaces de l'univers qui m'enferment, et je me trouve attaché à un **coin** [9] de cette vaste **étendue,** [10] sans que je sache pourquoi je suis plutôt placé en ce lieu qu'en 65 un autre, ni pourquoi ce peu de temps qui m'est donné à vivre m'est assigné à ce point plutôt qu'en un autre de toute l'éternité qui m'a précédé et de toute celle qui me suit. Je ne vois que des infinités de toutes parts, qui m'enferment comme un atome et comme une **ombre** [11] qui ne dure qu'un instant sans retour. Tout ce que je connais est que je dois bientôt mourir; mais ce 70 que j'ignore le plus est cette mort même que je ne saurais éviter.

"Comme je ne sais d'où je viens, aussi je ne sais où je vais; et je sais seulement qu'en sortant de ce monde je tombe pour jamais ou dans le **néant,** [12] ou dans les mains d'un Dieu irrité, sans savoir à laquelle de ces deux conditions je dois être naturellement en partage. Voilà mon état, plein 75 de faiblesse et d'incertitude. Et, de tout cela, je conclus que je dois donc passer tous les jours de ma vie sans songer à chercher ce qui doit m'arriver. Peut-être que je pourrais trouver quelque éclaircissement dans mes doutes;

---

7 *here it is not necessary to have*
8 *annihilated*

9 *corner*
10 *space*

11 *shadow*
12 *nothingness*

mais je n'en veux pas prendre la peine, ni faire un pas pour le chercher; et après, en traitant avec mépris ceux qui **se travailleront** [13] de ce soin, je veux aller, sans prévoyance et sans crainte, **tenter** [14] un si grand événement, et me laisser mollement conduire à la mort, dans l'incertitude de l'éternité de ma condition future".

Qui souhaiterait d'avoir pour ami un homme qui discourt de cette manière? Qui le choisirait entre les autres pour lui communiquer ses affaires? Qui aurait recours à lui dans ses afflictions? Et enfin, à quel usage de la vie on le pourrait destiner?

Qu'on s'imagine un nombre d'hommes dans les chaînes, et tous condamnés à la mort, dont uns étant chaque jour **égorgés** [15] à la vue des autres, ceux qui restent voient leur propre condition dans celle de leurs semblables, et se regardant les uns et les autres avec douleur et sans espérance, attendent leur tour. C'est l'image de la condition des hommes.

1. Lines 1–16 state that according to the author:
   A. religion teaches that man can see God clearly
   B. God is hidden from man
   C. the Church provides little evidence for the earnest seeker
   D. the Church is equally in the dark.

1. B **2.** Lines 17–23 state that:
   A. the immortality of the soul is of only academic importance
   B. the existence or non-existence of future eternal good is second in importance to current well-being
   C. man's first duty is to determine whether his soul is immortal or not
   D. those men who do not concern themselves with this point are just as well off.

2. C **3.** Lines 24–46 state that:
   A. the author is not concerned with those who have no interest in their own future well-being
   B. the end of the finest life is similar to that of the most wretched
   C. the believing man is happy in direct proportion as he approaches death
   D. the poor man is more likely to be enlightened than the rich man.

3. C **4.** Lines 41–54 state that:
   A. man is often happy in a state of ignorance
   B. if a man is in a state of doubt it is his duty to become enlightened
   C. if a man remains in a state of doubt, he should conceal this feeling from his fellow man
   D. the author disapproves of extravagance in display of belief.

4. B **5.** Lines 59–72 state that the author:
   A. is aware of the reason for his existence
   B. understands why he was placed in this world rather than in another
   C. realizes the eventual necessity of death
   D. has no conception of the nature of death.

13 *will bother with*   **14** *undertake*   · **15** *butchered*

5. D   **6.** Lines 73–80 state that:
 A. the author's condition is one of strength and joy
 B. to be concerned about the future is not necessary
 C. it is useless to look with scorn at those who search for truth
 D. one is foolish not to take a step to seek enlightenment.

6. D   **7.** Lines 83–91 state that:
 A. he who is unconcerned about the future deserves the trust of his fellow man
 B. no useful role in life can be assigned to the unbeliever
 C. the picture of the human condition is one of eventual bliss
 D. the average man is condemned to a life of hopelessness.

7. B

Reading Passages

INSTRUCTIONS: As you read the following practice passages, circle unfamiliar words. Read the entire passage for general understanding without looking up new words in the vocabulary. Verify your comprehension by taking the test at the end of the passage, and then work out the meanings of the new words more precisely. Review new vocabulary words often until you can recognize them immediately.

Un tremblement de terre

Extrait d'une lettre de M. Perrotin à M. Faye, *Comptes rendus de l'Académie des Sciences*, 1887, p. 666.

Le mercredi 23 février, à 5^h5^9 du matin, nous éprouvions une très forte **secousse**.[1] Ceux qui l'ont ressentie ne sont pas bien d'accord sur la durée du phénomène; pour moi, il a duré certainement près d'une minute. J'étais éveillé avant le commencement de la secousse et j'ai pu en observer toutes
5 les **péripéties**.[2] Faible d'abord, elle a été en augmentant avec une étonnante rapidité. Dès l'origine, j'ai voulu me lever, mais je ne pouvais pas me tenir debout: le plancher oscillait de l'est à l'ouest, d'une façon extraordinaire. Ces oscillations, à assez longue période, étaient accompagnées de trépidations d'une violence **inouïe**,[3] de très courte durée, mais néanmoins d'une amplitude
10 assez grande. Le tout était accompagné d'un bruit continu très intense, pareil à celui que produit le passage d'un train sur un **pont**[4] de fer. Il y avait dans tout cela des craquements provenant sans doute de la désagrégation des matériaux du sol et des murs des habitations, ainsi que des bruits métalliques très caractérisés.
15 La secousse principale a été suivie de plusieurs autres, mais de moindre importance; elles ont eu lieu aux heures suivantes:

Le 23 au matin: $6^{h·}10$, $8^{h·}30$ (cette dernière courte, mais assez violente);
dans la nuit du 23 au 24: $11^{h·}15$ et $1^{h·}50$;
le 25, à $5^{h·}15$ du matin.
20 En réalité, les secousses ont été beaucoup plus nombreuses, et, dans les quarante-huit heures qui ont suivi la secousse principale, il suffisait de **prêter** quelque **attention**[5] à ce qui se passait sous nos pieds pour constater qu'il se produisait de fréquentes trépidations du sol.

1. How long did the first earthquake last?
A. five hours and fifty-nine minutes
B. twenty-three minutes

---

1 *shock*	**3** *unheard of*	**5** *pay attention*
2 *vicissitudes*	**4** *bridge*	

C. about one minute, according to the author
D. about five minutes according to witnesses.

---

1. C   **2.** The earthquake:
A. began mildly and became more intense
B. was intense at the beginning and rapidly tapered off
C. was of about equal intensity throughout
D. was scarcely noticed by anyone except the author.

---

2. A   **3.** The author states that he:
A. wanted to get up but couldn't
B. couldn't hold himself in one place
C. waited until the earthquake ended before moving
D. oscillated between running to the east or to the west.

---

3. A   **4.** The shock:
A. was a peril for a train was passing through the town
B. was accompanied by an intermittent noise
C. was accompanied by an interrupted wind
D. was accompanied by a noise like that made by a train on a bridge.

---

4. D   **5.** The main shock was:
A. followed by a few more intense shocks
B. followed by several less intense shocks
C. followed by a two hour period of almost complete tranquility

---

5. B   **6.** the number of shocks was:
A. 25   B. 5   C. 6   D. undetermined but very numerous.

---

6. D

Le Delta du Chatt-El-Arab

Extrait de Robert Garry "Le Delta du Chatl-El-Arab," *Revue de Géographie de Montréal*, XIV (L'Université de Montréal, 1960), 20–21.

Le mot semble impropre. Nous sommes ici en plein désert et c'est plutôt oasis qu'il faut dire, une oasis **sise** [1] au bord de la mer, où l'eau douce fait des miracles et conditionne toute vie; venant de Bouchir, on aborde le delta par le sud. La vue est saisissante. Au bleu **uni** [2] et **foncé** [3] de la mer succède
5   brusquement un véritable kaléidoscope composé de **voies d'eau,** [4] lagunes, bancs de sable ou de **vase** [5] à demi submergés où **s'enchevêtrent** [6] et se superposent toutes les couleurs, avec une pureté et un éclat que seuls peuvent présenter les pays où il ne pleut presque jamais. La palette la plus riche de l'artiste à l'imagination la plus fertile ne saurait rendre cette **débauche** [7] de

---

1 *situated*   4 *water-ways*   6 *interlace*
2 *even*   5 *silt*   7 *profligacy*
3 *dark*

10 teintes où voisinent: couleurs vives et **crues,**[8] pastels délicatement ombrés
et **dégradés** [9] savants. Si vous ajoutez à cela les méandres les plus capricieux,
les labyrinthes les plus compliqués, un passage insensible de l'eau à la terre,
vous semblez avoir devant vous une plaque de marbre aux veines multicolores.
Ce paysage unique, merveille de la nature, s'interrompt bientôt pour faire
15 place à l'œuvre humaine moderne et voici Abadan la gigantesque raffinerie
de l'Anglo-Iranian Oil Co. qui étale ses tours de fractionnement et ses réser-
voirs sur des dizaines de milles de long d'un des bras du Chatt-El-Arab. Vers
l'est, le pipe-line de l'Aribistan **raye** [10] la plaine de son double trait noir.
L'Oasis de Bassorah apparaît bientôt dans sa radieuse beauté: une
20 forêt de **palmiers dattiers** [11] plantés dans un immense jardin. De petits
champs **accolés,**[12] bordés de canaux où croissent le blé, les céréales secon-
daires et les légumineuses des pays tempérés. Les habitations vues d'en haut
semblent avoir quelque allure, mais elles ne sont pour la plupart que de
misérables huttes de **boue** [13] séchée à armature de **stipes** [14] de palmier.
25 Quelques-unes, plus soignées, sont **blanchies à la chaux,**[15] mais le plus
souvent cet honneur est réservé aux mosquées dont les minarets percent **la
voûte** [16] des palmes.
Au milieu de cette oasis, la ville de Bassorah aligne ses rues et boulevards
bordés d'édifices utilitaires modernes et d'où s'élève, **obsédante,**[17] la senteur
30 acre du **naphte.**[18] Dans la **cuvette** [19] du Bas Delta l'eau est en abondance
et peut être aisément disciplinée, mais il n'en est pas de même plus au nord
où le désert semble avoir resserré son étreinte. C'est la lutte implacable pour
l'eau; contre son excès dans les parties basses où elle stagne, contre sa rareté
dans les parties hautes où elle manque. L'homme s'acharne à résoudre côte
35 à côte des problèmes de drainage et des problèmes d'irrigation. On aperçoit
de grandes dépressions aux formes les plus contournées, entourées de digues,
divisées en casiers [20] par d'autres digues transversales. On voit le sol **se
côlmater** [21] et s'assécher mais aussitôt réclamer de l'eau qui lui est apportée
par un canal d'irrigation. La vie se concentre le long des rives des fleuves
40 Tigre et Euphrate et le long des canaux. Au fur et à mesure qu'on s'avance
vers le nord, la bande de végétation **se cantonne** [22] le long des rives et expire
aux bords du désert. Parfois celui-ci s'approche et **côtoie** [23] le fleuve, là
où **la berge escarpée** [24] ne se prête plus à l'irrigation. L'oasis de Bagdad,
qui n'a ni la richesse, ni la luxuriance de sa rivale du bas fleuve marque les
45 confins du delta. Après elle, c'est le désert.

1.   In line 1, the context indicates that the word **impropre** means:
A. improper   B. inappropriate.

---

8 *raw*	**14** *stems*	**20** *checkered*
9 *off shades*	**15** *whitewashed*	**21** *to warp*
10 *streaks*	**16** *canopy*	**22** *hugs*
11 *date palms*	**17** *haunting*	**23** *borders*
12 *side by side*	**18** *naptha*	**24** *steepbank*
13 *mud*	**19** *basin*	

1. B   **2.** In line 2 the word **douce** would best be translated by:
A. soft   B. sweet   C. fresh.

2. C   **3.** According to lines 4–13 the area described resembles:
A. a surface of multi-colored marble
B. the palette of an artist
C. a huge lake of various shades of blue.

3. A   **4.** In line 16 the **tours de fractionnement** probably are:
A. oil wells
B. storage tanks
C. pipeline stations
D. cracking or refining installations.

4. D   **5.** The dwellings of the inhabitants of the region (lines 22–27) appear to be:
A. fairly rich and comfortable
B. wretched and poor, for the most part
C. white and well cared for, for the most part
D. made out of grass.

5. B   **6.** In line 32, if **étreinte** means *embrace*, **resserré** probably means:
A. tightened   B. relaxed   C. reserved.

6. A   **7.** From lines 31–37 we might assume that in this region there is:
A. an abundance of population
B. very little rainfall
C. extensive grazing of herds.

7. B   **8.** In line 39 **rives** must mean:
A. rivers   B. banks   C. rainfall.

8. B

Les comètes

Extrait de *L'Astronomie*, par Rudaux et de Vaucouleurs, Larousse, Editeur.

Le nombre des comètes reste inconnu; mais il est certainement considérable. C'est ce qu'exprimait très suggestivement Kepler en énonçant cette proposition que "les comètes sont aussi nombreuses dans le ciel que les poissons dans l'eau".

5   Des évaluations théoriques font estimer à plusieurs millions le nombre des orbites se croisant dans le système solaire. En supposant que les **périhélies** [1] se répartissent à peu près également, environ six mille comètes devraient **sillonner** [2] à tout moment l'espace, dans une sphère de diamètre égal à celui de l'orbite de Neptune.

---

1 *perihilia (points nearest to the sun)*   2 *to streak*

10   Quel nombre réel d'observations pouvons-nous aligner, en regard de
ceux-ci?

La plus ancienne observation dont les astronomes puissent faire état se
trouve consignée dans les annales chinoises, et remonte à l'an 2369 avant
J.C. Depuis, c'est à environ mille cinq cents que s'élève le nombre des
15   comètes aperçues, y compris les apparitions multiples de ceux de ces astres qui
sont périodiques. En réalité, ce chiffre devrait être beaucoup plus élevé. Il
y a, en effet, disproportion entre les nombres fournis par les observateurs,
avant et après l'invention des instruments d'optique. Dans le premier cas,
seuls ont été enregistrés ceux de ces astres visibles à l'œil **nu**,[3] et dont les
20   apparitions ne surviennent qu'à des intervalles de plusieurs années parfois;
avec, au contraire, les moyens modernes de l'optique astronomique et surtout
de la photographie, qui révèlent les pâles ou minuscules comètes **se dérobant
au regard**,[4] plusieurs découvertes, quelquefois une dizaine, viennent annuelle-
ment augmenter la liste des comètes.

25   D'un grand nombre de comètes on ne connaît pas exactement les éléments
orbitaux, soit parce qu'il s'agit d'apparitions qui, anciennement, étaient
simplement décrites à titre spectaculaire, soit parce que leur observation
n'a pas été effectuée avec toute la rigueur nécessaire. Ce manque d'informations peut encore s'appliquer, actuellement, à certains de ces astres trop
30   faibles et que des circonstances défavorables empêchent de suivre dans leur
marche.

En 1935, les éléments se rapportant à 663 apparitions seulement avaient
été déterminés, permettant de reconnaître, d'après le catalogue de Yamamoto,
467 comètes distinctes; parmi celles-ci, 170 ont des orbites elliptiques, 250 des
35   orbites paraboliques et 47 des orbites légèrement hyperboliques.

Bien entendu, ces nombres sont destinés à **s'accroître** [5] sans cesse. Aussi
bien, ne doivent-ils être retenus que pour donner une idée générale des
nombres de ces astres jusqu'à présent observés d'une manière ou d'une autre.

Des distinctions sont à établir parmi les comètes à orbites elliptiques, et,
40   par conséquent, périodiques: certaines ont été observées plusieurs fois, les
autres n'ont été signalées qu'une seule fois. Dans cette dernière catégorie
rentrent les comètes dont les éléments n'ont pu encore être déterminés avec
certitude, surtout lorsque le développement orbital entraîne des **durées** [6] de
révolution supérieures à deux cents ans. Il y a aussi celles qui, même d'assez
45   courte période, ne sont pas encore revenues depuis leur découverte plus ou
moins récente, ou bien encore, dont le retour échappa **par suite de** [7] circonstances défavorables. Il est aussi des cas où ces astres peuvent être considérés
comme "perdus", soit qu'ils aient été déroutés par suite d'importantes
perturbations planétaires, soit même qu'ils aient vraiment cessé d'exister,
50   victimes d'une désagrégation, événement dont il sera question tout spécialement un peu plus loin. Le terme "périodique" n'implique donc pas que ces
astres curieux viennent s'offrir régulièrement à notre contemplation.

---

3 *naked*   **5** *to increase*   **7** *as a result of*
4 *which are hidden*   **6** *continuance*

Enfin, on doit remarquer que les conséquences sont pratiquement les mêmes pour nous si une comète suit une course parabolique ou une course elliptique tellement développée que sa révolution **réclamerait** [8] plusieurs milliers d'années pour s'accomplir. La discrimination étant bien difficile à établir, nous l'avons vu, on reste en somme mal renseigné sur le nombre véritable des comètes périodiques.

55

1. Lines 1–9 state:
   A. the number of comets in the sky is equal to the number of fish in the sea
   B. theoretical estimates indicate six thousand comets within the solar system
   C. the number of comets is unknown
   D. several million comets travel in space through a sphere equal in diameter to the orbit of Neptune.

1. C   **2.** Lines 10–25 state:
   A. the oldest observations on comets have been found in ancient Chinese records containing a count of 2,369 comets
   B. thanks to modern methods of optical astronomy about ten new comets are discovered annually
   C. about one thousand comets have been observed
   D. since 1500 A.D. the number of observed comets, including the multiple appearance of periodic stars, has increased dramatically.

2. B   **3.** According to lines 26–32 the orbital patterns of many comets:
   A. can be calculated from early precise observations
   B. cannot be calculated because early observations were not sufficiently precise
   C. will probably be more accurately described in the future
   D. will probably never be predicted with complete accuracy.

3. B   **4.** Lines 33–38 state that:
   A. during 1935, elements pertaining to 663 comets were observed
   B. this number will increase to a peak and then gradually fall off as the limits of observation are attained
   C. this number is important because it is already approaching the maximum of potential observation
   D. Yamamoto catalogued the apparitions according to their orbital characteristics.

4. D   **5.** Lines 40–48 state that:
   A. comets with elliptical orbits are periodic
   B. the term "periodic" indicates reappearance of the comets at regular intervals
   C. the total number of comets can be ascertained by computers
   D. comets whose paths are elliptical will always reappear at stated intervals

8 *would require*

5. A   **6.** Lines 48–54 state that some stars are "lost" because of
  A. disintegration   c. solar holocausts
  B. interplanetary collision   D. completely unknown causes.

---

6. A

La médecine à la cour de Louis XIV vue par une princesse allemande

Extrait de la *Semaine des Hôpitaux* (Informations, 2 avril 1963), pp. 8, 9.

Le 16 novembre 1671, Elisabeth Charlotte, fille de l'électeur palatin, devenait princesse française par son mariage avec Philippe d'Orléans, frère de Louis XIV.

Elevée dans un milieu simple et rigide, la princesse ne s'adapta que très
5 mal à la vie brillante et dissolue de la cour de Louis XIV. Elle « **boudait** [1] souvent la compagnie, dit d'elle Saint-Simon, s'en faisait craindre par son humeur dure et **farouche** [2] et, quelquefois, par **ses propos,** [3] et passait toute la journée dans son cabinet qu'elle s'était choisi, où les fenêtres étoient à plus de dix pieds de terre, à considérer les portraits des palatins et d'autres princes
10 allemands dont elle l'avait **tapissé,** [4] et à écrire des volumes de lettres tous les jours de sa vie et de sa main, dont elle faisait elle-même les copies qu'elle gardait ».

Les éditions Plon viennent de publier de larges passages de cette correspondance, **étalée** [5] sur plus de 50 ans, qui retrace au jour le jour le règne de
15 Louis XIV et la Régence. Un de nos lecteurs nous signale quelques lettres particulièrement savoureuses qui donnent une description que n'aurait pas **renié** [6] Molière des maladies, des médecins et des thérapeutiques du XVIIe siècle.

1. Lines 1–12 state that:
  A. Elizabeth Charlotte became through her marriage, sister-in-law to Louis XIV
  B. she quickly adapted herself to the ways of the court
  c. she was lighthearted and friendly
  D. although she had an attractive retreat in which to write letters, she rarely spent any time there.

---

1. A

Luxation du coude

Saint-Cloud, 21 juin 1697.

« Il y a un mois, je fus avec **M. le dauphin** [1] à la chasse au **loup.** [2] Au moment où nous suivions un **sentier,** [3] il part un loup presque devant mon

---

1 *sulked*   3 *her words*   5 *spread over*
2 *sullen*   4 *hung, decorated*   6 *disowned*

1 *eldest son of French king*   2 *wolf*   3 *path*

cheval, qui **s'emporte** [4] et se **dresse** [5] sur ses deux pieds de derrière: il **glisse** [6] et **s'abat** [7] sur le côté droit; mon coude rencontre une grosse pierre
5   et je me **démets l'os.** [8] On cherche le chirurgien du roi, qui suivait la chasse, mais on ne le trouve pas, car son cheval ayant perdu **un fer,** [9] il avait été dans le village pour le faire remettre. Un paysan qui se trouvait là, dit qu'il y avait à deux lieues un barbier **fort habile,** [10] qui remettait tous les jours des jambes et des bras; lorsque je sus qu'il avait autant d'expérience, je montai
10   en **calèche** [11] et je m'y fis conduire, non sans éprouver de vives douleurs. Aussitôt qu'il m'eut remis le bras, je n'éprouvai plus aucune souffrance, je remontai en calèche et je revins promptement ici. Mon chirurgien et celui de **Monsieur** [12] vinrent pour examiner mon mal; je crois qu'ils éprouvaient un peu de jalousie de ce que **le paysie** [13] eut si bien fait la chose, et ils s'en
15   vont faire croire au pauvre homme que s'il n'examine pas aussitôt mon bras, **le sphacèle** [14] pourrait **s'y mettre.** [15] Le pauvre paysan se laisse persuader par les méchants chirurgiens, me met le bras à nu, tandis qu'il aurait dû rester dans l'appareil pendant neuf jours; ils font mouvoir le bras et me remettent l'appareil si mal que le lendemain il fallut tout rouvrir. Cela amena
20   une si **affreuse enflure** [16] de la main et du bras, que présentement encore je ne peux faire usage de la main ni la porter à la bouche, tandis que je pouvais tout faire avant que ces **maudits** [17] chirurgiens n'eussent ôté le premier appareil . . . je serais tout à fait guérie s'ils avaient laissé faire mon paysan . . .».

1.   Lines 1–8 state that:
     A. the writer when out hunting, was kicked by her horse
     B. the writer was thrown and received a dislocation of the elbow
     C. the King's surgeon was unable to set it
     D. a barber, reputedly very skillful, was brought on foot to the injured person.

---

1. B   **2.**   Lines 9–22 state that:
     A. the elbow was set by a court physician
     B. the elbow was set by the barber
     C. the King's surgeons were amazed and pleased with the barber's skill
     D. the writer soon regained full use of the elbow.

---

2. B

Convulsions de l'enfance

Versailles, 23 avril 1700.

«Vous aurez sans doute appris que Notre Seigneur Dieu, hélas! a déjà rappelé à lui mon petit-fils, le prince de Lorraine. C'est le médecin du duc

---

<table>
<tr><td>4</td><td>*bolts*</td><td>9</td><td>*a horseshoe*</td><td>14</td><td>*gangrene*</td></tr>
<tr><td>5</td><td>*rears*</td><td>10</td><td>*very skillful*</td><td>15</td><td>*set in*</td></tr>
<tr><td>6</td><td>*slips*</td><td>11</td><td>*carriage*</td><td>16</td><td>*bad swelling*</td></tr>
<tr><td>7</td><td>*falls*</td><td>12</td><td>*brother of the king*</td><td>17</td><td>*cursed*</td></tr>
<tr><td>8</td><td>*dislocate the bone*</td><td>13</td><td>*countryman*</td><td></td><td></td></tr>
</table>

qui a fait mourir l'enfant. Il était gros et fort. Il fut pris de convulsions parce que quatre dents voulaient percer **à la fois.**[1] Le médecin lui donna,
5 dans l'espace de douze heures, quatre **lavements**[2] d'eau de chicorée, avec de la rhubarbe, une poudre contre les convulsions, de forte **eau de mélisse**[3] en grande quantité et des gouttes d'Angleterre. Il faut que cela ait étouffé le pauvre enfant . . . Ma fille est **grosse**[4] . . .».

1. The letter states that:
   A. the young Prince of Lorraine was seized with convulsions because he started to cut four teeth at the same time
   B. the writer's grandson was small and puny
   C. the doctor within a twenty-four hour period gave him a quantity of medicine and bled him several times
   D. because of the doctor's efforts, the child's life was saved.

1. A

Un syndrome de Pickwick

Versailles, 12 décembre 1711.

« . . . Je ne veux pas **tarder**[1] davantage à vous écrire, car Dieu sait combien de temps je pourrai le faire encore: je ne vous cacherai pas qu'on me tient ici pour gravement malade; à la vérité, il ne me semble pas qu'il en soit ainsi, mais tous les médecins disent que moins je me sens malade, plus je
5 le suis. Et pourtant je suis grosse et grasse, je n'ai pas mauvaise **mine,**[2] j'ai bon appétit: seulement je suis toujours un peu **somnolente,**[3] je m'endors partout et c'est ce qu'on tient pour grave ici. C'est pourquoi hier on m'a tiré du sang, lundi et mercredi je prendrai médecine pour voir s'il n'y a pas moyen de me débarrasser de cette dangereuse somnolence. Je me résigne à la
10 volonté du Tout-Puissant et suis tout à fait calme, quoi qu'il arrive. Je ne **souhaite ni redoute**[4] la mort. Les deux premières **palettes**[5] de sang étaient hideuses, la troisième meilleure . . . ».

1. The letter states, among other things, that:
   A. the writer is considered by her doctors to be a hypochondriac
   B. she herself feels completely well and alert
   C. she neither dreads nor wishes for death
   D. the bleedings to which she was subjected proved inconclusive.

1. C

1 *at the same time*   3 *melissa cordial*   4 *pregnant*
2 *enemas*

1 *delay*   3 *sleepy*   5 *four ounce receptacle*
2 *appearance*   4 *wish for nor fear*

Epidémie de rougeole [1]

Versailles, 10 mars 1712–12 mars 1712.

« . . . Sans nul doute vous serez saisie de frayeur aussi en voyant que le malheur continue à nous **accabler.**[2] Les médecins ont commis la même faute qu'avec Mme la Dauphine, car le petit Dauphin était déjà tout **empourpré**[3] de la rougeole et en transpiration, qu'ils **lui ont fait une**
5 **saignée,**[4] puis donné de l'émétique, et au milieu de l'opération, le pauvre enfant est mort. Et ce qui prouve bien qu'ils l'ont tué, lui aussi, c'est que son petit frère était **atteint**[5] de la même maladie et les neuf docteurs étant occupé de l'aîné, les femmes du plus jeune se sont enfermées avec lui et lui ont donné un biscuit et un peu de vin. Hier, l'enfant avait une forte fièvre, ils ont voulu
10 le saigner, mais Mme de Ventadour et la sous-gouvernante du prince, Mme de Villefort, s'y sont fortement opposées et n'ont absolument pas voulu **le souffrir.**[6] Elles l'ont simplement tenu bien au chaud, et cet enfant a été sauvé, à la honte des docteurs. Si on les avait laissé faire, sûrement il serait mort . . .

. . . M. le Dauphin est très certainement mort de **chagrin.**[7] Il aimait sa
15 femme d'une manière inouïe et c'est le chagrin de sa perte qui lui a donné la fièvre. Pendant quelques jours, elle ne fut pas réglée, mais ensuite elle revint tous les quatre jours. On le saigna. Après la mort de sa femme, il lui poussa des **boutons**[8] au front, ce qui cependant ne l'empêcha pas de sortir. Il ne se mit au lit que le lundi soir. Il lui vint à la peau beaucoup de taches
20 violettes avec des boutons plus gros et d'une autre nature que ceux d'une rougeole ordinaire; on lui donna des cordiaux et on le fit transpirer, **mais cela ne voulait pas bien sortir**[9] . . .

Le lendemain, quand les vingt-quatre heures furent écoulées, on fit l'autopsie, on trouva tous les organes **pourris,**[10] le cœur **flétri**[11] et **dé-**
25 **primé,**[12] d'où l'on conclut qu'il est mort de chagrin . . .».

1. Lines 1–13 state:
   A. that an epidemic of measles which had overwhelmed the court was subsiding
   B. that the eldest son after being bled and purged by the court doctors died
   C. his younger brother, also ill with the measles, and who was taken care of by some ladies of the court, suffered the same fate
   D. the ladies of the court also advocated bleeding to reduce fever.

1. B   2. Lines 14–25 state that:
   A. the death of the Dauphin was indirectly due to the loss of his wife
   B. the Dauphin's fever was constant and high

1 *measles*	5 *afflicted*	9 *but it didn't work out*
2 *overwhelm*	6 *allow it*	10 *putrid*
3 *flushed*	7 *sorrow*	11 *withered*
4 *bled him*	8 *skin eruptions*	12 *feeble*

c. he was given ice packs in an attempt to reduce it
D. the autopsy showed no deterioration of the vital organs.

2. A

Hématémèse [1]

Marly, 3–6 mai 1714.

«Peu avant sa mort, le pauvre duc de Berry **a avoué** [2] qu'il en était la cause lui-même, car jeudi, il y a huit jours, il chassait dans la forêt, le sol était **glissant,** [3] car il avait plu un peu, son cheval glissa avec les pieds de devant, il le retint vigoureusement, si bien que le cheval se releva avec tant
5 de force, que le pommeau de **la selle** [4] alla frapper le duc entre la poitrine et l'estomac. Il ressentit immédiatement une vive douleur, mais il n'en dit rien. La nuit il perdit du sang en quantité, mais il **défendit** [5] à son valet de chambre d'en parler; il croyait qu'il avait la dysenterie. Il ne voulait pas le dire, de peur qu'on ne lui fît prendre beaucoup de drogues, croyant que cela
10 passerait de soi-même.

Vendredi, il commença à être très mal, il disait que cela ne provenait que de la diarrhée, et samedi il alla à la chasse . . . Dans la nuit de dimanche, ou plutôt lundi matin, avant quatre heures, il fut pris de fièvre et de **frissons,** [6] mais il **céla** [7] la chose, se leva et s'habilla; il voulait se rendre à la médecine
15 du roi. Les frissons le reprirent. Il ne put pas **s'en cacher davantage,** [8] les maux de tête étaient trop forts, il dut se coucher. La fièvre allait toujours en augmentant, accompagnée de forts vomissements. D'abord il rendit une matière toute verte et ensuite noire comme du charbon. Mais hier, en examinant les matières noires, on s'aperçut que c'est du **sang caillé.** [9] Il en
20 rendait par le haut et par le bas. Les docteurs étaient très contents et ils croyaient M. le duc de Berry hors de danger, parce qu'ils espéraient arrêter le sang. Nous allâmes tous à Versailles, pour nous réjouir avec Mme de Berry de ce que son mari était hors de danger; mais cette nuit, il lui a pris un vomissement **si affreux,** [10] qu'il ne peut plus rien garder dans le corps; il
25 est donc très dangereusement malade, bien qu'il n'ait presque plus la fièvre et que **les redoublements** [11] aient cessé. On vient à l'instant même de le saigner pour la cinquième fois; je suis persuadée que la forte dose d'émétique qu'on lui a donnée est cause de son mal, car on lui en a fait prendre neuf grains; cela peut bien avoir rompu une veine . . . ».

1. Lines 1–10 state that:
A. while out riding, the Duke of Berry fell from his horse and received a blow on the chest

1 *stomach hemorrhage*   5 *forbade*   9 *clotted blood*
2 *admitted*   6 *shivers*   10 *terrible*
3 *slippery*   7 *concealed*   11 *retching*
4 *the saddle*   8 *hide them further*

B. he did not immediately feel any ill effects

C. that night he lost considerable blood

D. his valet was considerably alarmed.

---

1. C   **2.** Lines 11–22 state that:

A. Friday he felt well enough to go hunting again the following day

B. Sunday night and Monday morning he took a turn for the worse

C. although he had neither headache nor fever, he was subject to attacks of vomiting

D. the doctors were baffled.

---

2. B   **3.** Lines 22–29 state that:

A. the writer, with a group of friends, went to Versailles to commiserate with the Duchess of Berry

B. that night he took a turn for the worse and his fever climbed dangerously high

C. the doctors were afraid to resort to bleeding

D. they gave him a heavy dose of emetic which the writer felt may have ruptured a vein.

---

3. D

La guérison des écrouelles [1]

Saint-Cloud, 25 juin 1719.

«On attachait autrefois en ce pays tant d'importance à la naissance d'un septième garçon, que les rois donnaient une pension au père; cela a tout à fait cessé, car on a reconnu que ce n'était qu'une superstition; quant à ce qu'on dit du pouvoir qu'a un septième garçon de guérir les écrouelles, je
5 crois qu'il en est de cette faculté comme de celle dont se vante le roi de France . . .».

1. This letter states that:

A. the birth of a seventh son in France was never considered especially important

B. a seventh son was supposed to have the ability to cure the disease of scrofula

C. the writer shared the belief that the seventh son had this ability

D. the writer believed that the King and his doctors alone could effect such a cure.

---

1. B

---

1 *scrofula*

Autopsie

Saint-Cloud, 23 juillet 1719.

«La pauvre duchesse de Berry est morte . . . Elle a passé comme une lumière qui s'éteint; elle s'est endormie. Hier on l'a ouverte. Je ne comprends pas qu'elle n'ait pas souffert davantage. Elle avait un ulcère à l'estomac, un autre à **l'aine;** [1] **la rate** [2] était entièrement pourrie, ce n'était plus qu'une
5   **bouillie;** [3] la tête était pleine d'eau, la **cervelle** [4] réduite de moitié: mon docteur pense que c'est pour cela qu'elle était si peu sensible à la douleur . . .».

1. This letter states that:
    A. the Duchess of Berry died after great suffering
    B. the writer did not understand why she suffered so much
    C. an autopsy revealed that the brain of the Duchess had shrunk to one-half its normal size
    D. this shrinking caused the brain to be more sensitive to pain.

---

1. C

De l'autorité scientifique

Par A. Bourguignon dans *La Semaine des Hôpitaux,* information du 26 mars 1963, p. 3.

L'histoire des sciences illustre bien le rôle de l'autorité scientifique dans le développement scientifique. Ce rôle est si important qu'il mérite que nous nous y arrêtions un peu longuement. Cette autorité peut être de deux ordres: individuelle—c'était surtout le cas d'autrefois—et collective.
5   L'autorité scientifique individuelle est celle d'hommes ayant une très forte personnalité: habituellement professeurs ou chefs d'école; ils ont ce que Bachelard appelle « *l'âme professorale,* toute fière de son dogmatisme, **immobile** [1] dans sa première abstraction, appuyée pour la vie sur les succès scolaires de la jeunesse, parlant chaque année son savoir, imposant ses démonstrations,
10   tout à l'intérêt déductif, soutien si commode de l'autorité, enseignant son domestique comme fait Descartes ou le tout venant de la bourgeoisie comme l'agrégé de l'Université».
     Aujourd'hui, l'autorité scientifique collective, diffuse, joue son rôle à **l'échelle** [2] internationale. En effet, le caractère de plus en plus anonyme—
15   parce que collectif—des travaux scientifiques a, proportionnellement, réduit le nombre des savants ayant une autorité internationale susceptible de rayonner au-delà du cadre étroit de leur spécialité. C'est donc un groupe culturel qui impose son autorité aux autres. Cette autorité, loin d'être usurpée, est

---

1 *groin*   3 *mush*   4 *brain*
2 *spleen*

1 *unchanging*   2 *scale*

légitimée par la puissance technique du pays, la richesse et l'abondance de ses
centres de recherche, le nombre de ses savants. On doit reconnaître qu'à
l'heure actuelle, le groupe culturel anglo-saxon et plus particulièrement le
groupe américain, occupe une place prépondérante dans le monde scientifique.
L'existence de ces deux formes de l'autorité scientifique n'est pas sans conséquence sur l'orientation et le développement des recherches.

L'autorité scientifique d'abord crée **la mode.**[3] Car il existe une mode en
science comme en art ou en littérature. Il y a les sujets de recherche à la
mode et ceux qui ne le sont pas. Et, comme toutes les modes, la mode
scientifique est changeante.

L'autorité scientifique et la mode qu'elle engendre ont pour effet positif
de **hâter**[4] les recherches dans le domaine sur lequel elles règnent, de multi-
plier les **recoupements**[5] et les contrôles, de fournir des thèmes de discussion
aux trop nombreux congrès et colloques internationaux.

Mais il ne faut pas oublier qu'elles ont aussi de **funestes**[6] conséquences.
Le groupe culturel jouissant d'une autorité prépondérante a tout naturellement
tendance à mépriser ou à négliger ce qui se fait **au sein**[7] des autres groupes.
Tel est le cas des auteurs anglo-saxons qui méconnaissent souvent **ce qui
s'écrit**[8] dans d'autres langues que l'anglais. Parfois, fait plus choquant
encore, les chercheurs qui appartiennent à un groupe méprisé ignorent les
travaux faits dans leur propre groupe. On a vu, en France, par exemple, des
travaux écrits en français n'être reconnus valables par les autorités scientifiques françaises qu'après avoir reçu l'investiture outre-Atlantique. Cette
prépondérance de la langue anglaise est telle que les zones d'influence des
langues française et allemande **se sont amenuisées**[9] depuis une vingtaine
d'années. Les travaux scandinaves, par exemple, autrefois rédigés en allemand,
le sont maintenant en anglais. Ces constatations ont depuis longtemps fait
envisager la création ou l'adoption d'une langue scientifique internationale.
Cette primauté scientifique de la langue anglaise fait qu'aujourd'hui un travail
rédigé en cette langue a plus de chance d'être connu qu'un travail rédigé en
allemand, en français ou en italien.

L'autorité scientifique en créant la mode provoque continuellement l'abandon immotivé de sujets de recherche ayant un intérêt égal à celui des sujets
à la mode. De même elle tend sans cesse à **étouffer**[10] les idées nouvelles ou
à laisser dans **l'ombre**[11] des travaux de valeur. De très nombreux exemples
pourraient être donnés de découvertes qui n'ont été connues qu'après la
mort de leur auteur. De tels cas n'ont d'ailleurs pas pour seule cause la mode,
ils sont parfois imputables au caractère confidentiel des revues dans lesquelles
ils furent publiés. Il est même certains auteurs qui, inconsciemment sans
doute, font tout pour que leur œuvre reste inconnue. Si l'autorité scientifique
peut, de façon passive, involontaire, **freiner**[12] le progrès scientifique, il

---

3 *fashion*   **7** *within*   **11** *shadow*
4 *hasten*   **8** *what is being written* **12** *slow down*
5 *cross-checks*   **9** *have diminished*
6 *deadly*   **10** *stifle*

60 arrive que, dans certains cas, elle intervienne activement, soit en suscitant une
véritable conspiration du silence autour de tel ou tel travail, soit même en
attaquant publiquement les travaux d'un homme ou d'une école.

1. The first four lines state that:
   A. scientific authority is principally collective
   B. scientific development illustrates the role of science
   C. the role of science is sufficiently important to warrant further study
   D. scientific authority may be collective and individual.

1. D 2. Lines 5–12 state that individual scientific authority:
   A. results from the constant search for truth
   B. represents the outgrowth of an open mind
   C. usually has an altruistic character
   D. is characteristic of strong-minded individuals

2. D 3. Lines 13–24 state that collective scientific authority:
   A. increases the reputation of internationally known scientists
   B. plays an important role in the direction of scientific research
   C. requires, to be successful, an increase in the number of scientists with extensive areas of knowledge
   D. decreases the need of specialists.

3. B 4. Lines 25–32 state that scientific authority:
   A. discourages professional meetings
   B. is the result of unswerving dedication to the furtherance of knowledge
   C. is comparable to art and literature in its susceptibility to changes in fashion
   D. is seldom the victim of fashion and popular demand.

4. C 5. Lines 33–49 state that:
   A. a strength of collective scientific authority is that it is not dependent upon what is going on in other scientific groups
   B. the majority of Swedish scientific works are still published in German
   C. the French language, because of its clarity and precision, is widely used for scientific expression
   D. a work published in English has a greater chance of becoming known than one published in Italian, French or German.

5. D 6. Lines 50–63 state that scientific authority:
   A. facilitates the development of new ideas
   B. actively encourages the publication of works of value
   C. occasionally conspires to stifle certain particular works
   D. is recognized for its impartiality in its judgment of scientific works.

6. C

La première guerre de Finlande (*30 novembre 1939-12 mars 1940*)

Extrait de Jacques Bariety, "La politique extérieure allemande dans l'hiver 1939-40," *Revue historique,* CCXXXI (1964), 147-149. (Presses universitaires de France, Paris)

La guerre de Finlande apparaît comme une conséquence de l'application de l'accord sur le partage des zones d'influence. Le 25 septembre, Staline fait savoir qu'il entend « s'attaquer à la solution du problème des **États baltes** »,[1] et pense pouvoir compter sur l'appui allemand. L'incorporation

5 progressive des États baltes et de la Lithuanie dans l'Union soviétique se fera sans de trop grandes difficultés. Le 28, Hitler ordonne le **repli**[2] immédiat sur le Reich de toute la population germanophone des pays baltes et laisse les gouvernements locaux en tête-à-tête avec les Soviétiques. En même temps que sur les États baltes, Staline exerce une pression très forte sur la Finlande,

10 demandant la cession de bases militaires. Les Finlandais refusent ce que les Baltes acceptent. Dans l'épreuve de force diplomatique qui s'ensuit entre Soviétiques et Finlandais, la politique allemande travaille à **faire le vide autour de**[3] la Finlande et les Allemands poussent les Finlandais à accepter les propositions soviétiques. Les Finlandais **s'entêtant**[4] dans leur refus et

15 la pression politique ne suffisant pas, ce fut l'attaque de l'Armée Rouge le 30 novembre. Au cours de la guerre qui suit, comme pendant l'épreuve de force diplomatique qui avait précédé, toute **équivoque**[5] est absente du comportement allemand.

En septembre, l'Allemagne refuse de servir d'arbitre dans le conflit qui

20 oppose Finlande et Union soviétique. Le 6 octobre, Weizsäcker, secrétaire d'État allemand aux Affaires étrangères, écrit: « Nous devons laisser la Finlande s'arranger avec les Russes. Nous recommandons un règlement à l'aimable, dans la mesure du possible ». Le 10, Ribbentrop repousse une sollicitation finlandaise de médiation. Le 11 octobre, les Allemands de

25 Finlande sont évacués. Après le début des hostilités, Weizsäcker ordonne, le 2 décembre, à la diplomatie allemande de soutenir le point de vue soviétique. Le Reich repousse le 5 une nouvelle demande finlandaise de bons offices. Le 10, Hitler et l'amiral Raeder donnent leur accord à la demande soviétique, formulée **la veille**,[6] de faire secrètement **ravitailler**[7] par des **navires**[8]

30 allemands les sous-marins soviétiques en opération dans le golfe de Botnie. Les autorités allemandes saisissent les armes en transit à travers l'Allemagne vers la Finlande. Le 4 janvier, la Finlande demande encore une fois en vain à l'Allemagne sa médiation et évoque la possibilité d'un appel à l'aide auprès des « puissances de la S.D.N. », c'est-à-dire la France et l'Angleterre.

35 Ici se pose l'une des questions les plus intéressantes de l'hiver 1939-1940.

---

1 *Baltic States*	**4** *persisting*	**7** *supply*
2 *withdrawal*	**5** *ambiguity*	**8** *ships*
3 *to isolate*	**6** *just previously*	

Y a-t-il eu un projet franco-britannique de profiter de la guerre de Finlande pour essayer de **faire basculer** [9] Finlande et Scandinavie dans leur camp, donnant ainsi aux Alliés des possibilitiés de manœuvre au nord de l'Allemagne, au risque même d'avoir à affronter un conflit avec l'U.R.S.S.? Seule une
40 étude des archives politiques et militaires françaises et britanniques, lorsqu'elle sera possible, permettra d'éclaircir ce point. Les archives allemandes révèlent du moins que cette crainte existe à Berlin et aussi à Moscou et contribue à la conclusion de la première guerre de Finlande en mars 1940. L'aide fournie à la Finlande par da Suède et la Norvège et **la montée** [10] de sentiments
45 antisoviétiques et antiallemands en Scandinavie inquiètent. Le 20 février, le ministre allemand à Helsinki annonce le danger d'un changement de gouvernement en Suède, la possibilité de l'occupation de la région de Narvik Kiruna par des troupes alliées et l'arrivée d'officiers alliés au quartier général de Mannerheim; il ajoute qu'une **parade** [11] allemande en Suède serait difficile,
50 la Baltique étant **galée**.[12] Le 1er mars, Hitler dicte le plan « Weserübung » d'invasion du Danemark et de la Norvège. Le 12 mars, la paix est signée entre Soviétiques et Finlandais.

1. Lines 1–11 state that:
    A. the incorporation of the Baltic states into the USSR was very difficult
    B. Stalin requested unsuccessfully that Finland grant him military bases
    C. Germany supported Finnish refusal
    D. Hitler ordered that the German speaking element of the Baltic states remain alert for future orders.

1. B   2. Lines 19–30 state that:
    A. in the ensuing Soviet-Finnish war, Germany's position was vascillating
    B. Weizsäcker, German Secretary of State of Foreign Affairs, offered to mediate the differences between the two countries
    C. Ribbentrop repulsed a Finnish request for mediation
    D. Hitler refused the Soviet request to allow Soviet submarines to be refueled by German ships in the Gulf of Bothnia.

2. C   3. Lines 31–34 state that:
    A. German authorities permitted the transhipment of arms for Finland through Germany
    B. on January 4, Finland alludes in a note to Germany to the possibility of calling on France and England for help
    C. the possibility of an English-French understanding was not cause for alarm either to Russia or Germany
    D. Swedish and Norwegian support to Finland and increased anti-Soviet and German feeling had no effect on Russian policy.

3. B

9 *to swing*   11 *show of force*   12 *frozen*
10 *rise*

L'effondrement d'un mythe politique

Georges Gurvitch, "L'effondrement d'un mythe politique: Joseph Staline," *Cahiers internationaux de
sociologie*, XXXIII (1962), 8–10.

Enfin, Staline a vigoureusement soutenu Trotsky dans ses projets concernant le « communisme militaire ». L'idée de Trotsky, après la fin de la
guerre civile, était que dans un pays techniquement sous-développé, comme
l'était la Russie, une expérience collectiviste ne pouvait se faire que d'en
5   haut, par un communisme militaire. « Mobilisons tous les fonctionnaires,
mobilisons tous les ouvriers dans l'Armée Rouge, affectons-les sur place
d'abord, et forçons-les ensuite, en les organisant en brigades de travail, com-
mandées d'une façon autoritaire, à réaliser le communisme ». Trotsky fut très
vivement critiqué pour son communisme militaire par Boukharine, ainsi que
10   par Kamenief et Zinoviev; ces deux dernières personnalités (futures victimes
de Staline comme Boukharine) ne jouissaient pas d'une grande autorité car,
comme Staline, ils s'étaient, en octobre 1917, montrés plutôt réticents quant
à la **prise** [1] immédiate du pouvoir par les soviets. Lénine était plein de
réserves à l'égard des « brigades du travail », puis il finit par céder à un
15   certain moment. Mais le plus grand propagandiste du « communisme
militaire » fut Staline.

Lénine mit fin au communisme militaire de Trotsky et Staline par la N.E.P.
(Nouvelle Politique Économique), en 1922. Et, pour un certain temps, il y
eut un **recul.** [2] Staline résistait pourtant, ce qui augmentait encore l'irritation
20   croissante de Lénine. Déjà souffrant, et ayant subi les premiers **accès** [3] de
l'hémiplégie qui devait **l'emporter,** [4] Lénine, s'adressant officiellement à
un Congrès communiste (je cite d'après le discours de Khrouchtchev au
XXIIe Congrès du Parti communiste, en octobre 1961), écrit en décembre
1922, à propos de l'élection de Staline comme secrétaire général du Comité
25   central du Parti: « Staline a concentré dans ses mains un pouvoir **sans
borne,** [5] et je doute qu'il puisse l'employer sans en abuser outre mesure. Il
est trop **grossier,** [6] et ce défaut devient intolérable lorsqu'il s'agit du secrétaire
général d'un Parti. C'est pourquoi, dit encore Lénine, je propose avec insis-
tance aux camarades de trouver un moyen de révoquer Staline de ce poste
30   et de nommer comme secrétaire général une personne qui serait très différente
de Staline, qui serait plus intelligente, qui aurait plus de discernement
politique, qui serait plus loyale, plus tolérante, plus aimable, plus attentive
à l'égard des camarades » (*Pravda*, 18 octobre 1961, p. 9, « Discours de
Krouchtchev »). Krouchtchev commente (je le cite): « Vous voyez que
35   Lénine comprenait combien les éléments négatifs du caractère de Staline
pourraient nuire au Parti et à l'État soviétique. Malheureusement, les somma-
tions de Lénine, ajoute Khrouchtchev, et ses conseils de prudence n'ont pas

---

1 *seizure*	**2** *relapse*	**3** *attacks*
4 *kill him*	**5** *unlimited*	**6** *vulgar*

été entendus à temps. Le résultat fut que le Pays et le Parti ont été éprouvés par de **néfastes** [7] difficultés engendrées par l'arbitraire absurde de Staline et le culte de son pouvoir personnel ».

Dans son discours de conclusion au même XXII e Congrès, Khrouchtchev a donné quelques exemples affrayants des méfaits de Staline, sur lesquels je vais revenir. Pour l'instant, je voudrais compléter les appréciations de Lénine par la citation de son *Testament*, mentionné par Khrouchtchev, mais publié intégralement par un trotskyste américain. Lénine écrit dans ce testament, au sujet de Staline : « C'est un grossier personnage, dont il faut **se méfier** [8] et chez qui l'intelligence et les convictions sont remplacées par la ruse, la haine et le désir de se mettre en avant à tout prix ».

Le disciple préféré de Lénine, Boukharine, quelques mois avant son procès et son exécution en 1936, a dit à l'un de nos amis communs (mort depuis et dont je ne voudrais pas mettre en cause le nom très connu), dans une entrevue qui eut lieu à Paris, ces paroles : « Staline est un criminel de droit commun, dont les désirs de vengeance par l'assassinat touchent à la **folie.**[9] La cruauté malsaine de Staline fait trembler tout son entourage ». Et, conclusion assez inattendue : « Cependant, c'est le Parti qui l'a mis en place. C'est un terrible malheur, mais l'autorité du Parti est plus importante que les crimes de Staline, et je refuse de fuir, car le maintien du Parti vaut que je sacrifie ma vie, qui d'ailleurs n'a aucun sens en dehors de lui ».

Comment, pourrait-on se demander, a bien pu s'effectuer, dans ces conditions, l'ascension **inouïe** [10] de Staline, et se développer la mythologie concernant son génie exceptionnel ?

La montée du culte stalinien, après la mort de Lénine et jusqu'à la guerre de 1940, a pour base la bureaucratisation du régime soviétique, la séparation de l'appareil du Parti de ses membres et l'isolement croissant du Parti lui-même par rapport aux masses ouvrières et paysannes. Trotsky, à qui Staline a emprunté l'hostilité contre toute autogestion des intéressés et **le mépris** [11] de toute démocratie, même à l'intérieur du Parti communiste, fit **volte-face** [12] en voyant les méfaits du stalinisme, dès la mort de Lénine, en 1924, et commença à combattre la sclérose bureaucratique du Parti comme représentant la menace la plus grave contre les acquisitions de la Révolution soviétique. Mais il était déjà trop tard ! La machine bureaucratico-policière du Parti devait écraser Trotsky lui-même et ses partisans. Si Trotsky fut expulsé et assassiné ensuite au Mexique par un **tueur à gages** [13] de Staline, et non pas exécuté en U.R.S.S. après un **procès,**[14] c'est qu'il avait gardé une immense popularité dans l'Armée Rouge dont il avait été le fondateur et l'organisateur, ainsi que le chef glorieux de la résistance victorieuse contre les invasions des troupes blanches. Staline n'a pas osé ouvrir un procès contre Trotsky, de peur de provoquer un coup d'État de l'Armée Rouge.

---

7 *fatal*	**8** *distrust*	**9** *madness*
10 *unheard of*	**11** *the scorn*	**12** *about face*
13 *hired killer*	**14** *trial*	

1. Trotsky pensait (lignes 1–16) que :
  A. dans un pays arriéré techniquement il fallait un communisme militaire
  B. a trouvé que Staline n'était pas de son avis
  C. fut soutenu par Boukharine et Kamenief
  D. s'est rendu compte que les idées de Lénine sur les "brigades de travail" étaient parallèles aux siennes.

---

1. A   **2.** Lénine (lignes 17–34) :
  A. supporta le communisme militaire
  B. s'opposa à l'élection de Staline comme secrétaire général du Comité central
  C. considéra Staline comme étant trop tolérant pour le poste
  D. ne s'aperçut pas des éléments négatifs du caractère de Staline.

---

2. B   **3.** Krouchtchev (lignes 34–48) :
  A. trouva que Lénine était trop sévère dans son jugement de Staline
  B. trouva que le pays et le Parti avait souffert sous le pouvoir arbitraire de Staline
  C. subventionna la publication du *testament* de Lénine par un trotskyste américain
  D. voulait se mettre en avant à tout prix.

---

3. B

Une exploration physique des mouvements de la **baguette**[1] de **coudrier**[2]

(*La Semaine des Hôpitaux*, No. 16, 26 mars 1963, pp. 4, 5)

Le problème que pose le **sourcier,**[3] et sa prétention de pouvoir **déceler**[4] à distance l'eau existant dans le sol, est vieux comme le monde. Pourtant, jamais il ne s'était trouvé un homme de science pour tenter d'y apporter une solution rationnelle.

5   C'est aujourd'hui chose faite. M. Yves Rocard, professeur à la Faculté des Sciences de Paris, directeur du laboratoire de physique de l'Ecole Normale Supérieure, vient de publier sous le titre « Le signal du sourcier » (Editions Dunod), un petit livre dans lequel il explique, expériences **à l'appui,**[5] pourquoi et comment la baguette du sourcier dévie au passage de l'eau.

10   Il faut ajouter que la courageuse tentative de M. Rocard n'a pas emporté l'**adhésion**[6] de ses collègues scientifiques. Déjà il se dessine un mouvement d'opposition, de la part de ceux qui refusent systématiquement d'aborder avec les moyens classiques de la science les problèmes classés « extra-scientifiques ». Pourtant, M. Rocard a reçu de la part des physiologistes un accueil plus

15   enthousiaste. Ce qui est réconfortant. Car, ainsi qu'on va le voir, la solution du problème n'est pas totale : pour la compléter, il faudrait poursuivre, sur le terrain de la physiologie humaine, les travaux de M. Rocard.

---

1 *wand*
2 *hazel tree*

3 *dowser, water witch*
4 *reveal*

5 *backed by*
6 *support*

Notre sens « magnétique »

A la suite d'un grand nombre d'expériences, le Prof. Rocard croit pouvoir affirmer que le mouvement de la baguette est provoqué par les variations, même faibles, du champ magnétique, elles-mêmes créées par les courants électriques suscités [7] dans le sol par les courants d'eau.

L'une des preuves qu'il avance est la possibilité évidente de détecter par la baguette de coudrier des masses métalliques où se trouvent de tels champs magnétiques : une automobile, par exemple, ou une locomotive.

« Dans une **gare de triage,**[8] dit M. Rocard, tout le monde est sourcier ».

La mise au point récente d'appareils susceptibles de mesurer avec précision des variations faibles du champ magnétique a permis au physicien d'apporter des preuves expérimentales claires de son hypothèse. Il a complété ce travail par des recherches à l'aide d'instruments spécifiques mis au point dans ce but, comme un plateau d'induction tournant.

Dans le pli [9] du coude [10]

Ceci lui paraissant clairement établi, le Prof. Rocard a voulu comprendre comment le sourcier était capable de ressentir ces variations du champ magnétique, et comment elles se traduisaient par les mouvements de sa baguette.

Tout d'abord, il a montré que si 50% des hommes sont capables de détecter ainsi de l'eau qui filtre dans le sol—la seule qui produise champ électrique et champ magnétique—quelques-uns sont **davantage doués** [11] que d'autres. Ils réagissent à des variations très faibles du champ magnétique, de l'ordre de 1 milligauss, soit le millième du champ terrestre.

Le Prof. Rocard s'est livré à une longue série d'expériences en plaçant en divers endroits du corps d'un sourcier de petits **aimants.**[12] Il s'est alors aperçu qu'en les mettant au pli du coude, toutes les réactions du sourcier disparaissaient.

L'explication lui semble claire : le champ magnétique de 100 gauss, créé par ces aimants, « sature » et bloque les réflexes sourciers. Il faut donc chercher au **niveau** [13] du pli du coude, conclut le Prof. Rocard, l'existence et la réalité physiologique de ce sens nouveau de l'homme, celui d'être sensible à de faibles variations d'un champ magnétique.

C'est à ce stade que le Prof. Rocard veut laisser la place aux physiologistes, refusant de s'aventurer plus avant dans un domaine qui n'est pas le sien. Il conclut en disant qu'il lui semble que l'homme ayant mis certains de ses muscles en position contractée, de la manière même dont il tient la baguette, devient sensible à un curieux stimulus, celui de l'inégalité magnétique.

L'organe récepteur est-il situé au niveau du pli des coudes ? Il aurait, de toutes manières, pour action d'empêcher l'exécution, en présence de cette inégalité magnétique, des ordres venus du cerveau et qui commanderaient normalement la position de la baguette : cette dernière, placée déjà dans une position instable, **file** [14] alors irrésistiblement vers le bas.

---

7 *set up*
8 *marshalling yard*
9 *the bend*
10 *elbow*
11 *more gifted*
12 *magnets*
13 *level*
14 *is attracted*

Les performances réelles du sourcier

En publiant ses résultats, fruits de plusieurs années d'expérimentation patiente, le Prof. Rocard ne prétend résoudre entièrement le problème des sourciers, ni apporter délibérément de l'eau au **moulin** [15] des radiesthésistes.

Au passage, il leur rend même le mauvais service de réduire considérablement leurs prétentions. Tout d'abord, il montre que le sourcier ne peut pas détecter toutes les eaux souterraines. Sa baguette ne réagit ni à l'eau qui dort, ni à l'eau qui court; mais uniquement à l'eau qui filtre, la seule qui produise des variations magnétiques.

Le sourcier n'a aucun moyen sûr de mesurer le **débit** [16] d'un futur puits, ou d'une source à dégager. Il peut avoir au plus une idée vague de la profondeur où se situe l'eau filtrante. Il peut aussi, sans que cela ait été expérimentalement établi, déceler des masses magnétiques **enfouies,** [17] comme certains **gisements** [18] métalliques, ou de gros objets de métal.

Quant à la radiesthésie, qui affirme souvent pouvoir **dépister** [19] les maladies, retrouver les enfants disparus, et faire des découvertes sur plans ou sur photographies, elle **réclame** [20] le scepticisme le plus grand, conclut le Prof. Rocard.

L'orientation des pigeons voyageurs

Dans un appendice, le Prof. Rocard étudie un autre phénomène tout aussi mystérieux: l'orientation des pigeons voyageurs. Faut-il envisager, ici encore, un sens « magnétique »? Cela n'est pas impossible.

On peut transposer au pigeon le phénomène « sourcier ». Il est prouvé que l'homme tenant une baguette est plus sensible lorsqu'il se déplace rapidement. D'avion, par exemple, le Prof. Rocard a détecté des variations magnétiques plus faibles. Ce qui correspond parfaitement à la théorie.

Le pigeon volant 30 fois plus vite que l'homme ne marche, pourrait donc percevoir de faibles variations magnétiques, donc « sentir » un trajet donné, savoir s'il se déplace à travers des « montagnes » ou des « vallées magnétiques », dont il pourrait garder le souvenir, ce qui l'aiderait à retrouver sa route.

Ceci n'est pas une explication. Car il arrive que des pigeons, emmenés par train à 100 km de leur lieu d'attache, le rejoigne par un vol qu'ils n'ont pas fait préalablement.

Le Prof. Rocard passe donc en revue d'autres hypothèses. Le pigeon apprécie-t-il la composante verticale du champ magnétique terrestre, dont il grade le souvenir, par exemple de celle de son pigeonnier? Est-il sensible à la rotation de la Terre, au fait qu'en volant il s'écarte plus ou moins de l'axe du globe? En attachant sous les ailes de pigeons de petits aimants, ils reviennent moins facilement à leur lieu d'attache.

La parole est maintenant aux neuro-physiologistes.

---

15 *mill*   **17** *buried*   **19** *detect*
16 *flow*   **18** *strata*   **20** *calls for*

1. In the first fifteen lines it is stated that:
  A. the question of locating water by a divining rod is as old as the world
  B. the explanations of Professor Rocard have received complete support among his colleagues
  C. Professor Rocard does not illustrate his explanations with proven examples
  D. the ideas advanced by Professor Rocard have not been well received by physiologists.

---

1. A   **2.** In lines 17–30 Professor Rocard claims that:
  A. the action of the divining rod is independent of variations in the magnetic field
  B. the perfecting of apparatus capable of detecting slight variations in magnetic fields have helped Professor Rocard support his hypothesis
  C. the use of the divining rod has failed in the location of buried metal
  D. the movement of the rod is caused by underground pools of water.

---

2. B   **3.** In lines 31–43 Professor Rocard states that:
  A. all underground water can be detected by the divining rod
  B. certain people are more sensitive to changes in magnetic fields than others
  C. the placing of small magnets in the bend of the elbow magnifies the action of the rod
  D. only 25% of any given group of people are sensitive to magnetic variations.

---

3. B   **4.** In lines 58–74, according to Professor Rocard:
  A. the presence of underground streams can be detected by the rod
  B. only water which filters through the ground sets up magnetic variations
  C. Professor Rocard feels that radio-electric detection holds promise for future development
  D. the depth and magnitude of flow can also be estimated from the action of the rod.

---

4. B   **5.** In lines 75–95 Professor Rocard states that:
  A. the carrier pigeon's ability to return to a given place may be due to magnetic phenomena
  B. there seems to be no relationship between speed and the ability to detect magnetic variations
  C. small magnets attached to the wings of pigeons do not seem to affect their homing ability
  D. he intends to refute the neuro-physiologists and their theories about magnetism and pigeons.

---

5. A

Dangers de la pollution atmosphérique

Extrait de J. Boyer et H. de Lauture, "La pollution
atmosphérique," *Annales de l'université de Paris*
no. 3 (1966), pp. 315-320.

Sur un plan général, le danger de la pollution atmosphérique est multiple,
atteignant[1] l'homme, les animaux, les plantes, les objets matériels. Nous
nous attacherons plus spécialement aux troubles aigus et chroniques observés
chez l'homme.

5   Dans certains cas, les accidents ont présenté une **allure**[2] extrêmement
brutale, et même dramatique, comme dans la vallée de la Meuse en 1930, à
Donora en 1948, à Londres en 1952. Entre Huy et Seraing, dans la vallée de la
Meuse, l'inversion de température permit l'accumulation de polluants provenant
des **usines**[3] de la région; on observa de multiples syndromes respiratoires

10   aigus, dont certains **aboutirent**[4] à la mort. Parmi les polluants, les composés
oxygénés du soufre semblent avoir joué un rôle primordial. A Donora, en
Pennsylvanie, les conditions météorologiques étaient très comparables et, dans
cette vallée industrielle, le brouillard persista quatre jours; les signes respiratoires étaient aussi **au premier plan,**[5] et dix-sept **décès**[6] furent notés. On

15   pense, sans pouvoir apporter de preuves formelles, que ces accidents avaient été
dûs vraisemblablement à des composés soufrés. Enfin, à Londres, le **tableau**[7]
clinique était le même, mais des décès furent observés à un **stade plus
précoce,**[8] dès le premier jour, et les foyers domestiques ont constitué la principale source de pollution, contrairement aux deux autres exemples à pré-

20   dominance industrielle.

Le problème médical le plus redoutable est posé par les *effets très prolongés
d'une pollution atmosphérique modérée.* Si la plupart des cancers humains
sont devenus un peu plus fréquents, en raison de l'augmentation de la durée
de la vie, par contre *le cancer du poumon a augmenté de façon considérable.*

25   L'usage du tabac n'explique pas tout. En effet, cette maladie survient plus
volontiers dans les grands centres industriels, comme l'ont montré en France
d'une part Gernez-Rieux, Gervois et leurs collaborateurs, d'autre part Truhaut.
A l'étranger il en est de même, et les experts de l'Organisation mondiale de la
Santé ont bien souligné que la pollution atmosphérique favorisait très nette-

30   ment l'apparition du cancer du poumon.

Comment l'expliquer? D'une part l'irritation chronique favorise le cancer.
Le gaz sulfureux qui érode le zinc des toitures, irrite aussi nos **bronches.**[9]
Mais surtout il existe des produits cancérogènes en quantité importante dans
les villes, notamment les benzopyrènes. Quand on veut provoquer un cancer

35   chez un animal, on emploie ce produit. Si l'on **badigeonne**[10] la peau d'un

---

1 *affecting*   5 *in the foreground*   9 *bronchia*
2 *aspect*   6 *deaths*   10 *brush*
3 *factories*   7 *picture stage*
4 *resulted*   8 *earlier*

animal avec des poussières provenant des cités industrielles, on peut provoquer **à la longue** [11] des cancers cutanés. Et l'on sait que d'autres produits cancérogènes que le 3-4 benzopyrène sont aussi présents dans l'atmosphère des grandes villes.

40   On a beaucoup insisté aussi sur la fréquence des affections respiratoires banales dans les grandes villes industrielles, et aussi sur l'augmentation de la mortalité par *bronchite chronique.* C'est un fait indiscutable. Les végétaux souffrent aussi de cet état, et certains arbres n'ont fleuri à Paris que pendant l'occupation allemande. L'homme en est aussi victime.

45   Rappelons enfin que certains polluants, chez quelques personnes, peuvent se comporter comme des allergènes et **déclencher** [12] des sensibilisations diverses, en particulier des crises d'asthme. Mais en milieu rural d'autres produits peuvent aussi les provoquer. Les inconvénients cités plus haut sont tellement grands qu'il est inutile de tenir compte de ces effets accessoires.

1. The first sentence states that:
- A. atmospheric pollution affects only man and animal life
- B. it seems to have a very minor effect on plant life or on material construction
- C. in this study, special attention will be given to the effect observed on man
- D. the chronic troubles undergone by man are relatively mild.

---

1. C   **2.** Lines 7–20 state that:
- A. polluting elements from factories, because of a temperature inversion, caused an accumulation of smog in the valley of the Meuse which resulted in several deaths
- B. atmospheric conditions in Donora, Pennsylvania, however, where seventeen persons died, were not at all similar
- C. oxygenized compounds of sulphur were not considered to have been to blame in the Donora deaths
- D. in London the atmospheric pollution is due to the heavy concentration of industry on the outskirts of the city.

---

2. A   **3.** In lines 21–30 we are told that:
- A. the most fearful medical problem is the result of prolonged exposure to mild atmospheric pollution
- B. substantial increases in the consumption of tobacco explains the increase in lung cancer quite adequately
- C. in the large industrial centers where the increased smoking per employee has risen sharply lung cancer has increased proportionately
- D. health authorities have pointed out, however, that different trends have been observed in foreign industrial centers.

---

11 *eventually*   12 *to set in motion*

3. A   4. Lines 31–39 state that:

    A. sulphur gas, which has an eroding effect on the exposed metal of roofs in the cities, seems to have little effect on our bronchial tubes

    B. cancer-producing agents in themselves are not present in any important amounts in the cities

    C. in order to produce eventual skin cancer in an animal it is sufficient to apply with a brush samples of the dust taken from industrial cities

    D. the only cancer-producing products found in large cities are the benzo-pyrenes.

---

4. C   5. Lines 40–44 state that:

    A. ordinary respiratory ailments have increased sharply in industrial cities

    B. no increase in the mortality rate attritutable to the increase in respiratory ailments has been noted

    C. plant life in the cities seems to remain unaffected

    D. during the German occupation of Paris, because of the type of fuel consumption, certain trees seemed to suffer more than usual.

---

5. A   6. The last paragraph states that:

    A. some people are allergic to certain polluting elements which can have the effect of triggering severe attacks of asthma

    B. in rural areas these same elements are necessary in order to produce similar effects

    C. the overall effects of atmospheric pollution have been widely exaggerated

    D. it is useless to compare the very great increase in convenience to industry with the relatively small inconvenience resulting from the side effects of the fuels used.

6. A

Une nouvelle antilope

Extrait d'une note de MM. de Rothschild et Neuville dans *Comptes rendus des séances de l'Académie des Sciences*, Vol. 144, pp. 98, 99.

Le nouveau Céphalophe dont nous nous permettons de présenter l'étude à l'Académie appartient au groupe du *Cephalophus sylvicultor* Afzel. Cette espèce, caractérisée surtout par la présence d'**une tache** [1] jaunâtre longitudinale dans la région dorso-lombaire, est assez variable quant à ce caractère

5   même. Son polymorphisme a été tout récemment limité par l'établissement d'une **coupe** [2] spécifique, M. Jentink ayant admis, pour certains exemplaires très différents du type, une nouvelle espèce à laquelle il a donné le nom de *Coxi*. Le spécimen d'après lequel cette dernière espèce a été décrite

---

1 *spot, streak*   **2** *demarcation*

provient du **N.-O.** [3] de la Rhodésie; le *C. sylvicultor* habite la côte orientale
d'Afrique, du Libéria à l'Angola, et celui que nous étudions est originaire du
centre africain proprement dit; leurs habitats sont donc fort différents.

Les caractères généraux de notre Céphalophe le rapprochent du *C. Coxi,*
mais plusieurs particularités l'en éloignent suffisamment pour que nous en
fassions une nouvelle espèce, dont nous allons signaler les caractères.

La coloration générale est notablement différente de celle du *Coxi;* elle
est d'abord beaucoup plus sombre, et, tandis que ce dernier est en quelque
sorte lavé d'une teinte gris jaune passant au gris pur dans certaines parties
claires comme les **joues,**[4] le nôtre est, au contraire, d'une coloration **fauve** [5]
noirâtre, passant à un gris assez clair sur les joues et le **menton,**[6] comme
chez le *Coxi,* mais se fonçant parfois jusqu'au noir. C'est ainsi que **le front** [7]
de notre spécimen est foncé au point d'être presque noir, tandis qu'il est
roux [8] chez le *Coxi;* il en est de même pour la partie dorsale du cou. La
touffe [9] frontale, au contraire, reste d'un roux **à peine** [10] mélangé d'un peu de
noir. Les **épaules,**[11] assez foncées et recouvertes de **poils** [12] courts, offrent une
transition entre la couleur noire médiane de la nuque et la couleur claire de
la tache dorsale, qui commence, sans limites bien nettes, en arrière des épaules.
Cette tache est très étroite, presque linéaire même; elle s'étend en arrière
jusqu'à 0^m, 06 environ de la queue; cet intervalle est occupé par une seconde
tache rappelant tout à fait le « disque » du *sylvicultor* ou du *Coxi;* sa forme
est plutôt celle d'un demi-disque assez bien dessiné.

Ces deux taches ne sont pas très nettement séparées; on les distingue
facilement cependant, d'après la différence des poils qui participent res-
pectivement à leur formation.

Tandis que ceux de la tache dorsale sont d'un blond très pâle, terminés,
et parfois aussi **annelés,**[13] de brun noir, ceux du disque sont noirs sur
presque toute leur longueur et terminés d'une pointe blanche. Il en résulte,
pour cette dernière tache, un aspect noir piqueté, **rehaussé** [14] par la présence
de poils assez courts, d'un blanc très pur, au-dessous de cette coloration.
La tache dorsale est bordée latéralement de poils un peu plus sombres que
le reste de la coloration, et cette bordure contribue à la faire **ressortir** [15]
et à la délimiter; son apparence, en raison de la terminaison brune de ses
poils, serait sans cela beaucoup moins nette et rappellerait encore moins ce
qui se passe chez les *C. sylvicultor* et *Coxi,* où sa coloration est entièrement
claire; cette bordure semble exister aussi chez le *Coxi.*

De part et d'autre de la tache dorsale ainsi bordée, les poils sont bruns
sur leur plus grande longueur et terminés de jaune. Cette coloration fait
place, insensiblement, à celle des parties inférieures, qui sont jaunâtres par
suite du développement de plus en plus grand de la terminaison jaune des
poils. La coloration générale est comme nous l'avons dit d'un fauve noirâtre. Tandis que **la lèvre** [16] inférieure, bordée d'un peu de noir, est, ainsi

---

3 *northwest*	**8** *red*	**13** *ringed*
4 *cheeks*	**9** *tuft*	**14** *accentuated*
5 *tawny*	**10** *hardly*	**15** *stand out*
6 *chin*	**11** *shoulders*	**16** *lip*
7 *forehead*	**12** *hair*	

que le menton et **la gorge,**[17] d'un gris noir très léger, la partie inférieure du cou et la poitrine se teintent de fauve, et la ligne médiane **du ventre**[18] se fonce légèrement par rapport à la coloration jaunâtre avoisinante. La région **inguinale**[19] est noirâtre. Les jambes, enfin, rappellent assez bien 55 celles du *Coxi.*

1. The first paragraph states that:
   A. the new antelope is characterized by an invariable yellow longitudinal stripe along the dorsal lombar region.
   B. the Coxi antelope inhabits the same area as does the one under consideration
   C. the habits of both are very different
   D. the appearance of the yellow streak can vary considerably.

1. D 2. Lines 12–14 state that:
   A. the general characteristics of both antelopes are practically the same
   B. the general characteristics differ sharply
   C. certain characteristics are sufficiently different to warrant the designation of a new species
   D. the author is going to point out the similarities.

2. C 3. The third paragraph (lines 15–30) states that:
   A. the color of the new antelope is lighter than that of the Coxi
   B. the coloration of the face of the new antelope is almost reddish
   C. the shoulders are covered with long hair
   D. both animals have a somewhat similar round spot at the base of the tail.

3. D 4. Lines 31–33 state that:
   A. the spots on both animals are clearly defined
   B. the spots are not clearly distinguishable from the dorsal stripe
   C. the hair from the dorsal stripe and the spot at the base of the tail is similar
   D. the difference in the hair permits making the distinction.

4. D 5. In lines 34–44 we are told that:
   A. the hair of the antelope with the disc-shaped spot is black tipped with white
   B. they have an undercoat of darker hair
   C. the hair of the dorsal stripe of the type under consideration is a light tan tipped with white
   D. this tipping with white intensifies the stripe and facilitates recognition.

5. A 6. In lines 45–55 we learn that:
   A. on either side of the dorsal stripe the hair is brown with yellow tips
   B. the lower lip is fringed with yellow hair
   C. the lower part of the neck and chest are of a whitish color
   D. the legs are considerably heavier than those of the Coxi.

6. A

---

17 *throat*   18 *belly*   19 *loin*

La conquête espagnole du Nouveau Monde

Extrait de Roland Mousnier, *Les XVIe et XVIIe
siècles: Les progrès de la civilisation européenne et
le déclin de l'orient (1492-1715)* dans *Histoire ge-
nérale des civilisations* (Presses Universitaires de
France, Paris)

Les Espagnols ont colonisé surtout les Antilles, de dimensions réduites
et rafraîchies par les brises de mer, le Mexique et les Andes du Pérou et de
Bolivie où ils retrouvaient des conditions analogues à celles des *mesetas* de
leur pays. Ils se sont moins occupés du reste de l'Amérique centrale et de
l'Amérique du Sud, défendues par la forêt tropicale. Ils ont quelque peu
négligé l'Argentine et la Patagonie d'une part, l'Amérique du Nord, de l'autre,
pays tempérés qui ne répondaient pas à l'idée qu'on se faisait des colonies.
Des hasards de l'exploration sur la côte nord du golfe du Mexique leur
firent considérer ces régions comme infertiles et sans intérêt.

Les grandes conquêtes furent celle de Cuba par Diego Velasquez, qui
comptait parmi ses hommes Fernand Cortès, celle du Mexique (1519-1522)
par Fernand Cortès, celle du Pérou par François Pizarre et Almagro (1532-
1536). La conquête et l'exploration furent pour les *conquistadores* une longue
souffrance.

Il fallut des marches interminables d'abord à travers des terres chaudes
exhalant la fièvre, sous des **nuées** [1] de moustiques, puis à travers des sierras
et des plateaux désertiques, très élevés, où la soif, la faim, l'air raréfié, les
sautes [2] de température, l'excitation nerveuse, **minaient** [3] vite les énergies.
Les **flèches** [4] empoisonnées des Indiens faisaient le reste. Alonso de Ojeda,
le brillant courtisan qui, pour amuser la Reine, faisait des pirouettes à Séville
au sommet de la Giralda, meurt abandonné, dans la dernière misère. L'on vit
un gentilhomme, Don Antonio Ossorio, frère du marquis d'Astorga, vêtu d'un
pourpoint [5] de mauvaise étoffe, déchiré, sans chausses, sans souliers, sans
coiffure, avec une épée sans **fourreau**,[6] demi-nu par un froid violent, cherchant sa subsistance avec ses **ongles**.[7] L'expédition de Hortal tourne au
désastre. Les chevaux deviennent enragés, les hommes sont atteints d'une
fièvre qui les plonge dans le sommeil. Lorsqu'ils rencontrent une rivière où
brillent dans le sable des **paillettes** [8] d'or, ils sont **épuisés**.[9] Ce n'est plus
l'or qu'ils veulent, c'est la vie. Dans la campagne de Veragua, parmi ceux
qui suivent Felipe Gutierrez, la vie est pour les cannibales. Même les gentilshommes tuent des compatriotes pour les manger. Les compagnons de
Navaez, abandonnés sur un **îlot**,[10] se tuent les uns les autres jusqu'à ce qu'il
n'en reste plus qu'un.

Même chez les plus heureux, que d'épreuves avant le succès, comme cette
« nuit triste » où les compagnons de Fernand Cortès, cherchant à fuir Mexico,
furent massacrés sur les **chaussées** [11] de la ville. Le matin vit sur les bords du

---

1 *clouds*	5 *doublet*	9 *exhausted*
2 *sudden changes*	6 *scabbard*	10 *small island*
3 *undermined*	7 *nails*	11 *streets*
4 *arrows*	8 *grains*	

lac une poignée de spectres couverts de boue et de sang autour du *conquistador* **pleurant** [12] sa fortune perdue, et la conquête européenne fut sauvée à cet instant par l'Indienne Marina, la maîtresse du chef, qui lui rendit courage.

40   Même le succès obtenu, que d'**amertume** [13] dans la victoire lorsqu'il fallut s'habituer sans espoir de retour à une terre étrangère, froide au cœur, loin du pays natal et des tombeaux des **aïeux.** [14] Bien des récits sont lourds de regrets et de nostalgie inavoués, comme celui qui nous montre Andres de la Vega, le père du **métis** [15] inca Garcilaso, réunissant ses vieux compagnons d'armes

45   pour partager avec eux une plante d'Europe, trois **asperges,** [16] les premières qui fussent venues sur le plateau de Cuzco.

    1.   Les Espagnols n'ont pas beaucoup colonisé (lignes 1–9) :
        A. l'Argentine   B. le Mexique   C. la Patagonie   D. les Antilles

---

1. A   2.   Pour les *conquistadores* la conquête et l'exploration furent (lignes 10–14) :
        A. faciles
        B. pleines de souffrance
        C. des expéditions paisibles
        D. des expéditions pour exploiter l'huile du Nouveau Monde.

---

2. B   3.   La force des Espagnols fut minée par (lignes 15–25) :
        A. les courtisans de la reine   C. l'air des grandes altitudes
        B. des maladies du foie   D. la volupté de vivre dans un pays nouveau.

---

3. C   4.   Hortal ne mène pas à bien son expédition (lignes 25–33) :
        A. à cause des attaques par les indigènes
        B. parce que ses hommes attrappent une étrange maladie
        C. parce que ses hommes s'entretuent pour de l'or
        D. à cause des cannibales.

---

4. B   5.   La conquête européenne réussit grâce (lignes 34–39) :
        A. aux compagnons de Cortès   C. aux exhortations des prêtres
        B. à la superstition des indigènes   D. à une très bonne amie du chef.

---

5. D

Les Espagnols résistèrent à toutes les causes de destruction et vainquirent.
La plupart étaient originaires de pays pauvres et rudes, des *sierras* d'Estramadure, des hautes terres du Léon, des Asturies et de la Castille, habitués de longue date aux étés torrides, aux hivers glacés, au vête-

5   ment mince, à la nourriture frugale, aux longues courses, beaucoup ayant une hérédité de bergers **transhumants.** [1] C'étaient presque tous de vieux soldats qui avaient lutté contre les musulmans à Grenade et dans les présides d'Afrique, plus tard contre les Français et les Allemands en Italie, et pour qui la guerre était la vie même. Bon nombre étaient réellement gentilshommes.

---

12 *bewailing*   **14** *forefathers*   **16** *asparagus*
13 *bitterness*   **15** *mixed blood*

1 *flock driving*

¹⁰ La plupart sans doute étaient d'origine **roturière,**² paysans, artisans, chassés
par la misère, mais tous se prétendaient et se voulaient *hidalgos.* Tous furent
comme **corsetés par**³ le vieil idéal chevaleresque de dévouement à une
grande cause, à leur chef et à leur Roi, par le sens de l'honneur, et de ce
qu'ils se devaient à eux-mêmes. C'étaient d'ailleurs des hommes de la Renais-
¹⁵ sance. Ils avouaient, non sans naïveté, leur désir de gloire, leur soif de sur-
passer les grands capitaines de l'Antiquité, Alexandre, César, Pompée, Han-
nibal. Un généreux **orgueil**⁴ les tenait debout dans les souffrances.

C'étaient des Espagnols graves, sombres, raides, tendus, brûlant d'un feu
intérieur, prêts pour toutes les entreprises folles pourvu qu'elles fussent
²⁰ grandes, insatiables, poussés toujours plus loin « à l'épée et au compas, plus
et plus et plus et plus » (devise du capitaine Bernardo de Vargas Machuca).
Au fond, dans la génération des conquérants, beaucoup méprisaient cet or
qu'ils croyaient chercher, et lorsqu'ils le possédaient, comme Fernand Cortès,
ils le **gaspillaient**⁵ aussitôt en de nouvelles entreprises. A peine installés, ils
²⁵ allaient ailleurs. « L'âme des Espagnols est inquiète et de grande entreprise »
(Michel Servet). Pour quoi brûlaient-ils, au fond, lorsqu'ils couraient vers tous
les pays de légende, celui des Amazones, celui des montagnes de diamants,
celui de la fontaine de Jouvence, ou vers les cloches d'or de la grande Quivira?
Peut-être pour ce que ce monde ne peut pas donner.

---

1. In lines 2–11 it is stated that in Spain the life of most of the *conquistadores*
had been:
A. comfortable   B. hard   C. usually luxurious   D. provincial.

---

1. B   **2.** They were strengthened in their hardships by (lines 11–17):
A. the desire for glory
B. the thought of their families in Spain
C. the fear of the King's displeasure
D. the desire for riches.

---

2. A   **3.** Lines 18–29 state that the conquest succeeded because:
A. they were naturally warlike
B. the conquerors administered their new riches wisely
C. the Spanish court supplied them with capable administrators
D. the restlessness of their temperament which led them to great deeds.

---

3. D

Tous étaient **mus**¹ par l'ardeur religieuse. En allant dans les terres
nouvelles, ils continuaient la croisade et l'œuvre de conversion. Et certes, il y
avait bien des contradictions entre leur foi et leur conduite, bien des inco-
hérences dans le comportement de ces natures ardentes et complexes, lancées

---

2 *of the common people*   **4** *pride*   **5** *squandered*
3 *bound up in*

1 *moved*

5 dans l'aventure. Mais celles-là sont parfois singulièrement révélatrices.
Fernand Cortès ne voulut avoir aucune relation avec l'Indienne Marina tant
qu'elle fut **païenne**: [2] dès qu'elle fut baptisée, il en fit sa maîtresse! Les
seules instructions de Diego Velasquez qu'il ne violât jamais furent celles qui
concernaient l'évangélisation: le premier but de la conquête est de servir
10 Dieu et de **répandre** [3] la **foi** [4] chrétienne; il ne faut pas perdre une occasion
de faire connaître la vraie foi de l'Eglise de Dieu. Sa bannière portait ces
mots en latin: « Amis, suivons la Croix et si nous avons la foi, en vérité par
ce signe nous vaincrons ». Tous pensaient ainsi. Tous avaient une fervente
dévotion à la Vierge, le culte de saint Jacques sous les traits d'un chevalier
15 **l'épée haute.** [5] Tous étaient conquérants « afin que toujours les Espagnols
combatissent contre les Infidèles et les ennemis de la Sainte Foi du Christ »
(Gomara).

Leur religion, relation directe de l'homme avec un dieu personnel, **tout** [6]
puissance et tout bonté, toujours présent, protecteur et bienfaisant, leur don-
20 nait, dans les pires dangers, un sentiment de force et de sécurité, que les
Indiens ne trouvaient pas au même degré dans la leur. La nécessité de plaire
à Dieu, en répondant à sa grâce par l'amour prouvé par les œuvres, avait
développé, malgré leurs **défaillances** [7] morales, leur sens de la responsabilité
et de l'effort personnel. L'examen de conscience, la prière dans les **tenta-**
25 **tions,** [8] avaient accru leur aptitude à conserver l'image mentale qui doit pré-
dominer et **entraîner** [9] l'acte voulu. Ils en tiraient une façon de **se raidir** [10]
contre les difficultés et les obstacles que n'avaient pas les indigènes. Ils devaient
à la religion un meilleur jugement des choses et un meilleur équilibre. Certes,
le *conquistador* qui, la nuit, traçait dans l'air un grand cercle avec son épée
30 pour éloigner les démons, pouvait paraître à ce moment au même point que
l'Indien qui allumait un grand feu pour les mettre en fuite. En réalité,
persuadé d'être protégé par le Christ invoqué au moyen du signe de la Croix,
l'Espagnol n'éprouvait pas les terreurs de l'Indien, **grelottant d'effroi,** [11]
et conservait l'esprit plus net et le cœur plus ferme.
35 Tous les Espagnols d'ailleurs en étaient arrivés dans leur conception d'ensemble de l'Univers au troisième stade mental, au stade du rationalisme quali-
tatif, certains parvinrent au quatrième, celui du rationalisme quantitatif, et
la pensée de tous, originaires de pays de technique supérieure, avait sur
nombre de points, des caractères de rationalisme expérimental et de positivité
40 qui **l'emportaient** [12] de beaucoup sur tout ce que l'on aurait pu trouver
d'analogue chez les artisans indigènes. Il en faudrait dire d'ailleurs autant de
tous les Européens.

1.   The main idea which comes out of lines 1–17 is that the faith of the *conquistadores* was:
A. reflected in the purity of their morals

2 *pagan*	**6** *all*	**10** *to brace themselves*
3 *spread*	**7** *lapses*	**11** *shivering with fright*
4 *faith*	**8** *temptations*	**12** *were superior to*
5 *raised sword*	**9** *bring about*	

B. one of the deepest forces which moved them

C. not much more than a facade

D. in most ways quite unlike that of the Crusaders

---

1. B   **2.** The effect of their religion was (lines 18–27) :

A. to encourage the habit of introspection among them

B. about the same as that which the Indian religions had on the Indians

C. to incur occasional moral lapses

D. to increase their warlike propensities.

---

2. A   **3.** Lines 27–34 state that in order to ward off evil spirits:

A. the Indians had special pipes and tobacco

B. the Spaniards waved their swords in the air in a special way

C. the Indians and Spaniards had basically similar ceremonies

D. invoked, in reality, the same God.

---

3. B

Un incident avant la Révolution

Extrait de Jean Robiquet, *La vie quotidienne au temps de la Révolution.* (Librairie Hachette)

Un curieux phénomène qui **secoua** [1] les nerfs du pays durant l'été de 1789 appartient plus à notre sujet. Je veux parler de la *Grande Peur* qui **se déchaîna** [2] brusquement par les campagnes à l'époque de **la moisson** [3] et dont une ordonnance royale, **affichée** [4] sur les murs et lue aux **prônes** [5]
5   des **paroisses,** [6] signalait toute la gravité:

« *De par le Roi.*

« Sa Majesté est informée que des troupes de brigands répandus dans le royaume s'attachent à tromper les habitants de plusieurs communautés, en leur persuadant qu'ils peuvent, sans s'écarter des intentions de Sa Majesté,
10   attaquer le château, enlever les archives et commettre d'autres excès envers les habitations et les propriétés des Seigneurs. Sa Majesté se trouve dans la nécessité de faire connaître que de semblables violences excitent toute son indignation. . . . **Elle** [7] ne peut voir sans la plus grande affliction le trouble qui règne dans son Royaume, trouble excité depuis quelque temps par des
15   gens malintentionnés et qui commencent par **semer** [8] de faux bruits dans les campagnes, afin d'y répandre l'alarme et d'engager les habitants à prendre les armes. . . . Sa Majesté invite tous les bons citoyens à s'opposer de tout leur pouvoir à la continuation d'un désordre qui fait le scandale et la honte de la France et qui contrarie essentiellement les vues bienfaisantes dont le Roi et les
20   représentants de la Nation sont animés pour l'avancement du bonheur et de la prospérité du Royaume.

---

1 *shook*   4 *posted*   7 *his majesty*
2 *was unleashed*   5 *sermons*   8 *propagate*
3 *harvest*   6 *parishes*

Fait à Versailles, le 9 août 1789.

Signé: « Louis ». Et, plus bas: « Le comte de Saint-Priest ».

Quelle est donc cette Grande Peur dont les pouvoirs publics semblent
25 s'inquiéter si fortement, à une heure où tant d'autres sujets réclameraient leur
attention? Une sorte de folie collective, un peuple qui se fait peur à lui-
même et qui voit des brigands là où il n'y a que des hallucinés.

Nous avons la chance de posséder deux documents, l'un officiel, l'autre
privé, sur les événements qui se déroulèrent alors dans la région du Beauvaisis.
30 Et, par une **rencontre** [9] assez rare, les deux pièces suggèrent des conclusions
à peu près semblables en ce qui touche la grande panique campagnarde.

La première est un rapport que Duguey, prévôt de la **maréchaussée** [10]
de Clermont, adresse le 28 juillet à Blossac, **intendant** [11] de Soissons. Il y
relate que, l'avant-veille, des **braconniers** [12] se sont pris de querelle avec des
35 gardes-chasse, sur le territoire d'Estrées-Saint-Denis, c'est-à-dire à quatre lieues
de Clermont. Les habitants de cette paroisse, toujours dans l'idée qu'on
en veut à [13] leurs récoltes, se sont empressés de donner l'alarme. Les paroisses
voisines ont également sonné le tocsin et le lendemain matin, à 7 heures, la
maréchaussée **s'est mise en branle,** [14] flanquée d'un détachement du Royal
40 Bourgogne. Pendant que le prévôt Duguey fait lui-même **seller** [15] son cheval,
des **exprès** [16] de Lieuville et d'Estrées-Saint-Denis viennent lui apprendre
que tout est ravagé chez eux. Il traverse la ville en ne voyant que des femmes
qui **s'enfuient,** [17] d'autres qui ferment leurs **volets.** [18] Tout le monde tremble
et se désole; car on annonce déjà que quatre mille brigands arrivent à
45 Clermont par la route de Nointel.

Le prévôt **a beau se répéter** [19] que la nouvelle est peu vraisemblable,
il n'en est pas moins fort ému quand il se met en route avec seize cavaliers et
dix bourgeois à cheval qui veulent bien lui **prêter main-forte.** [20] A peine
est-il sorti de la ville qu'il rencontre le capitaine des chasses de Monseigneur
50 le duc de Bourbon, accouru pour lui dire que le péril est imaginaire, qu'il n'y
a pas de grains coupés et que tout **se ramène à** [21] une querelle entre gardes
et braconniers et à un attroupement de curieux.

Voilà de quoi rassurer Clermont, mais pas pour longtemps, hélas! car
un autre bruit se répand: du côté de Paris et de Beauvais, des bandes en
55 armes sont signalées. Du coup, chacun se croit perdu; on se rassemble comme
on peut, on jure de mourir ensemble, jusqu'au moment où l'on apprend que
les soi-disant agresseurs sont de braves habitants des paroisses voisines qui,
armés de fourches et de haches, viennent au secours de leurs concitoyens.
Quelles effusions après une aussi chaude alerte! Les gens de Clermont **se**
60 **cotisent** [22] pour offrir un vin d'honneur à leurs défenseurs et, quand ils se
sont bien rafraîchis, on les emmène chasser dans la forêt de Neuville.

---

9 *coincidence*
10 *mounted constabulary*
11 *bailiff*
12 *poachers*
13 *covet*

14 *went into action*
15 *saddle*
16 *dispatches*
17 *are fleeing*
18 *shutters*

19 *vainly tells himself*
20 *lend assistance*
21 *boils down to*
22 *take up a collection*

1. The "Great Fear" (lines 1–5)
A. began rather suddenly
B. had long been anticipated
C. was caused by a severe reaction to arbitrary royal decrees
D. began in the rural churches.

---

1. A

2. The King's decree (lines 6–23) stated:
A. that ill-intentioned people were spreading false rumors
B. that all good people should assist the army against the troops of brigands
C. that the King and the representatives of the nation would oppose with all their power the disorders which were a scandal and a shame to France
D. that such disorders were being stirred up by foreign agents.

---

2. A

3. In lines 24–27 we learn that the "Great Fear" was due to:
A. the presence of bands of brigands which preyed on the countryside
B. the inability of the public powers to protect the people
C. self-induced fear fed by collective hallucination
D. the absence of other problems to occupy the attention of the people.

---

3. C

4. Lines 28–31 state that:
A. the panic is discussed in detail in two official documents of the time
B. the panic is explained by the events which took place in the Beauvaisis region
C. we find similar conclusions expressed in a private and an official document
D. occasioned a rather rare encounter between public and private investigators.

---

4. C

5. The first document (lines 32–45) is a report that
A. some poachers near Clermont got into an argument with the gamewardens
B. the inhabitants of Clermont nearly lynched some poachers
C. the provost Duguey went to inspect on horseback the ravages near Lieuville and Estrées-Saint-Denis
D. three thousand brigands were converging on Clermont.

---

5. A

6. The provost (lines 46–52) is
A. alarmed by the report of destruction made by sixteen noblemen and ten mounted citizens who came to lend him support
B. dubious about the truth of the report at first
C. informed by the captain of the Duke of Bourbon's hunt that only half as much grain had been destroyed as was reported
D. informed that the quarrel between the poachers and the gamewardens was aggravated by a group of curious onlookers who took sides.

---

6. B

7. The people of the town of Clermont (lines 53–61):
A. are reassured by the report from Paris
B. come face-to-face with a band of men armed with axes and pitchforks, intent on pillage
C. contribute individually in money and wine to buy off the invaders
D. take the newcomers hunting in the forest of Neuville.

---

7. D

Les émigrés au temps de la Révolution

Extrait de Jean Robiquet, *La vie quotidienne au temps de la Révolution.* (Librairie Hachette)

On se rappelle le passage des *Mémoires d'outre-tombe,* où Chateaubriand conte sa détresse en Angleterre à l'époque de l'émigration: « Je suçais des morceaux de linge que je **trempais** [1] dans l'eau; je mâchais de l'herbe et du papier. Quand je passais devant des boutiques de **boulangers,** [2] mon **sup-**
5   **plice** [3] était horrible. Par une rude soirée d'hiver, je restai deux heures planté devant un magasin de fruits secs et de viandes fumées, **avalant** [4] des yeux tout ce que je voyais: j'aurais mangé non seulement les comestibles, mais leurs **boîtes,** [5] **paniers** [6] et **corbeilles** ».[7]

Voilà de quoi nous apitoyer sur **le sort** [8] des réfugiés français durant ces
10   années lamentables. Encore les **hôtes** [9] de Londres comptaient-ils parmi les plus favorisés, puisque certains d'entre eux touchaient un shelling d'allo- cation par jour. Dans les villes allemandes, au contraire, Coblentz, Hambourg, Munich, Bamberg, pas de secours officiel à espérer, sinon pour les très grands **seigneurs.**[10]

15   Quand on se trouvait à bout de ressources,—et c'était le cas général puisqu'on ne touchait plus de revenus,—il fallait mendier par les rues ou exercer des métiers invraisemblables. Au coin d'une place d'Erlanger, le comte de Vieuville **cirait les bottes** [11] et faisait les courses des bourgeois; la marquise de La Londe **tenait la caisse** [12] dans un café; le marquis de
20   Montbazet était allumeur de **quinquets,**[13] le chevalier d'Anselme, acteur, Mlle de Saint-Marceau, fille de boutique, tandis que la comtesse de Virieu **ravaudait des bas**,[14] en plein vent, comme une simple Fanchon du Pont- Neuf. . . .

Et que d'autres métamorphoses encore! **Perruquiers,**[15] professeurs de
25   danse, garçons limonadiers, **frotteurs,**[16] ouvreurs de portières, tous les emplois, tous les rôles étaient bons pour ce monde **naguère** [17] si brillant, si préoccupé de son plaisir, et dont la dernière comédie de société se terminait par un drame de la faim.

L'épreuve [18] dut être effroyable, mais il est permis de penser qu'elle était,
30   pour certains, largement méritée. Le loyalisme **à rebours** [19] des promoteurs de l'émigration, de ceux qui étaient partis en masse, dès 1789, dans le **sillage** [20] du comte d'Artois, du prince de Condé, et des Vaudreuil et des Lambesc, ne pouvait avoir que des conséquences fatales.

Vouloir sauver la monarchie en déclarant la guerre à la France et en
35   appelant l'étranger chez nous, pas de procédé plus infaillible pour couper la Nation en deux, exaspérer **la lutte** [21] des classes, donner à la Révolution un

---

1 *dipped*
2 *bakers*
3 *suffering*
4 *swallowing*
5 *boxes*
6 *hampers*
7 *baskets*

8 *the lot*
9 *guests*
10 *nobles*
11 *shined boots*
12 *was cashier*
13 *street lamps*
14 *darned stockings*

15 *hairdresser*
16 *polishers*
17 *formerly*
18 *trial*
19 *in reverse*
20 *wake*
21 *struggle*

caractère de violence qu'elle n'avait pas à ses débuts, bref pour attirer sur l'aristocratie d'abord, et sur la royauté ensuite, de formidables représailles.

1. In the first paragraph we learn that when Chateaubriand was in England:
A. he had plenty to eat
B. he used to suck pieces of linen soaked in wine
C. he was very fond of the dried fruit and smoked meat he bought in the shops
D. he almost starved.

---

1. D   **2.** Lines 9–14 state that:
A. the life of the refugees during these years of exile was gay
B. those in London were better off than those in Germany
C. all of the refugees in Germany received official help
D. the higher nobility received no consideration in London.

---

2. B   **3.** Lines 15–23 state that:
A. when they received their allotments they gave gay parties
B. when they ran out of funds they had to resort to begging or to taking any available job
C. the Count of Vieuville shined shoes and bet on the horses
D. the Countess Virieu mended stockings in full regalia.

---

3. B   **4.** In lines 24–28 we are told that:
A. some of the prouder members of this group refused to accept just any role
B. this society formerly so brilliant, had yet to play its greatest role
C. the comedy played by this society changed into a drama of hunger
D. the roles of hairdresser, dancing master, soft drink vendor were the most sought after.

---

4. C   **5.** Lines 29–33 tell us that:
A. those who followed the Prince of Condé were the only ones destined to succeed
B. the loyalty of the promotors of the emigration was of the most idealistic kind
C. certain of the emigrants received no more than they deserved
D. those who followed the Count of Artois were the most loyal.

---

5. C   **6.** Lines 34–38 state that the result of the decisions made by the refugees was to:
A. assure the ultimate preservation of the Monarchy
B. bring about the Napoleonic Wars
C. achieve a temporary national unity
D. introduce the element of violence into the Revolution.

---

6. D

La transe chamanique

Extrait de Lucien Sebag, "Le chamanisme ayoréo,"
L'Homme: Revue française d'anthropologie, Vol. V,
numéro 1, (Janvier-Mars 1965), p. 7, 8. (Editions
Mountons)

La nuit tombe sur le campement: sur la place, vaste espace **nettoyé** [1]
entouré de maisons, se tiennent deux groupes séparés l'un de l'autre par une
vingtaine de mètres: hommes et femmes ne se mêlent pas. Chaque homme a
planté sa lance près de lui; assis, il s'y appuie parfois; tous fument, tirant
5 lentement de longues **bouffées** [2] de leurs pipes, pièces rectilignes d'un bois
dur, creusé dans le sens de la longueur. Les conversations **vont leur train:** [3]
elles s'animent et se colorent lorsqu'un des participants raconte certains
événements d'importance dont il a été témoin; le conteur se lève alors et imite
le comportement des divers protagonistes du drame, qu'il s'agisse d'êtres
10 humains ou d'animaux; il saisit parfois sa lance ou son **arc,** [4] reproduisant
le geste du chasseur qui essaye de tuer sa proie, ou encore il **rampe** [5] sur le
sol, comme un serpent vers sa victime. Il joue une véritable pièce de théâtre
et le public participe activement au spectacle: éclats de rire, exclamations,
cris d'effroi, soupirs, encouragements accompagnent les paroles et les gestes
15 de l'acteur. Tous savent que certains ont plus de talent que d'autres et c'est
aux **assistants** [6] de sanctionner les qualités et les défauts de chacun. Les
femmes, cependant, ne prêtent qu'une attention distraite à l'autre groupe; tout
en vaquant [7] à différentes occupations elles conversent entre elles, se font
part des multiples incidents de la journée; le ton des voix est plus aigu, les
20 rires plus fréquents que chez les hommes, mais la même animation règne d'un
bout à l'autre de la place.

Ainsi, chaque jour, les Ayoréo **veillent**[8]-ils tard; à mesure que la nuit
avance on voit des hommes se lever, aller chercher leurs épouses, à moins que
ce ne soit l'inverse, pour regagner leur cabane. Vers minuit, une heure, le
25 silence reviendra sur le campement; la place n'en sera pas déserte pour
autant: lorsqu'il ne fait pas froid, de jeunes couples temporaires y dorment
enlacés.

Cette nuit cependant revêt une importance particulière: un homme est
gravement malade et il a demandé les soins du **chaman.**[9] Celui-ci est assis
30 au milieu du cercle des hommes; il parle peu et ne **trahit** [10] nulle impatience.
Comme si de rien n'était, les hommes discutent; bien qu'elles sachent ce
qui va se passer, les femmes ne se sont pas approchées. Soudain le chaman
tire sa pipe du sac qui est à côté de lui et commence à fumer, aspirant à
pleins poumons [11] de grandes bouffées qu'il ne **rejette** [12] pas. Entre
35 chacune d'elles s'écoule un long intervalle au cours duquel, bouche fermée,
joues dilatées, il semble chercher à faire pénétrer la fumée en son corps

1 *cleaned*	5 *crawls*	9 *medicine man*
2 *puffs*	6 *audience*	10 *betrays*
3 *jog along*	7 *being occupied*	11 *great lungfulls*
4 *bow*	8 *stay up*	12 *exhale*

le plus profondément possible. C'est un moment très délicat: les lèvres sont
serrées, tous les muscles sont bandés, rien ne sort par le nez; il est couvert de
sueur.[13] Lorsque la fumée a pénétré jusqu'aux moindres recoins de son
40 corps et « imbibé ses os », il porte de nouveau la pipe à ses lèvres. Progressivement il commence à trembler: lorsqu'il est tout entier la proie de ce tremblement il **amorce** [14] son chant. Celui-ci commence très bas et ne dure au début
que quelques secondes; à plusieurs reprises le chaman l'interrompt pour tirer
une nouvelle bouffée. Il est encore assis mais le tremblement s'est accentué,
45 ses gestes sont devenus mécaniques comme si l'homme n'obéissait plus qu'à
une injonction étrangère. Le chant se fait plus fort et les interruptions
s'espacent. L'homme commence à se redresser et à mouvoir son corps. Tout
s'accélère: il chante, s'arrête pour fumer puis donne sa pipe à l'un des
assistants pour qu'il la recharge, sans jamais cesser de trembler; il appuie
50 sa main droite sur sa cuisse, **imprimant** [15] à tout son corps un balancement
d'avant en arrière, orienté dans les diverses directions de l'espace; **subite-
ment** [16] il se dirige vers le malade qu'il n'a jusqu'alors pas même regardé,
s'accroupit et, d'un geste sauvage, avec violence, sous le coup d'une impulsion
irrésistible, porte à ses lèvres la partie atteinte et commence à la **sucer.**[17] Puis,
55 sans lui prêter attention, il s'éloigne du patient de la même démarche automatique. Il recommence alors à chanter, mais des spasmes l'interrompent. Ill **est
aux prises** [18] avec l'objet porteur de maladie qu'il a extrait du corps du
malade et avalé; les bruits de **gorge** [19] se multiplient, car l'effort qui lui est
demandé pour vomir est grand. Puis dans un ultime sursaut il rejette le
60 mauvais objet, épine, **caillou,**[20] morceau de **caoutchouc,**[21] cheveu, petit
animal, etc. Il le montre alors à tous les assistants, mais son regard **figé** [22]
porte bien **au-delà** [23] des spectateurs et il ne prononce pas un mot. Enfin,
toujours de cette allure **scandée,**[24] il s'éloigne du groupe et va enterrer la
maladie à l'extérieur du village, derrière les maisons. Ceci fait, il revient vers
65 le cercle des hommes, reprend sa place et progressivement retrouve son
calme; les femmes que la cérémonie a attirées rejoignent leur groupe et les
conversations recommencent tandis que le malade, aidé par son épouse ou un
ami, reprend le chemin de sa maison.

Le chaman est fatigué; après sa cure il pourra rester plusieurs heures sans
70 souffler mot. Doucement la nuit s'appesantit sur le campement ayoréo. Les
jours qui suivent, on observera le malade pour voir si son état s'améliore et
on commentera le résultat de la cure qu'on attribuera aux qualités ou aux
défauts du chaman. Celui-ci **a engagé son prestige** [25] dans l'entreprise: s'il
réussit, il recevra de son client un cadeau important et on fera de nouveau
75 appel à lui **le cas échéant.**[26] **Échouer** [27] une fois n'a pas de conséquences
graves, mais il faudra veiller à ce que l'échec ne se reproduise pas trop souvent.
Le chaman a certes d'autres moyens de rétablir sa **renommée,**[28] mais si des
chamans existent, c'est d'abord pour guérir les malades.

---

13 *sweat*	**19** *throat*	**25** *risked his reputation*
14 *begins*	**20** *pebble*	**26** *in case of need*
15 *imparting*	**21** *rubber*	**27** *to fail*
16 *suddenly*	**22** *fixed*	**28** *fame*
17 *suck*	**23** *beyond*	
18 *is struggling with*	**24** *measured rhythm*	

1. Lines 1–22 state that:
A. the men and women mingle freely in the evening in the square
B. both men and women smoke and carry on animated conversations together
C. the men often act out important events in which they played a part
D. the women actively encourage these dramatic representations by exclamations of approval, sighs, or bursts of laughter.

---

1. C   **2.** Lines 21–37 state that:
A. The Ayoreo do not ordinarily stay up until the early hours of the morning
B. the sick person is seated, surrounded by a circle of men who talk to him quietly
C. the medicine man smokes his pipe, inhaling great lungfulls which he retains within his lungs
D. as he continues to smoke, the women approach the sick person.

---

2. C   **3.** Lines 37–56 state that:
A. as the medicine man becomes progressively more saturated with the fumes of tobacco, his body grows rigid
B. he becomes covered with sweat and starts his dance
C. he grasps the affected part of the sick person and sucks it to remove the cause of the illness
D. after dancing around the sick man he sits down again and resumes his sucking.

---

3. C   **4.** Lines 56–76 state that:
A. the body of the medicine man is wracked with his efforts to spit out the offending cause of the sickness
B. when he is successful, he carefully conceals the object from the tribe and buries it outside the village limits
C. after the cure is completed the medicine man returns immediately to his own house to rest
D. once a medicine man fails, he is immediately replaced.

---

4. A

Comment devient-on chaman?

Extrait de Lucien Sebag, "Le chamanisme ayoréo," *L'Homme: Revue française d'anthropologie*, Vol. V, numéro 1, (Janvier-Mars 1965), p. 9.

Ce chaman (*nainai*), qui est-il et comment est-il devenu ce qu'il est? *En buvant du jus* [1] *de tabac*. C'est là une action difficile: le tabac mélangé à l'eau donne un liquide épais et **écœurant;** [2] très souvent il arrive que l'apprenti médecin réussisse à boire ce qui lui est donné mais le vomisse
5   ensuite; il a, en ce cas, droit à un nouvel essai quelques semaines ou quelques mois plus tard. Lorsqu'il ne vomit pas, il ne recommence plus, à moins de

---

1 *juice*   **2** *nauseating*

circonstances exceptionnelles: on citait le cas d'un chaman patenté qui, après s'être intégré à un groupe différent du sien, se soumit une seconde fois à l'épreuve inaugurale afin de convaincre ses nouveaux compagnons de
10 la réalité de ses pouvoirs. Inversement, un double échec entraîne généralement le renoncement du postulant; recommençant une troisième fois, il ne serait pas pris au sérieux. Certains exemples, rares il est vrai, infirment cependant cette règle, quelques chamans ayant essayé à plusieurs reprises avant de réussir.

15 La double tentative est très fréquente: rares sont ceux qui supportent le jus de tabac **du premier coup,**[3] rares sont ceux qui vomissent une fois familiarisés avec le liquide. Celui-ci est normalement bu de nuit; son absorption est précédée d'un jeûne d'une journée; de la même manière elle sera suivie de restrictions alimentaires qui pourront se prolonger trois jours. Les
20 effets de la boisson et de la faim sont très spectaculaires: l'homme est plongé dans un état comateux qui le laisse comme mort; le terme ayoréo qui le désigne alors, *tossi,* signifie « mort un peu ». Cet état dure généralement toute la nuit, mais ce temps varie évidemment en fonction des individus et de la quantité ingurgitée. Celle-ci équivaut à la contenance d'une tasse moyenne mais,
25 très souvent cette limite est dépassée: on citait le cas d'un homme qui en but jusqu'à un litre et resta quatre jours endormi; on le porta dans sa cabane pour que le soleil ne le brûlât pas, on le couvrit de vêtements préalablement chauffés et on l'entoura de soins attentifs jusqu'à ce qu'il se réveillât.

Il arrive parfois que le candidat **mâche**[4] des feuillés de tabac; le résultat
30 est identique. C'est donc une véritable épreuve qu'il traverse: lorsqu'il perdra conscience, il sera sans défense, sans résistance. Aussi est-il aidé par un homme, l'*Iyodisoï* qui prend soin de lui, le reçoit lorsqu'il **s'évanouit,**[5] le couvre et fait un feu à son côté, les flammes ayant le pouvoir de réduire les effets **néfastes**[6] du tabac. Parfois un couple l'assiste à son réveil et lui donne
35 à manger, le jeûne n'étant pas absolu; l'homme ou la femme, après s'être **enduit les mains**[7] de salive, lui massera le corps afin de le réveiller, de lui redonner des forces. L'*Iyodisoï* n'est pas un chaman plus âgé mais un individu quelconque, particulièrement attaché à celui qui **tente**[8] l'épreuve. Certes ce dernier se fait souvent guider par un maître qui lui donne des
40 conseils et peut lui prodiguer des encouragements; mais, au sens propre, l'élève n'est pas introduit dans un univers nouveau par son maître. Celui-ci n'a rien à transmettre: tout le monde est au courant de la tradition chamanique, et apprendre à sucer le corps d'un malade ne pose pas de problème, puisque chacun l'a vu faire des dizaines de fois et a entendu les commentaires
45 que chaque cure suscitait. Le maître se contentera de donner quelques recommandations orales mais ne **se livrera**[9] à aucune démonstration pratique à seule fin d'enseigner.

1. In the first paragraph we find that the medicine man achieves his status by:
A. smoking a mixture of jungle herbs

---

3 *at the first attempt*	**6** *unfortunate*	**8** *attempts*
4 *chews*	**7** *coated her hands*	**9** *indulge*
5 *faints*		

B. drinking tobacco juices

C. performing healings as he travels from tribe to tribe

D. showing bravery in the presence of his peers.

---

1. B   **2.** The context of lines 15–19 suggests that the word **jeûne** means:

A. a fast

B. a kind of spiritual séance

C. a tribal dance

D. a nocturnal ceremony

---

2. A   **3.** The amount of liquid involved for the average candidate (lines 22–26) amounts to about:

A. one quart   B. one teaspoonful   C. just a few drops   D. about a cup

---

3. D   **4.** In order to awaken the sleeping candidate (lines 32–42) an attendant:

A. kicks him   C. massages him

B. beats upon the tribal drums   D. tries to give him something to drink.

---

4. C

L'Université de Paris au Moyen Age

From E. Durkheim, "L'Histoire de l'Université de Paris," in *La vie universitaire à Paris* (Librairie Armand Colin, Paris), pp. 7-11.

Les premières écoles du Moyen Age se constituèrent auprès des établissements religieux: monastères, presbytères et cathédrales. Bien qu'elles fussent surtout destinées à former des clercs, elles n'excluaient pas les **laïcs.**[1] D'ailleurs, comme on pouvait, après les avoir fréquentées, rentrer dans le

5   monde et se marier, leur action n'était pas limitée aux seuls milieux ecclésiastiques.

Une école de ce genre se forma très tôt auprès de l'église métropolitaine de Paris, consacrée à Notre-Dame. Elle se tenait sur le parvis même de la cathédrale. C'était **l'évêque**[2] qui nommait les maîtres et qui contrôlait

10   l'enseignement par l'intermédiaire de son chancelier.

Pendant longtemps, cette école ressembla à toutes celles qui existaient auprès des autres cathédrales du pays. Mais, à partir du XIIe siècle, un ensemble de circonstances vint lui donner un éclat extraordinaire qui la mit **hors de pair,**[3] et ainsi prit naissance un type d'organisation extrêmement

15   original, que l'antiquité n'avait pas connu: c'est l'Université de Paris.

La première de ces causes fut tout accidentelle: dans les premières années du XIIe siècle, Abélard vint enseigner à Paris. Nous avons aujourd'hui quelque peine à nous représenter ce que fut Abélard pour ses contemporains. Comme le dit un de ses biographes, il est peu d'hommes qui aient aussi complètement

20   connu toutes les joies de la gloire; son action sur son temps ne peut être comparée qu'à celle de Voltaire sur le XVIIIe siècle. C'est qu'il personnifiait

---

1 *laymen*   **2** *bishop*   **3** *unrivalled*

tout ce que le Moyen Age aimait: la dialectique brillante, la foi raisonneuse, ce curieux mélange d'ardeur religieuse et d'enthousiasme scientifique qui caractérise cette époque. Aussi, dès qu'il se fut établi à Paris, il y attira des 25 milliers et des milliers d'étudiants. Tout naturellement, Paris participa du prestige qui se dégageait de sa personne et de son enseignement. C'est vers Paris que la population studieuse de toute l'Europe prit l'habitude de se diriger, et, une fois que cette émigration périodique fut entrée dans les mœurs, elle survécut à la cause qui l'avait d'abord déterminée.

1. Lines 1–6 state that:
  A. only those preparing for the ministry were educated in the schools of the Middle Ages
  B. the first schools were established in completion with religious establishments
  C. the prime purpose of these schools was to prepare people for the clergy
  D. one could be married before entering one of these schools but was not permitted to get married thereafter.

---

1. C **2.** Lines 7–15 state that the University of Paris was:
  A. unlike all of its predecessors from the very beginning
  B. was organized along the lines of the famous schools of antiquity
  C. was born in the twelfth century
  D. changed radically after the twelfth century.

---

2. D **3.** Lines 16–24 state that:
  A. Abélard dominated his generation
  B. Abélard and Voltaire were fast friends
  C. the age of Abélard was strongly anti-scientific
  D. Abélard's faith was quite unlike that of his contemporaries.

---

3. A **4.** In line 24 **aussi** means:
  A. also   B. therefore   C. in like manner   D. however

---

4. B **5.** Lines 25–29 state that:
  A. Parisian authorities actively opposed the effect of Abélard's teaching
  B. Paris had been the intellectual center of Europe even before Abélard's time
  C. the flow of students toward Paris ceased after the death of Abélard
  D. Abélard was the great drawing card of the student world.

---

5. D

Mais une autre cause, plus durable, contribua à fixer ce mouvement. Le XIIe siècle est le moment où la vie politique française commence à s'organiser et à se centraliser. Sous les Carolingiens, la cour était ambulante et se déplaçait **au gré**[1] des événements. Sous les Capétiens directs, sans

---

1 *at the whim*

⁵ abandonner tout d'un coup cette habitude, elle élut de plus en plus fréquemment domicile à Paris, qui devint définitivement la capitale du royaume. Pour **se mettre à la hauteur**² de son rôle, Paris s'enrichit de palais, de monuments, et acquit ainsi une puissance d'attraction d'autant plus efficace qu'elle était sans contrepoids, car nulle ville n'était alors, en Europe, en
¹⁰ état de lui **faire concurrence.**³ Les étudiants eurent donc une raison de plus pour affluer à Paris de tous les pays du monde chrétien.

Ils vinrent même en si grand nombre que la seule école de Notre–Dame devint insuffisante pour les contenir. Il fallut autoriser des maîtres particuliers à ouvrir des écoles en dehors de la cathédrale. Ils enseignaient dans des
¹⁵ maisons privées, à leur domicile. Primitivement, l'autorité diocésaine, pour les maintenir plus facilement sous son contrôle, les obligeait à résider à l'intérieur de l'île que forment les deux bras de la Seine et dont la cathédrale occupe encore aujourd'hui le centre. Mais, à mesure qu'ils se multiplièrent, ils **s'affranchirent**⁴ de cette obligation, passèrent les ponts et vinrent
²⁰ s'établir, hors de l'île, sur la rive gauche du fleuve. Plus ils s'éloignaient de la cathédrale, plus il leur était facile de se libérer de la sujétion où les tenait l'évêque. Primitivement, ils n'étaient qu'une annexe de la cathédrale; en cette qualité, ils étaient soumis à la discipline ecclésiastique. Mais, une fois émancipés de cette tutelle, ils prirent conscience de leurs intérêts propres. Des
²⁵ idées et des aspirations nouvelles **se firent jour,**⁵ qui répondaient à cette situation nouvelle. Pour défendre ces intérêts et ces idées, ils se rapprochèrent les uns des autres et s'associèrent. La forme normale de l'association était alors la corporation. Ils formèrent donc, avec leurs étudiants, une corporation, une *Universitas;* ce mot était le terme technique pour désigner tout groupe-
³⁰ ment corporatif. Ainsi naquit l'Université de Paris: c'était la corporation des maîtres et des étudiants parisiens.

1. Lines 1–4 state that under the Carolingian kings the court
   A. was weak
   B. was strong
   C. changed location at rather regular intervals
   D. moved about from place to place at irregular intervals.

---

1. D   **2.** Lines 7–12 permit us to assume that:
   A. Paris experienced a building boom after the Capetian kings had come into power
   B. Paris became the capital city immediately upon the accession of the Capetian dynasty
   C. the University drew its students almost exclusively from France
   D. only a few other cities in Europe had the attraction of Paris at this time

---

2. B   **3.** Lines 13–26 state that the control exercised by the bishop was weakened because of
   A. internal dissension

---

2 *to prove equal to*   **4** *freed themselves*   **5** *were born*
3 *to compete*

B. subversive ideas being taught in private houses
C. the extreme intellectual ferment resulting from Abélard's teaching
D. the fact that the students no longer lived in a single community

3. D   **4.** According to lines 27–32
A. the quality of instruction was better when the students were subject to the bishop
B. the interest of the students and the faculty were generally in conflict
C. the word **universitas** meant *a corporation*
D. the conditions of the cathedral were primitive.

4. C

L'Université de Paris ne fut donc pas l'œuvre d'un jour. Elle ne fut pas créée à une date déterminée, par un acte de volonté. Peu à peu, des liens se nouèrent entre tous les maîtres qui enseignaient sur la rive gauche de la Seine, mais sans qu'il soit possible de dire à quel moment le corps se trouva
5 constitué. L'Université de Paris n'avait même pas cette unité qui vient d'un habitat commun. Chaque maître **louait** ¹ le local où il enseignait. Quand la corporation avait à délibérer sur une affaire commune, elle s'assemblait **tantôt** dans une église et **tantôt** ² dans une autre.

Cependant, avec le temps, cette masse, primitivement amorphe, fut amenée,
10 par la force des choses, à s'organiser. Elle se donna un chef, le recteur, qui la représentait au dehors, dans les rapports avec les pouvoirs publics. Comme tous les maîtres n'enseignaient pas les mêmes disciplines, ceux qui professaient sur les mêmes matières se rapprochèrent plus étroitement les uns des autres et formèrent, au sein de la corporation totale, des groupements particuliers. Ce
15 furent les Facultés: arts libéraux, **droit,**³ médecine, théologie. D'autre part, comme étudiants et maîtres étaient de nationalités différentes, ils se groupèrent par nations. Il y avait quatre nations: la nation de Normandie (qui comprenait les Normands et les Bretons) ; la nation de Picardie (les Picards et les Wallons) ; la nation d'Angleterre (Anglais, Allemands et Suédois) ;
20 enfin la nation de France pour tous les universitaires de race latine.

Dans la seconde moitié du XIIIᵉ siècle, apparurent les collèges.

A l'origine, les étudiants habitaient dans des sortes d'hôtelleries, appelées *hospitia*, qui appartenaient aux différentes nations. Chaque *hospitium* était administré par un principal, sorte de *primus inter pares*,⁴ élu par **les**
25 **pensionnaires** ⁵ de la maison. Mais il y avait à Paris un très grand nombre d'étudiants trop pauvres pour être logés dans une de ces hôtelleries. Des personnes charitables eurent l'idée de fonder pour eux des sortes d'*hospitia* où, grâce à une **dotation convenable,**⁶ ils pourraient être **hébergés** ⁷ gratuitement. Ces *hospitia* dotés et gratuits, ce furent les collèges. Ce n'étaient
30 donc, à l'origine, que des **pensionnats,**⁸ et qui ne recevaient que des **boursiers;** ⁹ l'enseignement continuait à être donné au dehors. Mais, à

1 *rented*   **4** *first among the peers*   **7** *lodged*
2 *sometimes . . . sometimes* **5** *boarders*   **8** *boarding houses*
3 *law*   **6** *suitable contribution*   **9** *holders of scholarships*

l'expérience, on s'aperçut que cette organisation offrait de grands avantages et qu'il y avait intérêt à la généraliser. Dans les collèges, l'étudiant était surveillé; ce qui était une garantie pour les familles. Aussi prirent-elles
35 l'habitude de faire entrer leurs enfants dans les collèges, en qualité de pensionnaires payants.

1. According to lines 1–8
    A. the University of Paris was given official existence by a royal decree
    B. it derived its unity from a geographical proximity of its component parts
    C. official meetings of the corporation were often held in various churches
    D. the date of the formal organization of the university was carefully recorded in its official archives.

1. C   **2.** The sub-divisions of the University were made along the lines of (lines 9–20):
    A. nationality   C. both of the above
    B. subject matter   D. neither of the above

2. B   **3.** The **collèges** of the University were in the beginning (lines 21–31):
    A. free boarding houses
    B. places where instruction was given
    C. restricted to the well-to-do students
    D. used to overcome the barriers between students of different nationality

3. A   **4.** Lines 31–36 state that
    A. the initial reaction of the families was unfavorable to the colleges
    B. some families put their children in the colleges as paying boarders
    C. most families felt the tuition in the colleges was too high
    D. the conduct of students in the colleges was often licentious.

4. B

L'Université elle-même favorisa le mouvement; elle y trouvait le moyen de prévenir les désordres de toute sorte dont les étudiants étaient coutumiers et qui lui **suscitaient** [1] à chaque instant des difficultés avec le pouvoir civil. Un jour vint où, pour cette raison, elle fit de la résidence dans les collèges
5 une obligation stricte pour les plus jeunes de ses étudiants, c'est-à-dire pour les étudiants de la Faculté des Arts. Tout naturellement, les maîtres suivirent leurs élèves; ils vinrent enseigner dans les collèges, puisque les étudiants y étaient réunis. Et ainsi la physionomie de l'Université se trouva assez gravement modifiée. Primitivement, elle était formée par une masse inorganique
10 de maîtres indépendants les uns des autres et sans hiérarchie d'aucune sorte; désormais, elle fut une constellation de collèges entre lesquels élèves et maîtres furent **répartis.** [2] C'est le collège qui devint l'unité scolaire et, à l'intérieur du collège, les élèves furent distribués systématiquement en classes, selon leur âge et leur degré de culture.

---

1 *created*   **2** *distributed*

15   Cette organisation fut le modèle que reproduisirent, sans modifications essentielles, toutes les Universités qui se formèrent ensuite, tant en France que dans les autres pays d'Europe. Toutes furent faites à l'image de l'Université de Paris; elles en furent comme des **filiales**.[3] Aussi disait-on de l'Université de Paris qu'elle était la mère des Universités, *mater universitatum*. Il y a plus:
20   la plupart des institutions qu'elle créa ainsi se retrouvent encore aujourd'hui, sous des formes diverses, dans les Universités des deux Mondes.

Mais l'Université de Paris ne fut pas seulement créatrice d'institutions: elle fut **le siège** [4] d'une vie intellectuelle d'une extraordinaire intensité. La discipline qu'on y enseignait de préférence à toutes les autres, et presque à
25   l'exclusion des autres, c'était la dialectique: elle était considérée comme l'art par excellence, la méthode qui résolvait tous les problèmes. Aujourd'hui, la dialectique nous fait l'effet d'une discipline singulièrement aride et **sèche**.[5] Mais les questions auxquelles elle était alors appliquée, étaient celles-là mêmes qui tenaient le plus au cœur des hommes: c'étaient les questions vitales de la
30   foi et les grands problèmes que, de tout temps, s'est posés la pensée humaine. Par la dialectique, on **entendait** [6] fonder une philosophie qui servît de base à la religion. Aussi la **docte** [7] population de la Montagne Sainte-Geneviève suivait-elle avec passion les grands débats qui illustrèrent alors l'Université de Paris. De là, pour celle-ci, un prestige incomparable, qui ne tarda pas à
35   en faire une grande puissance morale avec laquelle le pouvoir civil et le pouvoir ecclésiastique furent souvent obligés de compter.

1. Lines 1–6 state that professors started teaching in the colleges because
A. the civil powers tried to force the University to abandon the system of colleges
B. the University had no other facilities for the increased numbers
C. the students were encouraged or required to live there
D. they wanted to separate themselves entirely from the influence of the Church.

---

1. C **2.** Lines 6–14 state that the colleges
A. became the basic units of the University
B. soon outgrew their original usefulness
C. never really became organized
D. were often subject to serious internal dissension.

---

2. A **3.** According to lines 15–21 the organizational form of the University of Paris
A. was to be modified basically during the Renaissance
B. is reflected even in the universities of the present time
C. became widespread in France but not in other countries
D. is today highly archaic.

---

3 *subsidiaries*   **5** *dry*   **7** *learned*
4 *the seat*   **6** *intended*

3. B   **4.** According to lines 22–36 the art of dialectic
   A. sometimes created more problems than it solved
   B. seems sterile today
   C. was taught only to the most advanced students
   D. was one among many highly esteemed arts.

4. B   **5.** In line 33 the phrase **qui illustrèrent alors l'Université de Paris** means
   A. which the University of Paris displayed
   B. which the University of Paris held
   C. which made the University of Paris famous
   D. which the University of Paris engaged in.

5. C

La violation de la Pyramide de Chéops

Extrait de Georges Goyon: "Le mécanisme de fermeture à la pyramide de Chéops," *Revue Archéologique*
(1963), pp. 18-23. (Presses Universitaires de France)

Il existe dans la Pyramide de Chéops, à l'extrémité Nord de la Grande Galerie, une **issue** [1] dans le sol dont la dimension permet tout juste le passage d'un homme. Ce **trou** [2] devient une sorte de **boyau** [3] presque vertical **s'enfonçant** [4] dans la masse compacte de la maçonnerie, puis, vers le milieu

5 du trajet, fait un petit **crochet** [5] vers le Sud pour reprendre la descente et aboutir finalement dans le passage qui conduit à la salle souterraine abandonnée, à une distance de 20 m. au Nord de celle-ci.
   Quelle est la raison d'être de ce **cheminement?** [6]
   Certains archéologues et voyageurs ont voulu voir là la voie de retraite

10 des ouvriers qui avaient effectué la fermeture de la Grande Galerie, ne s'expliquant pas comment ils auraient pu sortir vivants après la fermeture du tombeau.
   D'autres ont pensé que les ouvriers destinés à être sacrifiés lors de la fermeture du tombeau, avaient préparé subrepticement leur chemin de retraite

15 afin d'échapper à la mort.
   Il est difficile d'admettre ces hypothèses.
   Tout d'abord, nous ne connaissons pas d'exemple de sacrifices de cette sorte, et l'**ensevelissement** [7] des personnes vivantes n'était certainement plus pratiqué à l'époque des Pyramides.

20 D'autre part, comment supposer que les Égyptiens—qui prirent tellement de précautions pour empêcher l'accès du cœur de la Pyramide, c'est-à-dire la salle contenant le corps du roi, en accumulant les obstacles—, firent un tel effort pour inventer et réaliser cet énorme mécanisme de fermeture, tout en

---

1 *outlet*   4 *penetrating*   6 *traversal*
2 *hole*   5 *hook*   7 *burial*
3 *passageway*

25 poussant finalement l'**inconséquence** [8] au point de ménager un passage aux éventuels **pillards** [9]?

La romanesque hypothèse du travail en cachette n'est guère plausible non plus.

Comment admettre en effet que les futurs condamnés, s'il en fut, aient pu de longues années au préalable, réaliser **à l'insu de** [10] la foule des ouvriers, 30 un travail si considérable? Et comment évacuaient-ils les débris?

Avec l'exposé du système automatique de fermeture que nous venons de présenter—système comprenant, comme nous l'avons dit, le procédé qui a permis au moment voulu l'évacuation du personnel—, l'explication de la présence de ce mystérieux boyau devient très aisée!

35 C'était le passage par où les premiers **larrons** [11] s'introduisirent dans la tombe royale pour la **piller.** [12]

Nous allons essayer de reconstituer le cheminement des voleurs.

Mais il conviendrait, en premier lieu, d'essayer de préciser l'époque probable de leur première visite.

40 Nous savons, tout d'abord, que malgré le respect et la crainte des dieux, qui caractérisaient les Égyptiens de l'Antiquité, malgré l'horreur des **châtiments** [13] posthumes auxquels étaient voués les profanateurs, on n'empêcha jamais que le pillage des tombes fut déjà commis dès l'Antiquité et peut-être même du vivant de Chéops.

1. The first paragraph describes:
    A. a serious issue concerning the pyramids
    B. a passageway leading to an abandoned room in the pyramid
    C. decorations in the *Grande Galerie*
    D. the treasure room of the pyramid.

---

1. B   **2.** Lines 9–15 conjecture that an exit was left in the pyramid:
    A. to permit the king's soul to depart
    B. to permit periodic inspection of the interior of the pyramid
    C. to permit the escape of the builders intended for sacrifice
    4. to permit access to the treasure room.

---

2. C   **3.** The writer does not admit the previous hypothesis because when the pyramids were built (lines 16–19):
    A. human sacrifice was not practiced
    B. slaves were sometimes buried alive
    C. a different type of hieroglyph was current
    D. such openings were common.

---

3. A   **4.** The question which next arises, however, is why the Egyptians:
    A. took such care to prevent access to the king's body
    B. went to so much effort to leave a passageway

---

8 *inconsistency*   **10** *unknown to*   **12** *plunder*
9 *plunderers*   **11** *robbers*   **13** *punishments*

C. put so many obstacles in the path of possible pillagers

D. were not more careful in their embalming processes.

4. B   **5.** The theory of the author (lines 26–36) is that the passageway:

A. was made by the king's order

B. was too small to permit human passage

C. was made by thieves intent on pillage

D. is inexplicable.

5. C   **6.** The ancient Egyptians believed (lines 40–44) that:

A. those who violated the tombs would be severely punished in the next life

B. the gods themselves respected the dead

C. the gods were pleased by the building of pyramids

D. Chéops would avenge himself on anyone who profaned the dead.

6. A

Le dernier acte de pillage eut lieu officiellement, au début du IXe siècle de notre ère. Il est probable que l'orifice du passage clandestin avait été perdu, remblayé par les décombres du **revêtement** [1] qu'on avait commencé à enlever.

Les auteurs arabes attribuent au calife Al-Maamoun (820 après J.-C.),
[5] fils de Haroum el-Rachid, l'initiative de la recherche du trésor de Chéops.

Cette attaque fut menée sur l'ordre du calife *après* que le revêtement externe de la Pyramide eut été emporté.

Le fait est prouvé par une tentative de percement exercée au-dessous de la **voûte de décharge** [2] de l'entrée vraie.

[10] En effet, on peut voir au-dessous de celle-ci les traces de percement qui, en raison de leur vague apparence de sculpture ou de ronde-bosse, ont fait beaucoup travailler les imaginations. Mais cette tentative de percement n'eut pas de suite parce que les ouvriers s'aperçurent bientôt que la voûte de décharge s'arrêtait là, et que leur tunnel allait se perdre dans la masse de la
[15] Pyramide.

Les chercheurs de trésors se résignèrent alors à vider la descenderie. Ils **butèrent** [3] ensuite sur l'extrémité du **bloc-bouchon** [3] en granit qu'ils démolirent en partie, puis après l'avoir contourné un moment, ils s'attaquèrent de nouveau aux blocs-bouchons qui obstruaient le couloir. Et quand ils
[20] atteignirent la Grande Galerie, ce fut pour s'apercevoir que le tombeau était déja violé.

Il est certain que le travail fut difficile et coûteux, et l'écrivain arabe qui relate le fait dit : « Quand les ouvriers parvinrent au centre de la construction, ils y trouvèrent, ô merveille! un bassin rempli de **dinars** [5] dont le montant
[25] était exactement celui qu'il avait fallu dépenser pour parvenir jusque-là ».

Mais cette allégation relève seulement du langage poétique. En fait, d'autres auteurs arabes ont dit plus prosaïquement qu'on ne retrouva dans la **cuve** [6] du sarcophage, que quelques os et chairs putréfiés par suite de la longueur des siècles.

---

1 *facing, veneering*   3 *stumbled upon*   5 *unit of currency*
2 *outlet, vault*   4 *plug*   6 *receptacle*

1. The last attempt to pillage the pyramid (lines 1–5) :
A. took place about 800 B.C.
B. was ordered by a ruler
C. was undertaken, ironically, by direct descendants of Cheops
D. was highly successful.

---

1. B   **2.** The **tentative de percement** (lines 8–15) :
A. was successful
B. was frustrated by the trickery of the workers
C. met a dead end
D. gave entrance into the treasure room.

---

2. C   **3.** According to the legend, the pillagers (lines 20–29) :
A. received poetic justice
B. met mysterious deaths
C. found nothing of value
D. found only three mummies.

3. A

L'esthétique industrielle

Extrait de Denis Huyman et Georges Patrix; *"L'esthé-tique industrielle"* (Presses Universitaires de France)

Il en est de l'esthétique industrielle comme du cinéma: là aussi on se trouve en présence d'une technique qui est à la fois un commerce, une industrie, et un art authentique. Etienne Souriau l'a fort bien dit: « Un art nouveau est né ». L'esthétique industrielle constitue un art nouveau, mais

5   qui est surtout **axé** [1] sur l'industrie (c'est là sa mission la plus fondamentale), et cet « art impliqué » **vise** [2] également une meilleure productivité, donc un but lucratif. L'on a donc eu tort d'opposer une esthétique industrielle française, **soi-disant** [3] désintéressée, à une esthétique industrielle américaine qui aurait été « **mercantile** ».[4] Ce caractère de spéculation commerciale qui, pour

10 certains, a pu desservir la cause des stylistes industriels, ne constitue nullement une **tare**.[5] Il nous apparaît au contraire comme la validité de l'esthétique industrielle, sa validation, sa justification, la promesse de son avenir. Si l'esthétique industrielle s'était contentée d'apporter je ne sais quel prestige gratuit, une noblesse de pure tradition, une grandeur sans puissance à l'in-

15 dustrie, elle serait restée **sans portée**,[6] comme le retour à l'artisanat **prôné** [7] au XIXᵉ siècle par Ruskin. Mais l'esthétique industrielle sert à vendre, à vendre beaucoup, à vendre toujours plus, à pousser le public le plus large possible à goûter de bons modèles à bon marché. Tout le XIXᵉ siècle se définit dans cette attitude d'un Emile Faguet: « L'art n'est jamais populaire. Il faut

1 *hinged*   4 *commercial*   6 *without effect*
2 *aims at*   5 *loss in value*   7 *extolled*
3 *so called*

20 en prendre son parti; la littérature et l'art ne sont populaires qu'à la condition d'être *médiocres* ». Le XXᵉ siècle, au contraire, s'est efforcé de plus en plus de **promouvoir** [8] cette expansion culturelle qui repose sur une élévation du goût du grand public et sur la formation d'une sensibilité esthétique des masses. Ici se rejoignent les préoccupations des démocraties populaires où
25 prolifèrent les Maisons de la Culture et les **visées** [9] des pays à économie capitaliste qui cherchent à satisfaire l'aspiration vers un progrès à la fois technique, scientifique et esthétique sans lequel l'existence humaine ne vaudrait pas la peine d'être vécue.

L'esthétique industrielle peut jouer ici un rôle très important en permettant
30 au monde moderne de triompher de cette inadaptation de notre civilisation et de notre culture à un progrès technique qui va trop vite pour ne pas déconcerter, par sa rapidité même, ceux qui voudraient vivre en harmonie avec lui. **Le malaise** [10] dû à ce **décalage** [11] entre un monde mécanisé, **trépidant,**[12] **survolté,**[13] et une humanité inquiète, en rupture avec ses habitudes tradi-
35 tionnelles de vie, pourra être guéri—en partie peut-être—par la politique esthétique des entreprises si **l'ambiance** [14] de travail, particulièrement sécure, donne un environnement tranquillisant pour l'homme devant sa machine. Si la machine est belle, si les produits sont réussis, l'harmonie renaîtra d'une « discorde accordée ». Ainsi le contrepoint de l'esthétique pourra bien être
40 l'éthique, selon le mot des *Prétextes* d'André Gide, lorsqu'il se demandait à lui-même au cours d'une interview imaginaire:
« Mais qu'est-ce donc, pour vous, que la morale?
—Une dépendance de l'esthétique! »
Sur ce point, Georges Combet rejoint André Gide, lorsqu'il écrit:
45 « La **laideur** [15] est toujours le signe d'un désordre . . . La mission esthétique qui **incombe à** [16] notre industrie est ainsi de nous aider à recouvrer notre équilibre et, par ses réalisations, de mettre de l'ordre dans notre civilisation, de contribuer à en éliminer les hasards. Elle vise à l'édification d'un monde à nos mesures, d'un monde où nos esprits soient rassérénés, où nous
50 vivions à l'aise, où nous n'ayons pas le sentiment de vivre en étranger ».
Ainsi la philosophie de l'esthétique industrielle est-elle liée au progrès de l'humanité en général et au perfectionnement du niveau culturel en particulier. Son rôle est loin d'être achevé. Il devra se poursuivre, bien au-delà de notre petite planète, jusque dans ces régions extra-terrestres dont l'avenir
55 nous trace les voies d'accès. Mais déjà l'ESTHÉTISATION progressive du monde actuel constitue le meilleur gage d'une première victoire de l'*Industrial Design*.

1. The first seven lines state that industrial aesthetics
    A. has no commercial purpose
    B. like the movies, has as its goal to enrich the experience of those who come into contact with it
    C. main function is to beautify industrial areas of work

8 *promote*	11 *split*	14 *surroundings*
9 *aims*	12 *vibrating*	15 *ugliness*
10 *uneasiness*	13 *stepped up*	16 *devolves upon*

D. is a new form of art revolving around industry and designed to increase productivity.

1. D   **2.** Lines 11–18 state that

A. the commercial aspects of industrial aesthetics detract from its value
B. industrial aesthetics has considerable prestige value
C. industrial aesthetics should be based on craftsmanship as extolled by Ruskin in the Nineteenth Century
D. the justification of industrial aesthetics lies in its money-making ability

2. D   **3.** Lines 18–28 state that

A. in the Twentieth Century, an attempt is being made to raise the aesthetic sensitivity of the masses
B. during the Nineteenth Century popular art and literature enjoyed a high aesthetic standard
C. industrial aesthetics is of little value in increasing the volume of goods sold
D. every day life is rarely affected by industrial aesthetics.

3. A   **4.** Lines 29 to 39 state that

A. industrial aesthetics can help bridge the gap between a culture based on technical progress and one based on material standards
B. industrial aesthetics facilitates man's living in harmony with the rapid increase in technology
C. the rapid rate of technical progress is due to industrial aesthetics
D. the worker in front of his machine does better work if he understands the purpose of his efforts.

4. B   **5.** Lines 38 to 50 state that

A. according to A. Gide, morality is independent of aesthetics
B. according to G. Combet the aesthetic mission of industry is to build a civilization tailored to fit the wants of mankind
C. industrial aesthetics emphasizes the lack of order in our civilization
D. industrial aesthetics exploits the ugliness of industry.

5. B   **6.** Lines 51 to 56 state that

A. the philosophy of industrial aesthetics is dependent on general progress and especially upon raising of the general cultural level
B. at the present time industrial aesthetics is at its highest peak
C. it is questionable whether industrial aesthetics can have any extra-terrestrial application
D. the implementation of industrial aesthetics is too expensive for wide-spread acceptance.

6. A

Appendix

GLOSSARY OF GRAMMATICAL TERMS

Adjective a descriptive or qualifying word applied to a noun: "a *white* horse" or "*une idée profonde.*"

Adverb a word which modifies a verb, an adjective or another adverb: "She sings *well*" or "*Il parle rapidement.*"

Auxiliary verb a helping verb, by means of which a compound tense is formed. *Avoir* and *être* are the most common: *Il est parti*—He *has* left; *Ils avaient oublié la date*—They *had* forgotten the date.

Conjugate to give the various tenses, numbers, persons, voices, moods of a verb. For example, the present tense of the indicative mood of *to be* is: *I am; he, she, it is; we are; you are; they are.*

Conjunction a word used to link together words, or phrases, or clauses: "Sue *and* Bob left early, *but* they arrived late *because* of the traffic."

Defnite articles In English *the*; in French *le, la, les.*

Determiners words which specify or point out: "*Those* students are late . . ." or "*That* idea is absurd."

Idiom an expression whose meaning as a whole cannot be derived from the combined meaning of the elements. For example, "to beat around the bush," means "to act or speak evasively." Idioms cannot be translated word for word into another language.

Indefinite Articles in English *a* and *an*; in French *un, une.*

Imperative a command or request form: "*Parlez plus lentement*" or "*Speak* slower."

Infinitive the form of the verb which does not identify the time or the performer of the

491

action. In English the infinitive is usually preceded by *to: to speak*. In French the infinitive is identified by the endings *–er, –ir, –re: **parler, finir, vendre***.

Irregular verb   a verb which does not follow one of the usual conjugation patterns.

An example of a regular verb is *trouver:*

je trouve
tu trouves
il trouve
*nous trouv**ons***
*vous trouv**ez***
*ils trouv**ent***

An example of an irregular verb is *aller:*

je vais
tu vas
il va
nous allons
vous allez
ils vont

Mood   the point of view from which the action is seen: factual (indicative), dependent on other conditions (conditional), subjective (subjunctive), or necessary (imperative).

Object   the word which receives the action of the verb. The **direct object** receives the action without a preposition (John hits *Mike*) and the *indirect object* receives it by means of a preposition (John threw the ball to *Mike*).

Participle   the form of the verb which indicates time but not the person. The **present participle** ends in *–ing* in English and *–ant* in French: *singing,* ***chantant***. The **past participle** often ends in *–ed* in English and *–é, –i, –u* in French: *opened,* ***trouvé, fini, vendu***.

Partitive   a construction indicating a part of a whole or an indefinite quantity: "I'd like *some* potatoes" or "*Donnez-moi **des** pommes de terre*."

Preposition   a word which locates a noun or pronoun in time, place, and so forth: *before* class, *to* the car, *on* the table.

Pronoun   a word which stands in place of a noun: "John lost his watch"—"*He* lost *it*."

Relative Pronoun   a pronoun which joins two clauses: "He spoke of the area *which* we had already visited."

Subject   the word denoting the person or thing that performs the action (active voice) or that receives the action (passive voice): The *student* broke the microscope. (active)—The *microscope* had been broken by the student. (passive)

Tense   the time of the action of the verb, such as present, future, or past.

Verb   a word which expresses action or state of being: "The weather *was* wretched," or "They all *caught* cold."

FALSE COGNATES

Below is a list of false cognates with which you should become familiar.

FRENCH	ENGLISH	ENGLISH	FRENCH
achever	to complete	to achieve	accomplir
actuel	current, present	actual	réel, véritable
assister	to attend	to assist	aider
attendre	to wait for	to attend	assister à
avis (m.)	opinion	advice	conseil (m.)
blesser	to wound, to injure	to bless	benir
but (m.)	purpose, goal	but	mais
cave (f.)	cellar	cave	caverne (f.)
chair (f.)	flesh	chair	chaise
chance (f.)	good luck	chance	occasion (f.)
			hasard (m.)
coin (m.)	corner	coin	pièce de monnaie
commodité (f.)	convenience	commodity	produit (m.)
crier	to shout, to cry out	to cry	pleurer
demander	to ask	to demand	exiger
dérober	to steal, to conceal	to disrobe	déshabiller (se)
éprouver	to test, to experience	to prove	prouver
fat	conceited	fat	gros
figure (f.)	face	figure (number)	chiffre (m.)
		figure (shape)	taille (f.)
franchise (f.)	frankness	franchise	privilège (m.)
front (m.)	brow, forehead	front	devant (m.)
			façade (f.)
glace (f.)	ice, ice cream	glass	verre (m.)
gros	fat	gross	grossier
habits (m. pl.)	clothing	habits	habitudes (f. pl.)
hâte (f.)	haste	hate	haine (f.)
ignorer	not to know, to be unaware	ignore	ne pas vouloir, reconnaître
injure (f.)	insult	injury	blessure (f.)
joli	pretty	jolly	gai, joyeux
journal (m.)	newspaper	journal	revue (f.)
journée	day	journey	voyage (m.)
large	wide, broad	large	grand, gros
lecture (f.)	reading	lecture	conférence
librairie (f.)	bookshop	library	bibliothèque (f.)
location (f.)	renting	location	situation (f.)
magasin (m.)	store, shop	magazine	revue (f.)
monnaie (f.)	change (in coin)	money (in general)	argent (m.)
nouvelle (f.)	news, short story	novel	roman (m.)
occasion (f.)	opportunity, bargain	occasion	moment (m.)
office (f.)	pantry	office	bureau (m.)
or (conj.)	now, well	or	ou
parent (m.)	relative	parent	père (m.) mère (f.)

FRENCH	ENGLISH	ENGLISH	FRENCH
passer un examen	take an exam	pass an exam	être reçu, réussir
peine (f.)	trouble, difficulty	pain	douleur (f.) mal (m.)
pièce (f.)	play (drama), room	piece	morceau
phrase (f.)	sentence	phrase	locution (f.)
place (f.)	seat, square (public)	place	lieu (m.) endroit (f.)
plat (m.)	dish	plate	assiette (f.)
prétendre	claim, assert	pretend	feindre, faire semblant
propre	clean	proper	convenable
quitter	leave	quit	cesser
réaliser	fulfill	realize	se rendre compte
remarquer	notice	remark, say	dire
rente (f.)	pension	rent	loyer (m.)
rester	remain	rest	se reposer
résumer	sum up	resume	reprendre
roman (m.)	novel	Roman	romain (m.)
rude	rough	rude	impoli
sensible	sensitive	sensible	raisonnable
sort (m.)	destiny	sort	genre (m.)
supporter	bear, stand	support	soutenir
sympathique	likable	sympathetic	compatissant
travailler	work	travel	voyager
user	wear out	use	employer, se servir de
vase (f.)	mud, slime	vase	vase (m.)
veste (f.)	coat	vest	veston (m.) gilet (m.)
ville (f.)	city, town	vile	vil
voyager	travel	voyage	voyage (m.)
wagon (m.)	car (train)	wagon	charrette (f.)

TABLE OF VERB TENSES

Indicative Mood

PRESENT

I speak, am speaking, do speak	I choose, am choosing, do choose	I answer, am answering, do answer
je parle	je choisis	je réponds
tu parles	tu choisis	tu réponds
il parle	il choisit	il répond *
nous parlons	nous choisissons	nous répondons
vous parlez	vous choisissez	vous répondez
ils parlent	ils choisissent	ils répondent

* Verbs in —re whose stem does not end in d have the personal ending –t in the third person singular: il rompt, he breaks.

IMPERFECT

I was speaking, used to speak, spoke	*I was choosing, used to choose, chose*	*I was answering, used to answer, answered*
je parlais	je choisissais	je répondais
tu parlais	tu choisissais	tu répondais
il parlait	il choisissait	il répondait
nous parlions	nous choisissions	nous répondions
vous parliez	vous choisissiez	vous répondiez
ils parlaient	ils choisissaient	ils répondaient

PERFECT

I spoke	*I chose*	*I answered*
je parlai	je choisis	je répondis
tu parlas	tu choisis	tu répondis
il parla	il choisit	il répondit
nous parlâmes	nous choisîmes	nous répondîmes
vous parlâtes	vous choisîtes	vous répondîtes
ils parlèrent	ils choisirent	ils répondirent

FUTURE

I shall speak	*I shall choose*	*I shall answer*
je parlerai	je choisirai	je répondrai
tu parleras	tu choisiras	tu répondras
il parlera	ils choisira	il répondra
nous parlerons	nous choisirons	nous répondrons
vous parlerez	vous choisirez	vous répondrez
ils parleront	ils choisiront	ils répondront

CONDITIONAL

I should speak	*I should choose*	*I should answer*
je parlerais	je choisirais	je répondrais
tu parlerais	tu choisirais	tu répondrais
il parlerait	il choisirait	il répondrait
nous parlerions	nous choisirions	nous répondrions
vous parleriez	vous choisiriez	vous répondriez
ils parleraient	ils choisiraient	ils répondraient

IMPERATIVE

speak, let us speak, speak	*choose, let us choose, choose*	*answer, let us answer, answer*
parle	choisis	réponds
parlons	choisissons	répondons
parlez	choisissez	répondez

Subjunctive Mood

PRESENT

(that) I (may) speak	*(that) I (may) choose*	*(that) I (may) answer*
que je parle	que je choisisse	que je réponde
que tu parles	que tu choisisses	que tu répondes
qu'il parle	qu'il choisisse	qu'il réponde
que nous parlions	que nous choisissions	que nous répondions
que vous parliez	que vous choisissiez	que vous répondiez
qu'ils parlent	qu'ils choisissent	qu'ils répondent

IMPERFECT

I spoke, I was speaking (that) I (might) speak	*I chose, I was choosing (that) I (might) choose*	*I answered, I was answering (that) I (might) answer*
que je parlasse	que je choisisse	que je répondisse
que tu parlasses	que tu choisisses	que tu répondisses
qu'il parlât	qu'il choisît	qu'il répondît
que nous parlassions	que nous choisissions	que nous répondissions
que vous parlassiez	que vous choisissiez	que vous répondissiez
qu'ils parlassent	qu'ils choisissent	qu'ils répondissent

Compound Tenses

PERFECT INFINITIVE

to have spoken	*to have arrived*
avoir parlé	être arrivé(e)-s

PERFECT PARTICIPLE

having spoken	*having arrived*
ayant parlé	étant arrivé(e)-s

PRESENT PERFECT

I spoke, I have spoken	*I arrived, I have arrived*
j'ai parlé	je suis arrivé(e)

PAST PERFECT

I had spoken	*I had arrived*
j'avais parlé	j'étais arrivé(e)

SECOND PAST PERFECT
  (**PAST ANTERIOR**)

I had spoken

j'eus parlé

I had arrived

je fus arrivé(e)

FUTURE PERFECT

I will have spoken

j'aurai parlé

I will have arrived

je serai arrivé(e)

CONDITIONAL PERFECT

I would have spoken

j'aurais parlé

I would have arrived

je serais arrivé(e)

PRESENT PERFECT
  SUBJUNCTIVE

I spoke
(that) I (may) have
  spoken

que j'aie parlé

I arrived
(that) I (may) have
  arrived

que je sois arrivé(e)

PLUPERFECT
  SUBJUNCTIVE

(that) I had (might have)
  spoken

que j'eusse parlé

(that) I had (might have)
  arrived

que je fusse arrivé(e)

Vocabulary

A

abaisser to lower, to reduce
abattre to knock down
abbé (*m.*) abbott, priest
abeille (*f.*) bee
abord(d') at first
aborder to take up a subject, to reach a place
aboutir à to lead to, to result in
aboutissement (*m.*) outcome
abstrait, abstraite abstract
accabler to overwhelm
accès (*m.*) access, attack, outburst
accessoire accessory
accoler to join side by side
accommodement (*m.*) settlement
accommoder(s') to make oneself comfortable, to get used to
accord (*m.*) agreement
  d'accord avec, sur in agreement with, on
accorder to grant
accouru (*past part. of* **accourir**) ran up
accoutumer(s') to accustom oneself, to become accustomed
accroire, (faire . . . à quelqu'un) to make someone believe, to delude
accroissement (*m.*) growth
accroître(s') to increase
accroupir(s') to crouch
accru (*past. part. of* **accroître**) increased
accueil (*m.*) welcome
accueillir (accueillant, accueilli, accueille, accueillis, accueille) to receive, to welcome
acharnement (*m.*) relentlessness
acharner(s') to work unceasingly
acheter to buy
achever to complete, to finish
acide acid, sharp, sour
acquérir (acquérant, acquis, acquiers, acquis, acquière) to acquire
acre acrid, bitter
acte (*m.*) action, deed, act
actuel, actuelle present

actuellement currently
adepte (*m.*) adept, supporter, convert
adhérent (*m.*) adherent, supporter
admettre (admettant, admis, admets, admis, admette) to admit
adorer to adore, to worship
adversaire (*m.*) adversary
aérien, aérienne aerial
affaiblir to weaken
affaiblissement (*m.*) weakening
affaires (*f. pl.*) business
affecter to feign, pretend, affect
afficher to post a notice
affiler(s') to join, to become affiliated with
affirmer to affirm
affliger to afflict
affluer to flow to
affranchir(s') to become free
affreux, affreuse horrible, frightful
affronter to face up to, to insult
afin de, afin que in order to, in order that
agir to act
  s'agir de to be a question of, to concern
agiter to agitate
agréable pleasant
agrégé (*m.*) certified teacher
aide (*f.*) aid, help
aider to help
aïeul (*m.*) grandfather
aïeux (*m. pl.*) ancestors
aigu, aiguë sharp, shrill
aile (*f.*) wing
ailleurs elsewhere
  d'ailleurs moreover, furthermore
aimable pleasant
aimant (*m.*) magnet
aîné (*m.*) eldest
aine (*f.*) groin
ainsi thus, in this way
ainsi que just as, in the same way as
aisé, aisée easy, well off financially
ajouter to add
aliment (*m.*) food
alimenter to feed, to nourish
allaiter to give milk
Allemagne Germany

allemand, allemande German
aller (allant, allé, vais, allai, aille)
    to go
allocation (f.) allowance
allumer to light
allumeur (m.) lighter
allure (f.) bearing, style, way of moving
alors then
alors que while, just when
altération (f.) deterioration
altérer(s') to change for the worse
amant (m.) lover
amasser to accumulate, to pile up
ambiance (f.) surroundings
ambulant, ambulante peripatetic
âme (f.) soul
amélioration (f.) improvement
améliorer to improve
amenuiser to minimize, diminish
amertume (f.) bitterness
ami (m.) amie (f.) friend
amiable friendly
amical amicable, friendly
amont (m.) upper waters, the head
    water
    en amont up stream
amorcer to begin
amour (m.) love
amour-propre (m.) conceit, self-love
amulette (f.) amulet, charm
an (m.) year
année (f.) year
analyse (f.) analysis
analyser to analyse
anatomiste (m.) anatomist
ancien, ancienne ancient, old, former
ange (m.) angel
anglais, anglaise English
Angleterre (f.) England
annelé, annelée ringed
annoncer to inform, to announce
anodin, anodine anodyne, mild
anonyme anonymous
anticiper to anticipate, to infringe upon
antiquité (f.) antiquity, the olden days
août (m.) August
apercevoir (apercevant, aperçu,
    aperçois, aperçus, aperçoive)
    to perceive
aperçu (m.) glimpse, insight, overview
apparaître (apparaissant, apparu,
    apparais, apparus, apparaisse)
    to appear
appareil (m.) apparatus, equipment

apparemment apparently
appartenir (appartenant, appartenu,
    appartiens, appartins, appar-
    tienne) to belong
appeler to call
appeler(s') to be called, to be named
appel (m.) call
    faire appel to call upon, to appeal
    to
appesantir(s') to become heavy, to
    weigh
appliquer(s') to apply oneself
appréciation (f.) appreciation, evalua-
    tion
apprécier to evaluate, to appreciate
appréhender to apprehend, to stop
apprendre (apprenant, appris, ap-
    prends, appris, apprenne) to
    learn
apprenti (m.) apprentice
approfondir to deepen, to study deeply
approuver to approve
approximatif, approximative approx-
    imate
appui (m.) support, aid
appuyer (s') to support, to be based
    on
après after
    d'après according to
après-midi (m. or f.) afternoon
arbitrage (m.) mediation
arbitre (m.) umpire, referee, arbiter
arbre (m.) tree
arc (m.) bow
archives (f. pl.) archives, records
argent (m.) silver, money
arracher to tear
arrêter to stop, to arrest
arrière (f.) rear, behind
artisan (m.) craftsman
asperge (f.) asparagus
aspirer to suck in, to inhale
assaillir to assail, assault, beset
assassinat (m.) assassination
asseoir(s') to sit down
asseoir to seat, to base
asservir to enslave
assez rather, quite, enough
assidûment assiduously
assidu, assidue assiduous
assistant (m.) member of an audience
assister à to be present at, to attend
assomer to fell, to knock down
assurer to assure

astronome (*m.*)   astronomer
âtre (*m.*)   hearth, fireplace
attacher   to tie, to attach
attacher(s')   to cling to
atteindre (**atteignant, atteint, atteins, atteignis, atteigne**)   to attain, to reach
attendre   to wait for
　s'attendre à   to expect
attendrir   to soften
attention (*f.*)   attention
　faire attention à   to pay attention to
attendu que   whereas
attirer   to attract
attitude (*f.*)   attitude, posture
attroupement (*m.*)   gathering
aube (*f.*)   dawn
aucun, aucune, ne . . .   no, not any
aucunement   not at all
audace (*f.*)   audacity
auditeur (*m.*)   listener
augmentation (*f.*)   increase
augmenter   to increase
aujourd'hui   today
aumône (*f.*)   alms
auparavant   before, previously
auprès de   close to
aussi   also, therefore
aussi . . . que   as . . . as
aussitôt   immediately
aussitôt que   as soon as
autant   as much, so much
　d'autant moins, plus   all the less, more
auteur (*m.*)   author
automate (*m.*)   automaton
automne (*m.* or *f.*)   Autumn
autoritaire   authoritarian
autour de   around
autre, d'autres   other, others
autrefois   formerly
autrement   otherwise
autrui   others, other people
auxiliaire   auxiliary
avaler   to swallow
avance, (en . . .)   early
avant   before
avare (*m.*)   miser
avec   with
avènement (*m.*)   accession
avenir (*m.*)   future
averse (*f.*)   rainstorm
avertir   to warn
aveugle   blind

avis (*m.*)   opinion
avoir (**ayant, eu, ai, eus, aie**)   to have
avoisinant, avoisinante   neighboring, joining
avouer   to admit
avril (*m.*)   April
axé, axée   hinged on

B

badigeonner   to brush over a surface, to paint
bagage (*m.*)   baggage
baguette (*f.*)   wand
bain (*m.*)   bath
baisse (*f.*)   lowering
balancer   to swing
baleine (*f.*)   whale
balle (*f.*)   ball, bullet
balte   Baltic
bambou (*m.*)   bamboo
bander   to bandage, to constrict
banlieue (*f.*)   suburb
bannière (*f.*)   banner, flag
banqueroute (*f.*)   bankruptcy
barrage (*m.*)   dam
bas, basse   low
bas (*m.*)   stocking
basculer   to rock, to swing
base (*f.*)   base, foundation
bataille (*f.*)   battle
bâtir   to build
battre   to beat
beau, bel, belle   handsome, fine, beautiful
beaucoup   much, a great deal
beauté (*f.*)   beauty
bénir   to bless
berge (*f.*)   steep bank
berger (*m.*)   shepherd
besogne (*f.*)   job, task
besoin (*m.*)   need
bête (*f.*)   beast, animal
betterave (*f.*)   beet
bibliothèque (*f.*)   library
bien   well, very
bien des   many
bien que   although
bientôt   soon
bienfaiteur (*m.*)   benefactor
bière (*f.*)   beer
bilan (*m.*)   balance sheet
biographe (*m.*)   biographer
blamable   blameworthy

blanc, blanche   white
blanchir   to turn white
   blanchir à la chaux   to whitewash
blé (*m.*)   wheat
blessé (*m.*)   wounded person
blesser   to wound
blessure (*f.*)   wound
bleu, bleue   blue
bloc-bouchon (*m.*)   the plug
boire (**buvant, bu, bois, bus, boive**)
   to drink
bois (*m.*)   wood
boisson (*f.*)   drink
boîte (*f.*)   box, container
bon gré mal gré   willy nilly
bonheur (*m.*)   happiness
bon, bonne   good, simple
bonté (*f.*)   goodness
bonsoir   good evening, good night
bord (*m.*)   bank (river), edge
bordé, bordée   bordered
bordure (*f.*)   border
borgne (*m.*)   one-eyed person
borner   to limit, to restrict
botte (*f.*)   boot
bouche (*f.*)   mouth
boucher   to close, to stop up
bouchon (*m.*)   cork
bouder   to sulk
boue (*f.*)   mud
bouffée (*f.*)   puff of smoke
bouillie (*f.*)   mush, porridge
bouillir   to boil
bouleversement   overturning
bouleverser   to overthrow, to overturn
boulanger (*m.*)   baker
bourgeois (*m.*)   middle-class person
bourgeoisie (*f.*)   middle-class
bourse (*f.*)   purse, scholarship
boursier (*m.*)   holder of a scholarship
bout (*m.*)   end
bouteille (*f.*)   bottle
boutique (*f.*)   small store
bouton (*m.*)   bud, button, pimple
boyau (*m.*)   passageway
boxe (*f.*)   sport of boxing
braconnier (*m.*)   poacher
branle (*m.*)   oscillation, motion, action
bras (*m.*)   arm
brave   brave, worthy
bref, briève   short, in short
brillamment   brilliantly
briller   to shine
brise (*f.*)   the breeze, wind
briser   to break

bronches (*f. pl.*)   bronchia
brosser   to brush
brouillard (*m.*)   fog
brouiller   to confuse, to blur
bruit (*m.*)   noise, rumor
brûler   to burn
brun, brune   brown
brunir   to tan, to turn brown
brusque   abrupt, sudden
bu (*past part. of* **boire**)   drunk
buche (*f.*)   log
bureau (*m.*)   office
but (*m.*)   aim, purpose, goal
butte (*f.*)   knoll
   être en butte à   to be exposed to

C

cacher   to hide
cachette (*f.*)   hiding-place
   en cachette   secretly
cadeau (*m.*)   present, gift
cadre (*m.*)   frame, cadre
cailler   to clot, to congeal
caillou (*m.*)   stone, pebble
caisse (*f.*)   cash-box
calcul (*m.*)   calculation
calculer   to calculate
calèche (*f.*)   carriage
canal (*m.*)   channel, canal
cantonner (se)   to be confined
caoutchouc (*m.*)   rubber
car   for, because
caractère (*m.*)   character, characteristic
carré (*m.*)   square
carrière (*f.*)   career, course
cas (*m.*)   case
   faire cas de   to value
casser   to break
casier (*m.*)   pigeon-hole
casserole (*f.*)   pan, saucepan
castor (*m.*)   beaver
cause (*f.*)   cause
céder   to give in, to surrender
célèbre   famous, celebrated
celer   to conceal
céleste   celestial, heavenly
cellule (*f.*)   cell
cendre (*f.*)   ash, cinder
cent   one hundred
centaine (*f.*)   about one hundred
centenaire (*m.*)   centenary
cependant   however
cerise (*f.*)   cherry

cerisier (*m.*) cherry-tree
certain, certaine certain, sure, particular
certes indeed
cervelle (*f.*) brain
cesser to cease, stop
cession (*f.*) transfer, surrender
chacun, chacune each one
chagrin (*m.*) sorrow, grief
chair (*f.*) flesh
chaleur (*f.*) heat, warmth
chaleureux, chaleureuse heartfelt, cordial, warm
chaman (*m.*) medicine man, witch doctor
chamanique pertaining to medicine man or witch doctor
champ (*m.*) field
chanson (*f.*) song
chanter to sing
chant (*m.*) singing, song
chapeau (*m.*) hat
chapitre (*m.*) chapter
chaque each
charbon (*m.*) coal
charbonneux carbonacious
charger to charge, to load
charge (*f.*) charge, load
chasse (*f.*) hunt
chasser to hunt
chat (*m.*) cat
château (*m.*) castle
châtiment (*m.*) punishment
chaud, chaude hot
  avoir chaud to be hot
  faire chaud to be hot (weather)
chauffer to heat
chausée (*f.*) street, cause-way
chausses (*f. pl.*) hose, britches
chauve-souris (*f.*) bat
chaux (*f.*) lime
chef (*m.*) chief, leader, head
chemin (*m.*) road
chemin de fer (*m.*) railroad
cheminement (*m.*) traversal
chemise (*f.*) shirt
chenal (*m.*) channel
cher, chère dear, expensive
chercher to seek, to look for
chercheur (*m.*) seeker, researcher
chérif (*m.*) Muslim official
chétif, chétive weak, puny
cheval (*m.*) horse
cheveux (*m. pl.*) hair

chez at the house of, among, in the work or thought of
chicorée (*f.*) chicory, endive
chien (*m.*) dog
chimie (*f.*) chemistry
chimique chemical
Chine (*f.*) China
Chinois (*m.*) Chinese
chirugien (*m.*) surgeon
  chirurgical surgical
choix (*m.*) choice
choquer to shock, knock
chose (*f.*) thing
chrétien, chrétienne Christian
christianisme (*m.*) Christianity
chuchoter to whisper
chute (*f.*) fall
ci-dessus above
ci-dessous below
ciel (*m.*) sky
cime (*f.*) summit, top
cinéma (*m.*) movie theater
cinquantenaire (*m.*) fiftieth anniversary
circonscrire (circonscrivant, circonscrit, circonscris, circonscrivis, circonscrive) to circumscribe
circonstance (*f.*) circumstance
cirer to wax, shine
citation (*f.*) quotation
citer to cite, quote
citoyen (*m.*) citizen
clair, claire clear, light in color
clarté (*f.*) clearness, clarity, brightness
cloche (*f.*) bell
clos, close closed
coeur (*m.*) heart
coiffure (*f.*) head-dress
coin (*m.*) corner
colère (*f.*) anger
collet (*m.*) collar
coloration (*f.*) coloration, discoloration
combattre (combattant, combattu, combats, combattis, combatte) to fight, oppose, combat
combien how many, how much
comestible (*m.*) anything edible
commandant (*m.*) commander, major, commandant
commander to order
comme as
comment how
communément commonly

compagnard, compagnarde pertaining to the country
compagnon (*m.*) companion
compétence (*f.*) competence, jurisdiction
comportement (*m.*) behavior
comporter to entail, involve, require, behave
composer (**se**) to compose, to be composed of
comprendre (**comprenant, compris, comprends, compris, comprenne**) to understand, include
compte (*m.*) account, reckoning
compter to count, to include
concentrer to concentrate
concevoir, (**concevant, conçu, conçois, conçus, conçoive**) to conceive
conciliable conciliatory
concitoyen (*m.*) fellow-citizen
conclure (**concluant, conclu, conclus, conclus, conclue**) to conclude
concours (*m.*) combination
concurrence (*f.*) competition
conduire (**conduisant, conduit, conduis, conduisis, conduise**) to lead, conduct, guide, drive
conduite (*f.*) conduct, behavior
conférencier (*m.*) lecturer
conférence (*f.*) lecture
confiance (*f.*) confidence
confins (*m. pl.*) confines, borders
confirmer to confirm
confluent confluence, junction
confondre to confuse
confrère (*m.*) colleague
confrérie (*f.*) brotherhood
confronter to confront
confus, confuse confused, embarrassed
congé (*m.*) leave
conjonction (*f.*) conjunction, union, connection
conjurer to plot, to avert
connaissance (*f.*) acquaintance, consciousness, knowledge
connaître (**connaissant, connu, connais, connus, connaisse**) to know
consciencieux, consciencieuse conscientious
conscience (*f.*) consciousness, conscience
conseil (*m.*) advice, counsel

conseiller to advise
consentement (*m.*) consent
conséquent, conséquente consequent
par conséquent consequently
conservateur, conservatrice conservative
conserver (**se**) to conserve, preserve
consister à to consist in
constamment constantly
constater to ascertain
constituer to constitute, to make up
construire (**construisant, construit, construis, construisis, construise**) to build, construct
conte (*m.*) story, tale
conter to relate
conteur (*m.*) story teller
contemporain, contemporaine contemporary
contenance (*f.*) capacity
contenir (**contenant, contenu, contiens, contins, contienne**) to contain
content, contente happy, glad, satisfied
contre against
contredire (**contredisant, contredit, contredis, contredis, contredise**) to contradict
contrée (*f.*) country
contrefaire (**contrefaisant, contrefait, contrefais, contrefis, contrefasse**) to mimic, imitate, conterfeit
convaincre (**convaincant, convaincu, convaincs, convainquis, convainque**) to convince
convenable suitable, proper
convenir (**convenant, convenu, conviens, convins, convienne**) to suit
corbeille (*f.*) basket, hamper
cordial (*m.*) stimulant, cordial
corps (*m.*) body
corps simple (*m.*) element
côte (*f.*) coast, rib
côté (*m.*) side
à côté de beside
cotiser to assess
coton (*m.*) cotton
cotoyer to border
cou (*m.*) neck
couche (*f.*) layer
coucher (**se**) to lie down, to go to bed
coude (*m.*) elbow

coudre (**cousant, cousu, couds, cousis,** **couse**)   to sew
coudrier (*m.*)   hazel-tree
couler   to flow
couleur (*f.*)   color
couloir (*m.*)   corridor
coup (*m.*)   blow
coupole (*f.*)   dome, cupola
cour (*f.*)   court
couramment   fluently
courant, courante   flowing, current
    au courant de   up to date with, aware of
courir (**courant, couru, cours,** **courus, coure**)   to run
couronne (*f.*)   crown
cours (*m.*)   course
course (*f.*)   trip, race, errand
court, courte   short
courtisan (*m.*)   courtier
coûter   to cost
coûteux, coûteuse   expensive, costly
coutume (*f.*)   custom
coutumier   customary, common
couvrir (**couvrant, couvert, couvre,** **couvris, couvre**)   to cover
craindre (**craignant, craint, crains,** **craignis, craigne**)   to fear
crainte (*f.*)   fear
cramponner (**se**)   to cling to
créer   to create
creuser   to hollow out, to dig
crochet (*m.*)   hook
croire (**croyant, cru, crois, crus** **croie**)   to believe
croyable   believable
croyant (*m.*)   believer
croiser   to cross
croissant   growing
croître (**croissant, crû, crois, crûs,** **croisse**)   to grow
croyance (*f.*)   belief
cru, crue   raw, crude
cruauté (*f.*)   cruelty
cuire (**cuisant, cuit, cuis, cuisis,** **cuise**)   to cook
cuisine (*f.*)   kitchen, cooking
cuisinier (*m.*)   cook
cuisse (*f.*)   thigh
cuivre (*m.*)   copper
culbuter   to topple
cultivable   arable, cultivatable
cuve (*f.*)   container
cuvette (*f.*)   basin

D

dactylo (*m.* or *f.*)   stenographer
dame (*f.*)   lady
dans   in
dater   to date
datte (*f.*)   date (fruit)
dattier (*m.*)   date palm
dauphin (*m.*)   eldest son of the King of France, dolphin
davantage   more, further
débarasser   to get rid of
débat (*m.*)   debate
débauche (*f.*)   profligacy
débit (*m.*)   flow
debout   upright
débrouiller (**se**)   to manage, to extricate oneself
début (*m.*)   beginning
décolage (*m.*)   shift
décédé   deceased
décéder   to die
déceler   to reveal
décerner   to award
décès (*m.*)   death
déchaîner   to unchain
déchirer   to tear
déclencher   to set in motion
décombres (*m. pl.*)   rubbish
découler   to derive, to flow
découvrir (**découvrant, découvert,** **découvre, découvris, découvre**)   to discover, to unveil
découverte (*f.*)   discovery
décret (*m.*)   decree
décrire, (**décrivant, décrit, décris,** **décrivis, décrive**)   to describe
dédain (*m.*)   disdain, scorn
dedans   inside
dédoubler   to divide, to split in two
déduire (**déduisant, déduit, déduis,** **déduisis, déduise**)   to deduce
défaillance (*f.*)   failure
défaut (*m.*)   fault
défendre   to forbid, to defend
dégagement (*m.*)   emission
dégager   to give off, to emit
dégâts (*m. pl.*)   damage
dégoût (*m.*)   distaste, disgust
dégoûter   to disgust
dégradé (*m.*)   shading off
déguiser   to disguise
dehors   outside, outward
déjà   already

déjeuner (*m.*)   lunch
    petit déjeuner (*m.*)   breakfast
délimiter   to demarcate, to define
demander   to ask, to request
demander (se)   to wonder
démettre (démettant, démis, démets,
    démis, démette)   to dislocate
demeurer   to live, remain
démission (*f.*)   resignation
démodé, démodée   out of style
démontrer   to demonstrate
dent (*f.*)   tooth
départ (*m.*)   departure, start
dépêcher(se)   to hurry
dépense (*f.*)   expense
dépenser   to spend
dépister   to track down, to throw off the
    track
déplacement (*m.*)   displacement, move-
    ment, change
déplacer (se)   to displace, to move
déprimer   to depress
depuis   since
déraisonnable   unreasonnable
dernier, dernière   last
    ce dernier   the latter
dernièrement   recently
dérouler   to unfold, to take place
derrière   behind
dès   since, from, as early as
dès que   as soon as
désagréable   unpleasant, disagreeable
désagrégation (*f.*)   disintegration
descenderie (*f.*)   incline
descendre   to descend, to go down
désespérer   to despair
désespéré   desperate
désespoir (*m.*)   despair
désigner   to designate
désirer   to wish, want, desire
désormais   from now on
dessécher   to dry out
dessein (*m.*)   design, plan, scheme
dessiner (se)   to take from
dessous   under, below
    au-dessous de   beneath
dessus   above, over
    au-dessus de   above
destinataire (*m.*)   addressee
destiner   to destine, to intend
destructeur, destructrice   destructive
détraquer   to put out of order
détresse (*f.*)   distress, misfortune
détrôner   to dethrone

détruire (détruisant, détruit, détruis,
    détruisis, détruise)   to destroy
dette (*f.*)   debt
deuil (*m.*)   mourning, sorrow
devant   before, in front of
devant (*present part. of* devoir)   owing
dévastateur, dévastatrice   devastating
devenir (devenant, devenu, deviens,
    devins, devienne)   to become
dévier   to deviate, swerve
devise (*f.*)   motto
dévoiler   to unveil, uncover
devoir (devant, dû, dois, dus, doive)
    to owe, to be obliged to
devoir (*m.*)   duty
dévouement (*m.*)   devotion
dieu (*m.*)   god
différer   to differ, to postpone
difficile   difficult
difforme   deformed
diffuser   to diffuse, to broadcast
digérer   to digest
digne   worthy
dignité (*f.*)   dignity, office, rank
diminuer   to diminish
dire (disant, dit, dis, dis, dise)   to say
direction (*f.*)   direction
dirigeant (*m.*)   leader
diriger   to direct, guide, lead
    diriger (se)   to proceed, to make
    one's way
discours (*m.*)   speech, talk, address
disparaître (disparaissant, disparu,
    disparais, disparus, dispar-
    aisse)   to disappear
dispendieux, dispendieuse   expensive
disposer   to dispose, to have at one's
    disposal
disposition (*f.*)   disposition, disposal
disputer   to dispute, to argue
disséminer   to scatter
dissolu, dissolue   dissolute
dissoudre (se) (dissolvant, dissous,
    dissous, *no past def.*, dissolve)
    to dissolve
divers, diverse   diverse, various
dizaine (*f.*)   about ten
docte   learned
doigt (*m.*)   finger
domaine (*m.*)   area, domain
domestique (*m. or f.*)   servant
dominer   to dominate
dommage (*m*)   damage, injury
    c'est dommage   it is a pity
don (*m.*)   gift

donc   therefore
donner   to give
donnée (*f.*)   datum
    données (*f. pl.*)   data, givens
dont   of which, whose
dormir   to sleep
dos (*m.*)   back
douane (*f.*)   custom office
doucement   softly, gently
doué, douée   gifted
douer   to endow
douleur (*f.*)   suffering
douloureux, douloureuse   painful
doute (*m.*)   doubt
douter   to doubt
douteux, douteuse   doubtful
doux, douce   sweet
drame (*m.*)   drama, theatre
dresser   to set up
dresser (se)   to rear
drogue (*f.*)   drug, nostrum
droit (*m.*)   law
droit, droite   straight, erect
droite (*f.*)   right (direction)
drôle   funny
dur, dure   hard
durer   to last
durée (*f.*)   duration

E

eau (*f.*)   water
ébranler   to shake, to weaken
écarter   to separate, to spread
écarter (s')   to move away
échantillon (*m.*)   sample
échapper   to escape
échéant   falling due
échec (*m.*)   failure
échelle (*f.*)   ladder, scale
échouer   to fail
éclairage (*m.*)   lighting
éclairer   to light up, to enlighten
éclaircir   to enlighten
éclat (*m.*)   glamour, glitter, burst
éclater   to burst, splinter
éclore (*no pres. part.*, éclos, éclos, *no past def.*, éclose)   to bloom, blossom, hatch
éclosion (*f.*)   blooming, the appearance
écoeurant, écoeurante   nauseating
école (*f.*)   school
économe   economical, thrifty
écouler   to run out

écouter   to listen to
écraser   to crush
écrier (s')   to cry out
écrire (écrivant, écrit, écris, écrivis, écrive)   to write
écriture (*f.*)   writing, handwriting
Ecritures saintes (*f. pl*)   Holy Scriptures
écrits (*m. pl.*)   writings
écrivain (*m.*)   writer
écrouelles (*f. pl.*)   scrofula
écrouler (s')   to crumble, to fall down
edifice (*m.*)   building
effectuer   to perform, to carry out
effet (*m.*)   effect
    en effet   in fact, indeed
efficace   effective
effiler   to taper
effondrement (*m.*)   collapse
effrayer   to frighten
effroi (*m.*)   fright
égal   equal
également   equally
égard (*m.*)   consideration, respect
église (*f.*)   church
électroaimant (*m.*)   electromagnet
élève (*m.* or *f.*)   student
élever   to raise up
élever (s')   to rise, to amount to
éliminer   to eliminate
élire (élisant, élu, élis, élus, élise)   to elect
éloigner   to put at a distance, to ward off
éloigné, éloignée   distant
embouchure (*f.*)   mouth of a river, the opening
embrouiller(s')   to become confused
émettre (émettant, émis, émets, émis, émette)   to emit
émigrer   to emigrate
empêcher   to prevent, hinder
emploi (*m.*)   use, utilization
employer   to use
empoigner   to grasp
empoisonner   to poison
emportement (*m.*)   transport (of emotion)
emporter (s')   to be carried away, to bolt
empourpré, empourprée   crimson, flushed
emprunter à   to borrow from
ému (*past part. of* émouvoir)   moved
en (preposition)   in
en (pronoun)   some, any

enchevêtrer (s') to become entangled
encore again, still, yet
endormir (s') to go to sleep
endroit (*m.*) place, location
enduire (**enduisant, enduit, enduis, enduisis, enduise**) to smear, anoint
enfance (*f.*) childhood
enfant (*m.* or *f.*) child
enfantin, enfantine childish
enfin at last, finally
enflure (*f.*) swelling
enfoncer (s') to penetrate
enfouir to bury
enfuir (s') (**enfuyant, enfui, enfuis, enfuis, enfuie**) to flee
engendrer to beget, to develop
enlacer to interlace
ennuyer to bore, to become tiresome
énorme enormous
enragé, enragée mad, enraged
enregistrer to register, to record
enseigner to teach
ensemble together
ensemble (*m.*) entirety, totality
ensevelissement (*m.*) burial
ensuite then, next
ensuivre (s') (**ensuivant, ensuivi, ensuis, ensuivis, ensuive**) to follow from, to result
entendre to hear, to understand
entendement (*m.*) understanding
entente (*f.*) understanding
enterrer to bury
entêtement (*m.*) stubbornness
entêter (s') to become stubborn
entourage (*m.*) circle of followers
entourer (s') to surround, to become surrounded
entrain (*m.*) spirit, liveliness, enthusiasm
entraîner to entail, to drag
entre between
entreprendre (**entreprenant, entrepris, entreprends, entrepris, entreprenne**) to undertake
envers toward
envie (*f.*) desire, envy
envier to envy
environ about, approximately
environs (*m. pl.*) surroundings, outskirts
envisager to face

envoyer to send
épais, épaisse thick
épaule (*f.*) shoulder
épeé (*f.*) sword
éperdument to distraction, madly
épine (*f.*) thorn, spine
épineux, épineuse thorny, spiny
épingle (*f.*) pin
éponyme of similar name
époque (*f.*) period, epoch
épouser to marry
épouse (*f.*) wife
époux (*m.*) husband
épreuve (*f.*) test, trial, hardship, proof
éprouver to undergo, to feel, to test
épuiser to exhaust
équipe (*f.*) team
équiper to equip
équivaler to be equivalent
équivoque (*f.*) ambiguity
ère (*f.*) era, apoch
erreur (*f.*) error, mistake
érudit (*m.*) scholar, learned person
escalier (*m.*) staircase
escarpé, escarpée steep, abrupt
esclavage (*m.*) slavery, bondage
esclave (*m.* or *f.*) slave
espacer (s') to become spaced
Espagne (*f.*) Spain
espagnol, espagnole Spanish
espèce (*f.*) kind, species
espérance (*f.*) hope
espérer to hope
Espéranto (*m.*) Esperanto, an international language
esprit (*m.*) mind, spirit, wit
essai (*m.*) attempt, essay
essayer to try
est (*m.*) East
estimer to estimate
estomac (*m.*) stomach
établir to establish
étage (*m.*) floor, story of a house
étaler to spread over, to display
étape (*f.*) stage (of a journey)
état (*m.*) state
été (*m.*) summer
été (*past part. of* **être**) been
éteindre (**éteignant, éteint, éteins, éteignis, éteigne**) to put out, to extinguish
étendre to extend
étendue (*f.*) extent, expanse
étincelant sparkling

étoffe (f.)   cloth, material
étonnement (m.)   astonishment
étonner   to astonish
étouffer   to smother, strangle
étrange   strange
étranger, étrangère   foreign
    à l'étranger   abroad
être (étant, été, suis, fus, sois)   to be
être (m.)   being
étreinte (f.)   embrace, grip
étroit, étroite   narrow
étude (f.)   study
étudiant (m.)   student
étudier   to study
évanouir(s')   to faint
éveiller   to awaken
événement (m.)   event
évêque (m.)   bishop
évident, évidente   evident, obvious
éviter   to avoid
évoluer   to evolve
exacte   exact, correct
examen (m.)   examination
exercer   to exercise, to exert
exhaler   to exhale, to give forth
exiger   to require
expérience (f.)   experiment, experience
explication (f.)   explication, explana-
    tion
expliquer   to explain
exposer   to disclose, to expose, to set
    forth
exposé (m.)   account, talk
exposition (f.)   exposure, exhibition
exprès   especially, on purpose
exprès (m.)   special order or messenger
exprimer   to express

F

face (f.)   face
    en face   opposite
facheux, facheuse   troublesome, unfor-
    tunate
facile   easy
facilité (f.)   facility, ease
façon (f.)   fashion, way, manner
facteur (m.)   factor, mailman
faculté (m.)   faculty, college
faible   weak
faiblesse (f.)   weakness
faim (f.)   hunger
    avoir faim   to be hungry

faire (faisant, fait, fais, fis, fasse)
    to do, to make, to construct, to
    perform
faisable   feasible
fait (m.)   fact
    tout à fait   completely, entirely
fameux, fameuse   famous
faqir (m.)   fakir
fardeau (m.)   burden
farine (f.)   flour
farouche   grim
il faut   it is necessary
faute (f.)   fault, mistake
fauve   yellow, faun, tan
fausseté (f.)   falseness
faux, fausse   false, wrong
faveur (f.)   favour
favoriser   to favour, to encourage
félicité (f.)   happiness
femelle (f.)   female
femme (f.)   woman, wife
fendre   to split
fenêtre (f.)   window
fer (m.)   iron, horseshoe
ferme (f.)   farm
ferme   firm, hard
fermement   firmly
fermeture (f.)   closing
fête (f.)   holiday, festival
feu (m.)   fire
feuille (f.)   leaf
février (m.)   February
fidèle   faithful, loyal
fidelité (f.)   faithfulness
fier, fière   proud
fièvre (f.)   fever
figer   to fix, set
figure (f.)   face, shape
fil (m.)   thread
filer   to spin, to go quickly
filial, filiale   subsidiary
fille (f.)   girl, daughter
fils (m.)   son
fin (f.)   end
fin, fine   clever, sharp
finir   to finish
fixé   fixed, firm
flatteur (m.)   flatterer
flèche (f.)   arrow
flétrir   to wither
fleur (f.)   flower
fleurir   to flower, to flourish
floraison (f.)   flowering, flourishing
fleuve (m.)   river

flotter to float
foi (*f.*) faith
fois (*f.*) time
folie (*f.*) madness, folly
foncé, foncée dark
foncer (se) to become dark
foncier, foncière fundamental
fonctionnaire (*m.*) official, civil servant
fonctionner to function, to act
fond (*m.*) bottom
fonder to create, to found, to establish
fondateur (*m.*) founder
formateur, formatrice formative
formation (*f.*) formation, education
fort (adverb) very
fort, forte strong
fortuné, fortunée fortunate, lucky
fou, fol, folle foolish, mad
foudre (*f.*) lightning
foudroyer to blast by lightning
fougère (*f.*) fern
foule (*f.*) crowd
fourche (*f.*) pitchfork
fournir to furnish
fourreau (*m.*) scabbard, sheath
foyer (*m.*) hearth, home
fractionnement (*m.*) division
frais (*m. pl.*) expense, cost
frais, fraîche fresh
franc, franche frank, free
français, française French
franchise (*f.*) frankness
franchement frankly
frappant, frappante striking, impressive
frapper to strike, to hit
frayeur (*f.*) fright
freiner to break, to slow down
fréquemment frequently
frère (*m.*) brother
frisson (*m.*) shiver
froid, froide cold
   avoir froid to be cold
   faire froid to be cold (weather)
front (*m.*) forehead
frontière (*f.*) frontier, border
frotteur (*m.*) polisher
fructueux, fructueuse fruitful
fuir (fuyant, fui, fuis, fuis, fuie) to flee
fuite (*f.*) flight
fumer to smoke
fumée (*f.*) smoke
funeste deadly, fatal

fur (au . . . et à mesure que) in proportion as
furieux, furieuse furious
fusée (*f.*) rocket

G

gage (*m.*) pledge
gagner to win, to earn
garçon (*m.*) boy, waiter
garde (*m.*) keeper, custody
garde-chasse (*m.*) gamekeeper
gare (*m.*) railroad station
gaspiller to squander
gauche (*f.*) left
geler to freeze
gémir to groan, to bemoan, to lament
gêner to bother
génie (*m.*) genius
genre (*m.*) kind
gens (*m. or f. pl.*) people
germanophone German-speaking
geste (*m.*) gesture, motion
gisement (*m.*) layer, stratum
glace (*f.*) ice, ice cream
glisser to slip, slide
gonfler to swell
gorge (*f.*) throat
goût (*m.*) taste
goûter to taste
grâce à thanks to
gracieux, gracieuse graceful, gracious
graminée (*f.*) graminaceous plant
grand, grande great, big
grandeur (*f.*) size, height, greatness
grandir to grow in size
gras, grasse fat, fatty
gratuit, gratuite free, gratis
grave grave, serious
gravité (*f.*) seriousness
grelotter to shiver
grès (*m.*) sandstone
grève (*f.*) strike, strand, shore
gréviste (*m.*) striker
gris, grise grey
gros, grosse great, fat, pregnant
grossier, grossière vulgar, crude
grotte (*f.*) cave
guère (ne . . .) hardly
guérir to heal
guérison (*f.*) healing, cure
guerre (*f.*) war

H

habile   clever
habileté (*f.*)   cleverness
habiller (**s'**)   to get dressed
habitant (*m.*)   inhabitant
habitation (*f.*)   house, dwelling
habiter   to live in, to inhabit
habitude (*f.*)   habit
   d'habitude   ordinarily
habituellement   usually
hache (*f.*)   axe
haine (*f.*)   hatred
haineux, haineuse   full of hatred
halle (*f.*)   market place
hasard (*m.*)   chance, luck, hazard
hâter   to hasten
haut, haute   high, tall, great, aloud
hauteur (*f.*)   height
héberger   to lodge
hectolitre (*m.*)   hectoliter (2.75 bush-
   els)
herbe (*f.*)   grass
héritage (*m.*)   inheritance, heritage
héritier, (*m.*) **héritière** (*f.*)   heir,
   heiress
heure (*f.*)   hour
   à l'heure actuelle   at the present
   time
heureux, heureuse   happy, lucky
hier   yesterday
histoire (*f.*)   history, story
hiver (*m.*)   winter
homme (*m.*)   man
Hongrie   Hungary
honte   shame
honteux, honteuse   ashamed, shameful
hors de   outside of, out of
hôtel (*m.*)   hotel, residence
hymne (*m.*)   anthem

I

ici   here
idiome (*m.*)   idiom, language
idolâtre   idolatrous
ignorer   to be ignorant of, not to know
île (*f.*)   island, isle
îlot (*m.*)   small island
image (*f.*)   picture, image
imbiber   to impregnate
immeuble (*m.*)   real estate
immotivé, immotivée   unmotivated

impérieux, impérieuse   imperious, imperative, urgent
impôt (*m.*)   tax
imprimer   to print, to impart
impropre   improper, unsuitable
imputable   attributable
inaltérable   unvarying
inaltéré, inaltérée   unchanged
inattendu, inattendue   unexpected
inavoué, inavouée   unconfessed
incliner (**s'**)   to incline, to bow, to yield
incomber   to devolve upon
incommode   inconvenient
incommodité (*f.*)   inconvenience
inconnu, inconnue   unknown
inconséquence (*f.*)   inconsistency
inconvénient (*m.*)   disadvantage
incrédule   unbelieving
incroyable   incredible, unbelievable
indépendamment   independently
indien, indienne   Indian
indienne (*f.*)   calico
indigène (*m.*)   native
indigne   unworthy
indiquer   to indicate
indubitable   indubitable, unquestionable
inégal, inégale   unequal
inférieur, inférieure   inferior, lower
infini, infinie   infinite
infirmer   to invalidate
infliger   to inflict
influer sur   to influence
infranchissable   impassable
infructueux, infructueuse   unfruitful
ingénieur (*m.*)   engineer
inguinal, inguinale   inguinal, loin
injonction (*f.*)   behest, request
innombrable   innumerable
inondation (*f.*)   flood
inonder   to flood
inoubliable   unforgettable
inouï, inouïe   unheard of
inquiéter   to disturb
   s'inquiéter   to worry
insensé, insensée   foolish, mad
insensible   insensible, indifferent
insensiblement   imperceptibly
installer (**s'**)   to install oneself, to move
   into
instruire   to inform, to instruct
insu (**à l' . . . de**)   without the knowledge of
insuffisant, insuffisante   insufficient
insupportable   unbearable, unendurable
intendant (*m.*)   bailiff, steward

interne   inside
intoxication (*f.*)   poisoning, intoxication
introduire (**introduisant, introduit, introduis, introduisis, introduise**)   to introduce, to show in, to insert
inutile   useless
isolement (*m.*)   isolation, solitude
issu, issue   descended from, born of
issue (*f.*)   outlet

J

jadis   formerly
jamais (**ne . . .**)   ever, never
jambe (*f.*)   leg
jardin (*m.*)   garden
jaunâtre   yellowish
jaune   yellow
jaunir   to turn yellow
jeter   to throw
jeu (*m.*)   game
jeûne (*m.*)   fast
jeune   young
jeunesse (*f.*)   youth
joindre (**joignant, joint, joins, joignis, joigne**)   to join
joue (*f.*)   cheek
jouer   to play
jouir   to enjoy
jouissance (*f.*)   joy, enjoyment
jour (*m.*) **journée** (*f.*)   day, light
faire jour   to become light
journal (*m.*)   newspaper
journalier, journalière   everyday, commonplace
juillet (*m.*)   July
jurer   to swear
jus (*m.*)   juice
jusqu'à   until, as far as
juste   correct, just, fair

L

lâche   cowardly
lacté, lactée   milky
laid, laide   ugly
laideur (*f.*)   ugliness
laisser   to leave, to allow
lait (*m.*)   milk
lancer   to throw

langue (*f.*)   language, tongue
large   wide
largement   widely, at length
larme (*f.*)   tear
larron (*m.*)   robber
lavement (*m.*)   washing, enema
laver   to wash
lecteur (*m.*)   reader
lecture (*f.*)   reading
léger, légère   light
legs (*m.*)   legacy
légitime   legitimate
léguer   to bequeath
légumineuse (*f.*)   leguminous plant
lendemain (*m.*)   next day
lent, lente   slow
lentement   slowly
lenteur (*f.*)   slowness
lèvre (*f.*)   lip
lever   to raise, to survey
libre   free
lien (*m.*)   tie, band, bond
lier   to bind, tie
lieu (*m.*)   place
lieue (*f.*)   league (unit of distance)
linge (*m.*)   linen, cloth
lire (**lisant, lu, lis, lus, lise**)   to read
litre   liter (1¾ pints)
livre (*m.*)   book
livre (*f.*)   pound
livrer (**se**)   to undertake, to indulge
loge (*f.*)   lodge
loi (*f.*)   law
loin   far
lointain   distant
longuement   at length
longtemps   long, a long time
lors de   at the time of
lorsque   when
louable   praiseworthy
louer   to praise, to rent
loup (*m.*)   wolf
lourd, lourde   heavy
lumière (*f.*)   light
lune (*f.*)   moon
lutte (*f.*)   struggle
lutter   to struggle
luxation (*f.*)   dislocation

M

mâcher   to chew
maçonnique   Masonic
maigre   thin

main (*f.*)   hand
main-forte (*f.*)   help, assistance
maintenant   now
maintenir   (maintenant, maintenu, maintiens, maintins, maintienne)   to maintain
mais   but
maison (*f.*)   house
maître, maîtresse   master, teacher, mistress
majdzub (*m.*)   Muslim official
mal   badly
mal (*m.*)   evil, misfortune
malade   ill, sick
maladie (*f.*)   sickness
malaise (*m.*)   uneasiness
malfaiteur (*m.*)   malefactor
malgré   in spite of
malheur (*m.*)   misfortune
malheureux, malheureuse   unhappy, unlucky
malsain, malsaine   unhealthy
mamelle (*f.*)   mamma, breast, udder
mammifère (*m.*)   mammal
manger   to eat
manière (*f.*)   manner
manquer   to miss, to lack
manquer à   to fail
marchand (*m.*)   merchant
marchandage (*m.*)   buying and selling
marchander   to bargain
marché (*m.*)   market
marche (*f.*)   march, step
marcher   to walk, function, move
maréchaussée (*f.*)   mounted constabulary
mari (*m.*)   husband
marier (se)   to marry, to get married
marine (*f.*)   navy
masser   to massage
matériaux (*m. pl.*)   materials
matière (*f.*)   material, matter
matin (*m.*)   morning, in the morning
maudire   (maudisant, maudit, maudis, maudis, maudisse)   to curse
mauvais, mauvaise   bad, spoiled
méandre (*m.*)   meander, winding
mécanisme (*m.*)   mechanism, machinery
méchant, méchante   bad, evil
méconnaître   (méconnaissant, méconnu, méconnais, méconnus, méconnaisse)   to be ignorant of, to misjudge

médecin (*m.*)   doctor
médecine (*f.*)   medicine
médicament (*m.*)   medicine, medication
méfait (*m.*)   misdeed
méfier (se)   to distrust
meilleur, meilleure   better, best
mélanger   to mix
mêler   to mix, to mingle
même   same, even
ménage (*m.*)   housekeeping
mendiant (*m.*)   beggar
mendier   to beg
mener   to lead
   mener à bien   to complete successfully
menton (*m.*)   chin
méprisable   despicable
mépriser   to scorn
mépris (*m.*)   contempt
mer (*f.*)   sea
mère (*f.*)   mother
mériter   to deserve, merit
merveilleux, merveilleuse   marvellous
mesquin, mesquine   petty
messe (*f.*)   Mass
mesurer   to measure
la métamorphose   the transformation
métier (*m.*)   trade
métis (*m.*)   person of mixed Spanish and Indian blood
mettre   (mettant, mis, mets, mis, mette)   to put, place
miette (*f.*)   crumb
mieux   better
milieu (*m.*)   middle, environment
millier (*m.*)   thousand
mince   thin
mine (*f.*)   mine, appearance
miner   to mine, to undermine
minerai (*m.*)   ore
minuit (*m.*)   midnight
minutieux, minutieuse   minute, detailed
mise (*f.*)   placing, launching
misère (*f.*)   poverty, misfortune
mode (*m.*)   mode, mood
mode (*f.*)   fashion, fancy
moeurs (*f. pl.*)   morals, customs
moindre   less
moins   less, fewer
mois (*m.*)   month
moisson (*f.*)   harvest
moitié (*f.*)   half
monde (*m.*)   world, society
   tout le monde   everybody

mondial of the world
mont (*m.*)   mount, mountain
montagne (*f.*)   mountain
montant (*m.*)   total, total expense
montée (*f.*)   rise
monter to go up
monticule (*m.*)   small mound
montre (*f.*)   watch
montrer to show
moquer (se . . . de) to make fun of
morceau (*m.*)   piece
mort (*f.*)   death
mort, morte dead
mot (*m.*)   word
moteur, motrice motor, moving
mouchoir (*m.*)   handkerchief
moule (*m.*)   mold
moulin (*m.*)   mill
mourir (mourant, mort, meurs, mourus, meure) to die
mousse (*f.*)   moss, foam
moustique (*m.*)   mosquito
mouvoir (mouvant, mû, meus, mus, meuve) to move
moyen, moyenne average
moyen (*m.*)   mean, means, way, manner
moyens (*m. pl.*)   means
mur (*m.*)   wall
musulman, musulmane Muslim
mutiler to multilate

N

nager to swim
naguère formerly
naître (naissant, né, nais, naquis, naisse) to be born
naissance (*f.*)   birth
naphte (*m.*)   naphtha, mineral oil
naturel (*m.*)   disposition, naturalness
naufrage (*m.*)   shipwreck
naviguer to navigate
navire (*m.*)   ship
né, née born
néanmoins nevertheless
néfaste inauspicious, of evil omen
neige (*f.*)   snow
neigeux, neigeuse snowy
nerf (*m.*)   nerve
net, nette clear, distinct
nettoyer to clean
neuf, neuve new
neveu (*m.*)   nephew

nez (*m.*)   nose
nier to deny
niveau level
nocivité (*f.*)   harm, noxiousness
noirâtre blackish
noir black
noircir to blacken
noircissement (*m.*)   darkening, blackening
nom (*m.*)   name
nombre (*m.*)   number
nombreux, nombreuse many, numerous
nommer to name
nonobstant que in spite of the fact that
notamment especially, in particular
note (*f.*)   note, grade
notion (*f.*)   notion, idea
nouer to knot, to join
nourriture (*f.*)   food, nourishment
nouveau, nouvel, nouvelle new
nouvelle (*f.*)   news
noyeau (*m.*)   nucleus, pit
nu, nue, bare, naked
nuage (*m.*)   cloud
nuance (*f.*)   shade of difference
nuée (*f.*)   cloud
nuire, (nuisant, nuit, nuis, nuisis, nuise) to be harmful to
nuit (*f.*)   night
nul, nulle no, not any
nullement not at all
nuque (*f.*)   nape of the neck

O

obéir to obey
obéissance (*f.*)   obedience
obligeance (*f.*)   obligingness
obséder to haunt
obstiné, obstinée obstinate
obstiner (s') to be obstinate, to persist stubbornly
obtenir (obtenant, obtenu, obtiens, obtins, obtienne) to obtain
occasioner to cause
occulte occult, hidden
oculaire ocular
    témoin oculaire eyewitness
odeur (*f.*)   odor, scent
odorant, odorante odoriferous
oeil (*m.*)   eye
oeuf (*m.*)   egg
oeuvre (*f.*)   work, works

offenser to offend
offrir (offrant, offert, offre, offris, offre) to offer
oiseau (*m.*) bird
ombre (*f.*) shadow
ombré, ombrée shadowed
omettre (omettant, omis, omets, omis, omette) to omit
omoplatte (*f.*) shoulder blade
oncle (*m.*) uncle
ongle (*m.*) finger nail
opérer to operate, to bring about
opposé, opposée opposed, opposite
or (*m.*) gold
or now
orage (*m.*) storm
oranger (*m.*) orange-tree
oreille (*f.*) ear
organisme (*m.*) organism, organization
orgueil (*m.*) pride
orgueilleux, orgueilleuse proud
orifice (*m.*) aperture
orner to ornament, decorate
os (*m.*) bone
oser to dare
ôter to remove
où where
ou or
oublier to forget
ouest (*m.*) west
outil (*m.*) tool
outillage (*m.*) tools, tooling, equipment
outre beyond, other than
  en outre in addition
ouverture (*f.*) opening
ouvrage (*m.*) work
ouvrier (*m.*) workman
ouvrir (ouvrant, ouvert, ouvre, ouvris, ouvre) to open

P

pain (*m.*) bread
paien, paienne pagan
paisible peaceful
paix (*f.*) peace
palette (*f.*) paddle, palette, small receptacle
palmier (*m.*) palm tree
panier (*m.*) basket
panne (*f.*) breakdown
papier (*m.*) paper
par by, through
parachever to carry out

parade (*f.*) display, show of force
paraître (paraissant, paru, parais, parus, paraisse) to appear
parapluie (*m.*) umbrella
parasol (*m.*) parasol
paratonnerre (*m.*) lightning rod
parcelle (*f.*) part
parce que because
parcourir (parcourant, parcouru, parcours, parcourus, parcoure) to travel, to skim over
pareil, pareille similar
pareillement similarly
parenté (*f.*) relationship
parfait, parfaite perfect
parfaitement perfectly
parfois sometimes
parfum (*m.*) perfume, fragrance, scent
parler to speak
parmi among
paroisse (*f.*) parish
parole (*f.*) word, speech, language
part (*f.*) share, portion
partage (*m.*) division
partager to share
partant leaving, consequently
parti (*m.*) game, match, party (political)
particulier, particulière private, special, peculiar, particular
partie (*f.*) part of a whole
partir (partant, parti, pars, partis, parte) to leave
  à partir de starting with, from
partout everywhere
parvenir à (parvenant, parvenu, parviens, parvins, parvienne) to manage, to succeed
parvis (*m.*) square in front of a church, parvis, court
pas (*m.*) step
pas (ne . . .) not
passion (*f.*) passion, enthusiasm
patenté licensed
patrie (*f.*) country, native land
patron (*m.*) employer
patronal pertaining to the employer or to management
patte (*f.*) paw, leg of an animal
pauvreté (*f.*) poverty, scarcity
pauvre poor, unfortunate
pays (*m.*) country
paysan, payse countryman, countrywoman
peau (*m.*) skin

pêche (*f.*)   peach
pêcher (*m.*)   peach-tree
peindre (**peignant, peint, peins, peignis, peigne**)   to paint
peine (*f.*)   penalty, sorrow
   à peine   hardly
pèlerinage (*m.*)   pilgrimage
pendant   during, for
pénible   painful
pensée (*f.*)   thought
penser   to think
penseur (*m.*)   thinker
percement (*m.*)   piercing, drilling
percer   to pierce, drill
percevoir   to perceive
perdre   to lose
père (*m.*)   father
perfectionner   to perfect
perfidie (*f.*)   treachery
péripétie (*f.*)   mishap
périphérique   peripheral
permettre (**permettant, permis, permets, permis, permette**)   to permit, to allow
permis (*m.*)   permit
   permis de conduire (*m.*)   driver's permit
personnage (*m.*)   personage, character
personne (*f.*)   person
   personne (**ne . . .**)   nobody
perte (*f.*)   loss
pesanteur (*f.*)   heaviness, weight, gravity
peser   to weigh
peu de   little, few
   un peu de   a little of, a few
peuplade (*f.*)   tribe
peuplier (*m.*)   poplar tree
peur (*f.*)   fear
   avoir peur   to be afraid
peureux, peureuse   afraid, fearful
peut-être   perhaps
petit, petite   little, small
   petit-fils (*m.*)   grandson
phénomène (*m.*)   phenomenon
phrase (*f.*)   sentence
physicien (*m.*)   physicist
physique (*f.*)   physics
physique   physical
pic (*m.*)   peak
pied (*m.*)   foot
pierre (*f.*)   stone
pieux, pieuse   pious
pigeonnier (*m.*)   pigeon-house
pile (*f.*)   battery

pillard (*m.*)   pillager
piller   to pillage
piqueté   dotted
pire   worse
pire (*m.* or *f.*)   the worst
pis   worse
place (*f.*)   place, square
plaindre (**plaignant, plaint, plains, plaignis, plaigne**)   to pity
plaindre (**se**)   to complain
plainte (*f.*)   cry, complaint
plaire (**plaisant, plu, plais, plus, plaise**)   to please
plaisir (*m.*)   pleasure
plan (*m.*)   plan, map
plancher (*m.*)   floor
plaque (*f.*)   slab, sheet
plateau (*m.*)   tray, disc, plate, plateau
plein, pleine   full
pleurer   to cry, to weep
pleuvoir (**pleuvant, plu, pleut, plut, pleuve**)   to rain
pli (*m.*)   fold
plier   to fold
plonger   to drive, to immerse
pluie (*f.*)   rain
plupart (*f.*)   most
plus (**ne . . .**)   more, no more
plusieurs   several
plutôt que   rather than
pocher l'oeil à quelqu'un   to blacken somebody's eye
poésie (*f.*)   poetry
poids (*m.*)   weight
poignée (*f.*)   handful, handle
poil (*m.*)   hair
poing (*m.*)   fist
point (**ne . . .**)   not, not at all
poire (*f.*)   pear
poirier (*f.*)   pear-tree
pois (*m.*)   pea
poisson (*m.*)   fish
poitrine (*f.*)   chest
polir   to polish
poli (*m.*)   polish
poli, polie   polite, polished
politesse (*f.*)   politeness
politique (*f.*)   policy, politics
politique   political
polluant (*m.*)   polluting element
pomme (*f.*)   apple
pommier (*m.*)   apple-tree
pommeau (*m.*)   pommel of a saddle or sword, knob
pont (*m.*)   bridge

porc (*m.*)   pork, pig
porte (*f.*)   door, gate
portée (*f.*)   import
porter   to carry, to wear
porte-parole (*m.*)   spokesman
porteur (*m.*)   bearer
posséder   to possess
poser   to pose, place
poste (*m.*)   post, position, job
postérieur, postérieure   posterior, rear
poumon (*m.*)   lung
pour   for, in order to
pour que   in order that
pourpoint (*m.*)   doublet
pourquoi   why
pourrir   to rot, decay
pourtant   however
pourvu que   provided that
pousser   to push, to grow
poussière (*f.*)   dust
pouvoir (**pouvant, pu, peux, (puis), pus, puisse**)   to be able to
prairie (*f.*)   prairie, meadow
pratique (*f.*)   practice
préalable   previous
précédent, précédente   previous, preceding
préciser   to specify
précoce   precocious, early
préjugé (*m.*)   prejudice
premier, première   first
prendre (**prenant, pris, prends, pris, prenne**)   to take
    s'en prendre à   to find fault with
    s'y prendre   to go about doing something
préoccuper   to preoccupy, to worry
près de   near to
presbytère (*m.*)   rectory
prescrire (**prescrivant, prescrit, prescris, prescrivis, prescrive**)   to prescribe, to command
préside (*m.*)   fortified post
presque   almost
pression (*f.*)   pressure
prêt, prête   ready
prétendre   to maintain, to claim
prétention (*f.*)   claim
prêter   to lend
preuve (*f.*)   proof
prévenir (**prévenant, prévenu, préviens, prévins, prévienne**)   to prevent
prévoir (**prévoyant, prévu, prévois, prévis, prévoie**)   to forsee

prévôt (*m.*)   provost
principe (*m.*)   principle
printemps (*m.*)   spring (season)
prise (*f.*)   taking, grasp, clutch
privilégié (*m.*)   privileged person
prix (*m.*)   price, prize
procédé (*m.*)   procedure
procès (*m.*)   trial
prochain, prochaine   next
prodige (*m.*)   prodigy, wonder
prodiguer   to be lavish with
produire (**produisant, produit, produis, produisis, produise**)   to produce
produit (*m.*)   product
profanateur (*m.*)   desecrator
profane   secular, profane
professeur (*m.*)   teacher, professor
profiter   to profit, to take advantage of
profond, profonde   deep, extensive
profondeur (f.)   depth
proie (*f.*)   prey
projet (*m.*)   project
projeter   to project, to plan
prolonger   to prolong
promener (se)   to take a walk
promenade (*f.*)   walk
promesse (*f.*)   promise
promettre (**promettant, promis, promets, promis, promette**)   to promise
promouvoir (**promouvant, promu, promeus, promus, promeuve**)   to promote
prône (*m.*)   sermon
prononcer   to pronounce, to declare
propos (*m.*)   purpose, subject
propre   clean, own
proprement   properly, appropriately
propreté (*f.*)   cleanliness
propriéte (*f.*)   property, characteristic, quality
prouver   to prove
provenir (**provenant, provenu, proviens, provins, provienne**)   to come from, to originate from
provisoire   provisional
prudemment   prudently
publier   to publish
puéril   childish
puis   then, next
puisque   since, because
puissance (*f.*)   power
puissant, puissante   powerful
puits (*m.*)   well

Q

qualité (f.) quality, position
  en qualité de in capacity of
quand when
quant à as for
quart (m.) quarter
que what, that, who, whom (cf. Chap. XXI)
quel, quelle what
quelconque any one, whatever
quelque a few
quelque . . . que however, whatever
quelquefois sometimes
quelques-uns, quelques-unes a few
querelle (f.) quarrel, dispute
queue (f.) tail
qui which, who, whom
quiconque whoever
quinquet (m.) street lamp
quitter to quit, to leave, to take leave of
quoique although

R

raccourcir to shorten
raconter to relate
rafraîchir to refresh
raide stiff
raidir to stiffen
raison (f.) reason
  avoir raison to be right
raisonnable reasonable
raisonnement (m.) reasoning
raisonner to reason
ramasser to pick up, gather
ramener to bring back
ramper to crawl
rapide quick, rapid
rapide (m.) rapids, express
rapidité rapidity, quickness
rapport relationship, ratio
rapporter to bring back, to report
rapprochement (m.) bringing together, proximity
rassembler to assemble
rate (f.) spleen
ravauder to mend, patch, darn
ravir to ravish, to delight
ravissant delightful, enchanting
ravissement (m.) abduction, kidnapping, ecstasy
ravisseur (m.) ravisher, abductor
ravitailler to provision
rayer to stripe, streak

rayon (m.) ray, radius, shelf, spoke
rayonnement (m.) radiation, radiance
rayonner to shine, radiate
réaliser to accomplish, to realize, to bring about
réalisation (f.) realization, accomplishment
réalité (f.) reality
rebours (m.) reverse side
récalcitrant, récalcitrante recalcitrant, refractory
récemment recently
réceptacle (m.) receptacle, repository
recevoir to receive
rechauffer to reheat
recherche (f.) search, quest
  recherches (f. pl.) research
récit (m.) account, version, recital
recoin (m.) nook, cranny
récolte (f.) harvest
reconnaissant, reconnaissante grateful, obliged
reconnaissance (f.) gratitude
reconnaître (reconnaissant, reconnu, reconnais, reconnus, reconnaisse) to recognize, to realize
reconstituer to reconstruct
recoupement (m.) cross-check
recourir (recourant, recouru, recours, recourus, recoure) to have recourse to
recours (m.) recourse, resort
recueillir (recueillant, recueilli, recueille, recueillis, recueille) to gather, to pick
recul (m.) relapse
redescendre to go down again, to descend again
redevenir (redevenant, redevenu, redeviens, redevins, redevienne) to become again
rédiger to write up, to draft
redouter to fear
redresser (se) to straighten up
réel, réelle actual, real
réfléchir to reflect
réflexion (f.) reflection
réformateur, reformatrice reforming
refouler to expel, to push toward or outward
refroidir to cool
refus (m.) refusal
regarder to look at
règle (f.) ruler, rule

réglé, réglée ruled, regular, in order
règlement (*m.*) ruling
régner to reign, rule
règne (*m.*) reign
regretter to regret, to miss (of persons)
rehaussé, rehaussée heightened
rejeter to reject
rejeton (*m.*) shoot, descendent
religiosité (*f.*) disposition toward religious feeling
relever to raise up
remarquer to remark, to point out
remblayé covered over
remercier to thank
remettre (**remettant, remis, remets, remis, remette**) to put back, remit, postpone
remonter to go up again, to reascend
remplacer to replace
remplir to fill
remuer to move, to shake
rencontre (*f.*) meeting
rencontrer to meet
rendre to render, make, cause, give back
   se rendre compte de to realize
renier to disown, repudiate
renommée (*f.*) fame
renseignement (*m.*) information
renseigner to teach
renverser to spill, tip over
répandre to scatter, shed, spread
répandu widespread
répéter to repeat
replier to fold over, to withdraw
repli (*m.*) withdrawal
réponse (*f.*) reply, answer
répondre to answer
reposer (**se**) to rest
repousser to repect, repulse
reprendre (**reprenant, repris, reprends, repris, reprenne**) to retake, to pick up again
représailles (*f. pl.*) the reprisals
répugner à to loathe
réputé, réputée reputed
résolu, résolue resolved
résoudre (**résolvant, résolu, résous, résolus, résolve**) to resolve
ressembler to resemble
ressentir to feel, to experience
ressort (*m.*) spring, energy, strength
ressortir tto go out again, to stand out
rester to remain
reste (*m.*) rest, remainder
restituer to restore

restreint limited, restrained
résumé (*m.*) summary
résumer to summarize
retard (**en . . .**) late
retardataire (*m.*) late-comer, backward person
retenir (**retenant, retenu, retiens, retins, retienne**) to retain, to hold back
retirer (**se**) to retire, to withdraw
retourner to return, come back, turn around
réunir to reunite, to gather
réussir à to succeed in
revanche (*f.*) revenge
réveil (*m.*) awakening
réveiller to awaken
révélateur, révélatrice revealing
revenir (**revenant, revenu, reviens, revins, revienne**) to come back
revers (*m.*) reverse side
revêtement (*m.*) revetment, sheathing
révision (*f.*) review
revoir (**revoyant, revu, revois, revis, revoie**) to see again
revue (*f.*) magazine, review, survey
rhume (*m.*) cold (medical)
richesse (*f.*) wealth
ridicule ridiculous
rien (**ne . . .**) nothing
rire (**riant, ri, ris, ris, rie**) to laugh
risible laughable
risquer to risk
rivage (*m.*), **rive** (*f.*) river bank
rivière (*f.*) river
robe (*f.*) dress
robuste robust, strong
roche (*f.*) rock
roi (*m.*) king
roman (*m.*) novel
rompre to break
ronde-bosse (*f.*) sculpture in full relief
roturier, roturière of the common people
rouge red
rougir to turn red, to blush
rougeole (*f.*) measles
route road, way
rouvrir (**rouvrant, rouvert, rouvre, rouvris, rouvre**) to reopen
roux, rousse red
royaume (*m.*) kingdom
rubrique (*f.*) heading
rude rough
rue (*f.*) street

ruelle (*f.*)   alley, bedside
ruiner   to ruin, destroy
ruisseau (*m.*)   stream
ruse (*f.*)   cunning, guile, trick
Russie (*f.*)   Russia
russe   Russian

S

sable (*m.*)   sand
sac (*m.*)   sac, bag, purse
sagesse (*f.*)   wisdom
sage   wise, good, well behaved
saigner   to bleed
saignant   bleeding, rare
sain, saine   healthy, wholesome
saint, sainte   holy, saintly
saisir   to seize, grasp, understand
sale   dirty
salle (*f.*)   room
sang (*m.*)   blood
sanglant, sanglante   bloody, bleeding
sans   without
santé (*f.*)   health
saper   to undermine
satellite (*m.*)   satellite, henchman
satisfaire (satisfaisant, satisfait, satis-
    fais, satisfis, satisfasse) to
    satisfy
sauf, sauve   safe, except
saute (*f.*)   jump (in temperature, price)
sauter   to jump
sauvage   wild, savage
sauver   to save
savamment   learnedly
savant (*m.*)   scientist, scholar
savoir (sachant, su, sais, sus, sache)
    to know
savoureux, savoureuse   flavorful
sayyid (*m.*)   Muslim official
scandé   rhythmical
science (*f.*)   science, knowledge
sclérose (*f.*)   hardening
séance (*f.*)   session, meeting
sec, sèche   dry
sécher   to dry
sécheresse (*f.*)   drought
secouer   to shake
secours (*m.*)   help
secousse (*f.*)   shock, jolt
sein (*m.*)   bosom, heart, middle
    au sein de   within
sel (*m.*)   salt
selle (*f.*)   saddle

seller   to saddle
selon   according to
semaine (*f.*)   week
semblable   similar
semblable (*m.*)   fellowman
semblant (*m.*)   semblance
    faire semblant de   to pretend
sembler   to seem
semer   to sow, broadcast
sens (*m.*)   sense, direction
sensé, sensée   sensible, sane
sensibilité (*f.*)   sensitivity
sensible   sensitive
sentiment (*m.*)   sentiment, feeling
sentier (*m.*)   path
sentir (sentant, senti, sens, sentis,
    sente) to feel, smell
septentrional, septentrionale   north-
    ern
serment (*m.*)   oath, pledge
serrer   to tighten, squeeze
servir de   to be used as, to serve as
seul, seule   alone, single
seulement   only, merely
si   if, so, whether, yes
si . . . que   however
siècle (*m.*)   century
siège (*m.*)   seat
siéger   to sit, to have a seat in
signaler   to signal, to point out
signe (*m.*)   sign
silencieux, silencieuse   silent
sillage (*m.*)   wake
singe (*m.*)   monkey
sinon   if not
sis, sise (*past part.* of seoir)   situated
soi-disant   so-called
soif (*f.*)   thirst
    avoir soif   to be thirsty
soigner   to take care of
soigneux, soigneuse   careful
soin (*m.*)   care
soir (*m.*)   evening, in the evening
    soirée (*f.*)   the evening, evening
    party
sol (*m.*)   soil, earth
soldat (*m.*)   soldier
soleil (*m.*)   sun
solidité (*f.*)   soundness, solidity
solide   solid, sound
sombre   sombre, dark
somme (*f.*)   sum, amount
    en somme   in short
sommeil (*m.*)   sleep, slumber
    avoir sommeil   to be sleepy

somnolence (*f.*) sleepiness
somnolent, somnolente sleepy, drowsy
son (*m.*) sound
songe (*m.*) dream
songer to dream, to think about, to imagine
sonner to ring, to sound
sort (*m.*) lot, chance
sorte (*f.*) kind
 de sorte que so that
sortir (**sortant, sorti, sors, sortis, sorte**) to go out
sot, sotte stupid
sottise (*f.*) stupid action
souci (*m.*) anxiety, care
soucieux, soucieuse anxious
soucier (**se . . . de**) to worry about
soudain all of a sudden
souffert (*past part.* of **souffrir**) suffered
souffler to blow, to whisper
souffrir (**souffrant, souffert, souffre, souffris, souffre**) to suffer, to allow
soufre (*m.*) sulphur
souhaiter to wish for
soulever to raise
soulier (*m.*) shoe
souligner to underline, to emphasize
soumettre (**soumettant, soumis, soumets, soumis, soumette**) to submit
soupçonner to suspect
soupir (*m.*) sigh
source (*f.*) source, spring
sourcier (*m.*) dowser, water-diviner
sourire (*m.*) smile
sous under
soustraire to subtract, remove
sous-marin (*m.*) submarine
soutien (*m.*) support
souvenir(**se . . . de**) (**souvenant, souvenu, souviens, souvins, souvienne**) to remember
souvenir (*m.*) memory
souvent often
spectacle (*m.*) spectacle, sight
spectre (*m.*) spectrum, ghost
sphacèle (*m.*) gangrene
spontané, spontanée spontaneous
squelette (*m.*) skeleton
squelettique skeletal
stade (*m.*) stadium, stage
stagner to stagnate
stationner to station, park

stipe (*m.*) stem of the palm tree
subir to undergo, to suffer
subite sudden
subjonctif (*m.*) subjunctive
subrepticement surreptitiously
succéder to succeed, to follow after, to inherit
sucer to suck
Suède (*f.*) Sweden
sueur (*f.*) perspiration, sweat
suffire to be sufficient
suggérer to suggest
suivant following, according to
suivant (*m.*) follower, following
suivre (**suivant, suivi, suis, suivis, suive**) to follow
suite (*f.*) following, sequence
 tout de suite immediately
sujet (*m.*) subject
sujet, sujette subject, dependent
sujétion (*f.*) control, subjection, servitude
sulfate sulphate
supérieur, supérieure superior, upper
superposer to superimpose
supplanter to supplant, to replace
supplice (*m.*) torture
supportable supportable, endurable
supporter to support, endure, to put up with
supposé que supposing that
sur on
sûr sure
surmonter to overcome, surmount
surnaturel, surnaturelle supernatural
surprendre (**surprenant, surpris, surprends, surpris, surprenne**) to surprise
sursaut (*m.*) sudden start, spasm
surtout especially, above all
surveiller to supervise
survivant (*m.*) survivor
survivre (**survivant, survécu, survis, survécus, survive**) to survive
susciter to raise up, to arouse
syndicat (*m.*) union, syndicate
syndiquer to syndicate, to unionize

T

tabac (*m.*) tobacco
tâche (*f.*) task
tâcher to try
tache (*f.*) spot

tacher   to spot, streak
tailleur (*m.*)   tailor
taille (*f.*)   figure, size
taire (**se**) (**taisant, tu, tais, tus, taise**) to keep silent
tandis que   while, whereas
tant   so many, so much
tant que   as much as
tantôt   soon, presently
tapis (*m.*)   rug
tapisser   to hang with a tapestry, to cover with a rug
tapisserie (*f.*)   tapestry
tard   late
tarder   to delay
tare   loss in value, stain
tartrique   tartaric (acid)
tasse (*f.*)   cup
tâtonner   to grope, to feel one's way
tâtonnement (*m.*)   groping
teinte (*f.*)   tint, coloring
tel, telle   such, such as
tellement   so much
témoignage (*m.*)   testimony
témoigner   to witness, to testify
témoin (*m.*)   witness
tempête (*f.*)   storm, tempest
temps (*m.*)   the time, weather
tendance (*f.*)   tendency
tendre à   to tend to
ténèbres (*f. pl.*)   darkness, shadows
tenir (**tenant, tenu, tiens, tins, tienne**)   to hold
tenir à   to desire, to insist on
tenir de   to resemble
tentation (*f.*)   temptation
tentative (*f.*)   attempt
tenter   to tempt, attempt
terminaison (*f.*)   conclusion
terrain (*m.*)   ground, field, terrain
terrasser   to knock to the ground
terre (*f.*)   earth, land, ground
terrestre   terrestrial
tête (*f.*)   head
thé (*m.*)   tea
thèse (*f.*)   thesis
tiers (*m.*)   third
tige (*f.*)   stem
tirer   to draw, pull
tissu (*m.*)   tissue, fabric
titre (*m.*)   title
tocsin (*m.*)   tocsin, alarm
toiture (*f.*)   roofing
tombeau (*m.*)   tomb, grave
tomber   to fall

ton (*m.*)   tone
tort (*m.*)   wrong
  avoir tort   to be wrong
tôt   soon
touffe (*f.*)   tuft
toujours   always, still, yet
tourner   to turn
tout, toute, tous, toutes   al¹, each, every
toutefois   yet, nevertheless, however
tout de suite   immediately
traduction (*f.*)   translation
traduire (**traduisant, traduit, traduis, traduisis, traduise**)   to translate
trahison (*f.*)   treason, treachery, betrayal
trahir   to betray
traîner   to drag
trait (*m.*)   line, streak, mark
traité (*m.*)   treaty
traiter   to treat
trajet (*m.*)   path
transhumer   to drive flocks of sheep
translucide   translucent
transmettre (**transmettant, transmis, transmets, transmis, transmette**)   to transmit
transpiration (*f.*)   perspiration
travailler   to work
travail (*m.*)   work
travailleur (*m.*)   worker
travailleur, travailleuse   hard working
traversée (*f.*)   crossing
traverser   to cross
  à travers   through, across
tremblement (*m.*)   trembling
tremblement de terre (*m.*)   earthquake
tremper   to dip
trépidation (*f.*)   tremor, trepidation
très   very
triage (*m.*)   sorting
tribu (*f.*)   tribe
tribunal (*m.*)   court
tromper   to deceive, to be unfaithful to one's spouse
tromper (**se**)   to be mistaken
trompette   trumpet
trop   too much, too many
trou (*m.*)   hole
trouble (*m.*)   confusion, disorder
trouver   to find
trouver (**se**)   to be found, to be located
tu (*past part. of* **taire**)   keep silent
tube à essai (*m.*)   test tube
tueur (*m.*)   killer

tuer to kill
turgescence (*f.*) turgescence, turgidity
tutelle (*f.*) tutelage, guardianship

U

unique unique, sole, only
univers (*m.*) the universe, the world
usage (*m.*) the usage, use
usine (*f.*) the factory, plant
usuel, usuelle usual, customary
utile useful
utiliser to utilize, use
utilité (*f.*) the usefulness, utility

V

vaincre (**vainquant, vaincu, vaincs, vainquis, vainque**) to conquer
vaisselle (*f.*) dishes
valeur (*f.*) value, worth
valoir (**valant, valu, vaux, valus, vaille**) to be worth
vanter (**se**) to boast
vapeur (*f.*) vapor, steam
vaquer à to be occupied with
varier to vary
vase (*m.*) vase, jar, receptacle
vase (*f.*) mud, slime
vedette (*f.*) star performer
végétal (*m.*) plant
veille (*f.*) previous night, previously
veiller to sit up late, to take care that
vendre to sell
vénérer to venerate
venir (**venant, venu, viens, vins, vienne**) to come
vent (*m.*) wind
ventre (*m.*) belly, stomach
vénusien, vénusienne pertaining to Venus
vérité (*f.*) truth
véritable true
vers toward, regarding
verser to pour
vert, verte green
vertèbre (*m.*) vertebrate
vertige (*m.*) vertigo
vertu (*f.*) virtue, quality
   en vertu de by virtue of
veston (*m.*) suit coat

vêtement (*m.*) garment, article of clothing
vêtu, vêtue dressed
viande (*f.*) meat
vide empty
vide (*m.*) vacuum
vider to empty
vie (*f.*) life
vieux, vieil, vieille old
vieillard (*m.*) old man
vif, vive quick, active, keen
vil, vile cheap, base, vile
ville (*f.*) city
vin (*m.*) wine
vinaigre (*m.*) vinegar
violer to violate
visage (*m.*) face
visées (*f. pl.*) aims, designs
viser to aim
vite quick
vitesse (*f.*) speed, velocity
vivant, vivante living, alive
vivement keenly, sharply
vivre (**vivant, vécu, vis, vécus, vive**) to live
voici here is, here are
voie (*f.*) line, way, track
voilà there is, there are
voiler to veil, cover
voir (**voyant, vu, vois, vis, voie**) to see
voisin (*m.*) neighbor
voisinage (*m.*) neighborhood
voix (*f.*) voice
vol (*m.*) flight, theft
voler to fly, to steal
volant (*m.*) steering wheel
Volapuk (*m.*) Volapuk, an international language
volet (*m.*) shutter, blind (window)
voleur (*m.*) thief
volonté (*f.*) will, wish
volontiers willingly, readily
volte-face about-face, turnabout
vomir to vomit
vouer to dedicate, pledge, devote
vouloir (**voulant, voulu, veux, voulus, veuille**) to want, wish
voûte (*f.*) vault, roof, arch
voyage (*m.*) trip, voyage
voyager to travel
voyageur (*m.*) traveler
vrai, vraie true
vraisemblable likely
vraisemblablement in a likely manner

vu   (*past part. of* **voir**)   seen
vu   because of, in view of
vue (*f.*)   view, sight
vulgairement   commonly
vulvaire   pertaining to the vulva

W

wali (*m.*)   Muslim official

Y

y (adverb)   there
y (pronoun)   stands for a clause governed by **à**
yeux (*m. pl.*)   eyes

Z

zèle (*m.*)   zeal

Index

(Numbers refer to pages)